Collected Essays of John Goode

TO CANDIDA

Collected Essays of John Goode

EDITED BY CHARLES SWANN
INTRODUCTION BY TERRY EAGLETON

KEELE UNIVERSITY PRESS

First published in 1995
Keele University Press
Keele, Staffordshire

Collected Essays of John Goode
© respective contributors

Composed by KUP
Printed on acid-free
paper by Hartnolls
Bodmin, England

ISBN 1 85331 068 9

Contents

Introduction by Terry Eagleton   vii

Bibliography of John Goode   xv

1   1848 and the Strange Disease of Modern Love   1

2   *Amours de Voyage*: The Aqueous Poem   27

3   *Adam Bede*   45

4   'The Affections Clad with Knowledge':
Woman's Duty and the Public Life   64

5   'Character' and Henry James   81

6   The Pervasive Mystery of Style: *The Wings of the Dove*   105

7   Hardy and Marxism   152

8   Sue Bridehead and the New Woman   171

9   Woman and the Literary Text   184

10   Feminism, Class and Literary Criticism   219

11   Gissing, Morris, and English Socialism   247

12   William Morris and the Dream of Revolution   272

13   Now Where Nowhere: William Morris Today   321

14   The Decadent Writer as Producer   336

15	Writing Beyond the End	355
16	Margaret Harkness and the Socialist Novel	375
17	Mark Rutherford and Spinoza	395
18	D. H. Lawrence	422
19	'The Uninteresting Actual Frog', or Is There Life After Postmodernism?	463
	Index	483

Introduction

John Goode first came to the public eye in 1966, as co-author with his University of Reading colleagues David Howard and John Lucas of a collection of essays entitled *Tradition and Tolerance in Nineteenth-Century Fiction*. Goode had two essays of his own in the volume, one on George Gissing, the other on Walter Besant and Henry James. The voice of the collection was radical, trenchant, briskly buttonholing, with the abrasive self-confidence of a set of young scholars who were hardly out of graduate school. It was casually iconoclastic but also impressively erudite: here was a firm of nineteenth-century critics who had read Schopenhauer as well as *Sybil*, and this interest in ideas, which Goode's contributions in particular evinced, was rare enough in '60s English criticism. In other ways, however, it was a puzzling performance – for where exactly were these writers coming from? When a new left-wing voice speaks out, one usually has some rough sense of its political pedigree; but with this volume such detection work was far from easy. It was not exactly left-Leavisite, though there were touches of that, nor was it from the Communist party stable of Arnold Kettle; Raymond Williams was an influence, but it was in no sense conventionally Williamsite; it was not especially 'New Left', in either its earlier Hoggartian or later Andersonian incarnations; Lukács hovered somewhere in the background, but these pieces were definitely 'criticism' rather than 'theory', a discourse which was then in any case no more than a gleam in the eye of Roland Barthes. What struck one about the book, in short, quite apart from its superb intelligence and *élan*, was its combination of political commitment with a brash, sometime chin-leading independence of judgement, as though these critics were at once unabashedly partisan yet doggedly determined to plough their own furrow.

A second collection from the trio, *Literature and Politics in the Nineteenth Century*, followed hard on the book's heels. Thereafter, John Goode published two full-length critical studies of his own, one on Gissing and one on Hardy, both books among the handful of best works on either author. But his more familiar mode was the essay, which he practised with rare expertise; and this is why it is more than some conventional obeisance to bring out this selection of his essays, now that their author is sadly no longer with us. For Goode was in my view the finest Victorianist we had in this country, a critic who combined the most formidable scholarship (he knew just how many columns *The Times* of 1886 devoted to novel reviewing) with a quite extraordinary fertility of perception; and since this work lay scattered in various journals and collections, some of them fairly obscure, it has not received the full attention, not least beyond the borders of Britain, which is clearly its due. A factor in this relatively low profile was the winning personal modesty of the man himself, who never lost touch with his modest beginnings and gave off the sense of a scholar quite unconcerned with celebrity. He was not particularly part of the conference circuit, not least in the days when his health was frail; and since he was not in the first place that most glamorous of all contemporary literary creatures, a theorist, the approbation he received was largely confined to the arena of Victorian studies. But he was not just a 'practical critic', any more than he was primarily an abstract thinker (his inaugural lecture in the Keele Chair on postmodernism, reprinted here, does not strike me as one of his more focused performances). He belonged rather to that rare species, the theoretically practising critic, one impressively *au fait* with the latest theoretical developments but able to absorb them effortlessly into the material practice of illuminating particular works. His work was densely empirical without being in the least empiricist, in a period when those two very different terms tended to be illicitly conflated. Few critics have combined such a beautiful sense of detail with such challenging generalities; he can argue his way up from Henry James's syntax through some knotty epistemological matters to the nature of the liberal subject in one breathtaking intellectual sweep. Indeed, his own critical style overcomes something of the opposition between 'common' and 'specialist' reader, by turns bluntly, even abruptly straightforward and adroitly intricate, conveying at a stroke the sensuous experience of reading and the activity of rigorous analysis. His essay on Henry James, reprinted here from *New Left Review*, is a marvel of sophisticated textual enquiry (has anyone written better on James than Goode?), but he is not afraid elsewhere to blurt out the bald opinion that Clough is a better poet than his Victorian *confrères*, to tell you what his *sense* of a trope or turn of syntax is, or to cut airily through some bit of received critical wisdom. If he is not in the first place a Jameson or Macherey, it is also because his readings are political before they are theoretical – because what passionately engages him are the political and ideological battles for which 'theory' has been too often some kind of metaphor or displacement in a politically becalmed epoch. Goode is first and foremost a *socialist* critic, a term one would be reluctant to use about many, even most, of the criticism which now offers itself as radical in a period when revolution or class struggle or material production have been forced to take a back seat to some more fashionable brands of political discourse. This resolute unfashionability is one of Goode's most attractive features, and belongs with the enviable integrity of his work, germinating as it does in what for the left was a politically more hopeful age, but unabashedly carrying these concerns across into the dark night of a Reagan-Thatcherism where they seemed to some increasingly notional and nostalgic. He was more interested in the destruction of the health service than he was in the floating signifier, and something of that ordinary social passion resonates in his deeply unmystified style, which manages to be subtle and upfront, artful and colloquial, at the same time. If he is a master of the pithy epigram ('there's no smokescreen without fire', he remarks in an essay not reprinted here), he can also be disarmingly direct: 'What Adam [Bede] really has to learn is not to marry beneath him' (p. 56); 'Milton, Blake and Shelley aren't people you would like to see sitting on the backrow of a branch meeting' (p. 323); 'Coleridge thought beauty grew on trees, as capitalists think that money begets money' (p. 341); 'What male readers find hard to take [about Will Ladislaw] is that he is actually pretty' (p. 238). It takes both exceptional insight and unusual good sense to speak, as Goode does in one of his essays, of the point of material wealth in Henry James being to have so much money that you don't need to think about it.

Goode was, I suppose, some kind of Marxist; but he differed from the orthodox literary Marxism of the 1970s in at least one crucial respect. He was enthusiastic about literature, which for the high-toned Althusserians of the day was the ultimate naivety. (There is, perhaps, something peculiarly Gallic about preferring to be thought wicked rather than simple-minded.) If he never entirely fitted into the Marxist methodologies of his period, it was partly because they (my own included) tended to practise a hermeneutic of suspicion, aloofly upbraiding the text for its ideological blindnesses, which was for him only part of a critic's responsibilities. He himself practised a kind of critical charity – note, for example, his proper admiration for that grandfather of all bourgeois liberals, John Stuart Mill – which was actually, in its historically grounded appreciation of the great liberal middle-class tradition, much more in tune with classical Marxism than the kind of tight-lipped semantic materialism which awarded Thomas Hardy four marks out of ten for trying. He is not embarrassed to speak of 'loving' William Morris (p. 323). But that charitable turn of mind was coupled with the keenest nose for cant and the most resolute anti-sentimentalism. Goode was a romantic in all the best rather than worst senses, alert to the utopian impulse of the movement and to the imagination as a politically transformative force, while steelily unconvinced by the simple motions of the heart. His readings were at once brisk and sensitive, sceptical of academicism while never for a moment mistaking themselves for the voice of the Common Man. Few were more disenchantedly aware of how literary works could be harnessed to an oppressive political power, but of those who held that faith he was one of a further minority who also saw just how they could round upon that power, frame, estrange and interrogate its force. He never, in short, surrendered to the left-pessimism of Foucault or the later Frankfurters, for which emancipation is just the latest ruse of the Law. He knew, as who of any nous could not, that there were political gains as well as political reversals, that Enlightenment could be liberatory as well as dominative, that writing could unleash as well as incarcerate. 'I resist', he writes in an essay here, 'the compression of knowledge and power into a single mode of oppression' (p. 232). But this eminently dialectical standpoint was growing increasingly unpopular by the time of his death, not least for those critics for whom everything seemed to have started with Saussure. Goode, by contrast, was both avant-garde and properly old-fashioned, unafraid to marvel aloud while not in the least averse to rapping his authors smartly over the knuckles. If there was something chronically subversive about his critical style, he was never that most tedious of beings, a card-carrying iconoclast.

Some of his most admirable achievements, in an age which sometimes grimly eschewed value-judgements, were bravely revaluative ones. In the course of this volume, he can be found rescuing George Eliot's *Romola*, insisting on the greatness of Arthur Clough's *Amours de Voyage*, boldly reassessing the status of Lawrence, disinterring Edward Carpenter, Margaret Harkness and William Morris's *Sigurd the Volsung*, speaking up for the subversiveness of Pater and aestheticism, redeeming Hardy for social radicalism and salvaging the political value of decadence. There is an authoritative confidence about his judgements, bracing but not bumptious, which extends to the most casual aside ('Houghton calls Claude's attitude to Rome vacillating, but I think there is a straightforward progression' [p. 31]). He has something of Leavis's trenchant autonomy of judgement, and would certainly have dismissed the vulgar caricature of Leavis as a mere 'élitist', even if his own particular judgements would often have made the Scrutineers wince. There are limits to this critical assertiveness, not least in his refusal to hear a bad word about Hardy; but it makes you want to read works you had casually dismissed, as well as feel guilty about too-eagerly endorsing certain revered reputations.

The so-called new historicism shuffles literary and non-literary texts into bizarre new constellations, but John Goode's essays indicate just how old-hat that controversial method is. His habit is to pull in the most unpredictable documents as a thick wadding around his chosen literary texts, wheeling Mazzini and Tom Arnold's *Equator Letters* into a discussion of Clough, juxtaposing Gissing and Positivism, George Eliot and Herbert Spencer, Rutherford and Spinoza, F.H. Bradley and Henry James, *Jude the Obscure* and *Marius the Epicurean* (the syntactical parallelism of whose titles he typically notes). If he was such a splendid critic, it is partly because he excelled in that most unEnglish of disciplines, the history of ideas, which is different from both literary theory and academic philosophy.

He had, in the traditional academic sense, a very definite 'period', which was indeed quite narrowly defined; he rarely strayed outside Victorian England, and made only brief forays into modernism, his judgement on which on page 336 seems to me questionable. But his critical passport took him through a number of intellectual frontiers, even if it did not thereby involve the kind of generalised conflation of the fictional and non-fictional so fashionable in an epistemologically sceptical age. On the contrary, his work becomes increasingly fascinated over the years by what one might call the 'fictional effect', its frames and mechanisms and specific devices, without for a moment succumbing to the illusion that the 'literary' is always and everywhere some uniquely privileged form of cognition. One can watch him fumbling towards this approach in his creative use of Macherey's complex dialectic of fiction and ideology, and indeed what one might call the ideology of form, a concept which in the act of attending to the peculiarities of the text grasps them simultaneously as a more general medium of social power, became in time the predominant motif of his writing. If Macherey appealed to Goode, it was because he seemed to promise to re-examine the text/ideology relationship in a way which precisely preserved the material specificity of the former. The literary work as 'mirror' is an apparently Marxist, in fact idealist model; the work as a 'mirror' which excludes, reorganises, frames, displaces, is a more promising trope altogether. Goode was a thoroughly historical critic who sprang to prominence in a left-formalist era, and when his historicism feels a little reductive it is usually provocatively, illuminatingly so, as in his audacious parallelling of the mood-swings of Clough's poetry with the fortunes of the 1848 French revolution. How many critics of Yeats, entranced as so many of them are by Byzantium and the *Anima Mundi*, would think it worth pointing out that he started writing at the time of the first English translation of *Capital* and died a few months before the Stalin/Hitler pact (p. 153)? If he starts off in fairly conventional fashion with a 'reflective' model of the literature–history relationship, as in his early treatment of, say, Gissing's *Demos*, he makes a transition in the middle-period work, doubtless under Althusserian influence, to a more 'productionist' paradigm of literary writing, in which the metaphors of staging, mounting and framing come powerfully to the fore. 'The novel', he writes of *Portrait of a Lady*, 'is not merely the conservative response to womanhood, not the realisation of a gracious lady, but a realisation of her picture. What we see in the frame alerts us to the excluded space outside it. The adorable object is not "nature" but a specific product within a specific system' (p. 194). Yet this shift from representation to production was never underpinned by the modish anti-realism of the 1970s, for which the form, implausibly enough, was somehow inherently reactionary. He had rescued the novel form from the clutches of the liberal humanists as early as '"Character" and Henry James', but he refused even so to indulge

in the Pavlovian dismissal of so-called liberal realism which marked the
'70s left in its most triumphalist period. He was not the kind of critic who
believed in one-to-one relations between literary forms and ideological
effects, though he is at his most persuasive in showing how Hardy in *Jude
the Obscure* – a work whose sheer offensiveness he retrieves for the contemporary reader – is pressing up more and more aggressively against the
conventional realist frame until it all but buckles in his hands. Other critics
may speak of pastoral England or the Immanent Will; Goode is more
engaged by just how awkward and unaccommodating a text *Jude* is from
a realist standpoint, or how this proto-modernist work is fascinated by
models of textual production. And when Goode does come to speak of
Hardy's unswerving pessimism, in his essays here as well as in his marvellous little book on the author, he enlists it convincingly for social
radicalism rather than fatalistic reaction.

The highpoint of English Althusserianism coincided, roughly speaking, with the emergence of feminist criticism; and Goode is not only one
of the notably few critics to pull these apparently incongruous discourses
constructively together, as in his pathbreaking reading of *Jude the Obscure*,
but one of the very few male critics one feels is personally enthused by
feminism, rather than dutifully tipping his hat towards it. The movement
permanently altered his interests and sensibility, as several of the essays
here will attest; it informs his moving, eloquent critiques of *Middlemarch*
or *Tess of the D'Urbervilles*. Yet he is not afraid to be critical of feminism
either, taking Kate Millett to task for using 'some of the most dangerous
of Anglo-Saxon literary orthodoxies' (p. 214), unlike those male pro-
feminists who allow correctness to triumph over candour. He is already
examining the complex relations between love, politics and sexuality in his
treatment of Clough's *Bothie* (a 'revolutionary poem about love', as he puts
it), some years before this became a received mode of critical enquiry. And
it is as though, in doing so, he deliberately, provocatively courts the risks
of being thought romantic in all the wrong senses, pointing to the redeeming power of sexual love, and the class-blindness of *Eros*, in ways which in
less deft hands could easily be mistaken as idealising, sentimentalist or
falsely utopian. Later, he will show how the intense sexual politics of *The
Mill on the Floss* cannot really be resolved within the terms of the novel's
own realism, and provides one of the most de-ideologising accounts of
Hardy's Sue Bridehead in modern criticism.

There are critics who are brilliant but largely predictable. You can thrill
to the intricate insights of a Leavis or Tate or Yvor Winters, but somehow
you generally know more or less what they are going to say, and part of the
enjoyment of reading them lies just in this pleasurable sense of recognition and attendant conservation of psychical energy. With Goode, you
can never quite guess what he will get up to; and this is not because he is
quirky or perverse – on the contrary, he is remarkably *sound* – but because

his work pulls off the unlikely feat of combining this soundness or plain good sense or quick sense of centrality with a striking idiosyncrasy. He always seems to come at a work left-handedly, as Walter Benjamin might have put it, slicing against the grain in a way which seems neither forced nor synthetic but simply true to his critical nature. You can share his beliefs, more or less, and still be astonished by what he conjures up from them on particular occasions. Anyone who has read, say, Fredric Jameson is likely to be struck by the depth and originality of his readings while being fairly quickly apprised of the kind of mind at work here, the habits and predilections built into it, the strategies it is likely to deploy. This is never true with John Goode, who surprises us again and again, and surprises us not least because this unpredictability is in no sense the upshot of a lack of consistent or coherent perspective. It is not, as T. S. Eliot insisted, just a question of being 'very intelligent', by which of course he meant (quite inconsistently with his own critical practice) having no sort of programme or agenda. Goode most certainly has a 'programme' of a kind – the project of a socialist criticism – and his work is marked like that of any major critic by the recurrence of a cluster of preoccupations. It is just that the relationship between this framework, and the specific insights to which it gives rise, is a peculiarly complex, flexible one, so that while one feels that his local readings are always informed by a controlling vision, they can never be simply read off from it. This is largely because of his devious practice of reading, which never rushes to premature totalisation but takes the pressure of each image or episode in the text without worrying, for the moment anyway, about some centre into which they will all finally merge. He responded sympathetically to Macherey's unmasking of the fetishism of aesthetic unity, as though this had always been part of his own reading practice, which indeed it had. (He was, however, rather less happy with the Machereyan or Freudian insistence on unconscious subtexts, given his willingness to believe that the writers whom he most admired knew more or less what they were up to. But this, in turn, belonged more with his view of the author-as-producer than with some old-fashioned intentionalism.) The point, anyway, is that Marxist critics are supposed to have a cavalier way with the actual words on the page, and are thus not expected to write sentences like 'the hesitant voice of the enjambement leads one to expect an important statement which materialises, in the downward curve of the intonation, as a hurry-scurry piece of evasiveness' (p. 37).

Goode's work on realism, of which he was a central theorist, naturally involved examining among other things how art can conceal art; and much the same is true of his own critical discourse, which sometimes has an air of rough, informal spontaneity about it while engaging under the cover of this inelegance in some wonderfully calculated rhetorical effects. 'Pope uses the heroic couplet to discriminate the antithesis of language and actuality: Clough uses the hexameter to discriminate the conflict of languages' (p. 42). George Gissing is 'one whose very pessimism gives comfort to bourgeois optimism' (p. 280). Indeed this kind of antithetical or chiasmic formulation is one of his stylistic trademarks, as a tortuous syntax strives to capture the dialectical nature of the object: '*The Ambassadors* is an intensely pessimistic novel because it portrays the destruction of the "liberal" concept of personality from within the framework of an ideology which bases itself precisely on that concept' (p. 92). The language occasionally becomes over-elliptical, but every sentence in Goode's writing earns its keep, and none is simply meretricious or archly self-conscious. Indeed, one of the paradoxes of his work is that you get all along the sense of an unusually strong, independent critical personality, but one which is oddly unaware of itself as such because it is perpetually to be seen in the process of submitting itself to the words on the page. There is, I think, an ethical as well as intellectual quality to this process, which recalls the real-left humility of the critic himself. John Goode was a brave, gentle and compassionate man, not without a dash of dark humour: when the interviewing committee for the Chair at Keele, nervous at the possibility of having to fork out sick pay to a man with a heart transplant, enquired politely after the state of his health, he is reported to have replied: 'Oh, you don't need to worry: either I'll be fine, or I'll drop dead.' His early death is a catastrophe for criticism, and a grievous loss to his political comrades.

Terry Eagleton

Bibliography

1. Books – as author, co-author or editor

Tradition and Tolerance in Nineteenth Century Fiction, with David Howard and John Lucas (London: Routledge and Kegan Paul, 1966): 'Introduction' (jointly written), pp. 1–7; 'George Gissing's *The Nether World*', pp. 207–41; 'The Art of Fiction: Walter Besant and Henry James', pp. 243–81.

The Air of Reality: New Essays on Henry James, edited and with an introduction (London: Methuen, 1972): 'Introduction,' pp. 1–4; 'The Pervasive Mystery of Style: *The Wings of the Dove*', pp. 244–300.

George Gissing: Fiction and Ideology (London: Vision Press, 1978)

Thomas Hardy: The Offensive Truth (Oxford: Basil Blackwell, 1988)

2. Chapters in books, articles, review articles

'Notes on the New Poetry', *Tamesis*, Summer 1963, pp. 4–6.

'Character and Henry James', *New Left Review*, Number 40, 1966, pp. 55–75.

'Gissing, Morris, and English Socialism', *Victorian Studies*, Volume XII, 1968, pp. 200–26.

Demos: A Controversy', *Victorian Studies*, Volume XII, 1969, pp. 432–40.

'Amours de Voyage: The Aqueous Poem', in *The Major Victorian Poets: Reconsiderations*, edited by Isobel Armstrong (London: Routledge and Kegan Paul, 1969), pp. 275–97.

'Adam Bede', in *Critical Essays on George Eliot*, edited by Barbara Hardy (London: Routledge and Kegan Paul, 1970), pp. 19–41.

'D.H.Lawrence', in *The Sphere History of Literature in the English Language*, Volume 7, edited by Bernard Bergonzi (London: Sphere, 1970), pp. 105–52.

'1848 and the Strange Disease of Modern Love', in *Literature and Politics in the Nineteenth Century*, edited by John Lucas (London: Methuen, 1971), pp. 45–76.

'William Morris and the Dream of Revolution', in *Literature and Politics in the Nineteenth Century*, pp. 221–80.

'The Egoist: Anatomy or Striptease?', in *Meredith Now*, edited by Ian Fletcher (London: Routledge and Kegan Paul, 1971), pp. 204–30.

'Stage Left', *Partisan Review*, Volume XXXIX, Number 2, 1972, pp. 276–81.

George Gissing, *The Nether World*, edited and with an introduction (pp. v–xiv) (Brighton: Harvester Press, 1974).

'Woman and the Literary Text', in *The Rights and Wrongs of Women*, edited by Juliet Mitchell and Anne Oakley (Harmondsworth: Penguin, 1976), pp. 217–55.

'The Decadent Producer', in *Decadence and the 1890s*, edited by Ian Fletcher (London: Edward Arnold, 1979), pp. 109–29.

'Sue Bridehead and the New Woman', in Mary Jacobus, *Women Writing and Writing about Women* (London: Croom Helm, 1979), pp. 100–13.

'The Moment of *Scrutiny*', *New Left Review*, Number 122, 1980, pp. 90–6.

'Margaret Harkness and the Socialist Novel of the 1880s', in *The Socialist Novel in Britain*, edited by H. Gustav Klaus (Brighton: Harvester Press, 1982), pp. 45–66.

'"The Affections Clad with Knowledge": Women's Duty and the Public Life', *Literature and History*, Volume 9, Number 1, 1983, pp. 38–51.

'Arnold, Baker, Culture: An Alphabet of the Repressive State', *News from Nowhere*, Number 5, 1983, pp. 38–51.

'A Reading of "Deceptions"', in *Philip Larkin: 1922–1985. A Tribute* (London: The Marvell Press, 1988), edited by G. Hartley, pp. 126–34 (written and first published in 1960 in *Tamesis*).

'E. P. Thompson and "the Significance of Literature"', in *E. P. Thompson: Critical Perspectives*, edited by Harvey J. Kaye and Keith McClelland (Oxford: Polity Press, 1990), pp. 183–203.

'Thomas Hardy and Marxism', in *Critical Essays on Thomas Hardy*, edited by Dale Kramer (Boston, Mass.: G. K. Hall, 1990), pp. 20–38.

'Mark Rutherford and Spinoza', *English Literature in Transition*, Volume 35, Number 4, 1991, pp. 424–53.

'Now Where Nowhere: William Morris Today', *News from Nowhere*, Number 9, 1991, pp. 50–65.

'"The Uninteresting Actual Frog", or Is There Life After Postmodernism?', Inaugural Lecture, Keele University, given on 19 February 1992.

'Feminism, Class and Literary Criticism', in *Critical Feminism*, edited by Kate Campbell (Milton Keynes: Open University Press, 1992), pp. 123–55.

'Writing Beyond the End', in *Fin de Siècle/Fin du Globe*, edited by John Stokes (London: Macmillan, 1992), pp. 14–36.

George Gissing, *New Grub Street*, edited and with an introduction (pages v–xxi) (Oxford: World's Classics, 1993).

'Remembering Anywhere: History and Retrospect in George Eliot and Arnold Bennett', *George Eliot – George Henry Lewes Studies*, Numbers 24–25, September 1993, pp. 163–74.

'For a Pilgrim of Hope' (an essay for Terry Eagleton's fiftieth birthday), in *The Year's Work in Critical and Cultural Theory*, 1991, Volume I, edited by Stephen Regan (Oxford: Basil Blackwell, 1994), pp. 294–301.

CHAPTER 1

1848 and the Strange Disease of Modern Love

The way in which any major historical event registers itself in the literature of the succeeding epoch is difficult to define. But 1848 has problems of its own. In the first place the Revolutions of that year have very ambiguous results. Both the English Revolution of 1688 and the French Revolution of 1789 are visibly linked, either causally or reflectively, with major changes in the political constitution and reorientations of the social structure. The Revolutions of 1848 don't have this clear historical status: in France, for example, the regime changes in content, but hardly at all in form, and the most obvious social change after 1848 is the re-emergence of the bourgeoisie in newly strengthened force. In actual terms, it is possible to speak, like Jacques Droz,[1] of the failure of the Revolution. Nevertheless, its significance is vast and undeniable, so that even a very conservative historian like Cobban describes the June days as 'a turning point'.[2] It is an event in which socialism first manifests itself as an active ideology, and one which leaves the proletariat ranged against the ruling classes. If it failed, it was because the social factor had become so important that the mere political overthrow of the existing régime was insufficient, and because the social structure remained resilient to the effects of political change. Political history had definitively become the explicit vehicle of social conflict.

The second problem is that as far as England was concerned, 1848 was a pathetic non-event. Even the 1789 Revolution, although it was purely national, constituted more of a threat to the English government than the Chartist Demonstration of 1848.[3] Indeed, Royden Harrison has convincingly argued that 10 April was really a theatrical performance engineered by the Government to give 'a form to the conflict which outstripped its real content'.[4] But this does not allow us to dismiss the event as insignificant. On the one hand, the demise of Chartism demonstrates the power of those forces behind the reform movement which had already been successful in 1846. And on the other, the working class movement underwent a complex but definite transformation after 1848. The Co-operative movement became more capitalist in outlook and in organization;[5] the Trade Union movement became deliberately less

1

radical, and political activity within the working class declined. In this sense, the working class pays tacit tribute to the triumph of the manufacturing classes. But equally, it meant that the various working class movements (particularly the unions) were becoming more skilled in organization and more professional in their encounter with employers.[6] We must link with this the reform movement of the fifties, which, as F. B. Smith has shown, is dominated by the 'incorporation theme':

> The radical manufacturing employers were concerned to extend the functions of the House because they agreed that if the workingmen were kept outside the electorate, they would come to believe that they held an interest independent of their masters, and would resort to strikes and coercion to gain higher wages and shorter hours.[7]

Of course, what Bright meant by incorporation was the assimilation into the *pays légal* of the labour aristocracy which meant leaving four out of five adult males outside (he was to refer to them as 'the residuum'), and so dividing the articulate workers from the masses. It would be ridiculous, naturally, to ascribe all these developments to the failure of the Chartists on 10 April. But what seems undeniable is that, after 1848, the relationships between political power and social organization begin to change. The manufacturing sections of the bourgeoisie became more dominant, but at the same time, at least on the continent, an alternative ideology to theirs had manifested itself closely linked to the industrial proletariat, which in England was making its articulate presence felt, and therefore the most farsighted manufacturers showed themselves responsive both to the need and possibility of transforming working class consciousness to their own. If the repeal of the Corn Laws and the fall of Chartism can together be seen as a sign of the supreme triumph of the manufacturing class against the landed interest on the one hand and the lower class on the other, the political history of the next twenty years demonstrates the paradoxes of its triumph.

It is undeniable too that the literature of the epoch following 1848 shows a marked change in its social consciousness. It displays no unity, of course, except that negatively there is a decreasing capacity to see historical change and the possibilities for historical change at all clearly. The writers who dominate the literary scene tend either to try to divorce literature from society altogether, or to seize on irrelevant analogies (notably the natural sciences) to mediate their encounter with the social world. The two writers whose work dominates both the forties and the fifties, Carlyle and Dickens, grow increasingly pessimistic. More specifically, there is an anxious acknowledgement of bourgeois virtues (Rouncewell, Doyce, Adam Bede) combined with a vigorous but often unco-ordinated portrayal of the oppressiveness of bourgeois convention. One of the most striking examples here is *Shirley*. When it is dealing with the Luddite disturbances the novel embodies a middle class myth (as Edward Thompson describes it). Yet it is also a painful and moving attempt to rescue sexual relations from the inequalities and dilutions of bourgeois marriage. As a result, *Shirley* remains two novels totally dissevered. Most of these generalizations are commonplace, though that doesn't mean that they are generally accepted, let alone self-evident. There is certainly no definitive way of relating them to 1848 even if we take that as a symbolic event. To link them to each other at all would involve an unwarrantable commitment to the concept of a *Zeitgeist*. What we can do, I think, is to gain a perspective on these themes and problems through the analysis of specific responses to 1848, to show that, in a general way, the despair, hysteria or mystification which appears in so much of the literature of the mid-Victorian period is encapsulated in works which respond to the Revolutions.

We can begin to define a framework by looking first at Bagehot's essay on the *coup d'état* of 1851. For this specifically political work displays many of the general features of social consciousness with which mid-Victorian literature has to cope. It is a highly intelligent and deeply cynical defence of the *coup*, and an attack therefore on the aspirations of the Revolution. Bagehot's premise is that 'the first duty of a Government is to ensure the security of that industry which is the condition of social life and civilized cultivation',[8] which is significantly committed to a capitalist sense of priorities, but which is on the face of it perfectly reasonable. What is striking about Bagehot is that he is under no illusions about the specific nature of industry's value: 'For this is the odd peculiarity of commercial civilization. The life, the welfare, the existence of thousands depend on their being paid for doing what seems nothing when done' (p. 9). Society depends, that is, on production for production's sake, on what Marx was later to define as commodity fetishism. This awareness is accompanied by a despairing mystification of the social process. The social fabric has come into being through a random coagulation of virtue, stupidity and mediocrity, and because of it people 'contrive' to go out to work, that is to keep themselves occupied until evening and to resist starvation. Society becomes therefore basically unalterable by any conscious human action. To change things radically is only to destroy the social fabric. Thus, 'the first duty of society is to preserve society' (p. 9). It is a familiar argument, but it is also unusually honest because it makes no attempt to rationalize man's social activity except in terms of an endless cycle of production and preservation. There is just one point at which the underlying naivety shows through the shrewd empirical exterior. And that is where Bagehot tries to explain the relativity of social institutions by 'national character'. This gives him a chance to justify the oppressions of Louis Napoleon by suggesting that the French need to be repressed because they are so rationally consistent that they are likely to overthrow their society completely in the interests of creating a more just system. Thus, having cited approvingly Burke's view that politics are 'made of time and place' (p. 25) (which Bagehot immediately reduces to 'politics are but a piece of business'), and cannot be judged by 'immutable ethics', he is able to sublimate the historicity of politics by a mystical and immutable concept. Hence, on the one hand, he portrays a social process which is meaningless except in terms of its own preservation, and on the other explains differences between societies by a pseudo-scientific absolute which determines the way in which society must preserve itself. There is a second myth on which Bagehot relies and which is significant for other writers. In spite of praising Louis Napoleon, he acknowledges that he is no Augustus, and goes on 'A feeble parody may suffice for an inferior stage and not too gigantic generation' (p. 20). The degeneration myth, like the national character, is a gesture of rationalization confronted with the opacity and apparently meaninglessness of the process of production.

There is one final point to be made about the world view the *coup d'état* reveals in an acquiescent mind like Bagehot's, and that is the way in which he views personality. He argues that Louis Napoleon is to be admired because he is an 'homme de caractère', but to prove this cites a view of him that describes him as completely dualistic: 'The President is a superior man, but his superiority is the sort that is hidden under a dubious exterior: his life is entirely internal' (p. 13). He is a shrewd operator in other words, the effective representative of a society which has defended successfully its meaningless social fabric. An opacity which reason can only undermine is best served by a man who is himself opaque and contradictory.

Bagehot's sense of the mystification of social relations and the implication that the best man to cope with such relations is a dualistic parody, is not exclusive to his conservative 'empiricism'. Leslie Stephen argued in favour of reform partly because he could see no threat to upper class supremacy by legislation since it depended on 'the occult and unacknowledged forces which are not dependent on legislative machinery'.[9] And in an entirely different context, that of 'liberal' theology, Jowett wrote in 1861:

> An ideal is, by its very nature, far removed from actual life. It is enshrined not in the material things of the external, but in the heart and conscience. Mankind are dissatisfied at this separation: they fancy that they can make the inward kingdom an outward one also. But this is not possible. The frame of civilization, that is to say, institutions and laws, the usages of business, the customs of society, these are for the most part mechanical, capable only in a certain degree of a higher spiritual life. Christian motives have never existed in such strength, as to make it safe or possible to entrust them with the preservation of

society ... For in religion, as in philosophy, there are two opposite
poles; of truth and action, of doctrine and practice, of idea and fact.[10]

Thus the dislocation between truth and society becomes inexorable. There
is no continuity between the individual and his world.

We should juxtapose this dualism against the work of the greatest
liberal of the age, John Stuart Mill. Mill, of course, defended the Revolution and even showed some limited sympathy with the Socialist ideas
it had brought to the fore. What is most interesting about his reply to
Brougham is that he contrasts what has happened in France with the
dualistic compromise on which the stability of the English social fabric
relies: 'The English are fond of boasting that they do not regard the
theory, but only the practice of institutions; but their boast stops short of
the truth; they actually prefer that their theory should be at variance with
their practice'.[11] On Liberty is surely a challenge to that variance, a challenge motivated partly by the failure of the triumphant middle classes to
give concrete expression to the theories which provided its rationale. For
what is most problematic about the essay is not what it says, but what
brought it about. After all, it is little more than a restatement of Locke,
and although one can see in it a challenge to socialist doctrines, and
although, as Packe points out,[12] the atmosphere of ideas in which it was
written was full of variations on a collectivist theme, the chief animus
in the essay is against the middle class itself:

> Already energetic characters on any large scale are becoming merely
> traditional. There is now scarcely any outlet for energy in this country
> except business. (f.n. 13)

It is important that Mill explicitly separates the principle of liberty from
the doctrine of Free Trade (p. 151), for what he is concerned above all to
affirm is the organic unity of the individual against the pressures of society
to conform to its demands: 'Human nature is not a machine to be built
after a model, and set to do exactly the work prescribed for it, but a tree,
which requires to grow and develop itself on all sides, according to the
tendency of the inward forces which make it a living thing' (p. 117).
The affirmative image of personal integrity sharply dissociates itself both
from the industrial revolution and the work ethic which was its moral
premise. It is not surprising that, a quarter of a century later, Hardy was to
take the opening sentence of the paragraph from which this comes as the
major intellectual referent of his novel of protest against middle class
conformism. On Liberty turns the bourgeois ideology on the bourgeoisie.
Before 1848 Mill had made himself the apologist of the new economic
world against feudalism (though admittedly a not uncritical apologist),
but once its triumph and its true nature had become clear, he became its

consistent accuser. And at the basis of the accusation is the threat that bourgeois society makes to the whole individual.

But equally, we are struck by the note of desperation in the essay. Underlying the charged affirmations there is a sense of having lost to the collective mediocrity of the middle class, and out of the almost pedestrian diligence of the argument there erupts an almost anarchist note of hysteria: 'In this age, the mere example of non-conformity, the mere refusal to bend the knee to custom, is itself a service' (p. 124). It grows out of a very positive sense that the real threat to individuality comes not so much from the state as from the pressures of public opinion which arise in a class-structured society. The tree image has to be taken in the context of the assertion (in *Utilitarianism*) that man is a social animal, and that his nature is to amend nature (*Nature*). It is not social action that Mill protests against, but social coercion, not collectivism but hegemony. And what the essay registers above all is that the vitality of man has been undermined by the triumph of bourgeois morality. Between Bagehot and Mill, at opposite poles ideologically, we have the acquiescent and protesting responses to a society based on the heroic individualism of industry become isolated from the individuals in it, and threatening to the organicism of conscious-ness. What I am primarily concerned to show in this essay is how the Revolution of 1848 seemed to offer other possibilities, and how its failure seemed to make for a world in which the individual had no place except as a function of the class he belonged to.

II

Clough is the writer whose work most dramatically responds to the Revolutions of 1848. It is well known that he went to Paris in May, and that he acquired such a radical reputation in Oxford that a mock proclamation of the revolutionary takeover of the university whose signatories were headed by 'Citizen Clough' was published.[14] But it goes much deeper than this. Clough's whole poetic career seems tied to the curve of events on the continent. His first major poem was written in 1848 before the election of Louis Napoleon, and it is his most affirmative work. *Amours de Voyage* is both thematically and tonally bound up with the ironies of the French siege of Rome in 1849, and his most bitter, unfinished work, *Dipsychus* was begun after the abandonment of universal suffrage in May 1850. After the *coup d'état* at the end of 1851, Clough's poetry withers. Naturally, there are purely personal factors here, but Clough himself was never able to think of his private affairs purely hermetically, and the enclosure of the strange eruption of his creative talent within the revolutionary period, and its clear development from affirmation to despair, cannot be dissociated from the political fortunes of the democratic movement.

Moreover, Clough's attitude to political events in the post revolutionary period is remarkably free of class-based fears and reservations. He was not, for example, sent into fits of hysteria by the June Days. He reported to Tom Arnold that the rumoured atrocities were 'unquestionably exaggerated', and went on to reveal an uncommonly radical attitude to the violence: 'I confess I regard it in the same light as a great battle – with, on the whole, *less* horror, and certainly more meaning than most great battles that one reads of.'[15] His letters of this period also, of course, are full of doubts and uncertainties, but these stem from the fear that the Revolution has not gone far enough because it has not created the basis for a new social structure. And what he specifically fears is the re-emergence of a triumphant bourgeoisie. On 14 May, two weeks after his arrival in Paris, he linked both of these points in a letter to his sister which creates a very clear and prescient perspective:

I don't expect much good will come of this present Assembly. – It is extremely shopkeeperish and merchantish in its feelings, and won't set to work at the organization of labour at all, at all. But will prefer going to war to keep the people amused, rather than open any disagreeable social questions ... The Socialist people are all in the dumps. (p. 16)

The last sentence suggests how much Clough's point of view was tied to that of the Socialists, and a letter of the same day to Stanley quotes a St. Simonian as saying, as Marx was to do, that the Revolution at that point was 'A Bourgeoisistic triumph'.[17] The famous 'glory is departed' letter of 19 May is motivated by the emergence of 'Well-to-doism' and the driving back of Liberty, Equality and Fraternity into 'dingiest St. Antoine'.[18] Clough grew disillusioned with the Revolution because of its failure, not because of its vision.

Nevertheless, it is true that by February of 1849 Clough seems to have accepted Matthew Arnold's much more sceptical attitude to the Revolutions. His letter to Tom Arnold of 15 February suggests positive as well as negative concurrence: 'The millennium, as Matt says, won't come this bout, I am myself much more inclined to be patient and make allowance for existing necessities than I was'.[19] On the other hand, the incompatibility between the two writers remains one of the most celebrated in literature. We only have Arnold's side of the quarrel, but it is clear enough why Clough was never able to accept Arnold's apparent poise. For even in this letter, Clough's patience has little to do with Arnold's cult of the inner self. Clough goes on to say that he has learnt from the fighting in the Revolution that there are worse things than pain and that therefore the less acute but more chronic miseries of society 'are also stages towards good'. I'm not so much concerned with the attitude here, which is neither logical nor consistently adhered to, as with what it shows us of Clough's bent of mind: it suggests a changed attitude towards social progress, not the recognition that there are more permanent human issues than are evident in the particularities of history. And in the poetry, as we shall see, Clough never relinquishes the sense that individual being can only be defined in its relationship to the social structure it confronts. Arnold's bitter denunciation of *The Bothie of Tober Na Vuolich* in 1848 surely recognizes the incompatibility in more objective terms than the moral browbeating he treated Clough to in later letters and in *Thyrsis*: 'Yes I said to myself something tells me I can, if need be, at last dispense with them all, even with him: better that, than be sucked for an hour into the Time Stream in which they plunge and bellow'.[20] The trouble with Clough, as far as Arnold was concerned, was that he challenged his own attempt to define himself apart from the *Zeitgeist*.

The attempt is riddled with contradictions, and the contradictions are manifest in the two sonnets Arnold wrote in 1848 to answer Clough's revolutionary commitment. The first sonnet seems to pay tribute to the motives of revolutionary sympathy, but the second line, 'and practised by too few'[21] quickly introduces a crucial reservation since it immediately drives a wedge between the sympathy and its object. This obliquely inserted opinion has, by the end of the poem become an accepted fact as the strong positive verbs of the octet ('but prized, but loved', 'despised') give way to trivializing and passive words such as 'sadness' and 'disquieted'. 'The long heart wasting show' becomes something which the great ones can do little about except feel sad, and the sadness is only a distraction anyway. 'Show' makes the great ones mere spectators of a theatrical illusion. This severing is completed by the clumsy syntax of 'If thoughts not idle, while before me flow/The armies of the homeless and unfed'. The crude assimilation of the great one's vision into his own by the sudden intrusion of the first person without any syntactical justification enables Arnold to evade any confrontation with their attitude as a different one from his, and the self detachment is managed by a purely connotative rhetoric as the implied inner freedom of 'thoughts not idle' is held apart from the undifferentiated necessity of 'flow'. The state of society which is the cause of the Revolution is assigned to a realm of necessity to which Clough, Arnold and the great ones generally are not subject. 'God knows it I am with you' is an empty rhetorical gesture seeking only to undermine rational argument.

The second sonnet is thus superfluous in terms of political debate. But it seems on the face of it to rebuild the link between the armies and the great ones by involving all in the same necessity. However, Arnold's use of the concept of necessity is here, as throughout his work, a rhetorical expedient whose purpose is to release the individual from the determinations of his epoch. For the mountains of necessity are not seen as having anything to do with the heart wasting show created by the coexistence of comfortable moles and hungry armies, but as the static boundaries of the individual landscape, uno'erleaped, it is true, but essentially apart from the life of the mind. Its margin is still there as a clearly defined space. Human history now seems to be 'A network superposed' and its relationship to the mountains is not clear. We only sense that it clutters up the margin which anyway is a dream-world. It is clear enough, I think, that Arnold uses imagery in a completely irresponsible way. Moles, armies, mountains, networks are all granting stern cover to a muddled and sentimental attempt to assert an absolute freedom from history within a mystified absolute determinism. It is also significant that Arnold needs to use two sonnets to make his point. The Petrarchan sonnet, because of its twofold structure, seems fitting for an argument which is based on 'if ... but', but Arnold can't fit his argument into its unity, for there is no unity in what he is thinking: he merely juxtaposes two levels of argument in order to make one seem irrelevant. He is compelled to acknowledge that Clough's sympathy for the Revolution is a genuine response to an aspect of human experience: he avoids engaging with it by asserting that it is not a response to another aspect. In one sense, Arnold, who usually convinces himself that he is uncontaminated by the conventional wisdom, looks forward to one of the most effective means of rationalization of the *status quo* of the generation that followed the 1848 Revolution: that social action is made irrelevant by biological necessity. It is ironic that in 1848 Arnold should have been attacking the *Times* for precisely the same rationalization.[22]

The continuing importance of the confusions we have noted here in Arnold's work does not require much demonstration. No-one uses the concept of the *Zeitgeist* more than he does, but his attitude towards it is profoundly ambiguous. Both in his letters and in his criticism (for example, the *Preface* of 1853 and 'The Function of Criticism at the Present Time') he takes refuge in the degeneracy myth that we have seen in Bagehot. But the *Zeitgeist* is something to be acknowledged primarily in order that it may be transcended: 'He will not, however, maintain a hostile attitude towards the false pretensions of his age; he will content himself with not being overwhelmed by them' (p. 606). There is no possibility of affecting the spirit of the age, only of proclaiming that one isn't contaminated by it. The noumenal thus becomes both a way of condemning the actual world and all attempts to participate in it by social action as illusory, and an escape from its intractability. The *Zeitgeist* is a totally deterministic concept – an epoch is what it is, and not to recognize this is to be immature – but to recognize its determinism is to be granted special dispensation from it. And because of this separation, the historical world becomes static in Arnold's work. So that, for example, the analysis of the three classes in *Culture and Anarchy* is more of a debased Platonic allegory than it is social criticism. It is not an analysis of class at all, but of something more like 'rank'. There is no essential difference between the classes – they only reduplicate each other's structure with varying specific contents, and they are not defined in any way by their relationship to each other. Arnold could only see the popular demonstrations of 1866 and 1867 as the populace's expression of *laissez-faire*. *Culture and Anarchy* springs from the need, defined in 'Democracy', to assert a national interest against class interest. But Arnold is so incapable of seeing the national spirit in terms of historical possibility that he fails even to consider that unbridled individualism may be specifically the product of one class, the class with supreme power. Yet a social critic with at least as much of an idealizing bent as Arnold, R. H. Hutton, had drawn the obvious conclusion from the overwhelming evidence of co-operatives, unions and so on: if a new loyalty to the state and to the social whole was to be sought, it had to be sought in the working class who were distinguished from other classes by their capacity for organization and their collectivist spirit.[23] Hutton's essay is sentimental and pervaded by a nervous assurance that the former political jealousy of the working class has gone, but it does at least look at the distinctive identity of the class. Arnold can get no further than the recognition that classes exist, and they are no more than agglomerations of that subjectivity which superposes an illusory network on the vale of life.

Paradoxically, the 'objectivity' which Arnold opposes to the network is defined primarily in terms of isolation. For culture is really no different from the buried life. Again, this is a paradox manifest in Arnold's poems to Clough. *Religious Isolation* accuses Clough of being childish in wishing to relate his inner life to the world outside (in this case not merely society but nature itself). What is startling about Arnold's poetry of these years is how complete the affirmation of isolation is. 'Live by thy light and earth will live by hers' is not simply an assertion of individualism, it denies the relevance of human relationship. To seek for continuity at all is a wish 'unworthy of a man full grown' (p. 104). The love poems of this period are really anti-love poems. He rebukes Marguerite for seeking her complement in him. 'Our true affinities of soul' (p. 127) are not in the man-woman relationship but in an identical search for the static, and this consummation is only to be found in death, 'All our unquiet pulses cease' (p. 128). When love is affirmed, as in *The Buried Life* it is because it works as a reminder of the inward knowledge of the buried self – 'The eye sinks inward, and the heart lies plain' (p. 275) – and even then it is not a way of being at all but merely a 'lull in the hot race'. Arnold never goes beyond this sense that the only objectivity is in the assertion of discontinuity with the stream of time. Culture, for all its connotations of wholeness, is a rationale of detachment adumbrating a mystical harmony beyond human history and human relationship. To change the actual world therefore is to tinker with a dream. Education might seem to be the exception. But Arnold's belief in the need for a national educational system is based on the need to provide a check to democratization by the creation of 'leaders' (significantly among the middle class). This is why he focuses not on elementary education (which is a force making for greater equality) but on secondary education. It is thus that the absolute isolation affirmed in the poems immediately after the revolution develops into a commitment to the establishment. For isolation is a resistance to experience, an assertion of the idea against the multitudinousness of life,[24] and this resistance bases itself on a transcendent reality, which is at once a subterranean necessity and a celestial harmony, a reality manifested in the shreds of authority resistant to human change and human desire.

It is precisely in the difference between their attitudes to the world's multitudinousness that the incompatibility between Clough and Matthew Arnold lies. For Clough too the chaotic intrusion of outer experience is problematic and threatening (see especially *Blank Misgivings of A Creature Moving about in Worlds Not Realised*), but for him finally there is no pseudo-Hegelian 'idea' to act as refuge. Multitudinousness, the immediacy of experience is therefore precisely what his poetry seeks to confront. And the confrontation explains the most obvious differences between his poetry and Arnold's, the concern in Clough with the contemporary and the decisive role in his three most important poems of sexual love. Arnold's defence of the use of subjects from the past seems to be just critical good sense. But he uses such subjects in a very ambiguous way. Empedocles is a modern intellectual given authority by his historicization. *Balder Dead* reads very much like an allegory of the class war, but since it is on a mythological plane Arnold can avoid defining the role of the individual in the creation of history, and Balder's new heaven is either a mental attitude (aestheticism) or a utopia for the educated. It doesn't have to be assessed in real terms at all. Love is just as problematic for Clough as for Arnold, but it is also an ineluctable force of continuity rather than at best a comforter of alienation and at worst a distraction. It is problematic for Clough because he accepts its impersonality (*Natura Naturans*), and impersonality is problematic not because it threatens a spurious individualism, but because it challenges the contractual relationship demanded by the social structure between the inner and the outer world. Love changes both – it destroys both the buried self and 'duty'. This recognition is inextricably bound up with Clough's involvement with the Revolution, for that too insists on a new concept of human unity: 'I contemplate with infinite thankfulness the blue blouses, garnished with red, of the garde mobile; and emit a perpetual incense of devout rejoicing for the purified state of the Tuileries'.[25]

We can define the link between sex and politics by looking briefly at Tom Arnold's Equator Letters. Arnold was probably the prototype of Philip Hewson and Clough is reported as having found the letters remarkable.[26] Certainly they have a clear bearing on *The Bothie of Tober Na*

Vuolich. Although they were written at the end of 1847, they clearly embody a revolutionary point of view, and it is obvious from Tom Arnold's letters of 1848 that he saw the Revolution as a potential fulfilment of the ideas he expressed in them; and even as late as July, 1849, he was writing to Clough: 'I always said before leaving England that I would return at once if there was a Revolution; and so I would' (p. 124). As a whole, the letters form an apologia for emigration, and what lies at the core is a sense of the total distortion of human relationships caused by the systematization of selfishness manifest above all in 'the class of capitalists' (p. 214). Emigration is the result of feeling 'the futility of all individual efforts to stem the stream'. The positive against which modern society is measured and found to be a systematic betrayer is specifically revolutionary, 'the sacred symbol, "Freedom, Equality, Brotherhood"' (p. 217). Arnold's view is pervaded by religious idealism, but for two reasons this idealism doesn't lead him to acquiescent patience. In the first place, although modern society has as its props the very inversions of the sacred symbol, 'The falsehood, the injustice, the inequality', there is no despair because they are the props of an 'unstable fabric' so that the religious idealism is never used as a substitute for the affirmation of historical change. Secondly, and it is clearly linked, there is no attempt to dissociate the subject perceiving the historical process from the process itself. Thus the sacred symbol is the source of personal emotion, 'inexpressible joy'. At the same time, the mental attitude which is critical of society in no way mitigates an oppressive social action:

> I am one of this rich class. I have *servants* to wait upon me; I am fed and clothed by the labour of the poor, and do nothing for them in return. The life I lead is an outrage and a wrong to humanity. (p. 218)

It is an outrage to humanity because it replaces 'brotherhood' with the social mediants of class relations. Tom Arnold is able to see himself as much a part of history as the armies of the houseless and unfed.

When the Revolution came, Arnold insisted to his sister that it was the penetration of the false social structure by the real basis of human relationships: 'It is not a class triumphing over a class, but a whole people getting rid of a *sham*, trampling under foot a lie' (p. 69). Behind this affirmation, it is true, there is an idealized concept of national unity which depends on a sentimental assertion of brotherhood ('And what allows us to be very hopeful of their success is that they seem to *love each other*'), and this assertion is debased by much post-revolutionary literature to become a rationale of patient reform and a counter to the antagonism provoked by injustice. Arnold even cites Disraeli in this letter. And the claim that class is a sham links with his brother's denial of the reality of class in *Culture and Anarchy*. But although it is a real intellectual limitation in Tom Arnold, the concept of 'ideal unity' and brotherhood is not, for him, a means of avoiding social conflict by arguing that there are buried bonds between men which no division can destroy, and that therefore inequalities do not need to be wiped out immediately. For Tom Arnold, the buried bonds must be manifested in the social actuality. Human solidarity is not a consolation for social oppression, it is a reality whose fulfilment demands the complete overthrow of the social structure, and the creation of a new society. The only means of effecting this is revolution, and if revolution is not available the only hope is to go away completely and start again.

Thus although Tom Arnold is, like his brother, dominated by an Hegelian idealism, it is an idealism which is, in a way totally alien to Matthew, historicistic. His belief in human continuity is critical rather than quiescent because it implies the manifestation of the Idea in time rather than in 'those elementary feelings which subsist permanently in the race and which are independent of time' (Allott, pp. 593–4). It implies it because Tom Arnold's vision of man's consciousness is antidualistic. His return to religious belief is described specifically as a recognition of the unity of spiritual and secular history, and the consequent sense of a continuity between man and nature:

> The history of Man and Nature then appeared like the seamless vesture, whole and undivided, enveloped in eternal beauty. Facts, institutions, characters, which had hitherto seemed to subsist independently of his being, and to draw their life and meaning from sources inaccessible to his thought, and unappreciable by his reason, yielded one after another to the test of the new idea, and from paradoxes and exceptions in Nature, became living realities, fraught with lessons for all time … There were not two orders of things – the natural and the supernatural – according to the Christian system, but one only, infinite and divine, – he saw that there was no fact, no institution, no doctrine, of which it could truly be said 'This is not governed by the ordinary laws of the world, and therefore the ordinary laws of thought do not apply to it' – but that all things that are, and were, and shall be, grow alike out of the one Soul which in Man has become conscious of itself, and recognizes throughout past history the work of its own hands. (p. 214)

Much of this is Carlylean, but there are significant differences. In the first place it affirms the unbounded potentiality of human reason, so that there is no leap of faith and commitment to 'duty'. Secondly, it recognizes that human consciousness declares itself in the whole of human history and not merely in the mind of the individual, so that history is not reversible, or escapable or marginal, but a total human creation continuous with nature. Because of this, inward development, with which Tom Arnold is as

much concerned as his brother, is not a self alienating process of intellec-
tion, but a continuing and coalescing encounter between consciousness
and experience: 'Reading and reflection had before this convinced him
that, for the individual, true knowledge was attainable only by encour-
aging and consulting the *spontaneous* movements of the mind ...' (p. 210).
Such movements, acknowledging the unity of experience, neither release
him to a higher plane, nor commit him blindly to the task at hand, but
take him back with critical awareness to the society he inhabits.

Take him back, that is, to seek in history the manifestation of that
joy he has found inwardly, for since its essence is continuity it cannot
be expressed except in terms of social relationships. And in the end, of
course, this process leads to contradiction. For the given social relationships are exact denials of this continuity, and to submit to them is to be
contaminated. Significantly, immediately after he has encountered directly
the poverty of London, Arnold declares the ineradicable hostility which
the progressive mind must feel towards society, and at the same time
reveals the thinness of the thread of faith to which it clings:

> Take but one step in submission, and all the rest is easy: persuade
> yourself that your reluctance to subscribe to Articles which you do not
> believe is a foolish scruple, and then you may take orders and marry,
> and be happy; satisfy yourself that you may honestly defend an unright-
> eous cause, and then you may go to the Bar, and become distinguished,
> and perhaps in the end sway the counsels of the State; prove to yourself,
> by the soundest arguments which political economy can furnish, that
> you may lawfully keep several hundred men, women, and children at
> work for twelve hours a day in your unwholesome factory, and then you
> may become wealthy and influential, and erect public baths and patron-
> ize artists. All this is open to you; while if you refuse to tamper in a
> single point with the integrity of your conscience, isolation awaits you,
> and unhappy love, and the contempt of men; and amidst the general
> bustle and movement of the world you will be stricken with a kind of
> impotence, and your arm will seem to be paralysed, and there will be
> moments when you will almost doubt whether truth indeed exists, or,
> at least, whether it is fitted for man. Yet in your loneliness you will be
> visited by consolations which the world knows not of; and you will feel
> that, if renunciation has separated you from the men of your own gener-
> ation, it has united you to the great company of just men throughout
> all past time; nay, that even now, there is a little band of Renunciants
> scattered over the world, of whom you are one, whose you are, and who
> are yours for ever. (pp. 215–16)

The end of this passage may not seem to be very different from Matthew
Arnold (poems such as *Quiet Work*, *Courage* and *Human Life* are making

similar points). But in its context it is very different. In the first place, since what underwrites this is a belief in continuity, Tom Arnold shows himself to be much more vulnerable to social experience ('you will be stricken with a kind of impotence'). Secondly, this is not the end, the final position, it is only the starting point of the decision to take social action by emigrating. And finally, even the end projects into the future, and we are reminded of his assertion to return to England if there were a revolution.

Nevertheless, we are confronted with an unresolved contradiction. The rational basis of integrity is the spontaneous recognition of human consciousness in human history. In the light of this claim, the passage is really affirmative: the discovered integrity cannot deny its basis in continuity by the acceptance of conventions which divide men from each other, and the enquiring mind from accepted belief. Yet the little band of renunciants seem to be those who are 'self reliant', who attempt to define themselves apart from their social being. The major difference between this and the contradictions we have noted in the work of his brother is that it is not an ideological contradiction, but one which grows out of the paradoxes of the specific historical situation – the personal predicament of the revolutionary mind in a non-revolutionary situation. And this too explains why Arnold is incapable of accepting accommodation while protesting his inner freedom. There is no choice for him between becoming an agent of social oppression and opting out altogether. And even then, opting out does not mean death but going to a new world. There is no refuge in your own light. In its starkness, this passage might stand as epigraph to Clough's major poetry.

But there is another, more specific reason for its relevance to Clough. The most surprising phrase in this passage is surely 'unhappy love' which clearly links with the sense of impotence the just man may feel. It is not merely a general philanthropic feeling that it is wrong to have servants which gives Arnold the subjective feeling of alienation and links him with the oppressions of the whole of society. What finally leads him to the realization that there can be for him no mid-point (not even the consolations of the community of just men) between submission and rejection, is his reading of *Jacques*, a novel about the thwarting of love by convention. Love is a mode of continuity, but the social structure imposes itself even on this: 'in the age in which we live, and in the society in which we move, there is a curse on love and marriage for those who will not bow the knee to the world's laws; those who have resolved to put away illusions, and to live for truth, be it at the risk of all that is held precious here below, rest, happiness, nay, of love itself which is the very life of life' (p. 217). Love is the life of life because it is what brings us to the unity of the universe. In a society based on division, love is cursed, distorted into the dualistic laws of the world. Love and revolution are thus brought together – their fates are bound up. If Tom Arnold's decision to emigrate is a collapse into an amalgam of evasion and utopianism, we should not underestimate the radical integrity which made it seem the only personal solution. His brother resolves the impasse of the confrontation between the free intelligence and a hostile society by ascribing the confrontation itself to a world of dream, so that he can submit in action asserting freedom of the mind as though thought were action. Clough's integrity, like Tom Arnold's, has no such comfort, and sexual love is what denies it, for it demands a wholeness of being that Matthew could do without.

III

The Bothie of Tober Na Vuolich shares the affirmative ambience registered in the Equator Letters, and if its tone is more exuberant it is surely in part because the instability of the social fabric which opposes Tom Arnold's sacred symbol had been revealed in European history. As we should expect in a major work of literature, its concern is not with vague generalities, but with concretely realized experience. It is not a poem about revolution, but a revolutionary poem about love, the personal emotion which existing society most directly challenges, and which, through its insistence on human continuity against social divisiveness, most immediately brings the individual consciousness into conflict with society. The poem celebrates the possibility of love, and defines its relationship to the contemporary social structure. Precisely because it is such an affirmative poem about love, and love cannot merely be seen as a relief or escape from the social structure, it necessarily becomes a radical critique of society and a vision of the possibilities of historical change. But, at the same time, because it is a celebration so concretely realized, its affirmations have themselves to undergo sharp scrutiny.

I am speaking here of *The Bothie* of 1848 which is a different, and, I think, more radical poem than that printed by Lowry, Norrington and Mulhauser, which is based on a posthumous edition of 1863.[27] Clough revised the poem in 1859, cutting out about 200 lines. It is the character of Philip which is most affected by the changes. His contribution to the debate in Canto II, his meditations in Canto IV and his letter to Adam in Canto IX receive the heaviest cuts. In the first edition, he is both more forceful and less callow. An index of this is the variation of Canto II, line 39. 'Never, believe me, revealed itself to me the sexual glory' becomes in 1863 'Never, believe me, I knew of the feelings between men and women'. Much of the revision is straightforward bowdlerization. At the same time, Adam is less dramatically realized in the later text so that he becomes more of a Socratic commentator and less of an actor in a drama of conflicting values. So, for example, in Canto II, when Adam has spoken with sympathy but detachment of Philip's praise of functional beauty, the 1848 edition has Philip retort that old men can speak with such detachment because they have lost the impulse which their wisdom rationalizes and accommodates to social inequality through 'duty'. Adam does not answer this until he has paused in emotional acknowledgement, and in his reply he admits that his own wisdom means discarding the original instinct that motivates one's continuity with others.

It is not simply that Philip is not allowed, in the later text, to be so damaging a critic of the conventional moral wisdom, it is also that, in this excised interchange, he introduces an image which gives coherence, throughout the poem, to the ideological significance of the love between himself and Elspie, and keeps its meaning completely distinct from Adam's wisdom. Philip has claimed that in the vision of sexual glory released by the peasant girl lies the most meaningful relationship with life:

> So women feel, not dolls; so feel the sap of existence
> Circulate up through their roots from the far away centre of all things,
> Circulate up from the depths of the bud on the twig that is utmost!
>
> (II. 12)

When Adam replies that what he really seeks is the good, and that this has nothing intrinsically to do with Philip's praise of the lower orders, Philip redefines the sense of this life-centrality (the Lawrentian phrase is relevant to the whole poem) in terms of magnetism:

> ... the grown-up man puts-by the youthful instinct,
> Learns to deal with the good, but what is good discerns not;
> Learns to handle the helm, but breaks the compass to steer by ...
>
> (II. 15)

The metaphor defines his relationship with Elspie; throughout the poem she acts as his compass, as he explicitly realizes, and she too, in another excised passage, defines what she feels for him in terms of the same metaphor:

> there in my dreaming,
> There I feel the great key-stone coming in, and through it
> Feel the other part – all the other stones of the archway,
> Joined into mine with a queer happy sense of completeness, tingling
> All the way up from the other side's basement-stones in the water,
> Through the very grains of mine: just like, when the steel, that you showed us
> Moved to the magnet, it seemed a feeling got hold of them both.
>
> (VII. 41)

The omission of everything from 'tingling' has an important effect on the image of the archway, for without the sense of process, the image becomes petrified, as though the completeness were a single unrepeated action. Thus what Elspie and Philip find becomes, in 1863, much more compatible with the ethical structure which Adam stands for. But more importantly, by playing down the magnetic image pattern, Clough takes out of the poem one of its most important affirmations, that of the Goethean concept of the elective affinity. In 1848 the poem grants love an independent coherence and validity: the spontaneous movements of mind discover their own image of continuity which is not merely accommodated by Adam's ethical commitment. Another of Philip's taunts is that in mastering the syllogism Adam has lost sight of the premise, and it is precisely the premise that he has to redefine for himself in terms of his own experience: 'Though I should like to be clear what standing in earth means' (II. 17). And the logic he discovers is radically different from Adam's – 'Only let each man seek to be that for which Nature meant him' (IX. 49) cuts completely across the social structure, while Adam's 'We all must do something, and in my judgement do it/In our station' (II. 16) is a rationale of accommodation.

Love is revolutionary because it penetrates the false dichotomies in which the characters are caught. Landscape and erotic joy are made one by Elspie's dream, so that love becomes the spontaneous movement of mind which recognizes the seamfree vesture of man and nature, soul and body, understanding and experience. At the opening of the poem, Clough creates a specious pastoral world in which the feudal community only thinly disguises the divisive capitalist reality, and in which masculinity is reduced to display with the ladies obscenely but harmlessly 'fingering kilt and sporran' (I. 5). Philip is critical of this world, and it is his refusal to participate fully in its pretences that draws David Mackaye towards him, for David, we note, has none of the bogus trappings of the feast – he is dressed as the Saxon. But initially, Philip's response is purely antithetical. He can replace one sham only with an equally false inversion, another false pastoral, the depersonalizing and socially mediated cult of the peasantry. So that it is psychologically apt that his love for Katie, though, in the 1848 text, it participates fragmentarily in the impersonality which he has found lacking in the self-regarding world of 'society', – 'Elements fuse and resolve, as affinity draws and repels them' (IV. 27) – should be full of contradictions. Though it is erotic, its physical realization would merely contaminate: it is opposed to the falsity of social marriage, and it thus becomes involved in marriage's social antithesis, sexual defilement. Katie and the Lady Maria stand for escape from and submission to the social convention, but the escape fails because the impersonality of love cannot be disentangled from social depersonalization, so that Philip is hurled to the opposite pole, the extreme and cynical cult of personality in the oppressive beauty of Lady Maria. Elspie is different from these in a quite radical way. Evoking the primacy of physical desire, paying tribute to the unconscious and impersonal forces of love, she makes sexuality mutual rather than acquisitive, and, recognizing it as a rhythm (the flood), she is able to disentangle sexual submission from its petrified societal image, inequality. It is no paradox that she acknowledges the impersonality of her desire for Philip, and yet that she chiefly educates him to penetrate the falsities of depersonalization: 'People here too are people, and not as fairy land creatures' (IV. 29). For this is the distortion in the social structure of the biological realities.

The poem as a whole is organized to reveal the continuous reality which is overridden by the fairy land of social forms. It moves primarily from mock heroic to heroic. In the opening cantos, the conventions of highland festivities and academic debate ironically manifest the tensions they gloss over. Knowledge, in particular, is severed from activity, so that the students' day is mathematically divided between study and physical recreation, and the vitality of the landscape is accommodated through mythologization and 'sport'. The debate about women in Canto II is concerned with genuine issues (above all the paradoxical conflict between social feeling and social form), but only inside the permitted convention which verbalizes harmlessly. So that, although Philip and Adam are serious, their respective attitudes are fittingly placed by the reductive parody of their supporters, Hobbes and Lindsay. The poem's development depends on Philip's capacity to break away from this atrophied world where community is servitude and sexuality is abstract ideology. Philip's colleagues, including Adam, serve as an index of his development, as they come to seem and to feel increasingly remote from the experience the poem is realizing. By the time Philip has found Elspie, we have seen them as amused spectators, as bewildered friends and as totally indifferent acquaintances. They recognize at a distance what has happened, but they are part of the old world Philip and Elspie are leaving behind, and if Adam is brought at the end into the relationship, it is only to rationalize a *fait accompli*. Hobbes registers this movement to a new immediacy in the development of his frames of reference. When Philip is opposing the distortions of society in a purely theoretical way, Hobbes is able to scale down his ideas to fit a fashionable intellectual system – Pugin's cult of Gothic architecture. Once Elspie and Philip are together, his analogy is to the elemental story of Rachel and Leah, and it is not a closed analogy, as the allusion to Pugin is; for he sees Philip and Elspie as resolving the conflicts of the story. He pays tribute at once to the depth of significance their love has, and to the millennial possibilities it portends. Rachel and Leah are one – the old conflict between romantic love and marriage is resolved through the new freedom and mutuality of affinity.

The political implications are made explicit in the final Canto. As we have seen, Philip redefines individuality in terms not determined by class. And if, to Adam's view that to follow our own instincts irrespective of the given social order is to be like soldiers in battle who ignore the commands of the Field Marshal, Philip replies with the Thucydidean image Arnold was to use at the end of *Dover Beach*, the implication is diametrically opposed. For it is not a rationale of detachment, but on the contrary an affirmation of the value of spontaneous action in a world motivated not by an opaque *Zeitgeist*, but by affinity. Significantly, Philip later describes the return of the 'old democratic fervour' in terms of the same imagery which Elspie had used to define her sense of his masculinity. Love and democracy are aspects of each other because they are visions of the unity of life beyond the false dichotomies of a class structured society.

Of course, like Tom Arnold's socialism, Philip's final affirmation is utopian, but I think the poem recognizes this. At the end, Philip is still a comically contradictory figure. If the flood of masculinity releases the old democratic fervour, the light of female responsiveness creates affinity with the populous city at dawn. To be sure, the image created is one of human potentiality – 'All its unfinished houses, lots for sale, and railway outworks, – / Seems reaccepted, resumed to Primal Nature and Beauty' (IX. 52) – but the acquiescence is seen as antithetical to the democratic fervour because it is a general faith in humanity, and not a specifically revolutionary faith. At the same time, the accepting light does not finally replace the democratic energy – both are forces in a continuing sexual rhythm. Clough is simply recognizing that the link between the sexual affirmations that the poem makes and the revolutionary fervour that grows from them is problematic in terms of human history. The human forces which make for revolution are realized in personal terms, but their manifestation in the social totality remains implicit. This necessary ambiguity is borne out by the ending of the poem itself. At the end of his letter to Adam, Philip directs his attention towards the bourgeois oppressiveness of marriage for the woman: 'How many are spoilt for wives by the means to become so, / Spoilt for wives and mothers, and anything else moreover' (IX. 51). The relationship between Philip and Elspie, despite its generalized implications, is thus placed as exceptional. Philip and Elspie come together partly because of the remote unpretentiousness of the Bothie itself, and their marriage is necessarily conditional on escaping from the society they transcend. Emigration is seen as a way of perpetuating the Bothie, of perpetuating its remoteness and avoiding contamination. The end of the poem necessarily reminds us of Gigadibs. He too remains mentally resilient to the acquiescent cynicism of Blougram, but the only answer he has in terms of action is to get out of the world in which Blougram's dualistic attitude seems to be necessary. Browning sees his idealist as slightly silly; Clough has too much integrity to be so

patronizing. But the ironies are there. Philip has become a more empirically motivated radical, but the experience finally takes him from the roots
of society.

I think that in spite of the ambiguities of its ending, *The Bothie* remains
affirmative: the actualization of love envisages the potentiality of revolution, even though the potential remains unrealized except in terms of a
private escape. It is as Europe appears to manifest again the triumph of
well-to-doism, that Clough begins in his poetry to scrutinize the curse
on love. One of the most significant poems of 1849, in view of what we
have been discussing, is *Jacob's Wives*. Rachel and Leah are not one, and
this poem is a bitter quarrel between them, always dominated by the
ethically superior and psychologically depersonalizing Leah. She doesn't
'win' because the conflict is endless, but she offers a compromise which is
a savage comment on bourgeois marriage:

> And Leah ended, Father of my sons,
> Come, thou shalt dream of Rachel if thou wilt,
> So Leah fold thee in a wife's embrace. (p. 84)

Sexual love is inexorably split between the romantic moment and the
social role of procreation – they are resolved only in dream. Jacob himself
speaks in another poem of this year, and it is clear that he is a pillar of
the community who has reached wisdom only by the sacrifice of personal
integrity and aspiration. The closing lines of the poem are a very clear
expression of what Lukács has called the *'malédiction tragique'*[28] which
develops out of the contradiction in the bourgeoisie between class consciousness and class interest:

> The stony hard resolve,
> The chase, the competition, and the craft
> Which seems to be the poison of our life
> And yet is the condition of our life!
> To have done things on which the eye with shame
> Looks back, the closed hand clutching still the prize!
> Alas! what of all these things shall I say?
> Take me away unto thy sleep, O God!
> I thank thee it is over, yet I think It was a work
> appointed me of thee.
> How is it? I have striven all my days
> To do my duty to my house and hearth,
> And to the purpose of my father's race,
> Yet is my heart therewith not satisfied. (p. 87)

In one sense this is more pessimistic than anything in Arnold because
there is no retreat into an ideal beyond historical necessity. Jacob's life is

full of distortion but it is the will of God. At the same time, the diction establishes this despair as a specifically class based one. The vocabulary is the vocabulary of Protestant self-help: 'chase', 'competition', 'craft', 'prize' are words of individualist enterprise. Yet this individualism is seen as a depersonalizing conformity to the will of God, and we note too the presence of 'resolve', 'work appointed', 'duty' as words that morally rationalize that enterprise and which are taken over as positives even by critics of mammonism, Carlyle and Arnold himself. The will of God prevails, but it is not compatible with the free light of reason. Personal love and work, in these two poems, turn against the individualism of which they are the primary affirmations.

For Clough there is no individuality without continuity, but continuity is manifested on the personal level by relationship and by action. In the world of the present, devoid of the immediate prospect of social change, the modes of continuity become agents of divisiveness both in the sense that they destroy human equality and fraternity in the cause of individualism and in the sense that they destroy liberty by turning that individualism into a conformity. I have already shown elsewhere how the elemental modes of continuity are seen, in *Amours de Voyage*, as factitious – bourgeois love, theatrical nationalism and romantic concepts of growth are only rhetorical gestures which rationalize experience in a way that can be contained by the social structure. In a world which seemed to hold the possibility of a renewal of society on the basis of free community, Clough is able to make concrete the personal experience of continuity. As the moment fades, he has to return again to a closer scrutiny of the treacherous affirmatives of bourgeois society.

Dipsychus is surely the product of this scrutiny, and not, simply, as has often been asserted, the confrontation of a fastidious intellect with an unethical but realistic common sense. Dipsychus is double minded because he has no concept of affinity with which to oppose the specious double morality of Cosmocrator. In Scene III for example, the Spirit's attitude to sex is not realistic, it is simply obscene and voyeuristic, but Dipsychus fails to oppose him because he is too urgently concerned to talk away his own terrifying desires with misty romantic clichés, and since the idea of mutuality doesn't enter, he can only offer social arguments which the Spirit can convert because he is social man. Dipsychus can see that prostitution is exploitation, but the only positive he has to offer is an equally reifying cult of virginity, so that the Spirit can counter with the idea that since virginity is unregainable, you aren't making matters worse by having a prostitute. Next, Dipsychus's affirmation against this is a depersonalizing philanthropism – the most degraded may be saved. The Spirit can accommodate this too, both with an Arnoldian assertion of ultimate necessity and with a brilliantly cynical epigram celebrating the Victorian salve of an exploiting conscience:

As women are and the world goes
They're not so badly off – who knows?
They die, as we do in the end;
They marry; or they – *superintend*:
And Sidney Herberts sometimes rise,
And send them out to colonize. (p. 536)

And Dipsychus then has to resort to an exaltation of marriage – which the Spirit immediately offers him. The comedy here, and throughout the whole poem, is that Dipsychus can never sustain values that the Spirit can't assimilate. The whole structure of the poem indeed is one in which, as Dipsychus resists one temptation after another, he finds himself with a choice between action and inaction. And the temptations too become more and more morally charged. The opening scenes are invitations to pleasure and self glorification – by the end, the Spirit is calling on him to submit. The only choice is between the abstract dissipation of energy (which anyway is not uncontaminated by the social structure – as the gondolier reminds Dipsychus, and as he himself realizes when he sees intellectual activity as the safety valve of 'the procreant heat and fervour of our youth'), and, on the other hand the sluicing out of the active self into canals. *Dipsychus Continued* merely encapsulates the many ironies of this predicament, for the returning prostitute not only undermines his respectability, she also complains that pleasure has been reduced to guilt. Society demands the total atrophy of the self from its desires. *Dipsychus* is the despairing protest of a man for whom the social structure has become the only reality.

And yet even in this poem other possibilities are glimpsed. The gondola episode affirms a vision of freedom which is only undermined because in the particular world of which Dipsychus is a product, it can only be freedom for an élite so that it becomes an oblivious idealism. And at the Lido too, Dipsychus' plunge into the elemental sea unnerves the Spirit completely. What makes such gestures futile is that there is no way of relating them to the given world without changing it, and the prospect of the given world being changed has gone. Clough is finally defeated by the world, and the defeat is deplorable, but I think also that it is informed by an exceptional integrity. He put *Dipsychus* aside, and he came to see *The Bothie* as 'childishly innocent',[29] but at the same time he never convinced himself that in accepting the social structure he could maintain a world of art uncontaminated by it. There is a letter of 1851, affirming the English tendency to moralize against the German genius for psychological insight, which is in one sense horrifying in its implicit philistinism, but in another profoundly aware of the intellectual dilemma of bourgeois consciousness:

The English fault therefore appears to me to consist, *not* in the propensity to apply a moral rule to all character and life, but in making their rule so narrow as to taking (sic) only a portion of our nature, and so purely external and mechanical as to misjudge the inner soul. The German reaction from this fault, – however fascinating as a deliverance from a thraldom felt to be oppressive, – seems to me to involve a far more dangerous falsehood. It treats all spiritual phenomena, all passions, all impulses, as mere developments of irresistible nature, which are to be accepted as being there, and among which we are not to demand any harmony, any subordination, or to recognize any obligatory ideal of perfection. As a kind of revolutionary assertion of the rights of a nature cramped by ungenial rigour, this anarchical doctrine may be generously borne with in individuals and in an age of transition. But, in itself it is, I must think, utterly false in philosophy, and most destructive in social tendency. Whenever the German Revolution works itself out into power, we shall see the effects of this faith in a divine Law-lessness, in terrible contrast to the English Puritan Revolution as an expression of faith in divine Law. For purposes of mere *Art*, the contemplation of life as a necessary growth from the spontaneity of nature, is perhaps the most favourable: but for the healthy action of individual men and the organic existence of the State, it is in my opinion fatal.[30]

Such illiberalism may tempt us to think nostalgically of Arnold's essay on Heine or even of *Culture and Anarchy*, but what is important here is the last sentence. Clough sees the inexorable conflict between the creative mind and accommodated man, and sees it specifically in terms of the implications of the middle class revolution. He found it better to keep silent than to go on pretending to himself that he could acknowledge the multitudinousness of life and still go on living in his own society. The volcanic eruption of his creative talent, and its total obliteration in the struggle for social survival, creates obvious and far reaching perspectives on the literature of the next two decades.

Notes

1.   Jacques Droz, *Europe Between Revolutions*, London 1967, p. 255.
2.   Alfred Cobban, *A History of Modern France*, London, 1965, vol. 2, p. 146.
3.   E. P. Thompson, *The Making of the English Working Class*, London, 1963, shows how widespread was the revolutionary movement in England in the 1790s.
4.   Royden Harrison, *Before the Socialists*, London, 1965, p. 79.
5.   Sidney Pollard, 'Nineteenth Century Co-Operation: From Community Building to Shopkeeping', in *Essays in Labour History*, ed. Briggs and Saville, London 1967, pp. 74–112.

6. E. J. Hobsbawm, 'Custom, Wages, and Work-Load in Nineteenth Century Industry', in *Essays in Labour History*, p. 114.

7. F. B. Smith, *The Making of the Second Reform Bill*, London, 1966, pp. 24–5.

8. Walter Bagehot, *Literary Studies*, London, 1898, vol. 3, p. 6. All subsequent references are from this edition and page references are indicated in parentheses. The 'Letters on the French Coup d'État of 1851' originally appeared in the *Inquirer* early in 1852.

9. Leslie Stephen, 'On the Choice of Representatives by Popular Constituencies', *Essays on Reform*, London, 1867, p. 106. A number of these essays are concerned to play down the effects of the Reform Bill. Cf. Cracroft, 'The Analysis of the House of Commons, or Indirect Representation', who notes that 'A Concurrence of causes has rendered Democracy in this country impossible', ibid., p. 190.

10. Benjamin Jowett, 'On the Interpretation of Scripture', *Essays and Reviews*, London, 1861, p. 356.

11. J. S. Mill, 'Vindication of the French Revolution of 1848', *Dissertations and Discussions*, London, 1859, vol. 2, p. 355. The essay originally appeared in the *Westminster Review*, April, 1849.

12. Michael St. John Packe, *The Life of John Stuart Mill*, London, 1954, p. 402. Packe undoubtedly exaggerates however. See J. C. Rees, *Mill and his Early Critics*, Leicester, 1956, p. 3.

13. J. S. Mill, *Utilitarianism, Liberty, Representative Government*, London, 1957, p. 127. All subsequent quotations are from this edition, and page references are given in parentheses.

14. Bertram, *The New Zealand Letters of Thomas Arnold the Younger*, Auckland, p. 221, reprints the proclamation. The joke is not without a serious basis. A letter to Stanley of May 28th, 1848, which cannot, in view of Clough's resignation, be taken as merely whimsical, proposes five 'Chartist' reforms of Oxford. See Mulhauser, *The Correspondence of Arthur Hugh Clough*, Oxford, 1957, p. 211. Hereafter referred to as Mulhauser.

15. Mulhauser, p. 215.

16. Ibid., p. 204.

17. Ibid., p. 206.

18. Ibid., p. 207.

19. Ibid., p. 243, 'Say Not the Struggle Nought Availeth' seems to be the poetic manifestation of this 'patience'. If, however, as two biographers of Clough have asserted, it is a political poem, the patience seems to be a strengthened faith in progress.

20. Lowry, *The Letters of Matthew Arnold to Arthur Hugh Clough*, London, 1932, p. 95. Hereafter referred to as Lowry.

21. This and all subsequent quotations from Arnold's poems and prefaces, is taken from Kenneth Allott, *Poems of Matthew Arnold*, London, 1965. Page references, where necessary, are given in parentheses. This sonnet and its sequel are printed pp. 102–3.

22. Lowry, op. cit., p. 68.

23. R. H. Hutton, *Essays on Reform*, London, 1867, pp. 27–44.

24. See his letter to Clough, Lowry, op. cit., p. 97.

25. Mulhauser, op. cit., p. 206.

26.   Bertram, *The New Zealand Letters of Thomas Arnold the Younger*, op. cit.,
      p. 207. All quotations from Arnold are from this source and I give page
      references in parentheses except where a quotation is from the same page
      as the preceding quotation. I follow Bertram in calling him Tom Arnold in
      order to avoid confusion with Thomas Arnold Senr.
27.   This is not to criticize their editing, since Clough revised it himself. They
      print the variants in an appendix. See the *Poems of Arthur Hugh Clough*, ed.
      Lowry, Norrington and Mulhauser, Oxford, 1951, pp. 496–511. Since it is
      so important to my argument that I use the first edition, I have taken all
      quotations from it (Oxford, 1848). References in parentheses are to Canto
      (Roman numeral) and page in this edition (Arabic numeral). Quotations
      from other poems are taken from the 1951 edition, and page references
      are given in parentheses.
28.   Lukács, *Histoire et Conscience de Classe*, Paris, 1965, p. 85. The general
      framework of this essay owes a great deal to this text of Lukács' and to his
      literary criticism.
29.   Mulhauser, op. cit., p. 338.
30.   Ibid., pp. 293 ff.

CHAPTER 2

Amours de Voyage:
The Aqueous Poem

'Here in Rome, we may not be moral mediocrities'
(Mazzini to the Roman Assembly, 1849)

'And there is no high-road to the Muses'
(*Homage to Sextus Propertius*)

I

Clough has been given a good deal of attention in recent years, but most of it seems to me to be of the wrong kind. Above all it shows a remarkable timidity of evaluation. Paul Veyriras *begins* his vast recent study (Paris, 1964) by disowning any great claims for Clough. 'Sa poésie,' he writes, 'n'a pas l'ampleur qu'on exige des chefs d'oeuvre.' John Jump calls *Amours de Voyage* 'a minor masterpiece', and so does Walter Houghton who places it a little lower than *In Memoriam*, *Empedocles on Etna* and *The Wreck of the Deutschland*. Such phrases and comparisons seem pretty uninviting to me. And if Clough does foreshadow Eliot (as Houghton claims), this really entitles him to no more than a paragraph in a history of Eng. Lit.

Obviously I think much larger claims have to be made, at least for *Amours de Voyage*. The fact that they haven't is due, I think, to the irrelevance and inadequacy of most of the scholarship. Too often even now the attention to the poetry is secondary to attention to the man who is seen to be little more than a set of conditioned reflexes vibrating in an eminently Victorian frame of mind. Chorley, Veyriras – and even Houghton – are cases in point here. Exposition of the poetry encourages this because it fails to come close enough to the language of the poem itself. And this too reduces the poem to a routine, if pleasantly witty, piece of honest doubt. Whereas it must be obvious to anybody who has read the poem that it is the product of a radically different kind of mind from those which produced *In Memoriam* or *Empedocles on Etna*. Not that I want to sell Clough on the cheap by claiming some specious 'modernity' in his poetry. The comparison with Eliot is just as damaging as the undiscriminating juxtaposition with Arnold and Tennyson. For although Clough's

27

dominant mode is, like Eliot's, an ironic one, it is, as I shall try to show, serving a very different, even antithetical, function. It is impossible to discuss Clough by lifting him out of the 1840s, but this doesn't mean that we should bury him in there. For the irony is extremely important, and it suggests a relationship to the reality which he shares with Tennyson and Arnold which is not their relationship.

To talk about difference any longer would be evasive. I mean superiority. The claim that must be made for *Amours de Voyage* is not just that it is a masterpiece, but a major masterpiece; indeed, for me *the* major masterpiece of high Victorian poetry. Naturally I can't conclusively prove this in an article on this scale, but after all the evasions, it seems time for somebody to be quite flagrant.

What I *can* hope to show is that *Amours de Voyage* demands the attention that we pay a great poem. And this means being aware of the fullest implications of its texture and its form. It isn't difficult to see why this has never happened. Everybody is conscious that Victorian poetry is overshadowed by the novel in its own time and by Romantic and Modern poetry in its historical position. This means that critics are anxious to assimilate qualities of the novel to some poems (as indeed were some of the poets) and *Amours de Voyage* is a likely victim because it has at its centre a 'character' carefully defined both socially and intellectually. Alternatively, Claude is a persona, like Eliot's Prufrock, recording with ironised objectivity the poet's own alienation from the contemporary world. Neither of these claims is false, both of them are inadequate. For we very quickly realise that Claude has nothing like the depth and complexity of, for example, Lydgate, or even Sir Willoughby Patterne. And, seeing Claude as an early Prufrock, we are likely to notice that Eliot's interior monologue has much more economy and honesty than a poem which is capable of 'Honour to speech! and all honour to thee, thou noble Mazzini!' Seen as a possum *avant la lettre* Clough trails pretty large clouds of the ineffectual angel.

However, a reading of the poem, unhampered by the habitual anxieties of the Victorian poetry specialist, will also reveal the inadequacy of such interpretations. For the most obvious quality of the poem is the richness of its verbal texture. Claude isn't primarily important as a 'character' (the absurdity of Veyriras's complaint that George, Georgina and Mary are insufficiently delineated should warn us against that kind of reading); he is a writer of letters. Nor is the poem an interior monologue, the letters are to particular people. And what we should be most conscious of is not the narrative of events or the revelation of character, but the patterns of words. I shall say something about the rôle of Claude later, but what must be immediately obvious is that the language and image patterns of the poem transcend his own social limitations. In order to understand the thematic content of the poem, we must attend to such patterns first, without reference to Claude. Only then will we be in a position to understand the radical significance of the poem itself.

II

The central preoccupation of *Amours de Voyage* is a search for continuity. This grows from a need to establish a viable relationship between self and world, but, more importantly, it demands a resolution of the conflict between the two empirically verifiable attributes of self, eyes and shadow – the self as perceiver and subject ('Though but to see with my eyes ...') and the self as phenomenon and object of others' perception ('Do I look like that? You think me that: then I *am* that'). What makes this tension so radical is that there is no assumed *substantial* self to be the source and thus the link between the attributes. The continuity with the outer world has to be effected on the basis of perception or of seeming rather than of 'being'. As we shall see, eyes and shadow propose different kinds of continuity which are rejected: through the perception of the real Rome, the eyes find continuity in time, but the social being which gives the eyes presence traps the spectator in isolation; through the acceptance of social identity, the shadow finds continuity in space through love, but this too comes to seem factitious, the uprooting of personality from time through the social lie about marriage.

The 'substantial' self disappears in Clough's work because, from the beginning, though it is so important in the preservation of an identity separable from the impinging social world, it is never more than an ambivalent metaphor. We can see this very clearly in the sequence of poems called *Blank Misgivings of a Creature Moving about in Worlds Not Realised* (1839–1841). In IX, Clough prays for preservation from absorption in the outer reality:

> Let me not feel, nor be it true,
> That while each daily task I do
> I still am giving day by day
> My precious things within away,
> (Those thou didst give to keep as thine)
> And casting, do whate'er I may,
> My heavenly pearls to earthly swine.
>
> (*Poems*, p. 33)[1]

Clearly there is here an inner sanctuary of self which is separate from the external world, but which mediates with that world ('while each daily task I do'). But even this bald antithesis is ambiguous. The inner sanctuary can only be defined in terms of a metaphor of which the vehicle is God

Throughout the sequence we are conscious only of negations of self (either the anti-self of the social mask or the pre-self of 'kind maternal darkness'). The landscape of self in IX is 'by hedge or tree unbroken' and is given meaning only by a few grey woods which in their 'unaltering impotence ... enhance the sovereign dulness'. It is a blank world, carrying 'nothing into reality' which only a vague and unnamed power beyond self can concretise into an image ('heavenly pearls').

But in *Amours de Voyage* there is no God, and therefore no available metaphor of self. What Claude finds in Rome is not the Christian image of heavenly pearls, but 'Aspirations from something most shameful here upon earth', and 'In our poor selves to something most perfect above in the heavens', but a 'positive, calm, Stoic-Epicurean acceptance'. Immediately after this the possibility of the shadow being all there is of substance is most nakedly confronted:

> Curious work, meantime, re-entering society: how we
> Walk a livelong day, great Heaven, and watch our shadows!
> What our shadows seem, forsooth, we will ourselves be.
>
> (I. 83–85)

This is the point from which the sense of continuity has to begin, and it conditions even the apparent antithesis of the societal self, the self as seer. For Claude's eyes are not the eyes of the Emersonian soul but the eyes of a social being, the English tourist. Emerson wrote: 'Travelling is a fool's paradise', and it is his voice which whispers in the prologue to Canto I. Tourism is an aspect of social man's failure in 'self-culture', and it is important that what most characterises Claude as seer is the social image, 'Murray as usual under my arm'. Murray defines Claude, even provides some of his comments on Rome.

Even so it would be wrong to see Claude's encounter with Rome as nothing more than a revelation of his lack of self-reliance. For initially it does provide for the possibility of the spectatorial self seeking a relationship with the external through a continuity in time (*'wherein gods of the old time wandered'*). It may seem odd to insist on this when the search for the more perfect earth is immediately countered in Letter I with 'Rome disappoints me much'. But careful discriminations need to be made here. Claude's word 'rubbishy' is not just pretentious, it is also precise. What disappoints him is the visible past available to the socially defined tourist. Its emblem is the Monte Testaceo which suggests the very opposite of continuity in time. The past seems to bury the present:

> All the foolish destructions, and all the silver savings,
> All the incongruous things of past incompatible ages,
> Seem to be treasured up here to make fools of present and future.
>
> (I. 21–23)

It is important to insist on the clutter, the heaped up rubbish which makes nonsense of the relationship between past and present: 'Things that nature abhors, the experiments that she has failed in'. Thus visible Rome operates against the central image of continuity in the poem – growth, the communication of past and present through a continually present nature:

> Somehow a tyrannous sense of a superincumbent oppression
> Still, wherever I go, accompanies ever, and makes me
> Feel like a tree (shall I say?) buried under a ruin of brickwork.
>
> (I. 36–38)

The solidity which has no splendour suffocates the soul in search of identity through the sense of history because the spirit of more perfect ages does not shine through it. It is brickwork not marble, it endures but it does not reflect. And this is because it embodies human failure not human ideals. Of the Coliseum, Claude writes:

> Doubtless the notion of grand and capacious and massive amusement,
> This the old Romans had; but tell me, is this an idea?
>
> (I. 46–47)

Nevertheless it is not as simple as this. The opening establishes an ambiguous relationship with Rome which becomes in the course of the first Canto a discriminating one. Houghton calls Claude's attitude to Rome vacillating, but I think that there is a straightforward progression. Visible Rome is rubbish, 'but I shrink and adapt myself to it'. It cannot be dismissed so easily, it inevitably impinges on identity, and though Claude recovers from this momentary shrinking to reassert his separateness from the seen world in the flamboyant inversion of the claim made about Augustus at the end of Letter II, a spirit of more perfect ages does emerge. At the end of the Canto, the question is not rhetorical:

> *Do I sink back on the old, or do I soar from the mean?*
> *So through the city I wander and question, unsatisfied ever,*
> *Reverent so I accept, doubtful because I revere.*
>
> (I. 282–284)

The reverence grows out of the perception of the true and false Romes. Even at the disillusioned opening Claude concedes that 'only the Arch of Titus and view from the Lateran please me'. The Arch of Titus belongs to the Rome of aggressive paganism (it is linked with the conquest of Jerusalem). From the moment at which Claude discovers not Christian neurosis but the Stoic-Epicurean acceptance, he is able to discriminate between the Horatian wisdom (in I. he celebrates the pagan survival with a version of lines from the Odes) and Jesuit repression. It is Loyola who becomes the focus of the superincumbent oppression:

> Innocent, playful follies, the toys and trinkets of childhood,
> Forced on maturer years, as the serious one thing needful ...
>
> (I. 80–81)

There is nothing distasteful about Claude's attack (as Houghton claims) – it is perfectly consistent with the interplay of growth and fixity which have already been established. 'Forced on maturer years' is a denial of growth, and the Jesuit responsibility for piling up rubbish (the Gesu, for example) and for 'overcrusting with slime' the true Rome fits in with this pattern. Through the rubbish and slime (Christianity), the continuing spirit of Rome emerges in the celebration of pagan monuments, the Pantheon (Dome of Agrippa), the immutable *manhood* of the marvellous twain (the Dioscuri), and the Vatican marbles. Inevitably bound up with this spirit is the spirit of the Renaissance (the Pantheon provides the link: Raphael is buried there, and Michelangelo's dome, St. Peter's, 'had hung the Pantheon in heaven'). Thus the epilogue to Canto I looks to Alba, birth-place of Romulus.

Of course this is not an unqualified illumination. It is rather a pro-gression – from disillusion through discrimination to a hesitant reverence. '*Do I sink back on the old, or do I soar from the mean*' probes questions which are unanswered in Canto I. 'I shrink and adapt myself to it' remains ambiguous because reverence may be immersion, the denial of growth; Emerson said of the tourist, 'he carries ruins to ruins'. But if the doubts are unanswered, they are not unanswerable. Claude precisely defines the condition which Rome can become a soaring from the mean in Letter X: 'Utter, O some one, the word that shall reconcile Ancient and Modern' – which demands a flow of time through the present into the future. The local 'some one' is Michelangelo, but we are already conscious that the Renaissance, as well as pagan Rome, is separated from the Modern by the Lutheran flood and the Loyolan slime. The reconciling word which gives continuity to the spirit of perfecter ages is the rhetoric of the historic defence of Rome. Looking back on 1849, Mazzini was to write: 'It was necessary that all should learn how potent was the immortality stirring beneath those ruins of two epochs, two worlds. I did feel that power, did feel the pulsations of the immense eternal life of Rome through the artificial crust with which priests had covered the great sleeper, as with a shroud.'

The sense of historic continuity in the historic act is important in the poem and we shouldn't be in too much of a hurry to point out the irony of non-commitment. In an unused but uncancelled passage in the main early draft of the poem,[2] this sense is explicit:

> Yet Politics, I will confess it,
> Yes, my political friends, I recant and acknowledge, have something
> Generous – something organic Creative and Art-like in them
>
> (*Poems*, p. 516)

Even here, of course, the assertion is ironically questioned: 'Politics, Art and Love – and the greatest of these is the purest'. But what is important is that it is possible to see the historical moment, the political act, as 'organic Creative'. Claude echoes the rhetoric of revolution.

Of course, the identification is only spasmodic and always absurdly sentimental ('Victory! Victory! – Yes! ah, yes, thou republican Zion'). However, this isn't a simple matter, because there is a complex relationship between subjectivity and objective truth in Claude's response. Of the French Revolution in 1848, Arnold wrote to Clough: 'Certainly the present spectacle in France is a fine one: mostly so indeed to the historical swift-kindling man ... Even to such a man revolutions and bodily illnesses are fine anodynes when he is agent or patient therein: but when he is spectator only, their kind effect is transitory.' Clough isn't capable of such predictably complacent irony (though in II. VI, Claude seems to be), but he is conscious of the historical vacuum of the tourist who can be no more than reporter. The verse of II. V, which records 30 April, exactly captures the interplay of presence and isolation:

> Twelve o'clock, on the Pincian Hill, with lots of English,
> Germans, Americans, French, – the Frenchmen, too, are protected,–
> So we stand in the sun, but afraid of a probable shower;
> So we stand and stare, and see, to the left of St. Peter's,
> Smoke, from the cannon, white, – but that is at intervals only,–
> Black, from a burning house, we suppose, by the Cavalleggieri;
> And we believe we discern some lines of men descending
> Down through the vineyard-slopes, and catch a bayonet gleaming.
> Every ten minutes, however, – in this there is no misconception, –
> Comes a great white puff from behind Michael Angelo's dome, and
> After a space the report of a real big gun, – not the Frenchman's?
>
> (II. 113–125)

The verse is vividly pictorial: the smoke, the gleaming bayonets and, rhythmically, the cliff-hanging 'and' of the penultimate line enact the movement and suspense of the battle with controlled narrative precision. But the accumulation of detail in the opening lines enacts a precise perspective too; Claude sees, but he sees from the Pincian, the favourite resort of the Northern tourist (who has been zeugmatically linked with Oudinot in the last line of the prologue to Canto II). And he stands among foreigners, including, ironically, Rome's enemies. Thus the whole passage is governed by the paralytic verbs of the raped spectator: 'So we stand and stare, and see', 'And we believe we discern', 'in this there is no misconception'.[3] The subjective disjunction implied here becomes more explicit in the following letters. II. VII makes it clear: 'So, I have seen a man killed! An experience that, among others!' 'Experience' is loaded with irony, for it is one which is seen and not lived. The hexameter allows for the juxtaposition of event and comment which undermines the event's immediacy and thus its meaningfulness. Later in the letter, Claude's paralytic isolation becomes farcically complete as he realises that, being dressed in black, he might be mistaken for a priest and so runs away from the crowd. The spectator is paralysed by what he *seems* to be, by his social shadow.

Thus, because he is a tourist, for Claude, the spirit of more perfect ages abiding in the historical event is an illusion. The perceptual self discerning the true Rome is unable to participate in the spirit's temporal continuity. Claude is able to share the rhetoric (the *Marseillaise*, for example) but not its realisation. But the irony is more complex than this. For the defence of Rome, as Mazzini admitted to Clough, was not undertaken in the hope of success, but in order to create a national consciousness. The flamboyant heroism throughout the siege was really a dramatised rhetoric itself. Claude's bitter '*Sanguis martyrum semen Ecclesiae*' is not inaccurate.[4]

The disengagement from the defence of Rome is not a refusal to act, but an awareness of the limitations of a particular rhetoric.

The farewell to Rome in III. XI, is, then, a rejection of a particular rhetoric, the 'ancient lyrical cadence' of Tibur and Anio, through an elaborate celebration and firm limiting. The opening lines (III. 214–219) evoke it only to comment on its unreality ('so not seeing I sang'). It is evoked a second time in terms not of literary convention but of narrative actuality ('here as I sit') but presence elicits rejection: 'so seeing and listening say I ... Tivoli beautiful is' only returns Claude to the unreality of the original invocation. So that the valley and villa of Horace is not the place to say farewell, but the Montorio, the key point for which the French troops were aiming in their last assault on Rome. The closing lines of the letter, bitterly but accurately, judge the spirit of eternal Rome, concretised in the Republic, to be merely a rhetorical illusion:

> But on Montorio's height, looking down on the tile-clad streets, the
> Cupolas, crosses, and domes, the bushes and kitchen-gardens,
> Which, by the grace of the Tiber, proclaim themselves Rome of the
>   Romans, –
> But on Montorio's height, looking forth to the vapoury mountains,
> Cheating the prisoner Hope with illusions of vision and fancy,– ...
> Waiting till Oudinot enter, to reinstate Pope and Tourist.

(III. 233–39)

The leisurely, end-stopped lines, the repetitive evocation of proper names, the accumulative Horatian rhetoric of the first twenty lines of the letter give way to the harsh enjambment and the perfunctory, generalised and plural catalogue of nouns, returning us again to the clutter of visible Rome. 'Proclaim themselves Rome of the Romans' clashes satirically with the last line (with its list of foreigners – barbarian invader, inheritor of the barbarian Spaniard, and barbarian tourist); the clash draws attention to the ambiguity of 'proclaim'. The Horatian wisdom and the spirit of more perfect ages depend on not seeing. Looking means seeing the defeat of Rome, and the word which links ancient and modern is merely declamation, doesn't relate to the actual: 'this Church is indeed of the purely *Invisible*, Kingdom-come kind'. The prologue to Canto III, it is true, momentarily offers a traditional refuge in an aesthetic contemplation of Rome but this exposes itself. '*Yet, at the worst of the worst, books and a chamber remain*' – we are thrust back to the whisper of doubt in the prologue to Canto I. The spirit of Rome can only live in its history – and its history is declamation.

Thus in Canto III, there is an increasing focus on the spatial continuity of love. Rome delusively offers continuity through the perceptual self; love begins in the social self, the shadow. I. XII moves from a jocular image of absorption in the language of the mercantile Trevellyns ('But I am in for it now – *laissez faire*, of a truth, *laissez aller*') into a series of images of sexual involvement (island of Circe, labyrinth, fissure). It is important to insist on this because critics have by and large tended to sentimentalise the theme of love in the poem. Naturally we are reminded of the *Roman Elegies*, in which, from the outset, Rome is meaningless without love: 'Oh, Rome, though you are a whole world, yet without love the world would not be the world, nor would Rome be Rome.'[5] The same point is made ironically in I. VII where Claude compares himself first to critical Iago, and then to 'poor critical coxcomb Adam!'. The exact echo of Genesis II. 20 ('But for Adam there is not found a help-meet for him') highlights the tension between the self as perceiver and the self as social animal. Adam the namer, Claude the topographical poet, is detached from the creation he celebrates (even if critically). Love offers the means of connection, as it does in Goethe.

But the *Roman Elegies* celebrate a very different kind of love. It is sexual, casual (the girl is a whore), and its object is Roman ('*Und der Barbare beherrscht römischen Busen und Leib*'). In *Amours de Voyage*, 'we turn like fools to the English'. Initially the communication is social, and Claude's connection is primarily an overcoming of class snobbery. If Goethe makes Rome meaningful through the lineaments of gratified desire, Claude merely finds a 'serene co-existence', a necessity simple, but one which can only be elaborated in a sentimental rhetoric:

Meat and drink and life, and music, filling with sweetness.
Thrilling with melody sweet, with harmonies strange overwhelming,
All the long-silent strings of an awkward, meaningless fabric.

(I. 172–174)

Claude himself assesses the rhetoric immediately by realising that the necessity simple could be fulfilled by nephews and nieces (the rational-isation here is significant: society isn't fair to Uncles, so they must fall in love). But it is important to note that it is the language which is treacherous. Claude muddles his metaphors: the long silent strings begin as strings of a piano which the harmonies strange of the female presence bring to life; but they end as the threads of a fabric which is incomplete (so that we move from musical strings to a warp and woof image). Thus the image changes from music/silence to meaning/meaninglessness. Treach-erously (because illogically) love (the love Mary offers) becomes more integral to being.

Claude is sliding from one cliché to another here, and this is bound up with the ambiguity of love in the poem. If we are conscious of Goethe (and we are obviously meant to be) we can see that Claude is not wrong to be indecisive about Mary: his mistake is to turn to the socially inte-grated English, when he really needs a Roman whore. 'Juxtaposition' accumulates ambiguities. The word on one level obviously associates with Goethe's sixth Elegy, which is a panegyric of the Goddess Opportunity (*Gelegenheit*) who is a goddess of the accepted moment. But Clough takes the word beyond its sexual connotations to something more sinister. 'But Allah is great, no doubt, and Juxtaposition his prophet' is more than an exasperated joke. 'Islam', Carlyle had said, meant 'that we must submit to God', so that it can become related to the social lie about marriage, the institutionalisation of a passing instinct through the myth of providence. It thus becomes associated with 'affinity' which can mean simply 'mar-riage'. The progression which Eustace initiates, and which becomes the agent of factitiousness, is 'juxtaposition', 'affinity', 'obligation', 'marriage'. Claude's hesitations are thus in the interests of truth. The socialisation of love is a lie. Juxtaposition is transitory: Mary in absence becomes 'a pale blank orb which no recollection will add to'. Affinity is extra-personal and pre-social. Lyell uses the word to describe the relationship between gradually differentiated species from a common stock, so that as soon as Claude is given the word in III. VII he explores its meaning in a recession through the stages of evolution, from mammals, through reptiles, to rocks and stones. The affinity of social love is no less a denial of self, than the affinity of biological origin, and it is more absurd because it is a lie. Claude ends the letter with a momentary desire to return to 'that perfect and primitive silence' – the pre-self is real, and anti-self ('duty') is hypocritical. The rhetoric of Victorian love is as factitious as the rhetoric of Italy.

There is a third mode of continuity in the poem which postulates a definition of being independent of the perceptual and the social selves. As we have seen immortal Rome is a tourist's delusion, and love a conventional lie: both lead back to the social self, the shadow without substance. Both are ultimately measured against a romantic image of self through growth. The most explicit introduction of this theme is in one of the first letters about love:

> There are two different kinds, I believe, of human attraction:
> One which simply disturbs, unsettles, and makes you uneasy,
> And another that poises, retains, and fixes and holds you.
> I have no doubt, for myself, in giving my voice for the latter.
> I do not wish to be moved, but growing where I was growing,
> There more truly to grow, to live where as yet I had languished.
> I do not like being moved: for the will is excited; and action
> Is a most dangerous thing; I tremble for something factitious,
> Some malpractice of heart and illegitimate process;
> We are so prone to these things with our terrible notions of duty.
>
> (II. 266–275)

The modulation of tone here is so precise that we can no longer ignore the function of Claude, and it is in connection with the theme of growth that Claude's rôle becomes most important. Clough firmly places him with 'and action/Is a most dangerous thing' in which the hesitant voice of the enjambment leads one to expect an important statement which materialises, in the downward curve of the intonation, as a hurry-scurry piece of evasiveness. But a careful equilibrium is created by the accuracy of the last line. It is an accuracy of social observation ('*we* are so prone') which contrasts with the pompous emptiness of the philosophic generalisation. The available social context *has* terrible notions of duty: we think of Eustace, of George, even of Mary who accuses Claude of being 'not quite fair to the party' and who is deeply conscious of the social advantage of only letting Claude know what it is 'right' to let him know. This balance allows us to take seriously the image of growth against which Claude is opposing the atrophy of convention. The attraction which disturbs and unsettles, is the kind offered by the socially defined Mary because it is bound up with the factitious choice of conventional action in the hope that it will furnish belief. Literally she *moves* him, and the comic justice of Canto IV punishes Claude with a frantic, meaningless pursuit. But punishes him partly, surely, because he has given in to the factitious at that point. The parody of *Julius Caesar*, 'there is a tide, at least, in the *love* affairs of mortals', places the pursuit as a kind of sexual opportunism: marriage might show a profit.

But in the passage I've just quoted, the marital lie is firmly placed against the imagery of growth. 'To live where as yet I had languished' suggests the casualness of *natura naturans* in which a momentary sexual encounter releases Spring. The pressures which drive Claude from Eden in the following letter are the pressures which institutionalise time through marriage: 'Bid me not venture on aught that could alter or end what is present'. I don't see how Houghton can talk of Claude's fear of sex. What he fears is the factitious rhetoric of institutionalised love; 'let love be its own inspiration'.

Only in the last canto does Claude associate his relationship with Mary with the possibility of growth:

> I, who refused to enfasten the roots of my floating existence
> In the rich earth, cling now to the hard, naked rock that is left me.
>
> (V. 66–67)

This certainly ironically rebounds on Claude. His refusal to accept the social lie inevitably becomes a refusal to accept *natura naturans* as well. But the ironies are more complex than this. The shrewdness of social observation comically recoils, but it does so because of Claude's philosophic inadequacy. In the passage I have just quoted from Canto II, we note the familiarity of the verbs describing the attraction which is *natura naturans*: 'poises and fixes and holds you'. It sends us back a hundred lines to the passage in which Claude meets the crowd which is about to murder the priest:

> Gradually, thinking still of St. Peter's, I became conscious
> Of a sensation of movement opposing me, – tendency this way
> (Such as one fancies may be in a stream when the wave of the tide is
> Coming and not yet come, – a sort of poise and retention);
>
> (II. 170–174)

In Canto III, the image of growth is rejected by the opposing imagery of chaos ('Let us not talk of growth; we are still in our Aqueous Ages'). But we can see that the image of growth has built into the rhetoric of chaos, (the unruly mob, the tidal wave). By an accident of language arising from Claude's own factitious acceptance of 'growth', the association of Mary with growth in V is already nostalgia for an image that never was, for a rhetoric which contains its own contradiction. The rootlessness of Canto IV is not a confrontation with his mistakes. The metaphor of growth with that of eternal Rome and love is cast on to the Testaceo.

Unless we admit that this is what is happening, the end becomes incoherent, whereas it is the enactment of incoherence. Claude in Canto V searches desperately for any means of continuity, reaching the depths of intellectual depravity when he finds comfort in a barrel-organ in Florence. Truly, he is not broken: the factitious comforts are rapidly rejected. Houghton rightly emphasises the importance of knowledge at the end of the poem. But we should recognise how limited the discovery is. The celebration of knowledge receives exactly the same ironic inflation as the other moral codes which are rejected: 'Faith, I think, does pass, and Love; but Knowledge abideth', and the letter ends with the transition from celebration to deflation which is the established modal movement of the poem: 'Eastward, then, I suppose, with the coming of winter, to Egypt'.

The knowledge that Claude finds it possible to believe in has nothing to do with routine Victorian refuges in knowledge (sweetness and light or positivism, for example). The least ironised affirmation comes immediately after Claude has seen through the falsity of religious comfort:

> What with trusting myself and seeking support from within me,
> Almost I could believe I had gained a religious assurance,
> Found in my own poor soul a great moral basis to rest on.
> Ah, but indeed I see, I feel it factitious entirely;
> I refuse, reject, and put it utterly from me;
> I will look straight out, see things, not try to evade them;
> Fact shall be fact for me, and the Truth the Truth as ever,
> Flexible, changeable, vague, and multiform, and doubtful. –
> Off, and depart to the void, thou subtle, fanatical tempter!
>
> (V. 95–103)

We can see how far Claude has gone beyond 'honest doubt'. There is *no* moral basis, not even self-reliance. In the following passage, Claude foresees himself admitting the fanatical tempter again in the face of death ('When the pulses are weak, and the feeble light of the reason/Flickers, an unfed flame retiring slow from the socket'). So that there is not even the morality of disbelief, since that too will perish before the ultimate absurdity. At the same time, this is a positive statement, because Claude uses the verb 'rest on' to describe his relation to the moral basis. Thus he pins it down as a psychological need: the initial search for continuity is itself specious. And what he thrust back on is the mere flux of the phenomenal. There is no continuity through memory, as in Tennyson, no consistency through stoic withdrawal as in Arnold, not even growth as in Wordsworth. Merely total empiricism: Clough has retreated from the reconstructive rhetoric of Romantic and Victorian poetry to the chaos of the multiform, to the honesty of David Hume.

III

Amours de Voyage is an experimental poem with no real precedent in English. Even its relationship with the *Roman Elegies* is as we have seen, by no means imitative (though Goethe obviously gave Clough the idea). To some extent, Goethe is to Clough as Virgil is to Pope. His poem is a referential ideal, in which Rome is discovered through love, ironically played off against the actual possibilities available to an intellectual Englishman. *Amours de Voyage* is in itself an ironic title: it is Goethe, not Claude who has an 'amour'. Yet the poem is much more than a decreative inversion (the strangling of romantic love by 'romantic' marriage), and it moves not towards total antithesis (as Book Four of the *Dunciad* does) but towards moral anarchy.

One wants above all to use the word 'wit' about Clough's best poetry, and by this I mean that we are aware of a sophisticated verbal mode of discrimination among values. It is not insignificant that Clough should have had so much admiration for the eighteenth century, for he alone among the most important Victorian poets is capable of maintaining the same detached ironic interest in language as an index of cultural values that Swift and Pope had. Yet there are obvious and vast differences. Pope's detachment is bound up with an assurance about the values among which he is discriminating (I don't mean this in a *simpliste* way, but in the sense that he knows that the languages which he is exploiting relate to systems of value which are coherent and stable). Clough doesn't have this assurance because by the 1840s the stability of relationship between language and meaning has disappeared. Thus in 'Duty – that's to say complying' there is a tension between two levels of irony. For the first 38 lines, we have an accurate and straightforward satire based on the antithesis of ideal and actual meanings of 'duty'. The final couplet, however, introduces a different tone:

> Moral blank, and moral void,
> 　Life at very birth destroyed,
> Atrophy, exinanition!
> Duty! –
> Yea, by duty's prime condition
> 　Pure nonentity of duty!
>
> 　　　　　　　　　　　　*(Poems, p. 28)*

The breakdown of metrical control, the enacted incoherence, throws doubt on the irony of the opening of the poem. The firm moral sense is there, but the assurance of communication has gone. And this takes us beyond the exasperated indignation of the single-word fourth line to the insoluble ambiguities of the fifth and sixth. Is Clough still contrasting real and actual meanings of 'Duty', or is 'Duty' itself a nonentity? How can a word which was originally something, however distorted, become pure *nothing*? We are thrust back on the literal meaning of the first line through a double irony. Thus the motive of Clough's irony is, like Pope's, related to the awareness of the threat to language as an accurate medium of communicating values. But its discovery is radically different: in the historical context, language itself is suspect.

In a more complex way, this sense of both the urgent need for an ironic verbal discrimination and of its impossibility dominates the experimentalism of *Armours de Voyage*. Light dies not only at the uncreating word of dulness but also of wit. This is why it is so important that Claude writes letters, because what matters is not experience itself, but the verbalisation of experience. The letters of Georgina and Mary offer a different, 'witless' language which challenges Claude's. Equally important is that the letters are one way. Originally Clough had one letter from Eustace, but rightly he abandoned it because it would have established a dialogue which would have distracted our attention from the act of verbalisation. In Canto V, Eustace even becomes an unknown God, and there is a good deal of comedy arising from Mary's letters to Miss Roper which spend a lot of time repeating Miss Roper's information, so that Clough goes out of his way to alert us to the *self*-exposure of the language. From this need, too, arises the social definition of Claude. He has to be '*very* clever' (though not very original) because he is to celebrate the available languages of coherence. Equally he has to be very inexperienced because he is to measure these languages against multiform fact. So it is that Claude is in pursuit, very often, of the phrase which will cope with what he is learning:

> Mild monastic faces in quiet collegiate cloisters:
> *So let me offer* a single and celibatarian phrase ...
>
> (III. 182–83: my italics)

Thus his way of coping with the superincumbent oppression of Rome is to offer a witty inversion of the bricks-and-marbles dictum; thus, at the moment of disillusion, he constructs a formal elegy for Manara and Medici and comments: 'All declamation, alas! *though I talk*'.

The primary attention to language explains the 'hurry-scurry anapaests' as well. Clough needs a metre which can accommodate and judge available rhetorics within the line. A simple example is '*Dulce* it is, and *decorum*, no doubt, for the country to fall'. The main structure exactly follows the Latin syntax through the postponement of 'pro patria mori' to the end of the line. But by splitting up 'dulce et decorum est', Claude adjudicates between the two virtues: dulce, yes, decorum, perhaps. Thus the possibility of the aphorism's factitiousness is built into an almost exact evocation: a tension is established between a subjective need and an objective value. Obviously too, 'no doubt' establishes an intonation of modern colloquialism which interrogates the objective availability of the Horatian language. The juxtaposition of the colloquial and the Latin makes the *latinate* syntax of the end of the line ambivalent. The irony works both ways: the aphorism is made to seem pompous through the casual deflation, and the

undergraduate intonation is made to seem unheroic. The narrative bears
this out: Claude is comically unheroic, but the heroism is merely
rhetorical. Only the hexameter could have achieved this complexity. A
pentameter would not have allowed for the necessary expansion, and an
iambic could not have balanced the rhetorically placed 'it is' against the
conversational 'no doubt'. Naturally the verse doesn't regularly work in
this way, but it always works to the same end which is the self-exposure
of language. Pope uses the heroic couplet to discriminate the antithesis of
language and actuality: Clough uses the hexameter to discriminate the
conflict of languages.

It is this which makes the poem a great one. Formally, it is not merely
experimental, it is an experiment. Its expansiveness gives us the opportunity
to watch available languages, metaphors and intonations work themselves
out and mutate into something else. At the beginning of Canto III, for
example Claude narrates quite historically his discovery of the imagery
of the Aqueous Ages first on the boat and then looking at the Triton in
Rome. 'Let us not talk of growth; we are still in our Aqueous Ages' is an
improvised epigram growing out of the collision of Genesis and Evolution
in a context of organic being and flux (the collision is only made explicit in
an unfortunately omitted passage). A little later he elaborates on the
improvisation through a formal restatement of alternative images:

> Not, as we read in the words of the olden-time inspiration,
> Are there two several trees in the place we are set to abide in;
> But on the apex most high of the Tree of Life in the Garden,
> Budding, unfolding, and falling, decaying and flowering ever,
> Flowering is set and decaying the transient blossom of Knowledge, –
> Flowering alone, and decaying, the needless, unfruitful blossom.
> Or as the cypress-spires by the fair-flowing stream Hellespontine,
> Which from the mythical tomb of the godlike Protesilaüs
> Rose sympathetic in grief to his love-lorn Laodamia,
> Evermore growing, and, when in their growth to the prospect
> attaining,
> Over the low sea-banks, of the fatal Ilian city,
> Withering still at the sight which still they upgrow to encounter.
> Ah, but ye that extrude from the ocean your helpless faces,
> Ye over stormy seas leading long and dreary processions,
> Ye, too, brood of the wind, whose coming is whence we discern not,
> Making your nest on the wave, and your bed on the crested billow,
> Skimming rough waters, and crowding wet sands at the tide shall
> return to,
> Cormorants, ducks, and gulls fill ye my imagination!
> Let us not talk of growth we are still in our Aqueous Ages.

(III. 79–97)

Clearly, the first two paragraphs express the transience of growth in terms of knowledge and love respectively. The first image ironises Genesis by making knowledge (which involved the fall) the high point of life, and ironises knowledge by making it a parasitic, fruitless and futile failure of growth to become anything more than process. The second, classical image makes the same point about love which also grows without achieving its end. But this image too relates to Wordsworth's *Laodamia* in which the trees are emblems of nature's participation in grief. The differences are immense. Wordsworth's last line fixes the process in a synoptically grasped pattern by containing it in the interplay of nouns: 'A constant interchange of growth and blight'. The 'interchange' is acted out in Clough, and what we have is not a contained pattern, but the syntax of a vicious circle. This is obvious from the refusal of the process to go beyond its continuing verbs ('withering' being a participle, and 'to encounter' being an infinitive). Rhythmically, the repetition of 'still' makes for a buffeting to and fro within the line. The finality of the necessarily heavy stress on 'upgrow' leaves the rest of the line to die out like a loosely swinging rope. Thus, within the hexameter, Clough enacts the moral anarchy of the image's refusal to achieve its purpose. The same is true of the first image, in which the repetition of 'flowering ... decaying' keeps the flower of knowledge in futile and incomplete movement. Both images are condemned to a Sisyphus-like striving after what they always just miss.

The elaboration is necessary because what is emerging is not just the inadequacy of love and knowledge, but the failure of the rhetoric of growth to achieve any finality. The 'Not ... or ... but' structure of the passage has no logical justification, but arises from the refusal of the first two images to focus properly. The literary images of growth press forward through their self-exposure to the natural image at the end. This is an image without fixity, without pretensions to coherence. There is no attempt to control the subjective distortions: 'Ye that extrude from the ocean your helpless faces' is viable only as a visual illusion and the violently active verb taken with 'helpless' implies an unresolved ambiguity in the relationship between freedom and necessity. In the anarchy of the sea, there is no defined and stable distinction between inner and outer. 'Cormorants, ducks, and gulls, fill ye my imagination' takes us into a nightmare world of invading flux. The important point, however, is that this is arrived at through a dramatic interplay of traditional metaphoric vehicles of coherence. Language itself is treacherous.

This is why comparison with Eliot is so irrelevant. In Clough there is no grasping of surviving fragments of tradition in a culturally sterile world. The tradition itself is what overwhelms and betrays: culture is a lie, anarchy the only truth. Any less elaborate structure would have been inadequate to enact the poem's radical discovery. Any more formal discipline would have been factitious (which is what we may feel about

In Memoriam after all, and even *Empedocles*). Clough creates a form which gives 'the strange disease of modern life' a local habitation and a name. The disease is a disease of language, the available rhetorics are shipwrecked on the ocean of protracted exposure. Many images are called, but in the end there are few left to be chosen. Only a form which is in itself an experiment which is prepared to float language and watch it become what it didn't set out to be, could have achieved this. For an aqueous age, Clough creates an aqueous poem, and I don't know of any English poet who has achieved so accurate an instrument of ironic openness. It is no use reviving Clough on a margin of minority. *Amours de Voyage* ought to be given major currency.

Notes

1.   Quotations from Clough's poetry are from *The Poems of Arthur Hugh Clough*, Oxford 1951. For poems other than *Amours de Voyage* page references are given, as are references to variant readings recorded in the notes. For *Amours de Voyage* reference is to Canto and Line number.

2.   Even a critique which has no pretensions to being scholarly has to make difficult decisions about the text of *Amours de Voyage*. Much of the variant material would obviously just clutter up the poem and Clough was clearly right to repress it in 1858. But knowing what we do about Clough's later years, are we right to trust him as an editor? Some passages seem to be rejected on grounds of prudence, and it is therefore necessary to exercise a local discretion.

3.   It is worth comparing this passage with the accounts in Henry James's *William Wetmore Story and his Friends*, pp. 133–155, which give exactly the same impression of excitement and remoteness.

4.   Trevelyan vividly re-creates the splendidly Romantic heroism of the Romans in *Garibaldi's Defence of the Roman Republic* (1907).

5.   David Luke's translation (*The Penguin Goethe*, p. 91). The German is:
   Eine Welt zwar bist du, o Rom; doch ohne die Liebe
   Wäre die Welt nicht die Welt, wäre denn Rom auch nicht Rom.

CHAPTER 3

Adam Bede

Adam Bede can be described as the first major exercise in programmatic literary realism in English literature. Yet most of the essays which approach it as a totality are content to treat it as a dramatic poem.[1] It is not difficult to see why this has happened. As Ian Gregor has argued, there is, despite the precision of dates, very little sense of the historical actuality of the vast upheavals in rural life which typify the 1790s.[2] The suggestions of historical change are marginal. If the Poysers are threatened by squirearchic tyranny, this is only to show their resilience. If Loamshire is ominously juxtaposed with Stonyshire, the relationship is merely symbolic and there is no sense of the new world really impinging on the old. Methodism is brought in only to show how unimportant it is as a social force in a rural community, and ultimately it serves merely as the particular 'clothing' of Dinah's humanitarianism. Time itself, in fact, is primarily a cyclical presence (naturally, Loamshire is bound up with the seasons), and it only has a linear existence in the context of purely personal histories. Loamshire is protected from time by the hills that surround it, for they are 'wooed from day to day by the changing hours, but responding with no change in themselves' (ch. 2). Thus the historical specificity seems merely decorative, a matter of giving the symbolic patterns a local habitation.

However, Ian Gregor has equally shown that an approach to the novel in terms of its symbolic patterns necessarily makes it incoherent: it is both pastoral, a celebration of the idealized past, and moral fable, looking forward to the great interior dramas of George Eliot's later work. I have no intention of resolving the duality that he perceives, because it is certainly there. What needs to be shown is that it grows out of an inner coherence which can only be fully defined by approaching the novel in terms of its explicit programme and the problems that it raises.

The most obvious rehearsal of the social reality of *Adam Bede* is in George Eliot's review of Riehl's *The Natural History of German Life*,[3] in which she describes, with details that are repeated in the novel, what she regards as the English equivalent of the German peasantry: 'we must remember what the tenant farmers and small proprietors were in England half a century ago'. The context of the passage is extremely important.

George Eliot begins with a didactic rationale of realism in art: 'Art is the nearest thing to life; it is a mode of amplifying experience and extending our contact with our fellow men'. Riehl achieves this, though he is not an artist, through his descriptions of the peasantry. The essay concludes with a statement of George Eliot's 'social-political-conservatism'. Approvingly, she summarizes Riehl's views: 'He sees in European society *incarnate history*, and any attempt to disengage it from its historical elements must, he believes, be simply destructive of social vitality. What has grown up historically can only die out historically by the gradual operation of necessary laws'.

'History' in this passage has a very specialized meaning which would be better covered by 'tradition' which *pervades* history. George Eliot focuses on the German peasantry and its English equivalent because 'it is among the peasantry that we must look for the historical type of the national physique', thus on an essence which transcends specific historical conditions, but which is more or less disguised by them. The German peasantry, then, approximates more nearly to the laboratory conditions necessary for the study of 'the popular character', because it is less prone to historical mutation than more sophisticated groups. Thus it serves more readily for the extension of sympathies with the populace because its portrayal is the nearest thing to a *natural* history of 'life'. Moreover, it is good evidence of the need for 'the vital connection' with the past which nourishes progress and makes it natural or organic (incarnate, in fact):

> The nature of European man has its roots intertwined with the past, and can only be developed by allowing those roots to remain undisturbed while the process of development is going on, until that perfect ripeness of the seed which carries with it a life independent of the root. This vital connection with the past is much more vividly felt on the Continent than in England, where we have to recall it by an effort of memory and reflection; for though our English life is in its core intensely traditional, Protestantism and commerce have modernized the face of the land and the aspects of society in a far greater degree than in any continental country ...

This makes it clear why, if George Eliot is to write a natural history of English life both to effect a real extension of sympathies and to illustrate a process of development which is organically related to the past, she has to choose an epoch in which 'the core' is still visible in 'the face of the land'. She has to choose an historical reality that she can dehistoricize, and which is not modernized by the Industrial Revolution. There are two reasons why she should choose the 1790s and not an earlier period. Firstly, she mentions that Protestantism as well as commerce has 'modernized' the face of the land. Unless she is going to write a medieval novel, she therefore has to choose a phase in which Protestantism has ceased to be protesting. In *Adam Bede* Anglicanism has become socially catholic, an integral part of a whole community and neither exclusive nor proselytizing. Moreover, it is morally organic: it no longer focuses on specialized activities (prayer, worship), but takes in the whole of man's activity. It is the nearest modern equivalent to the religion of Carlyle's Abbey of St Edmund, which is explicitly contrasted, in *Past and Present*, with Methodism. Thus, by choosing an era of 'catholic' Anglicanism which post-dates the Methodist Movement, George Eliot is able to emphasize its rootedness by contrast.

This leads to the second reason, which is that the choice of 1799 is a defiant one. The 'modernizing' influences of history are there in the novel. Arthur Donnithorne returns from Ireland full of plans for 'drainage and enclosure'. His grandfather tries to make the Poysers specialize as dairy-farmers, and, of course, Methodism is a force which sets Will Maskery against Irwine, which separates Seth Bede from his work, and which creates incipient hysteria in Hayslope. But none of these threats is realized, because George Eliot is concerned to demonstrate the intensity of tradition and the resilience of the core even in years of acute crisis. Against the factitious historical changes, too, there will be, in the presentation of Adam himself, a demonstration of the true, evolutionary process of development in which ripeness rather than severance creates a life independent of the root.

This defiant dehistoricization is borne out by the novel's technique. The early parts of the book show a persistent tendency to resolve the narrative into pictures. We begin with the static vision of the workshop, and when the men begin to talk it is as though a painting were to begin to move. Later, Dinah 'stood with her left hand towards the descending sun' (ch. 2), and our first view of Adam's home is equally pictorial: 'The door of the house is open, and an elderly woman is looking out; but she is not placidly contemplating the evening sunshine' (ch. 4). The whole community moves, in Book II, towards the stasis of the church scene: 'I beseech you to imagine Mr. Irwine looking round on this scene ... And over all streamed the delicious June sunshine through the old windows ...' (ch. 18). The comparison to Dutch genre painting is thus more than a plea for humble and rustic life: it really defines the procedure of fixing the core through the arrested moment. Hence the important emphasis on sunlight; E. H. Gombrich has said that Vermeer, through the use of light, gives his animate portrayals the stability of the still life, and George Eliot does the same – she fixes the world she describes through the creation of representative scenes. Thus the novel has the air of an anthropologist's notebook: 'Have you ever seen a real English rustic perform a solo dance? ... Wiry Ben never smiled; he looked as serious as a dancing monkey ...' (ch. 25). Even Mrs. Poyser is to be read as an 'original': 'Sharp! yes, her tongue is like a new-set razor. She's quite original in her talks too; *one of those* untaught wits that help to stock a country with proverbs' (ch. 33 – my italics). The 'pastoral' structure of the novel, with its fixed, cyclical rhythms and its illustrative 'types', is there not to idealize a past and to provide criteria for judging the present so much as to create a medium for the 'natural' historian. And if the medium is fixed, it is still part of a *process*. The animal imagery which is so prevalent in the novel is not merely serving an aesthetic function; it also establishes an evolutionary scale. And it is on this scale that human change bases itself. Thus the pupils of Bartle Massey: 'It was almost as if three rough animals were making humble efforts to learn how they might become human' (ch. 21).

We shall see that this evolutionary process, the struggle of the individual to adapt to the given medium, is precisely the basis of the moral fable. In the contrasting stories of Hetty and Adam we have an evolutionary drama of alienation and individuation which can only take place on a 'pastoral' stage. We shall see too that this involves an important transformation: social convention becomes natural law.

II

This transformation is enacted within the novel, and it only becomes clear with the wisdom of hindsight. Initially we have the sense of an appearance of stability ironically underscored by its historical limitations. Thus, though Hall Farm has the order and integrity of pastoral, its temporality is implied in our first view of it as though it were a manor 'in the early stage of a chancery suit'; however rooted the Poysers think themselves, the farm has a history to which they do not belong, so that they are themselves the instruments of change. The structure of the first three books as a whole moves ominously towards crisis. The first book moves spatially through the social totality to give a precise delineation of social distinction; the second, through the focus of the church service, brings together the society as an organic community. Both books have undertones of change (Methodism and the death of Thias Bede), but predominantly they establish the everyday life of the community. This prepares us for the unique, and therefore historical event of Arthur's birthday feast in the third book. Here the separate orders of society confront one another, so that from class-distinction we turn to class-relationship. Both the comedy of the arrangements, carefully organized so as to include the whole community and to preserve the social distinctions, and the satire of the upper-class incomprehension and intolerance of the lower orders (Lydia Donnithorne and Chad's Bess) illustrate the paternalist basis of human relationships. Irwine sets the tone when he says: 'In this sort of thing people are constantly confounding liberality with riot and disorder' (ch. 22), and Arthur dramatizes the paternalist ideal (liberality and order) in the feudal ceremony of Adam's promotion. At the same time we are conscious that the order is being destroyed by the hierarchic relationships it supports. The tributes of Poyser and Adam to Arthur are the central ironies of the book: we know that the class-gap is being closed by exploitation: the public liberality which goes with order is undermined by the private liberality, the locket and earrings that will disrupt that order. Book II opens with the Poysers making their way to church, a unified group which is a microcosm of the integrity of the community; Book III also opens with the Poysers' journey, but preluded by Hetty's secret, so that we have a sense of the group riding to its destruction.

That this should emerge in the very section which highlights the social structure through its special celebration emphasizes how much, in one perspective, the disruptive change grows out of the existing order. Arthur's feeling for Hetty is intensified by Mrs. Irwine's consciously class-based remark: 'What a pity such beauty as that should be thrown away among the farmers, when it's wanted so terribly among the good families' (ch. 25). Arthur's disruptive egoism grows directly out of his social situation. This is insisted on from his first appearance: 'If you want to know more particularly how he looked, call to your remembrance some tawny-whiskered, brown-locked, clear-complexioned young Englishman whom you have met with in a foreign town, and been proud of as a fellow-countryman' – the compliment depends on the Grand Tour. Everything about him suggests the paternalist psychology: he is keen on enclosure and admires Arthur Young; if he reads the *Lyrical Ballads* it is for *The Ancient Mariner*, not for the scenes of humble, rustic life, which he dismisses as 'twaddle stuff' (so that he is incapable of learning from *The Thorn*, for example). His evasion of moral responsibility recalls the explicit doctrine of *Tom Jones*: 'There was a sort of implicit confidence in him that he was really such a good fellow at bottom, Providence would not treat him harshly' (ch. 29), and when he is arranging his conscience to cope with his dishonesty by marrying Hetty off to Adam, he resorts to a note of aristocratic cosmic optimism which might come from the *Essay on Man*: 'So good comes out of evil. Such is the beautiful arrangement of things' (ch. 29). And, obviously, it is a class-psychology which allows him to destroy Hetty. The sin becomes a peccadillo because the gentleman can always compensate. Compensation creates a safe distance between offender and victim because it easily merges into another class notion, 'liberality'. The process is made explicit in Arthur's childhood: he kicks over an old man's broth in a fit of temper and repents by giving him a favourite pencil-case. He makes retribution for an offence against human relations with a *thing*; the thing has no relevance to the old man's needs, and its value is defined entirely by Arthur. The liberality and the solipsism are equally part of the same habitual process of reducing human relationships to a reflection of the social hierarchy. By the same class-psychology, he has to limit his relationship to Hetty to exploitation: 'No gentleman, out of a ballad, could marry a farmer's niece' (ch. 13). Thus the potential of social tragedy is certainly laid in the opening books of the novel: the order which seems pastoral, is threatened by its own basis in class-deference.

In one sense, this potential is realized. In his clash with Arthur, Adam momentarily crosses from deferential humility to egalitarian defiance: 'I don't forget what's owing to you as a gentleman, but in this thing we're man and man, and I can't give up' (ch. 28). Arthur tries to assert his class-privilege, but has to recognize his defeat and hide behind it afterwards: 'Even the presence of Pym, waiting on him with the usual deference, was a reassurance to him after the scenes of yesterday' (ch. 29). Nor is the private conflict merely a parable of possible social upheaval. The old Squire's threat to turn out the Poysers is, it is true, never fully realized, but this is precisely because structurally it is highly ironic. It is the new Squire, with his millennial promise, who is destroying the basis of the Poysers' world, and, immediately after the old man's threat has dissolved in gentle comedy, Hetty discovers her pregnancy and sets off to Windsor.

But, of course, in the end this does not mean disruption. The social group merely loses an unassimilable fragment, and the only result is that Adam joins the Poyser family, not on the false basis of marriage with the niece who doesn't love him, but on the basis of marriage with the sincere niece. The ending of the novel demands a different perspective on the total structure, and this means that we are conscious of a narrowing-down process which finally undermines the novel's potential for social tragedy. At the beginning the massively established world of Hayslope is threatened by three major possibilities of change, Methodism, the death of Thias Bede, and the affair between Arthur and Hetty, suggesting religious upheaval for Hayslope as a whole, familial disruption for the Bedes, and social exploitation of the Poysers. By Book IV the novel has been reduced to the last of these, which is also the most private. Dinah and Lisbeth appear at this stage of the story only as background, and the Poysers recede increasingly into the background (the structural gratuitous-ness of the chapter called 'The Bitter Waters Spread' is obvious). The seduction theme is severed from the social portrayal, so that, in so far as it has any social implication at all, Hetty's story is simply that of the outcast.

This change in perspective is implicit from the beginning in the ideological shaping of the social realism. Even Arthur, who is the most socially defined character in the novel, is also a moral case. His decision to conceal the truth about Hetty from Adam is partly a patronizing egoism (note the tone of chivalry in 'his first duty was to guard her'), but is also an immoral attempt to mitigate the law of consequences through the principle of expediency ('duty was become a question of tactics'). This is precisely the basis of Herbert Spencer's attack on the Utilitarians.[4] For him, the law of right is a law of perfection, and, though imperfect man is unable to fulfil it, to substitute an interim law of expediency is disastrous. Men have 'to give up their own power of judging what *seems* best' and act according to 'the belief that that only *is* best which is abstractedly right'. In Spencer's terms, Arthur is a moral infidel who doubts the efficiency and foresight of the Divine arrangements, and 'with infinite presumption' supposes a human judgment less fallible. This is the basis of Spencer's argument against ameliorative legislation: 'all interposing between human-ity and the conditions of its existence, cushioning-off consequences by poor laws and the like – serves but to neutralize the remedy and prolong the evil'. Arthur is to be condemned not only on the grounds of his own egoism, but because he wants, by exercising his social discretion, to miti-gate the consequences for Hetty of her folly.

The important phrase is 'conditions of existence'. It suggests both natural conditions and social environment. For Spencer there is no real difference. Although man's evolution is from pre-social egoism to social altruism (or, rather, enlightened self-interest), this is merely the exchange of one fixed medium for another. Progress is a matter of man's adaptation to the fixed laws of the social state: 'The social state is a necessity. The conditions of greatest happiness under that state are fixed. *Our characters are the only things not fixed.* They, then, must be moulded into fitness for conditions'. Thus, although Spencer would have agreed with George Eliot that the imperfections of society are 'the manifestation of the inher-ited internal conditions in the human beings who compose it', and that therefore it is folly to attempt to change society by legislation, he also argues that the individual must perfect himself by bending to the social law. The apparent contradiction is resolved by a belief in 'the operation of natural laws' and in particular the law of natural selection: 'He on whom his own stupidity, or vice, or idleness, entails loss of life, must, in the generalizations of philosophy, be classed with the victims of weak viscera or malformed limbs'. Society, then, is a natural law. He who fulfils its demands will inevitably contribute to its improvement. He who fails will also contribute, but by being expelled.

In Spencerian terms, Hetty is obviously a case of a 'fatal nonadaptation'. But this is not a simple 'example'. Mimetically, Hetty is a brilliant study in alienation. She has to mediate her relationship with her social reality by living in a dream of the luxurious future in which she escapes the present. We can put it this way because in two respects George Eliot remains dispassionately descriptive. Firstly, her dream world is given psychological definition: 'Young souls, in such pleasant delirium as hers, are as unsym-pathetic as butterflies sipping nectar; they are isolated from all appeals by a barrier of dreams (ch. 9). If 'unsympathetic' is rigorously judging, its context, 'delirium' and 'barrier', qualifies the sense of responsibility.

Secondly, the alienation has a social basis. Hetty's performance in front of the mirror (ch. 15) is primarily intended to show how she inhabits a world of appearances (she is, of course, a moral Duessa), but it is also clearly a response to a concrete reality insisted on by the blindless windows and the blotchy mirror with its tarnished gilding which, like Hall Farm itself, belongs to a world of faded gentility. The Poysers inhabit a middle-class no-man's-land which glimpses at, but never achieves luxury. There are moments when we feel that Hetty's is a sympathetic rebellion. 'Hetty would have been glad to hear that she should never see a child again' is supposed to be shocking, but surely only on the basis of a sentimental stock response. Totty *is* unbearable, and the pampering she gets from her mother doesn't suggest human love so much as lower-middle-class stupidity. Again, in a later episode, Adam gives Hetty a rose, which Hetty puts in her hair. Immediately 'the tender admiration in Adam's face was slightly shadowed by reluctant disapproval' (ch. 20), and he rebukes her for aspiring to the finery of the great ladies of the hall. The gesture is flippant, but it is hardly worthy of an instant sermon, and when, after this, Hetty dresses up as Dinah, we feel that it is a judgment on the ponderous morality of the Hayslope world as well as on Hetty. Later, in *Far From the Madding Crowd*, Hardy will see the vanity of woman as part of the indirect language with which she has to communicate her independence to a world of men, but in *Adam Bede* it means only isolation, and the isolated is a moral invalid.

For the fully realized alienation is subjected to an ideological framework. When we are told that 'Hetty would have cast all her past life behind her and never cared to be reminded of it again' (ch. 15), we have to see it as a biological deformity: she cannot shape herself to the medium she finds herself in. And in this respect, the authorial commentary has to work very hard. The evolutionary scale established in the descriptions of Massey's pupils and Wiry Ben becomes, in Hetty's case, overwhelmingly important. The lower orders are animals making efforts to become human. The Poysers are higher up the social, and therefore the evolutionary, scale, and thus the demands their environment makes are more sophisticated (the crucial test, as Creeger has pointed out, is the altruistic love of children). Hetty is, however, less than human. The animal imagery is bewildering but ideologically definitive: she is, at different times, a kitten, a duck, a lamb, a calf (all these on her first appearance), a butterfly, a pigeon, a canary, and a Brazilian monkey. She is also a rose-petal, a blossom, and a downy peach. At her most human she is a toddler like Totty. Obviously George Eliot is imitating the reifying language of men about women, but there is no attempt to distinguish between the language and the reality. Mrs. Poyser, who is shrewd, calls her a peacock, and Adam, who feels noble love for her, thinks of her in the same terms: 'he only felt a sort of amused pity, as if he had seen a kitten setting up its back, or a little bird with its feathers ruffled' (ch. 23). Hetty can hardly be other than an animal, but, of course, she has 'a woman's destiny', and thus, in the process of responding to its demands, she is necessarily destroyed.

The ideological pattern is coherent enough, but it is noticeable that, in working it out, George Eliot, like Spencer, dehumanizes social convention. For it is not nature that Hetty offends against (like Tess, she is 'a pure woman'), but the moral propriety which men have made. She murders her child because she fears social shame, and again *mimetically* George Eliot allows for the distinction. When Hetty at night finds straw to lie on she instinctively feels a return to life: she 'kissed her arms with the passionate love of life' (ch. 37). With daylight, she confronts social judgment ('that man's hard, wondering look at her') and life becomes 'as full of dread as death'. There is a bitterly ironic contrast between the interior presentation of Hetty's flight and the dry externality of the Court testimonies. Through this we achieve sympathy, but it is a sympathy which is halted before it questions social justice. Adam, naturally enough, wants Arthur to take the blame for what has happened: he sees her momentarily as the victim of social exploitation. Irwine, who is obviously George Eliot's spokesman, argues with him:

> you have no right to say that the guilt of her crime lies with him, and that he ought to bear the punishment. It is not for us men to apportion the shares of moral guilt and retribution. We find it impossible to avoid mistakes even in determining who has committed a single criminal act, and the problem of how far a man is to be held responsible for the unforeseen consequences of his own deed, is one that might well make us tremble to look into it. The evil consequences that may lie folded in a single act of selfish indulgence, is a thought so awful that it ought surely to awaken some feeling less presumptuous than a rash desire to punish.
>
> (ch. 41)

Reading this is to have the sense of a loss of focus. Who is apportioning Hetty's share of guilt if it is not 'us men'? Of course, the key word is 'moral', and the advice is against the 'rash' desire for punishment on the part of the individual. Arthur may have caused a crime; Hetty committed it. But it shows quite clearly how the ideological pattern of the novel prevents us from carrying the limits of moral enquiry beyond the merely individual to the social. Society's conditions, like nature's, are inexorable. And if our sympathy can go beyond that of the Court and see that Hetty is not a *cold-blooded* murderer, it cannot question the right of a society in which, in Hardy's resonant phrase, 'the woman pays', to exact its due. Such sympathy would deny incarnate history.

The moral doctrine is, however, less important than the terms of the vision which it embodies. In Mrs. Gaskell's *Ruth*, the voice of convention is personalized in the figure of Mr. Bradshaw, and thus the dramatic formation of social law becomes clear as the dominating Christian gives way, under the pressure of revelation about Ruth, to obscene hysteria. Though this leads Mrs. Gaskell into dissolving social problems in terms of individual reform, it also enables her to portray the psychological basis of class relations. The basis of George Eliot's realism is an acceptance of the abstract nature of convention because she is concerned with the individual *in* society rather than the individuals who make it. Society thus becomes a brown pond, separate from the cygnets and ducks within it, and inexorably fixed. The story of Hetty shows us the reification of society in process as the social tragedy becomes a biological parable.

III

Most critics accept what George Eliot instructs us to understand in the presentation of Adam – that through the suffering caused to him by Arthur and Hetty, he moves towards a 'higher feeling' of sympathy with those less morally gifted than himself. The trouble is that the language in which Adam's suffering is realized is so often inadequate. The first major reassessment in Adam's coming to self knowledge, for example, is his meditation during the service after his father's burial:

> 'Ah! I always was too hard,' Adam said to himself. 'It's a sore fault in me as I'm so hot and out o' patience with people when they do wrong, and my heart gets shut up against 'em, so as I can't bring myself to forgive 'em. I see clear enough there's more pride nor love in my soul, for I could sooner make a thousand strokes with th' hammer for my father than bring myself to say a kind word to him. And there went plenty o' pride and temper to the strokes, as the devil *will* be having his finger in what we call our duties as well as our sins. Mayhap the best thing I ever did in my life was only doing what was easiest for myself. It's allays been easier for me to work nor to sit still, but the real tough job for me 'ud be to master my own will … It seems to me now, if I was to find father at home tonight, I should behave different; but there's no knowing – perhaps nothing 'ud be a lesson to us if it didn't come too late. It's well we should feel as life's a reckoning we can't make twice over; there's no real making amends in this world, any more nor you can mend a wrong subtraction by doing your addition right.'
>
> (ch. 18)

In the presentation of Arthur and, to a large extent, of Hetty, George Eliot's normal mode of narration is to trace the dramatic curve of consciousness within a framework of moral judgment. In the case of Adam,

however, it is more frequently this kind of interior soliloquy, because, in
fact, he doesn't need authorial commentary – he can provide his own
judgment. And this means that the language has a striking lack of urgency.
The specific situation is immediately generalized: 'people when they do
wrong' reduces his father to one of a series, and, at the same time, despite
the 'humility' of the speech, carefully maintains Adam's moral superiority.
Despite the dialect, the whole speech has a logic and an eloquence ('What
we call our duties', 'It seems to me now', 'It's well we should feel') which
would be effective from the pulpit. And this is borne out by the movement
of pronouns from 'I' to the generalized 'we' to the impersonal 'you'.
Indeed, the final aphorism is a moral more applicable to Arthur and Hetty
than to Adam. Later in the novel, when the emotional pressure is much
stronger and George Eliot has to show us Adam incoherent with suffering, she is forced to be melodramatic and theatrical:

> 'No – O God, no!' Adam groaned out, sinking on his chair again; 'but
> then that's the deepest curse of all ... that's what makes the blackness of
> it ... *it can never be undone.* My poor Hetty ... she can never be my sweet
> Hetty again ... the prettiest thing God had made – smiling up at me ...
> I thought she loved me ... and was good.'
>
> (ch. 41)

The vocabulary is stagey ('curse', 'blackness', 'my sweet Hetty ... smiling
up at me') and the incoherence is engrafted – in fact, there is a clear
enough progression of thoughts ('but then', 'that's what'). It is clear that
George Eliot finds it consistently difficult to realize 'poor Adam's mad-
dening passions'. In the chapters following Adam's discovery of Arthur
and Hetty in the wood, it is significant that we learn very little of the
'scorching light' which comes to Adam and move quickly to the much
more assured dramatization of Arthur's consciousness.

The contrast in quality suggests that George Eliot's failure to be
convincing is more than a technical ineptitude. Adam is, in the first place,
always on the margin of suffering. The repentance of his intolerance of
Thias's wrongdoing seems gratuitous when it is set against Lisbeth's
finely realized misery. Her *whole world* is shattered by the destruction of
its central relationship: the only way out of her despair, as the careful
attention to the corpse and the satisfaction she feels in the tribute of the
Church service bitterly demonstrate, is through the embalming of the past.
Beyond that she is merely an obstruction. 'I'm no good to nobody now' is
an objective summary of her predicament, and, shortly after, we see Adam
pushing her away: ' "Well, well; goodbye, mother," said Adam, kissing her
and hurrying away. He saw there was no other means of putting an end to
the dialogue' (ch. 20). As this indicates, Adam does have a future beyond
his father's death; he is, in fact, released by it – 'the heaviest part of his

burden' has gone. Not only is he on the margin of Lisbeth's grief, but the suffering is marginal to him. The same is true of his relationship with Hetty: 'it was the supreme moment of his suffering: Hetty was guilty' (ch. 43). Something *outside* him has failed, and this too is ultimately a lucky break – he is spared marriage to Hetty by her 'guilt'. What Adam really has to learn is not to marry beneath him.

George Eliot is clearly embarrassed by the possibility of this reading, and she makes Bartle Massey its spokesman in order that we should see Adam angrily refuting it (ch. 46). But the events of the novel justify Massey's optimism, and she has to intervene directly, in a highly abstruse passage, to draw a distinction between benefits gained from one's 'own personal suffering' and the cynicism of supposing that one person's misery can be justified by another's resultant happiness. The speciousness of such moral economics, especially in a novel which insists on the communal interaction of guilt and sorrow, is obvious.

However, it would be wrong to suggest that, by being spared marriage with Hetty, Adam is spared the consequences of his own folly in loving her. Adam's love has a clear moral function; in order to ascend to the higher feeling of sympathy which is the basis of man's perfectibility, he has to have 'his heart strings bound round the weak and erring, so that he must share not only the outward consequence of their error, but also their inward suffering' (ch. 19). His love is *not* folly – it comes 'out of the very strength of his nature' (ch. 33). This clearly creates a problem, however, since Hetty is a deceptive appearance behind which is the reality of Dinah. (After his father's death, Adam dreams of Hetty and wakes to find Dinah; Hetty dresses up as Dinah.)

But Adam's love is a version of the Feuerbachian transformation: as the love of God is a sublimation of the love of humanity, so the love of beauty is a mistaken individuation. 'Beauty', we are told, 'has an expression beyond and far above the one woman's soul that it clothes ... it is more than a woman's love moves us in a woman's eyes – it seems to be a far-off mighty love that has come near to us ... The noblest nature sees the most of this *impersonal* expression in beauty' (ch. 33; George Eliot's italics). Although George Eliot mocks the horseman for judging Dinah by her physiognomy (ch. 2), she herself discriminates by physical appearances. Adam's strength is distinguished from Seth's passive mildness by a contrast of Seth's pale eyes with Adam's dark, penetrating glance. The clue is heredity. Adam, we can see, is a perfect blend of Celt and Saxon. Hetty's beauty is correspondent with a reality, but, because of heredity, the correspondence is indirect. Her eyelashes express 'the disposition of the fair one's grandmother' (ch. 15), and if we should think this ironic, the theory is stated less coyly later: 'There are faces which nature charges with a meaning and pathos not belonging to the single human soul that flutters beneath them, but speaking the joys and sorrows of foregone generations' (ch. 26).

Hetty, in short, is a moral fossil. Thus evolutionary doctrine gives the mystery of Adam's refining love a scientific basis.[5]

It is important to insist on this because the novel celebrates the superior evolutionary adaptability in Adam by showing that he is capable of an objective 'sympathy' which, through the punishment and destruction of Hetty, becomes rightly focused. But, as in the case of George Eliot's presentation of Hetty, it is necessary to discriminate between the mimesis and the ideology which frames it: the concrete realization defines the social basis of the idealization. We have already seen that Adam reifies Hetty. She is 'the prettiest *thing* God made' and his own explanation of the mystery of love is *sexually* impersonal – it is like 'the sprouting of the seed' (ch. 11). At the same time, it is carefully contained within his social awareness of duty: 'She's more nor everything else to me, all but my conscience and my good name' (ch. 28). This is more than moral limitation: his happiest reveries about Hetty are bound up with his vision of 'an opening into a broadening path of *prosperous* work', and he makes it clear to Arthur that she is something to be worked for: 'And I never kissed her i' my life – but I'd ha' worked hard for years for the right to kiss her' (ch. 27). The combination of reified sexual attraction and social advancement creates a very precise impression of the basis of the envisaged marriage which is borne out later when Adam confronts the future without Hetty: 'but now there was no *margin of dreams* for him beyond this daylight reality, no *holiday time* in the working-day world: no moment in the distance when duty would take off her iron glove and breast plate and clasp him gently into rest' (ch. 50). Woman is thus marginal, an escape from, the immediate reward of self-fulfilling work. It is a basis for marriage similar to that of Philip Hepburn and Sylvia in *Sylvia's Lovers*, but in Mrs. Gaskell's novel it is seen as class-based and thus it is an institutionalized and repressive love which crushes the woman's being. *Sylvia's Lovers* is also about the 1790s, but it is a truly historical novel. The marriage between Philip and Sylvia comes into being as the result of the riot which leads to her Radical father's death. Philip, the draper, is a new man, the *bourgeois* who integrates and therefore survives. The terms of the marriage grow out of the concrete historical situation.

Because George Eliot doesn't see the historical and human basis of institutions, she incorporates Adam's love in a metaphysical scheme justified by natural law. In these terms, there is no essential difference between Adam's relation with Hetty and that higher feeling for Dinah: the epilogue shows us Dinah's 'more matronly figure' in what has become Adam's timber-yard. She has given up Snowfield and accepted Conference's decision to ban women preachers (that this is *her* choice is emphasized by the fact that Seth hasn't accepted it, but has joined a break-away group). She is the model bourgeois wife, shaping her destiny through her prosperous husband's work. Ian Gregor suggests that if the love between

Arthur and Hetty is delusively Arcadian, Adam's love also looks back to a Golden Age. But they are different ideals, socially as well as morally, and they correspond differently to reality. The reality of Arthur and Hetty's relationship is aristocratic exploitation, and thus the Arcadian dream is directly antithetic to it, since Arthur and Hetty are neither children nor gods. Adam's love is based on the bourgeois mode of integration through work, and his love for Hetty is only delusive in so far as it is badly focused: socially and biologically, it adapts properly to the prevailing realities once beauty and soul correspond in the object.

I say bourgeois because I think that the doctrine of work as it emerges in the novel is related to the notion of the self-made man, the fittest survivor. This, of course, is far from explicit. Indeed, the concept of work is primarily integrative and it looks back to an ideal close to that celebrated in *Past and Present*. This is clear from the first chapter in the contrast with Seth. Seth is apparently more amiable but he is also ineffectual: he forgets the door-panels, he is unable to comfort his mother, he is unable to bring Dinah into direct relation with material reality. More importantly, he looks forward to the dreamers who are to precipitate the disasters of the novel – Hetty and Arthur. Thus Adam's materialism comes to seem a more truly religious activity, because through work he transforms egoism into creativity: 'All passion becomes strength when it has an outlet from the narrow limits of our personal lot in the labour of our right arm' (ch. 19). Work communicates with reality: it also communicates with other men: Adam tells Dinah that he likes to go to work through hilly country so that he can survey the land from a height, because 'it makes you feel the world's a big place, and there's other men working in it with their heads and hands besides yourself' (ch. 11). Physical integration with the universe, social integration with the community, and, besides these, self-integration through the provision of a moral absolute. At the height of his despair, when work has become momentarily meaningless, Adam says to himself, 'But tomorrow ... I'll go to work again. I shall learn to like it again some time, maybe; and it's right whether I like it or not' (ch. 48). In all this, he closely resembles Carlyle's Abbot Samson (who has 'a terrible flash of anger' at wrongdoing), and is thus a nostalgic figure in whom the true religion, as opposed to the 'diseased introspections' of Methodism, contrasts with the 'present' world of mammonism and dilettantism.

But work is much more than the expression of the community: 'a man perfects himself by working' – finds, that is, his individual destiny. The great individualists, the heroes, Wren and Columbus, are praised too, and Carlyle looks forward as well as back to the captains of industry and the aristocracy of talent. Mammonism is better than dilettantism and all it needs is a soul. In *Adam Bede* this forward-looking movement is present in the individuating process which ties up with the integrative one. Adam is not only defined by the moral contrast with Seth in the first chapter, but by the social contrast with the clock-watching workmen. Wiry Ben says to him, 'Ye may like work better nor play, but I like play better nor work; that'll 'commodate ye – it laves ye the more to do.' Although we are meant to despise Ben for this, he has a point. Adam is already a foreman, and however much he talks of pleasure and pride in work, he is paid to stop clock-watchers. Moreover, he already has his eye on a partnership, and, as Ben says, his success depends on being accommodated by the lesser mortals who work only for *immediate gain*. It is more than incidental that Adam's axiom, 'God helps them that helps themselves', is from Franklin's Preface to *Poor Richard's Almanack* entitled 'The Way to Make Money Plentiful in Every Man's Pocket'. Combined with the sense of community is a loyalty to the great individualists – Franklin and Arkwright.[6] And it is significant that Adam makes no fundamental distinction between Capital and Labour:

> 'For I believe he's one of those gentlemen as wishes to do the right thing, and to leave the world a bit better than he found it, which it's my belief that every man may do, whether he's gentle or simple, whether he sets a good bit o' work going and finds the money, or whether he does the work with his own hands.'
>
> (ch. 5)

Because of this, the clash between Adam and Arthur can never fully become a class issue, for the individualism is integrative, a matter of adaptation. 'Th' natur' o' things doesn't change, though it seems as if one's own life was nothing but change' (ch. 11). We are back to Herbert Spencer and the fixed social laws. Adam may be an idealization, but this is because he is a new man *unhistorically* realized as a more perfect man who moves up the evolutionary scale because adaptation is the double move-ment of individuation and integration: 'the ultimate man will be one whose private requirements coincide with the public ones'. Thus if his decision not to leave Hayslope is stoicism: 'It's all I've got to think of now – to do my work well, and make the world a bit better place for them as can enjoy it' (ch. 48) – it is also a good evolutionary policy: the unfallen Adam gets Dinah and a timber-yard.

IV

To see the novel as a process of transforming historical realities into ideological fable is not to underestimate its impressiveness. I am not arguing that *Adam Bede* is a fictional version of Herbert Spencer, but that the concrete realization of the empirical vision exists in tension with the historically specific ideology which shapes it. To use Belinsky's formula, art is necessarily a convex mirror – only a subjective distortion can enable it to reflect a totality. We should recognize, as criticism has tended not to do, that the convexity of George Eliot's art is more specific than a vaguely defined and classless humanism. Herbert Spencer is useful as well as relevant because it is more obvious in his work than in, for example, that of Comte or Feuerbach, that his ethic springs from class-interest: he moves towards the pervasive formula of 'man versus state'. The difference between him and George Eliot is that his work does not confront empirical reality at all in a direct way – he is all system. But it still remains true that George Eliot's realism does not escape its historical context, and the context emerges, naturally, most clearly in her first novel. Moreover, I am not merely concerned to establish limitations – the convexity is a positively important feature of George Eliot's realism. In particular, the reified and dehistoricized vision of the social law is a major premise of the 'original psychological notation' of *Middlemarch* and *Daniel Deronda*: the great interior dramas of Dorothea and Gwendolen depend on George Eliot's subjective participation in the appearance of the structure of the relationship between the individual and society to them as bourgeois consciences. And if, as I have implied, bourgeois abstractions play a more active role in George Eliot's realism than in Mrs. Gaskell's, this is not because Mrs. Gaskell's realism is more objective or less bourgeois, it is because George Eliot has a firmer grasp of a later, more alienated phase of development, in which the bourgeois vision has ceased to appear historical. And if this means the loss of a certain kind of objectivity, it also means that for George Eliot there is no escape into sentimental solutions through the 'one human heart'. Paradoxically, the apparent dehistoricization of social reality in George Eliot's work means that there is no escape from history.

Adam Bede, however, does witness an attempt to escape through the portrayal of historical forces as 'natural' history, and I have tried to suggest that George Eliot is too great a realist for this to be successful: in future the reifications will appear as reifications; individuation will be separation, not integration; the virtues of Adam will be divided between Caleb Garth, who is on the fringe of society, and Lydgate, who is in collision with it. Even within *Adam Bede* there is a radical questioning of the ideological pattern, though in a way which so fully probes the social basis of alienation that it is never fully repeated in the later work. This emerges in the portrayal of the relationship between Dinah and Hetty.

Most critics see Dinah as a wearyingly theoretical character. She is George Eliot's tribute to Feuerbach, the higher nature who sublimates her love of human beings through Methodism. Her sympathy, in the Spencerian formulas I have been suggesting, gives her a great potential for adaptability which is realized through her material participation in reality when she marries the integrated individualist, Adam. But, I think, George Eliot goes beyond Feuerbach in her portrayal of Dinah and undermines the adaptational pattern in her relationship with Hetty.

Marx's most obvious criticism of Feuerbach is that in dissolving the religious world into its secular basis, he fails to explain the detachment of the religious world in terms of the 'self-cleavage and self-contradictoriness of this secular basis' (*Fourth Thesis on Feuerbach*). This is precisely what George Eliot does achieve, through the precise delimiting of Dinah's religious emotion in the superbly structured sermon. Dinah begins in a social actuality: Christianity has a special relationship to poverty, and she returns again and again to the conditions of poverty. Combined with this is the personal concreteness of her story about seeing Wesley. The initial affirmation thus grows out of actuality – God looks after the poor and ignorant and provides their daily sustenance. Out of this grows, however, an encounter with doubt: 'It doesn't cost him much to give us our little handful of victual and bit of clothing; but how do we know he cares for us any more than we care for the worms and things in the garden, so as we rear our carrots and onions? ... For our life is full of trouble, and if God sends us good, he seems to send bad too.' With an effective candour, Dinah thus begins by registering the despair of poverty, and the sermon moves towards a far-reaching question: 'What shall we do if he is not our friend?' There is no other friend of the poor, but can we depend even on him?

At this point the narration changes from direct speech to *oratio obliqua*. This creates an obvious distance, for Dinah withdraws from her own question: 'Then Dinah told how the good news had been bought.' Actuality is exchanged for the story: the present is met with the past. Jesus *once* helped the poor. The move back to the present is achieved by a change from the historical to the suppositive: 'Ah! wouldn't you love such a man if you saw him?' The basis of Jesus's transcendence is thus wish-fulfilment. Again there is a change from direct speech to a narrative as we move from wish-fulfilment to the nightmare of sin. This is not to *oratio obliqua*, but to description of Dinah and the change that comes over her as she says, 'The lost! ... Sinners'. The religion of fear is a matter not of speech, but of dramatic projection which moves towards hallucination – 'see where our blessed Lord stands and weeps'. After the morbid details of the Passion, she wrestles with Bessy Cranage's soul. She thus returns to reality, but not to preach so much as to set up a real-life melodrama. The return is mediated by the series of transitions which has moved towards hysteria: reality, doubt, narrative, supposition, desire, fear, hallucination, reality. This is more than just brilliantly accurate: it brings out fully the connection between social alienation and its resultant dreams – desire and fear. There is no attempt to sentimentalize Methodism's ruthless exploitation of social injustice. Later, Dinah tells Irwine: 'I think maybe it is because the promise is sweeter when this life is so dark and weary, and the soul gets more hungry when the body is ill at ease' (ch. 8).

Thus, although Dinah is a sympathetic character, it is surely intended that she should be, as Barbara Hardy has described her, 'charmless'. What is sympathetic is the sense of human misery which is the basis of her Methodism, not the language in which that sense sublimates itself. But the radical limitation has a much more far-reaching effect. Dinah is a dreamer, and, as we have seen, the dream is a limited response to a concrete reality. Thus, the continual juxtaposition of her altruism in contrast with Hetty's egoism enforces as well a parallel between them in that both are alienated dreamers. If the primary function of the 'Two Bed-Chambers' scene is to underline the difference between them, it is also true that both are looking for a world beyond that in which they find themselves. The instinctive movement towards Hetty doesn't seem to me sentimental, because, in the first place, it grows out of a common withdrawal ('her imagination had created a thorny thicket of sin and sorrow'), and in the second, the communication between them is painfully limited by the inadequacy of Dinah's language: 'I desire for you, that while you are young you should seek for strength from your Heavenly Father, that you may have a support which will not fail you in the evil day' (ch. 15). Given the rigid formality and the lack of specific reference of this, it is not surprising that it merely creates a 'chill fear' which makes Hetty drive Dinah away. Nevertheless, beneath the failure, there is a communication which emerges in the prison scene much later. Irwine dismisses Hetty with a complacent insensitivity: 'some fatal influence seems to have shut up her heart against her fellow creatures' (ch. 41). We have already seen that Irwine, with his automatic acceptance of convention, is unqualified to communicate with Hetty (that 'some' is extraordinary – he has forgotten that Hetty has been shut up literally because of his mother's godson). Yet as soon as Dinah appears, we learn of Hetty that 'it was the human contact she clung to'. In Hetty's confession, it becomes clear that she sees Dinah as separate from the world of convention:

> 'I daredn't go back home again – I couldn't bear it. I couldn't have bore to look at anybody for they'd have scorned me. I thought o' you sometimes, and thought I'd come to you, for I didn't think you'd be cross with me, and cry shame on me: I thought I could tell you. But then the other folks 'ud come to know it at last …'
>
> (ch. 45)

It is a revealing moment, for we know how justified Hetty is – the reactions of Martin Poyser and Bartle Massey define a communal attitude. But, more than this, Adam, we have seen, suffers because she is not 'good'. From the moment he says to Arthur, 'tell me she can never be my wife' (ch. 28) he declares the limits of his sympathy. Only Dinah, with her limited and alienated way of coping with the world, is able to offer *human* contact. Both Hetty and Dinah live in a dream which questions the justice of the secular world, and it is a bitterly ironic commentary on the secular ideology which the novel celebrates that it is Dinah who humanizes Hetty, because, in the enforced confrontation with reality, she can offer another, more resilient dream to replace the one which has been destroyed.

Thus, though through the destruction of Hetty and the self-fulfilment of Adam, George Eliot insists on the natural basis of the social law and so reifies the social vision of the novel, she also realizes through Dinah the 'validity' of a religion which escapes the apparently unchanging secular world, and thus reveals its 'cleavage' by showing that reification is a psychological response to a particular situation. In Stoniton Gaol the fixed 'medium' of Hayslope is momentarily given an historical identity.

Notes

1. See for example: D. Van Ghent, *The English Novel Form and Function* (Holt, Rinehart & Winston, 1953); J. Arthos, 'George Eliot – The Art of Vision', *Rivista de Letterature Moderne* (1954); M. Hussey, 'Structure and Imagery in *Adam Bede*', *Nineteenth Century Fiction* (1955); W. M. Jones, 'From Abstract to Concrete in *Adam Bede*', *College English* (1955); C. Creeger, 'An Interpretation of *Adam Bede*', *English Literary History* (1956).

2. I. Gregor and B. Nicholas, *The Moral and the Story* (Faber & Faber, 1962), p. 16.

3. First published in the *Westminster Review* (July 1856), pp. 51–79. Quotations here are taken from *The Essays of George Eliot*, ed. T. T. Pinney (Routledge & Kegan Paul, 1963), pp. 260–99.

4. This and subsequent quotations from Spencer are from *Social Statics* (1851). Lewes said of this book: 'We remember no work on ethics since that of Spinoza to be compared with it' (*Letters*, i. 364).

5. Herbert Spencer, *On Physical Beauty* (1853), makes these points about beauty and heredity.

6. It is worth noting that, in her journal in 1857, George Eliot describes Samuel Smiles' *Life of George Stephenson* as 'a real profit and a pleasure' (*Letters*, ii. 369).

CHAPTER 4

'The Affections Clad with Knowledge': Woman's Duty and the Public Life

'The only ardent hope I have for my future life' Marian Evans wrote in 1849, 'is to have given to me some woman's duty – some possibility of devoting myself where I may see a daily result of pure calm blessedness in the life of another.' Much later, in 1877, Mrs. Lewes wrote that marriage 'holds the highest possibilities of our mortal love.' No one seems to illustrate so well the paradox of the 'feminine' writer as Elaine Showalter has identified it. Pursuing a vocation which is other than 'womanhood' itself, this group of writers services an antifeminist ideology, seeks heroines in their novels who believe or come to believe in womanhood as the only sufficient vocation. With George Eliot it is even more strange than with others. In the first place, for most mid-Victorian women novelists, the paradox is modified by the fact that writing fiction is an acknowledged female discourse: it is, therefore, a *licensed* mode of emancipation, and one of the roles of fiction in that society was to substantiate the patriarchal ideology. Marian Evans had no need of fiction as a way of liberating herself: her vocation by the mid-fifties was one which already placed her on an equal footing with men. Turning to fiction is a conscious act – an act of retreat into a safer discourse? Moreover, this turning to fiction takes place at a time when she is directly in touch with feminism. Barbara Bodichon's *Women and Work* appeared in 1857, and we know that Eliot did not want to take sides in the debate between Bodichon and Bray. Could it be that Dinah Morris's marriage to Adam Bede – the movement from preaching to partnership is an image of this new vocation? Wouldn't the next step after translating Feuerbach have been dangerously radical? In the letter I began with, she hopes for this woman's duty because she sees England only as 'a land of gloom, of ennui, of platitude' but at the same time of 'duty and affection' – the woman's duty is a way of returning to the fold. Writing novels may be a good compromise between the vocations of intellectual leadership and womanhood.

My paper addresses itself to this paradox recognising the peculiarity of George Eliot's case, and arguing that whatever psychological pressure there is behind Eliot's ambiguous relationship to the problem of sexual politics, it is inadequate to deal with it psychoanalytically. It is interesting that much good feminist criticism has addressed itself to Charlotte Brontë on the basis that the novels show the repressions of the ideology even if they finally submit to them, while Eliot is less attended to, probably because, as Elaine Showalter argues, she seems to be much less radical, much less *open* to interpretation. I think that the reason for this is not that she is more conservative, or more in retreat from radical questions, but because Eliot, unlike Brontë is aware of the question of women as a crucial feature of the whole of political life, and that she has to find a mode expressing this, has to push sexual politics beyond the domain of personal and domestic relations into the realm of the public life.

The paradox is starkly evident in *Daniel Deronda*. In one of the few statements Deronda makes which fully applies both to himself and to Gwendolen, he says:

> The refuge you are needing from personal trouble is the higher, the religious life, which holds an enthusiasm for something more than our own appetites and vanities. The few may find themselves in it simply by an elevation of feeling; but for us who have to struggle for our wisdom, the higher life must be a region in which the affections are clad with knowledge.'

(XXXVI)

'An enthusiasm for something more' is simply the ethos of all Eliot's fiction reduced to a commonplace: the specific importance here is 'the affections' being insufficient for those who have to struggle. The higher life is a region of knowledge, and the whole issue of this last novel is what constitutes that knowledge, and how it transforms the affections. Two essential points emerge from this. First, as far as Deronda is concerned, the higher life is not immanent in the given life. Zionism is a recovery of continuities but one which can only be made by the total break from immediate ties. What makes the novel so brilliant is that we are made aware of English society as one with which no compromise can be made. The best of those within it, Mr. Gascoigne and Sir Hugo Mallinger, for example, still endorse specifically the lies which enable Grandcourt to prosper. I am thinking of the moment in XIII when the rector is shocked by Gwendolen's lack of hypocrisy in her decision to marry Grandcourt ('He wished that in her mind his advice should be taken with an infusion of sentiments proper to a girl'). And Sir Hugo acknowledges the corrupt nature of politics but comments 'There's a bad style of humbug, but there is also a good style – one that oils the wheels and makes progress possible' (XXXIII). He adds 'There is no action possible without a little acting.' Just before he defines Gwendolen's refuge, Deronda has spoken of 'the small drama of personal desires'. Gwendolen's whole social identity is bound up with acting, gaming, playing the rules for one's own ends, and

'Grandcourt preferred the drama' (XXVIII). Mirah, who will be Deronda's choice, rejects the theatre, and Deronda's mother whom he will reject is an actress. The theatrical allusions and analogies which pervade the book point so insistently towards the impossibility of practising the truth within the old society that the Zionist theme is inevitable. Indeed that is one point about the prolonged treatment of zionism. Ezra Cohen the prosperous figure of orthodox Jewry compromising itself with the gentiles is offset as a good but impossible man against Mordecai, the true Ezra. Knowledge must have to do with truth. The unclad affections commit us to a world of lies.

The second point is simply that this logic is available as a programme of action only to Deronda. What he does here is to lead Gwendolen into the light of his own (and the novel's) perceptions and leave her stranded. In the passage from XXXVI he specifically refers to Gwendolen's attitude to music. Now music and Zionism are to some extent parallel. Klesmer acts on the opening of Gwendolen's conscience as Deronda does, and he too explicitly opposes the nature of English society, the lack of idealism in English politics and so on. And Miss Arrowsmith has to be prepared to opt out of her social world to marry him. To make this connection, however, is marginal after his marriage. Secondly, the relation of Deronda and Gwendolen to Zionism and music respectively is radically different. Although it is to a higher life that Deronda aspires it is to one for which his nature is eminently fitted: it is not merely an otherness to which he can submit but also 'some social captainship which would come to me as a duty.' (LXIII). And Gwendolen, of course, has to accept that she will not excel at music. At this late stage in the novel, Deronda is simply castigating her for not cultivating it as 'a private joy'. Music is the only alternative available to Gwendolen but it is not a total commitment. In any case it is one of the performing arts, like the real acting she thinks to undertake. And performance is precisely the corrupting factor in the small drama of personal desire.

More generally, what links Gwendolen and Deronda – the sense of a radical separation of consciousness from the social given – is ultimately what severs them. All the connections have an ironic disjunctive ambiguity. Mordecai's Zionism, the agency of Deronda's social captaincy, grows from a desire to 'revive the organic centre' (XLII). Deronda, a little later, tells Gwendolen that if she can see life as a debt she will find it 'growing like a plant' (the conjuncture of capitalist and organicist metaphors is interesting – debt, plant). Organic continuity is achieved through duty – social captainship is a duty, the higher life is a duty. But there are radically different concepts of duty. There is the duty of action (captaincy) and the duty of submission (life as debt). However, the first places the second as wrong. – Deronda does not submit even to the love of his mother. – Wrong, that is for the man. But for the heroine what else? Ironically

Zionism must of all available idealisms have the most subordinate role for women. Ezra Cohen notes that Jews thank God every Sabbath for not being a woman. The Princess asks Deronda whether Mirah has ambitions and is satisfied when he says no. Mordecai tells Mirah that women are 'specially framed for the love which feels possession in renouncing.' (LXI) And the following chapter ends with a passage from a Rabbi who said that 'The omnipresent is occupied in making marriages' and meant by it a metaphor for 'all the wondrous combinations of the universe'. Marriage, of course is Gwendolen's great crime against her own integrity. The final irony comes in the recognition Gwendolen has of her own place in a Zionist universe: 'the bewildering vision of these wide-stretching purposes in which she felt herself reduced to a mere speck.' (LXIX). The ontology is surely more like that of a Hardy than an Eliot protagonist. But it is reserved for the woman confronting the man's resolution. The end is desolate, but only for her.

I say that this illustrates the paradox of the feminine writer because, of course, through the agency of fiction-writing, by being George Eliot, Marian Evans is able to participate in the social captainship. To write *Daniel Deronda* is to engage with a duty of knowing and doing and educating in a way that is explicitly denied the feminine protagonist who must presumably return to the mediocrity of *her* mother and the triviality of drawing room music. Now I realise that *Daniel Deronda* is very different from the novels which precede it in the radical break it shows between the higher life and the small drama: Romola and Dorothea are enabled to find duty within an obscure daily round. However, it is only by force of the special circumstances each novel enacts. Her last novel ends so problematically not because Eliot has changed her ideas so much as that she does not allow special contingencies to mediate the gap between her own achievement and that of her protagonist. It is as though Deronda demands and finds an equivalent for the novelist's own higher life, leaving his heroine embedded in the daily social life with at best the possibility of obscure renunciation.

The negative aspect of my argument, then, is that, although Eliot's work is full of the paradox of the feminine novelist, it is not possible to see her simply as sharing it with other writers. Her late espousal of fiction, her stark representation of the double standard in her final novel both show that she knows this paradox *as a paradox*. There is no question for her as with Brontë or some lesser feminine novelists of groping towards subversive lucidity in the effort to vindicate an ideology. On the other hand, I want to argue that so far from being obscurantist, her fiction, taking cognisance of the levels of feminism available takes its specific form from questions that feminism raises but cannot adequately answer. I want to show the level of awareness of sexual politics in *The Mill on The Floss* to be too high to be resolvable within the terms of its own realism, and then to show how *Romola* forges a new, specifically Eliotesque realism in response to the issues unaccommodated by the form of the earlier fiction. The question of sexual politics in George Eliot is bound up with the specific realm of public, even political life, and that though this is what underlies the stark negation we have seen in *Daniel Deronda*, it is also what makes possible, necessary a feminist reading of George Eliot. Which is not to claim George Eliot as a feminist, but rather to argue that the issue of sexual politics and its place in the larger politics of nineteenth-century society remains central. Having discussed *Romola*, I shall be able to return to *Daniel Deronda* to show how it is most potently present precisely at the point it seems most marginalised.

II

The Mill on The Floss is the obvious focus for a discussion of Eliot's sexual politics. It seems the most autobiographical of the novels. It was written at the point when Eliot had most contact with the English feminist movement (Barbara Bodichon's *Women and Work* is a highly relevant text). It replaces the careful static realism of *Adam Bede* with a highly revealing interiority of narration and double edged use of metaphor (is there any equivalent of the Red Deeps elsewhere in Eliot?). It seems to be the most exposing text about the *experience* of being a woman in a patriarchal society. And yet in these terms, Elaine Showalter is surely right to see the novel as much less radical than *Jane Eyre*, and Maggie as a heroine supinely committed to renunciation. However I think we should also recognise how very different it is from *Jane Eyre* as well and how this difference moves Eliot into another phase of sexual politics for which the 'liberationist' question of woman having to throw off oppression and find her own personal nature, transcending the limitations of gender, is complicated by the recognition of individuality as a highly relative concept, subject to mystification and not merely to be clarified by psychoanalysis (which is how some feminist readings of Brontë 'produce' *Jane Eyre* and *Villette*, as texts for feminist consumption), but needing to be seen in terms of the real active relations between individuals and social groups. The very terms in which the novel is cast (scenes from provincial life) make it impossible for Eliot to portray this fully, but if the form of the novel is contradictory, it is not in my view because it is full of interesting fissures and silences, but because the issues are too big for its frame of reference.

The opening of the novel makes it clear that its project is very different from *Jane Eyre*'s. Maggie is not starkly alone narrating her life from impressions. On the contrary, Maggie is seen through a hallowed distance as part of a scene, and she is named by the familiar talk of her parents. Later Eliot is to speak of Maggie's destiny as an unmapped river (VI. 6) which implies that she is part of a whole terrain. Jane Eyre is set down in an alien world to find her place, like the protagonist of classical realism. Maggie is not individuated in this way: she is a member of a community and what separates her is the consciousness unaccounted for by this membership. This is explicitly a function of her being a woman. The second chapter opens with Mr. Tulliver wanting to give Tom an education and moves towards Maggie's entry with her parents lamenting her intelligence – 'an over cute woman's no better nor a long tailed sheep – she'll fetch no better price for that.' The whole novel is structured on this division: it is not about Maggie, it is about Tom and Maggie and their relationship to the family and the community. Maggie's introspection is a function of this differential membership:

> While Maggie's life struggles had lain almost entirely within her own soul, one shadowy army fighting another, and the slain shadows ever rising again, Tom was engaged in a dustier, noisier warfare, grappling with more substantial obstacles, and gaining more definite conquests. So it has been since the days of Hecuba, and of Hector, tamer of horses; inside the gates, the women with streaming hair and uplifted hands, offering prayer, watching the world's combat from afar, filling their long empty days with memories and fear: outside, the men ... (V. 2).

Both Tom and Maggie are placed in a situation of struggle, but there is an outside for men to relate to, unavailable to women. The only moment at which Maggie has the advantage over Tom in her membership is the moment of grief: 'Of those two young hearts Tom suffered the most unmixed pain, for Maggie, with all her keen susceptibility, yet felt as if the sorrow made larger roots for her love to flow in ... No true boy feels that ...' (III. 8). In other words it is only at a crisis of suffering that the woman can participate more actively in the community. But to be acute is useless, to be 'a *clever* woman' is to be 'a nasty conceited thing'. The contrast between Tom and Maggie is one between a 'character at unity with itself' and a 'consciousness of wider thoughts and deeper motives' (V. 2) precisely because the woman is intended to be within the gates:

> 'I have a different way of showing my affection.'
> 'Because you are a man, Tom, and have power, and can do something in the world.'
> 'Then if you can do nothing, submit to those that can.' (V. 5).

The explicitness of this motif in the novel first stresses that George Eliot is confronting sexual politics directly and consciously, but to do it in this way – as a question not of freedom and oppression, integrity and convention, but rather as one of the relative kinds of membership of social groups – is, I would argue, already to get beyond the level of discussion evident even in a text such as *The Subjection of Women*. This is already evident in the ideological formulation given Maggie's conflict in her discussions with Stephen towards the end of the novel. Her passivity, indecisiveness, embrace of renunciation are seen as the product of two contradictory modes of continuity – feeling and ties. In an excellent thesis soon to be [now] published, Sally Shuttleworth in *George Eliot and Nineteenth-Century Science* has shown how the novel juxtaposes two levels of organicist discourse (psychological and social) which contradict one another. What is important to my argument however is that what produces this contradiction is that Maggie is a woman. Stephen's response to Maggie's confusion is a mirror-image simplification of Tom's concept of duty in sexist terms 'what a miserable thing a woman's love is to a man's' and in fact it is not even a mirror image but a direct echo when he goes on to say: 'How can you go back without marrying me? You don't know what will be said, dearest. You see nothing as it really is' (VI. 14). Both Tom and Stephen have characters at unity with themselves: they follow a straight line between feeling and action. 'What will be said' and 'what really is' are the parameters within which they define themselves with a genuine integrity. Even Philip Wakem who is made more feminine by his invalidism challenges Maggie's renunciation by an absolute: 'It is narrow asceticism – I don't like to see you persisting in it, Maggie. Poetry and art and knowledge are sacred and pure' (V. 1). Like the other men, Philip is 'right' but for Maggie there is no way of simplifying – 'But not for me' she replies and this is ironic since what she is defending is *self denial*. We should not delude ourselves into thinking that Tom, Philip and Stephen represent choices for Maggie. Philip's insistence on the integrity of thought pushes Maggie as surely in the direction of Stephen's claim on her elective affinities (the allusion of the title of VI. 6 is clear, 'Illustrating the Laws of Attraction') as Tom's working for Guest and against Wakem parallels her movement from the cripple to the dandy. All three constitute an alien masculinity which demands part but never all of her womanhood. If Maggie is a heroine of renunciation it is not the renunciation of sublimated sexual submission. The commitment to Thomas À Kempis reflects this ('renunciation seemed to her the entrance into that satisfaction which she had so long been craving in vain' – IV. 3) and it is quickly destroyed by Philip. The renunciation she finally advocates to Stephen is not absolute but relative – 'whatever is opposed to the reliance others have in us' (VI. 14). Being a woman in this novel means being aware of complexity, and because of the contradictory demands made on woman, the complexity becomes inhibition.

'Being a woman' needs more definition because one of the features of the novel often noticed but not taken due account of is that the concept

of femininity is not confined to woman. Tom faced with an education
he cannot understand is 'more like a girl' (II. 1). Philip is 'by nature half
feminine in sensitiveness' (V. 3) and Stephen's first appearance as a social
being at the feet of Lucy is 'graceful and odoriferous' (VI. 1). All three are
required to assert themselves against the femininity which their social
position calls out (the pressure on Philip is the love of his father). So that
the difference between femininity and 'being a woman' is quite strictly the
difference between a psychological feature and the constitution of the self
as *identifiable subject*. Hence all the nonsense about curls at the beginning.
It is important to insist on this because we must understand the end in
its light. Elaine Showalter points out that one of the signs of Maggie's
passivity is that she does not make a break with her home town but tries to
compromise by finding a job within it. If we keep in mind the parallel with
Tom, I think we have a different perspective. Tom opposes the Wakem
power by becoming dependent on Guest's. He is also enabled to complete
his career by re-occupying the Mill. There is no question of this return
to origins being passive. On the contrary the Hectorian struggle thus
recovers a continuity. The self made man continues the tradition. The self
made woman, however, must be exiled. In this light, speculatively at least,
I see the end, not as satisfactory it is true, but neither as opiate. Rather, the
flood destroys the old buildings. The sex roles are reversed – Maggie
rescuing Tom, but only in an apocalyptic moment of the destruction of
the old order. Maggie doesn't die – Maggie and Tom die. What is finally
imaged is an equality which the social life cannot contain. How else can
Hecuba be outside the walls than by the breaking down of the walls?

Of course the ending is abrupt, confused, fanciful. But it is because
Eliot's awareness of sexual politics is too great for the domestic realism of
the novel itself, not because she retreats into religiosity. When Eliot is
describing Maggie's involvement in Thomas À Kempis at the end of Book
Fourth, she suddenly apologises for the 'tone of emphasis which is very far
from being the tone of good society.' The whole paragraph is a brilliant
ironic defence of 'emphatic belief' in terms of the cost of producing 'good
society' which floats on the gossamer wings of light irony. It is a passage
which foreshadows the *ennui* of the social world of *Daniel Deronda* and
links the obscure yearnings of Maggie to the opiates of the factory hand
because of the 'emphasis of want.' It reflects on the mediocre indolence of
Maggie's aunts and uncles as well as the laconic sensibility of Stephen
Guest. But it cracks the frame of the novel by asking questions about
Maggie's unnoted sorrows in terms of the class structure of an exploitative
society. In no way could Maggie ever be brought to such articulateness.
All she can see dimly is that life is more complex and more limited for her
because she is a woman. I turn to *Romola* next because it is precisely this
larger perspective that Eliot seeks to incorporate. That is, she seeks a form
which will politicise sexual politics.

III

There is nothing controversial in claiming that, whatever its limitations, *Romola* is the first of the mature novels. I would want to claim, however, that it is so because it offers the two primary structural features of what is specifically George Eliot's realism. The first is that when she says in *Felix Holt* that there is no private life that is not determined by a wider public life, she is not vaguely asserting the pressure of social factors, but actually asserting entanglement of the personal life with public affairs. What is common to her mature novels is the presence of an actual historical event which bears the weight of major social change – the rise and fall of Savonarola, the reform acts, the emergence of Zionism. Second, and in a sense by contrast, all the novels with the exception of *Felix Holt* have marriage as the central experience of the protagonist. I say, by contrast, because the first insists on the importance of wider issues while the second closes the protagonist round with a set of duties more precise than love. (I think of the famous letter to Sara Hennell of 1871 when, despising 'dog-like attachment' in women, she adds that 'married constancy is a different affair' – *Letters* V. 132). Thus at once the horizons become wider than *Mill on The Floss* as the walls become narrower and less penetrable. This offers a double determinism – the strain between feeling and ties is less negotiable, the gap between experience and historical knowledge less easily traversed. This is very different from identifying an ideological determinism *in* George Eliot. It is rather saying that her ideological deter- minism motivates her novels as fictions of the conjuncture of determinants. The first evidence of this is *Romola*: 'In Florence the simpler relations of the human being to his fellow-men had been complicated for her with all the special ties of marriage, the State, and religious discipleship' (69).

Romola is not popular. The historical setting (sometimes accused of being ahistorical) is said to be a mistake. Romola herself is too idealised. We can recover moments of intense 'psychological notation' in the accounts of Tito and Savonarola, but the best that can be claimed for it as a whole is that it is a massive fable. The most recent serious claim for it that I know is Felicia Bonaparte's *The Triptych and the Cross* (1979) which sees it as an epic evoking central myths of the whole history of Western Civilisation. Against this I would want to urge its specificity. Strangely, *Romola* while being dismissed as fable on the one hand has often been blamed for its erudition and heavy attempts at local colour on the other. I suspect that some of the difficulty is attributable to our own needs as consuming readers not to be shaken too explicitly out of the familiar unless the text is clearly labelled 'not to be confused with the knowable'. But that fifteenth-century Florence should be less engaging than the present is surely more a comment on our narrowness of interest than on George Eliot's 'mistake'. I speak of 'we' but I don't share the common appraisal of *Romola*. I find it an exciting, engaging text whose issues are made palpably alive and whose most interesting character is its heroine. I think I find it like this because I sense it to be a novel in which a writer whose understanding of the social conditioning of women gives her a specific historic sensibility. And although as in all Eliot's novels, there is an ideological project which can account for the shape of the book (and George Levine has defined that in terms of *Romola* as Terry Eagleton has in terms of Eliot as a whole), the shape is not the book or the sum total of its effect.

Romola is the earliest of a series of historical novels written in the 1860s which all have a female protagonist who in some way penetrates the male-dominated tissue of duplicities called public affairs – *Sylvia's Lovers, Emilia in England, Vittoria.* Meredith's texts significantly present this process in a context of Italian as well as English politics. Nicholas Rance has written of these texts and their bearing on popular politics but I think I ought to stress that they share a major difference from the industrial novel of the fifties in that through contact with popular movements the heroine learns not to placate social strife but to *take sides* (the contrast is with *North and South* and *Shirley* and equally in terms of form – whereas the industrial novel is an extension of domestic realism, the historical novel of the sixties is a break with it. The issues are not localised in the same way, even in the case of *Sylvia's Lovers* where the specific rebellion against the press gang is clearly seen in a context of the 1790s and government repression as a whole. The Italian connection is crucial, however, because Italian politics, especially in 1860 when the novel was conceived was poised on the edge of a choice between idealism and compromise – Garibaldi and Cavour.

Although it deals with fifteenth-century Italy, one major provocation of *Romola* was obviously the Risorgimento. The second part of the *Duty of Man* was published in 1858 and it is not insignificant that this text which shares so many of Eliot's own moral ideas should link nationalism both with the unity of humanity on the one hand and the importance of the family on the other. It ends by pointing out another duty than the liberation of a United Italy:

> Your emancipation can only be founded on the triumph of one prin-
> ciple, the unity of the Human Family. Today, half of the human family,
> the half from which we seek inspiration and consolation, the half to
> which is entrusted the first education of our children, is, by a singular
> contradiction, declared civilly, politically and socially unequal, and is
> excluded from this unity. It is for you who seek your emancipation, in
> the name of religious truth, to protest in every way and upon every
> occasion against this negation of unity
>
>   The *emancipation of woman* should be always coupled by you with
> the emancipation of the working man. It will give your work the
> consecration of a universal truth. (XII)

Another more local reason why the situation of women which is the immediate explicit concern of *The Mill on the Floss* should be given a new dimension by Italian politics is the figure of Jesse White Mario to whom George Eliot's attention was drawn by Barbara Bodichon in September 1857 (*Letters* II. 379). She had been refused entry to medical schools in 1856 and so went off to Genoa as correspondent of the Daily News, married a Mazzinian follower of Garibaldi and nursed the wounded in Garibaldi's campaign. The period between Eliot's two visits to Italy during the writing of the novel is, of course, the period of Garibaldi's greatest triumph. According to Trevelyan, Jesse Mario's work was praised in the *Morning Post* of August 1860. It is also interesting that on her way to research the novel in 1861, Eliot stopped to see the tomb of Harriet Taylor in Avignon where, at about that time, Mill was drafting the *Subjection of Women*. These are external facts. In the novel, sexual politics and politics are deeply linked, and the politics has many of the features of the Risorgimento – the idea of national feeling, the impact of a ruling family (Medici/Victor Emmanuel), church and state, humanism and theology). I don't mean that we should take fifteenth-century Florence as merely analogous. But Eliot never pretends that she wants to write about it simply: it is our vision of this past, as the mill is in our vision of the narrator's childhood. But here that past is European in its importance – the founding of modern culture, the source of Italian politics. Again, naturally politicians of the Risorgimento were concerned with reviewing the past (it is in this period that Machiavelli, for example, begins to be seen as more a patriot than a cynic).

'Thou hast withal the woman's delicate frame,' Romola's father tells her, 'which ever craves repose and variety, and so begets a wandering imagination' (6). As well as an indication of the 'humanist' scholar's sexist assumptions, this statement recognises the complex make-up of Romola's mind. Her relationship with Tito expresses itself as the product of psychological tensions which are linked with ideological choices which in turn determine political allegiances. The attraction of Tito which is realistically sexual is also related to a Hellenism which foreshadows Pater rather than Arnold: 'Strange, bewildering transition from those pale images of sorrow and death to this bright youthfulness, as of a sun-god who knew nothing of night!' (17). The whole passage from which this comes is a tissue of images of joy – wine, music, 'Nature revelling in her force'. The shift of loyalty from Tito to Savonarola picks up the Hebraic/Hellenic dialectic: 'Romola's life had given her an affinity for sadness which inevitably made her unjust towards merriment' (49). And at the end when she has fled from Florence for the second time and is disillusioned with the Frate, 'she longed for that repose in mere sensation which she had sometimes dreamed of in the sultry afternoons of her early girlhood, when she had fancied herself floating naiad-like in the waters' (61).

Equally, the cultural tension is one way in which the political struggle is expressed: the Medicean faction is linked with humanism, of course, as the Savonarola faction with Hebraic energy. The ordeal of Romola's daughterhood, sisterhood and marriage is a personal domain determined by and reflecting the historical struggles of Florence as it seeks to find its national identity, organic unity, moral value.

More importantly, the stages of Romola's experience are deeply bound up with the shifts in political power. If Tito is linked with certain psychological pressures acknowledged but repressed by Romola's father, her relationship to him is a working free from the images in which he tries to fix her. Eliot, of course, brilliantly delineates the coherent shape of Tito's attraction to Romola and his retreat from her. The early analysis contains the seeds of everything which follows: 'he felt for the first time, without defining it to himself, that loving awe in the presence of noble womanhood, which is perhaps something like the worship paid of old to a great nature goddess, who was not all knowing, but whose life and power were something deeper and more primordial than knowledge' (9). The 'awe' is linked with social status. The nature goddess is also the access to a world of ambition – 'for it was Romola and not Tessa, that belonged to the world where all the larger desires of a man who had ambition and effective faculties must necessarily lie' (34). That is why Tessa continues to be important – she is a refuge from 'a standard disagreeably rigorous' – and why she too must be confined to a given image ('Tito saved Tessa's charm from being sullied'). The double life is the product of a double standard: Romola must be worshipped but not be all knowing. The very Hellenic principle which commits him to a life of avoiding the unpleasant, commits Tito to a sexual politics which is even more repressive than Bardi's. As soon as they are married, we are told that he feels 'a certain repulsion towards a woman from whose mind he was in danger' (27) and a little later he counters her moral judgment with 'all the masculine predominance that was latent in him' (32). Worship, fear, repression – this pattern of patriarchal domination is clear in Tito, but what needs to be stressed is that it is deeply bound up with the political situation.

Connected as she is with his public life, Romola must have no part in it, because the public life for Tito is a matter of remaining flexible while maintaining a secret inviolability (the coat of mail is, of course, highly symbolic). Two points must be stressed. In the first place, the opening chapters of the novel, sometimes dismissed as redundant local colour, not only vividly establish the political conflicts in Florence, but establish them as an exclusively male domain. That is one simple point about the use of the barber's shop. Romola's entry into the world of public affairs coincides with her liberation as 'young wife' from Bardi's limited life and with her hearing Savonarola:

Romola had had contact with no mind that could stir the larger possi-bilities of her nature; they lay folded and crushed like embryonic wings, making no element in her consciousness beyond an occasional vague uneasiness.

But this new personal interest of hers in public affairs had made her care at last to understand precisely what influence Fra Girolamo's preaching was to have on the turn of events. (27)

I quote at length to note the transitions: stirring the larger possibilities of her nature is directly linked with an opportunity precisely denied Maggie, to enter public affairs. However, the second point is that 'nature' occupies a very strange position in the novel. She is for Tito a 'nature' goddess. Equally, Tito's devious politics which must, of course, exclude Romola except as image and passport, the politics of the barber shop, begins with his selling the jewels, rejecting the claims of Baldassare on the grounds that they are unnatural. Chapter 11 ('Tito's Dilemma') is crucial – it is about 'the proper order of things, the order of nature, which treats all maturity as a mere nidus for youth.' Nature here becomes identified with an egoism which defies 'the sentiment of society'. It is another version of the conflict between feelings and ties, but highly elaborated so that it is effec-tively a conflict between nature (defined practically as the survival of the fittest) and culture (defined as tradition). What is striking is the treachery of the natural and the apparently conservative clinging to the 'moral law restraining desire'. Given the treachery of the natural, the entry of Romola into the realm of public affairs becomes an hebraic 'cultural' commitment, but at one and the same time it is a defiance of Tito's sexual politics.

However, there is another stage to be gone through. Chapter 36, 'Ariadne Discrowns Herself' is initially the assertion of a *nature* against a *nature*: 'she felt that there could be no law for her but the law of her affections.' Romola's departure is 'the act of breaking an outward tie that no longer represented the inward bond of love'. It is simply an act of liberal feminism. The authorial comment which follows clearly questions the validity of the act in the name of 'that force of outward symbols by which an active life is knit together so as to make an inexorable external identity for us, not to be shaken by our wavering consciousness.' How-ever, this is not a negative or merely Arnoldian qualification. Romola's act makes her *free* and *alone*. Savonarola is to send her back in the name of the truth that commands you, but it is not to submission and retreat. Rather it is to a fuller political awareness: 'doubtless you were taught how there were pagan women who felt what it was to live for the Republic; yet you have never felt that you, a Florentine woman, should live for Florence. If your own people are wearing a yoke, will you slip from under it, instead of struggling with them to lighten it?' The 'idealisation' of Romola which is so often complained of, is something only acquired by the political status her integrity momentarily achieves. Savonarola offers renunciation, but it is not the same as Maggie's. It is a call to action, and one which embarrasses Tito: 'Romola had an energy of her own which thwarted his, and no man, who is not exceptionally feeble, will endure being thwarted by his wife' (48). I know that the chapters describing this energy, significantly titled 'Romola in Her Place', and 'The Visible Madonna' are full of references to 'sweet womanly forms' and 'womanly labours' and 'womanly sympathy' but what is important is that the place is not that of the young wife or Ariadne. The visible Madonna is another image but it is in contrast with the mystified invisible Madonna.

The analysis of the disillusion with Savonarola seems to me to be just as shrewd as the delineation of the renunciation. What lies at the root of the failure of Savonarola's personality is something which links him, ironically, with Tito: 'having once held that audience in his mastery, it was necessary to his nature – it was necessary to their welfare – that he should *keep* the mastery.' (25). Tito is also a man of the crowd. His 'nature' too identifies itself with that kind of mastery. It is Savonarola's moment of alliance with Tito which is the cause of his trap. It is the public bravura coupled with the secret knowledge of his own vulnerability which finally exposes him. It is the imposition of his own ego on the feelings he can master which sickens Romola. But note the word that Eliot naturally reaches for in that early analysis – *mastery*. It is one that hovers between sexual politics and politics. The ultimate breakdown of Romola's marriage, the dividing line between the sacredness of obedience and the sacredness of rebellion is linked with her recognition of the final contradiction of Savonarola's political stand. The 'tangled web' (36) which drives her to freedom is the 'web of inconsistencies' (69) which is her final image of the life of Florence. It is the web of marriage, the State and religious discipleship – sexual, political and cultural ties which are at once oppressive and essential. The novel does much more than acknowledge this, however. That is the final acknowledgement of *The Mill of The Floss*. What this novel does is to explore the modes of action within that entanglement and the demands made on the questioning consciousness not merely to survive but to develop.

IV

The transition between *Mill on The Floss* and *Romola* thus seems to me to be explicable as a transition from one level of awareness of sexual politics to another rather than a retreat into mystified concepts of the 'general life' and 'humanity'. These concepts, and the agency of their operation in a secular moral life *are* of course extremely important and it is certainly true

that they increasingly dominate the ideological shape of Eliot's fiction.
Such a commitment however does not negotiate the line between the
sacredness of obedience and the sacredness of rebellion, and it seems to
me to be the persistence of that problem which accounts for the desolation I have noted at the end of *Deronda*.

The question that remains is whether that desolation is a part of the
effect of the novel or merely a response I have because I don't share Eliot's
naive enthusiasm for mystical nationalism. The answer, at least speculatively is that if we understand the form of her novels to be based on a
specific conjuncture – the duty of woman and the public life, it is an
extremely *visible* desolation. To establish this it is first necessary to assert
the appropriateness of Zionism for the novel as a *whole*. The essay in
Theophrastus Such so often referred to in this context makes it clear I think
that to link Zionism with larger ideological forces such as racism and
imperialism is wrong (for George Eliot). She, on the contrary, ironises
British chauvinism and links Zionism with Greek and Italian and Irish
nationalisms, not to speak of 'proletaries and their tendency to form
Unions.' It is seen as a radical, anti-colonial movement whose specific
distinction is the specific contribution Jewish culture makes to the whole
race. It is defined against an English society whose main preoccupation
is sport – the recurrent word as of Grandcourt's relationship with
Gwendolen is *mastery*. We note as well how often the connection is made
between Zionism and the Risorgimento. Mirah sings a Leopardi song.
Deronda and the Grandcourts are in Genoa at a critical stage in the Italian
struggle. Recovery of the organic centre is identified with freedom from
oppression. If we ask why Zionism and not the Italian movement which
is present on the margins, I would ask that we note that in 1860 too it is
displaced, and I suspect here it is because Eliot needs a cause which has
no political organisation precisely like Mazzini who by now is more concerned with attacking socialism and materialism (including Mario) and
which is therefore totally apart from and separate from the compromises
of the social world. It has to be radical in that sense because only that
justifies Deronda's total break not only with those who love him but also
with the heroine who has struggled out of her egoism to find him gone.
Italian nationalism by the time of the setting of the novel, is already deep
into negotiation and compromise. Mazzini is on the fringe, Garibaldi
only head of a faction. monarchism and alliances prevail in the policies
of Cavour. The battle of Sadowa is crucial to Italian history, but it is a
Prussian victory. Only a *Utopian* movement, identifying progress and
recovery can offer itself as a new life.

However, whereas, as I mentioned, Mazzini regarded the emancipation
of women as important as the unification of Italy, there is no place in
Zionism for the woman who is not totally submissive. Our attention,
we must emphasise, is *explicitly drawn* to this. Deronda's discovery of his

'birthright' happens at the first meeting with his mother who has tried to conceal it. She has rejected Jewry because it oppresses women: 'I wanted to live out the life that was in me, and not to be hampered with other lives' (LI). What follows is an extremely eloquent feminist critique of Jewish culture: 'I am not a monster, but I have not felt exactly as other women feel – or say they feel about their children'. Deronda's rejection of his mother is not only shocking because it is his mother. It is also because it is in the face of the analysis she makes of the oppression of women. Moreover, if she is an actress ('all feeling ... immediately became matter of conscious representation') acting has been her mode of liberation, as it is the only immediate possibility for Gwendolen. We do not simply think of her as an egoist, but as a woman who has crossed the line from the sacredness of obedience to the sacredness of rebellion. It is not a question of whether Eliot approves of her: it is rather a question of whether she can be pressed into the service of the moral fable. She cannot and her interpretation of Deronda's Zionism is one that reduces it to a merely relative commitment: 'That separateness seems sweet to you because I saved you from it'. It is an unanswered point: Deronda is not only made to reject his mother for a higher concept of relationship, but also to reject her position without showing its inadequacy. This is coherent with the defence of Zionism in *Theophrastus Such* – Eliot's argument is not advocating it so much as pleading for a more sympathetic understanding. That it becomes much more positive in the novel is surely because of its fictional rather than its ideological function and its fictional function is to provide the possibility of a new and separate moral order. What it doesn't do is provide a universal possibility. Specifically it represses the female experience registered in the novel. The affections have to be clad with different forms of knowledge but these forms are so far from equivalent that the 'stronger something' to which Deronda and Gwendolen aspire is actually the source of their separation. I made this point at the beginning. What I am saying now is that it is a calculated effect of the novel, and the Princess and Gwendolen form a strange unspoken alliance. In fact, the most disturbing moments in the text are moments of unspoken female critique or aspiration. Gwendolen's response to Lydia's 'Medusa appearance' is not mere shock but awareness of 'the dark shadow thus cast on the lot of a woman destitute of social dignity' (XLVIII). The Princess' question about Mirah's aspirations links with Mirah's silence after Mordecai's fable about female devotion. They are merely incidents when unexpected affinities threaten the moral pattern. But they all question, like the Princess, the separation Deronda moves towards.

In one sense we have moved to an opposite position from that in *Romola*. In that novel the 'feminist' possibility of being free and alone is undermined by a 'truth' which turns out not to be able to sustain the light of feminine knowledge – Savonarola works by mastery after all. The wisdom Romola finally brings back is simply that life is more moral than death. The 'public life', the 'common' life of Florence is exposed as a web of inconsistencies. Here, the public life, the stronger something, is imaged as a separation, but that too, for all its pristine integrity is made personal by the unanswerable questions women pose against it. When I began working on this paper it was with a sense that Eliot's work would expose the limits of liberal feminism by insisting on the larger determinacy of questions of sexual politics. At the end I am as aware of the opposite point – that equally her novels never move away from the question of sexual politics, never *absorb* it in something else. It is always insistently posing questions about the higher life. And that is why, however much we explain Eliot s 'realism' in terms of available ideologies her fiction remains a way of seeing – her affections clad with a knowledge that embraces Deronda's vision and Gwendolen's bewilderment.

CHAPTER 5

'Character' and Henry James

In recent years the most influential critical approach to fiction in this country has been that of *Scrutiny* and F. R. Leavis. Briefly, this approach grew out of the rejection by Wilson Knight and the contributors to *Scrutiny* of A. C. Bradley's Shakespearian criticism. Bradley's emphasis on 'character' in Shakespearian tragedy was seen to have failed to take account of the 'spatial' totality of the plays, their existence as coherent linguistic and metaphoric structures. The search for this spatial totality was extended to the novel, and the famous series of essays in *Scrutiny* entitled 'The Novel as Dramatic Poem' expressed this desire to see a novel as a total 'structure'. In *The Great Tradition*, probably the most influential of books on the novel in England, Leavis extends the notion of spatial totality to an approach in terms of the totality of the writer's moral vision given concreteness through the form of the novel. He revised the phrase 'moral fable' and gave it a larger and more flexible meaning. His great tradition was the line of novelists whose spatial coherence was shaped by a moral coherence: this in turn was given validity through a fine discrimination and a life affirming energy. Thus W. J. Harvey's recent book *Character and the Novel* has become a major starting point for discussion of the novel in England, for reasons other than its intrinsic merit. He offers a direct challenge to the position formulated by Leavis and *Scrutiny*, to both the idea of 'fable' and to the narrowing features of the word 'moral'. More positively, he reasserts the primary importance of mimesis, of the novel's function as an imitation of life, rather than as an affirmation of it.

The second way in which Harvey's book is important is that his particular definition of mimesis relates to a developing ideology in English literary criticism, most elegantly represented by Iris Murdoch and John Bayley, and which we might call neo-liberalism. At the outset Harvey draws a contrast between the assumptions which lie behind 'the central, classic tradition of modern fiction'[1] (the 'realistic novel') and the theory which sees art as valuable 'because it has to do with order, and creates little worlds of its own possessing internal harmony, in the bosom of this disordered planet'.[2] 'The novel', Harvey says, 'is the distinct art form of liberalism' and he defines liberalism as a commitment to the 'manifold and discrete' rather than to a 'monistic' ordering of experience (such as you get with Christianity and Marxism). The novel is the product of negative capability rather than the egotistical sublime: 'Tolerance, scepticism, respect for the autonomy of others are its watchwords.'[3] Behind such a doctrine of art, of course, there lies a doctrine of life, one which is perhaps most conveniently, if schematically, stated by Iris Murdoch: 'Reality is not a given whole. An understanding of this, a respect for the contingent, is essential to imagination, as opposed to fantasy. Our sense of form, which is an aspect of our desire for consolation, can be a danger to our sense of reality as a rich receding background. Against the consolations of form, the clean, crystalline work, the simplified fantasy myth, we must pit the destructive power of the now so unfashionable naturalistic idea of character. Real people are destructive of myth, contingency is destructive of fantasy and opens a way for the imagination.'[4] Indeed, Murdoch's claim for the 19th-century novel is precisely that it provided the 'liberal' answer to 'romanticism' which liberal philosophy failed to do.[5]

Mimesis and Liberal Concepts

Although Harvey doesn't make a claim quite as extraordinary as this, his definition of mimesis is clearly and explicitly related to the liberal concepts elucidated in Iris Murdoch's essays; there is, above all, a very firm commitment to the centrality of character in any formal discussion. And the concept of character is openly a 19th-century one. 'The novelist', Harvey writes, 'must acknowledge, if he is to create a faithful imitation of mankind, that most human beings will always elude or overflow the categories of any human ideology'.[6] At the end of his book he even talks of the need for 'a surplus margin of gratuitous life, a sheer excess of material, a fecundity of detail and invention, a delighted submergence in detail for its own sake.'[7] Obviously James, at least the later James, is going to come off pretty badly in such a critique. Doesn't James precisely, in the novels after 1896, sacrifice the autonomy of self to the autonomy of form? Barbara Hardy writes: 'James is on occasion guilty of sacrificing human plausibility to economy and symmetry'.[8] Her statement is important because it formulates in a precise way what often underlies the irritation with the later novels in all the best criticism of James. Even Edmund Wilson, who can hardly be accused of an obsession with formal character, writes: 'his work ... becomes all a sort of ruminative poem, which gives us not really a direct account of *the internal workings of character*, but rather James's reflective feelings'.[9] And although Leavis explains James's later failure in terms of his lack of the 'nourishing intuition of the unity of life,' isn't it basically a need for 'human plausibility', even for an autonomy of character, which leads him to define part of his dissatisfaction with *The Golden Bowl* in terms of a frustrated desire for sympathy with Charlotte Stant?[10] These criticisms have to do with the fact that James reduces characters (the characters who often appear the most interesting) to *ficelles*. Even John Bayley's attempt to surmount the barriers to straightforward appreciation set up by James's formal commitments, in his essay on *The Golden Bowl*,[11] could only be conducted though ingenious distortion and careful evasion of the formal perversities of the novel. Such barriers *are* there: it is important that they are there: it is even part of James's greatness that they are there. They grow precisely out of the paradoxes of the 'liberal' concept of character.

The Autonomy of Self

The autonomy of form is something which James arrived at towards the end of a career which had begun with a firm belief in the autonomy of self. Two quotations will show this. The first is from *Washington Square* (1880). Sloper is telling Mrs Almond that Catherine is not going to break her engagement to Townsend as the result of her father's pressure:

> 'She is going to drag out the engagement, in the hope of making me relent.'
> 'And shall you not relent?'
> 'Shall a geometrical proposition relent? I am not so superficial.'
> 'Doesn't geometry treat of surfaces ?' asked Mrs Almond, who, as we know, was clever, smiling.
> 'Yes, but it treats of them profoundly.'
>
> (Chap. 21)

Sloper wins the battle of wits because he is cleverer: but his victory is only verbal, because if he treats profoundly, he treats surfaces that are fixed. Indeed Sloper fails because he tries to categorize personality like a Second Empire Positivist ('the sign of the type in question') – tries, that is, to cover the landscape of death which is in his heart with a 'scientific' confidence in his ability to diagnose and predict personality.[12] His use of the word 'geometry' here places him with a radical irony.

The second passage comes from James's preface to *Roderick Hudson* written for the New York Edition in 1907:

> 'Really, universally, relations stop nowhere, and the exquisite problem of the artist is eternally but to draw, by a *geometry* of his own, the circle within which they shall happily appear to do so.'

Admittedly James is talking here about art and not psychology, and he is aware that the geometry is a lie. Nevertheless the use of the same metaphor measures the extent to which his earlier work differs from the later. For here he seems to be committing precisely the same kind of error (an error of the unintelligent heart) that he had so brilliantly satirized 30 years before. Indeed, as Harvey implies, the cardinal sin in the fictional world of the early novels is precisely the refusal to recognize the autonomy of self. This is why Sloper, and Osmond (and, I think, Ralph) and Olive Chancellor are *seen to be* moral invalids. In the Prefaces of 1907, James seems, by his own criteria, to have become himself a moral invalid. 'Life being all confusion and inclusion, and art being all discrimination and selection, the latter ... sniffs round the mass as instinctively and unerringly as a dog suspicious of a buried bone.'[13] Again and again in the Prefaces, James comes back to an obsessive concern with the centre of consciousness, always in terms of the 'economy' of form gained by it. In fact, he even seems to make quite elementary mistakes: he talks, for example, of *The Portrait of A Lady* as though it were entirely structured around Isabel's consciousness, apparently forgetting the brilliant interplay between her introspections and Ralph's, and the direct insights we get into an Osmond totally unknown to Isabel.

Such a development has been explained in terms of James's estrangement from the public especially in the years 1886–96.[14] But it is not quite as simple as that, even in the prefaces where James's particular perversities seem so often to have hardened into total attitudes. The obsession with totality of form and the stifling talk of *ficelles* and *disponibles* is accompanied by a concern with mimetic viability, especially in the criticisms of the early novels. *The American* is criticized for being too much a Romance: 'The way things happen is frankly not the way in which they are represented as having happened.' And it is important to note that part of the failure is in the perfunctory quality of the Bellegardes ('the queer falsity' is James's phrase). *Roderick Hudson* is also criticized for being too crudely 'foreshortened', and James remarks of Christina Light: 'The determinant function attributed to Christina Light, the character of well-nigh sole agent of his catastrophe that this unfortunate woman has forced upon her, fails to recommend itself to our sense of *truth and proportion*.' If there is an antithetical relationship between the autonomy of self and the autonomy of form, James clearly didn't altogether recognize it in his theoretical writing. And it would be possible to show that he never did recognize it. We have only to think of the double charge made by Mark Ambient against his wife in *The Author of 'Beltraffio'* (1884), both that she is indifferent to beauty and the attempt to reproduce beauty, *and* that she has a conception of art which divorces it from truth, to see how closely the idea of form and the idea that art 'competes' with life are allied in James's theory. 'Form' may be consolatory in James, but the relationship between 'form' and 'character' is much more complex than Harvey suggests.

The Ambassadors and The Syntax of Experience

Harvey's definition of character is explicitly essentialist: 'we still think of (our own identity) as unique, isolate, discrete.' We can therefore know ourselves 'intrinsically' and others contextually. In the novel, the author, who has a god-like relation with his characters, is able to know his own characters both intrinsically and contextually.

Taken with the liberal, pluralistic resistance to fable, this commitment to character as unrelated substance puts the critic into a particular danger. Since characters are neither to be subsumed in a solipsistic alchemy nor fixed in a providential calculus, any doctrine of 'the eternal human heart' is easily going to be avoided, only, however, at the expense of historical relativism. Harvey attempts to overcome this by suggesting that there are constitutive categories of experience which, though they are not at all eternal, are relatively stable: stable enough to be regarded as unchanging for the epoch of the realistic novel. The categories he specifies are Time, Identity, Causality and Freedom, which taken together constitute a 'syntax' of experience: 'These categories control and regulate experience, so that if a novelist convinces us that his handling of them is truthful, then there is a good chance that the particular experience he portrays as the end-product of these categories will also strike us as true to life.' There are two important modifications of this thesis. In the first place, Harvey acknowledges that this syntax is presently undergoing a 'radical derangement' in the modern, experimental novel. Secondly, he deliberately produces the concept as 'a modest and rather commonplace rabbit out of the hat' so that we can take the assumptions it involves as read, at least for a discussion of the realistic novel.

Obviously any account of experience which assumes a self which precedes that experience is going to structure itself on the basis of this syntax. If from the concept of self as isolate and discrete we are going to extrapolate a sense of other isolate and discrete identities (which the novelist, in assuming his divine prerogative of intrinsic knowledge of his characters, necessarily does) then we must equally assume that our experience of the elements of this syntax is a common one. At this point Harvey's thesis becomes too vague to he tenable. Indeed the chapters of his book which discuss the categories are profoundly disappointing,[15] because, although his 'syntax of experience' is a necessary framework to the liberal concept of character, it is also self-contradictory. A discussion of *The Ambassadors* is crucial in a consideration of his thesis, because it is precisely about the power of the structure of experience to sustain the concept of an essential identity.

The Ambassadors is most obviously concerned with 'the pressure of the flight of time' in relation to 'the illusion of freedom'. The world of Woollett measures time as a unilinear duration in terms of abstract chronometrics (Mamie gives Strether 'sharpness, above all, to his sense of the flight of time'). Against this, in Paris, Strether has 'a rich conscious-ness of time – a bag of gold into which he constantly dipped for a handful.' This acquisitive sense, the sense that he takes time, rather than gets taken by time, is possible because Paris, the world in which the past is palpably present in its visible historicality, holds time in suspense, makes of it not a related and therefore determining recession from the richest array of possibilities, but a succession of replete moments. Experience and appre-ciation are not therefore wrenched apart but are unified in a world of vivid light: it is a Paterian world of art: 'for art comes to you proposing frankly to give nothing but the highest quality to your moments as they pass, and simply for those moments' sake.' (*The Renaissance*)

Modes of Identity

This confrontation between Woollett and Paris both in terms of time and in terms of freedom is a confrontation between modes of identity: between, to use Harvey's terms, contextual and intrinsic modes of knowl-edge. This distinction is made by William James who borrowed his terms (the empirical ego – self as known; the pure ego – self as knower) from James Ward. On one level, this can obviously apply to *The Ambassadors*. Coming to Europe for Strether means confronting his past in Woollett as a submergence in the empirical ego. His one scrap of identity is given him by the Review that he edits for Mrs Newsome: at the moment when he explicitly confronts the middle years he has crossed, the crisis in his iden-tity is stated precisely in these terms. 'He was Lambert Strether because he was on the cover, whereas it should have been, for anything like glory, that he was on the cover because he was Lambert Strether.' This is not merely the difference between a given and a self created identity, but also between a known and a knowing self: 'I come from Woollett, Massa-chusetts.' 'You say that', she said, 'as if you wanted one immediately to know the worst.' And, of course, the Americans in Europe seem to Strether exactly to reinforce this distinction between being known and knowing: Maria has, for example, 'just the air of having *seen* and chosen, the air of achieved possession of those vague qualities and quantities that collectively figured to him as the advantage snatched from lucky chances.'

In this quotation the verbs of freedom, 'seen' and 'chosen' are linked *in apposition* with the idea of possession. Paris offers freedom because it offers the possibilities of possessive appreciation. Strether's most intense moment of freedom is exactly like this. It comes in the visit into the French countryside shortly before he makes the discovery that Chad and Mme. de Vionnet copulate. He has the impression of walking into a landscape by Lambinet, 'he had admired, *had almost coveted*, another small old church, all steep roof and dim slate colour without and all whitewash and paper flowers within; had lost his way and found it again.' But this possession depends on a radical disjunction of time. He is reminded of Lambinet because of a picture he nearly bought in Boston but prudently refrained from indulging himself in. So that the present becomes pregnant not with the past, but with an isolated, replete moment in the past, the moment that *almost* made him a connoisseur: 'The oblong gilt frame disposed its enclosing lines; ... it was what he wanted: it was Tremont Street, it was France, it was Lambinet'. Strether has, at this moment, conquered the determinant role of time through this imaginative possession of the past in the present and in doing so has made the pure ego seem possible but he has not transcended time, he has merely transposed it to a spatial concept, and in doing this, he is able to celebrate the bygone future.[16]

Thus Strether is able to make up for what he has lost through imaginative apprehension, above all through being able to make experience immediate. But James is also insisting on the price that Strether has to pay for this freedom from the empirical ego. And one of the most obvious ways in which he does pay is that his vision is a romantic delusion. Here, for example, is the way in which he sees Mme. de Vionnet's flat: 'the whole thing made a vista, which he found highly melancholy and sweet – full, once more, of dim, historic shades, of the faint, far away cannon roar of the great Empire.' Here the temporality of time disappears in a word such as 'vista' and replaced by immersion in the 'full' moment. And this becomes ironic when Strether is immersed in the obvious delusiveness of Mme. de Vionnet. She is associated with Mme. Roland and Mme. Recamier, so that the Revolution and the post-Revolution era merge into a single anachronistic vision. In committing himself to Mme. de Vionnet, Strether commits himself to a 'vain appearance'. And so just as the white dress of Jeanne is used to blind Strether to the expressive blackness of Mme. de Vionnet's, so the light of Paris, which seems to illuminate so much, really, for the most part, dazzles. Because the past has already *given* Strether an identity, one created out of his own failure and Mrs Newsome's success, out of the death of his wife and child and the editorship of the Review, the past has to be displaced as past, and the pure ego has to create itself out of a past that never was, a past that knows neither succession nor consequence.

Strether's vision is, of course, an ironic one – his famous exhortation to Little Bilham contains within the affirmation the recognition that for himself it has come too late, and the slight note of absurdity in the metaphors Strether uses (the jelly of consciousness and the mould of circumstance) maintains an equipoise between the recognition of the necessity of his affirmation and its impossibility (at least for himself). But surely too, there is a second dimension of irony in the structure of the narrative which assesses Strether's awareness:

Did he live in a false world, a world that had grown simply to suit him, and was his present slight irritation – in the face now of Jim's silence in particular – but the alarm of the vain thing menaced by the touch of the real? Was this contribution of the real possibly the mission of the Pococks? – had they come to make the work of observation, as *he* had practised observation, crack and crumble, and to reduce Chad to the plain terms in which honest minds could deal with him? Had they come in short to be sane where Strether was destined to feel that he himself had only been silly?

(Book VIII, Chap. III)

This is not the final note of the novel – but the questions here are not just rhetorical. The touch of the real *might be* opposed to the work of observation and this entails a sharper irony than the one Strether recognizes. For it comes to mean that the touch of the real is what most challenges consciousness, and since it is only consciousness (knowing) that postulates the pure ego, it challenges the idea of essential character. And surely in terms of the plot, the touch of the real is efficacious. The moment of Strether's commitment to Mme. de Vionnet in the face of Sarah Pocock is a moment of high comic exposure:

He grew conscious, as he was now apt to do, of a strange smile, and the next moment he found himself talking like Miss Barrace.
'She has struck me from the first as wonderful.'
(And later).
'Ah dear Sarah, you must *leave* me this person here'.
In his desire to avoid all vulgar retorts, to show how, even perversely, he clung to his rag of reason, he had softly almost wailed this plea. Yet he knew it to be perhaps the most positive declaration he had ever made in his life, and his visitor's reception of it virtually gave it that importance. 'That's exactly what I'm delighted to do. God knows *we* don't want her.'

(Book X, Chap. III)

Strether is surely something of an Amis hero here, and it is Sarah who actually wins. And the reason is obvious enough: the work of observation has been harnessed by the vain appearance. Chad and Mme. de Vionnet have taken Strether for a ride and the Pococks give it precisely that perspective. The fine consciousness gets drawn further and further in by a light that never was.

Pure Ego and Empirical Ego

The ironic assessment of Strether's vision of Europe is confirmed by our inevitable impression of the novel as a whole – for although Strether's mind, which is the real content of the novel is switched on and vibrates there is no very certain sense in which it actually moves. This arises because the effort to affirm the validity of personal experience (and hence the reality of 'character') involves the demolition of the concepts which structure normal experience. Identity asserts itself only through the spatialization of time; freedom is only preserved through the displacement of causality. In other words the syntax of experience undergoes a radical dichotomy between idealism and determinism.[17]

But is it more complex than this. I have been using the terms 'pure ego' and 'empirical ego' to distinguish between Strether's consciousness and the identity which Strether is given by his past. Time and causality are seen to be a part of 'the touch of the real' that Woollett brings in other words belong to the abstractions that a conventional ordering of experience in terms of ethical absolutes uses to mediate 'the work of observation'. Against this which obviously makes for an empirical and therefore philistine self (because it is a mechanical non-curious imposition on experience) there is the immediate experience that Paris offers (that is to say unmediated by philistine convention). But the original distinction between the known and the knowing self was made by James Ward for a rather different purpose. The concept of the pure ego was an attempt to qualify F. H. Bradley's ideas about immediate experience. According to Richard Wollheim, Bradley's notion of immediate experience had two properties: first, it was presentational; second, it was 'non-relational.[18] As such for Bradley this 'non-relational felt unity' prefigured the highest form of thinking which was the Absolute. In such a scheme of argument the self was, like concepts of time, causality and so on, merely an abstraction imposed on this experience: 'Metaphysically your soul or Ego is a mass of confusion.' Ward's 'pure ego' was a way of differentiating between the self which is an abstraction from the non-relational felt unity, and the self which perceived this unity. It was a pretty tenuous idea and Bradley had little trouble with disposing of it.[19] Rather evasively in the *Principles of Psychology*, William James ducks metaphysical questions of the self altogether, although he assumes as a premise this very metaphysical notion.[20]

Immediate Experience

Quite clearly, the validity of immediate experience is as essential to the concept of 'personality' as is the concept of self. In a famous letter to Grace Norton in 1883, James wrote:

> You are right in your consciousness that we are all echoes and reverberations of the *same*, and you are noble when your interests and pity as to everything that surrounds you, appears to have a sustaining and

harmonizing power. Only don't, I beseech you, *generalize* too much in these sympathies and tendernesses – remember that every life is a special problem which is not yours but another's and content yourself with the terrible algebra of your own. Don't melt too much into the universe, but be as solid and dense as you can.

(1920 Ed. Vol. I, p. 101)

In somewhat different terms melting is precisely Strether's danger. The immediate experience offered by Europe undermines the syntax of experience which means both that the empirical ego is transcended *and* that the pure ego is in danger of immersion. And immersion is what happens to Strether. He gets further and further drawn in to the appearance embodied in Mme. de Vionnet, until towards the end of the novel he almost ceases to have a sense of his own identity: 'Strether paused anew, on the last flight, at this final rather breathless sense of what Chad's life was doing with Chad's mother's emissary. It was dragging him, at strange hours, up the staircases of the rich; it was keeping him out of bed at the end of long hot days; it was transforming beyond recognition the simple, subtle, conveniently uniform thing that had anciently passed with him for a life of his own.' So it would be wrong to see Paris and Woollett as antitheses. Caught between the measurement of Woollett and the immersion of Paris, Strether is exploited by both. Woollett impinges with the autonomy of ethical form, Paris with the monism of immediate experience: the syntax of experience stifles the intrinsic self: the intrinsic self, escaping its context threatens to lose itself in the universe.

Threatens to, but doesn't. What enables the pure ego to sustain itself determines the most obvious feature of *The Ambassadors*, the notorious cobwebby prose. The novel celebrates the supremacy of consciousness but obviously it isn't a *stream* of consciousness. The reason is that James is dramatizing the mind of Strether at the point before it becomes immersed and the prose is both attempting to overcome the determinant value of the abstract syntax of experience and to resist becoming an extra-personal flow. We can see this in the opening paragraph:

1. Strether's first question, when he reached the hotel, was about his friend; yet on his learning that Waymarsh was apparently not to arrive till evening he was not wholly disconcerted.
2. A telegram from him bespeaking a room 'only if not noisy,' reply paid, was produced for the inquirer at the office, so that the understanding they should meet at Chester rather than at Liverpool remained to that extent sound.
3. The same secret principle, however, that had prompted Strether not absolutely to desire Waymarsh's presence at the dock, that had led him thus to postpone for a few hours his enjoyment of it, now operated to make him feel he could still wait without disappointment.

4. They would dine together at the worst, and, with all respect to dear old Waymarsh – if not even, for that matter, to himself – there was little fear that in the sequel they shouldn't see enough of each other.
5. The principle that I have just mentioned as operating had been, with the most newly disembarked of the two men, wholly instinctive – the fruit of a sharp sense that, delightful as it would be to find himself looking, after so much separation into his comrade's face, his business would be a trifle bungled should he simply arrange for this countenance to present itself to the nearing steamer as the first 'note' of Europe.
6. Mixed with everything was the apprehension, already, on Strether's part, that he would, at best, throughout, prove the note of Europe in quite a sufficient degree.

The prose reflects both the ambiguities that I have been discussing and the particular way James tries to cope with those ambiguities. Some of the striking details in this passage quite obviously have to do with Strether's own self irony, one which derives from 'the apprehension' that Waymarsh is going to operate as a model of the empirical self which it is Strether's mission to affirm. Thus the litotes in 1 and 3 ('not wholly disconcerted'/ 'not absolutely to desire') and the shifting nomenclature of his compatriot ('friend' 1, 'dear old Waymarsh' 4, 'comrade' 5) together with the objectifying of himself in 'inquirer' combine with the comically elliptical syntax of (2) ('a room, "only if not noisy", replied paid') to highlight the contrast between the curious, tentative Strether and the rigid, hebraic Waymarsh, and Strether's bemused awareness of that contrast. But in (3) and (5) something more complex is going on. In (3) there is a syntactical displacement of time achieved through the use of the pluperfect. '*The same* secret principle' takes syntactical precedence over the clauses between which it is a relation, so that we are conscious of its sameness before we know what it is the same as. Thus the historical sequence is overcome, and this is emphasized as so often in James's late prose through the suspension of the syntax, subject and predicate being wrenched apart by the pluperfect clauses. Past and present are contained in one sequence of ideas. At the same time, there is something of a specious parallelism between the two subordinate clauses because the second is really a consequence of the first: 'that had prompted Strether not absolutely to desire Waymarsh's presence at the dock' is really *the reason why* he had postponed for a few hours his enjoyment of it. So that just as past and present are made to have a spatial relation, cause and effect are made to seem a parallel line of action instead of sequential ones. This is saved from becoming solipsistic through the very careful deployment of the conventions of syntax. So too with (5) where again we have the past (which is an instinctive thought) brought within the terms of the present (which is reflective), and a careful transition between the determined and the determining from 'it would be to find himself' to 'should he simply arrange'. But there is a further point to be made here, about the phrase 'with the most newly disembarked of the two men'. It is grammatically wholly superfluous, but it enables the sentence to reach out of its direct line of thought and capture an implicit sense of Strether's freshness of apprehension.

Experience and Language

These are particular points, and I hesitate to generalize from them. Obviously, however, the prose is tracing a highly subjective line (which, as we have seen, necessarily disposes with the 'syntax of experience') and gives it an objectivity through the syntax of language (meaning here rather what is possible in language than what is likely). Such an attempt tries both to recognize the flux of immediate experience and trying to hold it at a point of stasis, not through the conventional means (the setting up of abstract relations) but through the momentary structure of language.

The work of observation has to fortify itself through the careful maintenance of the gap between a consciousness and its dramatization. And this arises from the need to preserve essential being both from the abstraction which is ethics (to preserve the essential difference in Arnoldian or Paterian terms between being and doing) and from the annihilation present in the symbol. Between the monism of ethics and the monism of the transcendent there is only the structure of appreciation. The discrete self is paralysed.

The Self and Others in *The Turn of the Screw* and *The Golden Bowl*

The Ambassadors is an intensely pessimistic novel because it portrays the destruction of the 'liberal' concept of personality from within the framework of an ideology which bases itself precisely on that concept. By making an extreme, even perverse, effort to sustain the idea of self as unrelated substance, James provides the artistic answer to the question that inevitably arises in a consideration of Harvey's thesis that the modern experimental novel grows out of the dislocation of the 'constituent categories' which grant structure to the 'realistic' novel's rendering of experience. The question that he doesn't ask is why do these categories fail after about 1900? One of the answers is implied in the technique of *The Ambassadors*: they fail because of an inner contradiction between time and identity, causality and freedom which becomes beyond a certain point open warfare. The extreme defensiveness that James is thrust back upon, particularly in his special use of prose, is an index of how hard pressed his faith in essential self became.

I have argued elsewhere that the point of open warfare emerges definitively during *The Princess Casamassima* (1886), the novel in which James attempts unsuccessfully to confront the new reality of organized labour. From that point onwards, he becomes more specifically concerned with the inner structure of a particular class consciousness. This means inevitably that he ceases to offer an objective critique of society in terms of Balzacian realism and it is not unnatural, for example, that Maxwell Geismar in *The Cult of Henry James*, who approaches James in these terms, should see his work as a deceptive bourgeois fantasy. In the later James money plays a decisive role in the operation of social relationships but only through an immense critical dishonesty would anyone claim that its role is dispassionately rendered. Money in the later James becomes an attribute of innocence, blatantly offered as a magic wand in the capitalist fairy-tale. Certainly this is a serious limitation, but it doesn't undermine the real value of James's work. For what we are left with is a rich celebration of the inner nature of personality within a bourgeois ethical framework which in its extremity testifies to the corruption of that nature, a corruption inherent in the very affirmation of the value of 'experience' which emerges from Strether's vision. We can go further and say that this corruption is related to a *realized* social specificity in James's work, and that this too indicates the limitations of the 'reality' defined by the neo-liberal criticism.

Obviously, as a theory which insists on the primacy and opacity of character, neo-liberal realism lays great emphasis on 'love', on 'the deep initial sense of human differentiation'.[21] *The Turn of the Screw* is about this initial sense in a specific social context and an analysis of it demonstrates the specificity of James's exploration of 'character'.

In fact I am in total agreement with Marius Bewley about this tale and merely want to push his argument a little further.[22] Bewley rightly bypasses the famous debate about whether there are meant to be ghosts (as symbols of metaphysical evil) or whether the governess who relates the tale is suffering from pathological hysteria as the result of sexual frustration. The fact is that there is simply no way of telling from within the story. Clearly the governess is not to be trusted because she *is* in love with her employer and she is repressed. On the other hand, there is no real way of overcoming that fact that she describes Peter Quint accurately enough to Mrs Grose although she has never even heard of his existence (unless you also claim that she is lying to us, in which case, since we have no other evidence except hers, the whole tale collapses). Neither is there any help to be had from the preface: James makes a quite baffling distinction between the governess's 'crystalline *record*' and her '*explanation*' of the events. In fact the story seems to *demand* questions which are normally illegitimate in criticism – questions of the order of 'How many children had Lady Macbeth?' The governess went to the village the day before the first apparition of Quint; could she have learnt about him then? And so on. For Bewley it is not the answers that matter, but the need to ask the questions. Appearances and reality have become so wrenched apart that we no longer have any objective criteria of relevance. Thus we confront an improper chaos: the reader is forced to be totally subjective. The brilliance of the talc, like the brilliance of Strether's Paris, offers not an illumination but a dazzling, and this, of course, is a kind of darkness.

The Destruction of Character

But the darkness is visible, the chaos rendered. This is because it is presented in terms of the destruction of character as a factor in viable relationships. Bradley, in *Appearance and Reality*, was concerned partly to demonstrate the impossibility of a plurality of reals, and one of the ways that he does this is through knowledge. Knowledge is a relation, and relations must either be external (that is not affecting the substance or character of the reals) or internal (developing out of inherent properties which constitute the reals). Knowledge cannot form an external relation either to the knower or the known because knowledge in each knower makes a difference to the knower, and knowledge 'which touches, but does not change its object, does not contain its object, and so is not really of its object ... is not really knowledge at all.' On the other hand, if knowledge is an internal relation to the knower and yet is not *merely* inherent in the knower (in other words is objective) then the knower is modified from outside and therefore cannot be self contained. Similarly if the known is related internally to the knower, it is changed by being known and hence knowledge is merely relative. 'In other words, in the case of all true knowledge both knower and known are different in consequence of the knowledge that relates them, but if they are, then knowledge proves fatal to their mutual independence and hence their plurality.'[23]

James was not necessarily conscious of this line of reasoning, but, as we have seen he was certainly concerned to affirm the independence of reals and it is presumably this kind of argument that Bayley has in mind when he claims that in *The Golden Bowl* we find an antithesis between knowledge and love.[24] In other words, the idea of an intrinsic and discrete self can only be maintained in the face of the possibility of knowledge.

This is what is happening in *The Turn of the Screw*, but in a much more acute way because the idea of relationship is bound up with its particular social mediation. In the given social hierarchy, the employed is always likely to be empirically known. Thus Fleda Vetch, in *The Spoils of Poynton* becomes for Mrs Gereth her agent of communication, and finally the focus of Mrs Gereth's acquisitiveness. Owen too *knows* Fleda in this sense: 'You don't live anywhere do you?' This is his means of identification, and it is the one that Fleda confronts at the crisis of the novel when she recognizes her similarity to the girl who painted pictures that she sees lying for ever unsold in a shop window. The only way that she has of shoring up her own unmediated identity is by giving Owen his, that of her hackneyed ideal of manliness, and later by establishing her own fictive relationship of mental possession of the spoils.

Identity and Character

It is important to insist on Fleda's social deprivation: as the known object, her separateness becomes threatened by the knower, Mrs Gereth or Owen, but this is not countered with love, in Bayley's sense, because human differentiation is exactly what Fleda doesn't allow, for example, to Owen – she makes him into a 'character'. The governess in *The Turn of the Screw* is in a similar predicament. She too is poor, lonely and susceptible, and she is only given an identity through her role as employee. This is what gives her release from her 'small, smothered life', but it is also, and importantly a depersonalized role – she is a young and pretty governess in a line of young and pretty governesses. However she sees her employer, he clearly sees her as someone who will simply get on with the job without disturbing him. The depersonalized role is combined with a very sentimental, romantic disposition: 'Was there a secret at Bly – a mystery of Udolpho or an insane, an unmentionable relative kept in unsuspected confinement?' It is not unnatural that she should see her role as offering more than a job, as offering an identity through an unmediated relationship with the children.

At the same time, it is inevitable that she should define such a relationship in terms of her possession of the children: 'to watch, to teach, *to form* little Flora would too evidently be the making of a happy and useful life.' Above all this means that the children have to be for her blank sheets: 'I remember feeling with Miles in especial as if he had had, as it were, no history.' So they become symbolic of innocence, of what Robert Heilman has called 'the childhood of the race'.[25] Heilman takes the tale as a truly symbolic one and he gathers up the words and phrases used to describe the children to show how they do add up to this significance. He quotes, for example, 'brightly', 'radiant', dazzle', ' a lovely lighted little face', 'fairly glittered', 'extraordinary brightness', 'great glory of freshness', 'a positive fragrance of purity', 'a sweetness of innocence' and so on, as the significant comments on the children. But there is surely a very obvious point to be made here. Although these words coherently signify light and youth, they are all words of judgment rather than of description. We are not given a symbol, we are given an interpretation which we are forced to accept. But we cannot be forced to accept it as more than an index of what the governess is making of the children.

The Ghosts

This applies too to the question of the ghosts. Quint and Miss Jessel exist as real people in the past of the children. They thus stand for a part of the children's independent reality over which the governess can have no control. It is important that the governess' 'heroic' decision to stay as a matter of duty is made after the second appearance of Miss Jessel, when Miss Jessel occupies her own place in the schoolroom, in other words when she feels her own role to be directly threatened. She sees the ghosts as wanting to possess Miles and Flora, because that is the only kind of relationship she can conceive of. But it is not as simple as this. The real lovers are in the past, the ghosts may symbolize the past but are actually present. By producing the ghosts therefore, the governess overcomes the past of the children and makes it spatially present, and therefore symbolic. We note again and again in the tale how the governess prefers to induce from appearances rather than discover the truth (she refuses, for example, to inquire about the reasons for Miles' expulsion from school). The ghosts too are reduced to appearances:

> 'He has red hair, very red, close curling, and a pale face, long in shape, with straight good features and little rather queer whiskers that are as red as his hair ... He gives me the sense of looking like an actor.'

An actor indeed. Quint is here reduced to the level of a Victorian melodrama villain. Miss Jessel is constantly being described as haggard and beautiful, like the equally conventional fallen woman. The past is made apparitional, and the apparitions are reduced to romantic clichés. And the fictionalizing that goes on throughout the tale in the calling up of the ghosts grants its own kind of joy. In the final scene with Flora, the governess talks of 'my thrill of joy at having brought on the proof'.

This is the joy of the do-it-yourself novelist. The governess has created her own Udolpho. The imprecisely realized expansion of her experience grants freedom to her imagination and, according to her primitive lights, she is able to create an artefact in which she is both creator and heroine. Only this explanation can do justice to the elaborate and skilful modulation of the tale's formal existence. The prologue establishes a measured esca-lation of the tale's seriousness. The prologue's narrator firmly establishes a context of the Christmas 'amusette', the gothic horror story; Douglas, who presents the manuscript, raises it to a level of moral horror ('for dreadful, dreadfulness') and the governess herself makes it a story of a metaphysical struggle between good and evil. She does this, however, in melodramatic terms which allow all three perspectives to remain. The final scenes, in which, by summoning the ghosts to the children she destroys the childhood of Flora and the life of Miles, can be tableaux of the confrontation of good and evil, or they can be scenes of horrifying psychological pressure, or, since they are tableaux, simply *scenes*, spine chilling and entertaining. Importantly, it is the narrator of the prologue who gives the tale its title, and his perspective thus remains always possible.

Thus, though it is impossible to establish criteria of reality *within* the talc, there is a real enough tension between the events of the story and their presentation within the terms of the artefact. The governess has to combat knowledge not with love but with symbolism. In order to sustain an inner being which is not consumed by the identity she is given by her social inferiority, she has to create a world which can contain the identities of others within her own identity. She has to establish a relationship with the children which is 'internal' to them, but which does not change the structure of her own being. She becomes, then, the Absolute in her own creation, dispossessing Miles and Flora of any relationship which is not to her. The *object* of social knowledge attains *subjectivity* through art: this is her social revenge.

The Golden Bowl

In *The Golden Bowl*, there is no such obvious context of social victimization for here money becomes an attribute of innocence. Nevertheless what saves the novel from cloying, which it does on Bayley's reading of it in terms of an antithesis between knowledge (Charlotte and the Prince) and love (Adam and Maggie), is that the innocence embodies itself in exactly the same objectifying terms as the guilt of the governess in *The Turn of the Screw*. This is true less of what goes on in the novel thematically than of what goes on at the surface of the narrative. The surface is precisely what Bayley ignores, and, as a result sentimentalizes particularly the role of Maggie. At the moment of victory over Charlotte, we get something very different from love. Maggie notices that Charlotte is hurrying off to an obscure part of the garden to be alone, and she uses the feeble pretext of taking Charlotte a book to rush out and persecute her:

> Maggie had come out to her, really, because she knew her doomed, doomed to a separation that was like a knife in her heart; and in the very sight of her uncontrollable, her blinded physical quest of a peace not to be grasped, something of Mrs Assingham's picture of her as thrown, for a grim future, beyond the great sea and the great continent had at first found fulfilment. She had got away, in this fashion – burning behind her, almost, the ships of disguise – to let her horror of what was before her play up without witnesses; and even after Maggie's approach had presented an innocent front it was still not to be mistaken that she bristled with the signs of her extremity. It was not to be said for

them, either, that they were draped at this hour in any of her usual graces; unveiled and all but unashamed they were tragic to the Princess in spite of the dissimulation that, with the return of comparative confidence, was so promptly to operate. How tragic, in essence, the very change made vivid, the instant stiffening of the spring of pride – this for possible defence if not for possible aggression. Pride indeed, the next moment, had become the mantle caught up for protection and perversity; she flung it round her as a denial of any loss of her freedom.
(Chap. 38)

This is sufficient to indicate that the last thing Maggie has is any sense, initial or otherwise, of human differentiation. On the contrary, she is making of Charlotte a picture, a fixed surface about which she claims freedom to deduce inner facts. What we are aware of above all is an extreme dichotomy between language and event. The words 'doom', 'tragic', 'bristled' and 'stiffening' establish an extremely melodramatic tone, while all that is happening is that Charlotte, not unnaturally, is looking somewhat amazed at Maggie's breathless intrusion. Moreover, the metaphors reduce Charlotte to a theatrical figure; 'unveiled, and all but unashamed' indeed makes of her a figure in one of the crypto-pornographic paintings which had access to the Royal Academy in the 1880's and 1890's, and the image of 'pride' as 'the mantle caught up for protection and perversity' is from a context of Bernhardt. But these metaphors have nothing to do with the real Charlotte. Maggie induces this theatricality in order to be able to bring her conflict with Charlotte into the arena of metaphysical absolutes.

Possession

All the relationships in *The Golden Bowl* move monstrously within an ambience of possession: Adam of course, *acquires* the Prince, as a piece for his museum, the Prince acquires Maggie as a means of restoring his familiar dignity, and Charlotte acquires Adam as a means of staying close to the Prince. And Maggie too sees relationship in terms of possession: she visits the British Museum to study the Prince's ancestry, and importantly, her conflict with Charlotte is in terms of a battle for the possession of Adam – 'Not yet, since his marriage, had Maggie so sharply and so formidably known her old possession of him as a thing divided and contested.' She sees him not with any sense of mutuality but as an object: his very quietness, we learn, 'placed him in her eyes as no precious work of art probably had ever been placed in his own'. In fact what is opposed to knowledge in *The Golden Bowl* is not love, but appreciation; everybody deceives everybody else in order to preserve them from truth, from light, as one would preserve delicate museum pieces or, indeed, flawed golden bowls. The vast campaign for the preservation of human plurality goes on in the context of money, and hence goes on as an objectifying process. James is not consciously satirizing the limitations of relationship in such terms, but his exposure of 'love', so openly and so inextricably in a net-work of cash relationships, reveals a corruption that is ineluctable.

The value of James' later work gains in importance through its not being openly critical of such modes of relationship. He testifies to the radical contradiction in Harvey's notion of character as being intrinsically and contextually known. Harvey accepts the Marxist view that the realistic novel grows up initially with the development of modern capitalism. 'From this social process', he says 'derive the assumptions and values we may crudely if conveniently lump together as liberalism.'[26]

Only two pages later he is arguing that the realistic novelist sees the individual human being as eluding 'the categories of *any* ideology'. The work of the later James might have enabled him to avoid this evident contradiction, for James is saturated in the values of capitalism, in its metaphysical notions of the substantial self as well as its ethical notions of human relationship. The great point about the late novels is that they implicitly celebrate these notions at the point of head-on collision. The intrinsic self can only exist in the conditions in which others are contex-tual; to protect herself against the threat to her own intrinsic self, defined by its possession of her father, Maggie has to turn her back on Charlotte, on the Prince and even on her father as real, intrinsic others. In order not to be owned she has to become an owner, and what she becomes is the owner of the others in the same sense that the author owns his characters in a well made little drama: 'they might have been figures rehearsing some play of which she herself was the author: they might even, for the happy appearance they continued to present, have been such figures as would, by the strong note of character in each, fill any author with the certitude of success, especially of their own histrionic.' The opposing self opposes self.

Conclusion

The Ambassadors and *The Turn of the Screw* have been taken as showing the inner contradictions of two of Harvey's main concepts: the notion that it is possible to talk about a relatively stable 'syntax of experience' and the argument that 'character' – as an entity that can be both contextually and intrinsically known – is a concept that lies outside the categories of a particular ideology.

In *The Ambassadors*, Strether's contextual identity (his empirical ego) is related to a shared abstraction, time, imposed on him by the deterministic social world of Woollett. Paris offers a freedom from the empirical ego through a release of consciousness from the sequential nature of time, in which the past has a causal relationship to the present; Strether achieves a non-deterministic appreciation of the past which also enables him to possess the past. But this release constitutes a new threat to the pure ego, the knowing self, by offering more than appreciation, by offering immo-lation. Experience in Paris is no longer mediated by philistine convention, but insofar as it is immediate, it is also non-relational. The self can only be conceived of in terms of relations: it cannot exist if there is no non-self distinct from it. So that there is a double undermining of the syntax of experience. Insofar as the novel is a confrontation of Woollett and Paris, identity is affirmed through the destruction of duration, freedom through the denial of causality. Insofar as Woollett and Paris combine to threaten the plurality of self with alternative kinds of monism (ethical and epistemolog-ical), all the elements of the *syntax of experience*, time and space, freedom and causality make the identity structured on their bases seem a delusion. Identity finally has to sustain itself through *the syntax of language* in which the rules are exploited in a highly legalistic way in order to partake of the immediacy of experience without being finally immersed in it.

This is to say that Strether's bourgeois consciousness can only over-come the predicament arising from its confrontation with the destructive forces of outer experience by creating a kind of fictionalizing linguistic structure.

Fiction and Identity

This is related to a realized social specificity that gives *The Ambassadors*, and indeed the whole of the later James, a historical reference. A study of *The Turn of the Screw* makes this obvious. The governess creates a fictional world in a highly stylised mode in order to create for herself an identity which is separate from the identity given her by her social role. She achieves this through a kind of knowledge that is unable to change her and thus threaten her own separateness. This means that she has to induce facts rather than learn them, and has to keep them contained within a particular convention. Knowledge can become a form of possession, because what she learns becomes controllable by her. In terms of human relationships this means that she has to sustain her own identity against the destructive power of social inequality through a love for her charges which is entirely destructive of all their lives, which is outside her immediate experience of them. Like Strether, she spatializes the past, but in her case it is specifically a matter of social revenge. The antithesis between love and knowledge is thus a facile one: both become alternative modes of possession. The governess has to mystify us in order to compen-sate for her being known as a social being, but she has to love the children destructively – to make them part of her own opaque and fictional world.

We have seen too that this struggle to sustain the self by the destruction of other selves is built in to the very texture of the prose of *The Golden Bowl*. Given the very obvious domination of the major relationships in both of these novels by money, this theme of 'possessive individualism' is related to a very specific social structure. In the later James, 'character' is thus in an extreme crisis: it can only exist at all through possession, and so it becomes in itself a monistic concept. The choice is between buying others (as Adam Verver buys the Prince) or 'producing' them as attributes of a convincing illusion.

History and Absolute Judgments

A full answer to Harvey's thesis would require analysis of other writers he uses as examples, particularly Tolstoy and Sartre, *and* a discussion of writers who are omitted (above all, Lawrence).[27] But a complete answer is also impossible because it is hard to detect the ultimate implication of Harvey's thesis. The central contradiction here relates to Harvey's facile antithesis between 'the Scylla of historical relativism and the Charybdis of some form of absolute criteria'.[28] On the one hand he seems to be suggesting that the ideas of character are historically located in the 19th century, and that although they have been subverted in the 20th, they must be acknowledged for an understanding of the 'realistic novel'; on the other hand, at various points, particularly in his discussion of Sartre, he seems to be making a similar point to that of Iris Murdoch in 'The Sublime and the Beautiful Revisited' that, whatever the direction of modern philosophy, the liberal notion of character that we find in the work, for example, of George Eliot corresponds more closely with the world-view of 'the common reader'. 'Sartre is perhaps as good as any novelist can be without achieving real greatness; when we read his novels we say, "Yes, this is the Sartrian world"; but when we read one of the great masters we say, simply, "Yes, this is the world!"'[29]

The central doubt here is the word 'we'. Harvey means by it the 'common' reader, but it is difficult to imagine in what sense someone who reads *Middlemarch* is 'common'. What such readers are likely to have in common are precisely the liberal concepts of character inherited either from a bourgeois environment or a bourgeois education that a bourgeois novelist such as George Eliot takes for granted. So naturally Harvey's imaginary reader isn't going to find Sartre very congenial. And here we have to make a further point. To grant Sartre a whole chapter may look like a welcome penetration of the chauvinistic barriers that constrict most English criticism, but it is also a method of cheating. Naturally enough, most of Harvey's thesis is based on a study of English fiction of the 19th century. Sartre is both foreign and removed in time from this main body, so that he appears in a clearly antipathetic role. But to be fair to Sartre one would have to see his novels in the context of Balzac and Flaubert and Proust (none of whom he deals with at any length). Again, as Harvey fragmentarily acknowledges, the destruction of the liberal idea of character is something which takes place both long before Sartre, and in English fiction too. It is certainly evident, as Harvey admits, in D. H. Lawrence. Indeed the movement towards symbolism in Lawrence's work in a work as early as *The Trespasser* is precisely bound up with the failure of 'the old stable ego'. And Lawrence cannot be dismissed as a special case, both because he is the greatest English 20th-century novelist, and because the dilemma which his work is celebrating can be linked with the dilemma which informs *The Longest Journey* (1907).

Both novels are vital in any discussion of the English novel because they both bear witness to the oppressive quality of bourgeois convention and both seek solutions through myth, through the absorption of the isolated self in a larger unity outside the given conventions.

James and the Canon

This is where James comes in, even though he went to desperate lengths to maintain the old stable ego. Lawrence and Forster *place* James in a historical perspective: they necessarily alert us to the objective importance and limitations of his work. Equally, however, James, from his position within the liberal/bourgeois framework, places George Eliot. His work points to the limits of George Eliot's realization of character in a specific way. It is very noticeable, for example, that given a relationship with characters mediated through her own class limitations, George Eliot simply doesn't allow any kind of human differentiation. In *Felix Holt*, the mob is not a collection of people at all, but a natural phenomenon, and Felix himself is only differentiated in the crudest physiological terms (he is taller than the rest and has noble features – more racial purity really). In *Daniel Deronda*, the Jews have to be stage Jews in one way or another: they are allowed to be either pawnbrokers or prophets, but people never. Her most obvious failures point to the necessity of a fuller exploration of the self in a given society such as we get in James. Although George Eliot is supremely concerned with just this theme, she is compelled by the limitations of her concept of character to treat it in a rather static, antithetical way. James penetrates through the dilemma of the antithetical vision to a revelation of the corrupt nature of both the terms of the antithesis. Our imaginary 'common reader', however bourgeois, confronted, even appalled, by James, would hardly find George Eliot's vision more like life than Sartre's.

This will only lead us to underestimate George Eliot or overestimate the later James if we try to steer between the 'Scylla' and 'Charybdis' of historical relativism and absolute criteria. For certainly they are part of the same mode of thinking, a mode which judges literature in a fundamentally acquisitive manner. The relativism of a C. S. Lewis asks what charm there is in this or that piece in the literary museum; the absolutism of the New Critics or of Leavis asks what charm or good there is in this or that star in the literary firmament. Both, like the characters of a late novel of James, spatialize the past in order to consume it in possession: whether you see the past as spoils or as immediate experience, you are trying to subvert its relation to the present. Harvey recognizes this, and he attempts to overcome the inevitable and most pernicious consequence, which is that of seeing English literature as in some way a special discipline with a kind of magic that philosophy or history doesn't have, as the mainstay of 'culture'. But he ultimately does specialize the role of a literary work by making it a kind of utilitarian comforter of bourgeois values. The novels that I have been discussing are going to be unavailable (as truly *formal* structures) to any kind of acquisitive criticism: that is why I think it is important that they should be kept at the forefront of literary discussion.

Notes

1. *Character and the Novel*. Chatto and Windus, p. 28.
2. Forster: *Two Cheers for Democracy*, p. 59. Quoted in *Character and the Novel*, p. 12.
3. *Character and the Novel*, pp. 24–26.
4. 'Against Dryness', *Encounter*, Jan. 1961, Vol. XXVI, No. I, p. 20.
5. 'The Sublime and the Beautiful Revisited,' *Yale Review* Dec, 1959, Vol. XLIX, pp. 247–71.
6. *Character and the Novel*, pp. 25–6.
7. Ibid. p. 188.
8. *The Appropriate Form*, 1965, p. 6.
9. *The Triple Thinkers*, 1962, pp. 144–5.
10. *The Great Tradition*, 1962, pp. 171–91.
11. *The Characters of Love*, 1960, pp. 203–60.
12. Cf: Poirier: *The Comic Sense of Henry James*, 1960. My reading differs slightly from his.
13. Preface to *Spoils of Poynton*.
14. The classic discussion is L. C. Knights' 'Henry James and the Trapped Spectator'.
15. His discussion of Time (pp. 100–18) for example, resorts to boring distinctions between objective and subjective time. I assume, from his idea of the stability of the concept, that Harvey would reject the work of Georges Poulet. But he doesn't even mention Poulet, and this means that the whole section comes to seem naïve.
16. Cf. Poulet: *Studies in Human Time*, 1956, pp. 350–54.

17. Arnold Kettle's essay on *Portrait of a Lady, An Introduction to the English Novel* (1951–3) brings out this contradiction in an analysis of remarkable subtlety.

18. *F. H. Bradley*, 1959. Cf. p. 131: 'In other words, for Bradley the primary content of the mind was a continuum of flat, fleeting passive experiences.' The whole book offers a great deal of insight into the intellectual context of James's work.

19. Wollheim, *op. cit.* pp. 132–37.

20. James: *Principles of Psychology*, 1891, Vol. I, pp. 180–82.

21. Bayley: *The Characters of Love*, p. 7.

22. *The Complex Fate*, pp. 96–149.

23. Wollheim, *op. cit.* p. 192. I have altered the order of the argument slightly.

24. *Characters of Love*, p. 210 following.

25. Heilman: 'The Turn of the Screw as Poem': collected in Willen: *A Casebook on Henry James's The Turn of The Screw*, 1954.

26. *Character and the Novel*, p. 24.

27. Harvey does, of course, mention Lawrence, but with lamentable brevity. Significantly, Bayley is just donnishly and absurdly deprecating about him.

28. Cf. *Character and the novel*, p. 17.

29. Ibid. p. 182.

CHAPTER 6

The Pervasive Mystery of Style:
The Wings of the Dove

1 *Lifestyles and eyestyles*

'She died for you in order that you might understand her.'[1] Nothing seems clearer than the parabolic direction of *The Wings of the Dove*. Although it seems arbitrary to limit it to Swedenborg, we shall find it difficult to dissent from Quentin Anderson's general account of the plot of the novel. Structurally at least, Densher is certainly used as an Everyman whose character is unformed at the beginning of the novel, and Kate relates to him as an object of his earthly love which drives him towards mercenary gain. The dove's wings, victims of human rapacity, finally touch him with a transcendental grace, which brings him to an awareness of his guilt, Kate's limited nature, and the possibilities of redemption. Unable to bring himself to read Milly's letter, Densher is left wondering not about its intention but about the turn she would have given her act:

> This turn had possibilities that, somehow, by wondering about them, his imagination had extraordinarily filled out and refined. It had made of them a revelation the loss of which was like the sight of a priceless pearl cast before his eyes – his pledge given not to save it – into the fathomless sea, or rather even it was like the sacrifice of something sentient and throbbing, something that, for the spiritual ear, might have been audible as a faint far wail. (Bk. 10, Ch. 6)

'Died for you', 'pearl cast before his eyes', 'faint far wail' – it is no wonder that the joys of Kate's body are forsaken for the consecrated splendours of Brompton Oratory. Of course, the Christian imagery is used rather than affirmed for its own sake, and we are conscious above all of a variety of religious experience. The language never quite coincides. The substitution of 'understand' for 'save', and the theatricalization of 'still, small voice' into 'faint far wail' scale the experience down for the confines of human awareness and allow for its possibly overstated subjectivity. But it isn't completely humanized, as in George Eliot, because it seems to have no reference to secular values. We are not shown that Densher becomes a morally better person – only that his wasted passion divides him inexorably from Kate. It simply has to do with the affirmation of a level of reality beyond the phenomenal. The situation at the end of the novel is most closely paralleled by James's warmest praise of his father's ideas: 'it would absolutely not have been possible to us, in the measure of our sensibility, to breathe more the air of the reference to an order of goodness and power greater than any this world by itself can show which we understand as the religious spirit.'[2] Milly's triumph is the development of Densher's plastic consciousness to the point at which it acknowledges the 'religious spirit'. It is a concept which, precisely because of its syncretism and vagueness, dissolves many contradictions; and since it is one which, in a number of forms, as Brian Lee and Richard Poirier, among others, have shown, pervades American literature, we are missing the point if we ask for precise identification. In any case, if William James, with his philosophical training, can get no closer to explaining it than by the lugubrious image of the vivisected dog offered comfort because his suffering is of value to a higher level of life,[3] it is perhaps less dangerous for the suspension of our disbelief, that the novelist should give us no more than a solvent – a mild, dove-diffused air.

So if the moral fable is simple, it is also vague, and there doesn't seem to be much room for varying interpretations. The problem for the critic is very much one of evaluation, and that is going to depend not on the fable but on its realization. For with this novel more than most, we are aware, I think, that accounts of its structure do not coincide with our experience of the book, because the book is so much an expansion from a simple plan. If it has value, the value will reside in the significance and effectiveness of the texture which the frame holds. And the most difficult problem here is, of course, Milly. It is essential not to oversimplify. On the one hand, the novel is not about Milly. Two-thirds of it are concerned with the development of Densher's consciousness, and she is absent from both the beginning and the end. The title indicates her structural role – it is not a story about dove but about its wings, wings which act as an agent of evaluation for the other characters in the novel. In this respect, Milly is James's most important *ficelle*. On the other hand, we cannot go to the other extreme and say that the dove stands mute at the centre, the focus of other, foreground relationships,[4] since the middle of the book is concerned with her registration of English society. Neither is she a victim of a dehumanizing transformation, since we are only aware of her as discontented before she has elected to accept the sacrificial dove image. To treat her as a catalyst would be to ignore the centre of the novel, but since the novel isn't about her in the way *The Portrait of a Lady* is about Isabel, we are not given anything like the complexity necessary to dramatize her suffering and development. Milly has to be, as Lee has remarked, an insubstantial type.[5] And since she is to be an agent of Densher's metamorphosis, she cannot be presented with the 'satiric penalties'[6] which attend the line of Jamesian heroines, of which she is a late flower. We can imagine a *tale* in which Milly might be an inexplicable force ambiguously alienating Densher from Kate. But the novel is too extended, Milly too visible for her to remain a mystery, and the way she changes Densher is too fully explored for it to remain ambiguous. On the face of it, there are no ironic shadows thrown by the lights of Brompton Oratory, and critics who find Milly 'an irritating sentimentality'[7] cannot be facilely dismissed. On the other hand, I think that if we are as articulate as possible about the solidity of specification in the novel, words such as 'irony' and 'sentimentality' become difficult to use. The moral patterning is highly romantic, and, like William James's comfort for the dog, nauseating, but what is impressive about it is the detailed working of the prose, and the complexity of experience which the detail embodies.

The Wings of the Dove is the most panoramic of the three international novels at the turn of the century. *The Ambassadors* is Strether's novel, and its theme is his encounter with his own identity in the context of a liberated, fully subjective consciousness. *The Golden Bowl* is Amerigo's and Maggie's and its theme is marriage. *The Wings of the Dove* has four centres of consciousness, and its theme is social relations. It is striking how much of the novel is dominated by triangular relationships: at the centre, of course, there is the triangle of Kate, Milly and Densher, but there are others – Densher, Kate, Mrs Lowder; Densher, Lord Mark, Milly; Milly, Susan, Mrs Lowder; Densher, Sir Luke, Eugenio, and so on. The plot depends on the tensions in such relationships in which two people struggle for a third, or combine against a third, or in which the third struggles to square the other two. Moreover, the talk tends to be triangular – Lord Mark and Milly discuss mainly Kate, as do Mrs Lowder and Milly; Kate and Milly carefully don't discuss Densher, which comes to the same thing, and Milly and Densher, who come closest to a self-contained dialogue tend to discuss a fictional, all-American Milly. And much of the seeing in the novel follows the same tendency to refer both to an object of vision and a third referent which is invoked by mutual relationships. The most obvious case is the way in which Milly learns to see Kate as she imagines Densher might do; but also Densher learns about his relationship with Milly by seeing Lord Mark in Florians, and Milly learns the truth about herself by seeing Susan's face after the interview with Sir Luke. This triangularity emphasizes the social concern of the novel: it is not the other person which most matters, it is the other person's relationship to someone who is related to you, and the ultimate concern of the novel is the way in which one person's geometry squares with everybody else's.

We can also group the characters statically on a triangular classification of which the most important distinction is between plasticity and force –

we think of Densher as opposed to Kate and Mrs Lowder, Susan as opposed to Milly and Maud, Lionel and Marion as opposed to Kate. Secondly, there is an opposition between the kinds of relationship with experience that the various characters have. Many of them occupy fixed positions in the social scene and have distinctive lifestyles – obviously Mrs Lowder has with her florid expressive furniture, but so has Sir Luke with his surgery. And many of the others are felt to be sharply defined by the social position they occupy: 'His type', Milly feels of Lord Mark, 'somehow, as by a life, a need, an intention of its own, took all care for vividness off his hands' (Bk. 4, Ch. 1); and even the deliquescent Lionel Croy has been met halfway by life 'placing a hand in his arm and fondly leaving him to choose the pace' (Bk. 1, Ch. 1). All these characters, however forceful or passive they may be, play a distinctive role as a group in the novel, constituting a world in relation to which the main characters have to discover or invent the values by which they are to live, and the styles through which they are to express themselves. The novel's narrators don't have a distinctive lifestyle: neither Kate nor Densher have enough status to occupy a definite role; Susie has forsaken her previous role as lady author to watch Milly; Milly has only a decadent inherited lifestyle, symbolized by her expensive but obscuring dress, which is at odds with her desire to see life. But precisely because they don't have a distinctive lifestyle, they each have an individual way of looking at the 'world'. The complex texture of the novel is built up from the competing attempts of these 'eyestyles' to cope with and square the threatening lifestyles of the world.

2 The art of seeing things as they are

The most assured moment in the presentation of Milly comes early in Book 5, when she has been confronted with the image of how the English see her – as the dead woman of the Bronzino portrait. James has built up throughout the previous chapter both the sense of 'a high-water mark of imagination' – the rich, colourful social world – and at the same time its lurking ambiguities. These focus sharply as she is led by Lord Mark to the picture, made to run the gauntlet of the world's pity, and finally left to the mercy of Kate:

> A minute or two later the situation had changed, and she knew it afterwards to have been by the subtle operation of Kate. She was herself saying that she was afraid she must go now if Susie could be found; but she was sitting down on the nearest seat to say it. The prospect, through opened doors, stretched before her into other rooms, down

the vista of which Lord Mark was strolling with Lady Aldershaw, who, close to him and much intent, seemed to show from behind as peculiarly expert. Lord Aldershaw, for his part, had been left in the middle of the room, while Kate, with her back to him, was standing before her with much sweetness of manner. The sweetness was all for *her*; she had the sense of the poor gentleman's having somehow been handled as Lord Mark had handled his wife. He dangled there, he shambled a little; then he bethought himself of the Bronzino, before which, with his eye-glass, he hovered. It drew from him an odd vague sound, not wholly distinct from a grunt, and a 'Humph – most remarkable!' which lighted Kate's face with amusement. The next moment he had creaked away over polished floors after the others and Milly was feeling as if *she* had been rude. But Lord Aldershaw was in every way a detail and Kate was saying to her that she hoped she wasn't ill. (Bk. 5, Ch. 2)

James clearly uses the imperfect here to register a critical immediacy of consciousness. Milly only becomes aware of what she is saying and doing as she is doing it, and if it is the Aldershaws who are handled in the most obvious way, Milly's sympathy for them clearly arises from her own sense of vulnerability and exposure. Meanwhile all the social poise has become a threat; consideration becomes an index of one person's power over another. 'Pity would be no more / If we did not make somebody poor.'

That it should be Kate who is standing there, controlling a situation which for Milly has become such an exposure, is apt not only because the plot demands that Kate have special insights, but because it is Kate above all who understands the exploitative nature of society, and it is Kate from whom Milly is to learn about the way society works. Aunt Maud's patronage is the impress of wealth upon deprivation – her kindness merely making of Kate a 'sensible value' which is 'chalk marked for the auction'. The tension we feel before the Bronzino is derived from the comparisons we are bound to be making between the vulnerability of Milly's wealth and the vulnerability of Kate's poverty, as well as the contrast between the healths of the two women. The tension is very encompassing because by giving us, in the opening two books, such a full account of Kate's dilemma, we are bound to sense here not merely Milly's danger but also Kate's opportunity. And more than that: by giving the opening book to Kate's consciousness, James creates a moral world in which the most lucid values are treachery and exploitation ('the moral of which moreover of course was that the more one gave oneself the less of one was left'). From this moment, Kate begins to acquire a peculiar authority for Milly – but it is an authority which we already recognize. James establishes Kate's and Densher's situation so carefully that it is impossible to see whatever they do in the remainder of the novel as anything but a response to values deeply embedded in the human world.

Our starting point is her predicament and our initial perspective is one she provides. It establishes as the major criterion in the novel the success of a style, not its rightness in absolute terms. We are told, for example, that 'She saw, as she had never seen before how material things spoke to her' (Bk. 1, Ch. 2), but since we have just been given her father's house in Chirk Street and Marian's in Chelsea, we are unable to see this as a limitation. For James does more than enumerate the items of the hole she is trying to avoid collapsing into; he seems to insist on its utterly irredeemable quality by making what are normally positive attributes seem nauseating. Thus 'the small homely hum of Chirk Street' linked with the shabby sun and the cry of the costermonger becomes oppressive precisely because it is homely. So too, the worst feature of the dead Condrip seems to be his saintly profile, and his fatuousness seems to have been decisively demonstrated by his earthly death. In this deprived world, all the values become values of oppression or escape. Father and sister turn moral concepts into instruments marking her for the auction: 'duty', 'the bond of blood', become major threats to personality. The keyword is 'mark'. Mrs Lowder openly uses the reductive terminology which endorses Kate's estranged relationship to her world:

> ... Kate's presence, by good fortune, I marked early. Kate's presence – unluckily for *you* – is everything I could possibly wish. Kate's presence is, in short, as fine as you know, and I've been keeping it for the comfort of my declining years. I've watched it long; I've been saving it up and letting it, as you say of investments, appreciate; and you may judge whether, now it has begun to pay so, I'm likely to consent to treat for it with any but a high bidder. I can do the best with her, and I've my idea of the best. (Bk. 2, Ch. 2)

But it's not only Mrs Lowder who talks in these terms – Lord Mark does too. There is nothing in fact to suggest that social relationships are ever to be seen in any other terms. Kate is, in the context she finds herself in, right to see life as she sees it: 'life at present turned to her view from week to week more and more the face of a striking and distinguished stranger' (Bk. 1, Ch. 2). It pays its respects to what the wealthy social world has to offer – but it recognizes too that there can be no compact between the markers and the marked.

I am not trying to exonerate Kate – she doesn't need it, for she tries to be open with Milly ('oh you may very well loathe me yet') and Milly is not really deceived by Kate's pity ('She had felt herself alone with a creature who paced like a panther'). Milly accepts Kate's view of her as a dove because she sees a prospect of triumph in it. Kate's role is not so much to stand for a particular group of values as to embody a way of seeing life which is, on the face of it, an art of seeing things as they are. Nowhere else in the novel do we get the same density and sharpness of realization that we do in the opening chapter, and there is a clear reason for this. 'It was a medium, a setting, and to that extent, after all, a dreadful sign of life' – such phrasing, and the embodiment of its assumptions in the concrete creation of a medium for her father, remind us above all of Auerbach's analysis of Balzac: 'What confronts us, then, is the unity of a particular milieu, felt as a total concept of a demonic-organic nature.'[8] Lionel Croy is not realized simply as a pathetic old man but as a force, 'the force of his particular type' (Bk. 1, Ch. 1). The word, which is used about other characters too, seems to have a specific frame of reference. Taine, for example, wrote of Balzac: 'l'homme n'est point une raison indépendante supérieure, saine par elle même, capable d'atteindre par son seul effort la vérité et la vertu, mais une simple force, du même ordre que les autres, recevant des circonstances son degré et sa direction.'[9] Kate is, of course, a Balzacian character, a female Rastignac who throws down her gauntlet to society at the opening of the novel. But much more she is a Balzacian seer: her mode is the mode of consciousness of the *Comédie Humaine* itself. The image of society which she gives Milly is one in which everyone is working everyone else, and what she most fully acknowledges as a source of power is money (we might recall *Gobseck* in which the miser gains an artist's hold over the lives of his characters by their debts to him). She habitually sees individuals as types, 'espèces', which demonstrate the significance of forces and the milieux they take shape in (I'm thinking here particularly of her feelings about the Misses Condrip and Aunt Maud). More specifically, her habitual mode of imagery is from natural history: 'and she compared herself to a trembling kid, kept apart a day or two till her turn should come, but sure sooner or later to be introduced into the cage of the lioness' (Bk. 1, Ch. 2). And, of course, it is she who provides the title image of the novel, out of this naturalistic world view. Kate mediates our vision of the London scene as she mediates Densher's and, later, Milly's. The art of seeing things as they are is the art of understanding a social jungle.

However, of course, James certainly didn't regard Balzac as a novelist who could see things as they really are, and Kate's world view is as limited as that of the naturalist writer. Like Balzac, Kate has an obsession with things which derives from a money-orientated attitude to society. If life confronts Kate as a stranger, it is because her own force demands of the milieu she finds herself in that she should be able to work it without being worked by it: 'What she felt was that, whatever might happen, she must keep them, must make them most completely her possession, and it was already strange enough that she reasoned, or at all events began to act, as if she might work them in with other and alien things, privately cherish them, and yet, as regards the rigour of it, pay no price' (Bk. 2, Ch. 1). Possession without price here means without sacrifice, and the only way to achieve this is through the transcendent power of money. It doesn't take long for Milly to realize that it is money that Kate mainly sees in her:

> It was a fact – it became one at the end of three days – that Milly actually began to borrow from the handsome girl a sort of view of her state; the handsome girl's impression of it was clearly so sincere. This impression was a tribute, a tribute positively to power, power the source of which was the last thing Kate treated as a mystery. (Bk. 4, Ch. 2)

What is odd about this passage, however, is not that Milly should realize this fact, but that she should see it in Kate especially, whereas it is clear that everyone else, from Lord Mark to Susan Stringham, sees her wealth as the most important thing about her. The key phrase is surely 'tribute to power': it is the creative agency of money in Milly that Kate is so responsive to. It should be linked with the clearly Darwinian sense of her own vitality that makes Kate exercise it in pursuit of this power: 'She looked at him now a moment as for the selfish gladness of their young immunities' (Bk. 6, Ch. 4). One way in which the structure of the novel can be described is that of an attempt by a superior vitality to survive the unfit and usurp her inherited power: the upstart tries to overreach the final flower of a dying race. But something else is going on in the passage quoted above. Milly is borrowing a view of her own state, which means that she defines that view, and definition means limitation: she can assimilate Kate's vision of herself, and that enables her to scale the vision down. The art of seeing things as they are takes on a curious kind of *naïveté*.

In his first essay on Balzac, in 1879, James makes it clear that he regards Balzac's concern with money a limitation of his 'realism':

> There is something pitiful in the contrast between this meagre personal budget and his lifelong visions of wealth, and of the ways of amassing wealth, his jovial sensual colossal enjoyment of luxury, and the great monetary architecture, as it were, of the *Comédie Humaine*. Money is the most general element of Balzac's novels; other things come and go, but money is always there.[10]

The social observation is seen to be underwritten by a naïve obsession with the protagonistic potentiality of money, explained as the distortion made by the impact of great wealth on underprivilege. Kate's mode of vision is, for all its shrewd understanding, that of one to whom life presents itself as a distinguished stranger. The distortion is not incompatible with Milly's sense of the accuracy of Kate's view of London society. The point is that there are other societies (the international theme), and that the art of seeing things as they are has no real sense of the art of making things as they should be. In his later essay, of 1902, James speaks of the artist in the

Comédie Humaine being half smothered by the historian, and goes on to say that 'the reporter, however philosophic, has one law, and the originator, however substantially fed, has another'.[11] Kate's predicament is that the art of seeing things as they are has to be squared with her desire for possession without price, and she has no way of relating the two except through the highly intangible power of great wealth. Her feelings for Densher are, by her own term, 'romantic', but the romance has to remain within the 'real', the material world which speaks so eloquently to her. Given Lionel and Marian, Lancaster Gate and what it stands for cannot simply be placed – as it is by Densher's more plastic imagination – as a negation of the world of thought: it speaks too clearly of resolved contradictions, of a place in the social world which is neither on the counter nor in the shop window. Again we are reminded of James's criticism of Balzac:

> The romantic side of him has the extent of all the others; it represents, in the oddest manner, his escape from the walled and roofed structure into which he had built himself – his longing for the vaguely felt outside and as much as might be of the rest of the globe. But it is characteristic of him that the most he could do for this relief was to bring the fantastic into the circle and fit it somehow to the conditions.[12]

What is 'pitiful' about Kate is that the only way she has of escaping from the cage is by the pursuit of what has built the cage in the first place. The novel is to create an alternative vision, but the alternative is stated, rather sentimentally, in the 1902 essay:

> 'Things' for him are francs and centimes more than any others, and I give up as inscrutable, unfathomable, the nature, the peculiar avidity of his interest in them. It makes us wonder again and again what then is the use on Balzac's scale of the divine faculty. The imagination, as we all know, may be employed up to a certain point in inventing uses for money; but its office beyond that point is surely to make us forget that anything so odious exists.[13]

The Wings of the Dove is concerned above all with exploring the point beyond which imagination and money become mutually exclusive (it ends, after all, with Densher giving up money). But the difference between the essay of 1902 and the novel is that the novel traces, rather than asserts, that point. And it traces it primarily by the assimilation of the Balzacian art of seeing things as they are into a larger, more encompassing vision. In terms of the novel's central image, we are witnessing the movement from a creatural view of social identity (oh you're a dove) to a pragmatic symbolist one ('It gave her straightaway the measure of the success she could have as a dove'). The movement is complex and I think it is fully realized. Its starting point is an alternative view of money, and its pervasive irony is that the best way to escape the Balzacian limitation of the use of the divine faculty is to have so much money that you no longer have to think about it.

3 The real thing, the romantic life itself

Although she accepts Kate's image, Milly is immediately able to qualify it:

> 'Because you're a dove.' With which she felt herself ever so delicately, so considerately, embraced; not with familiarity or as a liberty taken, but almost ceremoniously and in the manner of an *accolade*; partly as if, though a dove who could perch on a finger, one were also a princess with whom forms were to be observed. (Bk. 5, Ch. 6)

The immediate context is obviously ironic. It makes it worse that Kate's humiliating image should be presented with so much apparent respect. But by the end of the scene Milly is to recognize the possibilities of success in it: and one of the reasons is that by this stage in the book there is already an alternative set of images made available for her, which she is able to take up and use later. The most important is the image of the princess who has it in her to command consideration. And the princess image is the most characteristic metaphor in the style of vision offered straightforwardly as an alternative to Kate's: that of the New England author, Susan Shepherd Stringham.

Susie is not easy to define in terms of a single aesthetic in the way that Kate is, partly because she represents a whole tradition that James knew intimately as a tradition, and which cannot therefore be disentangled without distortion; partly because she is a writer and therefore conscious of the sources of her imagery; but mainly because her enlightenment is one which enables her to assimilate fashionable writers – notably Maeterlinck and Pater – to a vision which is primarily transcendentalist rather than symbolist. Much of the third book, it is true, is taken up with the register of 'impressions', but the impressions have ultimately to take a secondary place to the significance that she places on them, and above all on her impression of Milly:

> She moved, the admirable Mrs Stringham, in a fine cloud of observation and suspicion; she was in the position, as she believed, of knowing much more about Milly Theale than Milly herself knew, and yet of having to darken her knowledge as well as make it active. The woman in the world least formed by nature, as she was quite aware, for duplicities

and labyrinths, she found herself dedicated to personal subtlety by a new set of circumstances, above all by a new personal relation ... (Bk. 3, Ch. 1)

It is surely a very New England predicament, having to darken knowledge of labyrinths – the predicament of the allegorist confronted with evil. Yet the allegorization, for all the disingenuous disclaimers, is not reluctantly undertaken, for the naked eyeball sees primarily to a world beyond the forms it registers. Through an accumulation of words such as 'real' and 'romantic' – a hyperbolic vocabulary of the enrapt imagination – and a tissue of potently dangerous illusion, James registers the fine cloud of observation as the thick veil of an obsession:

This was poetry – it was also history – Mrs Stringham thought, to a finer tune even than Maeterlinck and Pater, than Marbot and Gregorovius. She appointed occasions for the reading of these authors with her hostess, rather perhaps than actually achieved great spans; but what they managed and what they missed speedily sank for her into the dim depths of the merely relative, so quickly, so strongly had she clutched her central clue. (Bk. 3, Ch. 1)

The breathless, absurdly discursive syntax places Susie's eyestyle very firmly. But the fact that it is funny shouldn't detract from the fact that it is also very dangerous and destructive. The central clue she clings to is as reductive as Kate's art of seeing things as they are. The difference is that her typology is 'representative' in an Emersonian sense, rather than naturalistic. Like Kate, she attempts to possess through knowledge, and possession means defining the human as creatural, created not creative: 'the charm of the creature was positively in the creature's greatness' (Bk. 3, Ch. 1). 'Merely relative' defines the limits of her plasticity. Like Kate, she governs her vision by an absolute, and like her the absolute turns out to be money: 'it prevailed even as a *truth of truths* that the girl couldn't get away from her wealth' (Bk. 3, Ch. 1: my italics).

Matthiessen argues that Susie's 'literary' view of Milly is saved from being 'silly' because it is endorsed by Densher.[14] The logic of this is not apparent: surely we have to judge Susan's vision as it is given us, and our verdict will necessarily influence our final judgement on Densher. However, by the time Densher does endorse it, it has become transformed by the events of the novel. Like Kate, Susie offers Milly a metaphoric supply which she can assimilate into her own ultimate lifestyle. But also like Kate, the initial impact constitutes a clear threat to Milly: it is only not silly because it is so dangerous, and it is dangerous because, like Kate's imagery it is exploitative. Thus at the beginning Susan, even through her own exaggerated self-humiliation, reduces Milly: if she makes of Milly a great new steamer to whom she is as a little boat in the slipstream, she can become a tug pulling the new American miracle into London as a 'trophy'. The trophy is a way of overcoming the unmediated relationship between herself and Maud, which is one in which she is otherwise 'patronizingly pitied'. To be pitied is the novel's major criterion of failure. In taking her to London, Mrs Stringham makes Milly a function of her own relationships. And, for all her strident sympathy, this never really changes. She participates in the deceit of Milly at the end of the novel, and if it is through kindness, it only makes it worse. The significance of her middle name, Shepherd, has often been pointed out, but what is more significant is her real surname and Stringham goes all too well with Manningham. But it is not just a question of 'plot' – the whole hyperbolic sycophancy of the texture of Susan's prose sets Milly up as a set of 'strong marks'. In the first three books, the terms of war are set out: if you don't wish to be marked, first mark the markers.

It would be quite wrong, however, to see Susan's vision as simply a parallel threat to that of Kate's. If both reduce Milly to the product of her wealth and try to exploit her on that basis, Susan Stringham's way of doing it offers much more opportunity to Milly for counter exploitation. In the first place, whereas Kate's tribute to the power of money is entirely secular (it's the last thing she regards as a mystery), Susan's is mediated by a mystifying vocabulary which gives money a symbolic status. The fact of Milly's wealth is an absolute, the truth of truths, and her existence is the real thing, the romantic life itself. The juxtaposition of the two apparently contradictory adjectives is meaningful because the 'romance of wealth' is one of the clichés used about the New York millionaires who became such talking points in the last years of the century. 'There is a rich mine of romance, as well as solid reality,' wrote Walter Barrett, 'in the history of the merchants of the old time.'[15] And what is chiefly romantic about it is that it can supply for the United States an equivalent for the life of royalty: 'there is no nobility in this country. There is a class of princes, and they are the highest in the city ... princes of commerce.' James is never very clear about the kind of wealth Milly has, but though it is more likely to be akin to the real estate fortune of the Astors than the wealth of the Vanderbilts or Rockefellers, even this was hardly very deep-rooted. Nevertheless, as Gustavus Myers, a hostile historian, wrote, the tributes paid them were monarchical: 'the people were assiduously taught in many open and subtle ways to look up to the inviolability of property, just as in the old days they had been taught to look humbly up to the majesty of the king'.[16] Such regality is modified only by the tendency of such wealth to belong to families who are doomed to live, and decline, fast: 'For this country', Barrett writes, 'the continued existence of one house for fifty-four years is a long time.'[17] When Susan thinks of Milly's story as 'a New York history' she is imposing an order which is both more metaphoric and more local.

Her most potent metaphor is, of course, from an English text, but in its context this is equally apt. When she thinks of Milly as the 'potential heiress of all the ages', she is thinking also of Tennyson:

Mated with squalid savage – what to me were sun or clime?
I, the heir of all the ages in the foremost ranks of time.

What is important here is the way in which she adopts (and adapts) the image. Later, James writes of Susan's mother, using another famous phrase from the same poem: 'She had given her daughters the five years in Switzerland and Germany that were to leave them ever afterwards a standard of comparison for all cycles of Cathay' (Bk. 3, Ch. 1). At least Tennyson thought the ratio fifty years to one cycle. It points out the sharpness of James's irony in his presentation of Susan's consciousness: she has a mind that grabs at anything around to stick it into the discursive flow (it's an essayist's style, a debased echo of Emerson's omnivorous vigour), to inflate the moment and dissolve it into a generality identifiable only by its capacity to provoke ecstasy. It must make us wonder about the potential heiress of all the ages. On one level, it is a highly romanticized use of Tennyson's rather crudely racist and undiscriminating embrace of Western progress (the lack of discrimination is indicated by the fact he retained the image of 'ringing grooves of change' even when he learned that it was not accurate). Susan sublimates Milly's potential, but it is an acquisitive potential nonetheless: 'She was looking down on the kingdoms of the earth ... Was she choosing among them or did she want them all?' We wonder whether 'taking full in the face the whole assault of life' is anything more than the commitment Tennyson's hero makes to the mighty wind of social progress. If it is, it is because Susan does more than romanticize Tennyson – she updates it, and Americanizes it. For Tennyson's hero is talking about involvement with the foremost ranks of time, but Susan sees Milly as the potential possessor of the kingdoms of the earth. The morality of self-help is replaced by the power of the corporation; the decision to move on is here a decision to continue the tour. Milly is an heiress of all the ages because she is the heiress of New York millions. From an assertion, however crude, of cultural values, we have moved to an assertion of a single value – money. But, on the other hand, money has in the process been raised above time by a symbolizing imagination. The romantic life itself is possible because money is meaningful. And in making this claim, and making it available to Milly, Susan is being deeply responsive to an American tradition.

4 *What it was to be really rich*

James could hardly have ignored Howells's review of Veblen, 'An Opportunity for American Fiction'. Passages of it are so close to the novel that we cannot doubt that James is partly, in his own way, making a contribution to one of the major debates of the American nineties – the debate about 'plutocracy'. Howells claims that 'the flower of the American leisure class does not fruit in its native air, and perhaps cannot yet perpetuate itself on our soil.'[18] Milly is, of course, the final flower of her race and her career is close in many ways to the typical career for wealthy Americans defined in the article:

> They are only representations on a wider stage of the perpetual and universal drama of our daily life. The man who makes money in a small town goes to the nearest large town to spend it – that is, to waste it; waste in some form or other being the corollary of wealth; and he seeks to marry his children there into rich and old families. He does this from the instinct of self preservation which is as strong in classes as individuals; if he has made his money in a large town, he goes to some such inland metropolis as Chicago to waste his wealth and to marry his children above him. The Chicago, and San Francisco, and St Louis, and Cleveland millionaires come to New York with the same ambitions and purposes.
>
> But these are all intermediate stages in the evolution of the American magnate. At every step he discovers that he is less and less in his own country, that he is living in a provisional exile, and that his true home is in monarchical conditions, where his future establishes itself often without his willing it, and sometimes against his willing it. The American life is the life of labour, and he is now of the life of leisure, or if he is not, his wife is, his daughters and his sons are. The logic of their existence, which they cannot struggle against, and on which all the fatuous invective of pseudo public spirit lavishes itself effectlessly, is inter-marriage with the European aristocracies, and residence abroad. Short of this there is no rest, and can be none for the American leisure class. This may not be its ideal, but it is its destiny.
>
> It is by far the most dramatic social fact of our time, and if some man of creative imagination were to seize upon it he would find in it the material of that great American novel which after so much travail has not yet seen the light. It is, above all our other facts synthetic; it sums up and includes in itself the whole American story: the relentless will, the tireless force, the vague ideal, the inexorable destiny, the often bewildered acquiescence.

Were it not for the fact that he had touched on the theme so often before, James might almost seem to have taken up the challenge of that last paragraph in this novel. Certainly the logic of Milly's existence, at least for Susan and at first for Kate, is European marriage and residence abroad, and what drives the novel forward is her restlessness, her capacity to use up kingdoms of earth. Certainly the true home of a princess is in monarchical conditions, and tireless force, vague ideal and inexorable destiny sum up our first impressions of her. But if the novel shares some of Howells's sociological insights, its direction is completely opposite, of course. Howells's phrase 'bewildered acquiescence' is very close to Susan Stringham's phrase 'consenting bewilderment' except that Susan is using it about the effect Milly has on her associates. It implies a potentially positive role in opposition to Howells's wryly sympathetic portrayal of futile *naïveté*. *The Wings of the Dove* might be said to be a novel about conspicuous waste – except that it isn't certain that the waste is wasted (though the novel ends with Densher clinging to his 'wasted passion'). The novel's major paradox is that consenting bewilderment, the reversal of Howells's final note of failure, is achieved by taking the Howellsian process a step further – Chicago, New York, Europe and beyond that death. The inexorable destiny of American wealth is its transcendent immortality, which it achieves by its secret working on the plastic human soul. It is a paradox made possible by turning a dramatic social fact into a style. Even before they confront the dangerously considerate world of London, Susan implicitly recognizes that Milly only exacts consenting bewilderment as perceived object exposed to knowledge: 'She worked – and seemingly quite without design – upon the *sympathy*, the *curiosity*, the *fancy* of her associates ...' (Bk. 3, Ch. 1: my italics). By the end of the novel, the consenting bewilderment Milly exacts is a highly wrought aesthetic and moral system. What she does essentially is to make Susan's romance of wealth (which she doesn't at first share, thinking of herself as belonging only to 'the fashion'), and the traditional view of money which it assumes, come 'true'.

Like those in the psalm, the wings of this dove are covered in silver and gold. Rahv says that James is too immersed in personal relations to have any historical sense; but a full enough awareness, of the role of Milly's money reveals, in this novel at least, a remarkable sense of the historical implications of the personal relationships, and the ways in which they are expressed. We cannot hope to understand the way in which Milly achieves a lifestyle which will leave her free of the objectifying process of pity, unless we first recognize fully the potentialities and obstacles involved in being the heiress of all the progressive Western ages.

One of the obvious contexts is Emerson's essay 'Wealth' in *The Conduct of Life*. Its most important point is that wealth cannot be severed from the human energies and skills which possession of it signifies: 'money is representative'.[19] It is so because making money is a part of the individual's self-manifestation:

Man was born to be rich, or, inevitably grows rich by the use of his faculties; by the union of thought with nature. Property is an intellectual production.

But not only is it a valid representation of self, it is also a valid analogy for personal relations. With what James called that 'ripe unconsciousness of evil', he goes on to say:

> He is the rich man who can avail himself of all men's faculties. He is the richest man who knows how to draw a benefit from the labours of the greatest number of men, of men in distant countries, and in past times.

The Wings of the Dove seems to me to operate within these definitions and their assumptions. The wings vindicate the dove, and elevate her from the object of pity to the successful demander of consenting bewilderment. In a queer way she even gets everyone, Aunt Maud and Kate included, to work for her, to teach her and to act on her behalf for the gaining of Densher's soul. James also said of Emerson that 'he had a particular faculty ... for speaking to the soul in a voice of direction and authority ... it seems to go back to the roots of our feelings, to where conduct and manhood begin',[20] and this is the way in which Milly, and Milly's transcendent power, finally speak to Densher. This is not to say that the novel offers a simple affirmation of Emerson's bland *naïveté*. But neither, in the end, does it ironize or reject. It reassesses, in a concrete situation (one that reflects in some ways Emerson's other, and very different, essay on wealth in *English Traits*), Emerson's claims for the moral significance of money, and reformulates them in an historical situation, so that nothing is affirmed without attendant ambivalence. In *Notes of a Son and Brother*, James quotes his father's brilliantly accurate comment on Emerson, 'Oh you man without a handle', adding that the philosopher's answer always 'seemed to anticipate everything but the unaccommodating individual case'.[21] *The Wings of the Dove* offers an *accommodating* individual case, changing the details in the process and creating something more solid, if not more attractive, than that wide-eyed verbosity.

One of the reasons that he is able to do this is because the novel tacitly takes account of a changed social situation. Emerson was not of James's generation and his bewildering vagueness was felt not by him but by 'the passionately living of the earlier time'. The later time sees two developments, both of which give the novel opportunity to put a handle to Emerson. One is that in the world of cases there is a vastly increased possibility of wealth, and wealth becomes linked with a wide range of human activities – Morgan in Europe buying up paintings, the Astors coming to Cliveden. American wealth, as 'Covering End' programmatically demonstrates, is great enough to be able to underwrite European history. Secondly, the Emersonian view of wealth is under direct and extensive attack in the decade preceding the novel, so that any realization has a definite polemical base.

Throughout the eighties and nineties, much social writing concentrated on the influence, mainly evil, of 'plutocracy'. Henry Demarest
Lloyd radically challenged the Emersonian structure of thought by
insisting that wealth must be considered as an active and not representative phenomenon: 'Liberty produces wealth, and wealth destroys
liberty.'[22] And in 1899 the attack reached its climax in Veblen's great book,
The Theory of the Leisure Class. He relates the pursuit of wealth not to
any moral self-fulfilment but to the most primitive of urges, invidious
comparison which sees leisure as an index of superior prowess. Since, in a
sophisticated society, it is necessary to push the acquisition of wealth to
ever greater heights, the comparison tends to base itself on conspicuous
waste and vicarious leisure, so that the primitive urge from which the
pursuit of wealth derives is seen to pervade every manifestation of a
society's culture. Within the shadow of such concepts everything, from
professional football to institutions for the study of liberal arts, becomes a
function of invidious comparison. Even the intellectual whose role is
partly to criticize the accretions of wealth is a sign of conspicuous waste.
What is explicit in Veblen had long been implicit in Howells.

James praised *A Hazard of New Fortunes* in terms at once so excessive
and so carefully angled that we must regard his attitude to it as highly
ambiguous. 'As a triumph of *communication*,' he writes in a letter to
Howells, 'I hold the *Hazard* so rare and strong.'[23] The italicization of
'communication' sums up the care with which James makes his praise an
exercise in critical *disponibilité*: 'the novelist is a particular *window* ...' It is
hardly the sort of praise the novel is looking for – what is most characteristic of Howells's window is its claim to be plain glass looking on the
world from an objective viewpoint, and it is clearly to evade the issue not
to take up the sharp challenge the novel offers to the reader's political and
social intelligence:

> 'Such people as the Dryfoos are the raw material of good society. It isn't
> made up of refined or meritorious people ... All the fashionable people
> there tonight were like the Dryfoos a generation or two ago. I dare say
> the material works up faster now, and in a season or two you won't
> know the Dryfoos from the other plutocrats.'[24]

This may be one of the characters talking, but it is a statement about
actuality, not about the world of the novel: there is no qualitative difference, this is saying, between the Rockefellers and the Vanderbilts, and the
more established 'fashion' – the Astors and perhaps the Jameses. 'Plutocrat'
is the keyword: it suggests that money itself does the ruling. It isn't
representative but active, and what it purchases in the way of culture and
refinements of civilization is a very minor function of its hegemony. The
Dryfoos, after all, without the refinements, run the novel's intellectual and

cultural world. James is clearly as far from the social viewpoint of Howells as it is possible to be. Whatever the ambiguities of money, its potentialities are essentially good. The only really squalid and irredeemable people in *The Wings of the Dove* are Lionel and Marian – who are relatively poor.

But *A Hazard of New Fortunes* is especially important because, like James's novel, its primary concern is not with wealth in itself but with the role of the intellectual in relation to wealth. Howells's story is above all that of March's problematic relationship with his commercial masters, and its complexity foreshadows in a general way the complex relationship Densher has with the wealth he confronts a relationship which veers between satiric criticism and consenting bewilderment. The best moments of *Hazard* present this issue squarely and unsentimentally:

'I think,' said Mrs March, 'that city girls, brought up as she must have been, are often the most innocent of all. They never imagine the wickedness of the world, and if they marry happily they go through life as innocent as children. Everything combines to keep them so; the very hollowness of society shields them. They are the loveliest of the human race. But perhaps the rest have to pay too much for them.'

'For such an exquisite creature as Miss Vance,' said March, 'we couldn't pay too much.'

A wild, laughing cry suddenly broke upon the air at the street crossing in front of them. A girl's voice called out 'Run, run Jan! The copper is after you.' A woman's figure rushed stumbling across the way and into the shadow of the houses, pursued by a burly policeman.

'Ah, but if that's part of the price ...'[25]

Milly too is a wealthy city girl brought up free of the wickedness of the world, and March's attitude is basically that of James himself, for whom the flower of a civilization is its just measure. But March's consenting bewilderment is undermined by the cry of guilt on which such innocence is raised, and by the superior intelligence of his wife. The intellectual who tries to make some compact with the plutocracy is made to seem expediently sentimental. In *The Wings of the Dove*, James sets out to realize an unsentimental acceptance of the price of innocence by regranting money its mystery and its representativeness, by creating for the intellectual a relation to it which is not that of contract but of consent, as to a power greater than any this world by itself can show. In Regent's Park, Milly feels herself at one with the poor because she too has her rent to pay: it is as though Miss Vance and the laughing girl have been reunited in a single vision. Milly is the final flower of New York millions, but she has her own price to pay for it – flowers are the end point of a plant's growth; they are there to die. By making herself take on the suffering of guilt while remaining innocent, Milly replaces Howells's Manichean social vision with atonement. The result is a novel much more conservative, but also more profound, for James's realization is of the interpenetration of economic and metaphysical values. In spite of its occasional dry light, Howell's novel is finally dissolved in a cloud of milk and water socialism; whereas, for all its informing admiration for money and disease, *The Wings of the Dove* remains a convincing comedy about the ultimate mystification of the intellectual.

5 *A working view of the general case*

What I have been trying to suggest is that the novel is concerned with the connexions between ways of seeing and modes of relationship, in the context of the social role of money in general and large accretions of money in particular; and that in its concern it embodies highly representative visions and attitudes which are relevant to the historical situation out of which the novel grows. None of this, of course, resolves the problem of Milly's sentimentality, though it should help us to mark out that sentimentality which is being realized as part of the novel's texture.

The clearest statement is Bewley's: 'The guilt of the past,' he writes, 'so largely European, is revealed in all its musty squalor by the contrasting purity of a young girl who being American, has no part in that heritage of crime and misery that belongs in the old world.'[26] It is true, I think, that Bewley sees *The Wings of the Dove* too narrowly in terms of *The Marble Faun*, and in this statement fails to take full account of the connexion made in James's novel between being American and being rich. Nor does it take account of what ironies are there, such as the fact that the young girl's heritage is one which matches the squalor of Europe, and that if Milly remains innocent, she only manages it by being very clever. But some kinds of irony can be sentimental too, and elaborating the novel's many paradoxes doesn't answer Bewley's basic point. I don't think it will do, in the end, for example, to say that Milly adopts the dove image as a disguise under which her 'fullblown consciousness' is concealed for the remainder of the action: this assumes, in a very simplified manner, that 'you' can be different from the role you play, and although there are Jamesian protagonists who make that assumption (above all Isabel Archer), it is placed as an illusion.[27] And it only makes matters worse to suggest that James is trying to get away with making the dove image operate ironically on a social level and symbolically on an 'intuitional' one. Nor will it do to say that Milly is not allowed to strike through the pasteboard mask she adopts – since in that case we have no way of knowing that it is a mask.[28] The only hope for the novel's coherence is to resist injecting irony into the process of transformation just because it may be objectionable to humane sensibilities. Milly copes with the fact of her own disease and the destructive perception of it by the Europeans by cultivating an image supplied for her by those perceptions. And the image becomes a reality by operating on the consciousness of Densher and others: Milly, in other words, apotheosizes herself, conquering death by the impression she makes. The problem seems to me not that it is objectionable but simply that apotheoses don't happen: Bewley's point is important because it resists being palmed off with a simplifying fable. My argument is that we are given more – the whole process and conditions by which Milly can achieve her success.

Kate uses the dove image, as we have seen, as a creatural reduction. If she is thinking of any of its allusive referents, it must be those in Leviticus, where the dove is a sacrificial object used as a substitute for a lamb (Kate think of herself as a trembling kid). Milly receives the image as something that identifies what is wrong with her – the odd way people see her and judge her. It is only when she has felt that her exchange with Mrs Lowder is like dove cooing to dove that she sees the possibilities of success in the image. Mrs Lowder, of course, has money, and doves have wings. In Psalm 68, the dove's wings are used as a metaphor of triumph over humiliation: 'Though ye have lien among the pots, yet shall ye be as the wings of a dove covered with silver, and her feathers with yellow gold'; and in Psalm 55 they become the agents of flight from malicious tongues and are linked, as Sandeen has noted, with faith in God's revenging power.[29] Milly has turned the objectifying image she has been offered into an image of triumph and revenge, into a basis for subjective vision and detachment. It works at this point because of the multiple possibilities of the metaphor. But making a cliché viable in the face of complexity is not what makes a great novel; what happens to the image merely reflects the changing structure of relationships. What is asserted theatrically in the penultimate chapter of Book 5 is worked out in the novel's actuality in the chapter which follows it.

Throughout the book, Milly is coming to terms with exposure. The agent of exposure is pity: 'and when pity held up its tell-tale face like a head on a pike, in a French revolution, bobbing before a window, what was the inference but that the patient was bad?' (Bk. 5, Ch. 3). Just as specifically Christian virtues, such as Condrip's saintliness or Marian's turning the other cheek or even the homeliness of Chirk Street (which clearly has to do with humility) are part of the abyss that Kate has to escape from, so for Milly even the disinterested consideration of Sir Luke becomes a threat. It is true that she is sick, but she is also James's choice to register the impact of moral virtue. The effect of making Milly ill is to dramatize more acutely the potentiality of her wealth: she will overcome death itself. She can do this, however, only because she can embrace life in a very special way. After her visit to Sir Luke, she wanders through London confronted with a simple, existential either/or. On the face of it, it is a moral centre from which an embrace of being will radiate; but standing in the middle of Regent's Park, Milly seems to be in a remarkably empty world compared with Strether's. The reason, I think, is because Milly's concern is less with life than with the impression she can make on life – with 'success':

> Wonderments in truth, Milly felt, even now attended her steps: it was quite as if she saw in people's eyes the reflection of her appearance and pace. She found herself moving at times in regions visibly not haunted by odd-looking girls from New York, duskily draped, sable-plumed, all but incongruously shod and gazing about them with extravagance; she might, from the curiosity she clearly excited in by-ways, in side-streets peopled with grimy children and costermongers' carts, which she hoped were slums, literally have had her musket on her shoulder, have announced herself as freshly on the war-path. But for the fear of *overdoing the character* she would here and there have begun conversation ... (Bk. 5, Ch. 4: my italics)

The casual subjectivity of 'which she hoped were slums' both draws attention to the nature of the affirmative experience, which has little to do with actuality, and places it within the limits of Milly's wealthy experience. But the ironies are not only James's. Milly is quite conscious of acting out a character: the wonderments are not hers but those of the people who see her. 'Regions visibly not haunted by odd-looking girls from New York' is about as anti-impressionistic as it is possible to be. Lebowitz speaks of the struggle in this novel of the object to become subject, but we see in a passage such as this how inadequate such a description is. Milly's struggle is to become the subject of those to whom she is object, and to control what they see. Her self-irony is a part of this control. It has none of Strether's bemused self-questioning. 'Literally have had her musket on her shoulder' comically exaggerates, since she is only going for a walk, but with an intended 'charm' which we are supposed to admire – 'plucky little girl, able to admit her oddity and still go on walking'. Furthermore, the metaphor is clearly linked with the telltale pike. Milly is walking out to defend her regality: her musket harnessed to a counter-revolutionary struggle against the levelling-down process effected by the great leveller, death. If she feels herself to be like a poor girl with her rent to pay, she will obtain magnificent lodgings in return and, in the meantime, no local colour is going to outshine her sable plumes. Sir Luke speaks of Milly as having a great rare chance, and this seems odd since he is only offering her the common chance. But it is another tribute to her wealth. Dying will not matter. Already she is able to invade and assimilate the consciousness of others, recognizing Susan Stringham's 'positive need' to treat her as a princess, seeing that the way Kate looks sometimes 'was the peculiar property of someone else's vision'. Milly is able to create a lifestyle which is also a mode of vision, in which object and subject coalesce, and distinctions between life and death cease to matter.

The final chapter of Book 5 carries these potentialities of consciousness into the realms of actual relationships:

> She should have been a lady-copyist – it met so the case. The case was the case of escape, of living under water, of being at once impersonal and firm. There it was before one – one had only to stick and stick. (Bk. 5, Ch. 7)

Milly is escaping from two encounters – one with Susie and another with Sir Luke – by conflating them and withdrawing. She is allowing them to build their own image of her while she gets lost in the National Gallery. But she is not running away from difficulties – only from the sense of the unknown which she confronts when she becomes aware of 'the margin always allowed her' by others. She is opting for the known by becoming the oddity others are trying not to reveal they think of her. Rather than have an unknown margin, she fills it up according to Susie's image of her – 'and the proposal now made her – what was it in short but Byzantine'. Sir Luke, too, is deployed on the basis of her knowledge of what he will want – 'she knew him to desire just now ...' Anticipating others' knowledge, she can attain a kind of impersonality even in her very exposure. She can do it too because she can rely on the exposure being limited by human reticence and embarrassment: 'The worst would be that he was in love and that he needed a confidante to work it.' Nobody makes such sick jokes as Milly does about herself: it grants her a kind of firmness by overreaching the softness of others' pity. Ultimately, of course, it will not involve living under water (which I take to be an image of being submerged in anonymity) but quite the contrary, living high in the air; and only vicariously will she stick and stick – in personal terms she will take flight. But the lady copyists supply an initial image of retreat into adopted style.

The lady copyists serve two other functions. They link Milly with Densher – if she can't talk to them she can fall in love with one of their sons. But locally they serve as a distraction from the Titians and the Turners, and in this they are very important. Many critics speak of Milly's tendency to become a work of art; but the trouble is that people just don't become works of art, and James is not writing a fairy tale (or not one that can come true). Milly begins her triumph in the National Gallery, and this is certainly a world of art which she chooses as a refuge from the vulnerability of personal relationships, with the positive motive of 'overtaking' some of the great moments of history 'among the Titians and the Turners'. The utterly un-discriminating alliteration should put us on our guard.[30] Milly is not capable of aesthetic rapture, and is not to be overwhelmed –

as Strether is – by the resolution of reality into the consciousness which reproduces it. She finds herself too weak for the Titians and the Turners, but this is not merely because of her fatigue. The fatigue itself is the product of the motive. 'Pictures and things' are one of her 'general heads' connected with 'the continental tour'. She is less concerned with appreciation than getting her 'schools' right. For the purposes of this novel, the National Gallery is only secondarily the world of art: primarily it is the centre of tourism. Tourism and aesthetic appreciation are close in many ways, but you can be a tourist in a way you can't be a work of art. Milly's apotheosis is achieved not by becoming a picture, but by becoming a consummate tourist.

Tourism is, of course, one of the major themes of the chapter. Milly spends her time counting Baedekers until the American mother and daughter discuss Densher. Later, to help Densher over his embarrassment, Milly offers her 'unused margin as an American girl', and Densher is made to talk about his own tour of the States. The chapter ends with Milly metaphorically clinging to the Rockies to avoid the personal exposure of her forthcoming interview with Susan. The general theme mediates the dramatic changes of relationship which take place, and so socializes any subsequent triumph Milly has. Moreover it supplies an epistemological system in itself which destroys the dualistic subject/object relationship which makes Milly so vulnerable.

In the recognition paragraph, Milly studying the mother and her daughters becomes a subject of their subjectivity. They are looking at Densher, she watches them looking, and later becomes aware that Kate has been watching her watch them. But what is important is the way in which such knowledge is expressed. The American's knowledge of Densher is generic, 'in the English style', so much so that Milly thinks they are talking of a picture until she realizes that the description doesn't correspond with her knowledge of the styles of the pictures in front of her. Her knowledge of them, in turn, is in the same mode, for she sees at this point with less of her usual extravagant gaze and more of Kate's lucidity: 'She *knew* the three, generically, as easily as a schoolboy with a crib in his lap would know the answer in class.' The crib is, of course, herself – she later resents the fact that they don't know her. The tourists are seen as tourists by a tourist who herself, as she is recognized (that is, seen by Kate and Densher to be watching him), makes herself so much the tourist (the American girl) that she becomes, knowingly, the object of his tourism: 'She became as spontaneous as possible and as American as it might conveniently appeal to Mr Densher, *after his travels*, to find her' (Bk. 5, Ch. 7: my italics). Throughout Book 5, Milly has been escaping from her own objectification by understanding, knowing the subjectivity of others – knowing, that is, about the way they know her. The National Gallery creates the terms of reference by which she can make this not a painful and sporadic vision, but a successful system to cope with the undeniable objective facts of her existence – her wealth and her illness. The system is a style, and style closes itself against the contingent

Already, by the end of the chapter, Milly is working out a system of transcendence in two ways. In the first place, she reduces the relationship between Kate and Densher in her own mind to a romance of unrequited love: she stylizes it, even without being convinced by her own explanation. More importantly, she comes to terms with her own image by watching others watch it and learning to control it:

Whatever he did or he didn't, Milly knew she should still like him – there was no alternative to that; but her heart could none the less sink a little on feeling how much his view of her was destined to have in common with – as she now sighed over it – *the* view. She could have dreamed of his not having *the* view, of his having something or other, if need be quite viewless, of his own; but he might have what he could with least trouble, and *the* view wouldn't be after all a positive bar to her seeing him. The defect of it in general – if she might so ungraciously criticize – was that, by its sweet universality, it made relations rather prosaically a matter of course. It anticipated and superseded the – like-wise sweet – operation of real affinities. It was this that was doubtless marked in her power to keep him now – this and her glassy lustre of attention to his pleasantness about the scenery in the Rockies. She was in truth a little measuring her success in detaining him by Kate's success in 'standing' Susan. It wouldn't be, if she could help it, Mr Densher who should first break down. (Bk. 5, Ch. 7)

Everybody in this scene is playing the 'lively line', and Densher's way of playing it is to talk about his trip and neglect to talk about Milly. He is being 'kind' and this, as we have already seen, is the most destructive relationship. The crux is, of course, that Milly accepts it and remains detached at the same time, so that by the end of the passage she is positively using the Rockies, and the careful inattention to her they imply, to compete with Kate's self-control. From this point on, the novel will not be about the betrayal of Milly, but about competing lies. 'Glassy lustre of attention' emphasizes how much her capture of Densher will be a matter of role-playing. By allowing him his style of decent pity, she can offer him her pity, pretending to herself (and getting him to pretend to her) that he needs it. And a mutual pity will overreach the selfish gladness of young immunities.

What is important is that these paradoxes are growing out of specific contexts in a social comedy. We haven't suddenly entered some mysterious aesthetic realm. The possibilities for a stylized transformation of the relationships in the novel are thrown up by Milly's manipulation of the awkward social situation: the accidental personal encounter creates an opportunity for being impersonal and firm. Milly has her rent fixed: she cannot rescue Densher from the general view but she can, by accepting the general view, learn to keep him with her; and this will enable her to compete with Kate's manipulations, and, as the second half of the paragraph explicitly states, hold herself at a convenient distance from the inevitable confrontation with the facts that make the general view unavoidable. The effects on the language of this distancing are clear in the passage quoted: 'The defect of it in general – if she might so ungraciously criticize – was that, by its sweet universality, it made relations rather prosaically a matter of course. It anticipated and superseded the – likewise sweet – operation of real affinities.' The irony is hers, and again is self-admiring (how nice I'm being), and what it does is to flatten the comparison of the actual and the possible relationship by making sure that either way it will be sweet. Through a mannered verbalization, Milly has found a way to make his love, her disease and the real substance of their relationship irrelevant: 'I'll make it charming for you' she later tells Susan, and she does, beguiling all the forms of her relationships of any reality. The language in the chapters immediately before Venice has a strange rococo excess of flourish. 'Beautiful and good', 'the most charming person', 'a lovely acquaintance', 'a sight for the gods' – such phrases are uttered by Milly with a sickening glibness which is clearly her strongest shield against pity. Susie is 'wonder-struck', and this becomes the word to describe the effectiveness of Milly's strategy for the rest of the novel. It is a strategy which defies mere truth – she says, for example, that Kate has been 'gentle and nice' (Bk. 7, Ch. 1). Awareness and recognition become the major forfeits in an involved game of let's pretend: 'It put them again face to face, but it had wound Mrs Stringham up … She had risen by Milly's aid to a certain command of what was before them' (Bk. 7, Ch. 1). The charm also involves an accommodation of everybody else's vision. 'What was before them' turns out to be nothing more than a new idea which emerges from the gloom like a Maeterlinckian star. Sir Luke, too, is assisted in his need to offer kindness to his patient, and this isn't seen as just an aspect of Milly's love, but as a deft game: she has to be careful not to 'embarrass his exercise of a kindness that, no doubt, rather constituted for him a high method' (Bk. 7, Ch. 1). And the effect of this accommodation is a reversal process: 'the pledge of protection and support was all the younger woman's own' (Bk. 7, Ch. 1); 'what *was* he in fact but patient, what was she but physician' (Bk. 7, Ch. 1). Sweetness, accommodation, reversal – all add up to a sustained *trompe-l'œil*.

The proper perspective in which to see this transformation is offered by the apparently irrelevant scene between Susie and Mrs Lowder inserted in the middle of these pre-flight chapters. Aunt Maud is a butt for much of the satire in the novel; but this is only one of its finer ironies, for in the end she, more than anyone, gets what she wants – she parts Kate and Densher, and in some ways gets Densher for herself ('I like him for myself'). Her real dramatic value is to offer a brutal but comic commentary on the sentimental ambience being generated at this point in the novel: 'I might be crying now,' she says, 'if I weren't writing letters' (Bk. 7, Ch. 1). The remark, however revealing of her own philistinism, puts in its place Susie's ridiculous declaration 'I'm to be with her regularly sublime'. She sits like an earringed matron, knees apart at a market stall, while Susie tosses the 'truths' of the situation into her lap. It is an image which includes Susie as well, and it suggests the primitive nature of all the relations which are being struck up. All the sublimity, the benevolence, the consenting bewilderment would be nothing if it weren't that Mrs Lowder sees her own interest in the plan to get Densher for Milly – in this way she might 'handle' Kate. Milly has been making a takeover bid for the truths of those who threaten her with a personal relationship, but the bid only succeeds because the American millionairess has a common interest with Britannia in the Market-place. Suitably, then, it is Aunt Maud who sums up the whole situation at this point in the novel:

> 'I lie well, thank God,' Mrs Lowder almost snorted, 'when, as sometimes will happen, there's nothing else so good. One must always do the best. But without lies then,' she went on, 'perhaps we can work it out.' (Bk. 7, Ch. 1)

'Work it out' is a key phrase in this section of the novel (cf. 'the account of their situation that most showed it as workable', 'what would now make working for Milly such a general upward tug', 'though tactfully working', 'a working view of the general case', 'since she was to be worked for'), and it enables us to distinguish between the sentimental surface and its toughminded base. Susie is sentimental, to be sure, and her symbolizing and sublimating style is being worked for all it is worth to create what Sir Luke later defines as a beautiful show. But Mrs Lowder accepts here that lies won't do, and we have already discovered this to be the case with Milly: lies imply truths. What she has to create is something which can assimilate both lies and truths, which has its own inner logic and is immune to the law of natural selection which Kate is seeking to operate. The clue is offered by the National Gallery – recognition and awareness can be controlled by the all-embracing, subject/object conflation of the tourist. Tourism has to become a style, and its natural style is spatial totality and impenetrable representativeness. Milly has to become not merely a symbolist like Susie, but a symbol; and a symbol that, unlike Susie's romances, cannot be challenged by the lucidity of realism.

6 *How to be a symbol without really dying*

'Venice has been painted and described many thousands of times, and of all the cities of the world is the easiest to visit without going there.'[31] For the tourist, the image takes precedence over its actual source. In suddenly switching to Venice, Milly is able to 'become' the images the others have created for her, without being exposed thereby to their control. She can do this because Venice is the symbolic city where even the misery is part of the spectacle. Susan's metaphoric excesses can be taken over and given their own reality. But this is possible only because in moving to Venice herself, Milly brings everybody else onto its stage to act out their lifestyles around her, and because although she is in Venice, she has little to do with it. The palazzo is central and detached. She is not exposed to everybody else because they too become their images, and on the symbolic stage Milly is above them, watching. It is important to stress that James isn't suddenly writing a symbolic novel: we have seen that Milly's flight is carefully prepared within the terms of social comedy set up in the first six books. It is simply that she moves to a situation in which the symbolic life can triumph over the 'real' Darwinian world by affirming 'the religious spirit' – that level of human awareness that Balzac failed to do justice to, and that James never pretended was dissociated from the liberating effect of great wealth.

What most emphasizes the way in which symbolism is chosen as a mode to meet the modes Milly has found hostile is the conventionality of her situation and the way in which she manipulates it. There are many possible references in the last part of the book, but two are actually named by James – not because they are exclusively right, but as a reminder that a highly literary style is being wrought to 'compete with life'. 'Our consciousness,' Maeterlinck wrote, 'is our home, our refuge from the caprice of fate, our centre of happiness and strength';[32] and in her fortress above the dramatic world of the city, Milly finds that refuge in becoming in many ways like one of what Maeterlinck defined as 'the predestined'. The predestined are those who seem from the first marked out for an early death, and who appear at once completely innocent and strangely knowing: 'Why do they come to us like the bee to the hive, like the dove to the cote ...?'[33] The postulated answer is that they leave us 'the sadder and the more gentle' because they bring to mind something deeper and more obscure than human understanding normally encompasses:

It is as though they were on life's further shore, and the feeling rushes in upon us that now, at last, the hour has come for affirming that which is graver, deeper, more human, more real than friendship, pity or love; for saying the thing that is piteously flapping its wings at the back of our throat, and craving for utterance – the thing that our ignorance crushes, that we have never said, that we shall never say, for so many lives are spent apart in silence.

Both the remoteness and the affinity are what Milly sets out to achieve and does dying so meaningfully in her palace. The whole purpose of *Wisdom and Destiny* is to affirm consciousness as a way of overcoming the illusion of fate. Milly will overcome her fast-approaching doom by living on in the consciousness of Densher: 'There were times when they seemed to be looking down upon us from a lofty tower; and for all that we were the stronger, we dared not molest them.' The plot has faint echoes of *Pelléas et Mélisande* and *Aglavaine et Selysette*, and Susan recognizes the dim, symbolic atmosphere of Milly's Venetian home as a Maeterlinckian scenario. Moreover, Maeterlinck was very appreciative of Emerson, and Arthur Symons had stressed the connexion. His deliberately mystifying moral framework bridges the distance between European ambiguity and American innocence. Of course, Maeterlinck's dramas were very expensive to put on.

The other invoked presence is Pater who is also, of course, concerned with the primacy of consciousness. The Palazzo Leporelli recalls in several ways the house of Cecilia (the mystical German writer again makes the connexions with the older forms of transcendentalism that Susie inherits):

'The house in which she lives,' says that mystical German writer quoted once before, 'is for the orderly soul which does not live on blindly before her, but is ever out of her passing experiences, building and adorning the parts of a many-roomed abode for herself, only an expansion of the body; as the body, according to the philosophy of Swedenborg, is but a process, an expansion of the soul. For such an orderly soul, as life proceeds, all sorts of delicate affinities establish themselves between herself and the doors and passage-ways, the lights and shadows, of her outward dwelling-place, until she may seem incorporate with it: until at last, in the entire expressiveness of what is outward, there is for her, to speak properly, between outward and inward no longer any distinction at all; and the light which creeps at a particular hour on a particular picture or space upon the wall, the scent of flowers in the air at a particular window, become to her, not so much apprehended objects, as themselves powers of apprehension, and door-ways to things beyond – the germ or rudiment of certain new faculties, by which she dimly yet surely apprehends a matter, lying beyond her actually attained capacities of spirit and sense.' [34]

Milly becomes, of course, an orderly soul in a house 'all toned with time' where light reflects and flickers and where she can move 'aloft in the divine, dustless air'. Like Pater's Sebastian Van Storck, who is also wealthy, clever, detached and consumptive, she retreats to a room high above the contentious world, and in her death rescues another from it as Sebastian rescues the child from the flood.

Holland has noted that there are two rhythms in the novel – one of engagement and one of withdrawal. I think that really they are part of the same rhythm, the systole and diastole of the heart-throb which has to be pitted or preserved against the terminating drive of Kate's plot. Engagement and withdrawal come together, for example, in Sir Luke's room: 'She had come forth to see the world, and this then was to be the world's light, the rich dusk of a London "back", these the world's walls, those the world's curtains and carpet' (Bk. 5, Ch. 3). Pater's Sebastian manifests the same potentiality for 'going forth' before he finally retreats:

> There have been dispositions in which that abstract theorem has only induced a renewed value for the finite interest around and within us. Centre of heat and light, truly nothing has seemed to lie beyond the touch of its perpetual summer ... Sebastian Van Storck, on the contrary, was determined perhaps by some inherited satiety or fatigue in his nature, to the opposite issue of the practical dilemma. For him that one abstract being was as the pallid sun, disclosing itself over the dead level of a glacial, a barren and absolutely lonely sea.[35]

But Sebastian has had the first possibility – his tutor fancies that his power of determination means that 'his ultimate destination may be the military life'. Milly too, as we have seen, thinks of herself as a soldier when she walks out of the surgery to conquer life. In the Palazzo Leporelli she is tacitly recognizing that the abstract is in opposition to the phenomenal, but not merely to die but also to make a more systematic conquest. Just as Sebastian's detachment makes him strangely attractive to his fellow beings, so Milly in her retreat pervades more fully the consciousness of those around her. Like Poe's tell-tale heart, she will throb on long after she has retreated from the body.

But if we recall the affirmations of Pater's portrait in what happens to Milly in the Palazzo, we should note too its ironies. Sebastian dies for another, but an unevaluated comment by a physician suggests that this is a possibly meaningless gesture: he would have died anyway 'of a disease then coming into the world; disease begotten by the fogs of that country – waters, he observed, not in their place, "above the firmament" – on people grown somewhat overdelicate in their nature by the effects of modern luxury'. It reminds us that Milly was going to die anyway: living high above the flood, she cannot avoid the fogs which keep her under water, cannot avoid the ultimate depersonalization of the impersonal firm. And she is especially prone to them because, like Sebastian, she is over-delicate. Making herself into a symbol so metaphysically abstract that the borders between life and death cease to have meaning, she is only making a virtue of necessity. At the same time, she goes one better than Sebastian. Far from escaping from her wealth, she makes it the preservative of her ever-throbbing heart. She might offer a lesson to Sebastian in how to become a symbol without *really* dying.

It depends on her moving into the city where she is not an object viewed by others, but where all are tourists viewing one another. Venice is an extremely complex literary image and I can only hope to indicate some of its features. The most important is that it is a city of defiant appearance. Thus Ruskin:

> Well might it seem that such a city had owed its existence rather to the rod of the enchanter, than the fear of the fugitive; that the waters which encircled her had been chosen for the mirror of her state, rather than the shelter of her nakedness; and that all which in nature was wild or merciless – Time and Decay, as well as the waves and the tempests had been won to adorn her instead of to destroy.[36]

He goes on, it is true, to dismiss this as impotent romance and to describe the geological realities, but this is only to affirm God's miraculous and non-human wisdom. In this respect, as in the novel, Venice is the antithesis of England – a world of beautiful appearances and light, rather than one of dark ambiguity:

> Between that grim cathedral of England and this, what an interval! There is a type of it in the very birds that haunt them; for instead of the restless crowd, hoarse voice and sable-winged, drifting on the bleak upper air, the St Mark's perches are full of doves, that nestle among the marble foliage, and mingle the soft iridescence of their living plumes, changing at every notion, with the tints, hardly less lovely that have stood unchanged for seven hundred years.

But again, the analogy with what goes on in the novel is more exact. For if Venice contrasts with England in that it has doves and not restless ravens, it doesn't mean that it is a contrasting paradise. On the contrary, the stones of Venice need saving, like its glory; for under the arches where the doves nestle, the hurly burly of daily life, with its cheapjack traders, its idle middle classes and its Austrian occupiers, ignores the city's splendour. The doves link it with the past, but below them throats hoarse with cursing recall the ravens of England, archetype of the modern world. Below the dove-like Milly, Kate and Densher, Lord Mark and Mrs Lowder act out their shabby realities.

Ruskin makes a brief explicit comparison with England, but it is Gibbon, another of Susan's set authors, who makes possible an extensive analogy:

The policy of Venice was marked by the avarice of a trading and the insolence of a maritime power, yet her ambition was prudent; nor did she often forget that if armed galleys were the effect and safeguard, merchant vessels were the cause and supply of her greatness. In her religion she avoided the schism of the Greeks, without yielding a servile obedience to the Roman pontiff, and a free intercourse with the infidels of every clime appears to have allayed betimes the fever of superstition. Her primitive government was a loose mixture of democracy and monarchy ... The twelfth century produced the first rudiments of the wise and jealous aristocracy which has reduced the doge to a pageant, and the people to a cypher.[37]

Avarice, insolence, prudence, compromise, mixed constitution concealing an effective oligarchy – these surely define the features of the London Milly meets. This passage comes from a chapter describing the ransack of Byzantium. Milly is, of course, a Byzantine princess.

Venice then offers an ideal, lighted version of the London scene. Milly's viewers are themselves caught in a symbolic drama in which, for example, the secret love of Kate and Densher becomes a highly melodramatic sexual encounter, arranged at first as they stand highlighted in the Square of St Mark. Even the weather comes to symbolize the changing drama. And if it is all consummated in a Veronese scenario, it is worth recalling that Symonds, who also stressed the independence of Venice, wrote: 'Veronese was precisely the painter suited to a nation of merchants, in whom the associations of the counting house and the exchange mingled with the responsibilities and the passions of Princes.'[38] A city of mercantile integrity, built on swamps, destroying Byzantium, in which the doves express its true spirit presiding above the petty trading and hoarse aspiration – Milly could find no better symbol for the way in which her silver and gold could suffuse uncontaminated the dark world which is staring her out of life. And if it should seem incredible that a girl should become a dove, Pater has Socrates tell the story of the Halcyon and remind his pupils of a storm and calm and ask: 'Which do you think the greater and more difficult thing to do: to exchange the disorder of that irresistible whirlwind to a clarity like this, and becalm the whole world again, or to refashion the form of a woman into that of a bird?'[39] In the symbolist metaphysic, even meteorology is a supreme fiction – so it is not unconvincing that Densher after the storm should accept the dove.

I have dwelt on these references to emphasize how much, by just going to Venice and living and dying in a palace, Milly is adopting a style, a style in which the merely phenomenal world becomes a transcendable manifestation of hidden moralities. I don't think James is ironizing Milly, but I don't think either that he ever forgets that the ultimate symbol is money:

She was now playing with the thought that Eugenio might *inclusively* assist her: he had brought home to her, and always by remarks that were really quite soundless, the conception, hitherto ungrasped, of some complete use of her wealth as a counter-move to fate. It had passed between them as preposterous that with so much money she should just stupidly and awkwardly *want* – any more want a life, a career, a consciousness, than want a house, a carriage or a cook. It was as if she had had from him a kind of expert professional measure of what he was in a position, at a stretch, to undertake for her; the thoroughness of which, for that matter, she could closely compare with a looseness on Sir Luke Strett's part that – at least in Palazzo Leporelli when mornings were fine – showed as almost amateurish. Sir Luke hadn't said to her 'Pay enough money and leave the rest to *me*' – which was distinctly what Eugenio did say ... She was more prepared than ever to pay enough, and quite as much as ever to pay too much. What else – if such were points at which your most trusted servant failed was the use of being, as the dear Susies of earth called you, a princess in a palace? (Bk. 7, Ch. 3)

Eugenio, the servant who is too old to make love but not to make money, is the only person in the novel with whom Milly has anything like a trusting relationship, and we see the significance of this in the texture of the prose. Living is reduced to a metaphor based on money, because Milly has endless resources of money and no resources of life. Of course, her plucky little self-irony is at work again here, but what she actually does is to use her money as a counter-move to fate – both in the sense that she lives in a palace where all appears beautiful, and in the sense that, by creating an image of herself that overwhelms Densher, she can avoid the fate of being used to provide a means by which Kate's strength may express itself. She gets from Eugenio a metaphoric world, a world in which money replaces biological reality as the courier replaces the healer. Money makes for fiduciary relationships. In this sense, she really is a princess in a palace who can look down on the Susies of earth, play the game of sincerity with Kate, and pity Lord Mark for his failure to cope with her and her 'sinister light of tragedy'. And climactically, of course, she is able to purchase a Veronese party at which she appears transfigured, suited 'down to the earth' by a string of pearls. She purchases a 'perpetually charmed vision' because all are included in the 'candour of her smile, the lustre of her pearls, the value of her life, the essence of her wealth'. Innocence and wealth are completely fused in such an image, and together they are powerful. Her smile accepts her dove-like nature, but only so that it can precipitate the ravens of England towards their melodrama of lust and guilt in the 'drawing-room of Europe'. The Emersonian concept of money is triumphantly restored. Money is moral, representative. But what has restored it is the high sublime of the tourist lifestyle, and that is built on the *actual* value of money.

7 *The circle of petticoats*

The register of the high sublime is, of course, Densher, and our final estimate of the novel must depend on how we see his role in the novel, and how we judge James's success in portraying it. For if Milly is objectively dazzling the whole of society, her dazzling of Densher is the more intense because he is looking for a confrontation with the unknown. He has met, on his arrival in Venice, an atmosphere of stale familiarity generated by the cockneys of all climes, the tourists who pervade the respectable quarters of the city. He looks for more Bohemian lodgings, trying without success to lose his way. Initially the Palazzo is included in this ennui. Milly is after all the tourist of tourists, and the back-street lodgings are to serve to give privacy to his relationship with Kate. And yet, before he has actually got Kate into bed, his mind is paying tribute to the impression Milly can make, and soon he is to find the unknown, not in Kate's body but in the pervasive mystery of Milly's style. And this is going to appear to him as a superior knowledge: aware of how much Kate is 'under the impression of the element of wealth in her', he is able to see also that the pearls 'would uncommonly suit' Kate. Later, he is to give pearls the metaphoric sense they have in the Bible. Seeing what Kate sees he is able to see also what she doesn't: that Milly's wealth is dovelike 'only so far as one remembered that doves have wings and wondrous flights'. Milly, and Milly's power, is already becoming, quite strictly speaking, an objective correlative for Densher's pursuit of the unknown. Paradoxically it is precisely what Densher despises most at the outset, wealth and tourism, that becomes the medium in which he learns to love Milly. In fact, this most important of the novel's triangle simply gets turned on its head: a movement from pity to love is paralleled in the relationship with Kate by a movement from love to pity. In other terms, this is a movement from the admiration of lucidity to the admiration of mystery. This inversion is not difficult to perceive. The problem is that if we take it straight, it seems both incredible and sickening – the fairy princess with the thumping bank account, by dying decently (which really means not smelling of drugs) and forgiving all (which means being kind to a failed attempt to get some of the millions to whose excess her life is forfeit), obliterates the beautiful woman with the strength to live. If we take it ironically, which means seeing Densher as a super-subtle fool (like the narrator of *The Sacred Fount* or John Marcher), the novel becomes a terribly inflated authorial joke, exposing a mode of consciousness so specialized and ingrown that, for all its intelligence, it cannot see that it is being used by Kate to defeat Aunt Maud, Milly to defeat Kate, and in turn by Aunt Maud to defeat everybody. If the texture of the novel has the value I am claiming for it, Densher's experience has to have representative value. I think that it has, though its presentation is full of ironies, some of them satirically directed against him; but the most important *dramatic* ironies are features of the novel's universe manifested through him.

James is definite and specific about the kind of consciousness Densher has. Densher himself feels 'plasticity, within limits, to be a *mode of life* like another' (Bk. 8, Ch. 1: my italics). Plasticity is a formal commitment to a world of thought, of which the positive lifestyle of Mrs Lowder, with its 'immense expression of her signs and symbols' (Bk. 2, Ch. 2), is a 'portentous negation'. It negates because it speaks with a fixed and unimpressionable 'language' – '*solid* forms', 'wasted *finish*', 'general *attestation* of morality and money' (Bk. 2, Ch. 2: my italics) – so that plasticity is positively a mode of consciousness seeking another language than that of fixed signification. And seeking it, plasticity must necessarily be without objective identity: Densher is a citizen of the world, 'too probably spoiled for native, for insular use' (Bk. 2, Ch. 2). The ingenious discriminator, the *disponible*, Densher is an Everyman figure only to the extent that, in this novel, a particular world view is made a universal one. Significantly, he is contemplating an article when he is thinking of Mrs Lowder's furniture, for he has, above all, what St Beuve defined as the '*génie critique*' in his essay on Bayle. Densher's critical ability is very different from Kate's, however. We can see this most clearly when he is using a similar kind of imagery to Kate:

> The huddled herd had drifted to her blindly – it might as blindly have drifted away. There had been of course a signal, but the great reason was probably the absence at the moment of a larger lion. (Bk. 6, Ch. 3)

There is nothing naturalistic about the use of animal imagery here – herd and lion are stock literary metaphors used for purely moralistic distinctions. If Kate's vision is the aesthetic of estrangement, Densher's is the aesthetic of detachment – there is an overlap which draws them together, but a distinction which is destined to part them. Vision for vision, Densher's has more universality because it is not kinetic.

However, James is chiefly concerned to explore, in his portrayal of Densher, the 'mode of life' such vision implies. At the core of Densher's 'mode' is a fear of his own non-existence. Plasticity replaces doing with thinking ('his strength merely for thought'), and Densher contrasts 'life' with 'thought' so that it has to be a special mode of thought as well. The two marks on Densher's forehead (which he significantly thinks of as smudges) are impecuniousness and the facile verbalization of experience. The first is a negation – it makes him, in Mrs Lowder's eyes mediated through his understanding, 'a very small quantity' – and the second leaves him dependent not only on vicarious experience but on vicarious understanding. Both are present in terms of his own vocabulary when he senses that he has got beyond the 'reflux of the first emotion' of returning home:

His full parenthesis was closed, and he was once more but a sentence, of a sort, in the general text, the text that, from his momentary street-corner, showed as a great grey page of print that somehow managed to be crowded without being 'fine'. (Bk. 6, Ch. 1)

'Parenthesis' links Densher even at this stage with Milly, who has in the previous book felt the 'short parenthesis' of the crowded imagination close after her sense of Aunt Maud 'keeping the day'. It isolates, for each a moment of full consciousness, but is not a matter of mere subjectivity. Milly's parenthesis had begun with Lord Mark telling her that she was a 'success' – giving her, that is, the possibility of an unexploited objective existence. Densher's parenthesis closes when he feels that he himself is a sentence in the general text – when he is nothing but a purveyor of a predetermined structure of words. A little later, he feels himself *'relegated* to mere spectatorship' (Bk. 6, Ch. 3: my italics). In fact what most *threatens* Densher is mere subjectivity, because it also implies lack of will. He admires Kate because her intelligence is at one with her passion, and because she reveals 'a note of character that belittled his own incapacity for action'. It means that she not only mediates his relationship to the active world, but becomes the guide of his awareness – 'Kate's multiplied lights led him on and on'. To maintain that very plasticity which is his subjective mode, Densher has to try to achieve an objective existence.

In his attempts to achieve this, surely the ironies are heavily loaded against Densher. The attempt is self-contradictory, since it involves both an attempt to erect plasticity into a code and an attempt to overcome its will-lessness. Once he is involved in Kate's scheme, Densher becomes comically obsessed with 'how a gentleman would behave':

He had never known himself so generally merciful. It was a footing, at all events, whatever accounted for it, on which he should surely be rather a muff not to manage by one turn or another to escape disobliging. (Bk. 6, Ch. 5)

'Muff' gets exactly the right note of gentlemanly slang, a calculated minimizing of questions of moral integrity; and the proliferation of negatives and auxiliaries ('not to manage ... to escape disobliging') measures the passivity, the other-directedness of behaviour which is, with only mild irony, the subject for such self-congratulation. Henceforward, the key words of moral discrimination have to do with awkwardness, tact and delicacy. It reaches its climax in Book 9 when we get a sentence such as 'so that he best kept everything in place by not hesitating or fearing, as it were, to let himself go – go in the direction, that is to say, of staying' (Ch. 2). By escaping disobliging and not hesitating to hesitate, Densher constructs a whole ethical system which includes, as the high point of

complacency, feeling righteous indignation against Lord Mark because he
has told Milly the truth:

> Densher had indeed drifted by the next morning to the reflection
> which he positively, with occasion, might have brought straight out
> that the only delicate and honourable way of treating a person in such
> a state was to treat her as *he*, Merton Densher, did. (Bk. 9, Ch. 2)

As it turns out, of course, he is in many ways, from Milly's point of view,
right; but only because she has carefully prepared for everybody a web of
illusion. From his own point of view, of the man attempting to create
a mode of life from plasticity, Densher is placed as absurd: 'drifted' in
the first clause, which is indicative in mood, is contrasted wryly with the
determination of 'positively' and 'straight' of the subjunctive parenthesis.
Not being a muff, as Densher sporadically realizes, means standing quietly
in a circle of petticoats.

The second way in which he tries to achieve objectivity is the very
opposite – not the extension of plasticity as a mode of life, but a demar-
cation of it from immateriality through the assertion of will. We should
not sentimentalize the sexual relationship in the novel simply because it
seems refreshingly physical in a world pervaded by the 'spiritual'. Kate's
and Densher's young immunity is seen primarily in Darwinian terms: it is
what they have to oppose Aunt Maud with in the struggle for survival.
And that struggle is, in the last analysis, an individual one. The relationship is never something in itself, separate from its protagonists. Each
uses the other to mediate a relationship with life; each sees the other as
supplying a lack in the self; each seeks to possess the other. Kate feels of
his long looks – which stand for the world of 'mind' – that she 'must make
them most completely her possession' (Bk. 2, Ch. 1). Densher too has a
completely acquisitive attitude towards Kate:

> Having so often concluded on the fact of his weakness, as he called it,
> for life – his strength merely for thought – life, he logically opined, was
> what he must somehow arrange to annex and possess. (Bk. 2, Ch. 1)

We should note too that although Densher is recognizing here the
dependence of life on thought, the use of a word such as 'annex' keeps
them apart. Life is to be possessed so that thought shall not suffocate in its
withdrawal from the general text. It's a way of keeping the parenthesis
open. The problem is that it is *life*, with its integrity of passion and
intelligence, that is to annex him by the time he finds himself in Venice.
Again, he reacts to his 'so extremely manipulated state' with a metaphor
bringing his literary profession to bear on his impecuniousness:

There were things enough, goodness knew – for it was the moral of his plight – that he couldn't afford; but what had had a charm for him if not the notion of living handsomely, to make up for it, in another way? of not at all events reading the romance of his existence in a cheap edition. (Bk. 8, Ch. 1)

The final limitation of Densher's world view is surely clear in this: the facts of life have to be met with the fictions of thought. And if this means primarily squaring his conscience with his passivity ('he hadn't come all the way from England to be a brute'), it also means that he has to stop himself from feeling silly: 'There's nothing for me possible but to feel that I'm not a fool' (Bk. 8, Ch. 2). Foolishness becomes with awkwardness a major discriminating concept in Book 9. The sexual consummation is a 'test' on Kate of whether he has a will left at all, and of whether their contract entails obligations on her part as well.

It is also an episode in the struggle for epistemological survival. What spurs him on is that his plan is something that Kate can't see: 'It wound him up a turn or two further, none the less, to impute to her now a *weakness of vision* by which he could himself feel the stronger' (Bk. 8, Ch. 1: my italics). It is significant that not only does Densher gain strength from feeling that he is duping Kate, but also that he doesn't absolutely feel this but chooses to because it makes him feel better. Densher is a seer who has to see himself given definition within the picture. The definition he requires is that of the *bon prince*, capable of exerting a will and being seen to. In the significantly highlighted Piazza he makes his demand explicit for the first time, and James's prose registers precisely the nature of the demand and its determinations: 'For the knowledge of what she was he had absolutely to *see* her now, incapable of refuge, stand there for him in all the light of day and of his admirable merciless meaning' (Bk. 8, Ch. 2). There is a note of sadism, but it is essentially directed towards exposure. 'Merciless' echoes the 'merciful' of his feelings about obliging the circle of petticoats. Plasticity as a mode of life depends on an underworld in which the petticoats can be torn aside. Or at least seen to be torn aside: later Densher is struck by 'the vividness with which he saw himself master in the conflict'. The reflexive verb sums up the whole affair – we are concerned with a relationship of competing visions. Specifically this is the invasion of 'life' by thought – 'the fact of the idea as directly applied, as converted from a luminous conception into an historic truth' (Bk. 9, Ch. 1). The vocabulary in relation to the situation is almost Schopenhauerian. Getting Kate into bed is a triumph of idea over will.

The sex act is thus aptly only visionary – it exists only as future and past, as concept and percept. It is an act, not an entry into a new phase – they meet only once, and we know of it only as an 'arch of associations'. And it is precisely because of this that Densher moves so swiftly towards Milly.

The opening chapter of Book 9, particularly the second and third paragraphs, carefully track down Densher's development: the move from his feeling 'possessed' by the value of Kate's gesture, to his feeling taken up by Milly's imagination. The memory of the act is described first of all as something so intense that it is renewed for Densher each time that he unlocks the door; and because of this, by a deceptively natural transition, it is transcendent: 'it was in view as nothing of the moment, nothing begotten of time or of chance could be or ever would.' Once out of time, it becomes comparable to art – the act becomes the scene, and Densher who witnesses the scene again and again, occupies an ambiguous role between actor and audience, becoming like one of the 'fiddlers': 'He remained thus, in his own theatre, in his single person, perpetual orchestra to the ordered drama, the confirmed "run"; playing low and slow, moreover, in the regular way, for the situations of most importance.' It is a pornographic way to relate to one's sex life: the act, by its very intensity, has become distanced and stylized (ordered), and Densher has become a voyeur of his own past. Or rather, his sex life consists of nobody but Kate, who has performed *for* rather than *with* him. And if he feels a renewal of his fidelity as a result, the terms in which he feels it are highly significant: 'The force of the engagement, the quantity of the article to be supplied, the special solidity of the contract, the way, above all, as a service for which the price named for him had been magnificently paid, his equivalent office was to take effect – such items might well fill his consciousness when there was nothing from outside to interfere.' Article, contract, price – they are terms in which Milly is more likely to win than Kate. The forms of appreciation available to Densher (and I don't think there is any relevance in saying that James is just being old-maidish about sex here: Kate's gesture was objectively a price paid for a service) – timeless memory, faithful admiration – conspire in themselves to reduce the act to a *condominium* of aesthetics and economics which is actually the realm of tourism.

By the end of that paragraph, the intensity of impression is defeated not only because it creates no kinetic response, but because it fails aesthetically too – the vividness of the memory and the loyalty it inspires deprives it of 'the warmth of the element of mystery'. What is finally to defeat Kate is her lucidity. From this point on, Densher is more and more drawn towards the inscrutable and the oblique. The final turn of the screw is that the memory, being timeless, becomes so fixed in space that, from feeling that the act renews itself whenever he opens the door, Densher begins to feel that closing the door of his room is closing it on the memory too: so that 'before he reached the palace, much more after hearing at his heels the bang of the greater *portone*, he felt free enough not to know his position as oppressively false'. That composite verb, 'felt free enough not to know', brilliantly encapsulates both what Densher is and the way in which he fits with the general themes of the novel. The *portone* of the palace liberates him from knowledge, and liberation from knowledge is liberation from the oppression of falsity – not by emancipation into truth but by emancipation from real false dichotomies. So by the end of the paragraph he can feel that Milly's imagination purges the relationship of its guilt. 'Worse things than being duped,' wrote William James, 'may happen to a man in this world.'[40] The inscrutable has dissolved the lucid: 'Something incalculable wrought for them – for him and Kate; something outside, beyond, above themselves, and doubtless ever so much better than they.' That 'doubtless' fixes the terms of the novel – the moral superiority of Milly's imagination is chucked in as an asserted after-thought because it doesn't finally matter. What matters is that she wins, and the extent of her triumph is to be measured by the comic rout of Kate's memory – by the arrival at Densher's lodgings of New England Susie in a wet waterproof.

Densher's conversion can be usefully set in a context provided by Susie's eyestyle as well. In 'The Tragical in Daily Life', Maeterlinck writes:

> Its province is rather to reveal to us how truly wonderful is the mere act of living, and to throw light upon the existence of the soul, self-contained in the midst of ever restless immensities; to hush the discourse of reason and sentiment, so that above the tumult may be heard the solemn, uninterrupted whisperings of man and his destiny.[41]

Densher gets from Milly above all the metaphysical justification of his stillness, 'creating studiously the minimum of vibration'. When he finally leaves Kate it is to seek in his rooms not a memory but a stillness, 'so that it might prevail there till the inevitable sounds of life, once more, compar-atively coarse and harsh, should smother and deaden it'. The wings of the dove hush the discourse of reason and sentiment – that is of the intelligence and passion, the personal life offered with chill lucidity by Kate.

What it is replaced by is realized with a prose style hovering brilliantly on the border between comedy of manners and divine allegory:

> When one went on tiptoe one could turn off for retreat without betraying the manœuvre. Perfect tact – the necessity for which he had from the first, as we know, happily recognized – was to keep all intercourse in the key of the absolutely settled. It was settled thus for instance that they were indissoluble good friends, and settled as well that her being the American girl was, just in time and for the relation they found themselves concerned in, a boon inappreciable. If, at least, as the days went on, she was to fall short of her prerogative of the great national, the great maidenly ease, if she didn't diviningly and responsively desire and labour to record herself as possessed of it, this wouldn't have been for want of Densher's keeping her, with his idea,

well up to it – wouldn't have been in fine for want of his encouragement and reminder. He didn't perhaps in so many words speak to her of the quantity itself as of the thing she was least to intermit; but he talked of it, freely, in what he flattered himself was an impersonal way, and this held it there before her – since he was careful also to talk pleasantly. It was at once their idea, when all was said, and the most marked of their conveniences. The type was so elastic that it could be stretched to almost anything; and yet, not stretched, it kept down, remained normal, remained properly within bounds. And he *had* meanwhile, thank goodness, without being too much disconcerted, the sense, for the girl's part of the business, of the queerest conscious compliance, of her doing very much what he wanted, even though without her quite seeing why. She fairly touched this once in saying: 'Oh yes, you like us to be as we are because it's a kind of facilitation to you that we don't quite measure: I think one would have to be English to measure it!' – and that too, strangely enough, without prejudice to her good nature. She might have been conceived as doing – that is of being – what he liked in order perhaps only to judge where it would take them. They really as it went on *saw* each other at the game; she knowing he tried to keep her in tune with his conception, and he knowing she thus knew it. Add that he again knew she knew, and yet that nothing was spoiled by it, and we get a fair impression of the line they found most completely workable. The strangest fact of all for us must be that the success he himself thus promoted was precisely what figured to his gratitude as the something above and beyond him, above and beyond Kate, that made for daily decency. There would scarce have been felicity – certainly too little of the right lubricant – had not the national character so invoked been, not less inscrutably than entirely, in Milly's chords. It made up her unity and was the one thing he could unlimitedly take for granted. (Bk. 9, Ch. 2)

So many of the themes of the novel are brought together here. The opening sentences pick up the theme of what a gentleman would do, but we notice also that Milly can match his plasticity with an elasticity of role: without him having to assert himself, she is doing, being what he wants. She too achieves that impersonality she has desired from the time of her visit to the National Gallery. The conditions of this achievement are precise. Intercourse is to be in the key of the absolutely settled, and the musical metaphor is picked up again with 'keep her in tune' and 'Milly's chords', and echoed in 'without being too much disconcerted'. They are not having intercourse so much as playing together in concert, and James emphasizes this by the reflective self-consciousness of the game ('Add that he, again, knew she knew ...' – it is the epistemological equivalent of a French farce) and, startlingly by bringing 'us' – 'the strangest fact for us' –

into the prose as audience to admire their performance. The theatricality is not reductive because it is precisely what they are aiming at – producing between them a fiction which will not be spoiled by the fact that they know it is. What Kate's act becomes inevitably in Densher's mind is what Milly's style voluntarily is, in this sense. On the other hand, it survives because it offers not a lucidity, but a 'workable' line: a line which makes for decency rather than truth, and in making for it reaches a higher, vaguer, more obscure truth – a 'something beyond'. But, of course, the line itself is very precise – it grows out of the tourist role Milly is prepared to adopt, 'the great maidenly ease'. The metaphor at the end is important – the national character is a lubricant, and in the following paragraph a 'nonconductor' (i.e. an insulator). Both images are from mechanical contexts and have to do with the repression of forces (friction or electricity) in order to keep the machine going. James hasn't abandoned the ironies of that first sentence by the end, but he has certainly redirected them; so that instead of Densher rationalizing his malleability and tacit hypocrisy, we have Kate outmanœuvred by a machinery for eliminating the clash of interests in an innocent game of types, fact outmanœuvred by fiction, Milly's bewildered acquiescence transformed to our consenting bewilderment. James transcends his own ironies without losing their penumbral interrogations. Following Densher into the dark warmth of the element of mystery, we carry shreds of his satiric light.

8 *The mere money of her, the darling*

If then, Densher's conversion is to be seen as the intercourse between his flawed plastic consciousness and Milly's stylistic power (which is her wealth), it is also to be seen as an initiation into a vision which really overreaches the art of seeing things as they are, exposing it as a distortion capable of mere lucidity. There seems to be no system of values outside the grand alliance of Susie, Milly and Densher, who oppose their styles against Kate's. Densher occasionally recognizes that outside his circle of petticoats there are male witnesses – Sir Luke, Lord Mark, Eugenio – who might see the absurdity of his postures. But they do not represent an ideal other case, a potential male *ransome* of human vitality, because each of them is in some way on hire to the circle of petticoats. Eugenio has lost the ability to make love, though not to make money; Sir Luke is concerned only with a beautiful show of life, and gives tacit approval to the pretences of the Palazzo; and Lord Mark is merely an effect without being a cause, and his irruption of reality is merely destructive. The male witnesses are not male enough, because in this novel there is only one real source of power which is impersonal and firm, and that is hard cash. The final irony of the novel is that the satiric ironies, which are allowed full play in local details, are made to look ridiculous as we witness the power of Milly to survive, and exact, in death, even more consenting bewilderment.

This is emphasized, as is the transcendent power of wealth, by the fact that Densher's conversion is completed not by Milly herself, but by the two agents of her love who were most the butts of his satire mind, Susie and Aunt Maud (if he had felt sorrow for the first, and hatred for the second, it is merely because of their relative force). We have seen how much Susie contributes to the lifestyle Milly acquires, and how it is she, grotesque parody of pity like a naked new-born babe, who dissolves the lucidity of Kate's act. Densher finally speaks of her as 'a person who does see' (Bk. 10, Ch. 1). And, of course, for all her strident hyperbole, she does: for she sees the romantic potential of money, and the realization of that potential is what the novel is about. But the fact that Densher is saying this to Kate would make it one of the best jokes in the novel, if it weren't that the best jokes come from Susie's better half.

Mrs Lowder, as I have already suggested, offers brutally simple perspectives on the mystifying events of the novel, and these are too valuable to allow us to see her only as a comic butt. In the last book of the novel she is granted a positive dramatic role which is only hinted at earlier. The high mark of imagination that Milly has at Matcham is her awareness of Mrs Lowder's 'spiritual ebriety' – it is the climax of what turns out to be a parenthesis in which she enjoys a simple, unworked-for success as a veritable young lioness. When she loses this and is made a mere dove, it is Mrs Lowder who enters and is like dove cooing to dove, who gives Milly the idea of the success she can achieve after the lionizing has stopped. She is deeply bound up with Milly's triumph both in practical and thematic terms. With her nauseating amalgam of uninhibited avarice and sanctimonious sentimentality, she becomes the earthly spokesman of an unearthly power:

> What most deeply stirred her was the way the poor girl must have wanted to live.
>
> 'Ah yes indeed – she did, she did: why in pity shouldn't she, with everything to fill her world? The mere *money* of her, the darling, if it isn't too disgusting at such a time to mention that – !'
>
> Aunt Maud mentioned it – and Densher quite understood – but as fairly giving poetry to the life Milly clung to: a view of the 'might have been' before which the good lady was hushed anew to tears. (Bk. 10, Ch. 2)

Given the earlier placing of Aunt Maud, we cannot but turn the irony on Densher too, and yet it is only to acquiesce in the bizarre reality – the mere money is what gives her poetry. A poor girl dying wouldn't 'matter' in this way. And although Densher tries to dissociate himself from Mrs Lowder's sentimentality, he comes to feel more free with her than in 'the strange chill' of Kate's brightness. He dresses, on Christmas morning, quite as if for church', but it is Mrs Lowder who sends him there. She has become Milly's vicar, ensuring that the mere money continues to speak of the 'solemn, uninterrupted whisperings of man and his destiny'. The 'commendable fictions' of Susie, 'the wealth of sentiment' of Aunt Maud, and his own 'wasted passion' constitute a moral surplus generating a large gap between actual value and psychological value, which is what the world of thought lives off. The gap can be measured by Densher's adoption of Milly's counter-revolutionary image; during his reflections on Mrs Lowder's evocation of the mere money, 'Milly had held with passion to her dream of a future, and she was separated from it, not shrieking indeed, but grimly, awfully silent, as one might imagine some noble victim of the scaffold, in the French Revolution, separated at the prison-door from some object clutched for resistance' (Bk. 10, Ch. 2). It is a highly senti-mental image, since Milly died in luxury from natural causes, able to afford the most expensive surgeon, the most lavish apartments (which were the very opposite of prison), and bathed in a decent vagueness. But above all it is Milly's image – her style, invoked by Britannia in the Market-place. As though to make quite sure we don't miss it, James goes on in the next paragraph to describe Densher's feelings about Lancaster Gate: 'Before the fire in the great room that was all arabesques and cherubs, all gaiety and gilt, and that was warm at that hour too with a wealth of autumn sun, the state in question had been maintained ...' The state in question is the princely state in which Densher, responding to Susie's princess image, describes himself as having been received by Milly. The Palazzo is thus maintained at Lancaster Gate, and 'warm' places it firmly on Milly's side against Kate. But what is most striking is that we are witnessing a complete reassessment of Aunt Maud's 'medium' by Densher. It has the same vulgarity, but vulgarity is no longer a negation of thought. And the remainder of the paragraph describes him as playing a part for the sake of Lancaster Gate gossip, seeing its sentimental exaggerations, and accepting them. We almost have an image at the end of Mrs Lowder and Densher holding hands and gazing at the wonderful romance they have constructed. Certainly Mrs Lowder's most witty remark, 'I want him for myself', has been realized by the end of the novel. The liberal imagi-nation, the world of thought, the plastic consciousness has come to rest in the ample bosom of the mercantile matron. I was going to add 'and all on American capital' but, of course, it is finally without Milly's money, only with her credit. The will to believe keeps the churches full and the stock exchanges afloat.

I haven't, obviously, given a complete account of the novel's texture or of the contexts it invokes, but I hope that I have said enough to show that the deceptively simple, and simplifying plot is elaborated to become a coherent and wide-ranging study of the relationships between aesthetic and epistemological ideals and social relationships (specifically in a world which is becoming a plutocracy ruled by the corporation), and the trust which reinforces the establishment, not personally but in the ultimate impersonality of death. A right evaluation of the novel depends on seeing it, to the end, as comedy, instead of sentimentalizing it, as most critics do, as tragedy. The effects of Milly's death are very funny. More strictly, in the end the social world re-forms, and only the *idiotes*, Kate, the stranger who has tried to subvert it, is banished. I don't think necessarily that James made moral judgments on the world he was depicting, unless it was to endorse its structure by seeing in it the potential of aesthetic contemplation. What I claim is that his understanding of the dramatic relations between great wealth and the world of thought is deep enough for him to bring out all the complexities involved in experiencing those connexions. The simplicity of the plot not only permits the spatial presentation of these complexities, it is the direct reflection of the connexion: for money and language both seek to compose relationships into commendable fictions.

To demonstrate once more how great it is, we should put *The Wings of the Dove* into one final context, which is that of the fictional treatment of the millionaire. If we contrast, for example, Dickens's presentation of Merdle with Trollope's of Melmotte eighteen years later, we can see a significant development which corresponds historically to the increasing importance of large concentrations of capital, and a changing relationship of novelist to public. Dickens makes us sorry for Merdle – despite his iniquity he remains a pathetic old man, insignificant in all his personal relations. Trollope is even more morally indignant against Melmotte, who is seen as a crude, sadistic father, as well as an unscrupulous businessman in a world of unscrupulous fools. And yet Trollope obviously has terrific admiration for him as an artist. Most of the other characters are presented from a very cool, clinical distance unless, like Roger Carbury, they are woodenly idealistic. But he moves closer and closer to Melmotte; the scenes in the House of Commons, up to his death, are presented dramatically from inside Melmotte's consciousness. Clearly this is because, despite his moral fervour (which seems fairly routine anyway), Trollope can identify more easily with this crook than with any other character; and the reason for this is equally obvious. There are no other values realized in the novel than the ones Melmotte perpetrates – Carbury is not only fictionally dead, but his only substantial objection to Melmotte is that he is an upstart. Melmotte is close to the novelist because he is creative – his money and his morality determine the world of the novel as the novelist determines it also. What seems contradictory in Trollope is made explicit in Meredith's *One of Our Conquerors*: not only is the mind of Victor Radnor the centre of consciousness in the novel, it is also the entangled hiding-place of the transforming 'idea' which generates all vitality in the world of the book. The comic climax of the novel happens when Radnor is conducting the whole of high society as his orchestra at Lakelands. It is comic because of its incongruity: the financial whizz-kid has society in his hands, and this is a verdict on society; but on the other hand, the radical outsider has transformed society into a work of art. Meredith goes a long way towards making articulate the links between the millionaire and the artist: both aliens in the social world, they transform their perceptions into modes of life which assimilate other modes. For the financier, as for the novelist, there can be no self-realization which doesn't include the orchestration of all the other powers in the world. To go from Trollope to Meredith is to go from a secret, guilty complicity based on contempt of the rest of society, to a sophisticated attempt to sort out the artist's role in relation to the hegemonic consciousness.

But, finally, Meredith seems to shy away from his theme. Committed to a vitalistic liberalism, which in the later work is not sharply distinct from crude imperialism and racism, he scales Radnor down, limiting his mind to a flawed response to respectability; and *One of Our Conquerors* becomes an increasingly simple tale about the conflict between social and sexual interests. The conqueror does not, as he promises to do, conquer our imagination. But it is the conquest of imagination by accretions of money so large that they liberate the mind, both from money itself and from the shame of the lack of it, that underlies our culture. The illusion that there is a world of mind or a realm of art apart from the *merde* of the Merdles is the concern of *The Wings of the Dove*. 'The romantic stands, on the other hand, for the things that, with all the facilities in the world, all the wealth and all the courage and all the wit and all the adventure, we never can directly know; the things that can reach us only through the beautiful circuit and subterfuge of our thought and our desire.'[42] Wealth, no – but money? What operates a circuit if it is not currency? In his novels at least, James finds something so different from *merde* in the coffers of the millionaire that it becomes, in effect, the root of innocence and the flower of imagination. We meet the real, 'the things we cannot possibly *not* know'[43] with the lies we see by, and no other novel in English seems to me so honest, so dramatic about what purchases the lens.

Notes

*   In some modern editions, such as the Penguin, the chapters are numbered consecutively: those of Book 2 are numbered 3 and 4; Book 3, 5 and 6; Book 4, 7–9; Book 5, 10–16; Book 6, 17–21; Book 7, 22–5; Book 8, 26–8; Book 9, 29–32 and Book 10, 33–8.

1.   Quentin Anderson, *The American Henry James*, New Brunswick, 1957, pp. 233–80.

2.   *Henry James's Autobiography*, edited by F. W. Dupee, London, 1956, p. 335.

3.   William James, *The Will to Believe and Other Essays in Popular Philosophy*, New York, 1899, p. 58.

4.   S. Koch, 'Transcendence in *The Wings of the Dove*', *Modern Fiction Studies*, xii, Spring 1966, p. 94.

5.   B. Lee, 'Henry James's "divine consensus"', *Renaissance and Modern Studies*, vi, 1962, pp. 5–24.

6.   M. Bewley, *The Complex Fate*, London, 1952, p. 41.

7.   F. R. Leavis, *The Great Tradition*, London, 1962, p. 175.

8.   E. Auerbach, *Mimesis: The Representation of Reality in Western Literature*, New York, 1957, p. 416.

9.   H. A. Taine, *Nouveaux Essais de Critique et d'Histoire*, 8th ed., Paris, 1905, vol.3, p. 48.

10. *French Poets and Novelists*, Leipzig, 1883, p. 71.

11. Henry James, *Notes on Novelists, with some other notes*, London, 1914, p. 91.

12. Ibid., p. 110.

13. Ibid., p. 95.

14. F. O. Matthiessen, *Henry James: The Major Phase*, New York, 1963, p. 74.

15. 'Walter Barrett' (pseud. Joseph A. Scoville), *The Old Merchants of New York City*, New York, 1870, vol.2, p. 115.

16. *A History of the Great American Fortunes*, Chicago, 1910, vol.1, p. 187.

17. 'Barrett', op. cit., vol.2, p. 126.

18. C. M. Kirk and R. Kirk (eds.), *Criticism and Fiction, and other essays*, New York, 1959 ed., p. 340. In 1903, Howells was to write warmly and acutely about *The Wings of the Dove* itself: see 'Mr Henry James's later work' in F. W. Dupee (ed.), *The Question of Henry James*, London, 1947, pp. 26–39.

19. *The Complete Prose Works of R. W. Emerson*, edited by G. T. Bettany, London, 1889, p. 517.

20. *Partial Portraits*, London, 1911, p. 32.

21. *Henry James's Autobiography*, p. 347.

22. *Wealth against Commonwealth*, New York, 1894, p. 2.

23. *Letters*, vol.1, pp. 166–9.

24. W. D. Howells, *A Hazard of New Fortunes*, New York, 1965, p. 248.

25. Ibid., p. 223.

26. Bewley, op. cit., p. 53.

27. J. Kimball, 'The Abyss and *The Wings of the Dove*', in T. Tanner (ed.), *Henry James: Modern Judgements*, London, 1968, p. 279.

28. Naomi Lebowitz, *The Imagination of Loving: Henry James's legacy to the novel*, Detroit, 1965, p. 76.

29. E. Sandeen, '*The Wings of the Dove* and *The Portrait of a Lady*: a study of Henry James's later phase', PMLA, lxix, 1954, p. 1078.

30. The phrase, like that other joke epithet 'Britannia of the Market', comes in Ruskin (*A Joy for Ever* and *The Crown of Wild Olives* respectively). But that context is one of the 'accumulation' and 'distribution' of art.

31. Henry James, *The Art of Travel*, New York, 1958, p. 384.

32. M. Maeterlinck, *Wisdom and Destiny*, London, 1898, p. 26.

33. M. Maeterlinck, *The Treasure of the Humble*, London, 1909, pp. 45–58.

34. W. H. Pater, *Marius the Epicurean*, 2 vols., London, 1892, vol.2, pp. 99–100. Stuart Sherman in 'The Aesthetic Idealism of Henry James' (1917) emphasized the connexion with Pater in such a way as to yield some of the insights which the present essay explores – notably the importance of 'style' (Dupee, op. cit., pp. 86–106).

35. W. H. Pater, *Imaginary Portraits*, London, 1890, pp. 124–5. Subsequent quotations are taken from this edition, pp. 91–133.

36. *Complete Works*, London, 1902–12, vol.10, pp. 6–7.

37. *The Decline and Fall of the Roman Empire*, London, 1898 vol.6, p. 382.

38. *The Renaissance in Italy*, vol.3 of *The Fine Arts*, London, 1899, p. 273. See also L. B. Holland, *The Expense of Vision, Essays on the craft of Henry James*, Princeton, 1964, p. 306. Holland is generally very informative about James's use of the visual arts in this novel.

39. *Marius the Epicurean*, vol.2, pp. 89–90.

40. *The Will to Believe*, p. 19.

41. Maeterlinck, *The Treasure of the Humble*, pp. 97–8.

42. *The Art of the Novel*, edited by R. P. Blackmur, New York, 1960, pp. 31–2.

43. Ibid.

CHAPTER 7

Hardy and Marxism

For the purposes of this essay, I take *Marxism* to indicate an orientation rather than a specific doctrine. Most of the important issues raised by the term are continually debated and need to be so since Marxism is not merely or even primarily a theory but a program of action and must therefore be developed in relation to the historical change to which it is a response and a stimulus. I will therefore begin with a working definition that admittedly leaves many questions unanswered. First, Marxism entails historical materialism as the basis of its understanding of human society. Humanity is thus defined by its ability to reproduce its own means of existence, and all social formations are determined by (constrained and activated by) this basic characterization and its historical manifestations. The products of the social formations, material objects, and cultural events of ideological tendencies are therefore to be explained in relation to the productive forces and the social relations of production that together make up the identity of a concrete historical moment. There is no eternal social formation, and although there is a human nature it never appears in an abstract manner shorn of the historical variation that the material base determines.

Second, this historical variation is not meaningless. As productive forces and relations develop, they yield a surplus that at once leads to and intensifies a division of labor. This division tends to allot the surplus to the class that dominates the conditions of development. In crude terms, the main modern stages of this tendency are feudalism, which allots it to the class that controls the security of land (the overlords who conquer and/or defend it); capitalism, which allots it to the class that controls and finances the high level of technology necessary for the development of the industrial revolution; and socialism, which allots it to the class, the proletariat, that produces the surplus itself. The changes brought about by this reallocation of the surplus is neither gradual nor peaceful, since the dominant class never willingly hands over its power to its emergent successor. Thus Marxism has three related constituents: It is materialist, but *historically* materialist, and history is dialectical – that is, it moves through the conflict of opposites to revolution.

Marxism is relevant to Hardy in two distinct, though related, ways. First, Hardy wrote about the world he saw in the late nineteenth and early twentieth centuries. Marxism was the most powerful way of seeing that world to grow up in this period – because it was the intellectual system that had the most influence in changing it. This is the historical relevance of Marxism. There is also a theoretical relevance, in that Marxism is a recognizable orientation within literary studies and is thus as appropriate or inept to the study of Hardy as it is to that of any other writer. The historical relevance is more specific, in that there are many writers to whom it would not apply. Chronologically, if one takes the history of Marxism to begin with the date of the first appearance of the first volume of *Capital* in 1867 and to reach its first great practical success with the constitution of the USSR in 1923, it almost exactly coincides with the history of Hardy's literary career (his earliest poems are dated 1866; the last volume he saw through the press, *Human Shows, Far Phantasies*, was published in 1925). Second, there are other writers whose work falls within this same period to whom Marxism would not be so relevant, because if Marxism has any undeniable feature it is that it is preoccupied with the fate of the working class. And unlike, let us say, Henry James, whose literary career also begins in the 1860s and ends just before the Russian revolution, or Yeats, who started writing at the time of the first English translation of *Capital* and died a few months before the Stalin/Hitler pact, Hardy explicitly concerned himself in a large number of novels, stories, poems, and even, to some extent, *The Dynasts*, with sections of the working class in their specific social role as subordinate workers.

It is also equally clear, however, that this specific historical relevance to Hardy is problematic, for although Hardy wrote at the same time as the emergence of Marxism and although, like Marx, Engels, and Lenin, he was concerned with the condition of the working class, there is no evidence that he read Marx, read anything about Marxism, or had any ideas that can be shown to coincide with Marxism. On the contrary, if Hardy had a social vision at all it was probably subsumed in a larger metaphysical vision that owed more to the pessimistic Schopenhauer than to the (ultimately) optimistic Marx. When, at the lowest point of their social fate, Sue says to Jude that "there is something external to us that says 'You shan't!'" we can be almost certain that Hardy intended her to mean that there were forces in life itself conspiring to defeat their (restless) aspirations.[1] If there is a specific social doctrine at work in the novel, it probably has more to do with birth control than anything that could be related to Marxism. *The Dynasts* – on the face of it, at least – makes it even clearer that Hardy attributed human misery to the inept and uncaring universe. There is no sense that by uniting (to use the rhetoric of *The Communist Manifesto*), the workers of the world could throw off their chains. When, at the end of act 1, scene 2, of *The Dynasts*, the Shade of the Earth argues that "uncreation" would be better than the "tedious conjuring" that is history, the Spirit of the Years can only answer that "something hidden" urges matter to motion and that this history is as good as any. The Spirit of the Pities asks "why any" at all and is told that there is no answer. "I am but an accessory of its works," the Spirit of the Years says, "bounden witness of Its laws." The Immanent Will to which this refers never appears in the drama. In both senses of the word, it is unaccountable.[2] We shall have to come back to *The Dynasts*, whose ending is less clear than this opening position, but it is clear that this version of history is far removed from Marxism. However deterministic Marxism is, there is no doubt that, in Marx's own words, people make their own history. Nothing answerable or even voiced makes Hardy's history.

The pursuit of the specific historical relevance of Marxism to Hardy thus meets a very early resistance. We are left, weakly, with some idea that Marxism ought to be relevant in this sense, more relevant than to any other major nineteenth-century British author, but that it is only negatively so. Hardy deals with the working class, but never as a class, always as individuals experiencing "history" only as a meaningless manipulation thwarting their lives.

The more profitable way for the Marxist critic to proceed seems, therefore, to be through general theoretical relevance. Marxism is an intellectual position from which it is possible to investigate any historical social phenomenon, and Hardy, like any other writer, is a historical social phenomenon. This is indeed how most "Marxist" critics approach him.

Some remarkable criticism of Hardy has come from critics who are either explicitly Marxist or, like Raymond Williams, within terms of reference defined by Marxism. They are also highly various, but I can identify two major points that many of them have in common. First, there is what Terry Eagleton has termed Hardy's "recalcitrance."[3] Most of the great writers of the nineteenth century have to be demystified – there is always a level at which they are limited by the ideology of capitalism with which they work. Hardy is frequently seen to be different. Christopher Caudwell, whose few pages on Hardy in *Romance and Realism* remarkably forecast later interpretations, writes: "While all this was happening, the artist who as long as he lived in England could not be deceived by the ideology of capitalism's mercenary class was wrestling with the problems involved in that more profound motion of culture which had produced both the imperialising bourgeoisie, and its mercenary class."[4] This recalcitrance leads to a good ideal of critical self-identification. Raymond Williams's essay in *The English Novel from Dickens to Lawrence*, which is certainly one of the best criticisms of Hardy ever written, ends with the strong claim that Hardy is "our flesh and our grass."[5]

Now, as Charles Swann has pointed out,[6] there is a line that is crossed here between singling Hardy out and appropriating him into a socialist worldview that he palpably did not share. The concept of recalcitrance, though useful and important, is also in two ways distorting. First, Hardy is the isolated refuser of the dominant ideology only if one accepts the canonical versions of literary history taught in the institutions, within which, it is argued, Hardy cannot be contained. Hardy himself, however, feels that he belongs with a very strong radical literary tradition – Shelley, Browning, Swinburne, Meredith, and, in important ways, Pater. He is certainly very different from these writers but not as insulated from them as he seems to be, for example, from George Eliot and Arnold. More important, he is not the only figure in his own day to be unpacking the assumptions of dominant ideology – I think of Olive Schreiner and Mark Rutherford, as well as discursive writers such as J. A. Symonds and Havelock Ellis.

Moreover, this reading involves a conscious deformation of Hardy's project. Again Caudwell summarizes what others develop in different ways: "Blind unconscious bourgeois society is the antagonist of *Jude the Obscure* and also the real enemy of *The Dynasts*." Arnold Kettle in his first essay on *Tess of the d'Urbervilles*, which (let me add) in its time was vitally important for keeping Hardy out of the hands of second-rate philosophers, argued that that novel was really about the decline of the peasantry.[7] As Williams commented – and Kettle accepted the point – this could hardly be true when there was no English peasantry to decline. But Kettle's later essay still wants to defer Hardy's texts to a symbolic level, and even Williams, as Swann points out, reduces Hardy to a concern with his own "border country." Sherman's book is a classic and sad case of a writer whose warmth for and understanding of Hardy does not prevent him from failing to analyze what is actually there.[8] Two later accounts of Hardy – Boumelha's and Wotton's – are explicitly committed to the idea that it is on an unconscious level of the text, manifest in its gaps and slippages, that a materialist account of Hardy can take place.[9]

I am certainly not dismissing these accounts. I am merely arguing that they leave a great deal to be done, both about Hardy's place and about his project, both of which, in my view, are susceptible of materialist analysis. There is also a danger that a great deal of Hardy has to be left out in order to make him fit. Eagleton, for example, is so unwilling to take on Hardy's pessimism that he even, at one point, praises Roy Morrell's petit bourgeois, Boy Scout moralizing of Hardy.[10] Williams ends by saying that Hardy *mourns* what he sees. Both critics in this way emasculate the writer of the angry bitter endings of *Tess of the d'Urbervilles* and *Jude the Obscure* or even the sardonic "happy" endings of *Far from the Madding Crowd* and *The Mayor of Casterbridge*. Hardy was a lot less innocent and a lot more devastating than such critiques allow for.

Swann calls attention to the distorting effect, encouraged to some extent by *The Life*,[11] of seeing Hardy's career begin with *The Poor Man and the Lady*, which is supposedly a socialist novel, and end with the furor over *Jude the Obscure*. This account of Hardy's career ignores the fact that Hardy not only went on writing for thirty years after *Jude the Obscure*, but even published a second version of one novel, *The Well-Beloved*, and carefully revised most of his novels in 1911–1912 for the Wessex Edition. It is also not very likely that the first novel would have been "socialist" in any sense that would be accepted by Hardy's "Marxist" critics. Effectively, Swann says that we should pay more attention to Hardy's dismantling of organic form, so that we are concerned not so much with suppressed or underlying political issues but, rather, with the literary politics of the deconstruction of the coherent subject and the supplanting of depth, by narrative, by linearity within time. Such an approach at least restores to Hardy a level of consciousness that he manifestly has. But I think we have to go further. If we consider the question of how Hardy historically relates to Marxism instead of asking how he fits a coherent theoretical orientation, I think we shall find a writer who more than any other English novelist engages with its major concerns.

Let me stress, however, that we are not concerned with historical impossibility. At least when he was writing novels, Hardy would have had very little idea of and probably not much interest in a political ideology that had almost no adherents in Britain and no visible role in world history. Nor should we expect Hardy to arrive by his own route at insights comparable to those we find in Marx. Marx was effective precisely because he saw what nobody else *could* see, the mechanics of capitalism. It is still rare and difficult to read and understand Marx, and nothing can act as a substitute for the understanding he demands. What we shall, rather, find in Hardy is a series of thrusts in his writing that takes him to the impasse Marxism moves through. Hardy, I shall argue, gets nearer than any other nineteenth-century English novelist to defining the need for Marxist analysis, and has to move away from that need when he most closely approaches it.

2

Hardy himself thought that his novelistic career started with a "socialistic, not to say revolutionary novel," *The Poor Man and the Lady*, "a sweeping dramatic satire of the squirearchy and nobility, London society, the vulgarity of the middle class, modern Christianity, church restoration, and political and domestic morals in general" (*Life* 61). It is certainly true that not only what seems to have remained of this rejected text, the story entitled "An Indiscretion in the Life of an Heiress" (1888), but also all of the novels of the first phase (up to 1876) that deal with modern life, are preoccupied with the destructive effects of social inequality. *A Pair of Blue*

Eyes is a variant on the poor-man-and-lady theme. *Desperate Remedies* is about the exploitation of the social disadvantage of a young woman whose father is an impecunious tradesman. *The Hand of Ethelberta* charts the campaign of the daughter of a butler to conquer and enter the nobility. Class difference is both a spur and an inexorable barrier to the achievement of desire. Egbert Mayne, the hero of *An Indiscretion in the Life of an Heiress*, summarizes the sense of transgression that class imposes on love, as he watches his pupils go home after a visit from his Lady:

> Much as he loved her, his liking for the peasantry about him – his mother's ancestry – caused him sometimes a twinge of self reproach for thinking of her so exclusively. ... He watched the rain spots thickening upon the faded frocks, worn out tippets, yellow straw hats and bonnets, and coarse pinafores of his unprotected little flock as they walked down the path and was thereby reminded of the hopelessness of his attachment, by perceiving how much more nearly akin was his lot to theirs than to hers. [12]

Egbert's recognition of his true social identity is purely negative; it is the separation that matters, not the identification. The separation remains constant – "the madness of hoping to call that finished creature wife" (93). Moreover, it is shared by her as a fate in which she, too, is bound: "To be woven and tied in with the world by blood, acquaintance, tradition, and external habit, is to a woman to be utterly at the beck of that world's customs" (91). Egbert saves her from certain death, enlists enough of her love to put "in abeyance" the fine-lady position of her existence, so that they speak and act "simply as a young man and woman" (62), and even goes off for five years "to try to rise to her level by years of sheer exertion" (72), all to no avail. Only when she is forced with the direct prospect of marriage to Lord Bretton does she run to Egbert, and even in elopement she stops to appease her father, in whose arms she dies.

On the other hand, Egbert's awareness of the "peasantry" is totally vague. Even his grandfather, with whom he lives, is no peasant: As Williams said of Kettle's analysis of *Tess of the d'Urbervilles*, England has never really had a peasantry in the past few centuries. Intellectually and culturally, Mayne is at a voyeuristic distance from his own people. Stephen Smith in *A Pair of Blue Eyes* feels his distance from his parents more strongly than his distance from Elfride and her father, though her father will regard his birthright as more significant. Ethelberta takes her appropriate place in the ruling class only in disguise. How could a character of her intelligence and sophistication be a mere servant? In disguise, however, she is, of course, no longer herself and is thus the victim of a double bind. Cytherea Graye in *Desperate Remedies* confronts her existence as a figure on the labor market in a newspaper advertisement as "more material" than her real life, and at the height of her drama recognizes that she is completely alienated from her social image. Class allots us a place that we can only transgress as we become conscious of it.

It is clear, however, that if this recognition of the rigors of class division is radical in Hardy's early fiction, it is certainly not, in any modern or Marxist sense, socialism. Significantly, in a later reiteration of the "socialist" tendency of *The Poor Man and the Lady*, Hardy mentions Shaw's use of the disguise motif from *The Hand of Ethelberta*. Shaw is mentioned several times in the *Life*, and at the time Hardy was preparing it Shaw would surely be the most obvious example of a "socialist" writer. Shaw's social vision was at best radical. The class structure of society is for him a static obstructive milieu, which is disrupted and transformed by vitality and rationality manifest in a progressive individual. Class is an anachronistic survival. Hardy himself recognizes that this was not a socialist position when he wrote, apparently in 1884: "I am against privilege derived from accident of any kind, and am therefore equally opposed to aristocratic privilege and democratic privilege" (*Life* 204).

Class in the Marxist sense is not a system of social layers; it is the manifestation of a set of relations, specifically relations of production, "relations of effective power over persons and productive forces, not relations of level ownership."[13] Asa Briggs has shown that although this sense of *class* enters the language dramatically in the critical period between the first reform act and the repeal of the corn laws, *class* reverts to something much closer to the eighteenth-century idea of rank at around the time of the second reform bill.[14] This is clearly because arguments in favor of the extension of the franchise wish to widen the legitimation of social groups without altering the actual production relations. It is therefore in the interests of the dominant culture to speak of class as marginal, subject to internal divisions (especially within the laboring class that is divided into labor, aristocracy, and "residuum"), open to individual but not class mobility (the doctrine of self-help). Arnold in *Culture and Anarchy* illustrates the point very well. The classes to Arnold are a given. They do not exist in relation to one another but in parallel, each with a homologous structure. "Culture" is promoted by aliens within those classes who rise above their interests to promote a traditional esprit de corps, the best that is thought and done. Thus class is neither threatened as a mode of social division, nor allowed to be determinant. Its very marginalization ensures its persistence.

Hardy clearly adopts this agenda in these early socially conscious texts. Class is crucially important but as a system of layers. He identifies himself with a radical position simply by recognizing the existence of class (Tories, as Briggs points out, did not like to be reminded of it). But this radicalism goes one stage further than that of more orthodox radicals, for instead of regarding class as a barrier that can be transgressed by individual excellence, vitality, or even culture, Hardy's position is one that makes those qualities redundant. *The Hand of Ethelberta* absolutely confirms this point – only by disguising herself forever will Ethelberta be able to transgress. Even then it is a dangerous procedure. Neigh, for example, sustains his class position only by concealing the source of his wealth, the family knacker's yard.

This observation leads to further discrimination. In *Desperate Remedies*, *A Pair of Blue Eyes*, and *The Hand of Ethelberta*, the point of transgression and the guarantee of its ultimate failure are a relationship of work. Companion, architect, entertainer – these guarantee the access as by the same token they put the protagonist in the power of those who employ them. This relationship, it is true, is a very marginal feature of the class relations in these texts; but it is not merely a plot device to bring incongruities together, because this functioning is never really transcended. What makes it important, however, is that the most important text of this period, *Far from the Madding Crowd*, precisely does constitute the social relation as a relation of work. Hardy distances this from the actual world of the reader who belongs, presumably, to the madding crowd. But this distancing only clarifies the relationship. Gabriel is thrust into the subordinate position because he is undercapitalized and therefore inadequately insured (see Williams). His dependence on Bathsheba's employment is preluded by the series of disguises he has to adopt to try to acquire a social function, and, of course, he is really in disguise throughout until he resumes his true role as owner of the means of production. Other characters are classified only by the roles they play. Boldwood, for example, is not an aristocrat but only the nearest thing to it by reason of his economic position in the community. Troy ceases to be a sergeant and becomes a gentleman farmer as soon as he has access to the resources of the farm. Class and subordination are in this novel functions of the social relations of production. Society operates through work, and wealth – as Gabriel shows when he reckons wheat as the equivalent of gold after the storm – is expressed in the terms of a developed, wage-based capitalist economy. The reality of class relations is in this novel heavily disguised as idyll.

The Hand of Ethelberta reverts to contemporary life, and the class system is once more presented as rank. But there are enormous differences from the earlier works. First, as the visit to Neigh's family knacker's yard shows, rank has its actual economic basis. Second, by making herself indispensable to the upper world, Ethelberta turns herself from servant to mistress, which in turn makes her a slave of her own success. The master-servant relationship is, as shown in the parody Manlove practices, a two-way mirror (this is made explicit in *Indiscretion* [32]). More importantly, Ethelberta's manipulative success is challenged by the radical opposition of her stonemason brother, who stands for the class as an active process in opposition to the exploiting class. Gabriel Oak's economic subordination is brought into the urban, contemporary world and calls Ethelberta's mobility a form of treachery. This "comedy in chapters," unlike the Shavian drama it predates, turns into a potential class tragedy: the conflict between collective and personal modes of action that will finally reemerge with *Jude the Obscure*. But this is not merely a matter of representation. There are plenty of representations of this economic relation between classes. Hardy is, I would suggest, almost unique in the midseventies in recognizing this relation to be based only on exploitation. We have only to compare the presentation of class in *Far from the Madding Crowd* and *The Hand of Ethelberta* with Ruskin to see how far out on a limb Hardy is. In *Unto This Last* Ruskin defines wealth as a relationship giving power over others, and he recognizes that this power is the cash nexus that is produced by the division of labor. But in opposition to this view he offers two models of social relationship that are defined by something outside the nexus of cash payment: domestic service and military honor. Hardy seems to satirize this idea explicitly in his novels of the midseventies. Troy's exploitation of the labor relations at Weatherbury shows how effective military ethics are in social life. Ethelbert and Manlove show how domestic service is totally subordinate to economic need. Not only is the Arnoldian pattern of aliens within a hierarchy questioned by the Ruskinian bid to sustain inequality within a rhetoric of social justice; it is exposed as paternalistic nonsense. But after Sol the stonemason has confronted Ethelberta with her class treachery, where, in the portrayal of social relationships, is Hardy to go?

There is nothing either in Hardy's personal situation or in the general cultural situation in 1876 that would enable him to work out the issues raised in *The Hand of Ethelberta*. The most interesting novels of the same year, Eliot's *Daniel Deronda* and Meredith's *Beauchamp's Career*, show how even within the problematic arena of liberal values there is no visible solution to the political choice between self-fulfillment and self-survival. How much less for the class that has no access to resources except by individual mobility and class betrayal? In Hardy's next novel, *The Return of the Native*, social issues move to the margins. The Heathans are economically very primitive, mixing a marginal market activity based not on production but on collecting, with self-sufficiency, and they thus blend into the landscape, which becomes a generalized objective world for the children of outsiders, widow and retired sea captain, who have no personal economic activity at all. Hardy's concerns are, of course, equally abstracted from the actual historical conditions, resembling the confrontation of the romantic subject with no intractable and impersonal real of "Nature" that we find in Ruskin, Pater, and above all, Arnold. The "mind" is modern; the universe it confronts is supposedly "timeless." I have argued elsewhere that Hardy does not merely repeat this modern predicament but represents and goes beyond it, showing subject and object locked in paralytic opposition, but transcended by a necessity that is served neither by romantic rebellion nor by adaptation (which denies inner needs) and that is not available to consciousness separated from action.[15] This opposition is residually manifest in the landscape, which turns out to be not "nature" but, as Eagleton showed, nature as a language,[16] a text on which language is inscribed, its own morphology made up not of a dominant syntax but of many obscure dialectic operations. Opposition of this sort is dramatically evident in the mother's crossing (transgression) of the heath, by which action she confronts the objective world as not merely inscrutable but motiveless, and not therefore supplanting the need to act by wise passiveness.

I think Hardy in this phase is taking upon himself the predicament of what Gramsci would call that of the traditional intellectual with respect to the major discourses within which he can define his being, and shows him confronting an intellectual impasse that cannot be brooked except by transgression of the logical trajectory he confronts. Thus the astronomer of *Two on a Tower* is appropriately awed by the immensity of the universe, but viewing the southern skies, unmapped by his predecessors, he is disgusted by its meaninglessness. He retreats to the alternative discourse of romantic love (the subject as opposed to the object), only to find this no longer available either, to find instead a role as parent, protecting human life in all its insignificance, relating to it by a phrase that in itself is weak and probably borrowed from positivism, but central to Hardy's later development: "loving kindness."

The next phase of Hardy's novel writing – which begins late in 1884 as he starts to write *The Mayor of Casterbridge*, ends with the publication of *Tess of the d'Urbervilles*, and results in three novels as accomplished and powerful as the novels of 1876–1884 are confused and even contrived – coincides with the first phase of the socialist revival in England, when for the first time the influence of Marx was an important factor. In 1884 the Democratic Federation became the Social Democratic Federation, and although it was tiny and schismatic, it made a disproportionate impact on the public through the unemployed demonstrations in Trafalgar Square in 1886 and 1887. In 1888 Annie Besant, who was certainly not a Marxist but who was already sufficiently a heroine of revolutionary sexual politics through her divorce and her espousal of birth control, organized the successful strike of Bryant and May match girls. In 1889, the Dock Strike was the first major victory of unskilled organized labor.

Hardy records none of these events explicitly. But we should take note of a number of circumstances. First, even as Hardy left behind the class question in his early novels, his notebooks show him taking an interest in positivism, which prior to the emergence of Marxism was certainly the strongest intellectual system proposing social progress. The English positivists, as Royden Harrison has shown, befriended Marx and were in the seventies an important influence on radical politics.[17] Hardy's personal contact with Edward Beesley, the most left-wing of the positivists, is evident in 1885, when Beesley wrote to Hardy about his defeat at the Westminster election (though we must not make too much of this; Beesley had less contact with the socialist movement in the 1880s). Hardy would have had plenty of access to socialist theory from 1882 onward. Hyndman's *The Historical Basis of Socialism* leaned heavily on Marx, and Bax and Morris brought out *Socialism: Its Growth and Outcome* in 1884. Journals such as *Justice, Commonweal*, and *Today* rehearsed socialist issues. Hardy's two most distinguished rivals, Gissing and James, both brought out novels explicitly dealing with working-class politics – *Demos* and *The Princess Casamassima*. The note of 1884 without a context in *The Life* that I earlier quoted must surely be a response to this "democratic" upsurge. There are many writers to whom Hardy would have been sympathetic who were interested in the movement – Hardy himself mentioned the Belgian socialist, Laveleye. Carpenter, Symonds, Havelock Ellis, Shaw himself – all these writers recognized that the future of their enlightened ideology was bound up with the emancipation of the working class.

Most important, however, is the recruitment of William Morris in 1883 to the revolutionary socialist movement. Morris had been the leading member of the campaign against church restoration to which Hardy was so opposed. He was the heir of Ruskinian aesthetics and, as Hardy had done in *Far from the Madding Crowd*, he secularized Ruskin. Morris attracted great publicity to the socialist movement by getting arrested in 1887. Throughout the 1880s he lectured tirelessly, and produced two socialist stories, *The Pilgrims of Hope* and *A Dream of John Ball*, and many essays expounding socialism, some of which were collected in *Signs of Change* (1888). No writer could ignore the fact that this dreamy Pre-Raphaelite and guardian of traditional craft values was appearing vociferously and articulately on the barricades.

There is a second striking point about the revival of socialism in the 1880s: how bound up it becomes with feminism. Annie Besant is the obvious example, but Olive Schreiner and Margaret Harkness were both friends of Eleanor Marx, whose lecture on "Shelley's Socialism" in 1888 was as much concerned with Shelley's revolutionary sexual politics as with his democratic ideas. It is, of course, not possible to define how much Hardy would have been aware of any of this activity. I am trying only to define what might have been available; it helps to illuminate some of the features of the fiction Hardy wrote in this period. What is crucial is that class politics and sexual politics are part of the same ferment.

Both *The Mayor of Casterbridge* and *The Woodlanders* are, of course, resolutely distanced from these issues. The first is subjected to a precise displacement in time, and the second explicitly displaced geographically outside the gates of the world. Nevertheless, both have connections with the contemporary slum novels of Gissing, James, Besant, and others, as William Greenslade has shown.[18] Mixen Lane has all the marks of Gissing's Litany Lane (*The Unclassed*), and the woods of Little Hintock are repeatedly compared with slums, which in social discourse of the time are treated as natural deformations. In fact, it is common to make the urban working class, outcast London, darkest London, as displaced and exotic as Hardy's Wessex. One could speculate about the motives for Hardy's displacement, but certainly one of the effects is to shift attention from description to processes – that is, the distance creates a space in which histories take place.

The Mayor of Casterbridge is the story of a man of character, but character is conceived literally as bourgeois man, for what else is the mayor but the leading burgher? Hardy draws on Victorian degeneration myths, the nearest in time being Morris's own *Sigurd the Volsung* (1876), which has great similarities – that is, the original self-made man, whose character is unified by his subjective desire, loses to the adaptive divided man who can keep business and pleasure separate, calculate profit rationally, and deploy others effectively without owning them or taking responsibility for them. Henchard and Farfrae are opposed only within the various parameters of self-help – does one rise by overwhelming the objective world or by understanding it? It depends on the complexity of the objective world. What matters, however, from the viewpoint of this argument is that Henchard is reconstructed by the destructive experience of his evolutionary displacement, not as a new man but as one of a crowd, *les misérables*, and in the process, as Showalter has shown, feminized.[19] It is in the double "negation" of this individuality (and that no man remember me) and his masculinity that Henchard is reborn and that the triumph of Farfrae, Newson, and Elizabeth-Jane is so meaningless. The fall of Henchard replicates the original fall of Gabriel Oak, but the redemption is not a question of rising again; it is a question of embracing obscurity.

The Woodlanders was written between the end of 1885 and the beginning of 1887. Many of Morris's crucial essays appeared in 1885, including "How We Live and How We Might Live," whose title appears to be echoed in Hardy's second paragraph, and "Useful Work versus Useless Toil." Some of the Icelandic allusions in the novel, especially to the theft of Marty's locks by "Loki the Malicious" and the explicit comments about the division of labor in the production of Grace's skirt, which is, of course, what gets caught in the mantrap, seem to make this a novel that calls for comparison with Morris. More important than these local details, *The Woodlanders* inaugurates a general sense of social oppression, of which Marty's useless and piecework labor through the night is the first dramatic instance and the demolition of Giles's cottage the major narrative instance. This general level, however, is clearly abandoned once the story begins to focus on Grace and Fitzpiers. But this general level precisely brings into play the relationship between the social relationship and the gender relationships in the novel, for the economic oppression that is practiced on Marty and Giles by Melbury and Mrs. Charmond is repeated by the gender oppression practiced on Grace and in a sense Mrs. Charmond, and it is at this level that the tensions set up at the beginning of the novel are able to surface and issue in individual rebellion. Again there is a precise parallel to be drawn with Morris, whose *Pilgrims of Hope* shows the political energies of the commune demanding new attitudes toward sexual relationships and particularly toward monogamy. Divorce, which becomes the central issue of Hardy's novel, is a very central component of the Socialist League's manifesto issued in 1885 (Morris was a founding member of the Socialist League). The sexual politics of *The Woodlanders* have to be placed in a general world of alienation – all the characters are abstracted from their own lives because the circumstances of their lives are unresponsive to their desires. Hardy's pessimism in this novel, the sense of unfulfilled intention, is a utopian pessimism, deriving from a sense of what things might be. When Grace and Giles think that divorce laws will enable them to possess one another, they are like children in being taken in by lawyer Beaucock's claim that there is no longer one law for the rich and one for the poor. Sherman is right to see *The Woodlanders* as the novel in which the pessimism closely reflects the class struggles of the time. There is no reason, however, that we should not see it as strategic and conscious. The focus on Grace is a focus on the weakest link in the chain of bourgeois domination.

My intention here is not to provide an analysis of *The Woodlanders* but only to indicate how close Hardy has come to the same preoccupations as those of Morris, and hence how, indirectly, Marxism has become relevant to his project. *Tess of the d'Urbervilles*, I think, moves even closer. Its structure is actually best defined in terms of the Marxist model of the base and superstructure. That model is a means of describing the complex relations between the actual means of production (which are the material basis of a society) and the political and cultural structures that are raised on that basis. Of course, these structures do not simply reflect the base, and Marxists who (like Caudwell) tend to see every cultural manifestation as a metaphor for, let us say, capitalism tend to use it reductively. But if we recognize that the base itself is complex – composed not merely of technological resources but also of the social relations by which those resources are put to work – we shall also recognize that the superstructure must act on the base, that there must be levels of discourse more or less reflective of the base, and that the superstructure has its own history and rhythm, lagging behind in some respects, moving forward in others. Were this not so, the history of humanity would be a continuous marking of time.

I have argued in my detailed analysis of *Tess of the d'Urbervilles* that there are three related levels of discourse. There is first of all a complex and contradictory discourse about Nature, and human nature. The overall pattern of the novel denies that Nature has a holy plan. Tess is like a fly upon a billiard table. Her very excellence as a natural phenomenon, her sexual attractiveness, is her downfall. On the other hand, there is a strong sense in the novel – echoing Havelock Ellis and, among others, Morris – that Tess's downfall is only the product of a repressive attitude toward natural sexuality. Both of these approaches are "true" – that is, they are ways of describing reality – but they are dependent on positions of power within that "reality." When Angel feels the ache of modernism, he is merely thinking about the universe: When Tess says we are on a blighted planet, she is thinking about her drunken father and her numerous brothers and sisters. When Alec and Angel give way to desire, it is to destroy another being. When Tess and the other dairymaids run across the fields, it is to express their own generous vitality. The two sources of power in the novel are gender and class. Tess is finally made into a woman by violation and into a field woman by economic oppression. It is the interaction of modernism, sexual equality, and the demand for economic freedom that constitutes the "justice" that is deferred to the President of the Immortals and withheld from the pure woman hanged for being herself. Hardy sent a copy of the first edition of *Tess of the d'Urbervilles* to William Morris. It is a strange act – he did not know Morris personally and Morris almost certainly would not have appreciated the book. But the act tells us something about the project of the novel, as well as something more about the relationship not so much between Hardy and Marxism as between Marxism (in England) and Hardy.

I think it can be argued that if *Tess of the d'Urbervilles* permits and demands a Marxist reading, the texts that follow are much more problematic. *Jude the Obscure* is a novel about working-class experience as a subjective, isolated, and isolating ordeal. The whole point for both Jude and Sue is that there is no cultural home for them, no articulated class experience except that of the class from which they are by their economic position excluded. Accordingly, I do not regard it as any less radical a novel than *Tess of the d'Urbervilles*, but I think we fail to understand how deep it goes unless we acknowledge that it is a novel written by and about someone to whom Marxist answers are not available. I do not think it is difficult to see why Hardy's distance from a socialist analysis grew after 1891. Socialism itself in Britain was undergoing rapid transformation in the early 1890s after the successful resolution of the Dock Strike, the formation of the Independent Labour Party, and the marginalization of Morris himself. Hardy is no possibilist, and possibilism began to dominate the socialist agenda in these years. The radical "revolutionary" position was occupied by issues of gender and aesthetics. The response to *Tess of the d'Urbervilles* was to the idea of the heroine's purity rather than to her economic degradation. It is important to recall that while there was strong hostility to the novel, there was also very strong support for it, even to the extent of Grant Allen dedicating his "hill top novel," *The Woman Who Did*, to the author of *Tess*. Maverick and individualist as Hardy seems to be on the surface, he belongs to a social group as much as anyone does, and the group identified by his work is that of those disaffected intellectuals dominated by what was called the "new spirit." The group of stories written by Hardy in 1891 – which make up most of *Life's Little Ironies*, "The Son's Veto" for example, or "For Conscience Sake" – represents class as an agent of sexual respectability and repression. "The Fiddler of the Reels," the great story of 1893, combines a recognition of feminine sexuality (as subversive) with an emphasis on the liberating effect of music. Its ruralist guise does not cloak its affinity with George Egerton. "On the Western Circuit" ironically privileges the erotic as text.

But above all, the novel that intervenes between *Tess of the d'Urbervilles* and *Jude the Obscure* inaugurates a new dimension in Hardy's work. The two versions of *The Well-Beloved* – the serial published in *Illustrated London News* in 1892 and the book published after *Jude the Obscure* in 1897 – tell us a great deal about the politics of Hardy's writing. Hillis Miller discusses the two versions with his usual perceptiveness, but by implying that we should read the two versions together, he effectively depoliticizes the texts. In fact, he explicitly compares the novel to Fowles's ideologically pluralist *The French Lieutenant's Woman*.[20] But Hardy gives us two texts, not one text with two endings. The second text is intended to replace the first. That kind of replacement indicates a transition.

The serial version was, according to Miller, written as "something light" to replace the offensive *Tess* for the Tillotson firm. It is, of course, more outrageous than anything in the earlier novel, legitimating as it does an eroticism unrelated to affection or moral stability. At a deeper level, as Swann has suggested, it calls into question empiricist notions of identity, not only by implying that the object of Pierston's love can reappear in different women, but also by having interchangeable names, premarital sex as a custom, and generally a sexual politics that shows "morality" to be relative and historically variable (the lesson Angel Clare learns in Brazil). The serial version stresses Hardy's social message by having Pierston marry Marcia and Avice III. It also adds a long prehistory of well-beloveds through the letters he destroys before the story begins. This throws the focus onto the oppression of women. Marcia recognizes that "she was her husband's property, like one of his statues that he could not sell" (209); Pierston's development, which emerges dramatically after his marriage to Avice III, is primarily one of his recognition of the "barbarism" of the age in which marriage laws make it wrong to commit a simple "act of charity" by letting her go. The story in this version clearly foreshadows the relationship of Sue and Phillotson. Indeed, it makes more explicit the wrongness of the husband's imposing his subjective sexuality on the woman.

Two points emerge from this look at the serial. First, it is clear that the gender issue, particularly marriage, is the focus Hardy moves toward after *Tess of the d'Urbervilles*, because it is there that he has had most response. Class is very important in *Jude the Obscure*, but it is more inexorable than sexual politics. Sue and Jude are released from their marital bondage, but only into deeper economic oppression. There is a Marxist reading of *Jude the Obscure*, but unlike the reading of *Tess of the d'Urbervilles*, it is not a reading that fully accounts for the structure. No reading would. *Jude the Obscure* poses its questions at a level of insolubility that demands not a Marxist reading but (in my view) a Marxist answer. It is the lack of this answer that enables Hardy to write as he does. The nearest text available that proposes answers in Marxist terms, and a novel highly relevant to Hardy's text, is Morris's *News from Nowhere*. But that too is a text that raises more questions than answers. There are no easy answers. It is perhaps significant that Morris, too, ends his literary career in the nineties with stories about sexuality.

The second point is that when Hardy comes to revise *The Well-Beloved*, much of this instant social concern goes. The later text is much more the subjectivist and relativist inquiry Proust was to admire. It is much closer to the poetry. Hardy's poetry remains, of course, a vigorous challenge to the dominant lyric tradition that it deploys, making rhythm manifest as meter, metaphor as simile, "perception" as optics. *The Well-Beloved* in its final version still outrages the conventions of identity, love, and even time and place on which much nineteenth-century fiction is based. But it no longer does so in such an explicit, socially oriented way. To put it another way, while the first version is positively addressing a debate and an audience, the second, like the poetry, exists within a marked, marginal silence. We lose Hardy the hilltop novelist, the spokesman of an enlightened avant-garde, and gain the subversive sage (of course, a subversive sage is still a very paradoxical and disturbing persona).

The "social" as an explicit area of concern, though it reappears in more of the poetry than is sometimes acknowledged, is largely allotted to the epic drama. *The Dynasts* is a text that none of the critiques I have referred to really deals with, although it is Hardy's most explicit and sustained intervention in the public domain, and it is one that preoccupies him throughout his career. The total structure places Hardy very far from any Marxist analysis in the first sense that I have been pursuing. This is not so much because he refuses any notion of historical causality other than the voiceless and mindless will, but rather because there is in *The Dynasts* a radical disjunction between signifier and signified so great as to call in question the function of the signifying process itself. The history the text displays has immense detail and accuracy – if we did not have those daunting photographs of Hardy's Napoleonic library, we would still have an overwhelming sense of how much research is put into it. But it has no before and after. Nothing is changed by the Napoleonic wars; Europe is no different because of them. Neither are the wars really produced. The reader does not need to be aware, for example, that Napoleon is the product of a revolution, rather than just an upstart demagogue. Moreover, this history does not even exist as a moral milieu. It is not very rewarding to try to make discriminations between characters. Some are obviously fatuous (mainly the hereditary monarchs), some are efficient, some have a residual, marginal, private emotional life – but as none of these characters are really able to make choices, none of them are available for praise or blame. History is reduced to spectacle.

John Wain's perceptive comparison of the text to cinema in one sense confirms this view.[21] Not only does the language embody a vivid illusion, but it is an illusion safely on the screen. I think, though, that this idea precisely gives us a purchase on the text. Hardy, as we know, has not been miraculously prophetic by employing a cinematic technique. He would have seen dioramas and phantasmagorias, and some of the illustrations that he had known as a child have this same vivid illusory effect. Spectacle of this sort, however, like the *intention* of some Hollywood movies, is aimed at excluding the spectator from the illusion by awe. *The Dynasts*, I would argue, is a text much less about the Napoleonic wars than about their history. This point is confirmed for me by the overworld, which so far from being a superior consciousness is an excluded consciousness. The Spirits of the Pities, and the Spirits Ironic and Sinister in particular, are responses and postures of the intelligentsia doomed to understand and see but unable to alter in any way what has happened. History, for Hardy, is a text to be read, but not a text that can be altered. In this way, I think *The Dynasts* inscribes the history of the nineteenth-century intellectual. Poets are not, precisely and tragically, the unacknowledged legislators of the world. *The Dynasts* is the morning after *Prometheus Unbound*'s night before.

Critics of Hardy's drama make very little of its title, and yet *dynast* is a rare and strange word. The OED has few references for it; in fact, only one – Mahaffy's *Social Life in Greece* (which Hardy knew) – uses the word in the way Hardy seems to. Milton's "Tenure of Kings" talks of *dynasts* in the context of the *Magnificat*; and it is the Greek text of Mary's praise of God for overthrowing the mighty that Hardy invokes as the only explicit explanation of his title, *at the very end* of the work. *Dynasts* occurs through-out the text in the sense of a social group that has the "making" of history because its desires control the destinies of the lower orders. The high moments of drama are not the political debates, which are wooden and cynical, nor are they the royal passions or military stratagems. They are the moments of questioning – deserters, women, ordinary soldiers whose lives are wrecked on behalf of the dynasts. Warfare is "plied by the Managed for the Managers." Managers in the nineteenth century tended to be running workhouses, theaters, or boarding schools. But Hardy is using the term in a very much more modern sense because here it is not the managers who ply, but the managed. Finally, war is the most appalling and unjustifiable division of labor. Milton's text is, of course, antiroyalist. Mahaffy's, too, is also a very political text – not always radical, it is true. But Hardy feels that fiction, particularly Scott's fiction, is necessary because only by departing from the actual history (which is always the history of the rulers) can we enter an unrecorded plea for injustice, and mete out an unreal punishment for it. This is a comment on the repressive silence of the epic. Hardy's text registers the separation of the knowing intellectual from the process that silences the manipulated agents of history.

As noted, this consideration of lexicon is a long way from Marxism in one sense. And it is precisely that absence which *The Dynasts* is about. We have seen Hardy move close to a picture that accords with Marxist perspectives. We also see him move sharply away, into a kind of cosmic wisdom that leaves him in pain and leaves the world he portrays still full of injustice. Marxism was not, in nineteenth-century England, really an available answer. Hardy could not have gone on writing on its basis, because unlike Morris he could not postpone his vision to dream. Hardy is bereft, with a history that is meaningless and a consciousness that is sharp and unresting. What we have to ask is whether Marxism – and if so, in what form – would be an answer to the questions he asks. I believe it is. I will not have proved that point in this essay, but I hope to have shown, at least, that Marxism enables us to go on asking the questions that Hardy poses throughout his life and to which he would not allow answers that were either unrealistic or unjust. He wanted justice *and* realism, and that is a quest we are still embarked upon.

Notes

1. Thomas Hardy, *Jude the Obscure*, ed. Patricia Ingham (Oxford: Oxford University Press, 1985), 356.
2. Thomas Hardy, *The Dynasts*, ed. Harold Orel (London: Macmillan, 1978), 39.
3. Terry Eagleton, *Against the Grain: Essays 1976–1985* (London: Verso, 1986), 40. See also his introduction to *Jude the Obscure* (London: Macmillan, 1974), 9–20; and *Criticism and Ideology* (London: New Left Books, 1976), 94–95, 130–33. Also see nn. 10–15, below.
4. Christopher Caudwell, *Romance and Realism: A Study in Bourgeois Literature*, ed. Samuel Hynes (Princeton: Princeton University Press, 1970), 88–94. This was written, of course, before 1937, but was published too late to have been an influence on most of the other "Marxist" critics I discuss.
5. Raymond Williams, *The English Novel from Dickens to Lawrence* (London: Chatto & Windus, 1970), 95–118. There is a different version in *The Country and the City* (London: Chatto & Windus, 1973), 197–214.

6.   C. S. B. Swann, "Hardy's Fiction: 'An Attempt to Give Artistic Form to a True Sequence of Things,'" *Essays in Poetics* 9 (1984), 67–101.

7.   Arnold Kettle, *An Introduction to the English Novel* (1951; London: Hutchinson, 1961), vol. II, 50–64. See also his "Hardy the Novelist: A Reconsideration" (1966), in *The Nineteenth-Century Novel: Critical Essays and Documents*, ed. Arnold Kettle (London: Heinemann Educational, 1972), 262–73.

8.   George W. Sherman, *The Pessimism of Thomas Hardy* (Rutherford, N.J.: Fairleigh Dickinson University Press, 1976).

9.   Penny Boumelha, *Thomas Hardy and Women: Sexual Ideology and Narrative Form* (Brighton: Harvester Press, 1982); George Wotton, *Thomas Hardy: Towards a Materialist Criticism* (Dublin: Gill & Macmillan, 1985).

10. Terry Eagleton, *Walter Benjamin: or, Towards a Revolutionary Criticism* (London: Verso, 1981), 129.

11. Florence Emily Hardy, *The Life of Thomas Hardy* (London: Macmillan, 1962), 57–61.

12. Thomas Hardy, *An Indiscretion in the Life of an Heiress*, ed. Terry Coleman (London: Century Publishing, 1985), 49–50. All references are to this edition.

13. G. A. Cohen, *Karl Marx's Theory of History: A Defense*, rev. ed. (Oxford: Oxford University Press, 1979), 83.

14. Asa Briggs, "The Language of 'Class' in Early Nineteenth-Century England," *Essays in Labour History*, eds. Asa Briggs and John Saville (London: Macmillan 1967), 43–73.

15. John Goode, *Thomas Hardy: The Offensive Truth* (Oxford: Basil Blackwell, 1988).

16. Terry Eagleton, "Nature as Language in Thomas Hardy," *Critical Quarterly* 13 (1971): 155–72.

17. Royden Harrison, *Before the Socialists: Studies in Labour and Politics, 1861–1881* (London: Routledge & Kegan Paul, 1965).

18. W. Greenslade, "The Concept of Degeneration, 1880–1910" (Ph.D. diss., University of Warwick, 1982), 111–97.

19. Elaine Showalter, "The Unmanning of the Mayor of Casterbridge," *Critical Approaches to the Fiction of Thomas Hardy*, ed. Dale Kramer (London: Macmillan, 1979), 99–115.

20. J. Hillis Miller, introduction to Thomas Hardy, *The Well-Beloved* (London: Macmillan, 1975), 17.

21. John Wain, introduction to Thomas Hardy, *The Dynasts* (London: Macmillan, 1965), ix.

CHAPTER 8

Sue Bridehead and the New Woman

I

Criticism of *Jude the Obscure* usually takes it to be a *representation*; hence, however hard such analysis tries to come to terms with the novel's radicalism, it is inevitably ideological. Criticism of this kind necessarily dissolves the specific literary effect of the text, the author's 'production', into its component sources which are situated in 'reality' – that is to say, the ideological structure of experience by which we (including Hardy) insert ourselves into the hegemony. But *Jude* is such a truly radical novel precisely because it takes reality apart; that is, it doesn't merely reproduce reality, even as a 'series of seemings', but exposes its flaws and its mysti-fications. You cannot come to terms with the novel either as a moral fable or as an exhibition of social reality because it is the very terms of those structures, their ideological base, that it interrogates. After the death of her children, before she has, as they say, *broken down*, Sue tells Jude: 'There is something external to us which says, "You shan't!" First it said, "You shan't learn!" Then it said, "You shan't labour!" Now it says, "You shan't love!"' (VI. ii) This very precisely defines the overdetermined form of the novel. Learning, labour and love – the three human activities on which bourgeois ideology bases its libertarian pride – are shown to be denied by 'something external'. In most novels, in Hardy's own earlier work, these three are accommodated within 'the interstices of a mass of hard prosaic reality' (*Far from the Madding Crowd*, LVI); even Tess is left free finally to love. Here it really doesn't matter what the external is, whether nature's inexorable law or social oppression. What matters is that it is external; it might as well be God. But although Jude comments that this is bitter, he does not answer when Sue replies that it is true. Because he cannot answer, he has no way to stop her from seeking to pro-pitiate this external with the mortification of the flesh, the terrible flesh. A further precision is needed in our reading of this passage. Sue can say this because she is more articulate than Jude, who has *already broken down* by returning absurdly to the centre of his dream (Christminster). That is why he is horrified by her denial of love. Jude on his own account, even with Sue's aid, can confront and articulate what forbids learning and labour (and confront it as ideological). But it is only Sue who can demystify love and identify its determinants. And that is what most critics cannot take, and why criticism of the novel tends to sprawl from fiction to reality when it comes to Sue.

Most accounts of *Jude the Obscure* cannot cope with Sue except by reference to some ideologically structured reality. This usually enables the critic to say one of two things, both of which are demonstrably false representations of the text: either that Hardy's presentation of Sue is inconsistent, or that she is a neurotic type of the frigid woman. The most extreme version of the second reading is, of course, Lawrence's, which sees Sue as 'no woman' but a witch, whose attraction to Jude in the first place is in reaction to the incomprehensible womanliness of Arabella:

> And this tragedy is the result of over-development of one principle of human life at the expense of the other; an over-balancing; a laying of all the stress on the Male, the Love, the Spirit, the Mind, the Consciousness; a denying, a blaspheming against the Female, the Law, the Soul, the Senses, the Feelings.[1]

I don't need to stress the sexism of Lawrence's account; it is remarkably like that of the reactionary reviewers such as Mrs Oliphant and R. Y. Tyrell whom Havelock Ellis implicitly rebuked when he said that to describe Sue as neurotic was to reveal an attitude which considers 'human sexual relationships to be as simple as those of the farmyard'.[2] But I think that Lawrence is important because what he identifies as Sue's 'maleness' is her articulateness:

> That which was female in her she wanted to consume within the male force, to consume it in the fire of understanding, of giving utterance. Whereas an ordinary woman knows that she contains all understanding, that she is the unutterable which man must forever continue to try to utter.

What is unforgivable about Sue is her utterance, her subjecting of experience to the trials of language. Lawrence, underneath the hysterical ideology, seems very acute to me, for he recognises that Sue is destructive because she utters herself – whereas in the ideology of sexism, the woman is an image to be uttered. That is to say, woman achieves her womanliness at the point at which she is silent and therefore can be inserted as 'love' into the world of learning and labour; or rather, in Lawrence's own terms, as the 'Law' which silences all questions.

The most available feminist inversion of Lawrence's ideology makes the inconsistencies of Sue's character part of the limitations of the novelist himself. Kate Millett on the one hand affirms Sue's rationality ('Sue is only too logical. She has understood the world, absorbed its propositions, and finally implemented that guilt which precipitated her own self-hatred. Nothing remains to her but to destroy herself');[3] but on the other hand she clearly feels that Hardy loads the dice against Sue because of his own uncertainty, so that a woman who can be articulated by the feminist as 'an intelligent rebel against sexual politics' is presented to us as 'by turns an enigma, a pathetic creature, a nut, and an iceberg'. She complains that we are never allowed to see Sue's motivation and processes of change, but decides that the clue to Sue, as to Arabella, is that they both despise womanhood, and that in Sue's case, this makes her hold sexuality in terror. It is not that Millett doesn't recognise the validity of Hardy's representation; it is rather that Hardy himself doesn't understand what defeats her.

I want to try to show that both approaches to Sue are wrong, but more than this, that a significant silence in both critics indicates the way in which they are wrong – and that this, in turn, indicates where the fictive effect of the novel displaces its own ideology in a mirror. For it is quite remarkable how many critics either despise Sue or blame Hardy for the confusion without ever asking whether the difficulty resides in the ways in which we articulate the world. Perhaps the most revealing recent account is John Lucas's.[4] Lucas finds *Jude* a less achieved novel than *Tess*, because by making Sue so unrepresentative, and failing to place her against some concept of womanhood ('we need more in the way of women than the novel actually gives us'), Hardy fails to enable us to decide how much of the tragedy resides in the artificial system of things, and how much in the 'inexorable laws of nature' which make women what they are. Hardy, it is true, had already created a 'pure woman', but maybe we should ask whether the woman in *Jude* isn't precisely the question that is posed against that strange creation. Tess is the subject of the novel: that makes her inevitably an object of the reader's consumption (no novel has ever produced so much of what Sontag required in place of hermeneutics, namely, an erotics of art). But Sue is not the centre of the novel, she exists as a function of Jude's experience, hence as an object for him. It is surely possible that the questions come from her inability to take shape as that object. Lucas says that while we can understand why Sue shies away from Phillotson, the fact that she shies away from Jude makes her pathological, for although sex can be oppressive, it '*is*, or *ought to be* mutual' (my italics). Millett, we have noticed, says that Sue hates her sexuality; Lawrence, that she is sexless. First of all, as I shall show, this is not really true. What is true, however, is that Sue exposes the ideology of Lucas's statement. You can't, I think (as Millett says), be solid about the class system and muddled about sexual politics. These critics are muddled about both, and they are muddled because neither Hardy nor Sue will let go of the questions.

II

When Sue has retreated back into her marriage with Phillotson, Jude poses what I take to be the fundamental ideological question posed by the novel and found unforgivable by the critics who cannot take Sue:

> 'What I can't understand in you is your extraordinary blindness now to your old logic. Is it peculiar to you, or is it common to woman? Is a woman a thinking unit at all, or a fraction always wanting its integer?' (VI. iii)

If this question is asked in the novel it is surely naïve to ask it of the novel. What is more important is that this question should be asked; it poses for Sue only one of two possibilities – that the nature of her blindness to her own logic must be explained either by her 'peculiarity', or by her belonging to womanhood. Either way, she is committed to being an image, and it is this that pervades the novel. Nobody ever confronts Jude with the choice between being a man or being peculiar. The essential thing is that Sue must be available to understanding. We might want to deduce that Hardy feels the same way as Jude at this point, but I think to do so would go both against the consistency of the novel and against Hardy's whole career as a writer. Twenty years before he wrote *Jude*, Hardy had made Bathsheba Everdene say: ' "It is difficult for a woman to define her feelings in language which is chiefly made by men to express theirs" ' (*Far from the Madding Crowd*, LI). He built a career as a writer out of the very mediations that woman as subject has to create to define her own subjectivity. The plots that turn on caprice, the scenes which reach outside the interaction of manners, the images which embody contradiction, are all constructs made by the novelist to articulate those unspeakable (though not unutterable) feelings. In *Jude*, for the first time in his major fiction, the woman is no longer the vessel of those mediations, but the object of male understanding. Sue not only speaks for herself because she is an intelligent rebel; she is called on to speak for herself – to place herself in relation to other women and to their ways of feeling. She several times has to relate her particularity to what all women are like 'really'. In other words, she has to affirm that she is a *woman*, or admit her ethereal nature – her 'peculiarity'. If we think about the novel naturalistically, without any ideological idyllicising of love (it '*is* or *ought to be* mutual'), we might ask ourselves about the absurdity of Jude's lack of understanding. Sue has been driven around the country by prejudice and poverty, she is stuck in Christminster by Jude's obsession, and now all her children have been killed by Jude's son whom she has made her own. Our perfect union, she tells Jude, is stained with blood. But of course we don't consider it naturalistically, because we don't ever ask what is happening to Sue; because it is rather a question of Sue happening to Jude. So what matters is where this reaction puts her, rather than why it comes about.

Sue is more than anything an image; that is literally how she comes into Jude's life, as a photograph, and how she is continually represented to us throughout the novel – dressed in Jude's clothes, walking in the distance with Phillotson, looking like a heap of clothes on the floor of St Silas's church. But if she is an image, it is a vital part of this image that it has a voice, and hence a logic. Although logic and image play contrasting and reinforcing roles in relation to one another at different points in the novel, it is the relationship between them which calls in question the ideological alternative between peculiarity, on one hand, and the nature of woman, on the other. Sue thus has an instrumentality which makes it irrelevant to ask what kind of ordeal she is undergoing, at least until the novel moves towards the shared experience of Jude and Sue in the Aldbrickharn section. For example, at the very beginning Jude sees her haloed in the Christ-minster ecclesiastical art shop, while we see her buying pagan statues: a relatively simple juxtaposition of false image and conscious decision. But although Hardy presents her logic as having a potential subjectivity (that is, Sue's purchase of the statue is private, tentative, naïve and confused – it could be the frail start of an emancipation), by the time this logic has come to Jude's notice it is formed and decisive, something for him to understand and adjust his own attitude by. I don't think that this confusion entails confusion on Hardy's part, for it is as a confusing image that Sue is effective in breaking down Jude's illusions. Nor do I think that it is because she is in some way pathological. Sue has a potential coherence which is kept at bay by her function. If she is in any sense to be seen as abnormal, it is only in the sense that neurosis becomes normative in Freud because it exposes what a 'healthy' state of mind represses.

The question of her sexuality is crucial in this. It isn't an easy question. Jude himself calls her sexless before the consummation, then explicitly withdraws it when she gives in, only to repeat it in the last section when he is confronted with her return to Phillotson. And that seems to me what we are supposed to feel – an extreme confusion. But this confusion is not seen to reside in her personality; rather, it resides in the insertion of her dual role of image and logic into the world experienced by Jude. From the start this opens up a gap between what she actually says and the way that it is taken. When she tells Jude about the undergraduate who is supposed to have died of unrequited love, she cites it as an example of '"what people call a peculiarity in me"' but immediately goes on to affirm that her peculiarity lies merely in having no fear of men because she knows they are not always out to molest you. The differentiation here is cultural: '"I have not felt about them what most women are taught to feel."' Jude makes it biologistic. Equally there is no mystery about why she never became the undergraduate's mistress: '"He wanted me to be his mistress, in fact, but I wasn't in love with him"' (III. iv). It seems very straight-forward, and the undergraduate's claim that he died of a broken heart is surely intended to be preposterous. That is, until Jude's reception of the story is defined: 'Jude felt much depressed; she seemed to get further and further away from him with her strange ways and curious unconsciousness of gender' (III. iv). The only sexual terror in this seems to me to be Jude's – the sense that there must be something unnatural in a woman who won't give way to a man she doesn't love. And yet at the same time, what Sue affirms seems to offer very different possibilities: '"I suppose, Jude, it is odd that you should see me like this and all my things hanging there? Yet what nonsense! They are only a woman's clothes – sexless cloth and linen"' (III. iii). It seems to suggest, if only fragmentarily (though it goes with Aunt Drusilla's story of Sue as a child, her resistance to invidious comparison with Arabella, the adoption of Jude's son, and 'that complete mutual understanding' between her and Jude at the fair), a repressed version of a sexuality not possible in the novel itself.

That is all very well, but it is still true that Sue clearly doesn't want to consummate her relationship with Jude, and that she retreats into the most conventional guilt about their sexual relationship when the children are dead. But I think that if we take Sue's function into account, we cannot make the mistake of thinking that there is some inherent inconsistency in her characterisation. Again it is a question of the relationship of the image to the logic. For what teems to me to be most truly radical about this novel is that sexuality is not left as a kind of idyllic enclave to that external denial too. We have to bear in mind what the meaning of the marriage to Phillotson is. It comes out of that dislocation between logic and image which Sue enacts and which Jude never emancipates her from. Marriage has to do, as Phillotson makes clear, with the regularisation of the senti-ments, the ordering of sexuality in terms which will be socially effective. The evocation of Mill in thus context is not, as Eagleton says, bourgeois liberalism;[5] it is rather the taking of that affirmation into the area at which the ideology works most opaquely, the point at which the artificial system of things leagues itself with the laws of nature. Lucas quotes as an example of Hardy's muddle the passage about the young women in the dormitory:

> their tender feminine faces upturned to the flaring gas-jets which at intervals stretched down the long dormitories, every face bearing the legend 'The Weaker' upon it, as the penalty of the sex wherein they were moulded, which by no possible exertion of their willing hearts and abilities could be made strong while the inexorable laws of nature remain what they are. (III. iii)

Strictly theoretically, this might constitute an evasion (is it social oppres-sion or the laws of nature that make women the weaker sex?), but the same point has to be made about this that is made about Sue's representative-ness: it is the area of confusion between the two which constitutes the basis for the novel's question. Does Hardy mean to suggest the possibility that the laws of nature might change? Surely to do so calls into question the whole phenomenology of the narrative. This is a 'pretty, suggestive, pathetic sight', like the sleeping young women, an arena of understanding that slips out of our grasp as soon as it is glimpsed. Such contiguity of nature and society is exactly what constitutes the ideology of marriage. Sue's challenge to marriage is a challenge to the social structure itself, as Gillingham realises: '"if people did as you want to do, there'd be a general domestic disintegration. The family would no longer be the social unit"' (IV. iv). The Shelleyan counter to this is not marked by its sexlessness. *Epipsychidion*, which Sue invokes shortly after this, is about a love which evolves itself in transcendence of a prison, as some of the lines she omits make clear.

> High, spirit-wingèd Heart! who dost forever
> Beat thine unfeeling bars with vain endeavour,
> Till those bright plumes of thought, in which arrayed
> It over-soared this low and worldly shade,
> Lie shattered; and thy panting, wounded breast
> Stains with dear blood its unmaternal nest! (II. 13–18)

The last line surely reminds us of the blood-stained perfect union. Physical sexuality is continually implicated with marriage, and those early chapters in Aldbrickham are about the subject of marriage and 'the other thing' (sexuality) together, because sexuality is blood-stained. Once they have children, Jude and Sue have to live the economic life of the couple. In a sense Sue is right to see the children's death as retribution. It is the payment for a return to 'Greek joyousness'. Throughout the novel, what Jude and Sue aspire to is comradeship. This has to define itself against marriage, and thus against 'sexuality'. And yet, there can be no doubt that the real making of this comradeship comes in those few pages between the consummation and the return to Christminster. It is just, however, that it cannot descend into the world of actuality without being destroyed. And that is what Sue recognises in her mortification at the end. She and Jude were wrong to make their relationship physical because you cannot be comrades in a world of domestic gins.

As I have argued, Sue has to perform the function of articulating all this. The pattern of openness and retreat recognises the war between logic and image. But that is to put it too metaphysically; Sue is only bodiless in so far as the body of the woman is a basis of capitalist reproduction, and therefore not her own. At this point I should stress that I am not trying to find an apology for Sue. It is not a question of discovering a psychology or making her representative. What makes Sue effective is her function in the novel, which is the function of an exposing image – that is to say, of an image carrying its own logic which is not the logic of the understandable, comprising both what she utters and what she seems, the gap between them and the collusion they make. As this image she destroys the lives of the order-loving individuals who aspire out of their loneliness through her. It is this destruction, however, that uncovers the determinants of both their aspiration and their loneliness. The sexual fascination of Sue and its demand for comradeship exposes the very impossibility of sexuality. Outside the field of possibility which she calls attention to, there is always the external that limits the field. Where I think we can go so wrong in this novel is to treat it in terms of a representation which we then find incomprehensible. It is the incomprehensibility that constitutes the novel's effect; the incomprehensibility of Sue (who as an image is offered for comprehension) is one way at least in which the incomprehensibility of the world (i.e. bourgeois ideology) is offered. To seek to tie her down to representativeness, or to the explicable, would be to postulate that ideology is 'false consciousness'. But we are talking about a literary effect and it is the literary function of Sue as part of what Hardy produces in this novel that constitutes the basis of our understanding. And the case of Sue is relatively specific.

III

Hardy in the 'Postscript' of 1912 cites, perhaps disingenuously, a German critic who said that Sue was the first delineation in fiction of the woman of the feminist movement. In fact, as Elaine Showalter establishes, feminism is dominant in fiction already by the time Hardy writes *Jude*.[6] And more than this, Sue clearly belongs to a literary variant of the feminist heroine which became fashionable in English fiction after the first performance in England of *Hedda Gabler* in 1891, and which came to be known as the New Woman. A. R. Cunningham gives an informative account of this variant in 'The "New Woman Fiction" of the 1890s',[7] showing how other texts before *Jude* have heroines who cite Mill and Spencer and aspire to the emancipation which is doomed 'either through personal weakness or social law', and who even in some cases retreat like Sue into Christianity. While the better-known writers such as Grant Allen and Sarah Grand celebrate the New Woman largely as a figure of purity, other writers (most notably George Egerton) use the type as a means of confronting the displaced sexuality of woman. What I think characterises Hardy is that he uses this literary device not as a subject offered to the reader's amazement, but as an active force within the novel which answers to the buried ideology of the questing hero. In other words, whereas

Arabella limits Jude's dream, Sue translates his dream into questions, taking him beyond the bewilderment of 'the artificial system of things' into the bewilderment of nature's inexorable law. Nevertheless she does this as an image, and coherence is neither her consistency nor Hardy's, but the persistent way in which she exposes the limits of meaning. Although this is clearly a subject requiring elaboration, I want (rather than placing Sue in her immediate context as the New Woman) to see the novel in terms of the larger context of feminist literature at the end of the nineteenth century by relating it briefly to the best feminist text of that period, *The Story of An African Farm*.

Olive Schreiner's novel appeared in 1883 and there was a first edition in Hardy's library, though I have no idea whether he read it, and I am not trying to claim that it influenced him. More importantly, it seems to me, the relationship of Schreiner's novel to ideology shares a great deal with that of Hardy's. It is not accidental that Schreiner's text gets treated in very similar ways to Hardy's. Even Elaine Showalter says that matters of plot and construction were beyond Schreiner, and that what marks her writing is its ardour rather than its art. Schreiner as a writer, in fact, gets treated rather like Sue as a character – the talented neurotic who was unable to keep up any significant level of productivity. Of course there isn't much after *The Story of An African Farm*, but to have achieved that much seems fairly remarkable, and it is clear to me at least that it is a carefully structured text, positing many voices against one another, not – obviously – in a way that makes for an identifiable coherence or for a comfortably distanced fiction. But the relationship of Waldo to Lyndall is a liaison of speech, each of them stimulated into thought and given voice by a 'stranger' (the traveller who interprets Waldo's carving, the lover through whom Lyndall experiences the conditions of female sexuality); they are only able to communicate because they do not get entrammelled in sexuality: '"I like you so much, I love you." She rested her cheek softly against his shoulder. "When I am with you I never know that I am a woman and you are a man; I only know that we are both things that think."'[8] As well as this possibility of a comradeship making language the bridge which 'reality' denies to both of them, what is also important in relation to *Jude* is that Lyndall should define the difference between man and woman as the difference between expecting to work and being expected to seem:

'It is not what is done to us, but what is made of us,' she said at last, 'that wrongs us. No man can be really injured but by what modifies himself. We all enter the world little plastic beings, with so much natural force perhaps, but for the rest – blank; and the world tells us what we are to be, and shapes us by the ends it sets before us. To you it says – *Work*; and to us it says – *Seem*! To you it says – As you approximate to man's highest ideal of God, as your arm is strong and your knowledge great, and the power to labour is with you, so you shall gain all that human heart desires. To us it says – Strength shall not help you, nor knowledge, nor labour. You shall gain what men gain, but by other means. And so the world makes men and women.

'Look at this little chin of mine, Waldo, with the dimple in it. It is but a small part of my person; but though I had a knowledge of all things under the sun, and the wisdom to use it, and the deep loving heart of an angel, it would not stead me through life like this little chin. I can win money with it, I can win love; I can win power with it, I can win fame. What would knowledge help me? The less a woman has in her head the lighter she is for climbing. I once heard an old man say, that he never saw intellect help a woman so much as a pretty ankle; and it was the truth. They begin to shape us to our cursed end,' she said, with her lips drawn in to look as though they smiled, 'when we are tiny things in shoes and socks. We sit with our little feet drawn up under us in the window, and look out at the boys in their happy play. We want to go. Then a loving hand is laid on us: "Little one, you cannot go," they say; "your little face will burn, and your nice white dress be spoiled." We feel it must be for our good, it is so lovingly said; but we cannot understand; and we kneel still with one little cheek wistfully pressed against the pane. Afterwards we go and thread blue beads, and make a string for our neck; and we go and stand before the glass. We see the complexion we were not to spoil, and the white frock, and we look into our own great eyes. Then the curse begins to act on us. It finishes its work when we are grown women, who no more look out wistfully at a more healthy life; we are contented. We fit our sphere as a Chinese woman's foot fits her shoe, exactly, as though God had made both – and yet He knows nothing of either. In some of us the shaping to our end has been quite completed. The parts we are not to use have been quite atrophied, and have even dropped off; but in others, and we are not less to be pitied, they have been weakened and left. We wear the bandages, but our limbs have not grown to them; we know that we are compressed, and chafe against them.'[9]

That is what constitutes the unattainability of the woman; being expected to seem, she cannot talk unless she is able not to be a woman. In that gap between talking and seeming exists not only the character of Lyndall, but also the very form of the novel. The reality of the novel is more highly fragmented than many other texts of the period, and yet the writing itself acts out its ideological commitment to the Emersonian unity which is so often noticed in *The Story of An African Farm* – noticed, without its being seen as the instrument which makes possible the novel's own particular version of comradeship. Formally, this Emersonian unity comes to a head when Waldo's life is suddenly presented as phases of our life. In terms of the novel's meaning it is there in the final consolation of the hunter (a feather from the white bird of Truth) and the commitment Waldo makes to dreams. The form of the novel, that is to say, is instrumental.

But the instrumentality which the text achieves through its form must be defined in terms of its ideological recognition. When the stranger is telling Waldo of the hunter's search for truth, he makes it a precondition of that search that the hunter releases the birds of certain concepts from their cage: 'He went to his cage, and with his hands broke down the bars, and the jagged iron tore his flesh. It is sometimes easier to build than to break.'[10] The Emersonian commitment has to be seen in the context of this total demystification. Patiently the novel erodes all the ideological supports of the characters, so that it is the very fracturing of form that gives the novel its instrumentality. Now a fiction is a representation – it is itself an image, so that to provide a text which is a coherent representation would be the same as being understandable. And I have tried to show what constitutes Sue's effectivity is that she isn't – that she constitutes an image which breaks down the certainties through her own logic. This is, self-consciously, the aesthetic of *The Story of An African Farm*: the preface to the second edition clearly foreshadows the 'series of seemings' which follow ('the method of the life we all lead [where] nothing can be prophesied', as opposed to 'the stage method'). Significantly, both Schreiner and George Egerton move towards fragmented form. An Egerton story is not only short, it is chopped. And it is also strictly speaking incomprehensible. The heroine of 'A Cross Line', for example, is able to speak to the stranger, but what she says is enigmatic and she only goes to him because he accepts the enigma. The account of woman here picks up all the themes – image, enigma, liar:

> Then she fancies she is on the stage of an ancient theatre out in the open air, with hundreds of faces upturned towards her. She is gauze-clad in a cobweb garment of wondrous tissue. Her arms are clasped by jewelled snakes, and one with quivering diamond fangs coils round her hips. Her hair floats loosely, and her feet are sandal-clad, and the delicate breath of vines and the salt freshness of an incoming sea seems to fill her nostrils. She bounds forward and dances, bends her lissom waist, and curves her slender arms, and gives to the soul of each man what he craves, be it good or evil. And she can feel now, lying here in the shade of Irish hills with her head resting on her scarlet shawl and her eyes closed, the grand intoxicating power of swaying all these human souls to wonder and applause. She can see herself with parted lips and panting, rounded breasts, and a dancing devil in each glowing eye, sway voluptuously to the wild music that rises, now slow, now fast, now deliriously wild, seductive, intoxicating, with a human note

of passion in its strain. She can feel the answering shiver of feeling that quivers up to her from the dense audience, spellbound by the motion of her glancing feet, and she flies swifter and swifter, and lighter and lighter, till the very serpents seem alive with jewelled scintillations. One quivering, gleaming, daring bound, and she stands with outstretched arms and passion-filled eyes, poised on one slender foot, asking a supreme note to finish her dream of motion. And the men rise to a man and answer her, and cheer, cheer till the echoes shout from the surrounding hills and tumble wildly down the crags. The clouds have sailed away, leaving long feathery streaks in their wake. Her eyes have an inseeing look, and she is tremulous with excitement. She can hear yet that last grand shout, and the strain of that old-time music that she has never heard in this life of hers, save as an inner accompaniment to the memory of hidden things, born with her, not of this time.

And her thoughts go to other women she has known, women good and bad, school friends, casual acquaintances, women workers – joyless machines for grinding daily corn, unwilling maids grown old in the endeavour to get settled, patient wives who bear little ones to indifferent husbands until they wear out – a long array. She busies herself with questioning. Have they, too, this thirst for excitement, for change, this restless craving for sun and love and motion? Stray words, half confidences, glimpses through soul-chinks of suppressed fires, actual outbreaks, domestic catastrophes, how the ghosts dance in the cells of her memory! And she laughs, laughs softly to herself because the denseness of man, his chivalrous conservative devotion to the female idea he has created blinds him, perhaps happily, to the problems of her complex nature. Ay, she mutters musingly, the wisest of them can only say we are enigmas.[11]

The point about this passage is that it is a self-communing – it offers what the understanding of the good husband leaves out, what is inexplicable to the new lover. I'm here trying to talk about form and content at once: both the structure and the portrayal move towards that inconsistency which constitutes Sue's effectiveness. The New Woman is most effective in that sense, not because she reads John Stuart Mill, has reservations about the exploitation of her sexuality, or submits to the external (death, the lover, God), but because that dance opens up the ideological structure of reality. The end of *Hedda Gabler* sums up the challenge to intelligibility: '"People just don't do things like that."'

Notes

References in the text are to the chapter divisions of Hardy's novels.

1. 'Study of Thomas Hardy' in E. D. McDonald (ed.) *Phoenix II: The Posthumous Papers of D. H. Lawrence* (London, 1967), p. 509.
2. R. G. Cox (ed.), *Thomas Hardy: The Critical Heritage* (London, 1970), p. 311.
3. Kate Millett, *Sexual Politics* (London, 1972), pp. 130–4.
4. *The Literature of Change: Studies in the Nineteenth-Century Provincial Novel* (Hassocks, Sussex, 1977), pp. 188–91.
5. Introduction to *Jude the Obscure*, New Wessex edn. (London, 1975), p. 15.
6. Elaine Showalter, *A Literature of Their Own: British Women Novelists from Brontë to Lessing* (London, 1977), pp. 182–215.
7. *Victorian Studies*, vol. xvii (1974), pp. 177–86.
8. Olive Schreiner, *The Story of An African Farm*, 2 vols. (London, 1883), vol. ii, p. 94.
9. Ibid., vol. ii, pp. 39–42.
10. Ibid., vol. i, p. 301.
11. George Egerton, *Keynotes* (London, 1893), pp. 19–21.

CHAPTER 9

Woman and the Literary Text

I want to ask whether literary analysis can be valuable to women's studies. This is very different from asking whether 'literature' can be valuable. Obviously social historians can read play, novels and poems as well as anybody else, and there is no reason why they should not use them as documents that 'reflect' a reality – indeed, given the particular importance of the novel in the emergence of a distinct literature aimed at a female audience, that genre at least forms an unavoidable body of evidence. But they will be aware that what a novel reflects is mediated by its fictional nature, by the determination of its characteristics, by the history of forms, and by the highly specialized productive situation of the writer. And they will be aware of them as *caveats*. Literary analysis, on the contrary, has these very mediations as its object of study, for they constitute the 'literariness' of the literary text.[1] It is a question of whether such a study has anything to offer a programme of women's studies, and it is a question to which I do not have a confident answer. What I propose to do is to suggest a model of the way in which such analysis could be applied. If this has an arrogant, take-it-or-leave-it air about it, I should add at once that the context of women's studies itself seems to me to demand a radical revision of the procedures of literary analysis, and that what will be offered should not look like the literary criticism currently practised in the academies.

My starting point must be an apparently paradoxical one: that strictly a text illustrates nothing but what it is. To see it simply as a reflection of actuality (even allowing for distortions) or as a *response* to social realities postulates an interior, a removable essence which it does not have. If we can *interpret* a text, as Freud interpreted dreams, then we are either failing to represent its articulation (for texts are not dreams but the products of intentional work) or we are implying that the text has failed to transform its material, has failed to be irreducible. At the same time, the articulation itself is not independent of economic and ideological determinants, for it is made in a specific mode of production and the material it makes up (in both senses of the word) is a representation of 'reality', and a representation which is undoubtedly ideological in, at least, the largest sense of the term, in which it is axiomatic that all people, to live within society at all, must live in some relationship to whatever is the dominant ideology. In most cases a literary text will have a very particular relationship to ideology in general. What we have then is not a single relationship with ideology (illustration, reflection, response, or whatever) but a sequence of relations. First a text is a *project* which may be ideological (that is attempting to serve an ideology or oppose it from within it). Secondly, it is a project realized within determined circumstances which limit the questions it can ask, give it *margins* which rule it off from that about which it is compelled to be silent. Finally, it is an *object of production* which realizes the project, as a fiction whose specific effectivity is in making it *visible*, and in making it visible exposes it, in effect makes it *strange*, something new and unfamiliar in which the reader then rerecognizes the 'old and familiar' in new, surprising ways. Insofar as we become conscious not of an ideology trapped secretly 'inside' the text, but of the sense of ideology itself, motivating and shaping the representation, we are in the presence of a *fictional* coherence. On the other hand, insofar as the representation remains untransformed, unexposed, familiarized, we are in the presence of an *ideological* coherence. The decisive criterion is not what we are shown, but what we are allowed to see, which includes what we are not shown too.

The only formal device to be given extensive attention in English language criticism is that of the narrator. Although we should be aware of other structuring devices, it is useful to begin with this because it is precisely what articulates the relationship of the text to ideology itself (as opposed to a particular ideology). For ideology, in the phrase of the French Marxist philosopher Louis Althusser, 'interpellates' the subject: that is to say that it calls upon the free subject to subject itself freely to that to which it is subject. The use of the narrator in fiction constitutes that interpellation because it subjects the reader to a defined subjectivity, and thus, if it is successful, makes it visible. Now, as Kate Millet in her book *Sexual Politics* (1971) has shown, the ideological transformations within sexual politics in the nineteenth century raised to a high level of consciousness the relation of 'female' and 'feminine' and its manifestation on the levels of role, status and temperament. I have chosen for analysis texts which have the questions raised in these transformations as their project, and I have sought to analyse them at the point at which the narrative mode articulates, makes into fiction, that project. My model is an attempt to structure that analysis in terms of the structure of ideology itself.

There are two primary distinctions to be made. The first is between the project (the nature of woman) realized as the *object* of male subjectivity, and the same project realized as the *subject* of woman's own experience. Secondly, within each category of subject (male/female) there is a distinction between hegemonic and estranged subjectivity. That is to say that in the first category (woman-object) the object may be situated in a structure that affirms it, and is thus an *object of consumption*, or it may be a destructuring force, an *object in the way* of a quest for assimilation, an ordeal. In the second category (woman-subject) we can distinguish between the *'free' subject* (woman as subject of experience licensed at least partially by ideology to oppose it), and the *subjected subject* (woman as subject of and to her experience). Beyond this, there is a further distinction to be made (as I have already implied) between texts which articulate the projects fictionally, making visible the ideology which motivates both the project and its realization, and texts which remain fictionally incoherent because the particular ideological commitment to the material is too strong to make a full transformation possible.

We shall not find that there is any mechanical connection between these different sitings within ideology and distinctions of narrative mode, but we shall find that they are given their fictional status by the narrative mode as it is deployed at crucial moments in the novel. Above all this is determined by the *axis of distance* between the woman who is the novel's centre and the narrator (who is in each case identical with the woman but at crucial moments someone else) and the derivative *axis of distance* between the narrator and the reader. The distance may be one of sympathy or cognition or both, and it is thus difficult to state precisely how one measures it, in the abstract, but it is generated both by the events of the novel as they unfold, and by particular linguistic strategies, and in practice it is very precisely controlled. Thus a synthesis of ideological and rhetorical analysis should enable us to avoid reductionism.

Nevertheless it is only a model that I am offering. I do not claim to give a complete account of the texts that I am discussing, nor am I pretending that the model would need no modification confronted with a different range of texts. What I hope is that it will offer a way of going on.

The Girl of the Period

The first stage of the model in which woman is realized as the object of male consumption will obviously include, as its most representative examples, those texts which mythologize the conservative position in the debate about women. But we should be careful not to underestimate this position by seeing it as a merely sentimental idealization. In the late nineteenth century especially, we witness the emergence of a literature which is able to affirm the inferior status of women within a new awareness of the injustice of that status. It can do this because the traditional pieties are underwritten by a hard factual sense of the commodity situation of women. The crucial concept is 'womanliness' which is defined by its opposition to the epicene nature of the modern girl. Thus, for example, Mrs Lynn Linton:[2]

Possessed by a restless discontent with their appointed work, and fired with a mad desire to dabble in all things unseemly, which they call ambition; blasphemous to the sweetest virtues of their sex, which until now have been accounted both their own pride and the safeguard of society; holding it no honour to be reticent, unselfish, patient, obedient but swaggering to the front, ready to try conclusions in aggression, in selfishness, in insolent disregard of duty, in cynical abasement of modesty, with the hardest and least estimable of the men they emulate; *these women of the doubtful gender* have managed to drop all their own special graces while unable to gather up any of the more valuable virtues of men.

('The Epicene Sex', II. 236. My italics)

What is interesting here is not the ideas in themselves (except insofar as they neatly represent the commonest clichés) but the attachment of the moral virtues of 'the womanly woman' (II. 118) to sexual attractiveness. Mrs Linton is fully aware of the degradation of male idealization. In an essay called 'Affronted Womanhood' she writes that 'the idea of the sacredness of womanhood condemns woman to a "moral harem"' (I. 87) and she condemns in 'Feminine Affectations', as 'the real tyrant among women' not the feminist but 'this soft-mannered, large eyed, *intensely womanly* person who says that ... the whole duty of woman lies in unquestioning obedience to man' (I. 92–93 my italics). Nevertheless, even this condemnation makes it clear that the actual power of woman is confined to the one commodity she has – her womanliness. And throughout the book the assault on feminism is related to the economics of sexuality:

To most men, indeed, the feminine strong-mindedness that can discuss immoral problems without blushing is a quality as unwomanly as well developed biceps or a 'shoulder-of-mutton' fist. (I. 132)

The girl of the period is a poor imitation of the mondaine – 'Men are afraid of her and with reason. They may amuse themselves with her for an evening, but they do not readily take her for life' (I. 7). It is not merely an offence against the ideology for a woman to be unwomanly, but bad market research: 'she is acting *against nature* and her *own interests* when she disregards their (men's) advice and offends their taste' (I. 9). And when she moves from the level of temperament to that of role, the economic system is more clearly invoked. Arguing that it is for man to provide and for woman to dispense, she writes:

Any system which ignores this division of labour, and confounds these separate functions, is of necessity imperfect and wrong. (I. 38)

The moral argument which persistently has a theological rhetoric ('her consecration as a helpmeet for man' – II. 118) is always carried by a definition of what is sexually attractive, womanliness, and that in turn is made important because it is woman's only marketable commodity in a world where her only mode of production is marriage.

The potency of these connections can be illustrated by a radical and intelligent letter in Harry Quilter's collection *Is Marriage A Failure?* (1887)[3], signed 'Glorified Spinster, Reading'. It argues strongly that 'As a class women are oppressed and men the oppressors' and even that 'marriage is not essential to a woman's life'. Nevertheless, the declared aim of the letter is to protest against the desecration of 'the venerable sanctuary of wedlock'. 'I do not believe,' she goes on, 'that any woman with a spark of *womanliness* in her could honestly uphold such a doctrine'. And the reason is that it would only mean more 'degradation and oppression of the weaker sex' in 'the race of life'. Again it is notable how we pass from the quasi-religious rhetoric, 'venerable sanctuary' to 'womanliness' and from there to a metaphoric reference to the market economy, 'the race of life'. Most of the letter is a defence of the independent woman, but it is very much in terms of her 'compensations' and marriage is upheld because it offers some contract in a world in which '"might has been right" for long ages'. Quilter's own preface more blatantly stresses the hard economic reality that supports the traditional pieties:

> The purpose of happiness is really no part of the purpose of marriage ... marriage is what it is through the necessities of society; and that so long as society has the same necessities, and finds them fulfilled by marriage, the institution must be considered to be a success, though every married man and woman in the world were unhappy.

The proper study of the ideology of this period would need to analyse the complex turns of language in such texts as these, but I think I have quoted enough to show how the ideology sharpens itself into a religious rhetoric to mediate a hardening economism, and that 'womanliness' becomes the major commodity for women as a class, equivalent to labour in the working class, and thus the most vulnerable, most mythic part of the object. 'Grant that women are the salt of the earth, and the great antiseptic element in society' (I. 107) as Mrs Linton asks us to, and we expect to find in the fiction of the period not chivalry or piety as the major motive, but exchange value.

The texts that belong to this category do not, therefore, relate to ideology as a set of hidden values, but as an affirmative structure confronted with a specific resistance: the awareness of the injustice of the *status* of women. That which tends to meet and overcome the resistance is a realized dogma of *temperament* – the nature of woman or womanliness –

underwritten by economically determined prescriptions of *role*. The narrative mode, in order to dramatize the resisting awareness, must clearly summon the woman as subject, but must equally transform this subject through a strategic manipulation of the axes of distance, into an object of male epistemology so that it may appear as a valuable commodity. The male epistemology may realize itself in the text in a number of ways: as a dramatized male spectator in the text, or as implied male author/reader,[4] or, as in the case of many novels written ostensibly by and for women, as a reflected induction in the mediation of the novel by the implied female author, as though there were a shadowy overseeing audience beyond the immediate reader. We shall see all these means operating in the texts I have chosen to use as examples.

Mrs Oliphant's *Madam*[5] is a novel with a familiar motif: renunciation. The title itself alerts us both to the status and the temperament of the heroine, whose name, in case we miss the point, is Grace. The project of the novel is the continuance of the temperament through suffering and self-denial once the status has been denied. Madam is the second wife of a hysterical invalid squire who, besides being neurotically punctilious about time and dress, has imposed on her a cruel marital condition: she is to be so totally the wife and mother in his house that she is never to see the son she has had before their marriage. Compliant in everything, she only breaks this condition when the son gets into trouble, meeting him in secret in the park of the great house just before dinner. Not only is she late, she betrays her offence by a bramble which is caught in the train of her skirt. It is too much for the squire who is sent into a mortal paroxysm of rage. He lives long enough only to summon his lawyer to attach a codicil to his will disinheriting the children of their marriage if Madam ever sees them again. Forced to renounce her maternal role for a second time, she goes to live abroad with the reprobate son, suffers calumny and the bewildered disgust of her family, and lives out a fruitless devotion. She sees the other children only on her deathbed, the will is bypassed and they are safe from dispossession.

As this summary will suggest, it is a thin and sentimental novel but what is interesting about it is that the renunciation is motivated by an acceptance of rules that are openly seen to be capricious and cruel. This is not just a matter of romantic indignation: the home, which is the theatre of womanliness, is realized as a self-denying facade. Thus, Rosalind, Madam's stepdaughter, has to learn how to be a woman early in the novel by obliterating her own distress:

> She flew like an arrow through the hall, and burst into the sanctuary of domestic warmth and tranquility as if she had been a hunted creature escaping from a fatal pursuit with her enemies at her heels. Her hands were like ice, her slight figure shivering with cold, yet her heart beating

so that she could scarcely draw her breath. All this must disappear before the gentlemen came in. It was Rosalind's first experience in *that strange art that comes naturally to a woman of obliterating herself and her own sensations*; but how was she to still her pulse, to restore her colour, to bring warmth to her chilled heart? She felt sure that her misery, her anguish of suspense, her appalling doubts and terrors, must be written in her face; but it was not so. The emergency brought back a rush of the warm blood tingling to her fingers' ends. Oh, never, never, through her, must the mother she loved be betrayed! That brave impulse brought colour to her cheek and strength to her heart. She made one or two of those minute changes in the room *which a woman always finds occasion for* ... Then Rosalind took up the delicate work that lay on the table, and when the gentlemen entered, was seated *on a low seat within the circle of the shaded lamp*, warm in the glow of the genial fireside, her pretty head bent a little over her *pretty industry*, her hands busy. She who had been the image of anxiety and unrest a moment before, was now the culminating point of all the soft domestic tranquillity, luxury, boundless content and peace, of which this silent room was the home. (I. My italics)

Given that this is a house dominated by a shrieking little father supported by a scheming and spying housekeeper, the last sentence might seem to be heavily ironic. But it is not, because the woman somehow contrives to make it what it is, and Mrs Oliphant makes it clear that it is by her own self-obliteration: to be a woman is to be the culmination point of a silent room. That the 'art' should come 'naturally' is vitally important: it is an art that involves being what one is not, but, of course, within the ideology, the nature of woman is defined precisely in terms of being something *for others*. It is Rosalind's 'brave impulse' that provides the basis of the art, and it is her training as a woman, 'pretty industry' that makes it reliable.

So right from the start, we are aware that the situation of woman would be impossible if it were not for the 'nature' of woman which is an ideological concept. This is, to some extent, demystified by the harsh social realities. Madam's slight failure in the natural art of woman means that she loses her Madamish status which is her whole identity: 'She was pulled rudely down from the pedestal she had occupied for so long ... Though she had been supposed so self-sustained and strong in character, she was *too natural a woman* not to be deeply dependent upon sympathy' (XXXIX). The ideology is clearly operative again in the second sentence, but the word 'pedestal' should alert us to Mrs Oliphant's sense that it is woman's 'nature' to practice an *art* which is self preserving because it creates fictions. It is not woman's nature to be the culmination of a room, but to create the *illusion* that it is because she is nothing without it. Thus as well as an ideological programme (the self-obliterating nature of woman), there is an interrogative voice not letting us forget its fictionality. When one of Rosalind's suitors echoes Ruskin ('The kind of girl I like doesn't hunt, though she goes like a bird when it strikes her fancy. She is the queen at home, she *makes a room* like this into heaven'), she retorts that it is 'A dreadful piece of *perfection*' (XXIX. My italics). And when Madam is going away, she finds sanctuary in the very opposite of the stable, lighted, sociable drawing-room – a railway carriage – 'the protection which is afforded by the roar and sweep of hot haste which holds us as in a sanctuary of darkness, peace and solitude' (XXXVII). But the total movement of the novel leaves such challenges unconfronted and untransformed. The only coherent opposition to the self-obliteration myth is given to a ridiculous aunt and a strident younger daughter, and the novel is really nailed down by a benevolent uncle's wan comment: 'If this were a time to philosophize, I might say that's why women in general have such hard lives, for we always expect the girls to keep the boys out of mischief, without asking how they are to do it' (XVI). Rosalind ends by marrying her Ruskinian suitor without changing his views, and Madam preserves the drawing-room, remains its culminating point by an act of self-obliteration so complete that she is absent from what she makes.

An ideological coherence is then preserved despite the novel's subversive moments, and this is achieved by the manipulation of the point of view. From what has been said already, it can be seen that the cognition (the *awareness* of the art of woman's nature) is shared between Rosalind and Madam, so that the suffering that it brings is never sharply focused. The moment in the railway carriage is more a moment of collapse than of self-appraisal and the use of 'pedestal' is Mrs Oliphant's rather than Madam's. In fact we see very little of what Madam goes through: to see that would be to separate her (as subject) from her role and the novel maintains a religious integrity between them. When, near the end, after a long absence from the narrative, we see into her mind, it is only to see how she reflects on what has already happened, what she must accept: 'She had always known that sometime or other, these men would look at her so, and say just those words to her, and that she would stand and bear it all, a victim appointed from the beginning' (XXXVI). 'Always' and 'appointed' are words that bypass the actual experience of suffering and hold her subjectivity at a safe distance. It is Rosalind who undergoes the awareness of incongruity before it hardens into a given pattern, and she suffers only vicariously as the helpless and baffled spectator of her stepmother's action: and in terms of the events of the narrative, she is one of its beneficiaries. In spite of a number of authorial comments distinguishing between what happens in novels and what happens in 'real' life (which is of course claimed as the province of this novel), Madam is finally presented to us as explicitly a tragic figure: 'They are all gathered together again,' the dying Madam says, 'for the end of the tragedy' (XLIX). There could have been a bitter irony in this, but because Madam is kept by the narrative mode at a fictive remove, the fiction of her 'nature' is never made visible: she remains, to the end, Madam, admirable, culminating point of the domestic room, an object for our peace and comfort.

I want to contrast this text with Henry James's novel *The Portrait of A Lady*.[6] *The Portrait of A Lady* is the story of Isabel Archer, a young, faintly emancipated American girl brought to Europe by her aunt, the wife of a wealthy banker spending his retirement in England. The banker's heir, Ralph Touchett, a hypochondriacal aesthete, persuades his father to leave Isabel the bulk of his fortune so that she can be liberated completely from economic circumstances. After boldly rejecting the offers of a prosperous American businessman who pursues her through Europe (Caspar Goodwood) and an English lord, Isabel seems set for an exciting career. But she falls prey to the scheming of two more American exiles, Madame Merle and Gilbert Osmond who have a daughter Pansy, passed off implicitly as the child of 'widower' Osmond's first marriage. Conned by Osmond's aura of melancholy and aristocratic pride, Isabel marries him and quickly learns that she has married an empty and conventional tyrant. She defies him once by returning to England to see the dying Ralph but when Caspar Goodwood offers to take her away from her marriage, she refuses. Osmond is busy scheming for his daughter's prosperous unhappiness, and partly to protect the child, and partly to accept her fate, she goes back to Rome where her husband lives. James's novel offers a comparable programme to that propounded in *Madam*: the nature of woman as object of appreciation, realized as the story of the acceptance of a limiting and incongruous role, but realized, as I shall argue, with a coherence which makes visible the ideological shaping of the story. The programme is explicitly stated near the beginning of chapter XXXVII when Edmund Rosier, an ineffectual American connoisseur living in Europe, comes to Rome to see the heroine for the first time after her disastrous marriage to another American aesthete:

> The years had touched her only to enrich her; the flower of her youth had not faded, it only hung more quietly on its stem. She had lost something of that quick eagerness to which her husband had privately taken exception – she had more the air of being able to wait. Now, at all events, framed in the gilded doorway, she struck our young man as the picture of a gracious lady.

The image is fittingly pictorial not only because our young man is a collector, but also because Isabel has become what she is because of the connoisseur who liberated her with his father's money because he wanted to see what she would do with it, and the husband who plucked her as the prize of his collection. The ironies of the image are clear – the gilded doorway both embellishes her image and fixes her in it. We know that Rosier's appreciation is superficial, and five chapters later, in the rightly celebrated chapter XLII, we are to see direct into Isabel's mind and understand the suffering that underlies the image. Nevertheless the novel remains truly a portrait, and if the primary function of the portrait as a genre is to 'confirm one's position', in the phrase of the art critic, John Berger (*Selected Essays & Articles: The Look of Things*, Penguin, 1972), James's own criticism makes it clear that he sees portraiture as an image that invokes interpretation, a guessing of the unseen from the seen in the manner of Walter Pater's famous passage on the Mona Lisa in *Studies in the Renaissance*. What such interpretation does is not to contest the image but to use it so that a 'gracious lady' summarizes not merely an appearance, a status and a role, but also the expression of a nature brought to fixity by experience. And chapter XLII has exactly the same sense of completeness that we have noted in the presentation of Madam's consciousness: 'There was an everlasting weight on her heart – there was a livid light on *everything*' (my italics). The absolutes create the distance – that is where she is. We are witnessing a reflective awareness that comes too late for Isabel, though not for our appreciation. For this highly introspective chapter resolves itself into yet another picture, subject becoming object: 'she stopped again in the middle of the room and stood there gazing at a remembered vision'.

To see the novel in this way is to run counter to the accepted view on the way it works. James himself described its conception as that of 'a young woman affronting her destiny', and its method as that of 'placing the centre of the subject in the young woman's own consciousness'.[7] But the novel does not readily work in this way. In the first place, Isabel's consciousness works only in relation to the spectatorial and male consciousnesses around her – especially Ralph's – and it is Ralph who sets her up to meet 'the requirements of his imagination' (VXIII), which puts him in the position of the reader. Secondly, James only gives us Isabel's consciousness with a highly controlled authorial distance: 'The girl had a certain nobleness of imagination, which rendered her a good many services and played her a great many tricks' (VI). Increasingly, it is the tricks of her imagination that we are to watch marking out her destiny. And they are tricks because the author crucially maintains an air of bemusement which keeps Isabel's subjectivity slightly out of reach: 'The working of this young lady's spirit was strange, and I can only give it to you as I see it, not hoping to make it seem altogether natural' (XXIX). The crucial transition from her rejection of her former suitors on the grounds that they will limit her freedom, to her decision to marry what she admits is a nonentity is riddled with gaps during which she is travelling and emerging 'in her own eyes, a very different person' (XXXI). And the first three years of her marriage during which she learns of her mistake, is totally omitted. Rather than being a flaw in the novel this seems to be a deliberate repression in order to prepare the reader to accept the inexplicable (the fatal trick of her imagination) as the inexorable (the inescapable suffering reflected in chapter XLII). It enables James to limit her freedom to the level of awareness, so that the coda of the novel, when she is confronted with Goodwood's offer to help her escape her fate, represents no real free choice. His kiss 'like white lightning' is an image of death, and proffers only another 'act of possession'. She has only to choose between her identity (linked to the lights of the house from which she has come to meet Goodwood in the dark), which means too the 'very straight path' back to Osmond and her gilded frame, or obliteration in Goodwood's 'hard manhood'. What is important is not the choice she makes, but the energy she summons up to make it: 'She never looked about her but only darted from the spot' (LV). The narrative mode traces not so much a development from Isabel's innocence to experience, but from our bewilderment to our admiration. She meets the requirements of Ralph's imagination not by what she does, but by what she endures and represents, a higher graciousness than Rosier sees: "And remember this," [Ralph] continued, "that if you've been hated you've also been loved. Ah, but Isabel – *adored*."' (LIV).

The point of view is thus manipulated to keep the programme intact. But this already makes it a different kind of text from *Madam*. For there, as we have seen, awareness and suffering are kept glaringly apart because Mrs Oliphant has no way of transforming the subversive insights except by trying to keep them marginal. And this is not true of James's novel. For our very awareness of the limitations and interactions of the different axes of distance in the novel brings to the surface the unasked questions of its ideological commitment. Outside the circle of fine consciences, other commentaries question its assumptions – one thinks of the comic but never repressed American journalist, Henrietta Stackpole who has the novel's last word, and Daniel Touchett, another pristine American who is appalled by his son's idle fastidiousness, or even of the 'children of a neighbouring slum' who peer through the railings of a deserted West End square in the non-season, attracted by the animated conversation of Isabel and Ralph. These create other perspectives that alert us to the gilt on the frame of Isabel's portrait. So that when Isabel is allowed to reach a fully critical intelligence of Osmond's egoism we are compelled to see how she has been used by others, and has used them, as pictorial objects. In the end, it is the difference between 'tragedy' in Mrs Oliphant's debased ideological sense, and portraiture, because we can see the frame of the portrait. The novel is not merely the conservative response to womanhood, not the realization of a gracious lady, but a realization of her picture. What we see in the frame alerts us to the excluded space outside it. The adorable object is not 'nature' but a specific product within a specific system.

Most Dangerous of Playthings

Engels makes the point that monogamy does not exist on its own –
it is always underwritten by 'hetaerism' or various forms of the sexual
prostitution of women. One of the charges Mrs Linton brings against the
girl of the period is that besides being sexless, she is a bad imitation of
the mondaine:

> Men are afraid of her and with reason. They may amuse themselves
> with her for an evening, but they do not readily take her for life.
> Besides, after all her efforts, she is only a poor copy of the real thing;
> and the real thing is far more amusing than the copy, because it is
> real. Men can get that whenever they like; and whenever they go into
> their mothers' drawing rooms, with their sisters' friends, they want
> something of quite a different flavour. *Toujours perdrix* is bad providing
> all the world over; but a continual weak imitation of *toujours perdrix*
> is worse.
>
> If we must have only one kind of thing, let us have it genuine, and
> the queens of St John's Wood in their unblushing honesty rather than
> their imitators and make-believers in Bayswater and Belgravia. (p. 7)[8]

The link between feminist aggression and the idea of the other woman
may seem tenuous to us, but it is common enough in the late nineteenth
century, and it is what lies behind the literary convention of the *femme
fatale* who is at once the object of fear and the object of fascination in the
male epistemology because she represents a sexual relationship which is
outside the drawing-room, a rebel not 'content to be what God and nature
had made them' (Mrs Linton, p. 2). But that literary convention has to be
placed in a much wider category, which would include, as well as the
Gueneveres and Salomes of fantasy, such characters as Estella, in *Great
Expectations*, Hedda Gabler, and Gudrun in *Women in Love*, women whose
sexuality is a critical, self-realizing (and therefore within the ideology,
unnatural) mode of knowledge. At the same time, it is a category in which
the subjectivity of the woman becomes an object of man's ordeal, a force
which disorientates the given, hegemonic world-view. In Hardy's novel,
Far from the Madding Crowd, Bathsheba Everdene asks at one point
whether she is too mannish, and her confidante replies that rather she
is too 'womanish'. It is a word which usefully identifies the determinant
motif of the texts in this category, as different and yet closely bound up
with the determinant motif of the first category, 'womanliness'.

Although my examples are both taken from the genre of fantasy, it is
important to stress that they use the resources of the novel to elicit the
link I have made between the critical subjectivity of the woman and her
womanishness which is the object of a male ordeal. George Macdonald's

Lilith (1895) is a macabre romance which has gained some currency in recent years among what William Empson would call neo-Christian critics, such as C. S. Lewis, Tolkien and Auden.[9] It consists of the adventures of an orphan called Vane (the human soul whose name indicates the way the wind is blowing and the vanity of human wishes) in a dreamlike world which he enters through a mirror. His central act is to revivify the exhausted Lilith out of an impulse of naïve decency, so that she is thus released to attack the race of children (the Little Ones) whose cause he espouses. Lilith is, of course, a traditional conflation of the Hebrew demon who destroys children, and the supposed first wife of Adam, created independently from him, who quarrelled with him because she refused to have intercourse lying underneath him. From her brief appearance in Goethe's *Faust*, she becomes an archetype of the destructive woman. But whereas in, for example, a sonnet of Rossetti's, she is a static object of mystified contemplation ('And still she sits ...') in Macdonald's story she appears as a character with a rationalized motivation. Partly this is based on a will to power, the demand for a totally submissive love, but, more importantly, it is based on an assertion of self-creation:

> 'I am what I am; no one can take from me myself.'
> 'You are not the Self you imagine.'
> 'So long as I feel myself what it pleases me to think myself, I care not. I am content to be myself what I would be. What I choose to seem to myself makes me what I am. My own thought makes me; my own thought of myself is me. Another shall not make me.' (XXXIX)

She is thus not simply seen as a weaver of spells, and the creator of metaphysical evil, but as the representative of an articulate human position.

In Macdonald's vision, even Lilith, the destroyer of her own daughter (and thus the rebel against parenthood) is redeemable. But the process is portrayed with a cruelty that almost reveals the theological motivation (defiance, defeat, purgation, death, redemption) for what it is – an instrument of oppression. The passage I have just quoted occurs when Lilith is confronted with Mara, a daughter of Adam and protector of the Little Ones, who tries to persuade Lilith to allow the light of the creating will to enter her so that she will cease to will against her creator. When Lilith refuses, a white-hot 'worm-thing' crawls out of the hearth and enters the body of Lilith through a dark spot in her side: 'The princess gave one writhing, contorted shudder, and I knew the worm was in her secret chamber.' Mara comments 'She is seeing herself', and significantly Vane tries to put his arms round her, but is stopped: 'Her torment is that she is what she is. Do not fear for her; she is not forsaken. No gentler way to help her was left.' Lilith now blames God for what she is, and defies him again. 'I will not be made any longer', but she cannot unmake herself, and she 'will not be remade'. So once again, she suffers a violent assault, this time, 'naked to the torture of pure interpenetrating inward light'. The horror on her face makes Vane beseech for mercy again, but Mara says 'Self loathing is not sorrow. Yet it is good for it marks a step in the *way home*, and in *the father's arms* the prodigal forgets the self he abominates.' The process of reduction continues until Lilith finally repents (that is, wishes to die), but she cannot because one of her hands is the paw of a leopard (one of the forms she appears in during the novel) and she cannot open it. This final resistance of animal nature is not overcome until she persuades Adam, the husband she has wronged, to cut it off with a sword given him by an angel at the gate of paradise which will 'divide whatever was not one and indivisible' (XLI). The hand is given to Vane who is ordered to bury it with Adam's spade in the place where the waters that Lilith, in her war on the Little Ones, had caused to disappear from the face of the earth will flow again.

Summarizing it in this way makes the book sound quite mad, but this would be too charitable a view. Auden has correctly described it as allegory, and though it is tempting to present it as material for psychoanalysis, it would be wrong to miss the element of hard calculation. The nightmare of sexual symbolism has a clear ideological coherence. Lilith has denied motherhood, asserted herself and the will to power. Her animal nature (which is identified with self assertion) has to be taken from her by a series of phallic images, and buried in the life-containing earth so that the children can be fed.

Lilith's ordeal only becomes important at the end, and the novel is mainly concerned with Vane's attempt to make sense of his vision, to which the survival of Lilith is found to be the key. Thus what she is and what she suffers is truly the object of his ordeal. That is why his interventions on her behalf are so vital, for what he has entered through the mirror is the vision of a new life which turns to nightmare because of his guilt, and the guilt comes not from his intention, which is good, but the desire to work out the right action from his own experience. He gives Lilith life, and she sucks his blood. She dashes his loved one to pieces and he tries to save her from pain. He thinks that he will save the Little Ones through knowledge, so he seeks to know Lilith. He is guilty, in short, of humanism, [10] and it is his very individuality that, however well meaning, makes him vulnerable, and is indeed related to the evil that Lilith represents. Because of this, we have no fictional coherence in the end, merely a retreat into ideology. Vane's vision is an epistemological adventure insofar as Lilith represents an obstructive obstacle in his quest for meaning and reconciliation. And yet, finally, this adventure is made marginal. Vane's sense of reality is only destroyed to make way for another, already given reality which does not challenge the moral law he takes with him, but merely sanctifies it, and the only final discovery of his spiritual education is that education is undesirable. His ordeal is over when he no longer tries to participate in the struggle between good and evil, but is content, as Mara says, 'to watch and wait'. For all its apparent complexity, the novel has very simple designs on us. And it is the reduction of Vane from quester to spectator (and finally, undertaker to the primal family) – in other words a silent modification of the point of view from autobiography to eye-witness account – that enables these designs to be accomplished. For if Vane were still trying to understand at the end, the agony Lilith goes through would be heroic, and her defeat a defeat of free will. Whereas it is the triumph of mother Eve, and father Adam manifested in imagery that is meant merely to terrify us. What happens to Lilith can happen to you too, but it will not do so if you just watch and wait.

Fantasy is, of course, always vulnerable to its ideological project in a sense in which other, supposedly 'realistic' fictions are not, because they are governed at least by an ideological practice which is reflected *within* the story (by its commitment to the contingent 'reality'). If it has to be 'like life' the actual world-view shaping that life motivates the narrative and is therefore more prone to be visible. The ideological practice of fantasy is, however, confined to the act of writing itself, so that it can be much more invisible. Although the manifestation of the nature of woman as ordeal is not confined to fantasy, as I have suggested, it is a siting of the woman which requires a much greater narrative distance than that which presents her as an object of consumption, both because she is bound to be more powerful, a superwoman, and because there is a necessary distance between the subject who experiences the ordeal and the reader for whom the ordeal is an object of consumption. But I have discussed Lilith in order to show that its ideological coherence is still gained at the expense of its fictional coherence: the narrative is made irrelevant by its design. And this means that the opposite is possible, that even within the realm of fantasy, fictional coherence is possible and the project visible as a question which represses other questions.

The text that will best illustrate this from within the period I am discussing is Rider Haggard's *She*.[11] It is a novel often underestimated even by Haggard's admirers, although it is worth noting that Freud found it full enough of 'hidden meanings' to dream about it. What gives those meanings coherence is an ordeal of male sexuality of which Ayesha (She) is the primary cause. The story is narrated by Holly, a Cambridge don who is guardian to a beautiful male called Leo Vincey. Ancient documents, a palimpsest of remembered wrongs, send them on a journey to avenge the murder by Ayesha of an ancestor of Vincey, Kallikrates (the strong and the beautiful). It is a journey which yields a sequence of metaphors of sexual struggle: a squall in which the sea heaves 'like some troubled woman's breast' (IV), difficult penetration to an amphitheatre, an attack by a lioness, a feast which is set up by the rejected lover of their man-servant to avenge her humiliation, and, climactically, a treacherous entry into a cave which contains a life-giving pillar of fire, the womb of the earth whose cleft is only crossable with the aid of the flaming sword of the sun's rays.

The struggle is dominant because the attraction of woman is treacherous and destructive. The narrator is a misogynist who seems also fairly clearly to be homosexual so that he is, initially at least, on a crusade against the female power over man, and the tribe which She rules, the Amhagger, is matrilinear with the sexual pairings decided by the women promiscuously. So that female sexuality is a threat both to the lives and the values of the Europeans. But what is important is that the revenge/crusade motif is inverted when Ayesha herself appears, for she represents not unmotivated evil, but an alternative mode of knowledge. She is presented as the fatal woman, embodiment of the very diablerie of woman, likened both to Circe and Aphrodite triumphant, but this view has to be revised. This is partly because, like Lilith, she is allowed to explain herself ('If I have sinned, let my beauty answer for it': XX), but also because Holly is compelled to change his mind: he describes her at first as 'a mysterious creature of evil tendencies' (XXI) and then later relates her wrongdoings to her wisdom:

> And the fruit of her wisdom was this, that there was but one thing worth living for, and that was Love in its highest sense, and to gain that good thing she was not prepared to stop at trifles. (XXI)

She seeks the pillar of flame which will give her new life because she seeks to revolutionize the world, to conquer its laws with love. But the flame destroys her because her revolution goes against 'eternal law' – thus the ideological project, the survival of the ordeal and the conquest of its object by law is realized. The shifting perspectives of the fictional realization, have by the end, however, made this completion highly ironic. The glimpse into the 'possibilities of life' that Holly and Vincey have through Ayesha change them completely so that they are estranged from the world they have set out from and whose values they have seen triumph as 'eternal law'.

What makes this transformation possible is the dramatization of Holly. Ugly and rejected, in terror of woman, be comes to love Ayesha for the beauty and knowledge she represents. The ideological object of ordeal becomes for him, because of the vision she imparts, a supreme fiction. The journey outward becomes not a release from the past (the revenge intention) but a journey back to that past to reveal the puniness of male fear and its comfortable accommodation within the eternal law, so that there can be no return journey. The fatal woman is not here, as in *Lilith*, destroyed to make way for the eternal mother, but to affirm the law which becomes as a result unacceptable. Holly cannot accept that She has finally been destroyed: the unsought vision that he has gained compels him to challenge the eternal law as She challenges it. Thus she is not merely allowed to speak for herself: She is brought into relationship with the reader via Holly. Her subjectivity modifies his and ours because it affirms the unity of knowledge and love. *She* is a fine novel because it brings us to ask the repressed question of its project: what does the destructive woman destroy, ourselves, or ourselves' subjugation?

The Truth Shall Make You Free

So far we have been talking of texts that site the 'nature' of woman in the subjectivity of man, and this means that it tends to be something already constituted, revealed by the narrative rather than explored and challenged by it. Even in those novels in which we have seen the project made visible as ideology by the fictional realization, it is not the 'nature of woman' that is called into question so much as the nature of such a conceptualization itself and what exclusions it makes. Once we move to texts that site the woman as subject, the notion of woman's nature itself has to be openly questioned, for clearly there cannot be a subject which is not in itself problematic. Hence we turn inevitably to 'feminist' texts. 'What is now called the nature of woman is an eminently artificial thing', Mill writes in *The Subjection of Women* and this is really to call into question the very process of making the woman an object in ideology. Thus we can no longer deal with projects that have as their centre a concept such as 'womanliness' or 'womanishness', since the subject woman is called upon to ask: what am I? [12]

Nevertheless, it is still possible to distinguish between the hegemonic posing of that question and the estranged posing of it. For if there can be no assumption about what a woman is, the assumption about what constitutes a *subject* can still be made. Much of the early feminist polemic is of course made within the liberal ideology. The argument is that if women are accorded the same legal rights as men, they too will be free as men are. This tends to be the case with Mill's essay, and it can be seen rather crudely emulated in Mona Caird's proposal that marriage should be treated as a contract like any other, with the terms of the agreement decided by the two parties. I do not wish to underestimate the value of liberal feminism, but it is important for my purposes to establish clearly that it questions the traditional status and role of woman from within the ideology that insists on it. It sees a contradiction in bourgeois theory and tries to rationalize it, making woman as 'free' as man (which equally entails limiting that freedom as it is limited for man, as in the free contract concept). There is no contradiction of bourgeois theory. Thus the ideological programme of the fictions in this category has to do with the possible freedom of woman conceived as a rational application of the social contract.

Grant Allen's *The Woman Who Did* (1894) was, in its day, a *succès de scandale*.[13] It was clearly intended to be, since its polemical programme begins outside the novel with an authorial confession: 'Written at Perugia, Spring, 1893, for the first time in my life wholly and solely to satisfy my own taste and my own conscience'. This has a direct bearing on the story since the heroine's most important attempt to gain independence is to write a novel which fails because it is too serious and sincere ('the despairing heart-cry of a soul in revolt') so that the author identifies his own liberty with that of the protagonist. Both are rebels against what Allen himself would term 'philistia'. Herminia is the daughter of an Anglican dean who decides that it would be wrong to marry the man she loves because she has seen that,

> In a free society, was it not obvious that each woman would live her own life apart, would preserve her independence, and would receive the visits of the man for whom she cared – the father of her children? Then only could she be free. Any other method meant the economic and social superiority of the man, and was irreconcilable with the perfect freedom of the woman. (VI) .

So she has a child without getting married or living with its father, openly and programmatically ('the truth had made her free and she was very confident of it'). But, of course, she does not live in a free society, and the truth also makes of her a sacrificial victim. We see her forced into a closer dependence on her lover and, when he dies, into a single-minded concern with the economic and emotional demands of motherhood. Even this turned against her: the daughter grows up frivolous and conventional and when she finds out the truth about her birth, attacks Herminia with such bitterness that she leaves her no way out but suicide.

It is a superficial and sensationalist novel despite its air of apparent liberalism. The large and difficult question of woman's independence tends to be swallowed by the seemingly simpler one of illegitimacy, and Herminia's death, though it may appear from a summary to be distressing, is actually very comforting – a noble action succeeded by a noble martyrdom puts a definite end-point to the struggle. Our final attitude is foreshadowed in the dedication: 'to my dear wife to whom I have dedicated my twenty happiest years, I dedicate also this brief *memorial of a less fortunate love*' (my italics). Herminia's story is given, before it starts, an air of pious regret which mediates any anger or involvement it might have had. Grant Allen seems merely to be cashing in, without paying the price, on the difficult insights both into the situation of woman and the anomalies

of the writer's own productive conditions that emerge from the work of
Meredith, Hardy and Gissing. Allen's flirtation with radicalism and honesty
is guaranteed to remain at the level of flirtation.

Nevertheless, it seems to me an instructive text. Not only is it a fairly
lucid vulgarization of an aspect of female desperation which perforce
found expression as one kind of feminism; it also reveals the limitations of
this literary category – the way in which the ideology of the project can
demolish the coherence of its fictional realization. Truth and freedom are
mediated by a language that comes straight from the conventions that
are challenged. What is above all stressed is Herminia's *altruism*: the nature
of her love and her lover make it clear that for her, marriage would not be
oppressive. She rejects it for the sake of those who are oppressed by it (she
rather glibly contrasts herself with George Eliot and Mary Shelley and
others who practised marital irregularities merely because that was the
only way they could get what they wanted). In fact, she uses the very
vocabulary of the ecclesiastical father whose mores she is challenging: '"it
never occurred to me," she said gently but bravely, "to think my life could
ever end in anything but martyrdom."' (III). Since martyrdom is what she
consciously chooses, there can be no real development in the novel – there
is nothing to be learnt from her taken freedom. And, of course, it involves
a double distancing: she is distanced from her unnecessary predicament,
and we are distanced from her by her purity of motive. She is not changed
by what happens to her, and she changes nothing. And this is because she
is not in any sense revolutionary. She merely takes the vocabulary of bourgeois ideology and makes it consistent. She makes herself the free subject
of her experience and chooses actions according to her own readings,
but she is spared, both by her class-based confidence in a theological
vocabulary, and by the abstraction of her thinking, from the irrational
contiguities of economic and sexual forces – from being subjected to the
life she chooses. Naturally she suffers – martyrs must suffer – but she is
already armed against suffering. The point of view thus remains static.
Even the discovery that she cannot make money out of writing honest
novels does not sully her. We have in the end a bourgeois fable of the free
subject making its way. The only difference is that the free subject is a
woman, and the only difference that makes (and I do not deny that it is an
important one) is that Allen cannot bring himself to falsify the reality so
much that he lets her finally win. Even so what destroys her is not the conditions she has to face (she masters those with an ease that keeps the novel
very short) but a relationship conditioned at an ideological level the free
subject does not question – if marriage is dispensable, motherhood is not.
The truth shall make you free of all but 'the truth' (ideology manifests
itself as this, as well as in the form of 'convention').

Allen's novel is useful because it highlights the difficulty of a novelist
attempting to write programmatically feminist literature.[14] At the same

time it enables us to see by contrast the very great achievement of the writer who is closest to Mill in this period – George Meredith. Woman plays a special, and usually subversive, role throughout his fiction, and to give a full account of it would require analysis of many of the early works (notably *Rhoda Fleming* and *Vittoria*). But it is in a number of late novel that Meredith comes to focus most sharply on sexual politics: *The Egoist*, *Diana of the Crossways* and *The Amazing Marriage*. Of these, it is *Diana* that programmatically elaborates woman as the free subject encountering the social world:

> 'Oh! I have discovered that I can be a tigress!'
> Her friend pressed her hand, saying, 'The cause a good one!'
> 'Women have to fight.' (IV)

Diana, who is explicitly linked with the goddess of hunting and chastity, is an Irish wit and beauty who marries a churlish Englishman in hysterical reaction to the sexual advances of her best friend's husband. The marriage soon founders, and her husband sues her for adultery. The court vindicates her innocence, and Diana uses its verdict to justify her escape from the marriage. For much of the novel she lives as a single woman, making her living by writing novels, but she also becomes involved with a rising young politician. His sexual importunity angers her sufficiently to leak vital government information to a newspaper in order to obtain the money she desperately needs. Losing him, she is protected from further calumny by her devoted friends and admirers, the most solid of whom she marries.

Two motifs, sexual frigidity and sexual liberation, are obviously entangled, but Meredith keeps the first from providing an ideological distortion of the second[15] by the careful manipulation of point of view. Although she is realized as the free subject of her experience, it is only at crucial moments (mostly late in the novel) that we are allowed to see into her mind. Diana's wit and presence is also communicated through the diaries of 'contemporaries' (the novel is set in a past which has to be pieced together), by gossip and the anxious consciousness of her friends. Because of this, none of her actions can be seen as simple folly, nor even as gratuitous acts of emancipation – Diana's self is seen in a contingent world which even when it is friendly, provides a series of limiting conditions against which it is important for her to assert the motive power of her sense of freedom:

> She did not accuse her marriage of being the first fatal step: her error was the step into Society without the wherewithal to support her position there. Girls of her kind, airing their wings above the sphere of their birth, are cryingly adventuresses. As adventuresses they are treated. Vain to be shrewish with the world! Rather let us turn and scold our

nature for irreflectively rushing to the cream and honey! Had she
subsisted on her small income in a country cottage, this task of writing
would have been a holiday! ... The simplicity of the life of labour
looked beautiful. What will not look beautiful contrasted with the fly in
the web? She had chosen to be one of the flies of life. (XXX)

Even in such a passage as this, when Diana is rebuking her own extrav-
agance and regretting her own inability to conform to her 'sphere', her
mind moves inevitably towards the verb 'choose'. Meredith does not give
her a totally free situation, nor does he make her a paragon (as Allen
makes Herminia); she is 'a heroine of reality', but he does give her the
intelligence and energy to choose her entanglements out of the sphere to
which she is allotted, even by the high praise of others, and the practical
advice and love of her friends. Ultimately, however she may scold her
'nature', she is unable to deny it. 'Women are women, and I am a woman:
but I am I, and unlike them' (XLII). We must note too that her 'nature'
is not identified with an ideological concept, 'the nature of woman'. It is
not a given, but a problematic question raised by the free subject. In such
a context, the sexual frigidity, though it is not uncritically celebrated, as we
shall see, is not a 'defect' of 'nature', but part of the armoury against the
assault on her identity, a necessary stand against being reduced to the
'womanly'.[16]

There are several parallels with Allen's novel which are worth spelling
out because it will make the contrast clearer. In the first place, both
heroines make an explicit stand against marriage which places them
very much in the liberal feminist tradition (since marriage was seen to
be slavery and not a free contract). But Diana moves from theoretical
rejection to bitter experience, and the transition is important. Thus, for
example, before she marries, she sees a husband as a threat to freedom in
a coolly abstract manner:

> 'I cannot tell you what a foreign animal a husband would appear in my
> kingdom.' Her experience had wakened a sexual aversion, of some slight
> kind, enough to make her feminine pride stipulate for perfect indepen-
> dence, that she might have the calm out of which imagination spreads
> wing. Imagination had become her broader life, and on such an earth,
> under such skies, a husband who is not the fountain of it, certainly is a
> foreign animal; he is a discordant note. He contracts the ethereal
> world, deadens radiancy. He is a gross fact, a leash, a muzzle, harness, a
> hood, whatever is detestable to the free limbs and senses. (IV)

Although we are not invited to ironize this, she is made to pay for the
abstract and ethereal rhetoric by experiencing a grosser fact, the sexual
advances of a married man. And she does marry, not to discover that this
is more secure, but that a husband is more deadly than a foreign animal:

'Husband grew to mean to me stifler, lung contractor, iron mask, inquisitor, everything anti-natural' (XIV). Without collapsing her sense of freedom, Meredith makes Diana strengthen it against material existence. So the novel has no air of piety, and it does have a real suspense.

And like Herminia too, Diana is motivated by an idealism that can appear as sexual frigidity, as I have suggested. But the difference is that whereas in Allen's novel this is taken to be wholly noble, Meredith makes careful discriminations about it that foreshadow the ironies Hardy directs against Sue Bridehead in *Jude the Obscure*. That is, we are presented with it as armoury, but that in itself involves a complacency for which Diana is made to pay. Thus when her political lover, Percy Dacier, is demanding that their relationship be sexual, he says, 'I believe you were made without fire' and Diana's reply is nearly arrogant: 'Perhaps. The element is omitted with some of us: happily some think. Now we can converse'. What she has seen throughout the novel is not merely that marriage is a repressive institution but that it is one that is established by and for men, so that women may be placed as objects in the market (the most brilliant of the *obiter dicta* recorded by the diarists through whom she is first presented to us is: 'men do not so much fear to lose the hearts of thoughtful women as their strict attention to their graces' (I). But marriage which can be opposed with free thought and self-containment, is not the worst kind of degradation. She pays for the idealism of her chastity when she realizes that in the newspaper office where she sells her secret to avenge the male oppressor and stave off the economic reality, the status of woman drops 'from the secondary to the cancelled stage'. It is not the regression from freedom that challenges Diana's doing as it does Herminia's but the entry into it. This does not merely make for greater realism, it means that the fictional motivation of the novel is the freedom of the subject and that if is therefore exposed and not merely ideologically asserted.

But there is a third parallel between the two novels which demonstrates more decisively the difference between them. Both heroines are novelists, and, just as *The Woman Who Did* postulates an aesthetic commitment which identifies the freedom of woman with the freedom of the novelist from the pressures of the market, so Meredith's novel, at a much deeper level, incorporates his own sense of the social limitations and contradictory aesthetic potential of fiction. The subject woman is summoned to declare her own power to a world that wants only statues, and the subject novelist, very consciously the presenter of that problematic woman, claims the freedom to substantiate a truth that is neither 'rose-pink' nor 'dirty-drab' (Meredith's terms for romantic and naturalistic fiction) but 'wholesome, bearable, fructifying, finally a delight'. We have a double affirmation, woman/fiction, making a double negation, 'domestic decoration'/falsification. Whereas, in Allen's novel, the connection is merely, and gratuitously polemical, in *Diana* it is absolutely vital to the evolution of the novel. Its formal progression is from the diaries that memorialize her, to the crises that go on in her mind – the free subject as point of view is only won from the enigmatic records that cannot place her as object. And this is bound up with the progressive revelation of the contradiction between the nature of the subject and what the world expects of women – a progression that moves from the crude and legally contestable possessiveness of her first husband, to the more alluring and sophisticated image of Dacier, who sees her as his 'fountain of counsel ... the rosy gauze veiled more, than cold helper and advisor' (XXXIII). In the same way that we have seen how the contradictions of the work of art (portrait) exposes the contradictions of the woman-object, we see here how the problematic of the truth-telling artist exposes the problematic of the true woman subject.

The problematic for both novelist and woman is the relationship between knowing and contesting 'the dirty drab' of material existence. For the novel uses fiction to explore the limits of fiction: 'for nature will force her way, and if you try to stifle her by drowning, she comes up, not the fairest part of her uppermost' (I). When Diana frees herself from marriage, she escapes momentarily into a world of imaginative ecstasy, but this turns out to be merely a recovery of girlhood. In the material world she has to establish herself as a woman with an image, and this it is that poses for the character as for the novelist, what it means to be making something as a question. Her image is made through writing – 'metaphor was her refuge', and metaphor is explicitly linked with civilization itself, which is a curtailment of 'reality' (or so it appears in *The Egoist*). She is taken 'with a passion for reality' but she has also to be 'the actress of her part'. Caught in the shifting polarities of knowing and acting, the free subject knows its freedom only by knowing the limits of that freedom. She retains her independence from Dacier only by verbal betrayal – of the truth, but *to* the newspaper which counts her identity as nothing. And she is compelled finally to protect that identity by making it dependent, by accepting the compromise of inoffensive marriage.

The end of the novel is sometimes seen as a cop-out. Having created this free subject, the argument goes, Meredith hems her in with ironies that undermine that freedom. But the truth is that if Meredith had spared her the contiguities of her situation we would have been left with a novel that had no fictional coherence. Diana's freedom is legal and linguistic, but throughout the novel, the sexual situation has been linked with other political issues. The marriage of Diana and Warwick is likened by the diarists to 'another Union always in a Court of Law' (I) – that is England and Ireland. And Diana herself links the situation of woman to a recurrent topic in the novel, the growth of the railways:

We women are the verbs passive of the alliance, we have to learn, and if we take to activity, with the best intentions, we conjugate a frightful disturbance. We are to run on lines, like steam trains, or we come to no station, dash to fragments. (VI)

The passage exactly pinpoints the limits I am trying to define. Diana's first metaphor is linguistic, and it is radical (it exposes the oppression of women by making them passive verbs). The second is social and it is nostalgic (we are being overtaken by industrialism). Significantly, it is Redworth she marries, an Englishman ('They want the bridle-rein. That seems to me the secret of the Irish character': II), who makes his money out of railways. When he first seeks her at her house, the Crossways, to restrain her from leaving the country and making her legal position worse, he gets terribly lost because of the ambiguity of the directions he is given. Diana is safe only in the pseudonymic language of her independence. But outside, the larger social forces are at work. Confronted with the brute fact of being unable to survive without subterfuge, she is in the market for the strong capitalist. It only makes it more telling that Redworth is such a good man: the wedding yoke receives the sanction of grey toned reason, just as the rose pink is avenged by the dirty drab in fiction. 'I am going into slavery to make amends for presumption', Diana comments, and her confidante replies, 'Your business is to accept life as we have it.' It amounts to an ideological summoning. The free subject is summoned to subject herself freely. There is no paradox. The limits of the novel are in its language, and the limits of the free subject in what is licensed to it. Diana pays the price of not making a revolution: sexual politics is not apart from industrial oppression and imperialism, but if the only connections are linguistic, the free subject is only free within the limits of language. Meredith's is a great novel because the summoning of the woman's nature against the social image is a programme realized within the bounds of a narrative that recognizes the webbing of the liberated consciousness in the frame that marks off the questions it asks from the questions it silences.

The Woman Pays

In this essay I have so far been considering texts which have various forms of ideological programme. I have suggested that the narrative mode, the 'point of view', within which that programme is elaborated determines whether the text realizes the programme as an ideological or fictional coherence, which in turn distinguishes between fictions that reveal by accident the limitations of the programme and fictions which expose it by its very articulation. I have not tried to suggest that there is any difference in value between the categories, rather that it resides within them. But my last category is different. Here the woman is summoned to be the subject of her experience in order that she can be revealed as subject to it; the true subject of her experience, in other words, is that of being the object of other's knowledge. This is not an ideological programme at all: it incorporates all the others but goes beyond them in calling up the questions that they repress. Chiefly it articulates the relationship between role and status in such a way that the programme itself makes the break with patriarchal ideology. I am not claiming that such texts have no ideological content but that this content remains vestigial, a residuum which is a flaw in the realization. My examples are novels by Gissing and Hardy, and it is significant that in their work there is a prior break in the consciousness of the productive relations of the author himself. Before he wrote *The Odd Women*, Gissing had written *New Grub Street* which is the first novel in English to be devoted to the portrayal of literary production in a market economy. The evolution of Hardy's fiction is from playing what he called a 'scientific game' to the open rupture that is indicated in the 'Explanatory Note to the First Edition' of *Tess of the D'Urbervilles*: 'I would ask any too genteel reader, who cannot endure to have said what everybody nowadays thinks and feels, to remember a well-worn sentence of St Jerome's: If an offence come out of the truth, better it is that the offence come than that the truth be concealed.' There is no need for Gissing and Hardy to build connections between themselves and the subjects of their novels by making the protagonists novelists, because they have already as writers made their situation as members of an alien group the very basis of their art.

The Odd Women (1893)[17] does have an explicit programme but it is not a theme exemplified by a protagonist, rather it is simply the history of a group:

> 'But do you know that there are half a million more women than men in this happy country of ours?'
> 'Half a million!'
> Her naïve alarm again excited Rhoda to laughter.
> 'Something like that they say. So many *odd* women – no making a pair with them. The pessimists call them useless, lost, futile lives. I, naturally – being one of them myself – take another view. I look upon them as a great reserve.' (IV)

Rhoda Nunn is, of course, making a theme of it, but that is her *view*, her programme as a teacher in a school to train women to a wider range of jobs than the ones they have access to. But the novel's subject is only the factual group and other characters have other responses to their oddness. Monica, her interlocutor, for example takes marriage to a crusted middle-aged male chauvinist called Widdowson as her way out. And her older sisters take refuge in brandy and the Bible. Monica's colleague at the shop where she works becomes a prostitute, 'a not unimportant type of the odd woman' (XXVIII). Gissing's particular talent as a novelist is to create a group like this while limiting the consciousness of its individual members so that their interaction is marginal or accidental: essentially each woman confronts her shared predicament, which is precisely the question of her status outside her assigned role as wife and mother, in a felt loneliness. To summarize the plot would be to give a series of banal individual stories: this is an important feature of this double articulation. What matters is the dull dawn for each of the odd women that the choices they make as the subjects of their lives are both crucial and yet prescribed to the point of meaninglessness.

This is not to say that Gissing nails the novel down with the pessimism Rhoda rejects. The work of Rhoda Nunn and Mary Barfoot, her mentor, is seen as positive and valuable and it has its successes. But its limitations are also made manifest. In the first place, it is very much a class movement. 'I must keep to my own class,' says Mary and Rhoda agrees: 'as soon as we meddle with uneducated people, all our schemes and views are unsettled. We have to learn a new language for one thing.' (VI) And, beyond this, Rhoda recognizes that it is not just a social structure she is fighting, but the biological fact the structure exploits: 'I am seriously convinced that before the female sex can be raised from its low level there will have to be a widespread revolt against sexual instinct' (VI). This is not just a matter of talk: these difficulties in the woman's movement as portrayed in the novel dominate its elaboration in one direction – though it should be added that marriage is seen as more repressive. Rhoda necessarily becomes a specific kind of egoist, a Spencerian[18] survivor whose sympathies have to have strict limits: 'human weakness is a plea that has been much abused, and generally in an interested spirit' (XIII). She has little time for Monica's depressing sisters, and cannot allow herself to be disturbed by the pupil who commits suicide. Her affair with Everard Barfoot is a battle of egoisms: he demands that they live in free union, not because he believes in it but because he wants her submission – she, for the same reason demands marriage. They drift apart because of a misunderstanding that neither will clear up. And yet this tough egoism is vindicated if anything by the more terrible story of Monica who is trapped in a brilliantly realized tyrannical marriage and destroyed by trying to escape through a romance with a treacherous sentimentalist. At least Rhoda survives to make the last comment on the dead Monica's baby: 'Poor little child!' And maybe more than this – Rhoda's late meeting with Monica's tragedy gives her a larger sense of the group than that thematic statement I have quoted implies. Or at least we have it: for all the failure, material and emotional, in the novel, *The Odd Women* does not leave us resigned or hopeless about the women's movement. 'We flourish like the green bay-tree,' Rhoda says at the end, and because the range of consciousness is developed in the novel, we don't find this an ironic affirmation. The poor child may yet be 'a brave woman'.

Gissing can do this because he elaborates four autonomous but interdependent points of view in the novel. There is, of course, Rhoda's, which is one in which the need to make statements is increasingly brought into conflict with the recognition of motive in herself that those statements need to preclude. But this is no sentimental comedy. Rhoda goes through a series of rationalizations ('No longer an example of perfect female independence, and unable therefore to use the same language as before, she might illustrate woman's claim of equality in marriage. – If her experience prove no obstacle': XXVI), but what remains is the resilience of her ego. By twisting the plot to create suspicion of Barfoot, Gissing might be thought to be avoiding the full confrontation with love that Rhoda seems bound to make. 'Was he in truth capable of respecting her individuality?' is a question she is never brought to answer. But the episode supplies another answer: it reveals in both the lovers a final concern with power that goes beyond the level of misunderstanding. And because Gissing equally develops Barfoot's consciousness, we know that Rhoda's decision is necessary to her survival: 'Delighting in her independence of mind, he still desired to see her in complete subjugation to him' (XXV). Through Barfoot, and through making the distance between him and Rhoda's mind always present to us, Gissing elaborates Rhoda's 'independence of mind' as an object of conquest. She is not a fatal woman but she is to him an obstacle to be overcome, and when he fails he can turn to Agnes Brissendon who is an object in the marriage market.

Rhoda's story is only given meaning by the development of Monica's consciousness. Gissing carefully establishes her as a critical intelligence which can see further than the triviality of her shop colleagues and can demand more than the pathetic capitulation to circumstances of her sisters. It is in the light of such awareness that opportunities offered by the Barfoot school merely leave her depressed and the opportunity of a 'marriage of esteem' seems like the only possible escape. But again, Gissing elaborates the story by the interaction of her consciousness with that of her husband, Widdowson, who acquires her as an object, the reward of his years of labour and self-denial. Her subjectivity thus becomes to him a painful ordeal as his image of what a wife should be becomes an intolerable repression to her. So that their relationship too becomes a struggle, not fought out on the level of ideas and trials, but through forced stratagem and detection. Rhoda and Monica never really come together though their respective ordeals would be a mutual education. Barfoot and Widdowson hardly meet though the egoism of the first is defined and challenged by the sickening alliance of moral rigidity and appropriative desire of the second. Between them they constitute the object world of woman – just as between Rhoda and Monica the subject world is articulated. And it is because the male epistemology has at its disposal the double institution of monogamy and prostitution, that the struggle of the odd women is at best a series of pyrrhic victories.

The novel's strength is that it deploys interacting but finally uncommunicating points of view, and yet, paradoxically, it is this, that in the end prevents it from being a great work. For the price that Gissing pays for this double sense of the group and the isolation of its members, is that the full force of the contradiction in the woman's situation is dissipated: each of the protagonists experiences one fragment of it. It also prevents the novel from having any revolutionary potential: since the contradiction remains fragmented, it remains internal. Insofar as the struggle is turned outwards it is limited to polemic, to small pragmatic reforms (a small equalization of opportunity for middle-class girls with the right education) and to romantic subversion (which fails because it needs another man). I want to argue finally that it is precisely at the point of the limitation of Gissing's novel, that *Tess of the D'Urbervilles* begins to manifest its greatness. *Tess of the D'Urbervilles* is the story of the daughter of a poor and feckless country trader who is seduced by the scion of a *nouveau riche* family that has adopted Tess's aristocratic surname. She has a child which dies, and goes to work in a dairy where she meets and marries an agnostic intellectual, Angel Clare. On the night of their marriage Angel confesses to Tess about a former affair. Tess is encouraged to tell him about her past, but he turns against her because of it, and deserts her. After that she wanders from place to place in penury, working under appalling conditions until, to give some security to her now fatherless and evicted family, she goes to live with her first seducer as a kept woman in a near-by fashionable resort. At this point, Angel returns having learnt to regret his intolerance. In order to make herself free to go with him, Tess murders her keeper, and the pair wander off in vague flight from the police. She is arrested on Stonehenge, and the novel ends with her execution.

Hardy subtitled the novel 'A Pure Woman' and although in 1912 he said that it was added at the last moment and that the controversy it caused made him feel that it would have been better unwritten, he let it stand. And it is right, I think, because it makes clear the novel's project. But we need to be careful how we use the phrase. In the novel, he refers to her as 'an almost standard woman' which together with the fact that this discovery is made after she has ceased to be 'a maiden' makes it clear that purity is not innocence: Tess does not remain 'unsullied' by her experience, she becomes a woman by it – the first 'phase' of the novel is entitled 'Maiden' and the last 'Fulfilment'. Purity of the Christian-moral sort is demanded by Angel and his rejection of Tess is seen as a failure of sensibility. This is not an error likely to be repeated by modern critics, but another of Angel's mistakes is. He takes her as a 'visionary essence of woman', and although its etherealness is avoidable, we still have to beware of turning the project into a *theme* which pervades the novel. It is equally not a celebration of 'womanliness', that ideological absolute which is none the less ideological when it is softened with a little modern permissiveness.

'Pure woman' is a project: it is the object of a quest, not the subject of a demonstration. And that quest is Tess's who travels towards her fulfilment, and ours who see her life in 'phases'[19] (a word with many connotations, the most important of which is defined by John Stokes as 'non-teleological evolution' i.e. a structure for seeing an object of knowledge rather than the object of myth). In each phase we see a distinctive change in Tess (Maiden/Maiden No More (negation)/Rally (emergence)/ Consequence (withdrawal into illusion)/The Woman Pays etc.) and yet the lapse of time in the novel is much greater within the phases than it is between them. Hardy thus structures an evolution and since it is an evolution towards the destruction of Tess within the phase of her fulfilment it is an evolution without end. (As notorious as the subtitle is Hardy's ironic evocation of an 'ending': 'Justice was done'.) And if it is a structure, it is a structured *movement*. The evolution of Tess is measured against a system of coordinates on a rigid body – particularly against the double polarity of Alec (*Weltlust*/fanaticism) and Angel (theoretical unconventionality/appropriate morality).

I have briefly indicated the features of the text's articulation (which needs fuller elaboration) to emphasize how experimental the novel is. Hardy mediates our relationship with Tess in many ways but it is not appropriate to see him in a simple ideological situation. He is not simply a dispassionate all-knowing sage (when he presents the valley of Talbothays as a vast expanse, giving Tess the sense of new opportunity, and then withdraws to see her as a fly on a billiard table, he ironizes her subjectivity but doesn't take us with him, or stay in that cosmic overview himself). Nor is he – as modern sentimental critics see him – a 'stricken father' who 'mourns' her. The authorial view ranges from erotic appropriation ('her flower-like mouth and large tender eyes, neither black nor blue nor gray nor violet; rather all those shades together, and a hundred others, which could be seen if one looked into their irises – shade behind shade – tint beyond tint – around pupils that had no bottom; an almost standard woman') to 'naturalistic' description ('A bit of her naked arm is visible beneath the buff leather of her gauntlet and the sleeve of her gown; and as the day wears on its feminine smoothness becomes scarified by the stubble and bleeds') to admiration ('Tess, with a curiously stealthy yet courageous movement, and with a still rising colour, unfastened her frock and began suckling her child'), to identification ('a resolution which had surprised herself ... '). Each of these passages comes in the same chapter (XIV), and none of them are completely distinct from one another. What we are witnessing in fact is the objectification of Tess by the narrator which is acted out in the novel. At various points she is the object of consumption (for Alec and Angel, but she is also the self-sacrificing conscience-ridden girl for us), and the object of fascination (Alec cannot leave her alone, and she is finally, literally his *femme fatale*: but we have

seen what Hardy does with her eyes, for us) and she is even an emancipated woman (she makes more of Angel's liberal education than he does,
and the novel is partly structured around a sequence of gestures of liberation
against Alec, and self-asserting statements to Angel). These mediations
give substance to the subject experience of Tess herself, by making us the
subject of her, and thus guilty of the odd object images whose contradictions she is subject to.

The realization of the project is thus the evolution of a subject (Tess)
towards an object (which is also a contradiction-fulfilment/death). At the
beginning of the novel, it is accurate to see Tess's consciousness as 'alienated': subject, that is, to an 'inner contradiction' between 'conscience' and
'reverie' which responds to but does not correspond with, an external
contradiction in the social structure that demands individual integrity but
disintegrates the individual through labour and sexual exploitation. But the
movement of the novel is away from this inner contradiction towards
the rupture, open and articulate, of subject and the world of the subject.
In 'The Woman Pays' and 'The Convert' we see on the one hand the body
appropriated as a machine for economic and sexual usage (Tess is compelled to become part of the threshing machine and it is the episode in
which this happen which begins the sequence of events that precipitate
her towards prostitution). When Angel sees her after his return he is aware
that mind and body are separate in Tess. On the other hand, though Tess
has to withdraw from her body in order to sell it as commodity, she re-
enters it to oppose the exploitation. During the threshing episode she
strikes Alec D'Urberville with her gauntlet and this foreshadows her most
aggressive act, the murder of the man who owns her which happens at the
moment she is most completely appropriated – as the kept woman.

Just as the process is double (complete appropriation as object/complete
aggression as subject), so is its consequence. By her act she places herself
beyond the reach of the ideology which summons the subject to subject
itself to its determinants, but equally, she makes herself the object of its
retaliation. Hardy calls the last phase 'Fulfilment', and though it is heavy
with irony since the fulfilment is the execution of Tess (the moving in
to the kill of that which has had its 'sport' with Tess), it is also, quite
genuinely, a flowering. Tess lives inside time, and time is on the side of the
law which will destroy her for coming alive (re-possessing her own body).
But in the interval of time which is granted her, she lives outside its 'truth':
'I am not going to think outside of now' (LVIII). In one sense this is an
evasion, and it is left to Angel to do everything to prolong the interval, but
in another it is a triumph. In terms of attitude and tone, it is she who
dominates, gently educating Angel to live in the now where they have
space: she even welcomes its limits because she does not want to commit
their love to duration. And Tess has created this out of a class and sexual
killing. It is not a revolutionary act, and I would not want to argue that

Hardy ever thought of the possibilities of revolution, whether sexual or political, but it is an act of the kind of which revolutions are made, and it gives us a novel which creates in itself a revolution in form. For it is finally the story of her biological growth and its inevitable break with the exploiting world: its subject is larger than a word like consciousness can account for. The 'human' Tess and the non-human forces that motivate her make of her a subject whose subjection is at war with its subjectivity. And we can only be aware of this because we see Tess not as in a flat picture masquerading as depth, but from all the angles that are possible. And that is why, whatever Hardy's own ideological commitment, no frame will hold his novel in place.

Tess of the D'Urbervilles is not the latest of the novels I have discussed, but I hope I have been able to indicate that it is formally the most advanced, and that at the same time, *because of this* it is the most politically advanced. And this is the whole intent of my article. The model I have proposed is clearly tentative and needs much more elaboration, but if it has demonstrated convincingly that we can only see the political importance of a text by attending to its formal identity as the object of an act of production, it has achieved its main intention. And this has clear consequences for any movement which attempts to rescue our way of seeing things from the ideology that structures our response.

Notes

1. In this introductory section there are a number of influences, both negative and positive, that inform my thinking. For instance, the concept 'the literariness of a literary text' is the term Roman Jakobson uses to define the preoccupation of Russian Formalist critics, whose work in turn permeates this essay, as I think the formalists showed the possibility of a science of literary criticism. A crucial secondary source for rethinking this basic question is Pierre Macherey's *Pour une théorie de la production littéraire* (Paris, 1966). On the other hand, the influences I am opposing can be exemplified by the notion of a 'literary response' as it is used, for instance, by Kate Millett in her book *Sexual Politics* (Sphere, 1972). Despite its many excellences and despite its explicit opposition to traditional modes of academic criticism, I find Millett's book makes use of some of the most dangerous of Anglo-Saxon literary orthodoxies. It identifies the author with a character who then becomes a spokesman, it thus reduces literature to a response to social or ideological questions and forgets that literature transforms the material on which it is based, it forgets, in fact, that it is literature.

2. Mrs Eliza Lynn Linton (1822–98) was the author of many novels. Her book *The Girl of the Period* (Two vols. 1883) is a collection of essays originally published in the important weekly, the *Saturday Review*. It is a book well worth reading for its transparency. Some of the essays are

'Modern Mothers' (an argument against nurses on the grounds that they teach children 'class coarseness'), 'What is Woman's Work?', 'The Shrieking Sisterhood', 'Womanliness' and 'The Sweets of Married Life' ('a wife's first treat, and her greatest, is when her husband begins to leave off this kind of fervid lovemaking and settles down into the tranquil friend' – II. 128).

All quotations are from this edition and the reference in parenthesis is to volume and page.

3.   Harry Quilter, *Is Marriage a Failure?*, 1887. The preface states that it is a selection from the 27,000 letters received by the *Daily Telegraph* about an article by Mona Caird in the *Westminster Review* which argued that marriage should be a contract whose terms are drawn up by the agreement of both parties.

'Glorified Spinster's' letter is on pp. 53–5. The quotation from the preface is on p. 10.

4.   It will no doubt be noted with some scepticism that seven of the eight novels chosen as examples in this essay are by men. This had not struck me when I chose them but it may well not be accidental. But generally in the nineteenth century there is an important problem raised by the fact that a number of serious writers, the Brontës, George Eliot, Olive Schreiner (who used the name Ralph Iron when she published her remarkable *The Story of An African Farm* in 1883) and Vernon Lee (Violet Paget) used male pseudonyms. Of course, there is a simple enough explanation of this: it is a way of avoiding being classed among the writers of what George Eliot called 'Silly Novels by Lady Novelists'. But the effect of it on the narrative rhetoric would repay careful attention, especially in the cases of *Shirley*, *Adam Bede* and Schreiner's book. At the same time, the number of writers who created popular success as women novelists servicing the mythology of the feminine – Mrs Henry Wood (*East Lynne*), M. E. Braddon (*Lady Audley's Secret*), Mrs Humphrey Ward (*Robert Elsmere*), Marie Corelli, Mrs Oliphant and Mrs Craik, are the most obvious examples – is enormous, and clearly an important area of research.

5.   Margaret Oliphant (1828–97) is best known as the author of *The Chronicles of Carlingford* (1863–76), some of which have recently been reissued by Virago. She was also a prolific reviewer for *Blackwood's Magazine* and wrote a review of *The Woman Who Did* and *Jude the Obscure* called 'The Anti-Marriage League'. There is an account of her fascinating career in V. and R. A. Colby, *The Equivocal Virtue: Mrs Oliphant and the Victorian Literary Market Place*, Archon, 1966.

Madam was serialized in *Longman's Magazine* between January 1884 and January 1885, and published in three volumes in 1885. Quotations are taken from the serial version and references are to chapters.

6.   Henry James, *The Portrait of A Lady* (1881). Quotations are from the Penguin edition (1963) which is based on a later, revised text, but this is not important for the purposes of my argument. The original edition ended with what is now the penultimate paragraph of the novel and was thus slightly more ambiguous.

James's extensive use of the female protagonist makes him a writer of first importance in any consideration of literature in this area. One should mention especially *The Bostonians* (1886) which is concerned partly with the feminist movement in New England in the 1870s.

7. Henry James, *The Art of the Novel*, R. P. Blackmur (ed.), 1934, pp. 48–51.

8. Mrs Linton's logic seems absurd, though this is partly because I am juxtaposing different parts of the book. Nevertheless it is worth noting that such women are frequently presented as sexually ambiguous. In Meredith's *The Ordeal of Richard Feverel* (1859), the hero's other woman, Bella Mount, dresses up as a dandy as part of their sexual game, and she remains as 'cold as ice' (i.e. unromantic). Hedda Gabler's pistols are part of the same complex, and some of Moreau's versions of Salome are androgynous.

9. George Macdonald (1824–1905) was a Scottish Congregationalist Minister who retired at the age of twenty-six to write books. Between 1851 and 1897, he wrote more than fifty books, some of them for children. His first adult fantasy, *Phantastes* was published in 1858. The best account I know of the background to *Lilith* is an unpublished doctoral dissertation at the University of Reading by R. McGillis (1973).

10. By 'humanism' I mean a strictly agnostic commitment to the belief that the human mind can work out its own answers. Lilith is not a humanist – on the contrary, she exhibits a kind of Nietzschean will. By linking this with her commitment to liberty, Macdonald is clearly simplifying his task.

11. H. Rider Haggard (1856–1925) scored his first success with *King Solomon's Mines* (1886). *She* followed in 1887. Together with Robert Louis Stevenson, he opened up a vein of exotic romance which became one of the dominant forms of the eighties and nineties. He is also the first of the Imperialist writers, to be followed by Kipling and John Buchan. Both *King Solomon's Mines* and *She* have reached Hollywood. *Nada the Lily* is another of his novels that will be found relevant to this theme.

12. I have tried to show in the first two sections that the use of a woman as a centre of consciousness does not necessarily constitute her being sited as the subject of her own experience, since often her own nature as a woman is seen to be given. But I would not like to underestimate the importance of the female centre of consciousness in the history of fiction. The major instances – Richardson, Austen, Gaskell, Eliot – seem however to be exploiting the special aptitude of woman for registering the social limitations on the apparently free mind, and most of the narratives concern a movement towards accommodation. There are texts in which this accommodation is so precarious as to invite a radical questioning (for example, *Persuasion* and Gaskell's remarkable novel, *Sylvia's Lovers*), and Charlotte Brontë, as Kate Millett shows, uses her heroines in a much more radical way. What happens in our period is that a largely legalistic logic poses the question of woman's freedom as unanswerable by concepts of 'nature'.

13. Grant Allen (1848–99) was a popular novelist and writer on biology who dabbled in various branches of radical thought. One of his earliest novels, *Philistia*, contains a fictional portrait of Marx.

14. I think that *Shirley* and *Villette*, though there is no question of denying that they are much more serious works than *The Woman Who Did*, should be seen in the light of this discussion too. For though they are both 'feminist' texts, they are also very limited by the bourgeois conceptions of freedom that are revealed by Allen's novel. Which is why Charlotte Brontë can seem so reactionary when she is also so radical.

15. The conflation of the two is clearly a favourite myth of conservative ideology. We have seen it there in *The Girl of the Period*, and it is also very marked in James's *The Bostonians*. Lawrence also resorts to it, though it should not be forgotten that Clara Dawes, in *Sons and Lovers*, who makes possible the hero's sexual adulthood, is bound up with the suffragettes.

16. It is important to make this distinction, because, unlike Mill, Meredith uses nature as an affirmative concept. The point is that for him the 'nature of woman' is as eminently artificial as it is for Mill. Nature in Meredith always appear as a disruptive and radical force. I wouldn't argue that this is not an ideological concept, but it is very different from the idea that it is natural to behave according to social prescription. It means, for one thing, that one's 'nature' is not defined by the group (sexual, social etc.) of which one happens to be a member.

    Interestingly enough, in view of the first two sections, Percy Dacier who falls in love with Diana, and who tries in a sophisticated way to subordinate her to his own self-realization, dilates on her charms in a passage of absurd romantic rhetoric, in exactly the terms I have used to define the two aspects of the woman-object: 'She was dear past computation, womanly, yet quite unlike the womanish woman, unlike the semi-males courteously called dashing, unlike the sentimental' (XXVI). This is immediately after he has decided he can count on 'making the dear woman his own in the eyes of the world'. For the elaboration of male subjectivity, see *The Egoist*.

17. Gissing wrote a number of novels and stories which focus on the situation of woman in various ways. Most notable are *The Unclassed*, *A Life's Morning*, *Thyrza* and *The Emancipated*.

    The eighties and nineties saw the publication of several of more or less 'naturalist' fictions which are relevant to this section. We should mention George Moore's *Esther Waters*, and, although 'naturalist' is hardly an accurate classification, the stories of Mark Rutherford, *Miriam's Schooling*, *Catherine Furze* and *Clara Hopgood*. Ian Fletcher's *Selections from British Fiction 1880–1900* (1973) is a valuable anthology and guide.

    The best account of *The Odd Women* in its historical context is by Maria Chialant, *Annali*, vol. X, 1967, p. 155.

18. Herbert Spencer (1820–1903) was truly the originator of what has come to be known as 'Social Darwinism', although his major sociological principles were published before *The Origin of Species*. He it is who originated the phrase 'survival of the fittest'.

19. Stokes, *Resistable Theatres*, Elek, 1972, p. 155.

    The issue here is between two ways of describing Darwin's law of evolution. In the first edition of *The Origin of Species*, he used the phrase 'natural selection' and only later added Spencer's term 'survival of the fittest'. The first description, though it identifies an *immediate* cause of evolution by no means presupposes an overall pattern and a law of progression – but Spencer's phrase clearly does. Darwin's original idea could not be turned into a social programme since it tended if anything to deny any purpose in nature. The growth of Tess, though it is predictable to the extent that a 'phase' is clearly a recurrent period in life, has no social purpose. On the contrary it is anti-social.

CHAPTER 10

Feminism, Class and Literary Criticism

I: Droit de seigneur

In the interval talk during the 1990 Glyndebourne production of *Le Nozze di Figaro*, Simon Rattle, who was concerned to stress that the chief feature of the production was the use of authentic instruments which he felt clarified the score's dissonances, implicitly indicated an even more striking feature. He illustrated the relationship between score and singers first by discussing Marcellina, whose aria in Act IV is a strong protest against the oppressive perfidy of the human male. Then he showed how the matronly patience of the Countess could be turned into passionate anger. Susannah's performance was positioned in relation to those two, and neither Figaro nor the Count were mentioned. Thus the opera was to be derived from the apparently least important soprano part and focused on the women as a group. You would not think from the discussion that the dramatic world was ruled by its eponymous hero, or the social world by another man, Almaviva. It was certainly, though not explicitly, a production strongly influenced by feminism.

In part, to be sure, this reflects the opera (though one handbook at least asserts that Marcellina's aria is normally omitted in production). First, it is emphasized in relation to Beaumarchais' text. In the play, Marcellina's attack on men is split between the recognition scene (III. xvi) and the end of Act IV where it only briefly recurs. In the first of these, it emerges as a somewhat absurd outburst in three speeches which become increasingly passionate. Marcellina is said to be 's'échauffant par degrés' in the first and is 'exaltée' by the third (Beaumarchais 1957: 322–23) – 'carried away by her own eloquence' according to the English translator, who wants us to be under no illusion that there is any substance to Marcellina's rhetoric (Beaumarchais 1964: 176). So it is embedded in a display of character and arises out of the general *mêlée*. In Da Ponte, on the contrary, it is a much more startling and impressive outburst, for Marcellina only reveals her 'feminism' when she has to choose between loyalty to her new-found son and her belief in Susannah's innocence based solely on her solidarity as a woman. The effect of this in the opera is to reduce Figaro himself to the

219

same level of irrational absurdity as the Count, as his ironic air 'Aprite un po'quel' accui' emphasizes. In Beaumarchais, Figaro agrees with his mother and is allowed to hold the audience with general speeches about the times. In Da Ponte, he has become part of the dénouement in Act IV. Marcellina's address to the audience in Beaumarchais only ironizes women who, she says, will fight one another if there is cause for rivalry but when personal interest does not aim them against one another are drawn ('toutes portées') to support their poor oppressed sex. In the opera, Marcellina sings an observation about the perfidy of men. In the play she shows women passively carried by passion from one posture – rivalry – to another – solidarity. This contrast works through in other details. Thus the instant and unquestioned alliance between Susannah and the Countess is broken off momentarily in Beaumarchais by the servant's admiration for her mistress' ability to lie, a gift of 'l'usage du grand Monde' (III. xxiv, 1957: 304). Beaumarchais' target is the social system, not the war of the sexes. Da Ponte/Mozart are concerned also with hierarchy, but much more with the gap between the way women are construed and how they see things themselves. This is not surprising if we think that *Così Fan Tutte* is to follow.

But in one major respect play and opera coincide, and indeed the opera emphasizes what is less obvious in the play, and that is the relationship between the two comic resolutions of male *amour propre* and social oppression. The absurdity of male desire is exposed by dramatic intrigue on stage, and, in the final act, the Count, who has spent the whole play/opera thinking that he desires Susannah, gets turned on by his wife simply because he does not know it is her. Moreover, as I have said, the universalized jealousy of Figaro and the resentment of Bartolo are shown to be utterly subjective. These exposures take place through dramatic disguise, concealment, plot and revelation. Throughout the play male desire is shown to be ludicrous and childish by Cherubino (a complex case of cross-dressing made more imponderable by his/her soprano voice in the opera). A rich comic texture satirizes gender difference and resolves it in the provisional utopian manner germane to the genre.

The class issue, however, is different. This is a drama about the *droit de seigneur*; the fundamental concern is with the power of patronage. Figaro can only get his way through cunning and wit, and then only up to a certain point. However cleverly he tricks the Count into sticking to his decision to give up the *droit de seigneur* (voluntarily, of course – there is no question of it being taken away, and, as a result, no question of a loss of real power as all the praises sung in honour of his decision confirm), Figaro ultimately runs up against an economic determinant. He needs money to release him from his bond to Marcellina. The Count will only give that money in exchange for Susannah's favours. The feudal right which has been officially abandoned is continued by economic pressure. The resolution of this, especially in Da Ponte/Mozart, is not dramatic but narrative and romantic. In a scene of farcical unrealism, Figaro reveals the strawberry mark which discloses him as a gentleman and the son of Marcellina. The birthmark, the story of kidnapping and the parody of Oedipus are all stale romance devices. And whereas in Beaumarchais, Bartolo and Figaro are far from overjoyed by his discovery (thus qualifying it with a certain 'realism') Da Ponte/Mozart have all three – mother, father, son – sing a most happy trio while the Count stands by distraught by his exclusion. It is all absurd, and it occurs so soon and so abruptly that we are left in no doubt that the final dénouement, which is the exposure of the *amour propre*, is the serious concern of the drama. Thus whereas the women achieve equality (of a sort) *dramatically* by the development of character, the servants are only rescued by the fact that their chief spokesman turns out to be a gentleman after all. It is not surprising that Michelet found the play unrevolutionary, nor that it is said that Da Ponte plays down the political subversiveness. I do not actually think this is true, however. What he does is visibly abandon one half of the class/gender differential system which constitutes the dramatic basis of the opera. And the marginalization of Figaro in the fourth act confirms this. The Glyndebourne production brought this out very fully. Not only does Marcellina become the keynote woman, but Figaro is a much less dominant character than the Count whose passions are disclosed with an evil intensity. This was a production threatened with rape.

I draw two seemingly contradictory lessons from this. First, the fact that this production can be so recognizably feminist without, it seems, being conscious of it (since Rattle was concerned with its authenticity) tells us something about the degree to which feminism has altered cultural perceptions even at a level where 'establishment' values are pervasive. On the other hand the social implication seems to be less privileged: Peter Hall's staging was pretty and luxurious, and there was no sense of the *Ancien Régime* being oppressive. This is partly no doubt because the class issues in Beaumarchais are more related to feudalism than capitalism and indicate that gender difference works on a larger, longer time scale.

But the other possibility is that feminism has become the victim of a certain legitimation. For, after all, if the class relations of Beaumarchais have changed, so have the gender relations: oppression of women today is not the same as it was in the eighteenth century. What the Glyndebourne production was responding to was not the contemporaneity of the specific sexual mores of the *Ancien Régime* but the general and translatable fact that in late eighteenth-century society, as in ours, women are systematically oppressed. We could equally make the same transfer of class relations, and indeed the shift within the play from legal to economic power inscribes this on the surface. Beaumarchais, Da Ponte and this particular production each progressively weighs the scale of gender down in relation to that of class. The eighteenth-century authors maybe see it as only soluble through a history that cannot be presented, only represented through the intrusion of another time into the spectacle. The twentieth-century audience has less interest because the dissonances of actuality are more audible on the level of gender.

This, if it is true, is surely a new situation. Twenty years ago, the culture reflected a complex but intense concern with social inequality. From *Roots* and *Saturday Night and Sunday Morning* to *Cathy Come Home* the long revolution towards a society free of class oppression was the central issue. The oppression of women got on to the progressive agenda by a polemical rebuke – women, the *longest* revolution. Capitalism is not now on the wane, but has taken new forms which can accommodate a limited sexual equality. The television is full of advertisements which joke about equal opportunities. We must not exaggerate; opportunities for women may have increased but that is a long way from equality. There may be women on the stock market, and some men have been forced to dress in pretty uniforms and serve fast food. But in the two equal opportunity institutions in which I have recently worked, it is women who clean the male urinals, and the revived sweating system in the garment industry is dominantly serviced by female workers. The opportunities are more equal for some than others.

But this makes it important not to lose sight of the class issue, for the oppression is most effective when it is compounded by economic power. I am far from saying that middle-class women are liberated. The physical environment with its lack of child care facilities, its vast residual imbalance of gender distribution of responsibility and educational opportunity, is underwritten by a culture which still throws unwarranted psychic burdens on women of all classes. If I had to choose, I would rather be a (moder-ately) poor male than a rich female. Independent of each other as the two forms of oppression are they must both be kept in view. And that means not only not ignoring one of them, but not overlaying one with the other by metaphor or some other rhetorical link. It even means, as this is what happens in the real world, playing them off against one another as enemies. Literature is a privileged site of these issues because it rehearses them in a controlled space. Narrative and metaphor offer tempting connections which as readers we should be prepared to resist.

II: Men in feminism

I have probably already angered many feminists who will question my right to deliberate on these matters. I am trying to write about the oppres-sion of women, its relation to the oppression of the working class and the implication of this for literary criticism. I cannot claim any real experience of either form of oppression, though I have more direct links to the latter than the former. I do try to practise socialist and feminist criticism, but whereas socialists are nothing if not unfashionable, feminists have established a certain power base in academic life, and it is not surprising that men who ally themselves with the feminist movement are accused of a certain opportunism (for example, Todd 1988). So I had better account for the temerity of my intervention. I became interested in literature as a function of class displacement. Literary texts were both a means of entry into the dominant culture and a way of retaining a critical option. By 1964 when I got my first university post I was working within an ideological framework dominated by Lukács, E. P. Thompson, and Raymond Williams. The specific situation of women is something that barely crossed my mind (unforgivably, it has to be said, since there was plenty of evidence all around me including that provided by my own practice). By amazing good fortune, I worked in a Department of English which also had Juliet Mitchell and Margaret Walters, precisely at the advent of what Terry Lovell has called 'the second wave' of British feminist thought. One of my first publications appeared in the same issue of *New Left Review* as the original text of 'Women, The Longest Revolution'. It is not surprising that I assimilated some feminist ideas. In the 1970s, Juliet Mitchell and later Mary Jacobus invited me to write for collections they were editing. I accepted these invitations without really thinking that I was climbing on to a bandwagon, but I did benefit by being asked to talk at the George Eliot centennial at Rutgers in 1980. Here I met Elaine Showalter, Sandra Gilbert, Nina Auerbach and many others, and realized that feminist literary scholarship was already strongly developed, and that any participation of mine in this field from now on should be more in the nature of moral support than active intervention. This was certainly emphasized by the fact that when Women's Studies were set up at Warwick males were rightly, in the context, excluded from participation. On days of self-flattery, I like to think that as soon as feminism showed signs of being a bandwagon in literature departments, I got off. Obviously, feminism has continued to affect my criticism, but if I need feminism, it does not need me.

This embarrassing autobiographical digression seems necessary as general self-justification in the light of the self-conscious rhetoric of most of the male contributions to that bizarre text, *Men in Feminism* (Jardine and Smith 1987), and of the more excruciating appropriations which have happened in the last decade. I accept that the central preoccupation of feminist criticism should be, as Showalter defines it, 'gynocritics' (1979: 26) though as Lovell has pointed out (1987: 132) this needs to concern itself not merely with women's writing, but more specifically with 'woman to woman writing' that is liable, as she argues, to be 'coded out of "literature"'. Besides solidarity, men can contribute little to this. They can, of course, try to read male texts in a feminist perspective without critical cross-dressing. But there is another periphery here marked by women's writing which is not specifically 'to woman' but which is a meeting point – vexed and incomplete as all literary articulations must be – of competing forms of oppression. So that if here I am waving a banner saying 'what about the workers?', on its reverse, facing the other crowd, is 'the woman pays'.

III: An unhappy marriage

Revolutionary socialism, after the terrible trauma of 1956, experienced a revival during the sixties, which coincided with a feminist revival. By 1983 revolutionary socialism was beleaguered and on the edge of its present total (though temporary, as I believe) eclipse. The success of feminism was no more than a raft some socialists were trying to climb aboard. It is clear now that the socialist movement of the sixties and seventies failed to take account of the feminist movement in a productive way. The long series of debates between marxism and feminism were conducted almost exclusively from the feminist position and it is not surprising that the most potent, though disputed, image was of the unhappy marriage. Terry Lovell writes that marxism and feminism talk past one another (Lovell 1987: 161) and the impression created by her recent anthology is that the situation described by Sally Alexander in the opening essay, 'Women, Class and Sexual Difference in the 1830s and 1840s' is that not much has changed in the last 150 years (Lovell 1990: 28–50). Perry Anderson's magisterial review of the intellectual disciplines ghettoizes feminism in a section of its own (the last) and disposes of it with an embarrassed avuncular simile – 'something like a transverse current moving, as it were, across the wider flow' (Anderson 1990: 135).

But, of course, it is precisely the context of the *New Left Review* in which the debate in its present phase was inaugurated by Juliet Mitchell, 'the significance of [whose] work for British socialist feminism' as Terry Lovell puts it, 'cannot be over estimated' (Lovell 1990: 5). What began in 'Women, The Longest Revolution' as a rebuke to the exclusivity of class analysis, had become, by the time of *Psychoanalysis and Feminism* a much more direct challenge to classic socialist theory. Scrutinizing and revising Freud and rescuing him from biologistic appropriations or anarchist salvationism, Mitchell proposes that in kinship relations, patriarchy is a meta-discourse, within which capitalist ideology is but a particular expression. Our access to this meta-discourse is through psychoanalysis, whose main function is to establish gender difference (Mitchell 1974: 409). The strategic proposal is not that socialists should alter their politics to account for gender difference but that it is possible to pursue two autonomous revolutions – the social revolution in the economic base of capitalism and the cultural revolution in the superstructure of ideology.

This becomes known as dual systems theory (for example Sergeant 1981) and is vigorously debated on a number of levels. Much as I would love to enter this debate, I do not suppose anybody but me would benefit from it. There can be no doubt that certain positions are inscribed for men and women irrespective of the particular formation of their societies, and indeed it is precisely because borrowings can be made that these positions and the codes they are fixed by can seem to be (if not are) non-socially specific. Thus chivalry can be made to serve the sanctification of the nuclear family, a form within which it has no place historically. There is also no guarantee that a less oppressive mode of production will in itself alter the oppression of women. And this has to be because such values are constitutive of the self (which means the subject aware of itself as subject). Unless they are biologically determined (which would not make sense) they must be determined by a very deep-seated cultural transmission. Psychoanalysis, which postulates an unconscious in which all the desires which have to be repressed in order to serve cultural needs are deposited, must have a role in unmasking these strategies. I think the arguments that Elizabeth Wilson mounts against the exclusive privileging of psycho-analysis have some grounds but I do not find that they relate to what Juliet Mitchell actually writes. Mitchell does not argue, for example, that psycho-analysis shows gender to be so utterly determined that it might as well be biology. On the contrary, she is arguing that patriarchy, which is what psychoanalysis uncovers, is highly vulnerable. Psychoanalysis is not, after all, a process of knowledge. It is a practical activity. Nor, on the other hand, do I have any sense that it is thought that the 'cultural revolution' could come even if the social revolution were entirely abandoned (Wilson 1986: 157–161). Surely the lesson of Stalinism is rather the opposite. Slapping a different mode of production on an unchanged culture is both violently repressive and, as we now see, doomed to failure.

Nevertheless, I do not think that *Psychoanalysis and Feminism* was intended to be a bible. On the contrary, its conclusions are deliberately circumspect. The unravelling of patriarchy and capitalism is an analytic strategy motivated by the perception that in, say, writers as diverse as Engels and Marcuse, the welding of them together results in patriarchy always being seen within capitalism. This could no longer be said to be the case. There is a great deal of writing which now presents capitalism as merely a special case of patriarchy, the danger of which is that it emulsifies the relationship between them. Mitchell's later retrospective essay is explicitly alert to this: 'by setting up the opposition of the sexes as dominant, we helped to produce the ideological notion of a "classless society"' (Mitchell 1986: 45). It is not surprising that any marriage between marxism and feminism is likely to be unhappy. Both know only too well that it is an oppressive institution. A more abrasive relationship between the two might have more realism.

For this, in the present situation, we need to focus on what Juliet Mitchell strategically marginalized in 1974, the interaction of the two forces in a specific historic formation. This is indeed happening within British historiography. Barbara Taylor (1983) has unscrambled the gender/ class tensions within the working class in the age of Chartism. Mary Poovey (1989), in a remarkable sequence of specific studies of parturition, divorce and nursing, investigates 'the ideological work of gender' in mid-Victorian England. Above all, Leonore Davidoff and Catherine Hall (1987) have investigated the role of gender difference in the formation of middle-class culture in early Victorian England. These texts show that at specific historical points the categories of class and gender cut across as well as reinforce one another and that it is at those points of tension and repressive reconciliation that the complex interactions show themselves. They show that the closer you look at the actual history, the more variegated and volatile are the interactions of economic demands and ideological strategies.

But this does not invalidate a longer view in which cultural divisions transgress economic structures. A class structure needs but is tested by gender difference, and the residual patriarchy which forms the individual's psychic position is at once threatened and appropriated in the actuality of history and how people experience it. In this telescopic view, capitalism is the latest instance of what has motivated all known human history, strategies for dealing with scarcity. Among these capitalism, by its very nature, primarily selects accumulation. It shares with its predecessors, however, the need to deal with scarcity by forms of human selectivity – the most tried and trusted of which is oppression of specific groups. The most efficient and affable form of oppression is to activate one oppressed group against another, and nothing could be more convenient for the ecology of selective practices than that such groups should experience such oppressions in radically different and exclusive forms. This prescribes active solidarity, but language is too vulnerable to premature utopianism. It should also strive to recall the past and represent the present. On the level of theory, feminists and socialists should learn how to quarrel, and socialist feminists in particular have to learn how to quarrel among themselves. That this is a well-developed though highly-fraught area of intellectual debate, Lovell's anthology fully demonstrates (1990: 71–169). But it is important for the understanding of literary texts, which float up from variable depths and on different currents.

IV: Insisting on the letter

The first level of the problematic of reading is that 'literature' is a construct that arrives and is developed (dialectically, not genetically) with the developing domination of capitalism and the industrial bourgeoisie.

This gives rise to contested readings. The novel lies outside 'literature' for a long time but once it is incorporated, we can never again return to the primitive reading of the cultural production situation of novels in the eighteenth and nineteenth centuries. This is not a question of canonicity but of reading practices. Terry Lovell (1987: 133–150) has shown that 'literature' is linked with the extension of higher education to women (as in theory it was to have been for the working class as well). We can write general histories of the class/gender implications of extended literacy and its cultural significance, but our reading of these texts is always going to be within a definite institutional framework. Even non-canonical phenomena – popular fiction, movies, advertisements – are assimilated into the interpretive process, which assumes that the text does not really know what it is saying. Like analysands, they need to be interpreted. Both the texts that make it to the academic couch and the qualified readers who – whatever their origins – have the resources to study them are inevitably separated from working-class experience.

The question is whether such privileged texts can do more than embody the oppression of women as a specific class expression. There are two answers to this – one is basically 'no' but they can by their silence help us to translate the specific gender oppression to other specific gender oppressions. Thus, for example, Boumelha on *Shirley* does not try to challenge the Thompson/Eagleton position that for all its gender radicalism, it retreats into a bourgeois myth, but shows that it remains audibly silent at this barrier, leaving the last word to the servant (Boumelha 1990: 99). There is a second kind of answer, like Nancy Armstrong's, which argues that fiction displaces politics to domesticity and thus that in the gender conflict the real subtext of the plot is played out (Armstrong 1989: 4).

One way through this impasse is the further restriction that literary texts by their very nature tell lies. Boumelha complains, in her essay on George Eliot, that too much feminist criticism relies on a naive realism (Boumelha 1987: 25). One of the striking developments of the last decade has been to see the text less as representational than as functional. Texts do not embody real relations but display the imaginary relations by which those real relations call the subject into being. Thus it is not for what they represent that texts must be read but for what they omit or expose in a disturbed way (Belsey 1980:129). The dominant aesthetic of organic form has to be inverted. In this way there is first a departure from the classic realist text and a new evaluation of fantasy, but there is also within the 'realist' text a subtext which does not say what it means, but reveals the meaning it is designed to conceal.

There are two difficulties here. In the first place, far from inverting prominent critical modes this merely seems to me to confirm them. There never was a genuine canon of literary studies, though it is often convenient to deal with a recurrent body of texts as though it were so. We must not forget that an enterprise such as *The Great Tradition* which sets out to establish a body of sacred texts, is consciously contesting a perceived dominant category. Nor does it privilege representation and realism, though later Watt's *The Rise of the Novel* appears to (I say appears because Watt does not offer representation but a kind of readerly consensus as the mark of formal realism). The organic form or moral fable is also a kind of subtext and the more subversive subtext of later feminist criticism is only displacing one paradigm (of identity) into another (of difference). I say 'only' and it would be wrong to underestimate that inversion. One uneasy silence in my argument is about contemporary French feminism whose re-interpretative energies are undeniable, though whether we can resist what Janet Wolff calls 'any lingering essentialism' (Wolff 1990: 62), without resisting the whole enterprise, is not easy to judge. We see in American deconstruction how pluralism and openness can be depoliticized.

More importantly, it is not sensible to confuse representation with narrowly defined realism. If we see texts as merely expressive we have to move from the text to the author, which is a circular process – since how can we find the author except in the text? But we can usefully, though admittedly with analogical imprecision, think of a text as having margins, that is markers which identify the conditions on which a text distances itself from language in general. This relates to the specific mode of production of the text, and it is interesting that Wolff (1990: 108) has recently, in calling for a greater integration of textual analysis and the institution by which texts are produced and consumed, recalled Eagleton's phrase 'literary mode of production'.

But production does not stop. *Villette* has a marginal but concise place in *The Great Tradition* but, since Kate Millett selected it as the only female novel to discuss in any detail (1972: 140–147), it has become the patient of many readings. Is it produced in conditions of the Victorian novel or the Feminist Tradition?

The relativity of production may be, however, the way through the dilemma of representation and expressivity. Texts would not be expressive if they were not representative or even representational. Lovell has noted how the history of the novel is poised strangely between formal realism and the Gothic, but these two are not so far apart. The portrayal of unromantic daily life is of course completely illusionistic. Neither *Pamela* nor *Emma* represent anything that really happened. Instead it is the condition of realism that it contains a negotiable world within a definite frame – as Balzac, accusing his reader of sitting complacently in his armchair at the commencement of his obscure Parisian tragedy, acknowledges. It is only a kind of snobbery that suggests there is not this same mix of motives when we pick up *Emma* as when we watch *East Enders*. The recognizability is part of the pleasure. Equally fantasy is not escapist. If it did not represent something real it would lose its compensatory value.

Gothic terror is not merely a frisson but an education. The point is that both kinds of text offer narrative and the important point about narrative, as Boumelha, making a most useful distinction between Romance and *Bildung* suggests, is that they are teleological, offering 'socially ratified closure' to 'utopian expansion' (Boumelha 1990: 20). On this basis, feminist reading becomes a question of unmasking what is resistant to narrative closure. Boumelha's own reading of *Villette* is a subtle and expressive deconstruction of the way in which the novel forces upon its reader 'the strangeness of narration itself' (1990: 103).

This strategy reveals a site in which the divided discourses of class and gender can interact, but it has dangers. The most cogent argument against my claim that the 'literary text' is constituted as a fixed area within which class can be subordinated to gender is Kaplan's 'Subjectivity, Class and Sexuality', which precisely maintains that by its nature as 'a heterogeneous discourse' literature can be read as 'an imaginary though temporary solution to the crisis of both femininity and class' (Kaplan 1985: 164). Visibility and frailty thus open up the awareness of something (the class insistence on gender difference) otherwise 'absolute and impregnable'. How exactly does that 'both' get constructed? For Kaplan (who uses few examples), it is through a resort to the Althusserian appropriations of Freud – condensation and displacement. This arises from the general limitation of feminism to a function of the Enlightenment project. Wollstonecraft situates feminism within rationality and thus the liberal coherent subject. Literature demolishes that by the heterogenous admission of other discourses: 'Female subjectivity, or its synechdocal reference, female sexuality, becomes the displaced and condensed site for the general anxiety about individual behaviour which republican and liberal political philosophy throw up' (Kaplan 1985: 165). The number of hermeneutic steps that have to be taken here is very worrying. In the first place we have to assume that female sexuality (which in turn is mostly represented by 'romantic love') is a synechdoche for female subjectivity. I can only say that, as a man, I would never allow anybody to do this to me. My sexuality is obviously part of my subjectivity but I would strongly resent being identified by my capacity to fall in love. Indeed no *Bildungsroman* with a male protagonist would work in that way. Even the hero of *Le Rouge et le Noir*, who makes a career out of falling in love, has a second room in his ego for diplomacy. Secondly, that sexuality is colonized by general ideological anxiety, which in turn is truncated into individual behaviour. Interpretation of this kind fuses distinct factors whose relationship is never stable.

If gender is cultural, however, so is narrative. All novels use narrative but they are only a tiny manifestation of the totality of highly developed narrative practices. The clearest motive of narrative seems to be, as Levi-Strauss defined myth, to explain something in a culture which cannot be explained rationally. It is a just-so story – do not ask why, here is how.

Realism at its most abstract level is crucial to this – for our culture, gender is explained entirely by narrative. It has no cause other than the history of its formation. Eve, the mother of mankind, was made to be the helpmeet of man from his spare rib. Through her, mankind fell from his paradisal state and she was thus condemned to the pain of childbirth. In the Judaeo-Christian tradition which was widely believed well into the nineteenth century, no biological reason for gender is offered. Biology becomes important only when the narrative fails. Boumelha (1990: 13) writes that Darwin, Marx and Freud all offered narratives and although this is true, it is also true that they set out to demolish the more convenient narratives of bourgeois society genesis, Lamarckian teleology, supply and demand, the narrative coherence of dream and waking. The origin of species turns out not to be originary, the market turns out to be a specific historical structure not an eternal law.

This makes narratives by definition double-edged. They are modes of legitimation but they would not be necessary if they did not have questions to be answered; you do not need to make laws against acts that people are unlikely to commit. Thus, by their readability, they are also the means of recognition. It is not merely the *defects* of fictional coherence that open up the ideological closure, it is the fictionality itself that discloses a problematic in the ideology, otherwise you would not need to tell stories about it. That may be a reason, for example, why there is so little fiction about the labour process itself (indeed not much real documentation either) because there does not need to be a story about work. You work for a living if you need to because otherwise you would starve (this is ideologically, not absolutely true). Why women can't work for a living or only work at certain useless tasks like being a governess, why marriage has to be monogamous, permanent, and exogamous and why women have to take the name of men – these are not self-evident. They are matters of history. History, if it is indeed what hurts, is not a simple undialectical limit of desire. It is rather the set of conditions within which needs and desires may come to be partially accommodated. This is not to deny Boumelha's concept of excess, merely to take it structurally into the narrative project.

If this is the case, and I recognize that it resists a whole line of argument deriving from deconstruction and its penumbra, then we do not ask of bourgeois literature that it should somewhere reintegrate the abrasive contradictions of gender and class, not even in the transformed text of interpretation. Bourgeois culture can recognize rank but it cannot recognize class since class is part of the economic structure. Ideologically, a man's a man for all that, but of course it cannot think that a woman is a man too, though there is no reason why not. From at least *The Rights of Woman* to *Daniel Deronda* that contradiction is unmasked by argument and narrative. On the other hand, the woman's story in certain privileged texts meets its own class boundaries and it is in these that the relationship between class and femininity is deployed. They are the texts, I shall argue, that look back to childhood when gender is in the process of formation. This double instance makes *Middlemarch* the key text, though a comprehensive account would need to consider much debated precedents such as *Frankenstein* and *Wuthering Heights*.

V: It would have required a narrative

In her suggestive exploration of women intellectuals within Victorian patriarchy, Deirdre David writes: 'All intellectuals of both sexes can trace their genesis, in the most general terms, to a matrix of cultural and social values, but the woman intellectual in the Victorian period possessed a less firm sense of lineage and affiliation with a tradition than was the experience of the male intellectual' (David 1987: 226). As it happens, I do not think the sense of lineage and affiliation of most male intellectuals would stand much scrutiny. Carlyle, Ruskin and especially Arnold were after all desperately trying to construct such a lineage (what could be more minimalist than the touchstone?). But it is true as a relative statement – coherence is even harder for the writers David investigates than for their male counterparts. This implies that we should turn the statement on its head. Women intellectuals have a more strong sense of the disorganic forces within their situation.

I want to question the apparently transparent metaphor of the matrix, clearly used by David as a mathematical term but recalling by its contiguity its biological etymology. Yes, we have one mother, but it is not from her that we derive our cultural and social values. These not only do not come from a unitary source but specifically come from contesting sources whose task is to neutralize one another. The utopian function of the traditional intellectual (who, in the English case at least, is not assigned to but has to seek this role) is to organize that contest into an acceptable coherence (ritual, dance, catharsis). But s/he can only aspire to this through the recognition of the originating dispersal. This is why so many major Victorian male writers felt themselves prone to or threatened by their own femininity, and why the most knowing and unaccommodating of them, Arthur Hugh Clough, defrocked genesis, matrimony and masculinity. *The woman intellectual is the paradigmatic case.*

We must attend to texts that represent the class-specific expression of the gender division. These will expressly not be woman-to-woman texts but texts that inscribe femininity at the boundaries of class culture. Thus if *Villette* assumes a central place in feminist criticism, *Middlemarch* will have to be restored to its frontier. This is confirmed by its remarkable critical history. There is a certain point at which it might be seen as the canonical text – morally motivated, organically structured, naturally available for discussion. The two dominant tendencies in British criticism, Cambridge scrutinism and Oxford liberalism, both claimed it as their own. If Leavis thought of Eliot as 'a peculiarly fortifying and wholesome author' (1962: 139), thus making her the *All Bran* of English Literature, W. J. Harvey would also cite *Middlemarch* – along with *War and Peace*, and taking his authority from C. S. Lewis and Iris Murdoch – as one of the 'normal' novels of which the 'liberal' says 'Yes, this is the world' (Harvey 1966: 16, 182–83).

Middlemarch has paid the price of this assimilation. By the time Barthes' ideas arrived in England, McCabe had it as the example of the classic realist text, situating the reader as unproblematic subject in dominance with access to a metalanguage by which the mere minds within the text could be ironized (McCabe 1978: 16), and Zelda Austen was defensively trying to explain 'Why feminist critics are angry with George Eliot' (Austen 1976: 549). Showalter saw Eliot as less radical than Charlotte Brontë and proposed rescuing a woman's novel ('the fall of Dorothea') from *Middlemarch* (Showalter 1977: 131; 1980: 306). The end of organic form and the end of realism on the one hand, the rise of radical feminism on the other, both made *Middlemarch* look like a monument to dead ideas.

Of course that was in the 1970s. The last decade has seen a recuperation. Hillis Miller and Lodge have shown that the authority of the narrator is not unquestioned and various writers, notably Gillian Beer (1986) and Jennifer Uglow (1987), have reclaimed Eliot for the sisterhood. I think something has got lost in this double restitution, however. Certainly the pluralist text of Lodge – though it certainly is closer to what actually happens than McCabe's selective reading – does not pick up what for me is the most striking and positive thing about the novel, and that is its absolute concern for truthfulness and straight looking, within a strong awareness of its difficulty. In other words I certainly think there is an authority claimed by the text, though not the authority assumed in McCabe's understanding of realism. This is partly because I resist the compression of knowledge and power into a single mode of oppression. As for the feminist reclamations, I think that there is some wishful thinking involved even in Gillian Beer's meticulous contextualizing, which significantly focuses on the unrepresented history of feminism that closes the gap between the time of the story (the 1830s) and the time of the narrating (the 1870s) (1986: 147–199).

We must start from a text which does operate a hierarchy of discourses and does not concern itself with the emergence of the female subject. Penny Boumelha again anticipates my position here, showing that Eliot's novel eschews 'transcendence by the individual' and 'uses a relentlessly materialist vocabulary' to affirm this. I need however to develop this insight to apply to the whole structure of the text (Boumelha 1987: 30).

If 'Realism' is a useful term to apply to nineteenth-century fiction, following it is true the retrospective celebration of Lukács, it can be said to be identified with Balzac and Stendhal in France and Gogol and Tolstoi in Russia. In so far as it has an idea of itself, it is exactly opposite from the descriptions of McCabe and Belsey. In fact 'classic realist' must be a contradiction in terms since 'classic', if it means anything at all, must refer to the possibility of ahistorical aesthetic structures which realism, evolving at its simplest level, from Cervantes, actually seeks to subvert. Even *Anna Karenina* which seems to offer itself as an almost natural narrative, opens with a self-conscious comparison between happy and unhappy families and occasionally materializes Levin's reflections (as when he appears wrapped in furs early in the novel). Balzac is certainly challenging the reader's pre-disposition to literary convention in *Père Goriot* and when Stendhal asks whether the word 'hypocrite' surprises us he is questioning the whole basis on which we receive character.

'Realism' as a project undeniably posits an authorial distance but that distance is problematized and secular. When George Eliot in Chapter XV of *Middlemarch* contrasts her position with Fielding's capacity to involve generalizations in an armchair drawn to the front of a proscenium arch, she is disavowing three classical principles: a belief in human nature as a universal, a belief in the capacity of the author to speak in his own right as a man of sense, and a belief in the demonstrative capacity of the stage to show appearances that coincide with the reality. Lydgate's discovery of science, which is the subject of the chapter, exactly parallels this distance. He moves from the vapid generality of a gentleman's classical education to the dusty particularity of research which knows that neither sign nor category have any status in the object of knowledge. This particular web which has so often been taken for a totalizing principle in the novel has to be unravelled by the act of writing. Of course, like Darwin's tangled bank, it does not disclose *itself* as a set of connections. If there is an ecology, it must be researched.

This has two implications for the argument of this essay. Firstly, it suggests that *Middlemarch* is deeply suspicious of the lying discourse of literature, specifically metaphor and narrative. Both of these are related to the situation of woman in social organizations and are, of course, not merely literary but social. Lydgate here in Chapter XV is viewed by Middlemarch itself as 'a cluster of signs' and by himself as someone betrayed by woman, someone with a narrative already closed. Within the wider text, not only is Rosamund's swan-like neck conferred on her at a dinner party by gossip, but also the opening image of Miss Brooke is presented to us before she has any kind of history. More importantly, narrative is the unreliable chain that ties women into marriage since it is only through the necessary prolepsis of romance that marriage choices can be made. Both Dorothea and Rosamund make up stories of their future, but this is not a straightforward irony, since how else can they be expected to choose men?

> Dorothea's inferences may seem large but really life could never have gone on at any period but for the liberal allowance of conclusions, which has facilitated marriage under the difficulties of civilisation. Has anyone ever pinched into its pilulous smallness the cobweb of pre-matrimonial acquaintanceship? (Eliot 1986: 22)

This is a clear attack on the binding contract of marriage which makes an imaginative inference into an iron law: 'I am always at Lowick'. 'That is a dreadful imprisonment' (382).

The novel also deploys both metaphor and narrative in the interests of truth, but this leads us to its two specific conditions. First, its historicity. The only moment when the shared misery of the novel impinges on consciousness is when Dorothea appeals to Lydgate and he, years afterwards, remembers the cry from soul to soul, within that embroiled medium. Of course this recall comes too late to be of use to either of them, but it establishes the precise nature of the reader's privilege. We are not enabled to see the error and limitation of the protagonists because of some subject-engendered privilege, merely because we are no longer caught in that history. We have to make judgments on what the characters do – not to judge would be to treat the lives of people as objects of consumption (which, of course, is partly inevitable if we read about them) but judgment is at our peril for we live within our own embroiled medium and we only see the embroilment of others with any clarity. That is why, I think, for all its historical distance and its class boundaries, *Middlemarch* goes on bearing meaning to its readers, (who have more sense of actual life than some academic critics). When Eliot does come, at last, in *Daniel Deronda*, to write about her own time, she has given it up for lost.

Secondly, in so far as it claims for itself a certain scientificity, *Middlemarch* does not belong to the natural history discourse of Balzac but to the discourse of experiment. Experiment operates by exclusion. One of McCabe's demonstrations of the novel's arrogance is the end of Chapter XXXIX when Dagley, drunk, is dismissed to benightedness. McCabe fails to quote, however, the end of the chapter:

> Some things he knew thoroughly, namely, the slovenly habits of farming, and the awkwardnesses of weather, stock and crops, at Freeman's End – so called apparently by way of sarcasm, to imply that a man was free to quit it if he chose, but that there was no earthly 'beyond' open to him. (433)

The irony doubles back on itself. However unbenighted Dagley might become, there would be no earthly 'beyond' open to him. But the novel does not pursue this. What is more important is that it comes in the very chapter that, in reply to Ladislaw's 'that is a dreadful imprisonment', Dorothea answers 'I have no longings'. Clearly there is a connection between the economic and the ideological determinants here, but it cannot be said that the former substitutes for or displaces the latter since the connection is visibly repressed. There are other moments when the novel seems to encounter its own boundaries. Thus in the very chapter in which Mrs Garth questions Dorothea's womanliness (538), Caleb, confronted with the peasants' fear of railways, is reduced to silence for he 'had no cant at command' (546). All round the text is a silence that acknowledges a world beyond. Later in the novel, fraught with jealousy of Ladislaw and Rosamund, Dorothea looks out and sees a poor man and woman walking each with a burden, 'the manifold wakings of men to labour and endurance' (777). This will give her a general courage, but the 'manifold wakings' pass out of the story. Clusters of signs, narratives, are controlled by far-reaching enquiry, but it knows exactly how far it goes – not into the life of Brassing or the tenant farm or the nomadic labourer. The historical project is specific.

I have argued elsewhere that the specific movement in George Eliot's fiction from the dualistic pictorialism and memorialization of *Adam Bede* and *The Mill on the Floss* is in *Romola* because it makes marriage the narrative opening (Goode 1983: 44). Marriage for Eliot is not the privileging of the domestic over the public life but the arena in which public and private meet. We need, I think, to see a definite historical sequence which investigates this meeting: first, at the onset of the modern world, the Renaissance, in *Romola*, then at the emergent dominance of Eliot's own middle class, the 1830s, the time of the Reform Bill, and finally, her own time, the threshold of Imperialist expansion and extra-European consciousness. In this sequence, if I am right, it is not *Middlemarch* that is the anomaly but *Felix Holt*. This novel sets out most explicitly to deal with class relations and it is the focus of the most concentrated political complaints about her. Williams's critique, for example, focuses on *Felix Holt* a good deal (Williams 1970: 888). *Middlemarch* returns to the same period, and effectively cancels *Felix Holt*. What redeems the latter novel, of course, is the story of Mrs Transome. The issue of gender subverts the project, leaves it looking lifeless. The stated project, that there is no private life that is not determined by a wider public life, is never realized in the text since the question of reform is simply personalized, and change merely weathered. What threatens to disrupt this is the story of the critical wife and dominant mother. The relationship of political and gender issues is inverted in *Middlemarch*. Reform here is marginal, almost there merely to provide a seam connecting Miss Brooke to Middlemarch and a pretext for the presence of Ladislaw.

Davidoff and Hall have enabled us to see what a central and accurate historical decision this is. They show a number of things which illuminate the actual project of *Middlemarch*. First, that the question of marriage and the gender roles it displays is a new issue in the years 1780–1850. Second, that this question is constitutive of middle-class identity and that it is in process during that time, so that to deal with it is not to displace actual politics – it is a political sphere (and not in the dubious sense in which the personal is claimed to be political, but in the sense that it is an important public arena). Third, that it requires the redefinition of masculinity and femininity. This applies in a very detailed way to masculinity as it is perceived in *Middlemarch*. Davidoff and Hall register, for example, a shift in the evaluation of gambling as an index of manly occupation to accounting, and then argue that accounting is rooted in estate management. (Davidoff and Hall 1987: 20, 201). The story of Fred Vincy, who has to learn not only not to gamble, but also to keep books at the hands of the estate manager Caleb Garth, exactly fits.

But more important is the complex way in which femininity shifts from partnership to equality within separation, and how this is bound up with the pursuit of leisure and retreat. Out of this emerges a fourth crucial point and that is that there is no static class identity, that consequent culture includes rural and urban families and ranges from rich to middle income families. The remarkable coherence of the middle class is not to be found within the class-specific politics of the franchise, free trade and industrial development but within marriage.

This may lead to a revision of Juliet Mitchell's perception of the historical relationship of kinship ideology to the capitalist relations of production. On a detailed level, it confirms her point that liberation can be as limited by the freedom of consumerism as it can by the work ethic. Davidoff and Hall show that the work ethic and the cult of leisure are not contradictory but flow into one another. But at a deeper level it may show that capitalism and kinship are not contradictory of one another in the way she surmises though, of course, they are contradictory in so far as exogamy and the gift are redundant in a community which has mobility and the machinery of accumulation. Mobility and machinery of accumulation are not of course overnight blessings and in particular it would seem that only in a socialist society could you do without marriage in the base since it is necessary for the privatization of childcare, and the inheritance of wealth.

It does not need to be shown of course that marriage is at the core of *Middlemarch*. The first words of the novel proper, 'Miss Brooke', are a sign of the exchangeable identity of the woman: 'and how should Dorothea not marry?' What we have is a comparative anatomy of marriage in which various models – father/daughter, brother/sister, master/slave – are deployed against one another. We might even schematize this by seeing the two main marriages as manifesting a new ideology of partnership in old pre-bourgeois conditions (since Casaubon is both squire and rector) and the old ideology of wife as furniture in the new conditions of professional self-reliance. Certainly this social, class-specific inflection is related to an older resilient patriarchy. Eliot anticipates Mitchell, as she does Davidoff and Hall, in the opening pages which stress how Dorothea is constructed not by one absent father, but three, since not only is her biological father dead, but her social father effeminate, and her spiritual father, Mr Cadwallader, irresponsible, so that she does act as a dutiful daughter in seeking to seduce another father, Casaubon. Vincy too is notable for his absence of imagination, a coarse mirror in which the beauty of Rosamund cannot properly see itself. The cultural level, however, is manifest by the class-specific and historically distanced project which sets it in motion. I am far from suggesting that the text resolves the relationship of class and gender. Literary texts only ever resolve things rhetorically. In fact it is the refusal to fuse class and gender that makes *Middlemarch* such an uncompromised text.

But this does not differentiate my reading from the Boumelha/ Showalter rescue of the woman's novel from the text, which would finally have to rescue Dorothea from her second marriage, and may be not allow Mrs Bulstrode to return to hers without a sense of loss. I return to the absurd prolepsis, the pilulous smallness of the pre-matrimonial acquaintance which constitutes the ideological basis of the novel. The best marriage in the novel is Mary's and Fred's. It is, of course, very marginal and, consciously I think, made within visible literary conventions (Fred is the victim of great expectations, and the whole Rigg episode seems like a mystery not pursued). In two ways, Mary and Fred escape the constraints of the real patriarchal world. First, Caleb is far from absent, and can act as a substitute father for the incompetent Mr Vincy. Secondly, they have grown up together – they are siblings.

This gives marriage in the novel a dialectical possibility, since it is not merely a prison characters move into through lack of knowledge. Dorothea, who marries her 'father', learns through this to become the 'critical wife'. In the formation of middle-class, as opposed to aristocratic, domination, marriage has a potentially progressive as well as regressive role. Specifically, it is by the awareness generated by her bad first marriage – the realization that you cannot rely on fathers to teach you Hebrew, which would be access to the written secrets of the culture – that Dorothea learns to identify herself (by a written protest to her dead husband's instructions) and (as part of this) to recover her own childhood. For that is what her relationship with Ladislaw is, first that she is to him not a picture, image, portrait of a lady, but a voice (and a voice waiting to be released, as the Cleopatra is revealed to be the Ariadne), and secondly that the voice is contacted through an *exchange* of looks. The gaze of the opening, of Middlemarch, of the reader, is vicariously via Ladislaw returned. He is indeed one of the few visible males in fiction. What male readers find hard to take is that he is actually pretty – an attractive sexual object. But what is more important is that once they have found one another Dorothea and Ladislaw can become like children. There are many ironies here, to be sure, not the least of which is that Eliot with her historical distance as well as her historical imagination, knows that the mythic potential of the couple is sibling more than exogamous.

This sketchy account of the novel does not do justice to the complex textual realization which makes of marriage so dynamic a process working through the text. Thus on the margins of a feminist history proper of fiction – which focuses on the madwoman in the attic, on hysteria, on the incomplete suppression of female subjectivity – the history of the interaction of class and gender is inscribed not merely in the bourgeois novel but in the novel most consummately about being bourgeois. For the way to become fully part of 'the involuntary palpitating life' by which Dorothea sees her connection to the manifold wakings of men to labour and endurance is to enact the complex history of marriage by which the bourgeoisie institutionalizes its domination. The terms on which this development can take place include the suppression of that further class struggle between the bourgeoisie and the working class, but it is not a silent, naturalized suppression. It is marked at the boundary of Dorothea's consciousness and deferred by the novel's historicity.

VI: The tragedy of the dispossessed

Davidoff and Hall's research finishes in mid-century. When Eliot reached her own time in *Daniel Deronda* capitalism was already a world force, complicated by empire. The hegemony that both Gwendolen and Deronda have to deal with is a triplicate mastery of gender, class and race, and the objects of that mastery therefore are embroiled in their own divisive contestation. Daniel's bitter confrontation with his mother and the desolate last encounter of Gwendolen and Daniel are fraught with that internecine struggle. Class, gender and race are frequently cited as a totality, but this novel shows them to be opposed and athwart. The concept of a matrix of the subject is even more of a mask. Motherhood at the end of this novel is the source of nothing other than self-denial, unacceptable to the hero with new lands to occupy, redemptive for the heroine who is not a special case. I use 'redemptive' ironically, for what Gwendolen is told to return to is conformity to the image of motherhood that Daniel refutes.

We are entering with this novel the realm of the modern – urban, global, self-conscious, ironic. The frontier of women's history and class struggle is not merely complicated by the new boundaries drawn by globalization of capitalist exploitation, it is placed in another dimension. This does not mean, of course, that there are no texts which explore this frontier after 1880: Hardy's fiction, for example, can be seen as an uneasy negotiation of sexuality and class (see Boumelha 1982) and both George Egerton ('Gone Under', 'Wedlock') and Katherine Mansfield ('The Garden Party', 'Life of Ma Parker') explore this abrasive contiguity. Nevertheless, as modernity becomes more ineluctable, a certain aesthetic totality becomes less easy to sustain. This is not due to the loss of the unitary subject which one glimpse at the the first chapter of *Middlemarch* will show never existed. What is lost is the capacity of either mobility or pivotability to be agents of narrative continuity. If we take urbanization as the common denominator of modernity, mobilization and zoning are two contradictory conditions which make those forms of privilege unexceptional and therefore incapable of providing perspectives. What the great British modernists have in common is that they privilege obscurity (transitive and intransitive) in order to have access to modernized experience. So that whereas the functionality of the pre-modern protagonist derives from whatever provisional and contingent unity the plot confers on the subject, Clarissa Dalloway, Bloom and the separate generations of Brangwens owe their narrative agency precisely to their severance. That is why it is not difficult to marginalize any of them in an aesthetic derived from a totalizing politics. What is important about such texts is the productiveness of the transformation of ideological material they represent, and in these terms it is precisely the sense of the war between determinants that constitutes the basis of their effectivity. Thus while I don't think that Molly Bloom can be recuperated for feminism ('Penelope' is not feminine writing but a parody, though see Henke 1990: 126–163 for a different view), or that Clarissa Dalloway can be made an honorary member of the working class, I do think that the specific and limited agency constructed by these texts is one that socialists and feminists should hold precious.

The implications of modernism for feminism are analysed with remarkable succinctness by Janet Wolff. Arguing that the definition of the modern and the nature of modernism derived from the experience of men (to which we should add 'bourgeois') she goes on to say that women nevertheless had their own experience of the modern world and are as involved in the revolution of literary and visual languages as men. She concludes that modernist strategies are not intrinsically progressive, but that it is for us to insist on 'the radical potential of the deconstructive strategies of modernist culture' (Wolff 1990: 57, 63). We could make the same case for the working class, though its access to modernism is very limited. But they will not be the same case, and neither will the case of imperialist subjects. On the contrary, they will certainly contest one another, as Woolf contests Lawrence's phallocentrism, and Lawrence contests Joyce's petty bourgeois self-consciousness and Joyce contests their English imperialism. Needless to say (and it has already been said by others) each of these writers forces the reader to see what is being obliterated by the contestation, which is why you can see how important feminism is to Lawrence or how Woolf constantly brings the reader up against the working world in, for example, *Jacob's Room* (on this matter in general see Beer 1987). But what is just as important as these qualifying statements is that the texts of the modernist movement bear witness to the intractability of the contradiction between different levels of exploitation.

One way of handling this is to resort to cultural materialism, which I take to be a development of Althusser's relative autonomy. All levels of social interaction are grounded in material relations of power and exploitation and not in a way that can be reduced to a single paradigm, notably that of capital and labour. Gender and imperialism are therefore sites of struggle in themselves, and more significantly, the arena of cultural practices as a whole – even when making no direct reference to the three political arenas – is one in which the struggle can be unmasked; Lovell's study of fiction and her extension of the argument into the relationship of English studies to the containment of the emancipation of women is a notably valuable case. It is not difficult to show that the global and panoramic aspirations of nineteenth-century writers are at best illusory and, like all illusions, are sponsored by the hegemony. In this case, the modernist writers can be presented as carrying on their own cultural revolution rather than betraying someone else's.

I recognize the need to rescue modernism from the homogenized negation we find in Lukács and later variants on the one hand and some of the unremitting representationalist feminist critiques on the other, but it leaves me with a double anxiety. First, it is political. Capitalism is a more diverse and adaptable productive system than its predecessors, and it can therefore make space for many specific emancipations. During the immediate post-war period, when the Unions were strong, it enabled some improvement in the workforce. In the wake of advances in birth control and other advances in medical technology, it could adjust to the feminist revival. And it also handled decolonization without being radically damaged. All these adjustments, however, do not take away the fundamental condition on which capitalism relies – the production and exchange of commodities. Commodities can only exist as commodities on the basis of differential values and therefore of competition. There must always be, as the East Germans are now finding out, losers. The aggregate degree of oppression has never diminished under capitalism. It simply moves around. And it will always seek to displace itself, which is why class oppression is always passed on to gender or race and why gender and race in their struggle to ameliorate will always ignore economic misery if possible, and even create their own parodic exploitations. There is no sequence in this. There is a finely balanced ecology of misery. Only a society based on the exchange of use values in respect of human needs and abilities would change this. There is no site of struggle that has not been determined by a wider site of struggle.

The great classics of modernism eschew the panoramas of nineteenth-century fiction not because they have woken up to the illusory nature of the unitary subject (which was at best a transitive strategy and at worst always disintegrating) but because they need to speak for obliterated energies in search of different forms of totalization. But this leads to my second anxiety, which is methodological. It is certainly convenient to speak of the texts of 1910–1940 as radically different from their nineteenth-century forbears, because although the texts of Wells, Bennett and Galsworthy are also different, they are not different in the same way. That is why I use the term 'modernism'. 'Modernism', however, is sometimes opposed to 'realism' and sometimes to 'Victorian', and this must make us see immediately that it is at best a very leaky category. 'Modernity' to which 'modernism' is an aesthetic response is around from at least the 1840s, before 'realism' gets into English as a term applicable to the novel, and this latter does not have sufficient coherence to define either an aes-thetic programme, or even a retrospectively constructed category, without great elaboration. What needs to be stressed for the present argument is that the changes in literary method that we see in the development of the novel are continuous within parameters defined by an authorial project of demystification. In terms of the relationship between feminist criticism and class conflict this means looking more attentively at the origins of the feminist novel itself.

By 1910, there is, of course, a good deal of conflict between feminism and the labour movement. But this is not before the loss of a generation which held them together, and this is a significant moment in literary history. I am not only thinking of Beatrice Potter (later Webb) and Annie Besant, but of the remarkable group which centred on Eleanor Marx in the 1880s. Marx herself, of course, translated Ibsen and most significantly *Madame Bovary*, and her lecture on 'Shelley's Socialism' stresses the influence of Mary Wollstonecraft and Mary Shelley on the poet's 'percep-tion of woman's real position'. 'The woman is to the man as the producing class is to the possessing' (Aveling and Marx Aveling 1947: 13). But more specifically, for our purposes, we need to attend to two novelist friends of Eleanor Marx, one neglected, the other underestimated, who have to work their way through the given conventions of the broadly mimetic narrative in order to articulate the relationship defined in this comment.

The first of these is Margaret Harkness whose 'realistic story', *A City Girl*, was published in 1887, and whose even more extraordinary second novel, *Out of Work*, 1888, has recently become available from the Merlin Press (1990). Both of these texts – which come out of a critical reading of Zola – bring the issue of the exploitation of women into the immediate arena of, in the first case, urban poverty, and in the second that of unemployment and the unemployed riots of 1886 and 1887. *City Girl*, as the title signifies, seems the more obviously relevant since it takes a working-class girl as the focus of the double exploitation of women and the working class (see Goode 1982). But *Out of Work* is both more experimental formally and a more forceful illustration of my general point that the exploitation of women and the exploitation of workers are also in tension with one another. The pressures on 'the pretty methodist', Polly Elwin, to reject her pledge to the unemployed hero are fully realized, so that when he calls her 'little hypocrite' he also leaves the marks of his male violence on her wrist. More significantly, Harkness borrows the gamine convention in the Squirrel who ironically becomes, as Bernadette Kirwan observes, a substitute mother (Law 1990: xvii) to the hero. But before we are told that he has crawled back to his original mother's grave in the countryside to die, we are given a scene in which the Squirrel becomes aware of the cosmic but unfathomable female wisdom of the Sphinx and hears the song of 'the wraith Suicide' which echoes the last words on the cross. The Squirrel is drawn into 'the strong embrace' of Father Thames and is no longer 'a waif and stray' (Law 1990: 268).

What is remarkable about this novel is the way that the fragmented story embodies the relegation of what Kirwan terms 'sociable relations' (xvii) to the realm of the casual poor who by definition constitute no community – the Squirrel literally loses Jos in the stream of homeless poverty. Equally, Polly rejects him when she bumps into him on his way from a night in Bow Street police cell to 'the doss house' as she turns the corner of Commercial Street (218). This is in every sense an urban novel, a totally modern experience in which 'the utter loneliness' (267) is what men and women have in common. It is not a modernist novel and it is permeated by a strong but pessimistic Christianity, but it negotiates the boundary of gender relations and class relations in an important way.

The other text of this period which reworks the conventions of the novel in order to cross without negating the boundaries of exploitation is Olive Schreiner's *The Story of An African Farm*. This is not, of course, a neglected text and on the face of it it is less concerned with the interaction of feminism and socialism than that of feminism and Darwinism and feminism and imperialism. It is not trying to represent the formation of social relations: the farm is very isolated and more like the microcosmic world of *Wuthering Heights* than even a provincial world as distanced as St. Oggs. Nevertheless, the novel is situated in a larger political world, for the downfall of the precarious idyll is brought about by the parodically self-made Bonaparte Blenkins, who brings specious evangelicalism to the farm, and who reaches the height of his power after catching Waldo reading the chapter on property in Mill's *Political Economy*.

The critical questions that arise here are not about the importance of this text but about its pessimism and its incoherence. At the end of her chapter on 'The Feminist Novelists' which includes a strong account of Schreiner, Showalter quotes a story from *Lolita* of a monkey given an easel whose first painting shows the bars of its cage. I find the irony of this more telling against Nabokov than against the feminists who 'elevated their restricted view into a sacred vision' (Showalter 1977: 215), though there is no doubt that both Schreiner and Egerton, and, as we have seen, Harkness deploy the discourse of cosmic pessimism against what is perhaps a failure to see a clear programme of action. In this text, however, it is precisely the sacredness of the prison bars – or at least their unpassability – that generates its solidarity. It is because Waldo and Lyndall come together at the boundaries of their subjective experience that they articulate a totality that lies outside the individual life and outside the particular emancipations of religious doubt and feminist awareness. In this sense Gregory Rose, who begins as a courtier and ends as a transvestite nurse, is as much the embodiment of the novel's radical ideology as Waldo's stranger or Lyndall herself (a suggestion implicit in Showalter 1977: 152).

Because it deals with forms of oppression as separated experiences (Lyndall's question to Waldo is unanswered), and yet as coherent manifestations of oppression as a whole, the novel has to build itself not on subjectivity (which it parodies by inverting the pivotal, mobile agency of earlier novels, making the male pivotal, and the female mobile). Rather it has to build a structure out of gaps and barriers and occasional transmissions, whose only unitary source is the shared oppression of childhood. Doing this, it becomes not only the foundation novel of the African feminist tradition, as Holtby, Dinesen and Lessing recognize, but, certainly, one of the foundation texts of the modern novel in general. Gilbert and Gubar (1989: 53) correctly place it against the cultural agenda activated by imperialism, but still accuse it of incoherence, anachronistically dividing it between Victorian convention and modernist experiment. This makes experiment sound gratuitous or even wilful, and they tend to extract from the novel a new *Wuthering Heights* in which, strangely as cause for lament, male potency is lowered. Schreiner herself, however, made it clear that the 'incoherence' is programmatic. Echoing Eliot's dismissal of Fielding's generality as theatrical, she takes it further:

Human life may be painted according to two methods. There is the stage method. According to that each character is duly marshalled and ticketed; we know with an immutable certainty that at the right crises each one will reappear and act his part, and when the curtain falls, all will stand before it bowing. There is a sense of satisfaction in this, and of completeness. But there is another method – the method of the life we all lead. Here nothing can be prophesied. There is a strange coming and going of feet. Men appear, act and react upon each other, and pass away. When the crisis comes the man who would fit it does not return.

> When the curtain falls no-one is ready. When the footlights are bright-
> est they are blown out; and what the name of the play is no-one knows.
> If there sits a spectator who knows, he sits so high that the players in
> the gaslight cannot hear his breathing. (Schreiner 1889: vii–viii)

This is not the same as Eliot's 'embroiled medium' nor as Woolf's
'luminous halo', but it clearly comes between them. Of course it is marked
by the cosmic pessimism of its time, as Eliot is marked by positivism and
Woolf by Bergson. What is more important is that it shares with them the
need to break with previous supposedly realist practice in the interests of
the new realism, though the failure to finish *From Man to Man* suggests
that Schreiner found no way through the problems posed by the fractured
narrative of the earlier novel. A full analysis would show, however, that it
is not her incompetence which the provisionality of that text shows, but
her unflagging ambition to present new forms of female consciousness in
face of the evolving structure of global capitalism. It may be that we had
to wait for *The Golden Notebook* for that, a text that no one would accuse of
incoherence. Between them, Winifred Holtby, who also tried to find new
totalizations of competing forms of oppression, recognized in her review
of *From Man to Man* that the separate parts of Schreiner's work addressed
themselves to 'the tragedy of the dispossessed' (Brittain, Holtby 1985:
201). That tragedy is large, endlessly changing and rarely given to peripo-
etic unity, but it sometimes has reluctant spokespersons in literary texts.
It is for readers to make its voices heard, and to value those texts which
will not hide its discords.

References

Anderson, Perry (1990). 'A culture in contraflow', *New Left Review* 182, 85–137.
Armstrong, Nancy (1987). *Desire and Domestic Fiction: A Political History of the
    Novel*. New York, Oxford University Press.
Austen, Zelda (1976). 'Why feminist critics are angry with George Eliot', *College
    English* 37, 549–61.
Aveling, Edward and Eleanor Marx Aveling (1947). *Shelley's Socialism: Two
    Lectures*. Manchester, Leslie Preger.
Beaumarchais, Pierre Augustin Caron de (1957). *Théâtre Complet*, edited by
    Maurice Allem and Paul Courant. Paris, Bibliothèque de la Pléiade.
— (1964). *The Barber of Sevillè and The Marriage of Figaro*, translated with an
    introduction by John Wood. London, Penguin Books.
Beer, Gillian (1986). *George Eliot*. Brighton, Harvester Press.
— (1987). 'The body of the people in Virginia Woolf', in Sue Roe (ed.) (below),
    85–113.
Belsey, Catherine (1980). *Critical Practice*. London, Methuen.

Boumelha, Penny (1982). *Thomas Hardy and Women. Sexual Ideology and Narrative Form.* Brighton, Harvester Press.

— (1987). 'George Eliot and the end of realism', in Sue Roe (ed.) (below), 15–35.

— (1990). *Charlotte Brontë.* Hemel Hempstead, Harvester Wheatsheaf.

Brittain, Vera and Winifred Holtby (1985). *Testament of a Generation,* edited and introduced by Paul Berry and Alan Bishop. London, Virago Press.

David, Deirdre (1987). *Intellectual Women and Victorian Patriarchy.* Basingstoke, Macmillan Press.

Davidoff, Leonore and Catherine Hall (1987). *Family Fortunes, Men and Women of the English Middle Class,* 1780–1850. London, Hutchinson.

Eliot, George (1871–2). *Middlemarch,* edited by David Carroll (1986). Oxford, Clarendon Press.

Gilbert, Sandra and Susan Gubar (1989). *No Man's Land. The Place of The Woman Writer in the Twentieth Century.* II: *Sexchanges.* New Haven, Yale University Press.

Goode, John (1982). 'Margaret Harkness and the socialist novel', in Gustave Klaus (ed.), *The Socialist Novel in Britain.* Brighton, Harvester Press.

— (1983). '"The affections clad with knowledge": woman's duty and the public life', in *Literature and History* 9, 33–51.

Harvey, W. J. (1966). *Character and the Novel.* London, Chatto and Windus.

Henke, Suzette A. (1990). *James Joyce and the Politics of Desire.* New York and London, Routledge.

Jardine, Alice and Paul Smith (eds) (1987). *Men in Feminism.* London, Methuen.

Kaplan, Cora (1985). 'Pandora's box: subjectivity, class and sexuality in socialist-feminist criticism', in Green and Kahn (eds), *Making a Difference. Feminist Literary Criticism.* London, Methuen.

Law, John (Margaret Harkness) (1990). *Out of Work,* introduction by Bernadette Kirwan. London, Merlin Press.

Leavis, F. R. (1962). *The Great Tradition.* Harmondsworth, Penguin Books.

Lovell, Terry (1987). *Consuming Fiction,* London, Verso.

— (1990). *British Feminist Thought.* Oxford, Basil Blackwell.

McCabe, Colin (1978). *James Joyce and the Revolution of the Word.* London, Macmillan.

Millett, Kate (1972). *Sexual Politics.* London, Sphere Books.

Mitchell, Juliet (1974). *Psychoanalysis and Feminism.* Harmondsworth, Penguin Books.

— (1984). *Women – The Longest Revolution.* London, Virago Press.

— (1986). 'Reflections on twenty years of socialism', in Juliet Mitchell and Ann Oakley (eds), *What is Feminism?.* Oxford, Basil Blackwell, pp. 34–48.

Poovey, Mary (1989). *Uneven Developments.* London, Virago Press.

Roe, Sue (ed.) (1987). *Women Reading Women's Writing.* Brighton, Harvester Press.

Taylor, Barbara (1983). *Eve and the New Jerusalem.* London, Virago Press.

Schreiner, Olive (1889). *The Story of An African Farm,* by Ralph Iron [Olive Schreiner]. New Edition, London, Chapman and Hall.

Sergeant, Lydia (ed.) (1981). *The Unhappy Marriage of Marxism and Feminism.* London, Pluto Press.

Showalter, Elaine (1977). *A Literature of Their Own. British Women Novelists from Brontë to Lessing*. Princeton, New Jersey, Princeton University Press.

— (1979). 'Towards a feminist poetics', in M. Jacobus (ed.). *Women Writing and Writing About Women*. London, Croom Helm, pp. 22–41.

— (1980), 'The greening of Sister George', *Nineteenth Century Fiction*, 35.

Todd, Janet (1988). *Feminist Literary History. A Defence*. Cambridge, Polity Press.

Uglow, Jennifer (1987). *George Eliot*. London, Virago.

Williams, Raymond (1970). *The English Novel from Dickens to Lawrence*. London, Chatto and Windus.

Wilson, Elizabeth, with Angela Weir (1986). *Hidden Agendas. Theory, Policy and Experience in the Women's Movement*. London, Tavistock Publications.

Wolff, Janet (1990). *Feminine Sentences. Essays on Women and Culture*. Cambridge, Polity Press.

CHAPTER 11

Gissing, Morris, and English Socialism

The aim of this paper is to raise general problems about the relation of the novel to historical actuality through the discussion of a highly specific instance. Inevitably this entails a concern with the interpretation of the historical actuality itself, and I shall, at the end, point to the historical problems inherent in the nature of English socialism in the 'eighties, and in the ideas of William Morris especially. But primarily, I am concerned to highlight the literary problems which emerge from a study of George Gissing's presentation of that actuality with a view to raising three general questions about the nature of the novel as a mimetic form. It will seem that I am taking a very narrow, literal-minded view of "mimesis," and this is quite deliberate, for I think that discussions of nineteenth-century "realism" tend to be vague even where they are intelligent. At the same time, I shall be much less concerned with the "social reality" that the novel imitates than with the consciousness of that reality as it emerges in the history of ideas. It would be depressingly optimistic for me to offer even tentative solutions to the general issues: my concern here is to bring out their complex nature in a small instance, and perhaps offer an example of a methodology which tries to cope *critically* with the relationship between literature and history.

Two of the questions will be completely implicit. They both revolve around the ambiguities of the idea of realism. The novel I shall be mainly concerned with, *Demos*,[1] claims to be "a story of English socialism." It is, but it is an inaccurate one: it only partially coincides with the historical facts. Equally, however, its untruths are not meaningless: they coincide with a contemporary *consciousness* of socialism. Its unrealities in this way are as mimetic as its realities. How far is an awareness of this relevant to our judgment of the novel as a reflection of a particular phase of social development? The second question is the aesthetic aspect of this. Even if we decide that the novel can have a historical use because of its distortions as well as its reality, this doesn't justify it as a good novel. Nor am I going to argue that *Demos* is a good novel. But, as I shall try to show, in opposition to Raymond Williams, who has argued that it largely reflects Gissing's personal confusion,[2] *Demos* is confused partly because the situation, and the general consciousness of that situation, is confused.[3] Do we expect a novel somehow to transcend the limitations of its epoch? And how, exactly? What, without magic formulas about the artist, do we mean by "transcend?"

My third question is much less merely speculative and will be much more immediate in my paper. When we think about "the novel and society" we might be thinking about two quite distinct sets of problems. We may be thinking about the novel as, itself, a social product, defined by the economic and social situation of the writer (I'm thinking of the kind of problem discussed in Q. D. Leavis' *Fiction and the Reading Public*, or Kathleen Tillotson's *Novels of the 1840's*). Or we might be thinking about the novel as "mirror" of society. Naturally our main concern here is with the latter. But of course, logically, it is not possible to think about these aspects as isolated at all. Part of the aim of this paper will be, in specific ways, to suggest a relationship between the two.

Demos makes a useful case study for these problems. Gissing is an outstanding figure in the economic and cultural crisis in fiction in the 1880's and *Demos* has a special place in his career: it was written in years of acute poverty and misery (the story of *New Grub Street* [1891] takes place between 1882 and 1886), and by this time Gissing had clashed sharply with the arbiters of popular taste both in that his second novel, *Mrs. Grundy's Enemies*, remained unpublished by the timorous Bentley, and that in January 1885 *Punch* had lampooned him for advocating "open coarseness" in fiction. At the same time, *Demos* was a relative success, and we know enough about the circumstances of its composition and its reception to suggest that it was written to *be* a success. This means that the tension between the real Gissing ("Gissing the rod") and the anonymous implied author of *Demos* is rather transparent, so that the novel is a fairly clear case for the study of pressures on the novelist in the 'eighties.

Secondly, *Demos* is a good case for the study of the novel as social reflector because it deals with an amply documented actuality, the early development of the socialist movement in England, so that we are in a good position to assess its mimetic validity. Two further advantages stem from this in relation to the first point about *Demos* as a social product. The first I have indicated: the limitations of *Demos'* historical accuracy can be specifically related to anti-socialist ideological trends in the 'eighties. I shall be concerned with three especially: Mallockian aristocratic conservatism, positivism, and social Darwinism. The second point arises from the tension between Gissing and the author of *Demos* which I have just mentioned. The propaganda value of the novel is limited by a confusion in the anti-socialist case arising from the incompatibility between these three ideologies, and more importantly, from the incompatibility between these and Gissing's own position with regard to the relationship between character and society, which can crudely be described as being by Meredith out of Schopenhauer. Whatever other complications this may have, it means that the anti-socialist position is, on one level, affirmative of the status quo, and on another profoundly alienated from it. In specific terms, as we shall see, this results negatively in *Demos* in a strenuous effort to keep Morris' ideas, especially about art and civilization, well out of the novel, despite the fact that there is a character clearly based on Morris in the novel. Positively, it opens the way for a later, much better novel, *The Nether World* (1889), which, though it is not about socialism, reflects in very important ways ideas central to Morris' *Signs of Change* (1902).[4] We shall thus be in a position to see more fully the social pressures on Gissing by showing how the novel attempts to affirm the conventional wisdom of attitudes towards socialism, and at the same time how it can only do this in a confused way. This might have the additional advantage of offering an insight into the conventional wisdom too.

Equally, however, I shall argue that the confusion in *Demos* reflects a genuinely confused situation within the socialist movement. If *Demos* distorts, the distortion arises from the very attempt to be specific about socialism as a movement. The great distortion of *Demos* is that it *invents* socialism as a historical force, and can thus only produce a story strictly analogous to a pre-socialist epoch (*Demos* is really a novel of the 1840's cunningly disguised as a story of the 'eighties). At the end of this paper I shall suggest that this is a necessity: socialism has no historical identity in the 'eighties, except as possibility. Consequently, when Gissing comes to write "realistically" about the working classes, in *The Nether World*, he writes from a classically reified position: there are no signs of change. There are similarities to Morris' position, but there is this diametric opposition at the centre. Finally, I shall put all this in the perspective of *News from Nowhere* (1891), which I see as having to invent the history of socialism just as *Demos* does, and, in its consciousness of this necessity, sharing the despair of *The Nether World*.

I

Up until 1882, Gissing was, as is well known, very sympathetic towards Positivism, and this led him, by a natural process described generally by Royden Harrison,[5] to be something more than merely tolerant towards socialism. This is obvious in his first novel, *Workers in the Dawn* (1880) and explicit in two articles on Social Democracy published in the *Pall Mall Gazette* on 9 September 1880, p. 10. In the first of these, he writes, "Be the views of individual agitators what they may, it must not be forgotten that the theory of Socialism rests on the purely scientific inquiries of cultured minds. Recent German writers, such as Marx, Duhring, Schaeffle, Adolph Wagner, are neither mere enthusiasts nor demagogues; their convictions regarding the evil of our present economic system are the result of historical and practical knowledge which demands respect." It is clear then that at this stage Gissing's sympathy is reasonably informed, though putting Marx and Baron Albert Schaeffle together in this way suggests that there is some qualification to be made to this, which will become clear later. For a couple of years at any rate, Gissing seems to have become quite deeply committed. In April 1881, he tells his brother that he is preparing a lecture on the practical aspects of socialism.[6] And a year later, in April 1883, he writes to his sister describing Bank Holiday, in what is clearly an early note for the Crystal Palace episode in *The Nether World*. At the end of that letter (p. 16), he moves towards an analysis that closely resembles Morris:

> It is utterly absurd, this idea of setting aside single days for great public holidays. It will never do anything but harm. What we want is a general shortening of working hours all the year round, so that, for instance, all labour would be over at four o'clock in the afternoon. Then the idea of hours of leisure would become familiar to the people and they would learn to make some sensible use of them. Of course, that is impossible so long as we work for working's sake. All the world's work – all that is really necessary for the health and comfort and even luxury of mankind – could be performed in three or four hours of each day. There is so much labour just because there is so much money grubbing. Every man has to fight for his living with his neighbour, and the grocer who keeps his shop open till half-an-hour after midnight, has an advantage over him who closes at twelve. Work in itself is *not an end; only a means*; but we nowadays make it an end, and three fourths of the world cannot understand anything else.

It is difficult to believe that Gissing wasn't deeply involved with *Hopes and Fears for Art* (1882). And this seems to continue until at least 1884, when in February he makes what seems to me a pretty shrewd, and certainly sympathetic, distinction between Ruskin and Morris: "I would make a chief point of the necessary union between beauty in life and social reform. Ruskin despairs of the latter, and so can only look on by-gone times. Younger men (like William Morris) are turning from artistic work to social agitation just because they fear that Art will be crushed out of the world as things are" (*Letters of George Gissing*, pp. 135–136).

We shouldn't make the mistake of assuming that Gissing's letters reflect anything like a permanent position. Along with the social awareness there is in the early 'eighties a pose of aestheticism, and it is this that seems finally to determine his attitude towards Morris and the socialists. In a letter which was written shortly before he seriously embarked on *Demos* in 1885, he writes hysterically about Morris' appearance in the police court for assaulting a policeman: "But, alas, what the devil is that man doing in such a galley? It is painful to me beyond expression. Why cannot he write poetry in the shade? He will inevitably coarsen himself in the company of ruffians. Keep apart, keep apart, and preserve one's soul alive – that is the teaching for the day" (*Letters of George Gissing*, p. 169). So it is clear enough that, with the pessimism we are all familiar with in Gissing's work, he is clearly opposed to Morris and emotionally antipathetic to a working-class movement by the time he writes *Demos*. What is equally clear, however, is that he had acquired a more than casual knowledge of socialism, a fact that isn't always evident in *Demos*. Moreover, this same letter makes it clear that Gissing's opposition wasn't exactly based on a faith in the basis of society. "It is ill to have been born in these times," it continues, "but one can make a world within the world." *Die Welt ist meine Vorstellung*.

On one level, *Demos* shows signs of being written for commercial success: it has all the makings of a "Mudie" novel – languishing heroine with crypto-Lesbian friend, faithful working girl, pseudo-Broughton dark-past hero, lost will, and even a potential rape. At the same time there is a quite conscious attempt to repeat George Eliot's kind of popularity with Wyvern, the Irwine-like vicar, and Mrs. Waltham and the Wanley gossips. Moreover, it was extremely well advertised by Smith and Elder, usually at the head of their list, and often on its own (Harrison wrote: "the advertisements are phenomenal"). Published at the beginning of 1886, it had sold 500 copies by the beginning of May (which is good for a three-decker in the 'eighties), and a new edition appeared by the end of the year (see *Letters of George Gissing*, pp. 177–186).

Perhaps the most striking fact about the reviews is the amount of attention the book got. *The Times*, for example, gave it a whole column, a distinction it conferred on only seven other novels in the whole of 1886, the others being by well-established authors such as Stevenson, Anstey, Ouida, and Collins (*Demos*, as I've said, was published anonymously). The *Saturday Review*, the *Guardian*, the *Athenaeum*, the *Queen*, and the *Daily News* all had it at the top of their lists, giving it the most space. In the *Spectator* it was the only novel reviewed in the whole week. With the notable exception of the *Athenaeum*, the reviewers praised it pretty highly in their own terms. The *Queen* praised it because it wasn't *too* serious: "This ably written story, while it deals *incidentally* with many of the ideas and topics of the present day, contains enough of interest of the *usual* kind to suit the ordinary novel-reader" (LXXX [31 July 1886], 143, my italics). The church journal, the *Guardian*, while it regretted in passing that the novel "is too strongly coloured by sordid and painful elements," commended its moral – "which may be stated shortly as an illustration of the importance of keeping the two great commandments of Christianity in their proper order. Mr. Wyvern and Adela both cordially recognise the identity of the principle of socialism with that of the injunction to love our neighbours as ourselves: they only refuse to allow it precedence of the yet higher commandment" (XLI [14 Apr. 1886], 544). The *Saturday Review*, which had conducted a vituperative campaign against Morris in 1885, called it "almost a great work" and saw it as an affirmation of moral and intellectual beauty: "It is by the heart alone that social regeneration is possible; it is in the heart alone that its essential elements are generated. This the author of *Demos* has seen" (LXII [21 Aug. 1886], 261). Such praise, from philistine reviewers, is very striking to anyone who knows about Gissing's attitude to fiction and to "social regeneration." The very fact that the *Queen* wasn't too bothered by its seriousness, that the *Guardian* could rebuke Gissing gently and patronisingly for the sordidness of some scenes, shows how far from his normal habitual self Gissing had moved for this novel.

What is more striking is that only the *Athenaeum* seriously queried the reality of the story. "*Demos*," the reviewer wrote, "might as well have been written by the author of *Alton Locke*, or of *North and South*, or of *Shirley* as far as the freshness of its ideas on popular discontent or industrial mutiny is concerned" (10 Apr. 1886, p. 485). *The Times* recognised that Mutimer is really a beneficent capitalist, and claims that to be fair to socialism Gissing should have made Marx, St. Simon, or Proudhon the hero, but it goes on: "But *Demos* only purports to present us with a few *realistic* samples of modern Socialism. It would be rash to assert that Mutimer and other supporters of *The Fiery Cross* or *Tocsin*, are less sincere or more likely to be spoilt by good fortune than the socialist agitator as we actually know him in public life. If *Demos* suggests a practical moral, it is that the modern socialist is insincere. But on the general problem we get negative results, leaving us nowhere, and sadly bidding us despair of the future of the human race" (3 Apr. 1886, p. 5). So that it is not the mimetic validity that *The Times* questions but the pragmatic. *Demos* is right, but it isn't helpful. Most of the reviews speak of intimate knowledge, a judicial mind, and even impartiality. Even the *Daily News*, which advertised itself as the most widely read Liberal paper in the world, and had interviewed Morris sympathetically in 1885, recommended *Demos* without questioning its accuracy (1 Apr. 1886, p. 3).

A third point emerges from a study of these reviews. While most of them praised Gissing's portrayal of working-class characters, they were much less happy about those of the middle class. The *Contemporary Review* called Eldon "mere flat wash,"[7] and the *Guardian* found him "a great deal too sketchy." The *Saturday Review* commented generally: "but when the author comes to delineate middle-class life, his touch is far less powerful." This goes beyond a merely mimetic concern. Julia Wedgwood in the *Contemporary Review* was generally hostile to the novel on largely moral grounds: "The plans of the Socialist are, we are made to feel, mere poisonous error; but his rival has no plans at all, and merely wishes to undo what he has done. If we are invited to contemplate a problem, we should feel that there is a solution somewhere." The *Guardian* specifically felt that, though the moral of the story is commendable, it drifts dangerously near to aestheticism; particularly this is true of Adela: "We are not at all sure that a fourth volume might not in strict consistency show Adela travelling also to the goal of egotism – *her* route being the fairer but not less fatal one of aestheticism." The reviewer regrets that more isn't made of Wyvern, whose moral position he clearly approves. The reviewer in the *Spectator* shares the same unease about the moral positives within the novel. He also sees Adela as ambiguous: "the author hesitates, in his picture of her, between a merely refined nobility and true spiritual devotedness of character." He concludes: "What the story needs, besides a more vividly painted heroine, is some spiritual and intellectual background with which the dream of Socialism can be contrasted ... [again he regrets the marginality of Wyvern] ... Aestheticism appears to be the only alternative in the author's mind for the materialistic schemes in the realisation of which his Socialist hero so miserably fails" (LIX [10 Apr. 1886], 486–487).

The reviews thus confirm my introductory point about the tensions evident in *Demos* when we think of it as a work responsive to the pressure of taste. All of them recognised that it was a novel sufficiently striking to appeal to the "ordinary" novel reader. Even the hostile *Athenaeum* described it as "a really able and vigorous romance," and, on the other side of the coin, *The Times* excused its deficiencies on the grounds that it had to satisfy "the exigencies of modern fiction." Most of them accepted it as an accurate portrayal of English socialism, and predictably, the more orthodox among them were enthusiastic about its conservative critique of socialism. But equally they show that however far Gissing was prepared to go in his attempt to write a popular novel with an acceptable bias, he was unable to assert the values of that bias categorically enough to leave the orthodox complacencies undisturbed. At a crucial point, which became the starting point of his later work, Gissing's alienation from the conventional wisdom was involuntary.

Given this perspective, we are now in a better position, I hope, to understand the complexities which arise from a study of *Demos* as a mimetic form.

II

It would be specious to explain the attention given to *Demos* merely in terms of its concessions to the circulating-library subscriber and its confirmation of anti-socialist prejudices. *Demos* has a kind of accuracy which contrasts sharply with the vagueness of other novels about socialism of the period. W. H. Mallock's *The Old Order Changes* (1886), the most informed of these, is so much a matter of abstract debate that there is no concrete sense of the issues involved at all. At the other extreme, Henry James's *The Princess Casamassima* (1886), which is vividly pictorial, is defiantly ignorant of the underlying issues. And besides these we have a novel such as Grant Allen's *Philistia* (1884), which has a portrait of Marx in it, but which is really nothing but a hack romance, and Walter Besant's *The Children of Gibeon* (1886), which has a transparently specious realism and is concerned mainly with acting out Besant's philanthropic fantasies. Against these, *Demos* shows a real understanding of at least the external circumstances of working-class life, and a grasp of some of the issues in the socialist movement. Because of its specificity, *Demos* was praised by much more respectable men than a handful of hasty reviewers. Charles Booth singled it out as a greater source of information about poverty than non-fictional works,[8] and John Morley wrote to Frederic Harrison to ask him if Gissing was the writer: "There is some masterly work in it. One page, that describing the East End graveyard – contains a passage which is one of the most beautiful in modern literature. And there is genius throughout" (quoted in *Letters of George Gissing*, p. 185). Morley and Booth are praising what is an undeniable quality of the novel, its accuracy about working-class life in London in the 'eighties. It is outside the scope of this paper to go into this in detail, but a comparison of the details about the life of the Mutimers and the Vines with Booth's survey shows an impressive coincidence. Wilton Square, where the Mutimers live, really exists, and it occupied a social borderland between the abject poverty of Hoxton and the world of more comfortable artisans who lived north of Regents Canal. It is very near the canal and on the west side it adjoins Essex Road. Booth, in his description of this district, writes: "Two bad spots; one near the canal, the other off the Essex Rd. Many houses are farmed and have a family in each room; very poor and dirty. With these exceptions, the district is inhabited by fairly comfortable artisans" (Booth, II, 22). The house in Wilton Square begins as an artisan's house and is farmed out in the course of the novel. The realism isn't gratuitous; it is a concrete image of accurate social discriminations.

Moreover, as a story of socialism, *Demos* is close to the actuality. Richard Mutimer is a mechanical engineer, just as John Burns and Tom Mann were. Like Mann, he is very much concerned with conditions of work and especially the hours of work. Like both Burns and Mann, he is sacked for his socialist activities (Burns in January 1885, Mann in November of the same year). Like Burns, Mutimer is an outstanding orator, and like him too, he stands for Parliament with disastrous results. It is very difficult to get a clear picture of Burns as he was in the 'eighties, because most biographies can't escape the blindness of hindsight, but it is possible that Burns's conceit was evident already. H. M. Hyndman, who is not very reliable, wrote in 1911: "his colossal conceit was always in evidence."[10] It may not be irrelevant either, if Gissing had been attending meetings at which Burns spoke, that, according to Joseph Burgess, Burns had a very pretty wife (Burgess, p. 89). There are more obvious signs that *Demos* is partly intended to be a *roman à clef* in his portrayal of the Westlakes, who are clearly based on a not very close knowledge of the Morrises. Westlake is the author of *Daphne* turned agitator: "Long-haired, full bearded, he had the forehead of an idealist and eyes whose natural expression was an indulgent smile" (I, 103). Stella Westlake too bears a physical resemblance to Jane Morris, though the character Gissing delineates is highly idealised: "Black hair, cut short at its thickest behind her neck, gave exquisite relief to features of the purest Greek type. In listening to anything that held her attention her eyes grew large, and their dark orbs seemed to dream passionately. The white swan's down at her throat ... made the skin above resemble rich hued marble, and indeed to gaze at her long was to be impressed as by the sad loveliness of a supreme work of art" (I, 106). This may be ridiculously unlike Jane as she was, but we should recall that she was a cult figure (the young Henry James, for example, said that he didn't know whether she was a grand synthesis of Pre-Raphaelite paintings or whether they were just copies of her[11]). At the same time, it is true that Westlake's position in the Union is much more like Hyndman's in the Socialist Democratic Federation (particularly as editor of the *Fiery Cross*). But this is a confusion which leads to very significant distortions which we shall have to come back to. At the moment I simply want to make the point that *Demos* resembles the actuality *on the surface* to a degree which must have made it convincing.

At a more serious level, *Demos* is also partly accurate about the actual historical situation. The main points of Mutimer's policy for the New Wanley scheme, shorter hours, better housing, compulsory and free education, reflect the "stepping stones" advocated in the SDF manifesto *Socialism Made Plain*, as interim measures before the complete takeover of the means of production by the producers themselves.[12] Gissing is right about the tendency to schism which dominated the socialist movements of the 'eighties. The main one, of course, took place at the end of 1884 when, because of the authoritarian nature of Hyndman, a majority of the executive resigned to form the Socialist League. Moreover, the basic issues are grasped by Gissing: the split focussed on socialist strategy and the questions at issue are concerned with the justifiability of palliatives, the argument about whether to put up candidates for parliament and so on. I shall return to this, since if Gissing is generally accurate, there are important differences of detail. Moreover, Gissing seems to have foreseen the troubles of the Socialist League which, as Edward Thompson has indicated,[13] tended towards anarchism of the kind represented in Roodhouse's *Tocsin*, in its working-class branches, and academicism of the kind suggested by the change of the *Fiery Cross* into the *Beacon* among its more middle-class supporters. Finally, of course, the riot at the end of the novel bears some resemblance to the riots in Trafalgar Square of February 1886, which also seemed to have grown out of a loss of control on the part of the socialist leaders.

Thus, we have a novel which presented a close analogy of the socialist movement in a general way, and which seemed to be underwritten by a discriminating and detailed knowledge of working-class London. It may not now be so surprising that it was thought to be the product of deep knowledge.

But, of course, as the *Athenaeum* realised, *Demos* is not about *modern* socialism essentially. In the first place there is the New Wanley experiment itself. Here is how Mutimer explains his scheme to Westlake: "it will differ considerably from the Socialist experiments we know of. We shall be working not only to support ourselves, but every bit as much set on profit as any capitalist in Belwick. The difference is, that the profit will benefit no individual, but the Cause. There'll be no attempt to carry out the idea of every man receiving the just outcome of his labour; not because I shouldn't be willing to share in that way, but simply because we have a greater end in view than to enrich ourselves" (I, 107–108). It is true that the New Wanley scheme involves better working conditions, but two very fundamental points emerge from this. In the first place it involves industrialising Wanley, so that Mutimer has what is historically a bourgeois role rather than a proletarian one. I shall return to this in a moment. More immediately, the scheme as a whole is surely that of an Owenite co-operative rather than anything else. By not attempting to carry out the idea of every man receiving the just outcome of labour, Mutimer is dissolving what was seen by most socialists of the 'eighties as a central point of Marxist analysis, the theory of surplus value. What is truly inaccurate is that Westlake approves this scheme. "Co-operation," Morris wrote in a letter to Mrs. Burne Jones in 1884, "must be the rule and not the exception,"[14] and in "The Hope of Civilisation" (1885), he wrote, "Some see the solution of the social problem in sham co-operation, which is merely an improved form of joint-stockery."[15] Though he admired Owen, he wrote that his socialism fell short of its object because it did not understand that, as there is a privileged class in possession of the executive power, it will take good care that its economical position, which enables it to live on the unpaid labour of the people, is not tampered with (Morris, *Works*, XXIII, 71). Morris, it is true, was capable of being a little ambiguous about this. Thus in *Commonweal*, in September 1885, answering a letter advocating the setting up of socialistic communities, he seems to discipline himself with Marxist realism only with difficulty. First he writes, "In answer I beg to point out to him that it is not possible to establish a real socialistic community in the midst of Capitalistic Society, a social island amidst an individualist sea; because all its external dealings would have to be arranged on a basis of capitalistic exchange, and would so far support the system of profits and exchange" (I, 87). Then he goes on to say that he would welcome such communities as a kind of propaganda by example to raise the hopes of the masses and make them discontented with their useless toil. But this is not explicitly about industrial co-operatives, and there is no suggestion of the communities making profits themselves. Mutimer's scheme perpetuates the division of labour, accepts the middle-class notion of work not for the sake of the well-being of the producers but for profit, and, of course, in a way which would be unpalatable to Morris, intensifies industrialisation.

A possible source of the co-operative scheme is Schaeffle, who is mentioned in *Demos*, and who, in *The Quintessence of Socialism* (which is explicitly anti-Marxist), writes, "The spread of productive co-operation would not be, it is true, in principle a socialistic organisation, for associations of this type would still be only competitive businesses, the latest development of the capitalistic principle. But this would not be prejudicial to socialism; for such associations are organically more akin to collectivism, and therefore at a later stage will lend themselves to the introduction of socialism better than private businesses will do."[16] But even Schaeffle is really talking about state organisation, and of "the petty co-operative associations of a Schulze," he writes, "Such enterprises are based on the competition of separate capital; they have a disjointed system of production; they presuppose always an anarchical struggle of private interests" (*Quintessence of Socialism*, p. 62). The reason that Gissing seized on the co-operative idea seems rather to be that it gave him an opportunity to demonstrate the corruptibility of the working class as managers. A similar analysis can be found in Baron Émile de Laveleye's book, *The Socialism of Today* (1883). He uses co-operatives to illustrate the "flagrant injustice and manifest absurdity" of Marx's labour theory of value. If the head of a business is not remunerated exceptionally well, he will become corrupt: "Whenever co-operative societies have failed," he goes on, "it has always been through the fault of the managers."[17] We can thus see that Gissing is acting out an analogy which isn't really relevant, but which is used in a respected anti-socialist text. Laveleye's chapter on Lassalle contains a critique of co-operation which is remarkably like an abstract of *Demos*:

Co-operation as compared to individual enterprise is republican government succeeding to despotic rule. History, and even contemporary facts, prove that many qualities are needful in a people before republican institutions can succeed among them. In order to conduct a commercial or industrial enterprise properly, certain special aptitudes are indispensable; and if working men were to choose one of their number, these aptitudes would frequently be found wanting in him. His authority would be disputed, and his equals would not obey him properly. Enthusiasm for the work undertaken would keep the co-operators to their duty for some time; but sooner or later they would tire, devotion to their principles would cool down, incompatibilities of temper would manifest themselves, and dissensions or the incapacity of managers would finally lead to the dissolution of the society. In order to have a capable director, it would be necessary to pay him well; he would straightway become a bourgeois, a fact which at once would excite the jealousy of his colleagues.

(pp. 70–71)

In *Demos* we watch the development of Mutimer into a bourgeois industrialist. The definitive sign of the change is his dismissal of Rendal for insolence, for the threat to his authority, and one of the reasons why Roodhouse finds it easy to win over the old members of Mutimer's branch of the Union is that they are jealous of his affluence. Of course, there are important differences between Laveleye's prediction and what happens in *Demos* – we don't really see the co-operative breaking up from within because Gissing needs to keep the socialist ideal more or less intact so that he can present Eldon very specifically as a class antagonist, "an example of reaction" to use Eldon's own phase. But the comparison shows, I think, how far this distortion, which has some basis in some kinds of socialist theory, can transform the novel from a "realistic" story to a moral fable predicting the inadequacy of the best of the working class in a managerial role, not as Orwell does by creating a dystopia but by enacting the socialist theory in an inaccurate (because really pre-socialist) historical reality. And what Gissing ends up with is a portrayal of a process that most serious socialists of the 'eighties would have readily acknowledged as probable. In *Commonweal* in July 1885, Morris wrote, "I should like our friends to understand whither the whole system of palliation tends – namely, towards the creation of a new middle class to act as a buffer between the proletariat and their direct and obvious masters" (I, 61). It is as a buffer, or at least a focus of working-class discontent, that Mutimer finally meets his death.

The second effect of the nature of the New Wanley scheme is that it radically simplifies the class structure of the novel by making the proletariat responsible for the industrial revolution. By doing this, Gissing achieves three propagandist advantages. In the first place he focusses the socialist programme of appropriation specifically on the appropriation of land, avoiding the issue of the appropriation of the means of production. Secondly, he avoids any direct clash between proletariat and urban bourgeoisie, and presents the class war entirely in terms of the clash between the proletariat and the romantic aristocracy. Finally, he completely conflates utilitarianism and socialism and thus avoids taking account of Morris's arguments about art and society.

At the beginning of the novel, we are told that Wanley lags sadly behind the time: it is pre-industrial and, since its social structure is dominated by the Manor, it is distinctly eighteenth-century in its qualities. After his first meeting with Mutimer, Eldon proclaims: "I seemed to be holding a dialogue with the twentieth century" (I, 47). What, then, has happened to the nineteenth? The answer in terms of the novel is, of course, that it has died intestate in the figure of the first Richard Mutimer, who has miraculously been forestalled from bringing Belwick to Wanley, and his work is carried on by the socialist nephew. There can be no doubt, I think, that Gissing is aiming to enlist the support of conservative thinking by assimilating in his portrayal of socialism the important land question which arose in the 'eighties as the result of the popularity of the work of Henry George. George advocated as the root remedy of social evils the abolition of private ownership of land. On the one occasion when we are allowed to see Mutimer as a socialist orator, his speech is distinctively Georgist: "He spoke of the land; he attacked the old monopoly, and visioned a time when a claim to individual ownerships of the earth's surface would be as ludicrous as were now the assertion of title to a fee-simple somewhere in the moon. He mustered statistics; he adduced historic and contemporary example of the just and the unjust in landholding; he gripped the throat of a certain English duke, and held him up for flagellation" (I, 114–115). It is true that one of the favourite targets for socialist orators in the 'eighties was the Duke of Westminster (though I think he was a largely urban land-holder). It is true also that Henry George was extremely popular among socialists. Thus Tom Mann, in his memoirs, writes "it impressed me as by far the most valuable book I had so far read ... It enabled me to see more clearly the vastness of the social problem."[18] But this was in 1881, and from the beginning he wasn't satisfied with George's proposal. If the SDF welcomed the propaganda value of George's work, it was careful to dissociate itself from its positive policy. In *Socialism Made Plain*, the SDF called for the nationalisation of the land, but went on to say: "But private ownership of land in our present society is only one and not the worst form of monopoly which enables the wealthy classes to use the means of production against the labourers whom they enslave" (p. 4). Land nationalisation and the "organisation of agricultural and industrial armies under State control on co-operative principles," which, with the significant omission of the phrase "under State control," is the basis of the socialist experiment in *Demos*, were advocated as stepping stones in the manifesto, but only at the end of a long list. Hyndman himself explicitly rejected George's theory in *The Historical Basis of Socialism*.[19] Gissing makes the question much more basic than it was in socialist theory in the same way that Samuel Smith does in *The Nationalisation of the Land* (1884): George leads to the SDF and to Proudhonism which leads to Communism which leads to the death of liberty (which can only be defended by propertied classes). Land was not the starting point of socialist appropriation, but it was clearly the easiest issue to be sentimental about, and this is shown not only in *Demos* but also in *The Old Order Changes* and, insofar as anything is *shown*, in James's novel, *The Princess Casamassima*.

More important are the implications in terms of the class struggle. Gissing emphatically accepts the notion of class in the novel and quite clearly the notion of class antagonism. Mrs. Eldon, the noble lady who is to become the victim of the mob's brutality after the closure of New Wanley, talks very much in class terms: "What is this class distinction upon which we pride ourselves? What does it mean, if not that our opportunities lead us to see truths to which the eyes of the poor and ignorant are blind?" (I, 39). Her son is explicit that the relationship between classes is necessarily one of antagonism. "I have nothing of the enthusiasm of humanity ..." he explains to Adela, "You will clothe your workpeople better, you will give them better food and more leisure; in doing so you injure the *class* that has finer sensibilities and give power to the *class* which not only postpones everything to material well-being, but more and more regards intellectual refinement as an obstacle in the way of progress" (III, 32–33, my italics). Even the heroine, Adela, recognises her own alienation from her husband in purely class terms: "It was the face of a man by birth and breeding altogether beneath her ... He was not of her *class*, not of her world; only by violent wrenching of the laws of *nature* had they come together ... To be her equal this man must be born again, of other parents, in other conditions of life. 'I go back to London a mechanical engineer in search of employment.' They were the truest words he had ever uttered; they characterised him, classed him" (III, 54–55, my italics). In this way, *Demos* is truly a novel of the 'eighties. There is no attempt to discern a classless human reality beneath the accidents of social status (as for example in Mrs. Gaskell) and no attempt to find a definition of culture which transcends class (as in *Culture and Anarchy*). The battle for the prevailing of the best self is a battle for the domination of aristocracy.

But how relevant is this in specific terms to the 'eighties? It is obviously difficult to say in terms of the historical actuality. In terms of consciousness, the struggle between aristocracy and demos is surely a figment of the cultural/conservative imagination. I have already suggested that it is a dominant feature of other novels, though perhaps not so overtly stated as in Gissing. Gissing, in fact, seems to anticipate this kind of objection when he makes Eldon say that English socialism is "infused with the spirit of shopkeeping." It is inherently bourgeois in other words (as opposed to the romantic rebellion of nihilism). Later he asks, "How does it differ from Radicalism, the most contemptible clap-trap of politics, except in wanting to hurry a little the rule of the mob?" (III, 113). In an essay entitled "Radicalism: A Familiar Colloquy," printed in the *Nineteenth Century* of March 1881, Mallock wrote that radicalism was motivated entirely by hatred of the aristocracy; "Rank, birth, breeding, and any riches that are in excess of his own are distorted by his imagination into hateful or absurd abuses," and later he concludes, "English Radicalism is really a protest against aristocracy; it is not a protest in favour of equality" (p. 438). We have a distinct echo of this in Gissing's description of Old Mutimer: "Remaining the sturdiest of Conservatives, he bowed in sincere humility to those claims which the Radical most angrily disallows: birth, heredity, station, recognised gentility ... Such an attitude was a testimony to his own capacity for culture" (I, 53). This suggests that Gissing was conscious of what he was doing. The bourgeois figure in this novel is redeemed by his recognition of aristocracy and thus he gives back the estate that he has won from them in his own economic progress; the energies of the middle class are absorbed in the rejuvenation of a decadent aristocracy (Gissing doesn't attempt to suggest that the Eldons haven't brought their downfall on themselves). This runs directly counter to socialist arguments about the relation between the classes. Of course, the historical accounts of the development of society, such as Morris' and Hyndman's in *The Principles of Socialism* (1884) were primarily concerned with the increasing domination of the middle class, and, in 1885, Morris explicitly saw the aristocracy as a mere feature of the middle class: "the place of the old serf was filled by the propertyless labourer, with whom the middle class, *which has absorbed the aristocracy*, is now face to face."[20] Using a fictional special case, Gissing reverses the relationship acknowledged by socialist theory. Of course, he has it the other way round too. Richard Mutimer II, by becoming bourgeois himself, enables Gissing to transform the conflicts of the novel to something resembling *North and South* (without Mrs. Gaskell's delicate balance of sympathies). And at the end of the novel, Wyvern suddenly launches into the middle class in Carlylean terms (the cash-nexus) but his diatribe is necessarily irrelevant; the bourgeoisie is not really there in the novel at all.

Finally, and most obviously, the New Wanley scheme neatly bypasses Morris' ideas about art and society, fully expressed and explained in *Hopes and Fears for Art*. After his first meeting with Mutimer, Eldon says, "There will be not one inch left to nature; the very oceans will somehow be tamed, the snowy mountains will be levelled. And with nature will perish art. What has hungry Demos to do with the beautiful?" (I, 146). This clearly postulates an analysis of the relation between art and society totally different from that of Morris. The point is, however, that since Westlake is never really allowed to confront Eldon, the whole of Morris' analysis of the rottenness of an art which depends on a neurotic élite who feel themselves to be in enemy country is just not encountered. Art, in *Demos*, is merely a sentimentalised egoism (the poetry-fed soul at issue with fate). It is Wyvern who speaks for Westlake and he speaks in terms which allow for the utilitarian/aesthete antithesis to go unchallenged: "He has the mind of a poet; probably he was struck with horror to find over what pit he had been living in careless enjoyment. He is tender hearted; of a sudden he felt himself criminal, to be playing with beautiful toys whilst a whole world lived only to sweat and starve" (III, 114). Like much of *Demos*, this is very near to the truth, but far enough from it to be totally misleading.

Certainly, in *Hopes and Fears for Art* and in such lectures as "Art and the Beauty of the Earth," Morris contrasts his own conditions with those of "the residuum." But along with this goes a critique of the inanity of middle-class luxury (which is distinctly opposed to art) and both feelings are measured against the undivided labour of the gothic. This is too well known to need analysis here, and, as we have seen, Gissing knew well enough what Morris felt, and knew that the starting point was a criticism of modern art. The idea of art as a beautiful toy is certainly present in Morris (in his account of French art before the revolution, for example), but it is not so inherently, only in conditions alien to its proper development as the expression of man's pleasure in his labour. The effect of such a portrayal is to make Morris at once more utilitarian and more sentimental. We should add here that Morris certainly did envisage the possible destruction of art in the coming revolution (though this pre-dates his socialism, as the essay, "The Lesser Arts," of 1877 shows). But this was, of course, on a kind of phoenix basis. Gissing seems to share the view of Goddard H. Orpen, who contributed an appendix on "Socialism in England" to Laveleye's *The Socialism of Today*: "Mr. Morris says that we gave up art three centuries ago for what we thought was light and freedom, but that it has turned out to be light and freedom for the few alone. Does he really think that by surrendering such light and freedom as we possess we shall bring about a new renaissance in Art? The Socialist régime, whatever it may be, is certainly not calculated to encourage individuality" (p. 371).

Gissing's overall presentation of Westlake coincides in many respects with the journalistic image of Morris described by Edward Thompson (pp. 369, 470, and following). Eldon complains about the coarsening of "the author of *Daphne*" just as the *Saturday Review* talks about the "intellectual disaster" of the author of *The Earthly Paradise*. On the one occasion that we get any real indication of Westlake's positive views, Gissing idealises Morris' position so that it comes to seem less related to reality or to the rest of the socialist movement: "Their work, he told his hearers, was but just beginning. They aimed at nothing less than a revolution, and revolutions were not brought about in a day. None of them would in the flesh behold the reign of justice; was that a reason why they should neglect the highest impulses of their nature and sit contented in the shadow of the world's mourning? ... One loved the man for his great heart and for his gift of moving speech" (II, 132). If we put this against a passage from "Useful Work Versus Useless Toil," we can see how carefully Gissing has doctored what Morris would actually have said: "our own lives may see no end to the struggle, perhaps no obvious hope of the end. It may be that the best we can hope to see is that struggle getting sharper and bitterer day by day, until it breaks out openly at last into the slaughter of men by actual warfare, by "peaceful" commerce. If we live to see that we shall live to see much; for it will mean the rich classes grown conscious of their own wrong and robbery, and consciously defending them by open violence; and then the end will be drawing near" (Morris, *Works*, XXIII, 119). Revolution, for Westlake, is a harmless word, and the motive for action is crudely positivist ("highest impulses of their nature").[21] Gissing is using an image of Morris which emerges from both the hostile and the tolerant press. The *Echo*, on 8 October 1884, suggested that Morris was disguising "to himself the meaning of such a programme by clothing it in some beautiful form of language" (p. 2), and the *Daily News*, in "A Talk with William Morris," printed 8 January 1885, repeatedly tries to pass Morris off as a dreamy idealist who should nevertheless be admired for his sincerity: "His countrymen may regard his doctrines as impracticable and visionary, but there can be no doubt as to the purity and the loftiness of the aspiration" (p. 5).

This undermining sympathy distorts Gissing's portrayal of the schism. The Socialist League, as is well known, broke away from the SDF on the theoretical grounds of the necessity of what Morris called "purism." It was firmly opposed to palliatives (as we have seen), repeatedly scornful of parliamentary aspirations, and of course it was the schismatic group. Now while men such as Burns and Mann remained with the SDF, Morris left. On the face of it at least, Gissing is making Westlake more respectable than Morris, and again it has the effect of softening him and making him into a dreamy idealist. But here, I confess I am worried. In theoretical terms, Morris was "purist," Hyndman "opportunist." Yet, after the February riots of 1886 in which Hyndman took part, Morris, according to the *Daily News*, described them as "lamentable occurrences" and went on to say "the one thing necessary to bring about a revolution *in a peaceful manner* was a complete understanding of the question on the part of the working classes."[22] There are many complications here (Morris would, for example, see the riots as mechanical opportunism, premature and therefore pointless – as he seems to have seen the Commune). But it suggests that we need to look at *Demos* in another light – not merely as a reflection of a popular distorting image but as a reflection too of a confusion that was really there.

III

I shall return to this point at the end. It is necessary now to indicate the specific nature of the conventional wisdom which underlies Gissing's distortion of the socialist movement. Generally, as we have seen, Gissing's technique is to doctor the historical complexities so that his apparently realistic story becomes a moral fable acceptable to the middle-class audience for which he is writing. However, in order to do this he finds it necessary to justify four orthodoxies at once and none of them are compatible with each other. It is this, I think, which explains the dissatisfaction of the reviews. More than that, I would tentatively suggest that the resulting confusion is representative of the 'eighties in that it reflects first, that the response to working-class movements was hardening into ideological systems to a degree not evident in the 'forties, and second, that there is no consensus of conservative opinion but only rival rigidities. Gissing, in short, is trying to write an acceptable novel at a time when it is increasingly difficult to discover a widely acceptable anti-socialist ideology.

In the first place, as I have tried to suggest, Gissing is making a large gesture towards the conservative movement which attached more and more value to landed property and aristocracy, and whose most cogent ideologist was W. H. Mallock. Wyvern's belated attack on the bourgeoisie fits in with this: "What I made no secret of approving was their [the socialists"] substitution of human relations between employer and employed for the detestable 'nexus of cash payment,' as Carlyle calls it. That is only a return to the good old order" (III, 120). We are really back to *Sybil*.

Equally, however, *Demos* shows signs of retaining much of the positivism which had influenced Gissing so much early in his career. I have shown in *Tradition and Tolerance in Nineteenth Century Fiction* how *Demos* enacts a Comtist historiography with Mutimer representing the metaphysical polity (his Enlightenment reading-matter indicates this). Wanley has all the attributes of a village in a benighted "theological" phase for whom Wyvern is the spokesman. Of course, Gissing does not postulate a "positive" phase which will transcend them and there is no possibility of moralizing capital. Nevertheless the attack on socialism is not far removed from Harrison's essay, "The Radical Programme," which argued that, in positivist analysis, it was necessary to preserve a balance between conservative and radical elements, and more importantly, insisted that any change for the better would arise not from political action but from "spiritual power" defined as "public opinion moralized and organized, apart from political agitation."[23] Clearly Gissing's old patron would have warmed to the portrayal of the moral backslidings of the agitators illustrated by the figures of Cowes and Cullen.

Nevertheless there is, in the course of the novel, an explicit rejection of Harrison's ethical formula, "Everything for society." Eldon asserts that he has none of the "enthusiasm of humanity" and Wyvern offers an ecclesiastical blessing on his egoism when he tells him: "Altruism is doubtless good, but only so when it gives pure enjoyment; that is to say when it is embraced instinctively" (III, 118). Partly, at least, this surely reflects an anti-positivist conservative ideology, that of Herbert Spencer, whose *Man Versus the State* was published in 1885. This is, of course, an extremely individualist statement attacking all forms of social action with arguments derived from Spencer's earlier writing, in which he accepted the view that altruism was a stage towards which the evolution of man was working, but it could only be achieved by a change in nature which would arrive only through individual adaptation to circumstances and would only be thwarted through abstract legislation. We can see how clearly Gissing had Spencer in mind if we recall the philosopher's attack on philanthropism and compare it with Gissing's portrayal of Stella Westlake. "The kinship of pity to love," Spencer writes, "is shown among other ways in this, that it idealises its object. Sympathy for one in suffering suppresses, for the time being, remembrance of his transgressions ... Naturally, then, if the wretched are unknown, or but vaguely known, all the demerits they may have are ignored, and thus it happens that when, as just now, the miseries of the poor are depicted, they are thought of as the miseries of the deserving poor, instead of being thought of, as in large measure they should be, as the miseries of the undeserving poor" (p. 18). Stella is clearly guilty of this sentimentalisation: "when she spoke of the toiling multitude, she saw them in a kind of exalted vision; she beheld them glorious in their woe, ennobled by the tyranny under which they groaned. She had seen little, if anything, of the representative proletarian" (II, 220). On the one hand the socialists are attacked on a positivist basis because they lack "spiritual power" and on the other hand those with spiritual power (the Westlakes) fail to recognise the necessity of natural selection. If the working classes win (as Mutimer does at first) it is immoral; if they lose, it is natural.

But Spencer's influence goes much deeper than this. It dominates the class-consciousness of the novel. The working classes are simply lower evolutionary types, and Gissing's characterisation proceeds from this assumption. Compare Adela and Alice Mutimer: "Their contrasted appearances were a chapter of social history. Mark the difference between Adela's gently closed lips, every muscle under control; and Alice's which *could* never quite close without forming a saucy pout or a self-conscious primness" (II, 70, my italics). The difference is not merely aesthetic, it is clearly one of control over circumstances. The whole story, indeed, if it enacts a positivist historiography, has an adaptational structure: all the Mutimers are destroyed by new circumstances to which they are not able to adapt. When the "deserving" poor get their deserts, their undeserving nature becomes more apparent.

It could be argued that the contradiction between positivist and Spencerian conservatism is a minor one because Gissing never uses positivist formulas as more than convenient and incidental rhetorical devices. But this aspect of Spencer's influence makes for a much larger incoherence in the novel. In the first place, the aristocratic/conservative affirmation of class distinction, such as that voiced by Mrs. Eldon and rationalised by Wyvern, is clearly paternalist and hence includes philanthropy. The good old order, unsoiled by the cash nexus of which Wyvern speaks, is inconsistent with the social Darwinism implied in Gissing's portrayal of the working class. Class can be a matter of divine ordination or a reflection of natural evolution, but it can hardly be both. The sentimental conservatism of the heirs of Young England is exploited in the novel (it is evident in the divine innocence of Adela, for example) but it is equally ridiculed by the "natural" events of the novel and the impersonal struggle which precipitates the characters towards their destiny and towards a natural assertion of the social status quo.

Here again, however, we run up against a large-scale contradiction. Much of the novel is clearly calculated (as the reviewers were quick to notice) to appeal to aesthetes to whose position Gissing, as we have already seen, was very close. So that while Spencer's rigid and distorted Darwinism is applied ruthlessly to the lower orders, it has no real bearing on figures such as Eldon and Adela. They are not very good adapters either. Eldon is an "insurgent" who classes himself as a "wholly impractical man," and like Mutimer, he is a total egoist.[24] Adela too finds herself trapped in a fate against which she must rebel, and we are explicitly told that she has not enough character to subdue circumstances and only enough to endure suffering. They are clearly Schopenhauerian figures standing for the alienated "idea" in a world dominated by a destructive "will," and if the novel enacts, as far as the Mutimers are concerned, a Spencerian tragedy of natural selection, it also, in a contradictory manner, fulfils a fantasy in which the idea of art affirms itself against the will of progress. And just as Spencer ridicules paternalism in the novel, Schopenhauer denies Spencer.

At the same time, Schopenhauer's presence in the novel undermines even further the sentimental conservative ethic that the reviewers were looking for. It is difficult to believe in the highly "modern" sensibility of Eldon as "an example of reaction" when his whole life has been a rebellion against the conventions that, in the end, he sets about restoring. Moreover, if Eldon and Adela stand in the parable for "idea," what is "will"? Schematically, it should be "demos," but demos is taken care of by natural selection, and *dramatically* it is the middle-class world of Wanley with its malicious gossips, its narrow-mindedness and its money-seeking view of marriage. Adela's innocence in *this* perspective is part of the will which keeps her apart from Eldon ("the troubled fantasies of a virgin mind"). And Gissing seems to be *consciously* portraying the Wanley world as a ruthless fate; Adela feels, for example, that "a network was being woven about her by hands she could not deem as other than loving" (I, 246). The good old order is just as destructive as demos. The multiple contradictions involved here explain why Wyvern drops so much into the background. Like Irwine, he was clearly intended to be Gissing's conservative spokesman. But by the end, Gissing has undermined so many conservative positions that he has nothing for the spokesman to say. Indeed Wyvern's comment on Eldon's decision to deindustrialise Wanley is radical moral relativism: "you being you, I approve." It is little wonder that the conservative reviewers found little in the end to comfort them. Whatever he had exposed about socialism, Gissing had also exposed the chaos and contradictoriness of the opposing ideologies.

But if *Demos* reflects a confusion in the contemporary consciousness by its attempt to reflect that consciousness uncritically, it also, I believe, has a much more lasting importance if we consider it together with the novel to which it led, *The Nether World*. In the essay referred to earlier, I argued that between *Demos* and *The Nether World*, Gissing had resolved most of these contradictions. Henceforward all struggle is egoistic, all assertion of "character" is destroyed by the total social system And this leads to a very profound change in Gissing's relationship with Morris. *The Nether World* offers a portrayal of society which is very close to Morris's analysis of the capitalist system. At the centre is alienation: Sidney Kirkwood is condemned to the production of trivialities for a market governed by "abstract" demand. Bob Hewitt is made redundant by the decline of his craft and he is led to forging money as an ironic comment on that which has declared him superfluous – the profit motive. Above all, work is dominated by its relentless, pleasureless inhumanity, and, in terms of real human need, its futility. This is very close to Morris' analysis in "Useful Work Versus Useless Toil." Moreover, within the nether world, those who are oppressed are forced to intensify the oppression by the need to struggle among themselves, and this echoes the analysis of the formation of the proletariat and its failure to recognise its own essence (collectivity) in the struggle to survive in an individualist world that we find in "How We Live and How We Might Live," first published in 1885. Finally, Gissing's only answer to the nightmare world is the destruction of civilisation and a totally new beginning, and this too is an idea central to Morris. We have here, I think, a clue to Gissing's treatment of Morris in *Demos*: he *had* to make him impotent because *Demos* is so very nearly a condemnation of capitalism. Morris, of course, understood the despair of the "intellectual hanger-on group" whose sensibility civilisation had cultivated only to disappoint. Eldon, who is carefully spared a confrontation with Westlake, is too stupid to analyse his own disappointment in social terms. Gissing, I would suggest, wasn't, and in *Demos* he cripples himself trying to avoid the analysis.

At the same time, of course, it would be ridiculous to claim that Gissing was of Morris' party without knowing it. For Gissing the nether world *is* hell and there is no escape. The solution may lie in destruction, but there *is* no destruction except of individuals who try to escape. In *The Nether*

World, there is only miserable perpetuation. In "Misery and the Way Out" (1884), on the other hand, Morris said, "Friends, this earthly hell is not the ordinance of nature but the manufacture of man … and it is your business to destroy it: to destroy it, I say, not each man to try and climb up out of it as your thrift-teachers tell you, but to make an end of it so that no-one henceforth can ever fall into it."[25] Gissing's novel might almost be a reply to this. There is no consciousness within the novel of any way out except by individual assertion (not thrift, of course, but certainly a bitterly ironic version of self-help). In Marxist terms, Gissing's vision is reified: he has made a metaphysical reality out of a historical one. His novel is thus open to the same charge as that made by Engels in his famous letter to Margaret Harkness about her novel: it doesn't offer the potential of change; the seeds of revolution are not present within the realism (Marx, Engels, *Werke*, Bande 37, pp. 42–44).

This might seem to offer a neat formula for the difference between Gissing and Morris. But I don't think there is a neat formula. To complete this study we must glance briefly at Gissing's situation in the light of *News from Nowhere*. It is impossible now to see this work as crudely utopian: such a view ignores its careful structure and its most immediate context, Bellamy's *Looking Backward* (1888), which Morris reviewed in *Commonweal* in 1889. Two familiar points need to be reinvoked here. In the first place, Bellamy's utopia has no history. His state corporation just evolved naturally out of the gradual accumulation of capital. In reply to this, at the centre of *News from Nowhere*, there is a historical struggle embodying a lucid exposition of the Marxist dialectic. This makes for what Edward Thompson calls a "scientific utopia." Secondly, Morris, in his review, objected to Bellamy's pretence that his novel was objective. Utopias, he thought, could only be regarded as the subjective expression of their writers' temperament.[26] Thus we have the opening chapter with its emphasis on the *need* of the Socialist Leaguer to refresh his energy through dream, and, at the end, as he tries to get involved in his dream world, he is pushed out by Ellen, who sends him back to the nineteenth century. He can never be more than a voyeur in his own dream world. The ending is elegiac but realistic: Nowhere *is* nowhere, the vision remains merely visual. The argument is meant less to be convincing than therapeutic. Both of these points make the novel much more complex than appears on the surface. The trouble is that they don't quite go together. The historical basis makes for a greater ideological consistency for objectivity; the psychological realism emphasises its subjectivity. There *is* a coherence here, but a very limiting one. For the history is a history of the future: it, too, is part of the subjective dream world. Morris has to invent not merely a perfect dream world, but he also has to invent the history of socialism, not out of, but *in opposition* to the reality of the Socialist League. In a sense, *News from Nowhere* is as depressing as *The Nether World*.

And this brings us back to *Demos*. I've suggested that, in part at least, it reflects not only a confusion in the awareness of socialism in the 'eighties, but also a confusion in the actuality of socialism (English socialism, that is). It's a confusion voiced most eloquently in the bitter letters of Engels in this period. I would suggest that the essential confusion is that socialism in England at this period has no historical reality except as the subjective projection of its protagonists. It is an important but abstract force, and to be given any reality it has to be very much a fictional theme in a literal sense. In this respect, *Demos* is formally no more a distortion than *News from Nowhere*. The only alternative to invention is to write a novel in which the coming change is not apparent – as, for example, *The Nether World*.

The discussion inevitably goes round in circles for we are confronted with three imponderables. Either a reified vision, of the kind we get in *The Nether World*, is made necessary in the 'eighties because the only potential of change is not yet "there." Or the story of English socialism cannot be presented in a realistic medium, and a new kind of fiction is made necessary (*News from Nowhere* being the major example). Or, as I fear, we should have simply had a different kind of socialism. For it is possible to argue that socialism in England never has had a history – that it simply became absorbed into capitalist progress because of its "pragmatism." And this, after all, is not so very different from *Demos*. In inventing socialist history, Gissing portrayed socialism absorbing capitalist progress only to re-emerge again as capitalism on the one hand and utopianism on the other. The real horror of *Demos*, despite its local distortions, is that in essence it could be right.

Notes

1. *Demos: A Story of English Socialism*, 3 vols. (London, 1886). All quotations are taken from this edition.
2. *Culture and Society* (London, 1960), p. 179. Williams' section on Gissing is the best discussion I know of and it is in many respects definitive. I am certainly not attempting a total rebuttal of his general argument.
3. Valuable documentation of a particular aspect of this "consciousness" which in some respects qualifies what I shall have to say about the understanding of socialist theory, is contained in E. J. Hobsbawm's essay, "Dr. Marx and the Victorian critics," in his *Labouring Men: Studies in the History of Labour* (London, 1964), pp. 239–249.
4. For a detailed critical discussion of *The Nether World* see my essay in *Tradition and Tolerance in Nineteenth Century Fiction*, ed. David Howard, John Lucas, and John Goode (London, 1966), pp. 207–241. Since the present paper was delivered to a conference whose members were not, by and large, Gissing specialists, I felt that it would be an unwarrantable

complacency on my part to assume a knowledge of the earlier essay. In some ways therefore the two essays overlap, though what I have to say about *The Nether World* in this paper corroborates rather than repeats.

5. *Before the Socialists: Studies in Labour and Politics, 1861–1881* (London and Toronto, 1965), pp. 251–342.

6. *Letters of George Gissing to Members of His Family, Collected and Arranged by Algernon and Ellen Gissing* (London, 1927), p. 96.

7. Julia Wedgwood, "Contemporary Records I. Fiction," *Contemporary Review*, L (Aug. 1886), 295.

8. Booth and others, *Life and Labour of the People in London*, First Series, 4 vols. (London, 1902), I, 157.

9. Burns stood at Nottingham in 1885. Belwick is, in the novel, also a midland town.

10. Foreword to Joseph Burgess, *John Burns: The Rise and Progress of a Right Honourable* (Glasgow, 1911), p. viii.

11. *The Letters of Henry James*, selected and edited by Percy Lubbock, 2 vols. (London, 1920), I, 17.

12. *Socialism Made Plain, being the Social and Political Manifesto of the Democratic Federation* (London, 1883), p. 5.

13. E. P. Thompson, *William Morris, Romantic to Revolutionary* (London, 1955), pp. 494–498. "The evidence," he writes, "would suggest that Gissing was very close to the mark."

14. *The Letters of William Morris to his Family and Friends*, ed. Philip Henderson (London, 1950), p. 200.

15. *The Collected Works of William Morris, with Introductions by his Daughter, May Morris*, 24 vols. (New York, 1966), XXIII, 77. Hereafter referred to as Morris, *Works*.

16. *The Quintessence of Socialism*, trans. Bernard Bosanquet (London, 1889), pp. 21–22. Schaeffle is one of the German writers Adela has to translate for Mutimer.

17. *The Socialism of Today*, trans. G. H. Orpen (London, n.d.), p. 39. This first appeared in English in 1884.

18. *Tom Mann's Memoirs* (London, 1967), p. 16. Engels wrote to August Bebel in January 1884 that George was likely to "play a meteoric role" because of the traditional importance of the land question. But he added also that nationalisation of the land would not get very far in "the foremost industrial country in the world." See Karl Marx, Friedrich Engels, *Werke*, (Berlin, 1967), Bande 36, p. 88.

19. *The Historical Basis of Socialism in England* (London, 1883), p. 300.

20. Morris, *Works*, XXIII, 76, my italics. Compare p. 101: "Moreover, this class, the aristocracy, once thought most necessary to the State, is scant of numbers, and has now no power of its own, but depends on the support of the class next below it."

21. Morris made his contempt for positivism clear in "The Hopes of Civilisation" (1885); see *Works*, XIII, 78.

22. Report on a speech made at the Hammersmith Liberal Club, *Daily News*, 11 Feb. 1886, my italics.

23. *Contemporary Review*, XLIX (Feb. 1886), 264–279.

24. "For him the world contained nothing but his passion and existence had no other end" (II, 6).

25. May Morris, *William Morris, Artist, Writer, Socialist*, 2 vols. (London, 1936), II, 162.

26. Thompson, pp. 802–808. Thompson makes both these points in his excellent discussion of *News from Nowhere*. He gives them a different relative emphasis, however, and draws conclusions very different from mine.

CHAPTER 12

William Morris and the
Dream of Revolution

Morris takes the insights into industrial capitalism offered by the tradition whose major figures are Carlyle and Ruskin and gives them coherence through his theoretical understanding of Marxism and saves them from impotent hysteria by his persistent involvement in political action. E. P. Thompson definitively establishes his stature as a social critic in these terms, and Raymond Williams rightly describes his undeniable distinction when he says that Morris's socialism announced the extension of that tradition his book invokes 'into our own century'.[1]

But there is a major problem of value in Morris's work, and this too is brought to our attention in *Culture and Society*:

> For my own part, I would willingly lose *The* (sic) *Dream of John Ball* and the romantic socialist songs and even *News from Nowhere* – in all of which the weaknesses of Morris's general poetry are active and dis-abling – if to do so were the price of retaining and getting people to read such smaller things as *How We Live, and How We Might Live, The Aims of Art, Useful Work versus Useless Toil,* and *A Factory as It Might Be.*[2]

This certainly suggests the right order in which to read Morris, but it seems also to offer itself as a critical judgement and as such it needs to be challenged. For although Williams recognizes that his discrimination would mean a change in Morris's status, he does not seem to realize how great that change would be. Since the distinctive feature of Morris's socialism is, as he argues, the fact that he sees it as a cultural 'recovery of purpose' through the granting of a proper social role to art, it is important that Morris should be able to create work which isn't merely the reflection of the marginal futility to which the arts are reduced in a capitalist society. If we reject Morris's creative writing, we must call into question the whole social criticism – it relies too much on what seems to be a bad conception of art.

I wish to make claims for the imaginative writing of the years of Morris's socialism by seeing it as a formal response to problems which are theoretically insoluble, except in terms of metaphors which are unsatis-factory and intractable in the actual historical situation. Art is obviously the creation of the human mind responding to values and insights which participate in continuity; socialism is a theory of change which perceives the determinant factors of change in forces outside immediate individual and conscious control. In his excellent chapter on the cultural theories of English Marxists, Williams shows how muddled any attempt to explain the relationship between economic forces and cultural events in terms of an 'infrastructure' and 'superstructure' can become. The effect of the muddle, he argues, is to make many Marxist theorists revert to a discredited romanticism, and assimilate Marx's teaching to it, rather than to transform romanticism by Marxism. I don't want to argue that Morris overcame the acute difficulties inherent in Marxist attitudes to the arts in his theoretical writing, but that the imaginative works attempt, with much success, to find a mode in which the creative mind can be portrayed in its determined and determining relationship to historical actuality.

The proper context for the recognition of this is that of Morris's non-socialist contemporary writers. Thompson discusses this in some detail, but his account leaves an unresolved problem. On the one hand, he rightly criticizes Morris's aesthetic theory because it failed to take account of the importance of the work which was being created around him. 'In general', Thompson writes, 'Morris was blind towards the great achievements of bourgeois realism.'[3] On the other hand, in moral terms, he sees this as a basis for praise:

> The best and most honest of the literature at the end of the nineteenth century is marked by a profound disillusion, a searching for private reassurance, limited personal objectives, in the midst of a hostile social environment ... Against this tide, Morris stood alone with full assurance, with conscious confidence in life. The rock he stood upon was his Socialist convictions, his scientific understanding of history. The name which he gave this rock was 'Hope'.[4]

The split between aesthetic and moral judgements again reduces Morris's creative work to a marginal role. But it also makes the ideological assurance look almost complacent. The metaphor is dismaying. Socialism ought not to be a rock, but a creative current in the historical tide; it ought not to stand against the cultural life of the time it finds itself in but to transform it into a revolutionary consciousness. Yet this is the most common image of Morris – an intelligent man of heroic but blind faith. Certainly in his criticism, Morris's socialist faith seems to have blinded him to what was best in the literature of his own time. But a close analysis of his imaginative writing establishes that the difference between his commitment and the disillusionment of his contemporaries is not one of simple antithesis, of rock and tide, but one which signifies radically different solutions to shared tensions. Morris's formal experiments of the 1880s demonstrate a concern to create an historically possible revolutionary literature, and this involves a creative programme which goes in a different direction from those of such writers as Gissing, Hardy and James. We can only understand the validity of that programme if we see first how the tendency of their fiction is towards the contradiction of what they were trying, in their different ways, to achieve, an art which would cut through the complacencies of bourgeois consciousness to the truth.

II

The classic statement of the central problem in fiction of the late nineteenth century is Engels's famous letter to Margaret Harkness of 1887. He is criticizing her novel, *City Girl*:

> If I have any criticism to make, it is only that your story is not quite realistic enough. Realism, to my mind, implies, besides truth of detail, the truthful reproduction of typical characters under typical circumstances. Now your characters are typical enough, to the extent that you portray them. But the same cannot be said of the circumstances surrounding them, and out of which their action arises. In *City Girl* the working class appears as a passive mass, incapable of helping itself or even trying to help itself. All attempts to raise it out of its wretched poverty come from the outside, from above ... The revolutionary response of the members of the working class to the oppression that surrounds them, their convulsive attempts – semiconscious or conscious – to attain their rights as human beings, belong to history and may therefore lay claim to a place in the domain of realism.[5]

Engels is discussing the central problem of a realist aesthetic which is the relationship between specificity and typification particularly in the context of fiction's response to historical movement. Peter Demetz who has discussed the letter in detail wilfully misreads it in a way which precisely emphasizes the importance of this context. Demetz argues that the concept of typification derives from two traditions, the normative (which is theological in motivation and aspirational in aim) and the classificatory (which is scientific and descriptive). He applies this simple formula to Engels and decides that he is criticizing Margaret Harkness for failing to provide typification of the first kind: 'obviously Engels ... was aiming at a dogmatic conception that would compress the raw material of reality into a form of the typical predetermined by partisan considerations'.[6] He thus ignores the fact that Engels explicitly rejects the notion of a *Tendenzroman*, and that, in a letter to Minna Kautsky, he criticizes her for creating a character in which 'personality is entirely dissolved in principle'.[7] Demetz assumes that Engels' view of the historical process is automatically wrong.[8] Yet what Engels is actually asking for is not the satisfying of partisan considerations, but the reflection of what is there, not just as a feature in the surface reality, but as an active force which gives that reality a historical identity, a potential for change. The letter is simply saying that Margaret Harkness does not portray completely the reality imitated by her novel, because she does not realize in the situation she describes the potential for change. Depiction of circumstances is particularized and static and thus unrealistic. What Engels means by typicality of circumstances is made clear in the letter to Minna Kautsky:

> ... a socialist-biased novel fully achieves its purpose, in my view, if by conscientiously describing the real mutual relations, breaking down conventional illusions about them, it shatters the optimism of the bourgeois world, instils doubt as to the eternal character of the existing order, although the author does not offer any definite solution or does not even line up openly on any particular side.[9]

The danger of 'realism' is that it can lose focus because it becomes overwhelmed by the phenomena it imitates and comes to see them as a permanent system of reality unconditioned by history. The voice of protest against the existing order of things may become the voice of despair through the intensity of its realization of that order; and despair is more comfortable than protest. Typification involves the realization of 'real mutual relations' which do not allow for pessimistic but consoling 'realities'. It is something that the late Victorian novelists could hardly achieve: overwhelmed by the complexities of the present, they come to write of it as a hell from which they cannot escape.

But this does not entitle us to a facile dismissal of the later Victorian novelists. The reality which Engels is talking about is very difficult to realize in concrete terms; to portray the inexorable is inevitably going to be like portraying the eternal. Engels himself almost undercuts his criticism at the end of his letter to Margaret Harkness: 'I must own, in your defence, that nowhere in the civilized world are the working people less actively resistant, more passively submitting to fate, more depressed than in the East End of London.'[10] To present the reality of historical change would mean, especially for the English writer, an abandonment of immediate realism.

The best illustration of these problems is in the work of Gissing. We can see in him both a remarkable effort to assimilate the social actuality with which he is confronted, and a final incapacity to face up to its implications in formal terms. The limitations declare themselves early on, in *Demos*. Gissing simply isn't able to understand socialist psychology (not in concrete terms: in explicit comment in letters, he shows himself much more understanding of, for example, the stand Morris takes). Westlake, the artist and socialist, is portrayed in terms of a simple antithesis, dreamer and philanthropist in guilty reaction to the dream, although Morris was able to reject both terms of the antithesis very clearly. It is clear that Gissing can only create characters in terms of withdrawal or absorption. Because of this, his working-class hero necessarily has to be portrayed as becoming bourgeois because engagement with society must be seen either in terms of condescension (the philanthropist) or conquest. The distinctiveness of Gissing's later fiction is that he is able to present this dichotomy as a subjective viewpoint which leads to the defeat of the protagonist. There is no actual escape from economic realities: however reluctant and intellectually apart a character is, his withdrawal is reduced to a rhetorical gesture. In *New Grub Street*, Reardon confidently asserts the distinction between his real self and his social being: 'If I had to earn my living as a clerk, would that make me a clerk in soul?'[11] But when Reardon does take a post as a clerk and his wife protests, his challenge to her to maintain the distinction brings out the inexorable reality:

'Amy, are you my wife, or not?'
'I am certainly not the wife of a clerk who is paid so much a week.' (p. 188).

The whole discussion from which this comes prevents us from trivializing Amy's remark with the word 'snobbery'. It is a scene in which the sexual breakdown of a marriage becomes inextricably involved with the necessities of lower middle class life and its aspirations. Amy ends in the arms of the 'strong man', the man of success: Reardon's failure in social terms is inseparable from his failure in moral and physical terms. Against this social Darwinism, an Arnoldian inner self is maintained, but it is one which has become purely nostalgic. The best self, the inner world which holds itself apart from the force of circumstance, no longer has the capacity to build a bridge which will find compatibility in the outer world: it reduces itself to a recessive desire which hangs on to fragments of a world it cannot have. When, later in the novel, one of the characters contemptuously talks of the working class reading public, he says: 'The working classes detest anything that tries to represent their daily life. It isn't because that life is too painful; no, no; it's downright snobbishness' (p. 314). This comes shortly after a pathetic discussion between Reardon and Biffen at the top of Pentonville Hill in the fog about 'a metrical effect in one of the Fragments' (p. 311). The snobbishness of the working class is not more absurd than the culture-hunger of the hero. Defeat is inevitable and total.

Gissing's understanding of the epistemology of this defeat is profound, but the price to be paid for the understanding is the stabilization of the historical process in order to create a sense of the permanently antithetical relationship between the self and society, and this means further that he is compelled to share that epistemology to accept its limits even in the portrayal of its inadequacy. We can see this in the critical scene where Reardon tells his wife that he has gone back to a clerkship:

> He had foreseen a struggle, but without certainty of the form Amy's opposition would take. For himself, he meant to be gently resolute, calmly regardless of protest. But in a man to whom such self-assertion is a matter of conscious effort, tremor of the nerves will always interfere with the line of conduct he has conceived in advance. Already Reardon had spoken with far more bluntness than he proposed; involuntarily, his voice slipped from earnest determination to the note of absolutism, and, as is wont to be the case, the sound of these strange tones instigated him to further utterance of the same kind. He lost control of himself; Amy's last reply went through him like an electric shock, and for the moment he was a mere husband defied by his wife, the male stung to exertion of his brute force against the physically weaker sex.
>
> 'However you regard me, you will do what I think fit. I shall not argue with you. If I choose to take lodgings in Whitechapel, there you will come and live.'
>
> He met Amy's full look, and was conscious of that in it which corresponded to his own brutality. She had become suddenly a much older woman; her cheeks were tightly drawn into thinness, her lips were bloodlessly hard, there was an unknown furrow along her forehead, and she glared like the animal that defends itself with tooth and claw.
>
> 'Do as *you* think fit? Indeed!'
>
> Could Amy's voice sound like that? Great Heaven! With just such accent he had heard a wrangling woman retort upon her husband at the street corner. Is there then no essential difference between a woman of this world and one of that? Does the same nature lie beneath such unlike surfaces?
>
> He had but to do one thing: to seize her by the arm, drag her up from the chair, dash her back again with all his force – there, the transformation would have been complete, they would stand towards each other on the natural footing. With an added curse perhaps.
>
> Instead of that, he choked, struggled for breath, and shed tears.
>
> Amy turned scornfully away from him ... (p. 189)

Reardon is not spared in this passage. The sexual reality of his marriage is torn apart by his social weakness. 'Stung' into male assertion, his dominance is almost comically confined to the verbal gesture. The physical superiority has become merely a matter of memory – in the present it is Amy who takes the psychological and sexual initiative, and her scorn at the end of this passage is completely justified. If it weren't so much felt to

be the product of a continuous and relentless social pressure, Reardon's
bursting into tears would be farcical; as it is, it is presented as an absurd
anticlimax, the farce of nightmare. He is at a remove from his own male
nature: the performance is a conscious effort to recapture something
that is lost. He is in reality the feminine partner. Of course, the passage
beginning 'Great Heaven' tries to rescue his dignity, but it is done entirely
from his point of view, and it is totally irrational since it is he who has
deliberately transformed the social struggle to a sexual one in the first
instance. Unmanned by his failure, Reardon tries to hold on to the form
of the marriage after its substance has changed; accidentally revealing the
true substance by his stridency, he retreats from it into a kind of moral
aestheticism. Later in the scene, he rationalizes his own failure by whining
about Amy's lack of faith in him. She retorts, 'Instead of saying all this, you
might be proving that I am wrong' (p. 192). We assent to her comment –
the gap between protest and action is paralysing. On the other hand, what
she means by proof is the refusal of the clerkship, the maintenance of
social dignity. There is no escape for Reardon from the whirlpool of his
economic being – but there is no specious pity for him either. He collapses
because there is no adequate sense of identity available to cope with the
outside world. The values that Reardon retreats to are openly those of an
absolute sense of class – 'natural' is identical with 'brutal', and 'brutal'
with the woman of the street corner. At the same time, the notion of his
'soul' is supposed to be separable from class – the true Reardon is not a
clerk. The escape from class is through class-snobbery. Reardon's understanding of the world around him is seen to be the product of what he
most wishes to escape from.

All this is clearly there, judging Reardon, but we feel that Gissing's
presentation of this process is limited because the language of presentation is inadequate. It cannot bend away from Reardon's conscious
vocabulary towards one which will affirm the unconscious forces at work
here (Amy *Victrix*). 'He meant to be gently resolute, calmly regardless of
protest' is elegant and inert, and this more or less describes Reardon's
mind. The trouble comes with the remark that 'tremor of nerves will
always interfere with the line of conduct he has conceived in advance',
which is obviously an authorial comment since it is accounting for the
unconscious factor which 'interferes' between intention and action, but
which is equally elegant and inert. 'Always' dilutes the concreteness of the
situation by veering off towards aphorism, and 'interfere' is a ludicrously
inadequate verb. On the other hand, it is difficult to see how Gissing could
have solved this problem within the terms of the realistic novel. In order
to portray a consciousness which is alienated in the way that Reardon's is,
it has to accept the world-view of that consciousness. Gissing can 'place'
Reardon but only in terms in which Reardon could, when he wasn't under
stress, place himself. This means that the narrative has to enact in itself

the confusion between the response to a genuine social issue (the unmanning of the artist by penury) and an absolute but subjective opposition of
values (self and other). At the same time, since this opposition is purely
vestigial (significantly it is Amy who wants Reardon to go on with his
intellectual work – he is merely asserting his right to accept defeat and
become 'a harmless clerk'), what mainly emerges from the novel is its
inadequacy as an epistemology. The insights Gissing portrays seek a style
which goes beyond that of the individual consciousness.

The formal limitations link with what is, in the end, a failure on
Gissing's part to achieve a major confrontation between his protagonists
and the social order from which they recoil. At his best, Gissing can
dramatize this failure and bring out clearly its representativeness as a
cultural phenomenon. At its worst it can become a comfortable rationalization. 'Keep apart' is a constant theme of Gissing's work, but it can blind
him, as it does in his most dubious work such as *Born in Exile* and *Henry
Ryecroft*, to what he is so competent to see, the impossibility of keeping
apart. One of his few specifically political novels, *Denzil Quarrier*, clearly
illustrates this tendency. It is a story about the election which followed
Gladstone's Midlothian campaign which in itself is a significant point in
the democratization of political discussion.[12] Gissing seems at first to have
a real concern with connecting the psychology of his characters and the
potential transformation of political life seen in the Liberal successes of
that election. The hero is a man of means without any focus of interest
who nevertheless registers a personal protest against middle class convention by living in a successful ménage with a married woman. Asked to
speak at a Liberal stronghold, he preaches a moderate feminism and
is immediately adopted as a radical candidate. The novel becomes then a
study of the conflict between the political career and the private life. But
the actual emergence of this conflict becomes lost in a much less explicable struggle between the warring egoists who try to control Quarrier's
life. The quality of his radicalism in any case forestalls any real link being
made between progressive political attitudes and sexual affirmation:

> So long as nature doles out the gift of brains in different proportions,
> there must exist social subordination. The true Radical is the man who
> wishes so to order things that no one will be urged by misery to try and
> get out of the class he is born in.[13]

Politics become reduced to specious accommodation while the real struggle is pushed to the margin of social life despite the emphasized social
origin. Even in this one novel where Gissing sets out to confront a changing
social world as one in which the protagonists play an active role, the protest
becomes a social rationalization and, by qualifying the term 'radical' out
of existence, and creating a dramatic structure in which the effective

characters are almost motiveless mystifications, Gissing at once dehumanizes the impinging reality and absolves his characters from being anything other than victims of circumstance. The pessimism comforts the beneficiaries of the *status quo*.

Gissing is obviously a minor novelist, but his work illustrates clearly the dilemma confronted by greater contemporaries. James, for example, does transcend the determinism of realist 'antithesis' but he does so by the creation of a special language which creates its own rules and terms of triumph not unconscious of the economic realities which underwrite the subjective awareness of the protagonist, but taking possession of those realities and making of them moral dramas. Thus Milly Theale overcomes Kate Croy through the triumph of her moral perfection, but the agency of this perfection is her money. The real terms of the antithesis remain – Milly is rich and can control reality, Kate is poor and must struggle to dominate it before it dominates her. It is simply that the destruction of the individual consciousness by the impinging world is averted by turning the whole world into an image of consciousness.

The basis for the transformation of realism by the rediscovery of the integrated self is not in either of these writers but in Hardy. Hardy stands not, like Gissing, at the opposite extreme from Morris, as one whose very pessimism gives comfort to bourgeois optimism, but as one who affirms an aggressive role for human personality in the social world from which it is isolated – though, unlike Morris, Hardy is not supported by a coherent political theory. The subversive nature of his fiction is clear from the earliest novels, and it is clear that their subversiveness rests on a very clear sense of what can be affirmed. *Far from the Madding Crowd* is a drama of the quest for modes of expression which take account of the unaccommodated self. What Bathsheba and Gabriel find is physical contact on the hayrick in the storm – a discovery of work not as duty, the mode of accommodation to social law which is celebrated in *Adam Bede*, but as a physical rhythm, the fundamental expression of man's relation to the world around him. They are able to affirm this against the social status of Boldwood and the social duplicity of Troy because of what Joseph Poorgrass calls 'the gospel of the body'. The renewed community, purged of its overlord and its romantic hero, gains a new integrity of body and mind.

But it is a community which is far from the madding crowd. At the other end of his career, Hardy is compelled to confront the disintegration of human individuality in a society which does not belong to the past. For Jude there is no community to underwrite the integrity of body and soul. He stands in his field unaware of the past. The gospel of the body is caught in a meaningless confrontation with a dehumanized society and indifferent nature. There will only be a place for Jude if he denies either his intellectual aspirations or his capacity for love. To survive in this world is to be inhuman. But this is not a collapse into determinism. Jude is a very affirmative hero because he refuses to give up the search for integrity, and he only lies down in death. When he speaks to the crowd at Christminster, we are conscious of his triumph: 'But I don't admit that my failure proved my view to be a wrong one.' Success is not rightness, and Jude speaks with what Scott Fitzgerald was to call 'the authority of failure'. It is an authority which has revolutionary potential, yet it cannot be brought to the surface inside the novel itself. The halo round Christminster is Jude's individual delusion, and it is also a response to a collective experience of deprivation, but it cannot be realized as a collective experience. For that to happen would mean moving out of the world of the present and into the world of vision. Hardy was right to send his novels to Morris, and Morris should have recognized their real possibilities. But his inability to do so is understandable – for he has to move away, not from the personal delusion to the magnificent failure, but into the delusion so deeply that its basis in collective experience becomes clear. As he puts it at the end of *News from Nowhere*, 'And if others can see it as I have seen it, then it may be called a vision rather than a dream.'[14]

III

If Morris was blind to the achievements of nineteenth-century realism, he was nevertheless shrewdly aware of its problems. In *News from Nowhere*, Clara says:

As for your books, they were well enough for times when intelligent people had but little else in which they could take pleasure, and when they must needs supplement the sordid miseries of their own lives with imaginations of the lives of other people. But I say flatly that in spite of all their cleverness and vigour, and capacity for story-telling, there is something loathsome about them. Some of them, indeed, do here and there show some feeling for those whom the history-books call 'poor', and of the misery of whose lives we have some inkling; but presently they give it up, and towards the end of the story we must be contented to see the hero and heroine living happily in an island of bliss on other people's troubles; and that after a long series of sham troubles (or mostly sham) of their own making, illustrated by dreary introspective nonsense about their feelings and aspirations, and all the rest of it; while the world must even then have gone on its way, and dug and sewed and baked and built and carpentered round about these useless animals.' (XVI. 151)

Although this is, in many ways, philistine, it also points to a central problem in nineteenth century fiction – the ambiguity of the relationship between the generalized social picture and the particularity of the protagonists who are chosen to embody its features. Gissing is only able to cope with the discrepancy through a reduction to blind determinism on the one hand and a factitious coherence of language on the other. And although Hardy is acutely conscious of the discrepancy, and is able to discover new orders of consciousness which take account of this tendency to isolate the particular and bring it into relation to the life in which it grows, he is unable to discover a social medium in which such orders can survive except one which is not available in time. One of the few novels of the period which is specifically concerned with the portrayal of historical popular movements, *The Revolution in Tanner's Lane*, becomes the register of the diminishing scale of the radical mind as it transfers itself from the great historical moment to the life which continues after it. We move from the genuinely revolutionary sensibility of the Blanketeers to a quite starkly disconnected story in which the hypocrisy of the new generation of dissenters is exposed by a *theoretical* revolution with the result that the 'respectable' minister is replaced by an academic one. Not only do we see dissent itself becoming conservative and conformist, but the surviving radical spirit manifesting itself in an almost entirely private way, gaining a moral victory and a highly doubtful improvement of personnel. The Tanner's Lane revolution is a farcical shadow of the forces displayed in the first half of the novel, and it does not change the course of history at all. The radical protagonists of the first part are recalled in the closing words of the novel only to remind us that what they stood for has really been driven underground: 'What became of Zachariah and Pauline? At present I do not know.'[15] Rutherford certainly affirms the reality of the revolutionary mind but he is hopelessly sceptical about its possible field of action.

Morris's whole literary effort in the eighties is to affirm the reality of the revolutionary mind and to see it in possible fields of action. 'It is the province of art', he wrote towards the end of his life, 'to set the true ideal of a full and reasonable life before him [i.e. the working man]' (XXIII. 281). What underwrites the possibility of this is the consciousness of historical change: 'Until recently,' he wrote in collaboration with Belfort Bax, 'amongst cultivated people, enjoying whatever advantages may be derived from civilization, there has been an almost universal belief, not yet much broken into, that modern or bourgeois civilization is the final form of human society. Were this the case, we should be pessimists indeed ...'[16] It is this sense which differentiates him from Gissing, Hardy and Rutherford, but we need to define carefully its distinctive nature, because it participates in their pessimism before separating out from it. In a lecture of 1884, 'Misery and the Way Out', Morris said:

> Friends, this earthly hell is not the ordinance of nature but the man-
> ufacture of man; made I will believe not by their malice but their
> stupidity; and it is your business to destroy it: to destroy it, I say, not

each man to try to climb up out of it, as your thrift-teachers tell you, but to make an end of it so that no one henceforth can ever fall into it.[17]

Morris here anticipates the pessimism of a novel such as *The Nether World* which sees the earthly hell as a permanent state and escape only in terms of an ironic version of self help, and even of *Jude the Obscure*. The separation is in the words 'not nature ... but the manufacture of man' and this gives the judgement on the present, which is no different from that of Gissing and the later Hardy, temporality. The historicism is informed by two firmly grasped concepts which are the basis of all Morris's socialist writing – the class struggle and its historical consummation, revolutionary change. It was the need to cope with the sense of the first and the despair of doing so except by revolutionary theory that drove Morris to socialism initially. In a lecture of 1886 he picked up a word made current by John Bright in the reform debates of the sixties; 'there is an ugly word for a dreadful fact which I must make bold to use – the residuum: that word since the time I first saw it used, has had a terrible significance to me, and I have felt from my heart that if this residuum were a necessary part of civilization, as some people openly, and many more tacitly, assume that it is, then this civilization, carries with it the poison that shall one day destroy it' (XXII. 65). The imagery is deterministic and its sense of class is merely negative, but 'destroy' carries a definitive sense of change, and this means already that Morris is differently situated from those who imagined the present world to be indestructible. In the following year, Morris moves towards a much more active sense of change via an intensifying despair. He writes to Mrs Burne Jones, about the trial of Johann Most, 'These are the sort of things that make thinking people so sick at heart that they are driven from all interest in politics save revolutionary politics: which I must say seems like to be my case'.[18]

It is thus out of despair rather than vision that Morris moves towards the recognition of the class struggle and its necessary outcome in revolution. What Marxism gives him is an historical coherence which re-orders the relationship between visionary conceptions of man's possible existence and the despair of seeing the piecemeal progress of liberalism preventing those conceptions from becoming less and less likely. To move from the vague and emotive remarks that I have just quoted to the discussion of class in *How We Live, and How We Might Live* (1885) which leans heavily on Chapter XXII of *Capital*, is to move into realms of coherence that would be quite alien to the dualistic mind of Gissing. Morris now sees the class struggle not as something which is merely dangerous and deplorable but as something which is necessary, and he sees change, therefore, not as a matter of improving the moral and material standards of a helpless residuum, but as one of that proletariat recognizing its own essence, combination:

The working-classes or proletariat cannot even exist as a class without combination of some sort. The necessity which forced the profit-grinders to collect their men first into workshops working by the division of labour, and next into great factories worked by machinery ... gave birth to a distinct working-class or proletariat: and this it was which gave them their *mechanical* existence, so to say. (XXIII. 11)

It is precisely this coherence that gives Morris his aesthetic. The potential of historical change predates the consciousness of its agents. Despair of change is merely a false consciousness which itself tends towards revolution: 'all history shows us what a danger to society may be a class at once educated and socially degraded' (XXIII. 79). But if this danger is to be transformed into the possibility of revolution the false consciousness must be transformed into a consciousness which recognizes the reality of social change. To set the true ideal of a full and reasonable life before the working class is not, therefore, to be idealistic. It is merely to bring into articulate consciousness progressive forces at work in history on preconscious, or 'mechanical' levels.

At the same time, Morris's use of the earthly hell metaphor suggests how sensitive he is to the social pessimism arrived at by his most intelligent contemporary writers. This is because although Marxism gives his vision an historical basis, the central concept of his socialist ideology is one which has been with him from the beginning, alienation. But he never lets go his ability to enter into the alienated consciousness of the individual aware of social injustice, and this provides the basis of all his creative writing. Taking up the antisocialist argument that the working class is better off than savages, Morris points to its absurdity because it takes no account of social relationships, and he goes on to define his own version of alienation: 'but for us, for the most of us, civilization has bred desires which she forbids us to satisfy, and so is not merely a niggard but a torturer also' (XXIII. 105). In another essay he demonstrates that his sense of alienation has a very forceful subjective meaning: 'all civilization has cultivated our sensibility only to disappoint it, and ... we suffer ... from the consciousness of the mass of suffering and brutality which lies below our lucky class, ugliness all about us, the world made for naught.' Although such sympathy is a rhetorical device and is placed by an abrasive irony, 'we discontented ones of the intellectual hanger-on group', it also acknowledges the difficulty of others in attaining his belief in change. It suggests that there is a tension in his work, which is what the creative writing is concerned with, between the vision of the historical potential which he had learned from Marx and the degree to which it is manifest in the historical actuality.

This is not the place to discuss Morris's involvement with English socialist groups but it is impossible not to recognize that underlying much of his work there is a profound unease about their historical role. Activism is central to Morris's socialist thinking and it comes out almost automatically in *How I Became a Socialist*:

> So there I was in for a fine pessimistic end of life, if it had not somehow dawned on me that amidst all this filth of civilization the seeds of a great chance, what we others call Social-Revolution, were beginning to germinate. The whole face of things was changed to me by that discovery, and *all I had to do then* in order to become a Socialist was to hook myself on to the practical movement ... (XXIII. 280)

The italicized phrase is an index of how closely Morris regarded theory as wedded to practice, but, written as it was in 1894, this must be seen as a difficult statement of faith. Very early on, he saw that the SDF had no genuine historical reality; it was, he said, a 'theatrical association in a private room with no hope but that of gradually permeating cultured people with our aspirations'. 'Theatrical', 'private', 'gradually', 'cultured' – the words add up to a socialist nightmare.[19] The sense of unreality is important again in his explanation of his break with the SDF: 'the revolution cannot be a mechanical one, though the last act of it may be civil war ... why then should we swagger about violence which we know we cannot use?'[20] And yet it cannot be said that the Socialist League discovered any more valid role: it was less active in events such as the Trafalgar Square riots of 1886 and 1887 and it was indifferent to the Dock Strike.

Socialist action in the eighties does not seem to have given Morris much sense of the way things were changing. His vision of the immediate future is, in fact, very subdued:

> ... our own lives may see no end to the struggle, perhaps no obvious hope of the end. It may be that the best we can hope to see is that struggle getting sharper and bitterer day by day, until it breaks out openly at last into the slaughter of men by actual warfare instead of by the slower and crueller methods of 'peaceful' commerce. If we live to see that, we shall live to see much; for it will mean the rich classes grown conscious of their own wrong and robbery, and consciously defending them by open violence; and then the end will be drawing near. (XXIII. 119)

It is true that the date of this, 1885, may mean that the modesty of the prediction is determined by the gloom which followed the split, but it points to an important feature of Morris's writing throughout, and that is the disciplined refusal to allow the historical actuality to be flushed with the light of the historical potential. This potential is seen as offering only struggle in the foreseeable future. The realism of this is complex in its effect. On the one hand, it prevents Morris from short circuiting the revolutionary process; on the other, in the light of the spontaneous movement from commitment to activism that is registered in *How I Became a Socialist*, it makes for a tension – between the need to act and the recognition of the limited possibilities of action – limited, that is, not merely quantitatively but qualitatively: English socialism doesn't offer a confrontation with reality. We shall have to come back to this, but we need to take note immediately of Morris's alertness to the predicament of the socialist intellectual. Looking back on the early days of socialism in *News from Nowhere*, Hammond gives us an exact diagnosis:

> When the hope of realizing a communal condition of life for all men arose quite late in the nineteenth century, the power of the middle classes, the then tyrants of society, was so enormous and crushing, that to almost all men, even those who had, you may say *despite themselves, despite their reason and judgment*, conceived such hopes, it seemed a dream. So much was this the case that some of those more enlightened men who were then called Socialists, although they well knew, and even stated in public, that the only reasonable condition of Society was that of pure Communism (such as you now see around you), yet shrunk from what seemed to them the barren task of preaching the realization of a happy dream. (XVI. 104)

The paradoxes are acute. There is no suggestion that the enlightened men are anything but right: pure Communism is here. Nor is there any suggestion that their aspirations were anything but 'reasonable'. Yet they conceive such hopes *despite* themselves, *despite* their reason and their judgement. It means that the socialist vision is in some way beyond immediate consciousness although in theoretical terms it is conceivable. The believer is conditioned as much by his alienation as the pessimists who see the earthly hell as a law of nature are by theirs.

This is the starting point of Morris's socialist aesthetic. His awareness of alienation comprehends a sense of the radical dislocation of consciousness from historical reality (with its potential for change). Art has therefore to create a new consciousness which moves away from the immediate towards the possible. Realism has to be transcended: 'as for romance, what does romance mean? I have heard people miscalled for being romantic, what romance means is the capacity for a true conception of history, a power of making the past part of the present.'[21] It also becomes a power for seeing the future in the present. But its form is determined by alienation. Art is ineluctably the creation of the individual socialism is the recognition of collectivity. Such a recognition can only be registered through the transformation of individual epistemology, and the transformation has to take place within the individual through an entry into dream. Socialist art does not transcend alienation: it transforms it into revolutionary consciousness by the recognition of the collective possibilities of the mind's curve away from actuality. For Morris, in dreams begins responsibility.

IV

The affirmation of the responsibility of dream in a world in which consciousness has become ineradicably dislocated from the field of its existence is an assumed feature of all of Morris's socialist writing. But the most exploratory treatment of the theme predates his socialism and is the subject of *Sigurd the Volsung*. It is an acutely frustrating text because its thematic importance and narrative skill are almost obliterated by Morris's adoption of a style which is passively the product of the very alienation the story is about. The language is opaque and frequently inept – a combination of pseudo-anachronism trying to escape from the realities of modern English and an inert obedience to the demands of metre, as though all that keeps it communicating is a reflex response to a machine. The poem records the development of the extreme disaffection of the inner mind from the outward life in terms of a highly modernized myth. True, Morris writes out the worst physical brutality of the original myth, but what we have instead is a psychological drama which is more violent and inexorable – *Sigurd the Volsung* is much nearer to *Women in Love* than to the Saga, and translated into English it could have been a great Victorian degenerative myth of social alienation and the breakdown of sexual relationships.

In the story, power moves from the Volsungs to the Niblungs and finally to Atli. The first stage signifies a transference from a race in whom desire and action are unified to one in whom desire can only be fulfilled through duplicity (both that of Grimhild in doping Sigurd and that of her sons in plotting the murder). This leaves open the possibility of redemption through self-sacrifice, but the final stage, in which Atli has become the ruling power, is one in which the divorce between desire and action has become a social system in which the ruler employs retainers to sustain his power: he is, himself, physically insignificant. We have moved to the lord of the city, and only destruction of the whole society can atone for the evil nature of the ruler.

Three interconnected motifs contribute to this evolution of alienated man. The first is that the values of the Volsungs, which include heroism, community and equality ('For the man was a mighty warrior, and a beater down of kings' (XII. 19)) become outlawed. By their very heroism, the Volsungs are unable to cope with the duplicity of the Goths. Sigmund scornfully rejects the offer of Siggeir to buy the sword he has drawn from the Branstock because he has no conception of trading one's actions for acquisitions. By the same token, however, the Volsungs have no conception either of conspiracy, the closed, indirect pursuit of revenge, and so fall prey to Siggeir's stratagem. The Volsungs' story is one of 'How a mighty people's leaders in the field of murder fell' (XII. 16), and murder is a mode of action that the integrity of giants, who know no dichotomy between the values they seek and the means they will employ to achieve them, cannot cope with. Sigmund survives only through the cunning his sister has learnt, and the race is perpetuated only through her secret incest with him. Sinfiotli is the progeny of a race doomed to conserve itself through secrecy and crime, and he and his father, though they are of heroic stature, are doomed to outlawry. They become for a while werewolves, and, though they recover from this, it seems to declare the potential for brutality that their isolation breeds in them. And this is confirmed when Sinfiotli murders Siggeir's children: the moment is presented with a calm brutality which reduces both murderer and victim to something less than human:

> but Sinfiotli taketh them up
> And breaketh each tender body as a drunkard breaketh a cup.
>
> (XII. 36)

Sigmund lives to return to the land of the Volsungs, and his heroism survives in community, but his last years are without the creative vitality that we had been made to feel present at the wedding of Signy earlier. Sinfiotli has nothing to do but become a pirate, and he is in the end murdered by Sigmund's wife. Sigmund banishes her and takes a new wife who is virtuous, but in the battle he has to fight against his chief rival, as he feels himself becoming 'king of the world at last' (XII. 53). His sword is destroyed by Odin and he is killed. The Volsungs are to survive, but not as leaders of their own community. Sigurd, with whom Sigmund's new wife is pregnant, is to be brought up in a strange country. Thus an historical rhythm is established at the outset in which 'Earth grows scant of great ones, and fadeth from its best' (XII. 5), so that greatness in its social manifestation comes to seem naive and can only survive outside the social law as individual greatness.

This idea informs the second motif: we move from the saga of the heroic community to the romance hero, and thus the second book is chiefly concerned with the dynamics of individuation. The land of Elf where Sigurd is brought up is a gentile utopia – 'There no great store had the franklin, and enough the hireling had' (XII. 61) – but Sigurd, educated by Regin, the man of skill and knowledge, is given a consciousness which grows beyond accommodation in a static society:

> For this land is nought and narrow, and Kings of the carles are these,
> And their earls are acre bidders, and their hearts are dull with peace.
>
> (XII. 68)

The specific focus of the aspiration becomes, of course, the rhinegold, and this is the third motif in the degenerative myth, the development of the acquisitive mind. The story of Andvari, the original guardian of the gold, invokes the possibility of a mind being changed by the situation it finds itself in, so that the elf of the Dark, whose knowledge had been universal, becomes narrowed by its contact with the gold and is unable to concentrate on anything but the counting of the gold which it knows will not bring happiness. Fafnir, the brother of Regin, who takes all the gold for himself, turns into a dragon fully conscious of his despair. Both characters present powerfully the determination of consciousness by money, but their role is more than incidental. When Sigurd kills Fafnir (through stratagem), it is a triumph for his heroic personality – 'I, Sigurd, knew and desired, and the bright sword learned the way' (XII. 3), and thus it is an assertion of values which are not determined by circumstance. But his triumph is ambiguous, accompanied by 'sounds of a strange lamenting' (XII. 112). For although Sigurd's heroism is unquestioned, we note as the poem progresses that it is not one which creates a social world out of the triumph. His mother's prediction – 'all folk of the earth shall be praising the womb where once he lay' (XII. 51) – only comes true insofar as he achieves personal glory. Sigurd meets what confronts him – there is no sense of specific objectives. The attainment of the gold turns him into an episodic hero. More than this, once he has tasted the heart of Fafnir and become through it aware of the conspiracy of Regin against him and taken action to forestall it, we have moved completely, with the hero, into a world in which the main task of life is a struggle for existence by the isolated individual through cunning or violence or both. From that point on, the major impetus of the poem derives from the complete dislocation of the inner and outer selves manifest above all in the distortion of sexual relationships.

Sigurd is granted a vision of transcendent love in his first meeting of Brynhild (who mediates between fate and humanity). But this is outside the realm of human life, and their resolution to recreate this vision in the world of men is thwarted first by her inaccessibility and then, as Sigurd drifts away inevitably towards where war takes him, by the drug of oblivion which Grimhild administers. What Sigurd gains is not the love of Brynhild but the complex of love and hatred which Gudrun gives him – a complex which in its destructiveness and violence looks forward to Lawrence's Gudrun. Gudrun, whose psychology is one of the most remarkable things in the poem, feels for him in terms of individual aspiration rather than any sense of mutuality underwritten by social integration: she is mainly silent in his presence, feeling both admiration and envy for his heroic deeds. This dualism is a comment on what the integrity of the Volsungs has been brought to. Sigurd's death is brought about by the same destructive ambiguity: Gudrun's brothers do not break the blood-bond they have made with Sigurd, they circumvent it, and what remains in the poem is the fullest working out of the complex interplay of law, desire and stratagem which this situation sets up. Gudrun lures her brothers to their deaths at the hands of Atli. The moment when she sits in the hall where the battle is raging, withdrawn and dressed in white, and remains passive as drops of her brother's blood stain her dress, is not Swinburnian, but one where the suppressed will takes command of the life around it by its very withdrawal. The Niblungs do achieve an heroic stature in their struggle against Atli and their sacrifice of themselves and the gold to prevent the ruler of the city from securing final power. But it is the heroism of reparation for guilt, and the guilt derives from the thrust of man's heroic energies into isolation and the withdrawal of the will into cunning. It is the mythic version of 'modern love' seen as the creation of an acquisitive society.

But it is more than this, because Morris's chief concern is the structural relationship of the dichotomy in consciousness which this theme adumbrates. Although Sigurd is made to lose his love for Brynhild, Grimhild cannot recreate him anew. His face becomes emotionless and he rides off aimlessly into the deedless dark: although the vision of transcendent love is untranslatable into the world of men, it is equally undeniable. Sigurd does make contact with Brynhild in the world of men twice, and the contact is highly ironic. Before he reaches the Niblungs, he finds her by accident in Lymdale, another earthly paradise like the Land of Elf, wearing a dress depicting the past history of the Volsungs. We have seen already that such a world is unavailable to Sigurd, and it is realized here as an echo of what has been: 'For fair they are and joyous as the first God-fashioned Kings' (XII. 141). She too is a figure who belongs to the past of the Volsungs – and soon Sigurd is to be drugged into forgetfulness, not of its aura and importance, but of its coherence. Sigurd's accommodation is not that of the historically rooted hero but that of the leader of warlike people who is also the outsider. But this first meeting is also given positive value by the second meeting which comes after Sigurd has been drugged and has married Gudrun. Grimhild sends her eldest son, Gunnar to take Brynhild as wife. Sigurd and the second son, Hogni go with him. They find that Brynhild's castle is surrounded by a wall of fire, and Gunnar's horse refuses to go through it. He takes Sigurd's horse, who also shies away in spite of a career of unalloyed fearlessness. Hogni then makes the two men hold hands and Sigurd sees Gunnar disappear and reappear again in the body of himself. He realizes that he has assumed the body of Gunnar and rides through the flames, swears a troth to Brynhild and sleeps with her, laying a sword between them. Brynhild marries Gunnar but remains pale and unsatisfied as Gudrun seems 'dreamy with the love of yester-night'. When Gudrun in triumph reveals the truth of the change of identities, Brynhild begins to die of grief. Neither Gunnar, nor Sigurd who offers marriage, are able to recall her to life, and she demands Sigurd's death before she dies herself.

The significance of this is very plain. The first meeting adumbrates the lost possibilities of the vision of love in the actual world. The second depicts, mythically, its actuality. Body and mind are asunder. Sigurd can only reach love through inhabiting the body of Gunnar. Gunnar gains love (the acquisitive verb needs to be emphasized) only through employing the consciousness of Sigurd. Man must seem to lose his identity to bring love into this world. Marriage thus becomes a lie – 'And the lie is laid between them, as the sword lay while agone' (XII. 204). The realities of sexual love are distorted by the dislocation of identity and the trickery of the societal witch. Equally, however, though the realities of sexual love eventually insist on being recognized, it is not as love but as murder. The sword between Sigurd and Brynhild is as real as the lie between each of them and the Niblung they have been duped into marrying. The love has to be unconsummated – remaining a dream which can only be actualized inversely in death. Sigurd will die in Gudrun's arms.

This account doesn't pay tribute to the realization of these themes. For Morris manages to bring out through the linguistic fog the dramatic sense of what Grimhild does to Sigurd's mind by destroying its relation with the past, and, later the grimness and violence of the struggle for domination between Brynhild and Gudrun. Both features point to what is affirmative in this inexorable destructiveness of sexual distortion. The entry into man's primeval greatness of deceit and greed transforms the heroism which is the heritage of that greatness, and the love which is its vision, into the heroism of the outsider and the lie of marriage. Sigurd is successful in action but he is finally unable to hold the integrity of the Volsungs together in his mind, so that his very identity becomes the agent of other, debased forces. But Sigurd remains, even in defeat, isolated and withdrawn, unable to participate in his own wedding ceremony. And Brynhild remains apart from the world she is trapped in, holding the vision of Sigurd together separate from her marriage. Finally Gudrun, the woman of the repressed will and the withdrawn aspiration, will bring revenge on all those who are agents of destruction. She will draw her brothers to their death, and she will burn the court of Atli. Her alienated sexual violence will ensure that the saga does not come to rest in the lowest level of degradation. Her dramatic act affirms the ultimate freedom of mind which is postulated throughout the poem. Grimhild can divorce Sigurd from his vision of love but she cannot put it completely from his mind, and only by divorcing his mind from his body can she take possession of love for her son so that the possession is limited to the duration of the divorce. Both Sigurd's vision and Brynhild's knowledge of him ensure that finally love can only be destroyed by the acquisitive society and cannot be assimilated by it. In their dream world, and in the retreated consciousness of Gudrun, there remains an unviolated force which emerges in each of them in turn as a chain reaction which will come back into society to destroy it.

Consciousness may be split in two, but it cannot be remade in the image of what splits it. In the recognition of the responsiveness of this division to a cleavage in the outer world, the mythic division of labour, the revolutionary mind begins its growth.

V

Sigurd the Volsung necessarily ends in destruction. The unviolated consciousness can only issue in the recoil of the individual: once Gudrun has completed the process of vengeance, she has nothing to do but to walk into the sea. The isolated mind is a sepulchre within which the lost echoes of the values of the past reverberate, and it bursts open to history only to spread death. Socialism enables Morris to envisage its withdrawal not merely as responsive but as capable of becoming a possible social experience. The inexorable historical rhythm which he creates in relation to the unassimilated consciousness in *Sigurd the Volsung* is not pervasively triumphant, but it is always hostile. A dialectical view of history grants the opposing consciousness a role in the ongoing dynamic. It means that the task of the disaffected mind is not to destroy all that is outside it, but to seek out the forces in the historical rhythm which are its objective equivalents. The relationship between subjective and objective is difficult to grasp in conceptual terms but it can be best defined *vis-à-vis* Engels:

> And this conflict between the productive forces and modes of production is not a conflict engendered in the mind of man, like that between original sin and divine justice. It exists, in fact, objectively, outside us, independently of the will and actions even of the men who have brought it on. Modern Socialism is nothing but the reflex, in thought, of this conflict in fact; the ideal reflection in the minds, first, of the class directly suffering under it, the working class.[22]

We shall need to emphasize later that Morris's attitude to the role of the human mind is much less deterministic than the use of a word such as 'reflex' implies, but what socialism gives him is the realization that the laws of change may only be grasped by the individual in terms of his alienation – that is, in terms of his response to the thwarting of his desires by the world of actuality. The determining role of consciousness begins in the recognition of the nature of its determination by objective contradictions. Dream, the freed consciousness, thus becomes a major, though expendable, register of the antithetical forces invisibly operating against the perceptible reality.

Thus there is nothing facile about Morris's use of dream as a convention within which to realize concretely socialist insight. Above all, it is not polemical but exploratory. Despite the intensity and commitment of Morris's social vision, and his talent for coherent argument, his fictional works are not didactic. In the first place, the lucid and confident prose of *Signs of Change* demonstrates that Morris has no need of parable to give specious support to his theory. Secondly, it is obviously absurd to expect anybody to be converted to socialism by reading *A Dream of John Ball* or *News from Nowhere*, and Morris clearly did not intend that they should be. The rightness of Socialist theory is a *donnée* of such texts, and their major concern is to explore in dramatic terms what it means to the experiencing mind to bring socialist values to an understanding of historical change. And underlying the exploration is a deep tension between the need to create a viable relationship between dream and perceptible reality, and the recognition that the fulfilment of this need is an agony as great as Jude's.

The theme of *A Dream of John Ball* allows for a highly compressed portrayal of the struggle to achieve a meaningful relationship between human aspiration and the historical process. The rebellion of 1381 had become an important event in the work of historians contemporary with Morris, particularly those whom he admired.[23] Stubbs describes it as a 'revolutionary rising' and goes on:

> The rising of the commons is one of the most portentous phenomena to be found in the whole of our history. The extent of the area over which it spread, the extraordinary rapidity with which intelligence and communication passed between the different sections of the revolt, the variety of cries and causes which combined to produce it, the mystery that pervades its organization, its sudden collapse and its indirect permanent results, give it a singular importance both constitutionally and socially.[24]

It clearly has great relevance to Morris's own situation in the eighties. Green makes a more precise point which is also important in its implications. Talking of the system of slogans and catchphrases for which the uprising is famous, he writes: 'In the rude jingle of these lines began for England the literature of political controversy: they are the first predecessors of the pamphlets of Milton and of Burke.'[25] The Kent uprising in particular reveals the possibility of a concerted political action on the part of the people which is not a protest against oppression on a narrow basis. 'Their discontent', Green writes, 'was simply political'.[26] Thorold Rogers, whose work was an obviously useful document for socialist writers, emphasizes as well that it is a revolt which shows a sophisticated organization and that it is the product of prosperity as well as oppression: 'How can men combine and organize when their one thought is for their daily bread, and that is only secure for the day?'[27] Thus it is an *articulate* uprising with real possibilities of victory. It has its literature and its ideology – its longing for justice as well as its immediate grievances (Rogers differentiates it from the peasant war in Germany and the Jacquerie on these grounds). It is a movement which expresses a definite change in the level of consciousness of the common people. Morris is therefore right to stress the real qualities of material and cultural life of the men who were in revolt. The strength of social identity is an important feature in the articulation of single grievances into political action.

But it is not merely the rebellion's formal qualities that make it relevant to the Socialist movement. 'Priests like Ball', wrote Green, 'openly preached the doctrines of communism'.[28] Rogers goes further and suggests that not only the ideas but the reaction of the people to their situation made them open to socialist thought. The Statutes of Labourers are for him important because the serfs reacted to them by forming combinations: 'in plain modern English, the serfs entered into what are now called trades unions'.[29] The poor priests who provided their ideology 'had honeycombed the minds of the upland folk with what may be called religious socialism',[30] and Tyler and the other leaders were concerned with much more than the redress of grievances; their concern was for 'the reconstruction of English society'.[31] C. Edmund Maurice, who wrote a composite biography of Tyler, Ball and Oldcastle in 1875, went so far as to head a section of his book 'The Class Struggle in Richard II's Reign'.[32] Not surprisingly, John Ball was already a major figure in socialist mythology. Hyndman, with a note of that chauvinism which was to play such a destructive role in the history of the socialist movement, wrote, in *The Historical Basis of Socialism in England*: 'It is well to show that the idea of socialism is no foreign importation into England. Tyler, Cade, Ball, Kett, More, Bellers, Spence, Owen, read to me like sound English names: not a foreigner in the whole batch.'[33] Morris would hardly have subscribed to this kind of vulgarity (though he may have felt the need to redress the Germanocentrism of Engels) but since he is attempting to define the basis of the historical change of consciousness it is clearly important for him to show that the aspirations of his own socialist comrades are linked with aspirations which lie deep in the inherited past.

Morris's story is thus deeply responsive to issues emerging in history in his own time. The rebellion of 1381 is a moment of great significance to the socialist movement because it is a coherent rebellion which looks forward in its aims to socialism itself. Nevertheless, Morris could not, of course, have been satisfied with the vague labels of Stubbs, Green and Rogers. Nor could he fail to be acutely conscious of the gap between what may have been the socialist aims of the rebellion and its most important effects. All of the historians I have mentioned agree that the ultimate focus of the rebellion was the end of villeinage, and that, although the charters granted by Richard II to buy the rebels off were revoked, the long term results of the rebellion were to cause the end of feudalism. 'They had struck a vital blow at villeinage',[34] Stubbs writes, and Green, as usual more dramatic and specific, concludes, 'serfage was henceforth a doomed and perishing thing'.[35] Predictably, the picture they give has been heavily demythologized by later historians, but, if this dates Stubbs and Green, it does not affect Morris, whose concern is to evoke a dramatic concentration of a changing awareness, and not to set up a mechanical cause and effect relationship. But Morris goes beyond the historians in a more basic way. He would know from Marx that the major precondition of capitalist production is the freeing of labour. Thus whatever 'communism' Ball was preaching was dialectically opposed to the direction his rebellion took. The release from serfdom was part of a process which retarded 'fellowship' by disruption of a sense of community. Though its ideology has socialist content, the peasants' uprising is, in its effect, part of the process by which society becomes capitalist.

This is reflected very accurately in the text. There is a marked contrast between the political consciousness of the peasants and that of Ball: the people who are actually going to create the rebellion are much more conscious of the struggle for liberty than the struggle for community. The stave of Robin Hood, for example, shows this:

> ... it was concerning the struggle against tyranny for the freedom of life, how that the wildwood and the heath, despite of wind and weather, were better for a free man than the court and the cheaping-town; of the taking from the rich to give to the poor; of the life of a man doing his own will and not the will of another man commanding him for the commandment's sake. (XVI. 224)

The remark about rich and poor is much more routine than the evocation of the importance of liberty, and it is, in any case, not one which suggests that the rich man has to be abolished. By contrast, Ball's sermon has a text which goes much further: 'fellowship is heaven, and lack of fellowship is hell' (XVI. 230). Even Ball's attack on feudalism is on its inequality rather than its restriction of individual liberty:

> ... ye know who is the foeman, and that is the proud man, the oppressor, who scorneth fellowship, and himself is a world to himself and needeth no helper nor helpeth any, but, heeding no law, layeth law on other men, because he is rich. (XVI. 234)

Thus Morris realizes not merely the positive value of the rebellion but also its final contradictory nature. Those most directly involved in the concrete situation, the peasants and craftsmen who do the fighting, see the cause in libertarian terms. Ball, the theorist, raises the level beyond that of liberty to that of equality. But his language is revealing – his rhetoric is religious. The vision of what lies beyond the immediate objective (which comes to mean the fight to obtain a free market) demands a terminology which is not confined to the world of concrete activity: 'the change beyond the change' can only be dreamt of in terms which are bound up with 'the glory of the heavens which is worshipped from afar'. Morris's realization is close to Engels' analysis in *The Peasant War in Germany*, where Engels draws a distinction between middle class heresies which were simply anti-clerical, and the insurrectionary heresies of plebeian and peasant classes, of which John Ball's is one:

> This position of the plebeians is sufficient explanation as to why the plebeian opposition of that time could not be satisfied with fighting feudalism and the privileged middle-class alone; why, in fantasy at least, it reached beyond modern bourgeois society then only in its inception; why, being an absolutely propertyless faction, it questioned institutions, views, and conceptions common to every society based on division of classes. The chiliastic dream visions of ancient Christianity offered in this respect a very serviceable starting-point. On the other hand, this reaching out beyond not only the present but also the future, could not help being violently fantastic. At the first practical application, it naturally fell back into narrow limits set by prevailing conditions.[36]

Engels offers here a precise equivalent of the balance between consciousness and actuality in the peasant uprising. What is important is that his use of the words, 'fantasy', 'dream visions' and 'violently fantastic' alerts us to the title of Morris's story. What mediates the gap between aspiration and possibility is the conceivable – dream.

A Dream of John Ball contains a threefold ambiguity on which the whole tension of the story depends. In the first place, it defines the tale itself – the narrator's dream of the past (itself historically aware since the mode is a mediaeval one). But it also means John Ball's dream, which has to be interpreted in two ways. In the first place, his dream is his fantasy of fellowship. It is a romantic vision, linked with the moonlight, but which has to be set against the gloomy truth that the narrator reveals to Ball among the dead. And this revelation too is a dream – not of aspiration but of consequence. As daylight replaces the moon, a second, more objective dream replaces the fantasy: 'scarce do I know', says Ball 'whether to wish thee some dream of the days beyond thine to tell what shall be' (XVI. 286).

The drama of Ball's coming to knowledge is acted out against the coming of day. It begins in church with the moon providing the only light and the two men confronting the dead and being compelled to assert against the fact of death the only source of life's meaning, human community: 'This', said I, 'That though I die and end, yet mankind yet liveth, therefore I end not, since I am a man; and even so thou deemest, good friend ...' (XVI. 265). Such an assertion involves coming to terms with history, and so John Ball has to confront his own death with the knowledge of what it will bring, the division of labour as the most direct consequence of the destruction of feudalism and the most important factor in the development of capitalist exploitation. As the narrator explains, the moon image of John Ball's dream fades. At last, his hope is merely that the population under such a grim system will diminish so that there will be fewer people to suffer. Once even this has been denied, Ball reaches despair and moves out of it again at what is the turning point of the narrative:

> 'I have but little heart to ask thee more questions,' said he, 'and when thou answerest, thy words are plain, but the things they tell of I may scarce understand. But tell me this: in those days will men deem that so it must be for ever, as great men even now tell us of our ills, or will they think of some remedy?'
>
> I looked about me. There was but a glimmer of light in the church now, but what there was, was no longer the strange light of the moon, but the first coming of the kindly day. (XVI. 276)

The glimmer of light comes because John Ball has answered his own question. Every speculation about the future reduces itself to this final one of determinism, and although there is no specific answer, by the very fact that Ball identifies in his own age the doctrine of total irrelevance of human will, taken with the fact that he is about to go out and change the course of history by the remedy he has sought, he discounts the validity of any future determinism. Determinism is a recurrent response in any age. Morris shows in this how firmly he grasped the socialist vision of man in shaping his own future. In the *Theses on Feuerbach*, Marx had written:

> The materialist doctrine that men are products of circumstances and upbringing, and that, therefore, changed men are products of other circumstances and changed upbringing, forgets that it is men that change circumstances and that the educator himself needs educating.[37]

Although the tale makes rigorous distinctions between fantasy and possibility, it affirms also the creative role of the revolutionary consciousness in a way seemingly excluded by Engels' word 'reflex'.

Nevertheless, we have passed from the light of the moon to the glimmer of the dawn, and thus got beyond the fantasy. Moon, linked with the antithetical and subjective dream world of John Ball's personal vision, gives way to the sunlight which is primary, objective and social – the community's vision which is to make possible the next phase of history.

So that what follows John Ball's moment of self-discovery and self-evident affirmation is not the reassertion of his vision but a dry and bitter account of the mechanical forces of progress, ending with the most stark manifestation of alienation when the proletariat denies its very identity: 'their eyes shall be blinded to the robbing of themselves by others, because they shall hope in their souls that they may each live to rob others: and this shall be the very safeguard of all rule and law in those days' (XVI. 283/4). At this point, in order to be able to face the reality of the daylight, Ball has to seek a new vision which will not be confined to the assertion of the active role of man's consciousness, but needs to see the grounds on which it can be asserted. It is no longer enough that a remedy should be sought because the possibility of total alienation has been confronted; it is now necessary that Ball should know the kind of remedy: 'Canst thou yet tell me, brother, what that remedy shall be, lest the sun rise upon me made hopeless by thy tale of what is to be?' (XVI. 284).

The terms on which Ball may be given hope are rigorously controlled by his historical situation. Morris very carefully organizes the narrative in order to demonstrate the relationship between necessary insight and inevitable ignorance by creating a dramatic moment of developing distance between Ball and the narrator. The latter sees the dawn 'widening', and the poppy which he had plucked at the house of his fourteenth-century host is withering: he is being gathered back into his own reality as John Ball moves from the private dream world of the moonlit church to the public world of the battle. So he talks 'loud and hurriedly' as though he can only assert and not demonstrate: the affirmation is to be a different, more emotive rhetoric than the closely argued disillusioning of Ball. What he affirms is, simply, that the 'Fellowship of Men shall endure' so that he returns to Ball's visionary ideology, and he tries to explain the relationship between that affirmation and the prolonged negations of the preceding dialogue by an explicit and developed use of the moon and sun imagery:

Look you, a while ago was the light bright about us: but it was because of the moon, and the night was deep notwithstanding, and when the moonlight waned and died and there was but a little glimmer in place of the bright light, yet was the world glad because all things knew that the glimmer was of day and not of night. Lo you, an image of the times to betide the hope of the Fellowship of Men. Yet forsooth, it may well be that this bright day of summer which is now dawning upon us is no image of the beginning of the day that shall be; but rather shall that daydawn be cold and grey and surly; and yet by its light shall men see things as they verily are, and no longer enchanted by the gleam of the moon and the glamour of the dreamtide. By such grey light shall wise men and valiant souls see the remedy, and deal with it, a real thing that may be touched and handled, and no glory of the heavens to be

worshipped from afar off ... The time shall come, John Ball, when that
dream of thine that this shall one day be ... (XVI. 284/5)

The bright light of the moon only emphasizes the darkness of its sur-
roundings; its subjectivity has to be transcended by its extinction in the
daylight. Yet, though John Ball goes to his personal death in the bright
sun, his mind cleared of the illusory link between freedom and fellowship,
he goes illuminated by what of his vision his comrades share with him, and
this, the sun, is validated by the rebellion's long term success. But sunlight
too can delude. The ultimate reality is grimmer and less comforting.

On the other hand, it does not offer the possibility of distortion either.
In the grey light, the remedy will be seen not as an aspect of heavenly
glory but as something secular and immediate. At this point, the structure
of images has turned a complete circle. The remedy perceptible in the
grim daylight of the historical consequence of the rebellion is exactly
the same as the remedy sought by John Ball in dream:

And what shall it be, as I told thee before, save that men shall be
determined to be free; yea, free as thou wouldst have them, when thine
hope rises the highest, and thou art thinking not of the king's uncles,
and poll-groat bailiffs, and the villeinage of Essex, but of the end of all,
when men shall have the fruits of the earth and the fruits of their toil
thereon, without money and without price. (XVI. 285)

Thus it is precisely what, in John Ball's vision, *isn't* taken over by the rebels
in explicit terms which is the truly revolutionary force in men's minds.
What John Ball has to learn is not that his dream is subjective and impossible but that it can only have articulate meaning when it replaces, as a
shared and immediate objective, the aspiration of his followers. But this
too commits him to death in the cause of that aspiration, since his dream
can only begin the process of becoming vision by entering at once into
the world of action. For, if the ideology of the rebels is what makes for the
opposite of John Ball's dream, the spirit of solidarity which he inspires
among them is a recognition in action of the change beyond the change.
'The philosophers have only *interpreted* the world, in various ways; the
point, however, is to *change* it.'[38]

Going out to create this change, Ball says to the narrator 'thou hast
been a dream to me as I to thee' (XVI. 286). It gives us the proper perspective in which to see all this, for the primary purpose of the narrative is the
education of the present through its dialogue with the past, an education
which reveals the role of mind in the historical process and which therefore demands the creation of an equilibrium between knowledge of the
inevitability of the past and hope for the future. The encounter with Ball
finally validates that hope in the context of historical inevitability, but

it can only do this through insight and symbol and not through discourse. The value of the symbolism is that it reveals the education of the educator – the narrator's grasp, in the face of historical inevitability and on the basis of historical insight, of the essential rightness of vision, and of its assertion in the real world through revolutionary action. It is a grasp given force by its emergence from a coherent drama of consciousness.

The drama is latent above all in the intensity of narrative. It completely misses the point of the story to say glibly, as G. D. H. Cole does, that it is a story of a past that never was because it is merely a fable.[39] For what is most striking about the narrative is its careful attention to visual detail and its attempt to relate the particular event to a concretely realized sense of the everyday life of the community which experiences the event. The story has no point at all if it does not convey with great exactness the vision of the narrator. However, it is necessary to distinguish between the visual detail and the dramatization of the social world, because they operate on two different and contending planes of the narrator's experience. Most of the visual description comes at the beginning when the narrator wakes up to find himself in a strange world. As soon as he begins to experience the social rhythms of that world, the strangeness drops away. As soon as he is challenged to account for himself, the narrator instinctively becomes a fourteenth-century man, not one of the Kentish rebels, but an accommodated visitor confirming by his presence and acceptance the national solidarity of the movement. From this point onwards, the dramatic immediacy of the vision is much more apparent than the visual detail. Although there is a cinematic vividness about the battle-scene, it is presented not as something strange but as the activity of men whose world we are inhabiting. The involvement is disrupted by John Ball's invitation to talk privately. Again we are primarily aware of visual detail, and, with it, the recognition of distance:

> So we turned away together into the little street. But while John Ball had been speaking to me I felt strangely, as though I had more things to say than the words I knew could make clear: as if I wanted to get from other people a new set of words. Moreover, as we passed up the street again I was once again smitten with the great beauty of the scene; the houses, the church with its new chancel and tower, snow-white in the moonbeams now; the dresses and arms of the people, men and women (for the latter were now mixed up with the men); their grave sonorous language, and the quaint and measured forms of speech, were again become a wonder to me and affected me almost to tears. (XVI. 257)

The withdrawal is an important structural feature. The narrator has just been asked to play a more definite, active role by the leader of those who are to change the world, and immediately his consciousness reverts to the spectatorial estrangement of the beginning of the story; the key terms in this passage are 'strangely', 'become a wonder' and '*smitten* with the great beauty', and they push the narrator back into the nineteenth century. It is precisely with this distance reinvoked that the narrator has to play his role in the tale. He cannot escape his historical knowledge, which means that he cannot become part of this world (partly because what is most valuable about the world is what is making it disappear).

Only when we are aware of the complexities of the fictional structure are we free to discuss the relationship of the tale to historical actuality. Obviously the presentation of fourteenth century society is highly idealized, not because of escapism, however, but because of Morris's alert responsibility to the socialist vision of history. The genre itself demands the purification of phenomena so that the potentialities of a situation emerge from the actualities. If Morris is to show the emergence of the revolutionary consciousness at a given historical moment, then he has to concentrate on what, in the life of the community at the time of its formation, makes it possible. And, as Thorold Rogers asserted, it is just the sense of a prospering communal culture which does make its formation possible. We have to see, not what this society was (naturalism is capable of making its object exotic), but what it was capable of becoming if we are to see it participating in the historical process. Morris, in fact, takes care of the realities of mediaeval life much more effectively by placing this prosperity in a process of change than he could have done had he concentrated on naturalistic detail. The battle itself shows exactly how the relationship between picture and movement defines the relationship between value and historical reality. We are, of course, conscious of its historic significance – battles are moments in which the processes of change are accelerated. At the same time the realization of the battle scene is very much a matter of the realization of a moment of creative and undivided labour, the community working together in its own defence and each individual occupying a complete role. The conduct of the battle pays tribute to the society it is demolishing. The idealization brings out the values which underwrite the historical moment as an agent in a dialectical process: such values define the basis of the consciousness which brings nearer the immediate future of free and divided labour and at the same time looks beyond that future to socialism.

The dream vision structure is thus not only historically apt (since it is essentially a mediaeval genre) but the right register for the awareness of these potentialities and their role in history, because it makes for a purification of phenomena. But it is used dialectically both as affirmation and negation, and careful discriminations have to be made. We are conscious first of all of the psychological pressures which make for dream; it is the refuge of the alienated man: 'Sometimes I am rewarded for fretting myself so much about present matters by a quite unasked-for pleasant dream'

(XVI. 215). The dream world which is described to exemplify this opening sentence is one of architectural beauty and it relates to the present merely as the juxtaposition of statically realized abstract values. The concept of dream as relief and antithesis is, however, radically revalued already by the end of the first paragraph; 'All this I have seen in the dreams of the night clearer than I can force myself to do in dreams of the day' (XVI. 216). 'Force' suggests that dream, though an alienated activity, is one which is open to discipline, and 'clearer' implies that the relief which is sought still has a responsibility to truth. Dream is given a positive intellectual role. More importantly, however, the sentence makes an important distinction between the involuntary dream of night and the willed 'dream of the day': not only do dreams have specific responsibilities but these responsibilities are fulfilled better by the proper assessment of the involuntary invasion of consciousness than by the conscious effort to bring these values into the mind. The fullest possibility of vision is available only to the dream which is beyond the individual will.

These discriminations reassert themselves at the end of the story with, of course, our understanding of the role of dream for the creative revolutionary mind giving them a new urgency. Like John Ball, the narrator has come to a dream of truth, and he too has to carry that dream into the actual world, not as antithesis, moon-vision, but as dialectically engaged consciousness. John Ball has, however, a battle to go to, a moment of revolution in which to transform his interpretation of the world into an agent of change. For the narrator, there is only the continuing present and so the daybreak involves a more complex process of coming to terms with vision:

> I got up presently, and going to the window looked out on the winter morning; the river was before me broad between outer bank and bank, but it was nearly dead ebb, and there was a wide space of mud on each side of the hurrying stream, driven on the faster as it seemed by the push of the south-west wind. On the other side of the water the few willowtrees left us by the Thames Conservancy looked doubtfully alive against the bleak sky and the row of wretched-looking blue-slated houses ... the road in front of the house was sooty and muddy at once, and in the air was that sense of dirty discomfort which one is never quit of in London. The morning was harsh too, and though the wind was from the south-west it was as cold as a north wind; and yet amidst it all, I thought of the corner of the next bight of the river which I could not quite see from where I was, but over which one can see clear of houses and into Richmond Park, looking like the open country; and dirty as the river was, and harsh as was the January wind, they seemed to woo me toward the country-side, where away from the miseries of the 'Great Wen' I might of my own will carry on a day-dream of the friends I had made in the dream of the night and against my will.

> But as I turned away shivering and downhearted, on a sudden came the frightful noise of the 'hooters', one after the other, that call the work-men to the factories, this one the after-breakfast one, more by token. So I grinned surlily, and dressed and got ready for my day's 'work' as I call it, but which many a man besides John Ruskin (though not many in his position) would call 'play'. (XVI. 287/8)

He has been cut off from the dream by 'a white light, empty of all sights', and what we have here initially is the defeated landscape of the dawn of actuality after the triumphant dawn of the day of rebellion in the dream. The vestigial life, however, creates a rhythm of return and the first of these paragraphs carefully plots the most obvious relationship of the dream to actuality – that of cherished antithesis. The residual affirmations of the river and the wind are enough to involve the perceptual mind in a retreat not from reality but into a world beyond perception, a world whose existence is testified to but only as imagination. Within such a world, the values of the dream can be wilfully kept alive in day-dream, away from the city and the inexorable process of urbanization and exploitation. The rejection of this relationship is prepared for by the ironic separation of the imagination from the eye which begins its operation: he moves from the part of the river he can see to the bight he cannot but which he can think of as offering, beyond houses, a view of Richmond Park which in turn offers an illusion of the country. Already, by the time we get to day-dream, we are conscious not only of the illusory nature of the withdrawal but of its remoteness from his own range of experience. The only possibility is to turn back to the city, and turn towards his own and others' misery. Equally, because the dream is not the product of the individual will, it can only be kept alive at all by a return to the conditions which gave rise to it – the fretting over modern life. Only by turning back into his own alienation, the source of the dream, can the narrator make his dialogue with the past meaningful. What happens in the last paragraph is that the values for which John Ball and the men of Kent stood, are kept alive by the negation of the present not in withdrawal but in irony. 'Grinned surlily' is a gesture of acceptance of the actuality which does not acquiesce in it. What dominates the final paragraph of course is the sense of the division of labour which is in direct antithesis to the whole presentation of the fourteenth century community. And yet, as we have noticed, it is also what the rebellion most immediately achieved. So that at the end we are made both to measure the distance between human possibilities and the actual world, and to acknowledge the necessity for those possibilities to be worked out in the historical process. We know that the dream of John Ball is not a nostalgic dream of the past, held apart from the Great Wen, but John Ball's dream, that which made him participate in the history that created the Great Wen and which brought him, in fantasy, to a conception of the change beyond the change, the revolutionary future which the surly grin does not resign to the depressing present.

The tale thus pays full tribute to the determinants of history, but it refuses to collapse into a defeated pessimism, and it equally avoids the dangers of 'economism'. But we need to emphasize how limited the claims which are made are. For John Ball there is a dream both of the possible and the actual, and he is able to relate the two in the action by which he goes out to his death united with the community which is changing the course of history. For the narrator the gap is not to be bridged through action. Nothing fills the white light between dream and actuality. All that we can claim is that the dream, becoming through the careful interplay of its psychological possibilities a formal literary genre, offers a vision of the mind and its values which creates man's destiny. What remains is the problem of recognizing the precise basis of the transformation of that mind in action.

VI

In an essay which sets out to explore the relationship between theory and practice in Marxist thought, Antonio Gramsci identifies mechanical determinism as the 'aroma' of a particular phase of the socialist struggle, and in explaining it he states very clearly the problem that Morris was faced with in his life and which his creative writing coherently portrays:

> When one does not have the initiative in the struggle and the struggle itself is ultimately identified with a series of defeats, mechanical determinism becomes a formidable power of moral resistance, of patient and obstinate perseverance. 'I am defeated for the moment but the nature of things is on my side over a long period', etc. Real will is disguised as an act of faith, a sure rationality of history, a primitive and empirical form of impassioned finalism which appears as a substitute for the predestination, providence, etc., of the confessional religions.[40]

Morris doesn't, of course, entirely escape the charge of 'impassioned finalism', and *A Dream of John Ball* ends ambiguously, rejecting the concept of dream as retreat but not offering the means by which it participates in the socialist narrator's programme of action. The revolutionary consciousness cannot be passive and withdrawn, but neither can it impose itself mechanically on events when it does not have the initiative.

And whereas, after his dream acknowledging the historical limits of his achievement, Ball goes forward to a changed situation and a change-creating act, the narrator *returns* to the daily routine, strengthened in his mind but without the prospect of choosing action. The contrast is too marked not to be deliberate. And this recognition of his own limitation of consciousness to the disjunction of thought and action in the present informs the choice of mode in the stories which follow *A Dream of John Ball*, the German Romances. The role of Morris's art seems increasingly to be one which combats the tendency to collapse into a deterministic act of faith by presenting the potentialities of human growth in a situation in which it is enabled and compelled to take the initiative. The German Romances base themselves on an epoch in which the choice between involvement and retreat is a real one between two ways of defining personal identity rather than between self-isolation and self-abnegation in an act of faith. Dream becomes both an agent of change and a doorway of withdrawal; it offers itself as the stasis of atrophy or as the starting point of the transformation of consciousness into revolutionary and collective action.

Morris's choice of a society which resembles that of the early teutonic tribes demonstrates, as does *A Dream of John Ball*, a fine awareness of contemporary historiography. Maine, Freeman, Morgan and Engels himself had all given a good deal of attention to this epoch since it seemed to offer a point in time when the needs of the individual for private freedom were balanced with maximum equilibrium against the coherence of the community. There is a frequent contrast with Rome, most fully worked out by Freeman in *Comparative Politics*, in which he argues that the Roman and the German concepts of society represented respectively 'two great ideas of the State, the conception of the State as city and the conception of the State as a nation'.[41] The essence of the Germanic state for Freeman, as for Morris, was that it made for the maximum distribution of power: 'For the whole history of our land and our race will be read backwards', he wrote, 'if we fail always to bear in mind that the lower unit is not a division of the greater, but that the greater is an aggregate of the smaller.'[42]

Freeman's concern is primarily with the external structure of society. Morris goes much deeper than this and portrays the consciousness of the people who create such a constitution. Above all, the Germanic nation is built on the free acknowledgement of kindred as against the legalistic acquiescence in the realm of the Roman *res publica*. Morris, in fact, closely resembles Marx whose *Pre-Capitalist Economic Formations* is concerned to distinguish between three attitudes to the individual's consciousness of his social existence, the Asiatic, the Greco-Roman (both defined in the following passage in the first paragraph) and the Germanic:

> Community is neither the substance, of which the individual appears merely as the accident, nor is it the general, which *exists and has being* as such in men's minds, and in the reality of the city and its urban requirements, distinct from the separate economic being of its members.
>
> It is rather on the one hand, the common element in language, blood, etc., which is the premise of the individual proprietor; but on

the other hand it has real being only in its *actual assembly* for communal purposes; and, in so far as it has a separate economic existence, in the communally used hunting-grounds, pastures, etc., it is used thus by every individual proprietor as such, and not in his capacity as the representative of the state.[43]

It is thus the moment in society when the individual is least divorced from the conditions of his existence and most closely linked with other men in the struggle against nature and hostile forces. The salient feature is dramatically presented in *The House of the Wulfings* when, on the eve of battle, Thiodulf goes into the woods to meditate and becomes spontaneously caught in his own affirmativeness, building a small dam as a token of his creative link with his own world:

> As he sat, he strove to think about the Roman host and how he should deal with it; but despite himself, his thoughts wandered, and made for him pictures of his life that should be when this time of battle was over; so that he saw nothing of the troubles that were upon his hands that night, but rather saw himself partaking in the deeds of the life of man. (XIV. 105)

There is no tension here between personal aspiration and a sense of belonging to the community: even reverie returns him to its acknowledgement. And yet this can be precisely because this personal life is neither possessed nor divided by society but accepted by it as of a contributing individual. The whole story is pervaded by this sense of integrity, and when it emerges explicitly at the end, we acknowledge its validity:

> For to the Goths it was but a little thing to fall in hot blood in that hour of love of the kindred, and longing for the days to be. And for the Romans, they had had no mercy, and now looked for none: and they remembered their dealings with the Goths, and saw before them, as it were, once more, yea, as in a picture, their slayings and quellings, and lashings, and cold mockings which they had dealt out to the conquered foemen without mercy, and now they longed sore for the quiet of the dark, when their hard lives should be over, and all these deeds forgotten, and they and their bitter foes should be at rest for ever.
>
> Most valiantly they fought; but the fury of their despair could not deal with the fearless hope of the Goths. (XIV. 189)

For the Goths, the battle is a campaign for their own individual being as well as for the community's integrity. For the Romans it is their tribute to the 'separate economic being' of the city, against whose claims they can only advance those of pessimistic resignation.

But if the Romances respond to features of contemporary historiography, they do not, of course, make any attempt to portray an actual
historical situation – not even in the mediated way *A Dream of John Ball*
does. They couldn't, since the documentary portrayals of such a period
have to be extremely vague and lacking in decisive 'event'. The historians
themselves approach the period in a highly conceptualizing way, presenting the structures of different societies rather like archetypes of social
structure. The starting point of Morris's work is an idea of what men can
conceive society to be rather than what they have achieved. And this too
relates to an essential feature of the historiography, for the Germanic *gens*
is used ideologically as an example of what is good or might be good in a
social structure. Freeman uses the concept of state as nation rather than
as city in order to explain why England is 'more just and free than the
other'.[44] Morgan argues that this kind of *gens* is what will be the model of
the future, and, not surprisingly, Engels concluded *The Origin of the Family*
by quoting this passage:

> Since the advent of civilization, the outgrowth of property has been so
> immense, its forms so diversified, its uses so expanding and its manage-
> ment so intelligent in the interests of its owners, that it has become, on
> the part of the people, an unmanageable power. The human mind
> stands bewildered in the presence of its own creation. The time will
> come, nevertheless, when human intelligence will rise to the mastery
> over property, and define the relations of the state to the property
> it protects, as well as the obligations and the limits of the rights of
> its owners ... The dissolution of society bids fair to become the
> termination of a career of which property is the end and aim; because
> such a career contains the elements of self-destruction. Democracy in
> government, brotherhood in society, equality in rights and privileges,
> and universal education, foreshadow the next higher plane of society
> to which experience, intelligence and knowledge are steadily tending.
> It will be a revival, in a higher form, of the liberty, equality and frater-
> nity of the ancient *gentes*.[45]

Morgan's judgement offers the exact terms of the rationale of Morris's
Romances. In *A Dream of John Ball*, we see man's desire for change as a
potent but almost imperceptible thread in an historical process which he
cannot foresee. Only through irony does the tale prevent itself from
becoming a mechanical antithesis of dream and necessity, and the irony
secures itself against complete immersion in the actual through the creation
of a Chinese box of dreams: if my faith is a dream based on the past, it is
also a dream of that past's dream which is validated partly by what it
achieved, my actuality, and partly by its ability to communicate with my
dream, which is a negation of my actuality. In order to escape this eternal

reflection, Morris has to dramatize the revolutionary mind in a world in which it has not lost the initiative, has not become bewildered by its own creation so that its beginning must be in negation. The individual consciousness has to be seen in the situation in which it has mastery over the society which mediates its relationship with others. Only such a mind can be a determinant in direct forms of action. The world of the Germanic tribes represents the closest model for that situation, but it is impossible to pretend that the revolutionary mind can be realized through a simple historic recreation, because that realization would have to contain the seeds of degenerative change. The real significance of the *gentes* is that they look forward, as Morgan suggests, to the future, to the next 'plane' of society. So that we are confronted with a *projection* of the Germanic nation, a concrete realization of what it portends. And this is not an escape from the exigencies of the present, but from the possible comfort to be gained from a too passive awareness of those exigencies. The Germanic Romances, especially *The House of the Wulfings*, give us the moral ordeal of the revolutionary mind unprotected by determinist rationalization.

This particular tale can achieve as much, because a great deal of it is successfully devoted to establishing a social world in which freedom means integration. The people are united with the objective conditions of their existence: 'and they worshipped the kind acres which they them-selves and their fathers had made fruitful, wedding them to the seasons of seed-time and harvest' (XIV. 29/30). We are reminded of the description of the Brangwens at the beginning of *The Rainbow*, and the rhythms of Morris's prose, when they are not crippled by the oddity of his notion of a fit language, anticipate Lawrence. But whereas in *The Rainbow* there is an inevitable aspiration away from the gentile culture, in Morris's Romance the process of achieving individuality is not seen as antithetical but as realizable within the social structure. Hence one of the major episodes in the story is the election of Thiodulf as war leader. It both acknowledges the individual capacity for choice in each of the members of the commu-nity, thus endorsing Marx's point that community takes its existence from assembly, and it grants a social identity to the exceptional man without placing in his hands the social existence of the individual members. The sense of the world beyond which, in *The Rainbow*, destroys community, in this tale, as we shall see, endorses it.

All the tensions of the tale, nevertheless, stem from the recognition that the individual consciousness takes its existence from outside the com-munity as well as within it. But the resulting conflict between individual and social selves is seen not in terms of social determination, but purely in terms of psychological growth. Thiodulf, leader of the Wulfings, has a child by a semi-divine creature of the woods, Wood-sun. Within the house, the child, Hall-sun, is passed off as his foster child. Wood-sun tries to isolate Thiodulf from the Community by a series of temptations, which offer not so much moral conflict as psychological strain. First she tells him that he is not by birth a Wulfing, but a stranger; later, she persuades him to wear a hauberk which will protect him in battle, but which dissolves his attention to the fight. Her hold over him is specifically linked with dream. Wearing the hauberk, he swoons and dreams of his childhood and his old mentor. It is a dream of joy until first the mentor turns to stone and then he feels himself to be turning to stone. He stirs himself from the dream and finds 'a white light empty of all vision' (XIV. 150). He can return to life and the battle because his friends have taken off the hauberk to look at his wounds – 'and the joy of waking life came back to him, the joy which but erewhile he had given to a mere dream' (XIV. 150). He returns to the fight, but he is again given the hauberk, and this time withdraws into a dream world in which Wood-sun seems to be by his side and the battle becomes a resented distraction. He remains withdrawn at the next council and a spokesman has to speak for him. Later, he explains this withdrawal to Wood-sun:

> But now must I tell thee a hard and evil thing; that I loved them not, and was not of them, and outside myself there was nothing: within me was the world and nought without me, Nay, as for thee, I was sundered from thee, but thou wert a part of me; whereas for the others, yea, even for our daughter, thine and mine, they were but images and shows of men, and I longed to depart from them, and to see thy body and to feel thine heart beating. And by then so evil was I grown that my very shame had fallen from me, and my will to die: nay, I longed to live, thou and I, and death seemed hateful to me, and the deeds before death vain and foolish. (XIV. 169)

There is a withdrawal into the self of the same kind that we have seen in *Sigurd the Volsung*, but here it is not the social conditions which determine it, but love itself, which in turn is characterized as man's meeting with the divine (again, a repetition of the Brynhild motif). The hauberk is clearly a symbol of personal relationships which isolate the self from the community. It creates a dream world, but one in which the self becomes involved in the past and in which, in turn, the past begins to petrify, having no organic relationship to the present. As in *A Dream of John Ball*, the return from dream is bridged by an empty light, but here, in the actual world, there is a possibility of joy asserting itself outside dream. It is not that the past has to be made meaningful by the creation of a fictive participation, a leap of the imagination, but that it has to be accepted as growth rather than as fixity. Earlier, Thiodulf has said that whenever he tries to recall his childhood, he always finds his mind moving towards a larger sense of the past, 'the tale of the Wulfings', and to see himself, not as a single life but as a participant in the ongoing life of the race: 'and I amidst it ever reborn and yet reborn' (XIV. 109). The petrifaction image is an exact reversal of the image of stone and stream in *Easter 1916*: for Yeats, the stone is the image of the committed self, 'hearts with one purpose alone', enchanted by the external political world, troubling the living stream of the personal life. For Morris, on the contrary, the personal life becomes a petrifaction, a refusal to accept growth and a fixated dream of childhood, unless it participates in the world 'outside myself', that is, both community, the free acknowledgement of the social relation, and the future, 'the kindred and the days to be' (XIV. 145).

But if this is, in ideological terms, an opposite affirmation from that of Yeats, it is not a factitious escape into 'duty'. The tale has to create a relationship with 'outside myself' which does not deny selfhood. Wood-sun singles out Thiodulf because she is divine; her divinity disables her from understanding the communal reality of human nature: 'such is the wont of the God-kin, because they know not the hearts of men' (XIV. 171). In positive terms, this means that Thiodulf's encounter with the world beyond, that which Wood-sun represents, is an encounter with that which recognizes his own *excellence*, the excellence which, within the community, makes him leader. The basis of his social relationship is thus in his belonging to what is outside the society. The story of the hauberk is an attempt to resolve this paradox through total individuation. The account of its origin offers the projection of one potential of selfhood, that which isolates itself from the community. The hauberk is the creation of a Dwarf who desired a Goddess who loved a mortal. The Dwarf offered her the hauberk which would save her beloved in battle in return for her body. She agreed but at the moment which he was about to take his pleasure, she paralysed him, and in revenge he put a curse on the hauberk so that although its power of protection remained, its wearer, saving his life in battle, would have also the battle's shame.

The allegory is a highly compressed account of the development of the individualistic consciousness. The Goddess seeks to isolate the excellence of the mortal by granting him immortality: she is prepared to *bargain* in order to achieve this, so that there is a concept of *price*, and hence the beginning of the division of labour. The price she is prepared to offer to satisfy her love for another man is the gift of her body to the dwarf, so that love becomes dualistic – body and soul are potentially separable. And finally she withdraws from her bargain, keeping her body intact, so that the concept of sexual exploitation is also involved: sex becomes a commodity, but it finally becomes an intangible commodity. The real price that is paid is the severance of the mortal from the life which surrounds him. Reduced to romantic love and religious aspiration (towards immortality), man's encounter with the divine, with what singles out his individuality, comes to be estrangement from the community, and, finally, therefore from the conditions of his existence. Furthermore, it denies the possibility of growth (because death is the inevitable effect of growth), and joy turns inward to a dream world. We have reversed the situation in which we find ourselves in *A Dream of John Ball*: dream vision and the prose of actuality have changed places. Morris establishes a society in which the severed self is glimpsed as a *potential* but not *inevitable* manifestation. He affirms the necessity of a new order of consciousness, but he realizes its possibility in the context of the alternative if realized in capitalist society, that context convincingly rendered as nightmare.

This is possible and unsentimental because there is no simple antithesis. The psychological process which lures Thiodulf into the dream world of severed individuality is precisely that which grants him an ineluctable relationship with the community. The child of the divine encounter, Hall-sun, is also a dreamer, but her dream is prophesy: the child of loneliness brings knowledge greater than her consciousness can retain for the community: 'Also she perceived that she had been weeping, therefore she knew that she had uttered words of wisdom. For so it fared with her at whiles, that she knew not her own words of foretelling, but spoke them out as if in a dream' (XIV. 41). She is the result of man's solitary encounter with divine love, but in the world of the kindred, which contains the possibility of the perfect cohesion between the individual mind and the social field of action, there is accommodation of that experience. Hall-sun, in her prophetic role, acknowledges a double recognition. On the one hand, the divine aspirations of the individual only make for truth within the community (so that dream is vision and not daydream). On the other hand, what knits the community together is not its blood ties (the undynamic dictatorship of the past over the present), but the continuous homage paid to man's outsider reality. In her dramatic role, Hall-sun realizes the possibility of a much greater integration than this. Recognizing what is wrong with Thiodulf, she goes to Wood-sun and argues that the way in which she is trying to save Thiodulf is a form of possession which will destroy his identity: Wood-sun cannot save the real Thiodulf, only a thrall who is his shadow. Only in heroic death, committed to the cyclic rhythms of the kindred, can Thiodulf be himself. The totally individuated individual loses his individuality. Selfhood, in such a world, is the recognition of the collectivization of experience and commitment to the kindred and its future. Thiodulf is not a Wulfing, but only through the continually renewed process of becoming a Wulfing through action is he truly Thiodulf. It is this that makes the story a *revolutionary* Romance rather than a reactionary one. We are given the forces which made for the destruction of the gentile community in a transformed relationship – on the one hand as reduced to the world of nightmare, and on the other transformed from their destructiveness into precisely what makes for its defence.

VII

I have been trying to show that Morris's literary work cannot be seen as a mere relief from or appendage to his directly active work as a Socialist in the eighties. It constitutes a formal response to the realities of his own situation which can be validated in terms of the historical consciousness with which he came into contact (both Marxist and non-Marxist). Specifically, he invents new worlds or reinvokes dream versions of old worlds, not in order to escape the exigencies of the depressing actuality but in order to insist on a whole structure of values and perspectives which must emerge in the conscious mind in order to assert the inner truth of that actuality, and give man the knowledge of his own participation in the historical process which dissolves that actuality. We have seen that this insistence needs to take full account of the particular moment and that this demands a remarkable sensitivity to the responsiveness of form. The moment is one in which, for whatever complex of reasons, the individual is seen more and more to be totally circumscribed in his actions by an apparently self-acting social law. Confronted with such hopelessness, the socialist is likely to be forced back on an elaborate determinism in which the forces of progress inevitably assert themselves irrespective of the action of individuals, so that the socialist mind becomes merely reflexive (some of Engels' comments on the English scene seem to me to show a marked defeatism which resembles this). This is contradictory because it must take as its starting point the divorce of man as a conscious being with a subjective sense of his own reality from the conditions of his existence in which he finds his objective reality; and it must take as its end the moment at which this divorce is repaired through the reconciliation of the mode of production with the forces of production: in other words, the moment in which man takes hold of his own life. Yet this has to be achieved by forces outside himself: man's alienation will be brought to an end by alien forces.

The very act of creating fictions which will take account of the historical movement of forces in society, however, implies resistance to this contradiction. Fiction can only depict people – it cannot depict forces of production: it is committed therefore to the portrayal of the operation of the historical processes by which it is informed in the minds of its protagonists. It is this very confinement of the fictional mode to the concrete and perceptible which leads us to say of a work born in an era when the possibilities of change are extremely distant that its acceptance of the inexorability of the social law makes it more 'realistic' than a work which strives to bring to the fore those possibilities. The most obvious way of escaping this is to present the accomplished change as a utopia existing in antithesis to the present. *Looking Backward* is this kind of novel and despite its specious evolutionism, it has no sense of the change as a process. And, of course, it is as equally deterministic as a Gissing novel because its

characters are *products* of the resolved society as Gissing's are of a contradictory one. Morris's work, on the contrary, attempts to recognize in
concrete terms that the reconciliation of man with the conditions of his
existence will be a process in which both man and the conditions change
in their relationship to one another and in which man can be seen as
a determining as well as determined force. Inevitably this places on the
creative writer the obligation to create forms in which the forces of change
are portrayed as they appear in the conscious minds of the characters
he creates, and it means also that the created world of his characters must
have a relationship carefully defined within the generic significance of the
work – to the 'unchanged' instant which does not escape irresponsibly
from its epistemology. It means creating forms which neither accept
as eternal man's alienation, nor retreat into worlds in which it has no
relevance, but which provide for both its recognition and its assessment
by realizing it as a subjective response to an objective condition which is
not only valid as subjectivity in recoiling from the objective world, but
which is also capable of returning to that world as a subversive force.
It means the recognition of the estranged mind of man not merely as an
escape, but also as a revolutionary agent. The dreamer of dreams has to
recognize that he is born in his due time. This includes recognizing, as in
The House of the Wulfings, a time when dreams will have to be turned away,
but it does not mean that dream can be transcended in the present.

Estrangement is subversive in Hardy too, but only by reference to
defeated social values. Morris's Romances are attempts to give concrete
expression to values which are best seen in possibilities offered by defeated
social orders, but also to recreate those orders so that they speak to the
dreams of the estranged man not merely as something gone but as something containing values that must be striven after, and can be attained
only by the transformation of dream into vision. This transformation is
portrayed in *The House of the Wulfings* as the entry of the individual,
recognizing the true nature of his self in the community, into action for
the community – Thiodulf's storm. Beyond that, however, and extremely
important in forging a relationship between the realized revolutionary
mind and socialist practice, is the discovery of the potential for transformation of vision into collective action. It is a discovery enacted in *The
Roots of the Mountains*.

Here too we are concerned primarily to make discriminations about
the historic role of dream. The hero is caught in a dream world by his very
satisfaction with the gentile community until the dream leads him to the
broken community which lies beyond the Burgstead, and from this to a
direct confrontation with the Romans, so that the values of the kindred
become affirmed by its ability to face what are, in fact, bourgeois structures
of society. Although the tale is therefore one of education, leading the
protagonist to discover in his personal aspiration a dynamic role within

his society, it becomes finally a romance about revolutionary strategy. The key episode of the last section is the war council in which Face-God and Folk-might (man's personal divinity and his power of association linked in revolutionary war) plan their assault on the territories beyond the vale which are already occupied by the Romans. They plan on a basis of combining permeation with invasion so that we are alerted to the need for the revolutionary act of the leaders to be taken up by the participation of the masses. Collectivity means not only the integration of personal intelligence and the sense of community but also a new collectivity of mind. The relevance to the present moment is clear. In a world where man's alienation seems to be complete, only my dreams are my own, and so it is through my dreams, and my attention to them, that I shall take hold of my life again. Yet, insofar as my dreams *are* my own, they are in danger of enclosing themselves in a sea of blankness and isolation, becoming perpetual islands whose refuge enables me to make my peace with the alien world. Only insofar as my dreams push outward into action, only insofar as they claim the understanding of other people through my commitment, can they become creative and revolutionary.

The Romances enact the events which dramatize in an actualized world this need and this possibility, but Morris needs to go further than this. The Romance looks back to potentialities vested in the past but unrealized in the present: ultimately, the socialist writer needs to push forward the consciousness of his readers directly towards the responsibility of creating community. Romance also celebrates the hero and his revolutionary consciousness. Although *The Roots of the Mountains* dramatizes the encounter of this consciousness with the oppressed masses, it does not portray that mass consciousness, because, of course, as soon as it is portrayed, as soon as it becomes explicit in the minds of the people, we have reached a totally changed world. The only form which portrays the revolutionary consciousness of the people is one which looks forward and invents a new society – Utopia.

News from Nowhere has received a good deal of intelligent attention from A. L. Morton and E. P. Thompson, and so I shall deal with it very briefly, giving what is really only a reemphasis of their points to make the text relevant to the main concern of this essay. They stress the importance of seeing *News from Nowhere* in its generic tradition: it is itself conscious of the limitations of the dream vision. What it sets out to portray is not what the future will be like, but how a nineteenth-century socialist might conceive of it in order to communicate the rationale of his faith in his socialist activity. We have seen already that dream plays a definite but limited role in the formation of the revolutionary consciousness. In these terms, *News from Nowhere* has the same structure as *A Dream of John Ball* except that the narrator is now in the same position as John Ball, looking to the change beyond the change. And like *John Ball*, it is partly an affirmation of the particular intelligence of the perceiving consciousness. So that at the centre of the tale is the socialist commitment to the role of historical necessity which makes no attempt to by-pass the class struggle, and, at the end, the narrator is thrust back into the nineteenth century to take up his role in history, by bringing the values of the new world into the minds of those who are to fight to bring it about.

However, if this were all, then *News from Nowhere* would be a much simplified account of the historical role of the revolutionary consciousness compared with *A Dream of John Ball*. For, in the earlier tale, we are concerned with the dream of John Ball's dream, so that we have the sense of the dynamic role of knowledge as well as aspiration: the narrator's imaginative leap into the past's possible imagination of the narrator's present and the assessment against the actual present bring the revolutionary mind into focus with the historical process. The past can inform the present to make its conception of the future more clear. In *News from Nowhere*, on the other hand, the narrator is dramatically powerless. He can comfort only himself, and he can change nothing in the future with which he holds a dialogue, so that we can only be aware of that future as antithesis, as a static world different from ours – at best, the historical account can only be a bridge which links present and future but which in itself remains a separate entity belonging to neither.

What prevents *News from Nowhere* from becoming gratuitous and dehumanized like, for example, *Looking Backward* in which the new world which inspires Bellamy's sickly optimism is significantly like that which now feeds the witty despair of J. K. Galbraith, is that it never tries to become objective by creating a social system of a totality of institutions. Utopia is the collectivization of dream, as opposed to Romance which is the transformation of individuality through dream into leadership. We are presented with, above all, the shared dream: the personal aspiration is actualized as a whole society. All the figures in the land of perfection are aspects of the dreamer himself: all must voice his attitudes and responses. This is true even when there are disagreements, since the major psychological affirmation of Morris's utopia is that the world can contain a fully free individualism. In terms of the narrator's own consciousness, the discussions are simply the free play of temperamental inconsistencies, so that although the characters have their basic differences they are all sympathetic. Thus Dick's historical philistinism isn't challenged by Hammond's scholarship but lives in peaceful coexistence with it, and even the acerbity of Ellen's grandfather can exist in balance against the sometimes priggish sanity of Ellen herself. We are in a world where human flexibility does not become involved in destructive conflict: the essence of collectivity is freedom, and by the same token, the peak of individuality is the open community in which individuality has ceased to be aggressive. This emphasis is, I think, a right one. Although the discursive bent of the novel brings

out the inextricability of the unalienated mind with the conditions which
can allow it to grow, the dramatic emphasis is always on the attitudes
rather than the conditions. We don't have, as we do in Bellamy, a sense
that human beings have become superfluous particles in a perfect system,
and although we don't, and couldn't get involved in the story any more
than we can get involved in Adam's labour in the Garden of Eden, we do
get a very real sense of what human values might be liberated in a communist society.

But if the pressure of the dreamer's personality on the shape of the
'future' makes the novel more open about its subjectivity and therefore
more accessible to the readers' participation than *Looking Backward* which
manifests so distinctly aggressive a complacency that in the end Bellamy
can't even bring himself to admit that the narrator was dreaming, it also
must radically limit its scope. What is remarkable about its achievement is
its articulateness about these limitations. We have an heroic effort to
present imaginatively those values which the socialist mind is working
towards as part of a social experience. But questioning that presentation is
a concrete realization of the psychological pressure which thrusts the
narrator towards his vision of those values. And although the major aim of
the utopian form is the collectivization of dream, as the closing sentence
implies, what we are mainly aware of is that those pressures derive from a
radical sense of isolation, of the man who is lost and can only find himself
by the projection of his personality into a dream community. The opening
of the story carefully establishes this. We begin, not with the oppressiveness of modern life, but with the centre of the activity which is to
change it, the League. What most characterizes the League is precisely
the destructive individualism which the story escapes from: 'For the rest,
there were six persons present, and consequently six sections of the party
were represented' (XVI. 3). The oppressiveness of modern life is there as
well, in the tube train and the ugly suspension bridge. Nowhere will be set
up in direct opposition to this 'civilization'. But not before the League,
the agency of socialist activity in the present, has been already precluded
as a valid response to the civilization which is to be rejected. The narrator
dismisses his comrades as 'fools' and, although this reflects on his own
intolerance as well, it does mean that there is no prospect of the communication of dream, the creation of vision, within the party. On the contrary,
it is as a relief from the despair of working within the party that the
narrator moves towards utopia: he needs 'an epoch of rest'.

This is all perfectly clear, but if we press it a little further, we have to
challenge Morton's description, 'scientific utopia', which is based mainly
on the historical section. Chapter XVII shows very clearly Morris's grasp
of the meaning of Revolution. But it is still an *invented* history, and whatever the clarity of the account as a whole, the account of its beginning,
that is of the present, is extremely vague: 'When the hope of realizing a

communal condition of life for all men arose, quite late in the nineteenth century' (XVI. 104). The syntax is betraying. 'Arose' evades a human subject so that we are uncertain about whose hope it was – was it, for example, one fostered by the six Leaguers who do little but squabble but who are presumably more conscious of the hope than those outside the League? And that 'quite' is inexcusable: has it happened already or is it to be even later than the present? This is the phrase which establishes the link between present and future in historic terms but it is a link which does not come into focus, and it is in marked and significant contrast with the clearly delineated chain of events which follows. In this chain, the League has no part, nor does any other socialist organization which would be recognizable from the eighties. It is an invented history as much in antithesis to the present as the statically realized future. The alienation which produces the dream of Nowhere is a response to the present, both recoiling and subversive. But equally there is a recoil from what, in the present, is the most coherent and collective register of the subversiveness. 'How the Change Came' is as much a dream as Nowhere itself. It does touch on the actuality in a way which suggests continuity rather than antithesis, but it is a very special continuity: 'Looking back now, we can see that the great motive-power of the change was a longing for freedom and equality, akin if you please to the unreasonable passion of the lover; a sickness of heart that rejected with loathing the aimless solitary life of the well-to-do educated men of that time' (XVI. 104). 'The unreasonable passion of the lover' links Morris much more closely, surely, with Hardy than with any socialist movement. It makes the change related to the eruption of unconscious forces into the individual consciousness of the contemporary mind.

The Utopia itself becomes therefore primarily not so much a picture of enacted values as a reversal of the rejected values of modern life. The novel is essentially one of protest (and frequently personal protest, as the mediaevalism suggests). In such a context, the ending is extremely subdued. The narrator remains a spectator figure until the feast at the end. The feast opens up the possibility of integration, but before the narrator has participated in the communion, he becomes invisible. It is a remarkable passage because the effect is not to distance the scene from the narrator, but to withdraw the narrator from the scene: 'I turned to Ellen, and she *did* seem to recognize me for an instant; but her bright face turned sad directly, and she shook her head with a mournful look, and the next moment all consciousness of my presence had faded from her face' (XVI. 209). Confronted with the social realization of the values by which he affirms commitment, the narrator loses his own reality. The gap between the present and the future becomes a nightmare of one's own non-existence. The narrator can be no more than voyeur in his own dream; there is no way of realizing how he can speak to it through his own life as John Ball had spoken to the present. Nowhere is nowhere except as a conceptual antithesis in the mind of the exhausted activist. And although the end cannot be taken as ironic, it cannot be seen as offering much consolation for the immense sense of the distance between the dream and the actuality which made it necessary. It is all very well for Ellen to seem to be saying 'Go back', but go back to what? To the League? The only specific identification of a role for the narrator is deterministic: 'you belong so entirely to the unhappiness of the past that our happiness even would weary you' (XVI. 210). It is difficult in the end to see how this affirms values on a much more social basis than the death of Jude. The collectivity of dream is not brought into relationship with the possible collectivity of the present.

But beyond *News from Nowhere*, there is *The Story of the Glittering Plain* which suggests a revised account of the role of dream in the revolutionary consciousness. The plain itself is a timeless paradise offered to the hero as consolation for the loss of his betrothed, but although old men seek it as the answer to their senility, he escapes back into a world where time and age are active to seek his beloved. 'I seek no dream', he says, 'but rather the end of dreams' (XIV. 273). We have seen that in *News from Nowhere* dream is the product of a twofold disaffection: from the society of the late nineteenth century (the revolutionary alienation) and from the community of those who meet to discuss hopes of change. For this too is rigorously circumscribed by its historical situation. I am not, of course, implying that Morris's faith in socialism was deteriorating, but that *News from Nowhere* registers acute doubts about the mode of action that socialist theory had to take. Running away from the feast, the narrator is recognizing his own imprisonment in disaffection, but he is also perhaps running away finally from dream, holding within himself the knowledge of values other than those manifest in the present. It seems to me that we have, in this novel, much less a Utopia than an account of the agony of holding the mind together, committed as it is to the conscious determinants of history and the impersonal forces of change – united only in conceptual terms. But more than that, it is the fullest recognition that dream itself insists on isolation, and that it can only become a collective experience in terms of history – a history which is not communicable in articulate terms.

This means that the difference between Morris and Hardy is not one of the former's greater affirmativeness so much as his greater insistence on the compulsion of the isolate self to seek a collectivity in the historical world. We may need to say that finally Morris fails to carry this insight into the world of action and that his writing has no way of coping with this failure in the context of the nineteenth-century experience. But this is much more a judgement on the Socialist League than it is on Morris. For what is truly important about his achievement as a creative writer is that his work attests to the need to create a revolutionary sense of community in order to reflect fully the estrangement of the disaffected mind, and that in its confrontation with this need it portrays the intensity of conflict which is inherent in the effort to relate it to the historical situation. Morris creates a revolutionary literature because he discovers forms which dramatize the tensions of the revolutionary mind. And I don't know any other writer in English who does that.

Notes

1. Raymond Williams, *Culture and Society*, London, 1958, p. 158.
2. Ibid., p. 155. It should be *A Dream*. I think it makes a difference.
3. E. P. Thompson, William Morris: *Romantic To Revolutionary*, London, 1955, p. 763.
4. Ibid., p. 779.
5. Marx and Engels, *Literature and Art*, Bombay, 1956, pp. 36–7.
6. P. Demetz, *Marx, Engels and the Poets*, London, 1956, p. 138.
7. Marx and Engels, *Literature and Art*, op. cit., p. 39.
8. It is obviously absurd for Demetz to say that what Engels means by reality is the 'realities postulated by his ideology', since this is true of anybody.
9. Marx and Engels, *Literature and Art*, pp. 39–40.
10. Ibid., p. 38.
11. George Gissing, *New Grub Street*, London, 1967, p. 163. All references are to this edition. Page numbers are given in parentheses.
12. See H. M. Lynd, *England in the Eighteen-Eighties*, London, 1968, p. 200.
13. George Gissing, *Denzil Quarrier*, London, 1892, p. 35.
14. William Morris, *The Collected Works*, New York, 1966, vol. XVI, p. 211. All references to the works of Morris are to this edition unless otherwise stated. Quotations are followed by their locations in parentheses, the volume number in Roman numeral, followed by the page number in Arabic numeral.
15. Mark Rutherford, *The Revolution in Tanners Lane*, London, 1887, p. 388.
16. Morris and Belfort Bax, *Socialism, its Growth and Outcome*, London, 1893, p. 16.
17. May Morris, *William Morris*, Oxford, 1936, vol. II, p. 162.
18. William Morris, *Letters*, London, 1950, p. 149.
19. Ibid., p. 202.
20. Ibid., pp. 228–9.
21. May Morris, *William Morris*, op. cit., vol. I, p. 148.
22. *Socialism, Utopian and Scientific*, translated by Edward Aveling, London, 1892, pp. 47–8.
23. Morris and Bax, *Socialism, Its Growth and Outcome*, op. cit., p. 76.
24. Stubbs, *The Constitutional History of England*, 3rd edn., Oxford, 1887, vol. II, p. 471.
25. Green, *History of the English People*, London, 1878, vol. II, p. 475.
26. Ibid., p. 476.
27. Rogers, *Six Centuries of Work and Labour*, London, 1949, p. 271.
28. Green, op. cit., p. 474.

29. Rogers, op. cit., p. 252.
30. Ibid., p. 254.
31. Ibid., p. 262.
32. Maurice, *Lives of the English Popular Leaders in the Middle Ages*, London, 1875, p. 128.
33. Hyndman, *The Historical Basis of Socialism in England*, London, 1883, p. 4.
34. Stubbs, *The Constitutional History of England*, op. cit., p. 485.
35. Green, *History of the English People*, op. cit., p. 486.
36. Engels, *The German Revolutions*, ed. Lionel Krieger, Chicago, 1967, p. 38.
37. Marx and Engels, *On Religion*, Moscow, 1955, p. 70.
38. Eleventh thesis on Feuerbach. Marx and Engels, *On Religion*, p. 72.
39. G. D. H. Cole, *William Morris*, London, 1948, p. xviii.
40. Gramsci, *The Modern Prince and Other Writings*, London, 1967, p. 69.
41. Freeman, *Comparative Politics*, London, 1893, p. 86.
42. Ibid., p. 76.
43. Marx, *Pre-Capitalist Economic Formations*, London, 1964, p. 80.
44. Freeman, *Comparative Politics*, op. cit., p. 81.
45. Morgan, *Ancient Society*, Cambridge, Mass., 1964, p. 467.

CHAPTER 13

Now Where Nowhere:
William Morris Today

As the title of this journal [*News from Nowhere*] indicates, William Morris continues to engage the left intelligentsia, separated from him though it is by a century whose history has been beyond the wildest Victorian imagination. This is undoubtedly in part because he is the only major British writer before E. P. Thompson and Raymond Williams to engage seriously with Marxism. But Morris is not available as the origin of a tradition except within a contest of rival claims to his historical support, and this is complicated by the kind of writer he is and the cultural group from which he emerges. For the strangest thing about Morris is that in a culture which produced Paine and Godwin, he should come, not from the enlightenment liberal/utilitarian tradition that culminated in J. S. Mill, but under the aegis of its conservative antagonist, John Ruskin. Our first major transmitter of Marxist values is neither philosopher nor economist but an artist and writer working within 'literature', the grand narrative of the appropriated surplus. Socialism is about practice – reading Morris do we overlook the literariness which makes for distance and ambiguity in order to extract useful ideas? The American collection of essays celebrating the centenary of *News from Nowhere*, Boos and Silvers' *Socialism and the Literary Art of William Morris* is, as its title demonstrates, alert to this tension even if the conjunction leaves it unresolved. Coleman and O'Sullivan's subtitle, *A Vision for Our Time*, is unashamedly pragmatic.

There are exceptions. Both Christopher Hampton and Jan Marsh pay attention to the generic and figurative meanings that lie within the text Hampton places the story within the tradition of dream vision, while Marsh analyses the book's 'erotic thread' by which she shows Morris's vision to be deeply imbued with male desire (p. 121). She also rescues it by arguing that lust operates as a metaphor or carriage for utopian desire (p. 124). I find the analysis more convincing than the rescue. You could equally well argue that utopian desire was the vehicle for male passion, especially as poor Ellen, in Marsh's account, has to stand as a personification of the new age, at once alluring and unobtainable' (p. 124). But at least, like Hampton, she gives us an essay we can debate (there is no doubt that Morris himself was very conscious of the uncertainty of his own gender attitude). So too does Ray Watkinson, though his essay on the contexts of 'work' in the book is more informative than interpretive, and more historical than literary, which, in a volume that makes as little recognition of Morris's historical distance from us as of his discursive practice, is certainly not a limitation.

On the whole, however, while very laudably trying to produce a non-academic book for non-specialists, the editors have assembled a collection which simply contemplates this late Victorian romance as contemporary discussion document. For the most part this has meant dragging Morris back from the dead and making him speak direct to our needs. Not surprisingly, since the collection is published by Green Books, the 'vision for our time' is mostly to be valued because it is ecologically sound and benevolently anarchist. Paddy O'Sullivan argues that the central thesis of Morris's book is that 'by abolishing the production of surplus value, the new society was able to lessen its impact on the rest of nature' (p. 179). Adam Buick uses the text to advocate a Kropotkinian, decentralized, steady state economy based on relative abundance. Mark Pearson uses it to attack totalitarian modernist architecture in the name of 'the need to establish a dwelling upon this earth, beneath these skies' (p. 148). This is all certainly ahistorical, even glaringly so. Buick, for example, concludes with a remark that would have bewildered Morris: 'sooner or later, humanity must establish a stable, sustainable relationship with the rest of nature' (p. 168). Although Morris is very critical of industry, he shows almost no sign of ecological consciousness, even envisaging an increase of mechanisation (the force). The return to simplicity is not to do with the planet but with people. Man exists, Hammond tells us, 'in reasonable strife with nature' (*CW*, 16.58).[1] England has become 'a garden where nothing is wasted' and its architecture reflects a people who 'won't stand any nonsense from Nature in their dealings with her' (*CW*, 16.72/73). Morris is not only, as we might expect, not fully aware of the ecological dangers of human history because of his historical position, but actually less concerned than some of his contemporaries – Ruskin himself, Richard Jefferies, and W. H. Hudson for example.

But this is not the most important point. A selective reading, especially one that lifts individual ideas from the text and rearranges them, can certainly produce a green Morris, just as it can produce a bolshevik Morris, a Trotskyist Morris and an anarchist Morris (see Thompson, 1977, on this). There is a frisson of sectarian anxiety both in Buick and in an essay on 'How the Change Came' about whether Morris mistakenly meant state capitalism by 'state socialism'. And Stephen Coleman has no hesitation in taking Morris's and Bax's description of Robert Owen's 'theory of the perfectibility of man by the amelioration of his surround-ings' (p. 84) despite the clear indications that even in Nowhere murder can still arise.

This desire to find our own values in Morris is understandable. To read Morris extensively is for any socialist an experience much like love. He is the only radical writer in English towards whom one does not feel awe (Milton, Blake, and Shelley aren't people you would like to see sitting in the backrow of a branch meeting). He uniquely addresses the practical issues of building a better society without becoming arrogant and techno-cratic like Shaw or Wells. It is such a relief to read him. And like all loved ones, we would like him to be perfect and in our own image. But there are things he couldn't see, and things he wouldn't see. Although, for example, he assumes that there is going to be a European war as early as the 1880s, and although he understood the meaning of imperialism as an economic buffer to internal decline, *News from Nowhere* fails to address the interna-tionalisation of conflict, as Crump points out, nevertheless measuring the accuracy of this imaginary text against a historical perspective derived from the present time – although to be fair to him, he does, at the last minute, recognise that this is 'incongruous' (p. 72).

The nation state has collapsed in Nowhere but the 'change' has been brought about entirely in one country, and we know only too well the con-sequences of socialism in one country. The arrival of the global village, the capacity of capitalism to deploy war as a means of economic 'recovery', the evil co-existence of international finance with repressive nationalism or communalism, these make taking Nowhere as a possibility, even with the discipline of 'how the change came', more or less self-indulgent. This is not to blame Morris. He would have been the first to say that the future is very hard to predict.

But there are also things that he should have been able to see and did not, either because his class origin left him too immune to the harsh realities of working-class life, or because he was too much in awe of Engels whose understanding of the local situation was limited. Thus, for example, Morris was too dismissive of 'palliatives', particularly the campaign for the eight-hour day. Of course, such stepping stones were very limited. But you don't have a working-class movement without working-class power, and power does not exist if you do not have surplus energy. If there is a lesson for modern socialists to learn from Morris, it is that too many mod-ern socialist intellectuals, especially those who come from public school backgrounds, regarded the welfare state as a mere emulsifier, propping up capitalism. Of course, this is partly true. But the destruction of state welfare and the undermining of the unions has left the working class in a weaker position politically now than it was even in the 1930s. Again it is hardly Morris's fault that he was born rich, but it is a limitation on his unmediated value.

I am as prone as anybody to want Morris to be right about everything. But it is nevertheless from his own time that he addresses us, and, more-over in the terms of his own imaginative discourse, which in the case of *News from Nowhere* is narrative fiction, and more specifically as the subtitle, alluding to Edward Bellamy's preface, alerts us, utopian romance. If you look in the text for a blueprint of a socialist future, you end up feeling that it is either impossible or unpalatable, but if you pay attention to its rhetorical strategy on the one hand, and its ideological function on the other, you have a more deeply fascinating and problematic text, and a better chance of accounting for why, long after other future narratives, such as *Looking Backward*, have come to seem dystopian, it continues to demand our response. What Coleman and O'Sullivan's collection does not recognise is that if you are to deal with Morris both as a socialist and as a writer, you have to get beyond the idea that texts are the objects of consumption, even if the consumption is designed to make a better world rather than merely to satisfy an immediate taste. Socialist reading recognises that all discourse is pragmatic, and socialist writing is designed to be and therefore appear pragmatic. But this means you cannot discuss a Morris text in terms of what it represents. Although depiction is an important rhetorical strategy for Morris, its task is not to give you pictures even of a life better than the one you know – of course there is no life better than the one you know, even if the one you know requires radical improvements. Jumping into a new world as Guest jumps into the salmon-crowded Thames means losing the critical reader.

It is best to approach all Morris's writing by comparing it to his design work. Much of his design is based on the depiction of natural forms, but this is not to create an illusion of those forms' presence in the way that a Wedgwood pot depicts classical scenes to give you the illusion that you possess a glimpse of another life. Morris transforms the natural images into a pattern that he thinks will improve the immediate environment. You don't look at a Morris wallpaper to have the feeling that you might still be outside. He made it plain in his 1891 'Address on the Collection of Paintings of the English Pre-Raphaelite School' in Birmingham that although naturalism was the most important feature of its art, naturalism was itself a kind of convention, designed to overcome the conventionalism of academic art, 'a genuinely *natural* convention' (*AWS*, I. 301). It is part of its definite revolt against 'Academical Art' (297). The function of the representation is pragmatic. It is to displace dominant ways of seeing, and to be sure, the conservative response to this naturalism was to say 'they are not like nature' by which, Morris wryly adds, it meant 'they are not like pictures' (299).

Now if we look at Morris's writing, this pragmatic dimension is manifest in two ways. First, from the beginning there is a marked and specific intertextuality. Each of the major poems from *The Defence of Guinevere* to *Sigurd the Volsung* is a specific reworking of already ideologically available myth, or the supply of a new or undiscovered myth in order to change the literary environment. Even the unfinished contemporary novel started in

1872, the so-called *Novel on Blue Paper*, with its remarkable prelude, offers itself self-consciously with the words 'our story begins' and defines the environment of the narrative as it might appear to the dreamy wanderer in the London streets as one in which 'the common place people ... must deal in a different code of right and wrong (Morris, 1982, p. 1). This intertextuality does not disappear with Morris's conversion to socialism. *The Pilgrims of Hope* is manifestly a novel of adultery whose centrality in nineteenth-century bourgeois fiction Tony Tanner has shown. But it is a reworking in which the revolutionary events of history do not leave the personal relations untouched but enable them to break free of conventional possessive love (see Boos's excellent analysis of this poem in Boos and Silver, pp. 147–166). And, of course, *A Dream of John Ball* and the German romances are specific interventions in medieval historiography and anthropology.

But these texts show a second and complicating discursive function which does reflect Morris's new political vision. It is worth recalling that there is a long gap between *Sigurd the Volsung* and *The Pilgrims of Hope* (1876–1886) and that, although the latter is still verse, thereafter Morris moves into prose for all his subsequent narratives. *Pilgrims of Hope* itself has a more prosaic diction than earlier texts, though it has to be said that Morris uses archaism (or rather imitates archaism) in some of the later prose works. The conversion to socialism gives Morris a completely new sense of the political importance of narrative derived from a Marxist sense of history.

Morris has from the beginning a strong sense of the past which he gets from Carlyle and Ruskin. A sense of the past is different from and even an obstacle to the sense of history. It is basically metaphoric – the past is juxtaposed as contrast or parallel. This is not the only way the past is dealt with in Carlyle and Ruskin but their impact on Morris is of this kind. He does not abandon this contrastive structure as soon as he becomes a socialist, but only eventually, through the practical and theoretical lessons of the mid-eighties. Thus, in 'Art under Plutocracy' (1883), he brings the middle ages to witness that 'this claim of labour for pleasure rests on a foundation stronger than a mere fantastic dream' (*CW*, 23). Later, in 'Art and Socialism' (January, 1884), he says 'think of a piece of history and so hope' – this is the decline of Rome, 'this tale of the past is a parable of the days to come'. The past is thus static, its lessons demonstrative. The dynamics of change are absent ('decline' because of its overtones of Gibbon suggests a stable state overtaken by something beyond its control; change came, Morris says, 'like a thief in the night'). Moreover, history is almost entirely a movement of mind in this lecture. Since the end of the middle ages, he writes, Europe has gained freedom of thought, increase of knowledge, and a huge talent for dealing with the material forces of nature. So it becomes possible to designate history as optional – 'Society

... has bought these gains at too high a price ... the death of Art was too high a price to pay for the material prosperity of the middle classes'. History has been a mistake. The past is pastoral. But the voluntarism does not make history anything but mechanical. Because it is a movement of mind nobody is really responsible for it – 'Creation is no longer a need of man's soul'.

Within eighteen months, this view of past and present has given way to a surer sense of process. In 'The Hopes of Civilisation', which appeared in June 1885, the move from the middle ages is no longer a cultural shift, but a moment in the emergence of the class struggle from the dismantling of feudalism. Nor is the arrival of capitalism a mistake but a revolutionary process with its own hopes and aspirations. Most importantly, this is not something external to human nature. On the contrary, the historical survey begins with a sense of the strangeness of human nature in the medieval period. When he makes utopian projections as he does in 'The Society of the Future', it is as a self-conscious 'chapter of confessions'. Historical change has become larger than the individual will but absolutely internal to it. When, in 1888, Morris explained his political position to the Reverend George Bainton, he defined socialism as a theory of life taking as its starting point, the evolution of society; or, 'let us say, of man as a social animal' (*CL*. 2.282).

These changes coincide with the return to narrative after ten years. The difference in the function of narrative distance in *Sigurd the Volsung* on the one hand, and *The Pilgrims of Hope* and *A Dream of John Ball* on the other, reflects this change in the understanding of history. For *Sigurd* is both heroically contrastive and analogical – its myth of loss clearly figures the alienating effect of the division of labour (Goode, 1972). The later texts engage with the meaning of particular historical moments in which human agency and historical process are related by a complex interaction – in which, in other words, men make their own history but not in the manner in which their actions had intended. By the time we get to *The House of the Wulfings* and *The Roots of the Mountains*, we are clearly dealing with a sense of history very different from that which ascribed the decline of Rome to the 'Northern Fury' since the alternative social structure of the *gens* is portrayed in detail.

The new sense of history, however, does not merely make narrative a more attractive form of discourse, but puts Morris in a radical situation in terms of the constitution of that discourse. And this operates on two levels, each of which has received considerable critical attention though not much as a single network of issues (Wilding, 1980, is the exception). Both levels are evident in the generic subtitle, 'Chapters of Utopian Romance'. 'Utopian' and 'Romance' are both highly charged words, and Morris held strong views about the discourses they invoked. Moreover, both relate to the nature of history since they extrapolate unseen alternatives to the present. Specifically, they have to do with the relationship of structure and agency, since utopias are about what people want, as opposed to what people find themselves in, and 'Romance', in its broadest sense (which is how Bellamy used it in his preface), is about how the human agent deals with or endures the world he finds himself in. Utopian romance combines an interest in political programmes with an interest in stories. Given that we have been alerted to this double discourse, we cannot treat *News from Nowhere* simply as a utopia or as a romance: it must also be a discourse about these genres and about their relationship to one another.

I will take 'Romance' first. A number of critics, most notably Brantlinger (1974) and Sharratt (1980) have developed the allusions made in the text to the nineteenth-century novel to suggest that the text inscribes an anti-novel or a critique of 'realism'. There is much to support this in the text. Boffin is described as writing 'reactionary novels' with antiquarian interest (an avenging echo, according to Brantlinger, of the Victorian critique of the Pre-Raphaelites). Ellen later accuses Guest of wanting to nurse a sham sorrow as in nineteenth-century novels, and her longer comment on nineteenth-century fiction (*CW*, 16.151) spells out the excessive privileging of private bourgeois emotion even in texts which deal with the lives of the poor. They generally end, she says, with the hero and heroine on an island of bliss being supported by precisely those poor whose lives have been sympathetically portrayed. These allusions create a level of textual self-consciousness which signal, according to Brantlinger, the hostility of all utopian art to non-utopian art, and anticipate, according to Sharratt, the pragmatic, self-conscious aesthetic of Brecht.

I agree with the general thrust of these arguments that *News from Nowhere* contains a critique of the dominant literary form of its own era. But this critique should not be confused with total rejection. It is not true as it is sometimes asserted that Morris was blind to the achievements of nineteenth-century realism. Throughout the letters and *Commonweal*, there are comments which show a strong and sympathetic interest in the novel. For example, in 1885, he wrote to Fred Henderson that George Eliot was 'the cleverest Englishwoman of our time, having established a well deserved reputation for her novels'. In the following year, he reports that being at a loss for a book to read in the train, he took up *Mansfield Park*. This hardly confirms the impression that Morris only read Scott and Dickens, and only read them for entertainment. In March, 1886, he reported reading *War and Peace*, 'which I find I can get through with much approbation, but little enjoyment, and yet, (to take the horse round to the other side of the cart) *with a good deal of satisfaction*' (my italics). He goes on to say that he did not think he would go on to 'tackle *Anna Karenina*', but by March 26th he had, according to a letter to May Morris, nearly read it (*CL*, II. Letters). The reaction is mixed (though the lack of enjoyment is understandable if we remember that no good translation from the

Russian would have been available in English). But you do not read both *War and Peace* and *Anna Karenina* within a month out of mere piety or curiosity. In 1888, in *Commonweal*, he made a spirited defence of Zola's *Germinal* against British Grundyism (which got Zola's translator imprisoned twice) on the grounds of its realism, 'a true picture', as he puts it, 'of the life which our civilisation forces on labouring men and I hold that "what is not too bad to be done, is not too bad to be told about", though I find no difficulty in imagining our rulers and masters take a very different view of the subject' (*Commonweal*, 25th August, 1888).

This critique of realism is not motivated by essentialist aesthetics such as those that surround recent debates about 'classic realism' but about the social function of a mode of writing. This comes out in a very sharp comment on Hardy, in the Birmingham Address, sometimes cited as yet another sign that Morris did not appreciate his contemporaries in spite of the fact that the observation is made to defend the turning away from modern subject matter by the Pre-Raphaelites: 'Let us take the novels of such a man as Hardy ... They are supposed to represent scenes of modern life in their novels. But do they? I say they do not: because they take care to surround those scenes with an atmosphere of "out of the way" country life, which we ourselves never by any chance see. If you go down into the country, you won't see Mr Hardy's heroes and heroines walking about I assure you' (*AWS*, I.304/305). This is, of course, true, and if Hardy had been discussed in terms of dominant and subversive conventions rather than mimetic absolutes, his work would not have had to wait so long for its just appreciation. More importantly, we can see that Morris understands the historical determinants which make an aesthetic at one time subversive and at another reactionary.

The problematic of the novel in *News from Nowhere* is specific, and we can understand this if we consider Morris's review of G. B. Shaw's *Cashel Byron's Profession*. Praising its dramatic quality, its keen observation and vivid representation, he adds nevertheless that like all those novels of 'this generation which have any pretence to naturalism', it lacks the power that 'accumulation gives' (*Commonweal*, 17th July, 1886). He contrasts this with Scott and Dickens not because the older authors are more entertaining but because they have the unity and completeness of great drama. It is the lack of historicity of modern fiction that he is criticising – the isolation of its scenes, the undynamic quality of its vividness. This is precisely the thrust of Ellen's attack on the nineteenth-century novel. We see the hero and heroine living happily in an island of bliss after a long series of mostly sham troubles while the world must even then have gone on its way: 'and dug and sewed and hacked and carpentered' (*CW*, 16.151). Introspective illusion, lack of historical significance, lack of materiality: these are charges that could be made against the novel by critics committed to realism – Engels and Lukács, for example. But this leaves us with a problem – if Morris felt that the novel was lacking 'accumulation', why write texts that are even less substantial than those they despise?

Part of the answer is that we should not take Ellen to be Morris. Novels continue to be written even in Nowhere. And Clara makes the suggestion that there is no art about the Nowhereians because they are too uninteresting to write about. Morris's lecture to the Fabians, 'How Shall We Live Then?', having begun by suggesting that the reason for setting out his personal view of the Promised Land of Socialism is the hope of provoking others into giving their views, goes on to say 'I am almost prepared to deny that there is such a thing as an individual human being: I have found out that my valuable skin covers say about a dozen persons' (Meier, 1971, p. 223). The debates in *News from Nowhere* are not bogus as they are in much utopian writing, certainly in Bellamy. So the novel that Ellen describes and dismisses is always threatening to enter the text. The structure of the book highlights the psychology of the narrator – the pressure towards dream at the beginning leaves its trace even as Guest becomes inquirer and observer on our behalf. If the story comes as a response to his alienation in the world of the present, it also causes him moments of alienation from the unalienated new world. Hammond's 'inverted sympathy' with the past is 'a blanket for me against the cold of this very new world' which leads him to ask how the change came (CW, 16.103). Hammond's ironical response to Guest's (unconsciously ambiguous?) description of the new world as a 'second childhood' is a 'scarcely veiled threat' (102). Towards the end of the novel, he is shaken when Dick says to him 'you had better consider that you have got the cap of darkness, and are seeing everything, yourself invisible' (155). Each of these moments problematises the relationship between Guest the narrator and Guest the protagonist until Ellen pulls them negatively together: 'you belong so entirely to the unhappiness of the past, that our happiness even would weary you' (210). He cannot both enter the new world and still mediate it for us. Thus there is always a shadowy margin between Nowhere as vision and as experience. The utopia is marked by the ordeal of Guest's seeing. That is why, for all the simplification of sexual relations in the book, the central story comes to be Guest's falling in love with Ellen.

But this redoubled alienation (which I briefly noted in 1972 when I too thought of texts simply as representations) is the basis of the historic sense which the text transmits. For it deconstructs the two central aporia of the realist project. The first of these is – in the words of the cleverest woman of Morris's generation – that there is no private life that is not determined by a wider public life. I call it an aporia because although it appears to be a precondition, it poses questions (how?, how far?) rather than answers them. The two great realist writers Morris mentions in his letters, Eliot and Tolstoi, return to it again and again, only to find a stalemate. Character, formed by the social world, finds itself alienated from it. The public world demands sacrifice or suicide (even if the suicide in the case of Dorothea, Deronda and Levin is intellectual). But, and this is the second aporia, the novel privileges experience over desire – it is the story of lost illusions. The only positive the novel can offer is compromise or the recovery of origins (or an uneasy truce between the two).

News from Nowhere does not abandon this problematic – it historicises it. The meaning of Guest's experience is not merely to enjoy an 'epoch of rest' (which is what limits the vision), but by being thrust forward in time to uncover his own historical identity. Nowhere does not merely have a different order of things by which the discontents of civilisation wither away, but a different human nature: '"Human nature!", cried the old boy impetuously, "What human nature? The human nature of paupers, of slaves, of slave holders, or the human nature of wealthy freemen? Which? Come, tell me that!"' (*CW*, 16.86/87). This transforms the boundaries of public and private. Revolutionaries long for freedom with 'the unreasonable passion of the lover'. Through the process of learning from the decline of capitalism and the struggle to institute state socialism, the longing becomes a way of facing up to reality. Passion, the motive of nature in human nature, becomes the basis of reason. The evolution of society is the evolution of man as a social animal.

This means that values in Nowhere itself are not at rest. Several times the utopian world shudders with its own temporality. Hammond falls into melancholic reverie; Ellen's father complains about the new world's mediocrity and, although she answers him, Clara's eager response to his complaint keeps the doubt in play. These are minor recognitions that history does not stop and that its changes are located in the psyche more than they are ironic challenges to the utopian nature of the new world. Neither is it merely a matter of the past still flowing in to the present: when Guest asks Henry Morsom what is to come after this (an intensely loaded question given all the allusions to a return to childhood in the text), Morsom is evasive but does not deny that change will come.

Finally, Ellen herself, who, unlike her grandfather or Hammond, or Morsom or even Clara, is not on the edge of the picture, but fully part of the new world, is both conscious of history, and conscious of the need to recall it. Guest, she explains, finds her so strange because in his own epoch, she would have been one of those who escape the slavery of poverty and the oppression of women by becoming a prostitute. This vindicates the new world because her individuality is accepted and embraced, but she knows that this cannot be taken for granted: 'I think sometimes people are too careless of the history of the past ... who knows, happy as we are, times may alter; we may be bitten with some impulse towards change' (*CW*, 16.194). When she accuses him of 'wanting to nurse a sham sorrow, like the ridiculous characters in some of those queer old novels' (198), she is inviting him to slough off his own historicity. But she has recognised within a few pages that he cannot come fully into her present, and soon even she will find him invisible. For he, like them, is social man, bound up with the evolution that teaches him to know himself and holds him off from the future whose history he has to live through. The insertion of the historical chapters, 'How the Change Came' and 'The Beginning of the New Life', accounts in detail for the coming of the new world through the interaction of necessity and human agency (in contrast with Bellamy who sees historical struggle as a mere distraction from smooth evolution, or with Hudson's *The Crystal Age* which has suffered a single, practically forgotten catastrophe). I wrongly saw this as a limitation in 1972, because the history had to be invented and this was a sign that socialist representations of the real world could not be made. This was not to blame Morris, but to comment on the immaturity of the socialist movement in 1890. I was wrong because I failed to see the narrative function of these chapters and as a result the function of the narrative.

For as we have seen, the narrative function of these chapters extends far beyond their own public domain. Morris gives us a detailed and conflict-ridden history which, because it changes human nature, can only be experienced by Guest as a kind of return, the future the past might have held but did not deliver. Thus the journey up the Thames is a recovery which at its most intense moments seems like a return to childhood. This recidivism is why Ernst Bloch dismissed it, but it is part of the text's whole thrust. Guest does not lost his illusion: his illusion loses him (literally, he becomes invisible). Thus he is forced to return only because his dream world cannot be realised without effort (as it is for the hero of *Looking Backward*). He returns with a future whose function is not representational, but pragmatic.

In a short article in *Commonweal* in November 1890 – that is immediately after the end of the serialisation of *News from Nowhere* – Morris reviews the achievement of the seven year old socialist movement. Rejecting both the routes of palliation (the new Trades Unionism and the Fabians) on the one hand, and of 'future, inconsequent revolt' on the other, he argues that the real task has been and must continue to be 'to make socialists' (*AWS*, II.517). What he means by this is explicit in a later essay, 'Communism', in which he argues that the test of socialism is its capacity to win the minds of the working class. *News from Nowhere* is a contribution to that task, as Meier argues (1978, p. 269), turning longing from negation to a prospect of order because it gives discontent not an origin, but a history. To move from the present to the future, Guest feels, is to move from 'blind despair' to 'hope', not from utter loss (since the despair is blind) to happiness (*CW*, 16.204). And that, of course, is the final note of the book, to hope that the dream, personal, embarrassing even, 'akin to the unreasonable passion of a lover' (*CW*, 16.104) and hence frail and open to dispute (even from within the many selves who constitute the author), will become, by being shared, a vision.

But there remains the question of how much is to be shared and by whom. Simon Dentith, in *A Rhetoric of the Real* (1990, pp. 121–133), looking at the original appearance of the text in *Commonweal* displacing and then following the 'Notes on News' column, shows how its 'negative pragmatics', that is the double effect of its inverted realism and the self-exposure of its substitutions for the abolished actuality, fulfills a specific strategy in the task of 'making socialists'. In this context it is less general propaganda than a way of reminding the faithful of what lies beyond the daily battle. This does not give us an open work by which each reader is called upon to dream his own dream, but rather a discussion text whereby the specific contents of the dream are offered to socialist analysis. If this emerges mainly as the dream of abolition of alienating structures, it is on the basis of specific negations, first of the distinction between town and country and then, through the Dick-Clara story and the vision of the children in the woods, the abolition of the family as a device for the securing of private property. But as to what such an abolition would result in, Morris, by his realisation of a world imagined without such structures, risks exposing his own dream in order to show that these basic institutions are not without the possibility of negation.

Dentith calls attention to the difference of the effect of the book as it appears in serial and then various book formats. For in *Commonweal* it is much more directly pragmatic than it will be in later formats, locked in as it is to the party debates and juxtaposed to the 'real' news which motivates the originating discontent on which Morris's dream is founded. Once it reaches book form, it is both more crystallised (because it is no longer serial and loses its air of improvisation) but also more open to interpretation and finally, Dentith argues, becomes wholly ambiguous, available to readerly consumption once it is lavishly printed. This compels us to look at the utopianism of the text in a more complex way.

The most interesting analyses of *News from Nowhere* in recent years have stressed either its pragmatic (Meier, Dentith) or its heuristic (Thompson, Williams), function. Both approaches are better than seeing it as a negotiable blueprint, or my own original view of it as the representation of the tensions of the revolutionary mind, since the first is unworkable by Morris's own admission, and the second, as Thompson pointed out, fails to account for the text's effect. But they aren't strictly compatible since the first sees it as rallying the faithful by giving them some long-term target, while the second sees it as the education of desire and this clearly argues a radically different view of the way Morris sees the utopian impulse (at its extremes, either as a 'topic' to be exploited, or as a deep, intrinsic and revisionist need).

On the one hand, it is not difficult to argue that Morris is not utopian.

His text begins as a dispute with Bellamy which Morris himself says is a utopia and therefore personal, just as he writes that Sir Thomas More's *Utopia* tells us more about More's own era than it does about a possible ideal world (*AWS*, 1.291). Taking this to a reading of the text which sees it primarily as a contribution to the daily life of the revolutionary party, the utopian drive of the text would seem to be to expose the bad utopianism (partly because concealed under a cloak of possibility) of Bellamy, and to replace it with a revolutionary vision that would lift the heads of the party above the immediate horizon. Morris seems to be taking on this role in 'The Society of the Future', a lecture originally given on Bloody Sunday, but published for the first time in March 1889, when he contrasts himself as one of the 'visionaries or *practical people*' (*AWS*, 2.455), with the analytic. The secondary function, which would justify the text as book, would be to challenge debate beyond the party circle, as Morris is doing in 'How Shall We Live Then?', a lecture delivered to the Fabians in March 1889 when he offered 'my personal view of the Promised Land of Socialism, with the hope of eliciting an account of the views of several of this audience' (Meier, 1971, p. 222). In both of these cases the utopian text is purely instrumental. It is not promoting utopian values but opportunistically commandeering those values for right socialist positions.

The heuristic view, however, constitutes a positive value for utopia. arguing, as Thompson, following Abensour does, that *News from Nowhere* constitutes a critique of Marxism's limitations (Thompson, 1977, p. 806). The text then offers no mechanical blueprint but 'the education of desire', which encourages the dream as a way out of mechanical Marxist prescriptions. The attraction of this reading is that it enables us to read the text less reductively than Meier who sometimes decomposes its questions to fit the already existing arguments in Marx. Equally, however, it encourages a very open text. For desire must be pluralistic on one level since any sign of its collectivism must turn it into a semblance of necessity. *News from Nowhere* is certainly not an open text. It lays down a very definite historical programme and addresses questions of social relations with specific principles. On the other hand, its psychological accuracy does not allow us to extricate those issues from the total experience. Thus, if it is not open, it is undecided (between dream and vision, free choice and necessity, for example, or in the most general sense between theory and practice).

I think that there are two ways to approach this which will bring us back to my original point that the questions of ideological position and literary understanding cannot be separated. The best recent account of the utopian context of Morris's text is by Ruth Levitas. Although her definition of utopia includes 'desire for a better way of being and living', she resists the associated idea that this entails a 'utopian impulse' intrinsic to human nature:

> Utopianism ... has as a precondition a disparity between socially constructed experienced need and socially prescribed and actually available means of satisfaction ... there is every reason to expect that societies will differ both in the extent to which a gap between needs and available or potential satisfactions is experienced, and in the extent to which there are cultural hypotheses about the potential closure of this gap as well as in the nature of these hypotheses (Levitas, 1990, p. 183).

The key to understanding *News from Nowhere* in this respect is to recognise the tension between analysis and experience not – as Perry Anderson sees it – as 'irrationalism' but as a claim for the non-rational (p. 128). Summarising the Abensour/Thompson argument that *News from Nowhere* is about the education of desire, Levitas writes, 'Utopia does not express desire but enables people to work towards an understanding of what is necessary for human fulfilment' (p. 122). Morris thus offers a heuristic text but not one that enables desire to become, in Williams's phrase, 'a mode of living with alienation' (Williams, 1980, p. 203, quoted Levitas, p. 125). Morris's closing antithesis of dream and vision is picked up at the end of her book when she briefly takes up the 'political question' of the judgment between utopias. If utopia arises from desire, the transformation of reality depends on hope. Utopia can keep dissatisfaction alive but it is not the source of hope, for the dream becomes vision only when hope is invested in an agency capable of transformation' (p. 200).

That, as she affirms, is our political problem still, but it is clear that an historical understanding of *News from Nowhere* enables us to address it with more clarity. Levitas's argument about the complex relationship of utopian thought to agency, how we live and how we might live, brings us round again to the pragmatic function of the text with which Dentith is concerned. What is endlessly fascinating about Morris's text is the way in which its transparency does not simplify the process whereby its ideas feed back into life. It rescues desire from the unhistorical origin in unchanging human nature, so refusing to abstract the constructive urge in socialism from living experience. *The Communist Manifesto* criticises the utopian socialists because they tried to substitute their contrived organisation for the gradual, spontaneous class organisation of the proletariat. *News from Nowhere* challenges the 'realism' of mere experience which is so constantly marked in the novel as a form of illusion, not in order to contrive the future, but rather to remind us of the need to make it.

This negative interaction – utopia challenging experience, experience historicising utopia – is crucial to the aesthetic of Morris's text. In a discussion of naturalism early in the story, Hammond argues, as Morris does in the lecture on the Pre-Raphaelites, that writing about modern life is no more a direct transcript than writing about the pharaohs. Dick immediately converts this into a positive point: 'surely it is but natural to like these things strange' (*CW*, 16.102). Guest soon after feels the need of a blanket 'against the cold of this very new world where I was, so to say, stripped bare of every habitual thought' (103). This is the point at which Hammond begins to tell him how the change came. The strangeness demands naturalisation through the filling up of the historical gap, but that gap is itself the celebration of agency. And that is how the text as a whole works for us. The strangeness of its dream startles us and reminds us of the gap between blind despair and hope. Whatever happens we should go on reading *News from Nowhere* not because it will tell us what we want but because it will tell us that wanting it is not enough and that if we want it enough we will have to make others want in equal measure. This is a truly socialist utopia, but its precondition is not its dream but the recognition that we need to make socialists.

Notes

1. I use the following abbreviations in the essay:

AWS: *William Morris, Artist, Writer, Socialist*, by May Morris, two vols, New York, Russell and Russell, 1966.

CL: *The Letters of William Morris*, Norman Kelvin (ed), Princeton, Princeton University Press, 1984.

CW: *The Collected Works of William Morris*, New York, Russell and Russell, 1966.

References

1. Anderson, P. (1980), *Arguments within English Marxism*, London, Verso.
2. Boos, F. S. and Silver, C. G. (eds) (1990), *Socialism and the Literary Artistry of William Morris*, Columbia, University of Missouri Press.
3. Brantlinger, P. (1974), '*News from Nowhere*: Morris's Socialist Anti-Novel'. *Victorian Studies*, 19, pp. 35–49.
4. Dentith, S. (1990), *A Rhetoric of the Real*, London, Harvester Wheatsheaf.
5. Goode, John (1972), 'William Morris and the Dream of Revolution', John Lucas, ed., *Literature and Politics in The Nineteenth Century*, London, Methuen.
6. Levitas, R. (1990), *The Concept of Utopia*, London, Philip Allan. Meier, P. (1971), An Unpublished Lecture of William Morris, *International Review of Social History*, Vol. XIII, part 2, pp. 217–240.
7. Meier, P. (1978), *William Morris: The Marxist Dreamer*, Brighton, Harvester Press, 1978.
8. Morris, W. (1982), *The Novel on Blue Paper*, edited and introduced by Penelope Fitzgerald, London, The Journeyman Press.
9. Sharratt, B. (1980), 'News from Nowhere, Detail and Desire', Ian Gregor, ed., *Reading the Victorian Novel, Detail into Form*, London, Vision Press.
10. Thompson, E. P. (1977), *William Morris: Romantic to Revolutionary*, London, Merlin Press.
11. Wilding, M. (1980), *Political Fictions*, London, Routledge and Kegan Paul.
12. Williams, R. (1980), *Problems in Materialism and Culture*, London, Verso.

CHAPTER 14

The Decadent Writer
as Producer

I

'Was it that we lived in what is called "an age of transition" and so lacked coherence, or did we but pursue antithesis?'[1] Yeats's question is still no easier to answer, even though it is generally recognised that the tragic generation foreshadows modernism: for modernism itself seems largely to inherit élitist and organicist tendencies which site it, if antithetically and problematically, within the late capitalist ideology.[2] Generally this essay makes larger claims for what I shall term, following Symons, the decadent movement: what I shall set up as a 'materialist' perspective reveals a 'break' with the hegemony (crucially restricted) that modernism only repairs by assimilation.

But to begin with, it is necessary to identify a negative answer to Yeats's question, and it is Sartre, I think, who makes it most significantly:

> Thus, whereas literature ordinarily represents an integrating and militant function in society, bourgeois society at the end of the century offers the unprecedented spectacle of an industrious society, grouped round the banner of production, from which there issues a literature which, far from reflecting it, never speaks to it about what interests it, runs counter to its ideology, identifies the beautiful with the unproductive, refuses to allow itself to be integrated, and does not even wish to be read.[3]

He sees possibilities in this spectacle: it constitutes the writer's transgression and fall; the excesses of its formal displacement might have been an adolescence out of which emerged not merely an open break, but a *déclassement* from below, a new content and virtual public. It never went beyond the antithetical assertion of autonomy because of the danger of the writers becoming '"a white collar proletariat" on the margin of the real proletariat, suspect to the workers and spurned by the bourgeois' (p. 89). The consequence was that Marxism, in a triumph without glory, became the Church, 'while the gentlemen writers, a thousand miles away, made themselves guardians of an abstract spirituality'. It is hard to resist this account of the transition from 'decadence' to modernism, 'autonomy' to 'abstract spirituality'. Especially in England, where a distinction between even 'the avant garde' and modernism proper can be made.[4]

If Sartre defines the spectacle, it is Poggioli who provides the concepts with which to explain it. The term 'avant-garde' itself, he argues, only becomes applicable to the arts as it begins to lose its political significance.[5] It is only from within a hermetic field that the arts enact analogous revolutionary moments. Notoriously, the most progressive artists have been at best naive in their descents into political actuality. Even Walter Benjamin, who goes further than most critics in understanding the political significance of technical change, argues that it is better to see Baudelaire not from the perspective offered by his appearance on the barricades, but as a 'secret agent in the enemy camp'. Poggioli makes a further distinction between the 'intelligentsia', which, as Herzen realized, is capable of a proletarianization, and the actual public of the avant garde which he calls the 'intellectual élite' (pp. 84–8). Sartre's whole analysis stems precisely from the perspective of an intelligentsia which recognizes the irrecoverable *incorporation* of the intellectual élite. The domination of English intellectual history by the élite explains the containment of modernism. For the struggle to organize the traditional intellectual, as Eagleton has shown, ends in victory for the hegemony precisely because the whole concept of his alienation (stemming from Arnold) is based on the felt need of a totalizing unity (the State, tradition, culture, organic form, organic community, etc.) produced by the fissures in utilitarian ideology as it has to cope with a higher organization of the capitalist production process. Almost literally, the modern intellectual organizes himself on behalf of monopoly capitalism, becoming the guardian of an abstract spirituality duplicating the corporation of the imperial state, and actually making possible 'literature' as an ideological form – that is, as a canon available to the academy for the intellectual training of the ideological managers.[7]

I wish to affirm the achievement of the decadent movement both on the basis and in the face of this analysis. For already a contradiction emerges: how, if modern literature offers the spectacle of a non-integrating, isolated form, can it become organic in Gramsci's sense? It can only do so if, in achieving its 'coherence' the transition has lost the main thrust of its antithesis. The decadence thus becomes important not in so far as it prepares the way for modernism, but in so far as it rebukes its betrayal. This is not a matter of overturning the analysis, but of reminding ourselves of another statement of Benjamin's which is not, like the first, a tentative footnote, but a firm principle: 'Sundering truth from falsehood is the goal of the materialist method, not its point of departure. In other words, its point of departure is the object riddled with error' (p. 103). The first stage of any analysis has to be the identification of what riddles the object, and in this case it is a principle of Benjamin that enables us to perceive it: that the first question we have to ask about a work of art is not what is its situation *vis-à-vis* the relations of production, but what is its situation *in* them. The analysis I have compiled from Sartre, Poggioli and Eagleton poses the question of the *ideological relationship* of the modern movement to social change. But if we pose the question of the *production relations*, we can see that the decadent movement in particular, if it frequently voices ideas that flow into the organicism of the intellectual élite, and if, as in Yeats's essay 'The Autumn of the Body', it can be subsumed into it, distinguishes itself by being a specific resistance to coherence, the resistance of the producer to the guardian. If this only emerges in restricted and distorted ways, it may be because it could be no more than a white-collar proletariat, but it nevertheless met that risk. The coherence of the transition may mask a break which demystifies the text.

II

'Decadent, decadent, you are all decadent nowadays. Ibsen, Degas, and the New English Art Club; Zola, Oscar Wilde, and the Second Mrs Tanqueray.'[8] Hubert Crackanthorpe thus neatly exposes the absurdity of the meaning of the word. Even within a single writer it had no stability: Symons, for example, sees it as an inclusive term in 1893, a marginal one in *The Symbolist Movement.* It embraces Henley and Pater in the magazine version of 1893, but not in the reprint of 1923; while in the interim, Symons has applied it to Meredith (again specializing its meaning from the term offered in 1893). Yet, even its bewildering semantic diversity, the fact that it needs to be used, acknowledges that if it is ridiculous to generalize the innovatory forms in art in the 1890s, it is also natural and meaningful. The most obvious variation is not so much one of meaning but one of levels of meaning. Symons sees it as the pursuit of *la vérité vraie* in 1893, but confines it to 'that learned corruption of language by which style ceases to be organic' in 1897.[9] It can thus be taken to signify a total ideological commitment or else a stylistic character, and it is notably as the former that the outstanding polemics against 'decadence' attack it, while its most notable defence assumes it is the latter. Le Gallienne sees literary decadence as a break with vital literature:

> In all great literature, the theme great or small, is considered in all its relations, near or far, and above all in relation to the sum total of things, to the Infinite, as we phrase it; in decadent literature, the relations, the due proportions, are ignored. One might say that literary decadence consists in the euphuistic expression of isolated observations.[10]

And he goes on to cite the Arnoldian criterion of seeing life steadily and seeing it whole. Lionel Johnson, in his book on Hardy, also stresses the break with universality that decadence brings ('the great books and utterances tell all one story under diverse forms').[11] In decadent writing, literature becomes 'the private toy of its betrayers', and the universality it must lose, though it is not Le Gallienne's 'infinite', is still a totalizing conception, 'its humanity'. Both writers, in other words, see decadence as a break with some form of organic whole, with culture. On the other hand, not only Symons, but also Havelock Ellis, see this as a specific *stylistic* development – for Ellis, it is the inversion of the classical subordination of the parts to the whole.[12] These and other definitions may make it useless to define decadence as an idea, yet they make it clear that it is possible to identify a movement which can be classified by its structural relation to the literature of the past – as a break with that past which disintegrates it from the reaction of ideology (that is, of an expressive totality, whether it is the Infinite or Humanity) and insists on the break-up of stylistic totalities, 'a revolt from ready-made impressions and conclusions, a revolt from the ready-made of language, from the bondage of traditional form, of a form become rigid'.[13] The precise importance of Symons's negations (and their negativity) can be seen if we see Crackanthorpe's essay as a whole. For although he rejects the umbrella word, he is nevertheless affirming a movement: not only is he envisaging the time when the 'battle for literary freedom will be won' but basing this on the fact that 'a new public has been created', one that has 'eaten of the apple of knowledge' – that is, understands the nature of artistic production.

But Crackanthorpe takes us a stage further. His polemic is directed not against the philistine, the moral objector, but against a new phenomenon, the artistic objector, the aesthetic philistine who opposes the innovatory in terms of the art of the past. Arthur Waugh, against whom the polemic is addressed, had tried to distinguish between 'nakedness' and 'nudity':[14] 'that universal standard of good taste that has from the days of Milo distinguished the naked from the nude.' Implicitly, at least, this escapes the utilitarian opposition by incorporating art within a totalized mode of seeing, and it is this that Crackanthorpe attacks in the name of productive excellence. In other words, he is concerned to expose the élite. Although it is right to see a break in the productive relations of literature in the 1860s, the concept of the artistic objector suggests that we must distinguish between kinds of break. On the one hand, Arnoldian Hellenism, which constantly makes application to the hegemony (as Swinburne put it, David, son of Goliath); on the other hand, the paganism of the aesthetic movement which demystifies art and sets it resolutely outside the walls. The break at this level is best studied through Pater's major confrontation with romanticism, the essay on Coleridge. For in that essay, the intelligentsia and the intellectual élite oppose one another not as knowledge and art but as the knowledge of art and the ideology of art.

The essay is usually cited as an example of modernist relativism, and relativism is very important to it, but not the liberalism of indecipherable pluralities. For Pater's relativism is linked again and again specifically to the positive method: 'The idea of the "relative" has been fecundated in modern times by the influence of the sciences of observation.'[15] And it is derived not from a helpless confrontation of idealism and empiricism (the rage for order whistling and smiling in the rich mess) but from an awareness of the material determinants of consciousness: 'The truth of these relations experience gives us; not the truth of eternal outlines effected once for all, but a world of fine gradations and subtly linked conditions, shifting intricately as we ourselves change'. It is not to a factitious totality that we resort to contest this: on the contrary 'to the intellect, to the critical spirit, these subtleties of effect are more precious than anything else'. To stress this is not necessary merely to rescue Pater from the capitulations of modernist ideology, but also to emphasize how much his theory of art depends not on a defensive élitism (the constitution of an abstract spirituality) but on an endorsement of the most advanced epistemology of his time. In fact, his critique of Coleridge's ideas bears a marked resemblance to Foucault's history of forms of knowledge.[16] The 'esemplastic power', for example, is seen to be more 'valid' because of the 'charm ... in the clear image' than because of its ability to 'bear a loyal induction'. In the realm of poetry, therefore, Coleridge struggles against the coming of the relative with an epistemology of signification which Foucault sees as characteristic of the Middle Ages and surviving as literature. Equally, however, Pater is sceptical about what Foucault would term an epistemology of representation: 'Ancient philosophy sought to arrest every object in an eternal outline, to fix thought in a necessary formula, and types of life in a classification by "kinds" or "genera".' Both ways of knowing, the connecting sign and the fixating table, are rejected in the name of an understanding of natural laws and determinants – the epistemology of nineteenth-century science. It is this positive sense that underlies the total rejection of any attempt to explain men's activities and consciousnesses by anything outside themselves and the historical determinants of their lives. The consequences for the theory of art are radical. Since there is no absolute, no expressive totality, art cannot embody any ideological function. Above all, it has to be disseevered from the romantic unity of art and the universe. Pater quotes Coleridge's famous comment on Shakespeare: 'The organic form is innate ... Such as the life is, such the form', and comments:

There 'the absolute' has been affirmed in the sphere of art; and thought begins to congeal. Coleridge has not only overstrained the elasticity of his hypothesis, but has also obscured the true interest of art. For after all, the artist has become something almost mechanical;

instead of being the most luminous and self-possessed phase of consciousness, the associative act itself looks like some process of assimilation. The work of art is sometimes likened to the living organism. That expresses the impression of a self-delighting, independent life which a finished work of art gives us; it does not express the process by which that work of art was produced.

It would be astonishing, if we didn't know the ideological necessity of it, that the notion of organic form has survived Pater's clear perception of its *mechanical* (i.e. in modern terms, *reified*) nature. But the passage not only points this out; it explains its persistence. Organic form expresses the *reader's* impression: that is, it explains an effect in the sphere of circulation (which Marx also termed 'realization') which precedes and follows the productive process. As in Marx, so in Pater, it is not a question of denying the phase of reception, but of not allowing the phase of production to be mystified out of existence. For it is production that creates value, and it is the historical determination of the mode of production which makes a work of art what it is. Coleridge thought beauty grew on trees, as capitalists think that money begets money. In the realm of theory, Pater accomplishes a demystification which would make it impossible for art to subserve the ideology that supports it. The most achieved moments of the decadence not only break with received ideas in ideological antithesis, but do so by affirming the productive source of value – I think primarily of Huysmans's railway engines, but also of a poem like *La Mélinite* where the mirror dislocates the dancer from the chorus, or Gray's *The Barber* where the produced beauty of the dream moves to an encounter with madness. Such texts are not mere antithesis, but make for a transition to the contradiction of the producer. If this is the case, why is it that a theoretical revolution in art, not merely analogous to, but also with the same consequences as, the theoretical political revolution – the affirmation of the productive source of value – remains a series of moments that are betrayed? An answer must be speculative. But it is possible to argue that as in politics, so in art, the exposure of ideology is insufficient to effect a revolution in practice because the base is not motivated by the superstructure. What Poggioli neglects, in his brilliant distinction between the intellectual élite and the intelligentsia, is that art has a very definite situation in the economic base. Significantly, Pater is housed in Oxford, but even he found it necessary to censor himself. The 'actual' relations of production, however, not only retain a capitalist form but intensify it. Or to be more precise, the economic practices of book production demand an ideological commitment that runs so counter to the theoretical demystification that the latter has to site itself, in order to survive, in an élite within the élite.

III

I can best stress the extremity of the contradiction between the base and the superstructure by considering the case of the Society of Authors. It is not merely that the progressive thrust of the decadence grows up within an increasing commercialization of the kind indicated by Q. D. Leavis. It is rather that a more complex market situation demands a more mystified ideology of literary production. The Society, by its very attempt to clarify and rationalize the relationship of the writer to the economic realization of his work, offers the most obvious example of this mystification.

Founded in 1883, the Society[17] reached a membership of nearly a thousand within a decade. It quickly gained prestige and respectability. Tennyson became its first president, and Meredith succeeded him; Collins, Reade and Yonge were among its first vice-presidents. The Lord Mayor of London gave it a banquet in its first year. Seeking to obtain greater legal recognition for literary property, and to place the relations between authors and publishers on a basis of 'equity and justice', its activities were diverse and coherent. It issued information on the technicalities of publishing and distribution, to enable its members to form a realistic view of the value of their work (e.g. S. Squire Sprigge's *The Methods of Publishing*, 1890, and *The Costs of Production*, 1891). It arranged three conferences in 1887 on the grievances between authors and publishers, and drafted bills to consolidate the law of copyright. From 1891, it had its own journal, *The Author*. In 1894, it took a formal decision to oppose the continuation of the three-decker novel, bound for the circulating libraries. In addition to public activities such as these, it acted as an advice bureau to authors, and eventually began its own literary agency. In short, it worked as an organization to give secure professional standing to an occupation riddled with amateurism, romantic vagueness and apparent unpredictability. It is not insignificant that it is founded in the era of the New Unionism, that movement to provide a structure of industrial relations to the casualized labour of the unskilled. Walter Besant, its leading figure, wrote novels about the working class, and was indeed the brother-in-law of Annie.

And yet to make that connection is to see immediately how little the organization of the casual intellectual has to do with that of the casual worker. For fundamentally it inverts the recognition of his productive role. The 'leading principles' of the society, according to a declaration of 1889, were:

First that literary property needs to be defined and protected by legislation, and the relations between author and publisher to be placed upon a basis of equity and justice. Secondly, that the question of copyright, especially between this country and America, is one which requires to be kept steadily in view and persistently attacked.[18]

Productive relations are thus made a function of the legal status of 'property', and this not only subordinates the concept of literary work, but even
of professional service. Writing becomes the creation of a property which
must not be 'used' without the owner receiving what he demands for it.
Sprigge, the Society's secretary, began his book with a chapter entitled
'Literary Property', and wrote of the literary work in terms which reveal
how far the mystification goes:

> A man's literary work is, though the fact is too often forgotten, his
> personal property, which he may use absolutely as he chooses, over
> which he alone has control, to sell, to lease, to lend or to give away. (p. 9)

In order to make the literary work a property, Sprigge has to postulate a
'use value' (may use as he chooses) which a moment's thought will show to
be non-existent. It is true that, as he says later, 'there is nothing illogical in
the author's wish to benefit by his work', but he can clearly only realize
this benefit by the exchange of his work as a commodity. He has no choice
therefore in the disposition of a thing (his manuscript) since the only value
this has is that of his objectified labour power, an objectification which
only has exchange value as the means of production of a book. Significantly, Sprigge does not imply that the author has, among his choices, the
power of witholding it from the process of production. The only 'choice'
he has is in the kind of contract he accepts. Of course, this is more variable
than the kind of choice open to all productive workers (because, unlike
them, he is able to work without the aid of the owners of the means of
production, though that is a useless privilege since without their aid
the work must remain unproductive). The mystification is not one that is
confined to Sprigge. Matthew Arnold, for example, in an essay on copyright, wrote that 'a man has a strong instinct making him seek to possess
what he has produced or acquired, to have it at his disposal'.[19] Production
and acquisition thus confer the same rights (and of course the copyright
issue, as it has to do not only with the remuneration of the writer, but also
with a value persisting beyond his death, is an index of the transfer of
the value created by work into the object as an innate property). John
Hollingshead spoke of the laws concerning dramatization explicitly in
terms of the laws protecting land-ownership,[20] and Wilkie Collins called
his article on American piracy 'Thou shalt not steal'. Thus, although
literature is the product of work, and although, in the realm of aesthetic
theory, the recognition of the productive role of the artist is the most
important advance, here, in the realm of the actual relations of production, literature is seen, by those who seek an equitable status for it, not as
a function of the productive process but as a property, protected by law,
which in effect acts as a barrier to capitalist investment by demanding a

kind of rent – in Marx's terms, a monopoly rent, subject only to the laws of demand. Clearly the Society would do little for the writer who had not the forces of the market to increase the exchange value of his commodity.

But the mystification goes much further. For since a literary manuscript is not really like a piece of land, it has to be regarded as well as an equivalent for money capital exacting interest. When George Smith (of Smith and Elder) produced a suggested pro-forma account sheet, he was taken to task by the *Law Journal* (which was quoted as authoritative by the Society) because he had included in the account a five per cent charge for the advance of the publisher's capital, as well as a charge for risking bad debts and offering discounts. These charges were invalid, the *Law Journal* argued, because the cash advanced, the risks taken, the incentives offered, constituted the publisher's investment in the partnership between himself and the author and so he had no right to charge for what he had only undertaken to do. In this argument, the manuscript becomes an equivalent for money capital, although its money value is not realizable until the actual money capital has set in motion the productive process which will convert the book into a consumable commodity. The manuscript is thus given a magical ability to operate in in the phase of circulation before it becomes a commodity. Besant was to take this illusion to amazing lengths in a lecture at one of the 1887 conferences entitled 'The Maintenance of Literary Property':

> What would be said in the City, if, when two men had agreed on sharing the profits of an enterprise, the one who kept the books were to make a secret profit for himself by setting down the expenses as greater than those actually incurred ...
> What would be said in the City, when two men went shares in an enterprise, should the one who did the active part refuse to let his accounts be examined? [21]

Not only has the point of reference become the centre of mercantile speculation, the City, but so mystified into 'investment' has literary work become that the writer is seen as a sleeping partner, the publisher as the only one who does the active part. It is true that these points are being made about a phase after the completion of the manuscript; but that that should be the centre of attention reveals how ill equipped the Society, and their supporters, were to see the capitalist production of books as the confrontation of capital and labour.

When Flaubert was in the midst of writing *Madame Bovary* (a text in which both author and protagonist are seen to produce the 'reality' they need to expose), he wrote to Louise Colet that he detested the French equivalent of the Society of Authors *'bédouin tant qu'il vous plaira; citoyen jamais'*.[22] He added that he would like to inscribe in front of his books that reproduction of them is permitted. The concept of a literary property right, the role of citizen in that sense, is precisely what forces what I have termed the 'decadent' writer into the desert of his own autonomy. In 1895, Gissing made the same complaint to Edouard Bertz: 'The extent to which novelists are becoming mere men of business is terrible.'[23] He blamed Besant for this, but he also went on to praise him 'for his efforts to improve the payment of authorship'. The whole contradiction of nineteenth-century authorship lies in these letters. For the writer is no longer faced with a simple market situation, as Byron and Scott and Dickens were. They could be professional writers by being capitalist writers. They made the market their works reflected. Once the writer is a producer – not the secretary of reality (nature or society) – he is confronted either with total isolation from the productive relations of his society, or the possibility of becoming the deviser of a form of capital. There is no way for his work to be integrated into the capitalist process. When Hardy was asked whether he thought that writers should receive national recognition, he replied, with characteristic irony:

> I daresay it would be very interesting … But I don't see how it could be successfully done. The highest flights of the pen are mostly the excursions and revelations of souls unreconciled to life, whilst the natural tendency of a government would be to encourage acquiescence to life as it is. However, I have not thought much about the matter.[24]

This shifts the discussion into another area, the relation between the writer and the state, but it is deeply bound up with the analysis we have been considering. For what Hardy is saying is that the writer by his very nature has to oppose ideology (that is, the apparatus for enabling the free subject to subject himself to 'reality'). We have seen how, on the one hand, this break is at the very centre of the progressive theory of art at the end of the century, and how although this most significantly expresses itself as the recognition of the productive role of the artist, the very form in which that productiveness has to realise itself is one which remystifies the literary process for a market economy. There is a real connection between Coleridge's organicist displacement of art into the realm of realization and Besant's spiriting away of the writer's work into an equivalent of money capital. We have to produce the state at this point because the way out of the difficulty in real terms is to re-organize the writer, not for the market, but for the institutions of social control, to make the work in other word's the means of production for another production, literary criticism. Hardy is relevant here because in his own practice he recognizes the contradiction of the decadent producer in its class implications.

IV

Jude the Obscure was published in 1895: the boom novel of the mid-nineties is Du Maurier's *Trilby*. *Trilby* is an appropriate context for Hardy's novel in the terms of this essay, not only because of its success, but also because it is about the nature of artistic success in itself; and it offers a clever version of what Crackanthorpe identified as aesthetic philistinism. The bohemian idyll, history of the lily bred of corrupt soil, of the artistic vision bred of unrequited love and resistance to 'philistine hate', is cleverly distanced, so that what in fact is a lucid portrayal of the conditions of artistic production is presented at once as something belonging to a world richer than the reader's (and author's) tame normality ('The present scribe is no snob. He is a respectably brought up old Briton of the higher middle class – at least he flatters himself so. And he writes for just such old philistines as himself'),[25] and at the same time as belonging to a very definite past and so placed as an adolescence ('and now having really cut our wisdom teeth': p. 447). So that if we are, like Billee's mother, incapable of entering that world, we can also love it, as she does Trilby, on its deathbed. It is a classic instance of the best-seller having it both ways: the world of value displaced into nostalgia and therefore enclosable within the 'real' world: the flower of the dunghill, in Renan's image, entering the drawing room on promise of an early death.

Nevertheless, Du Maurier is knowledgeable enough to understand that the Parisian world of art is more than a world of vision. If Billee's inspiration is a romantic memory that reproduces itself through him, as though his canvases had been made with Trilby's foot, the other version of art, that presented through Svengali, is that of beauty produced against nature. Honorine, whose voice is naturally talented, is ruined by his training: Trilby is tone deaf. The art that he trains in her is an art of acute transformation, of a trivial ditty made to bear tragic passion, of an impossible Chopin piano piece vocalized ('And there is not a sign of effort, of difficulty overcome': p. 318). To achieve this, Svengali has to make another Trilby – 'an unconscious Trilby of marble' (p. 441) – who reflects back 'as from a mirror' his own love of himself. Against this, Billee's 'old cosmic vision of the beauty and sadness of the world' (p. 311) is a tired romantic cliché, acceptable on precisely the same terms as Waugh's distinction between nakedness and nudity – 'all beauty is sexless in the eyes of the artist at his work' (p. 95).

It is, of course, precisely because Billee's sexless naturalism reflects the sad reality that it can be accommodated. Svengali, who changes his material through a productive process (significantly manifest as theatre), is evil, poor without pathos, a visitation destroying innocence. It is such a clever novel because Svengali's power is repressed in the story itself: it is only after the story is over, when Svengali has shown himself as destructive and is safely dead, that we actually learn about what he has been doing. So it never challenges the romanticism of Billee, and the Paris world can be forgiven in a vale of tears because the actual process of artistic production is placed as a strange gap within it. *Trilby* is the myth of aesthetic philistinism.

Hardy's novel, which is the very opposite kind of sensation from *Trilby*, can also be seen as its mirror image. For Jude is also an artist who tries to emerge from his utilitarian field to materialize his aesthetic image – the impression of a halo in the light of Christminster, the photograph of Sue. But, unlike Billee, this is no contained nostalgia, and, unlike Svengali, there is pathos in his poverty. The Jew is a deliberately contrived absence ('Nobody knew exactly how Svengali lived': p. 52), whereas Jude is at the very centre of his own experience, which is the novel itself so that the struggle to materialize a vision is not mystified. And Jude is no strange pariah, but a member of a class – 'the voice of the educated proletarian' as *The Saturday Review* put it (*Critical Heritage*, p. 83). The whole of the Christminster episode is the ordeal of Jude confronting his own proletarianization, knowing his real place according to the terribly sensible advice of the Master of Bibliol, but knowing also the reality of his productive role, as when he realizes that the mechanistic bits of reproduced masonry are probably no more factitious than the weather-worn originals, or when he recognizes the greater centrality of working-class Christminster. Equally the sexlessness of the beauty that he desires, the impenetrable walls of Christminster and Sue, is not a condition of his achievement but the annihilation of it.

A. J. Butler's review of *Jude* was entitled 'Mr Hardy as Decadent', and in the terms of this essay he was surely right. The decadence of the novel for him lay in its denial of the law which the earlier novels affirmed, and which is at 'the base of social existence',[26] that 'you can't have everything'. He rightly sees the novel as an explicit exposure of ideology itself (all the terribly sensible advice, the 'perception' of contradictory truths), seen in terms of what Althusser[27] has called 'the ideological couple' of the capitalist state, the family and education. The protagonist is not only displaced from the totality (the buried organic continuity of the brown field), but is forced by this both to seek to reconstitute it for himself as a secret mystery he can journey towards and to confront the implications of his failure (the grammar books foreshadow the whole process: the access to the privileged world of vision that they promise is replaced by the repressive insistence of the letter, a rote learning that will keep him in his place). The only access offered by the series of repositories of cultural value is that of emulation, repairing the crumbling masonry of its exclusivity. The aesthetic image, the hazy light in the distance, materializes itself only as denial. The nearest Jude gets to self-realization is modelling Christminster in cake. 'You can't have everything', the base of social existence, is denied because Jude in his obscurity cannot have anything that corresponds to that light.

The original notes for the novel were made in 1887, the scheme laid down in 1890, the detailed writing began in 1893. It can be no accident, surely, that the most vital work to emerge from Oxford in those years was that of Pater. *Marius* was·published in 1885; and not only does the syntax of Hardy's title (which is so unlike any of his previous titles) echo Pater's but Lionel Johnson's description of *Marius* (in a review of 1894) might also do as a description of *Jude*: 'Youth, confronting this very visible world, yet upon a quest for some interpretation, harmony, absolute truth, which should make the vision, if not beatific, yet somehow divine.'[28] Equally, the Conclusion to *The Renaissance* was restored in 1888, and it is surely this that is echoed in Hardy's preface: 'Like former productions of this pen, *Jude the Obscure* is simply an endeavour to give shape and coherence to a series of seemings, or personal impressions, the question of their consistency or their discordance, of their permanence or their transitoriness, being regarded as not of the first moment.' To give shape to impressions that have *in themselves* no shape or value – this is surely decadent production as we have defined it: the preface might almost have been written in defiance of Lionel Johnson's book. But not only is the organic coherence disavowed, and thus the novel programmatically disengaged with the totality, but it reflects a historical determinism. The serial version, of course, appeared in *Harper's New Monthly*, which in November 1893 printed Symons's 'Decadent Movement', in which he quotes a phrase of Ernst Hello's to define decadence which accounts for one dimension of Jude's obscurity: 'desire without light, curiosity without wisdom'. The novel is thus a 'decadent' production, and its protagonist the hero of a 'decadent' displacement. We find many incidental features of the decadence incorporated into the text: Jude's time-travelling appreciation of Christminster, Sue's paganism (she buys the statues of Apollo and Venus, and later declares that she is not modern but older than medievalism) and her androgyny, even her final retreat into ritualism, Father Time's Schopenhauerian pessimism ('the coming universal wish not to live'), the text's massive allusiveness, particularly the double quotation from the 'Hymn to Proserpine'. If, on the one hand, it is the first truly working-class novel in English (not the first novel about the working class, but the first to articulate a working-class voice), it is also this because it confronts the world of value with a decadent disaffection. In more than one way, Jude is of the white-collar proletariat.

And this is not merely a matter of portrayal. If Jude's dream is materialized as an excluding totality, he has also the possibility, which is the basis of decadent art, of producing that dream as an opposing materiality. Where he returns to Christminster, Sue tries to remind him that it has done nothing for him, but he replies that 'it is the centre of the universe to me because of my early dream'. What we have in the last section is not a helpless spectatorship but a theatrical production of the ironies and dislocations. Jude in this sense is outside his own predicament. He enjoys the irony of living in Mildew Lane; he announces his failure and celebrates it in a speech to the Christminster crowd. And if Father Time theatricalizes his superfluity by suicide, and Sue theatricalizes her theoretic unconventionality by mortifying the flesh, Jude, who may seem to take another decadent way out by getting drunk, goes further by reciting Job to an audience that cannot hear him, bent on cheering the festivities. More than this, however, that last section is not only Jude's theatre (ultimately the mirror theatre, opposed to the audience like *La Mélinite*), but Hardy's too: his farewell to the novel, that 'scientific game' whose organic realism his text despises. For here, in this last part of the last novel, his most offensive assaults on the reader's credulity, particularly the grotesque joke of Father Time's death, are made. The proletarian hero and the literary producer make an alliance to affirm their autonomy, but in order to do so take their place in a cultural struggle. For true autonomy, the completeness of dislocation, cannot rest content with an independence.

V

Hardy's novel offers a perspective on the whole situation of the writer in the late nineteenth century, and it also marks a point beyond which it would be necessary to make literary production revolutionary in more than an *analogous* way. That point is never moved beyond. Henley, Gray, Davidson and Symons all in their way shared Jude's obscurity and the best of their work stands opposed, as form of production, to the hegemony. But none of them cross the barrier reached in *Jude* – on the contrary, for all of them there is an expressive totality – Imperialism, Catholicism, vitalism, mysticism – in which to take refuge. More importantly, the journey from decadence to modernism, is no road forward. On the contrary, the way out of literary production and its contradictory identity, is literature – the text for an ideological practice, education, the training of the agents of social control. Let me end by suggesting the way this happens in a seminal work such as Symons's book, *The Symbolist Movement in Literature*.

Most critics would agree that this text represents a radical development in Symons's world that can best be expressed by saying that he got to know Yeats.[29] It may be less acceptable to assert that this development represents more of a loss than a gain. 'The Decadent Movement in Literature' really has the sense of a movement, a sense of a new phase of consciousness embodied in various, but related forms. By the time 'symbolism' has come to replace 'Decadence' as the comprehensive word, this sense of a movement, the change in the relations of literary production signalled by the word 'revolt', is dissolved in a vaguer assertion of continuity –

all poetry is symbolic, symbolism is merely the self-consciousness of the symbol. The key concept is no longer revolt but 'ancient lights'. In 'The Autumn of the Body' (1898), Yeats had seen the decadence as a faint light on a transcendent world denied by positive science: it was in other words a seasonal return to an abstract spirituality. Symons hovers uneasily between this – which is affirmed by the overall argument, beginning as it does with Carlyle's organicist definitions of the symbol and reaching a climax with the essay on Maeterlinck with its blurring of the lines between symbolism and mysticism – and a residual grasp of the specific new movement. This latter feeling emerges, for example, in the realization of the cult of the actress and its implications in Nerval, of the strategic pose of aristocracy in Adam, of the function of travesty in Laforgue and above all of the programmatic and *logical* research of Mallarmé. All these points recognize the specific productive nature of Symbolism, whereas the presence of mysticism, the assertion of the eternal quality of symbolism, together with the sentimentalization of Verlaine (the poet as child) and the total failure to come to terms with Rimbaud, all these have to do not with the production of the symbol but with the realization of the symbolic as the sign of an expressive totality, 'the once terrifying eternity of things about us' (p. 95). Thus, in however bizarre a way, Symbolism becomes not a movement, but a Romantic continuity. Symons travels an inverse journey from Jude. Beginning with the recognition of the separation of the producer, the need for him to produce his own revolt, he comes to rest in the aesthetic image as vision: 'We find a new, an older sense in the so worn out forms of things' (p. 74). It is because Symbolism came to England not as the making of new forms, but as a new light on an organic, if occult, tradition that modernism could site itself within the ideology. We could pinpoint the whole issue by reminding ourselves that Symons has to write off Baudelaire, and when Eliot comes to embrace him it is merely as the ideologue of damnation.

Symbolist – symbolic; aesthetic – occult; autonomy – abstract spirituality. These are the terms of the transition, but they constitute a reversal – the dislocation becomes a relocation; Of course, such terms only locate an ambiguity. No one would want to claim, for example, that Yeats makes himself the scribe of a vision: on the contrary, he invents a vision to provide material for production. But ambiguity, irony, mask, if they make for an exposed margin, and enable us to treat modernist writers as secret agents in the enemy camp, also form part of the specific condition of the insertion of the writer in that camp. I have argued that aesthetic theory, which is above all a theory of production, is in contradiction with the ideology demanded by the market, an ideology necessarily of realization in which literary work becomes capital. But we must go further. With very few exceptions (the major instance is Bennett) there is no way back into the market for the writer, but there is a back road through the occult, an expressive totality which, however eccentric, can oppose itself to positivism (I think of Eliot and Bradley, Lawrence and Haeckel, Joyce and Aquinas as well as Yeats and Swedenborg), can become independent (because it is a thousand miles away from capitalism) but not autonomous (because like capitalist ideology it reflects the transcendent creation of value, whether through the Golden Dawn, tradition or the phallic consciousness). And this back road leads to the University which neither Jude nor Symons entered, and of which Pater, though he worked within it, saw the walls (see *Emerald Uthwart*). It makes possible, that is, literature at the point beyond which literary production must confront the terms of its possibility. Yeats's flirtation with Gentile is not a local event – it represents the claim of the writer on the hegemony to be housed within its institutions as an abstract spirituality whose coherence mirrors the mysteries of the capitalist state, opposed to science, to historical relativity, to, in the end, literary production. If we have to demystify literature, to rescue it from its role as realizable value, the constant capital of critical practice, we must begin by recognizing that it expelled itself from the market not, in the first instance, to enter the cloister, but to expose the market and its bases. The tragic generation lived, to be sure, in an age of transition, but that they lacked coherence is not their limitation but their very potentiality, for it is a transition, not to modernism, but to the new forms that wait to be made.

Methodological Note

This paper has been usefully criticized on two grounds, both of which relate to its apparent Althusserianism. I don't think I am an Althusserian, and though I borrow ideas both from Althusser and Macherey it is because I find them useful for specific purposes. This is not eclectic: the sources for a materialist account of literature are, I believe, Benjamin (and to some extent Brecht) and Gramsci. Althusser and Macherey seem to me to be elaborating a theology based largely on a system of analogies. But I think that to deny their contribution of usable vocabularies and unavoidable negations is foolish.

The first ground of criticism is of my use of the term 'production'. The point is made that I use the term in three different ways – as a concept of aesthetic theory, as a material fact (the production of books as commodities) and as a form of generalized social description (the mode of production which Jude encounters). The connections between these levels are not made clear. I hope I have improved the matter a little by deleting from my text any suggestion of a fourth use, 'ideological production'. This term seems to me to be entirely analogical: education and 'communication' are not 'productive' except peripherally though their forms are determined (in a highly complex way) by the demands of a mode of production (the need of a class domination, the need of managerial and bureaucratic supervision of developed phases, etc.). The literary text, however, is different. What differentiates a poet or a novelist from other types of intellectual is precisely that he makes an object which can be consumed. You can be an intellectual without producing a book: but a poem is not written until it is written, and does not function until it is readable. Therefore, although the connection between a Paterian sense of production and the actual production of commodities is difficult (that is precisely the subject of this essay), it has to be made. I wrote this essay precisely to find a concrete way of elaborating the problems of that connection. Furthermore, in any mode of production, except one in which there is no surplus, or possibly in which the surplus is consumed by the producers (this is not so impossible as it might appear), there will be many non-productive people, and their social membership will be defined precisely by the manner of their non-productiveness, that is, their relations to the mode of production. Priests, professors and prostitutes, in Marx's phrase, are all consumers of an appropriated surplus, but if they had no function then they either would not exist, or their existence would not have to depend on their specific roles (they could simply be consumers). Writers belong to that category precisely by making certain objects which are seen to have a use value. The whole problem is historically specific, because it is not until the development of a literary market, in which the writer can insert himself into society as the producer of *commodities* (that is, use values that are distributed as exchange values, that realize themselves ultimately as the universal value, money) that the literary text as a production, as the object of a determinate productive process, becomes truly visible. As Marx points out in *Theories of Surplus Value*, Milton produced *Paradise Lost* not really for £5 but as a silkworm 'produces' silk. But the form and tendency of that poem is not natural all the same: it is generated by the social situation of the writer who *works* at it. So there is a gap between the writer's activity (which resembles productive labour) and his effectivity (which lies outside the actual mode of production). As soon as the market becomes dominant, it is possible to make an equivalent between a writer and a piece of cheese: *The Corsair* equals *x* pounds of cheese in a way that, in its time, *Paradise Lost* did not equal it. Once you have the concept of the text as commodity, the question of its use value then becomes crucial since the gap opens up between use value (measurable by its necessary labour) and its exchange value. Baudelaire, Flaubert and Pater, among others, are so important because the problems they expose are not merely abstract. From them, any theory of literature which is not ideological has to begin. There is then every need to relate the theory of production to the actual relations of production within a social totality, the mode of production. The present essay only tries to get to the problematic that faces us. This problem is interestingly treated by

Nicole Gueunier in 'La Production Littéraire: Métaphore, Concept ou Champ Problématique', in *Littérature* 13.

The second criticism was of my use of 'expressive totality'. It is argued that I merely oppose to this a negation: the break-up of totalities. Obviously this is partly the limitation of the decadent movement. But I am trying to argue that behind such an antithesis is an attempt to make a totality which is not expressive but effective. The expressive totalities opposed by decadent art the mystified systems that lie beyond it: but the displacing mirror of decadent art has itself as a total commitment, and in *Jude*, at least, tries to relate that commitment to the possibilities of a more advanced mode of production. I see the decadence as leading not to Dada or mere self-consciousness, but to the possibilities of proletarian art, Tatlin's dream and Brecht's theatre. This probably seems wayward, but I have the example of Benjamin, and Trotsky's attack on the Futurists ends with seeing it as 'a necessary link'.

Notes

1. Yeats, *Autobiographies* (1956), p. 304.
2. Eagleton, 'Ideology and Literary Form', *New Left Review* 90, pp. 81–109.
3. Sartre, *What is Literature* (1950), p. 108.
4. Kermode, *Modern Essays* (1971), p. 71.
5. Poggioli, *The Theory of the Avant-Garde* (New York, 1971), p. 12.
6. Benjamin, *Charles Baudelaire: A Lyric Poet in the Era of High Capitalism* (1973), p. 104.
7. Balibar and Macherey, 'Sur la Littérature comme Forme Idéologique – Quelques Hypothèses Marxistes', *Littérature* 13 (Février 1974), pp. 29–48.
8. Crackenthorpe, 'Reticence in Literature', *Yellow Book*, Vol. I, 1894, p. 266.
9. Symons, *Studies in Prose and Verse* (1904), p. 149.
10. Le Gallienne, *Retrospective Reviews*, Vol. I, pp. 24–5.
11. Johnson, *The Art of Thomas Hardy* (1923), p. 2.
12. Ellis, 'Huysmans', reprinted in Stanford, *Critics of the Nineties* (1970), pp. 142–71.
13. Symons, 'The Decadent Movement in Literature' in Beckson, *Aesthetes and Decadents of the 1890's* (New York, 1966). p. 137. I have used this text because it is based on the magazine version of 1893.
14. Waugh, 'Reticence in Literature', *Yellow Book*, Vol. I (1894), p. 218. The whole essay is an example of the kinds of arguments against decadence that I have been discussing. Unity, tradition, restraint are its keynotes.
15. Pater, *Essays on Literature and Art*, edited by Jennifer Uglow (1973), p. 2.
16. See Michel Foucault, *The Order of Things* (1970).
17. The most accessible source on the Society's history is Walter Besant's *Autobiography* (1902), Chapter XII (written in 1892).
18. Reprinted in Sprigge, *Methods of Publishing* (1890), p. 113. The declaration reveals that subscriptions were a guinea a year, that the Secretary was

available for advice Monday–Friday, and that among the council members were Edward Arnold, Alfred Austin, Augustine Birrel, R. D. Blackmore, Edward Clodd, Marion Crawford, Edmund Gosse, Rider Haggard, Hardy, Meredith, G. A. Sala, H. D. Traill and Edmund Yates. Haggard and Gosse were on the Committee of Management.

19. Arnold, *English Literature and Irish Politics*, ed. Super (Ann Arbor, 1973), p. 118.

20. *Grievances between Authors and Publishers* (1887), p. 94.

21. *Ibid.*, p. 25.

22. Flaubert, *Correspondance*, 4e Série, p. 17.

23. Gissing, *The Letters of George Gissing to Edouard Berz*, ed. Young (1961), p. 204.

24. Hardy, *Life of Thomas Hardy* (1965), p. 240. The question was put to him by Robertson Nicoll in November 1891.

25. Du Maurier, *Trilby* (1896), pp. 151–2.

26. Cox, *Thomas Hardy, The Critical Heritage*, p. 287.

27. See 'On The Reproduction of the Relations of Production' in *Lenin and Philosophy* (1972).

28. Johnson, *Post Liminun* (1911), p. 26.

29. See the excellent essay by Richard Ellmann, 'Discovering Symbolism', *Golden Codgers* (1973), pp. 101–12. Reference to Symons's book is to the edition introduced by Ellman (New York, 1958).

CHAPTER 15

Writing Beyond the End

'Even the New is historical'.[1]

Introduction

One reason, surely, why there was a fin de siècle at all is because the only end in sight was calendrical. The cataclysmic possibilities of the mid-century passed by, and a strong discourse of social evolution seemed to have all the terms of debate within its grasp. The Commune left Third Republican France hardly less bourgeois than the Second Empire; the Civil War did not make reconstructed America any more egalitarian; Reform Acts did not damage the class fences of Britain, and Prussia had Bismarck. In the immediate perspective of the nervous eighties Britain, which promised some turmoil in mid-decade, went through the pain barrier of a mass strike without the power structure falling apart, and Americans felt more threatened by 'new fortunes' than 'anarchists'. The dominant capitalist structure must have looked as though it was here to stay: history, one might have thought in 1890 as well as 1990, was over.

Of course, this would turn out to be delusion within a generation. But if the dominant structure filled you with anxiety or despair, you might need to excavate a distant end to reinstitute diachronicity in a world seemingly in place. Degeneration is one such teleology. There is also an upsurge of social dreams proposing a better future but having much in common with the darker prophesies.

To call them 'Utopias' is to throw them into a taxonomic black-hole which will only be necessary because William Morris raises that term for good strategic reasons when opposing his own vision of the future to that of the American social democratic prophet, Edward Bellamy. For what characterises them, as A. L. Morton, in his pioneering study, noted, is not their alternative geography but time travelling.[2] The major narratives are positively not nowhere. Richard Jefferies' *After London*, W. H. Hudson's *A Crystal Age*, Bellamy's *Looking Backward*, and Morris's *News from Nowhere* are recognisably the place of the present transformed. Morton explains it externally, so that the filling up of the map makes it necessary to find new narrative machinery. But it is not true that the map was filled up, as *Heart of Darkness* will make clear, and 'place utopias' return in the twentieth

355

century as Charlotte Perkins Gilman's *Herland* and, in effect, H. G. Wells's *Men Like Gods* indicate. The time-travelling texts of the late century have transition rather than the more centrally utopian contrast as the narrative motivation.

But it is not simply, I think, because of the arrival of historicity, as Frederic Jameson argues.[3] Although Bulwer Lytton's *The Coming Race* (1872) is spatial (the coming race is underground), its title ambiguously foreshadows later proleptic preoccupations. On the one hand, its social state contrives 'to harmonise into one system ... the ideals of a Utopian future'[4] but, on the other, 'a thousand of the best and most philosophical of human beings ... would either die of ennui, or attempt some revolution' (p. 230). Although human, their evolution has made them a different species. Nevertheless when they emerge into the sunlight, they will be 'our inevitable destroyers' (p. 248) because of their anti-individualist perfectionism. As Raymond Williams shrewdly points out, the coming race bears all the marks, literal and metaphoric, of Arnoldian culture.[5] But what really makes its members alien is that the female is dominant morally and physically. The discourse is of natural not social history: evolution, shadowed perhaps, as George Levine shows, as marking the ideology of scientism in general, by its seeming contradiction, by the second law of thermodynamics.[6] This text sets a biologistic agenda which only Morris, and only by strenuously managed aesthetic strategy, contests.

Thus the neutralisation effect elaborated by Jameson[7] does not stand opposite mythic complexity (as it does in spatial utopias) but has to be unravelled from within the mythic given (all the more so since evolutionary plots obviously identify themselves as natural law). So that they become the other side of the coin of the fitness/degeneration discourse – take their origin in it, as we shall see.

Not only are they contrasted with the utopia properly speaking (that is, 'islands and trenches') but also with utopianism as Marx and Engels discuss it. Saint-Simon, Fourier and Owen are said to superimpose a future on a present which will be unproblematically transformed once humanity sees reason.[8] Our texts look to the future for relief, evolution from or overthrow of the present. Like the degeneration discourses they mirror, they try to confer diachronicity on a closed synchronic model – the modern city, globalised as Empire – must be presented not as future, but as future perfect, specifically not as 'no-place' but as the present visibly transformed. The transformation then must be seen to be immanent, an already completed growth waiting to unfold.

Morris, taking a slight enough cue from Lytton, raises for good tactical reasons, the spectre of utopia around these texts which do not offer themselves as political critiques of the present but as forecasts of a future generated either by catastrophe or evolution. Of course, they are inevitably readings of the present, but there is a certain repression in the project which confers determinacy as a mask on desirability. If this seems to be, as it is, an aggressively assertive strategy by writers who are conscious of their marginalisation, it also leaves room for ambiguity. If you translate what should be into what will be, you leave open the prospect of it turning out to be far from desirable. That is why we need to begin with a text clearly not utopic, *After London*, which announces the possibility of recuperation from catastrophe. After considering two writers who follow directly in its wake, I will then try to show that evolutionary utopia is not less grounded in the degenerative present, so that we can see more clearly how *News from Nowhere* separates itself from both by a precise articulation of a conditionality the time travelling utopias refuse.

After London and After: Jefferies, Carpenter

After London appeared in 1885 and Morris, writing, as it happens, from Milnthorpe, the home of Edward Carpenter, responded strongly to it. 'Absurd hopes curled round my heart as I read it,' he wrote.[9] It is a highly reactionary text, with Felix Aquila becoming a strange Arnoldian King Arthur to regenerate the race by leading a tribe of shepherds, resembling the gens of Morgan and Engels. But it also establishes the possibility of an anarchist agenda. The primary image, that of a London submerged under a swamp of its own cloacal excess leaves open the possibility of a recuperative utopia. Alienated from the barbarism of the residual feudalism, Felix seeks his fortune as a mercenary in a city of double identity, and double entrance where he unknowingly dines with a slave: 'Should he adhere to the ancient prejudice, the ancient exclusiveness of his class, or should he boldly follow the dictate of his mind?'[10] After this, and after rising and falling in arbitrary fashion in the military camp, he is morally equipped to engage with the swamp of modern civilisation: 'he had penetrated into the midst of that dreadful place, of which he had heard many a tradition: how the earth was poison, the water poison, the air poison, the very light of heaven falling through such an atmosphere poison' (p. 206).

This is both history of the future and analogy. Future London is also 'darkest London', the swamp is an ecological disaster and a metaphor for the moral degradation of a divided society proleptically announced by the double world of the unnamed paradigmatic 'city'. 'The relapse into barbarism' with which the story opens is thus finally understood not only to be the residual world of the future, but the Arnoldian barbarity of the contemporary English aristocracy who abhor reading and the intellectual life.

Escaping the evil of the swamp is 'like awaking in Paradise' (p. 211). Roger Ebbatson rightly points out that the novel returns from acute pessimism to a subdued hope for renewal which makes comparison with *News from Nowhere* relevant.[11] Felix comes upon a tribe of shepherds, uncontaminated primitives to whom he brings know-how, protection and the possibility of a new kingship. He goes to claim the bride his earlier discontent kept from him, and though the story ends inconclusively we are certainly invited to think that a new reborn feudalism will be built. Morris's 'absurd hope' is of a civilisation destroyed, 'the game played out' taking the text's licence to opt out of this specific closure. By the time he comes to write *News from Nowhere* he will have written *A Dream of John Ball*, which fully historicises the medieval world, and so enables him to portray any change as political.

Jefferies' novel opens up the possibility of a reactionary utopia, however, as W. H. Hudson's *A Crystal Age* (1887) shows. This bizarre, neurotic text is by no means the innocent idyll that both Jameson and Darko Suvin say it is.[12] Hudson himself seems to have thought it a utopian project because in the preface to an edition of 1906, he writes that we cannot help asking one another, 'What is your dream – your ideal. What is your *News from Nowhere*?'[13] Moreover, with its combination of the most negative ideas of Arnold and Schopenhauer, it fits a precise enough ideological position which in representational fiction is visible in Mallock, Gissing and James.[14] Gissing, recording his first meeting with Hudson (with whom he became good friends) in 1889 described him in his diary as 'the man I have wished to see for two or three years'.[15] Later, Lewis Mumford, proponent of organic community theories, regarded it as important.[16]

Hudson is vaguer about the catastrophe than Jefferies. Smith, the protagonist who falls off a cliff and wakes into an unrecognisable future world, only knows at the end that there has been 'a sort of Savanarola bonfire' which has destroyed everything valued in modern civilisation. But the causes of the change are inwardly present in that civilisation, echoing both Arnold's 'strange disease of modern life' and the spiritual landscape encountered by Browning's Childe Roland: 'In the wilderness of every man's soul was not a voice crying out prophesying the end?' (p. 294). The father who governs the crystal age says that in the past knowledge was sought without asking whether it was for good or evil. Civilised men were like shipwrecked men, drinking sea water that drove them mad until 'they hoped by knowledge to possess absolute dominion over nature, thereby taking from the father of the world his prerogative.' Worms bred in the corrupted flesh of these men flew from body to body, filling 'the race of men in all places with corruption and decay' (pp. 78–80). The processes of scientific progress are thus also the processes of degeneration.

The survivors do not return to nature but create a society focused on patriarchy and the sacred space of the great house, 'for the house is the image of the world and we that live within it are the image of the Father who made us', the earthly father says, and although in the irrational world 'there reigns perpetual strife and bloodshed, the strong devouring the weak and incapable' and this is necessary for renewal, man who has reason does not slay and is therefore respected by the animals who serve him. It comes as no surprise to learn later that the protagonist had been a self-proclaimed Philistine who is now encountering sweetness and light (p. 248) or that the distinguishing mark of the different houses in the crystal age is their excellence in specific arts. Reason is not rationality but making the will of God prevail. The age is crystal because it reflects the Father, the phallocentric heaven on earth.

But the most important effect of reason is to liberate mankind from sexual desire. The whole story is concerned with Smith's erotic passion for the daughter of the house, who can only return angelic affection. Reproduction has been dissevered from normal human relationships and confined to the single selected father and a mother who thereby sacrifices her own happiness for the sake of prolonging the race. Hudson later made it clear that this was the key to his novel. 'The sexual passion is the central thought in the Crystal Age,' he wrote in 1917, 'the idea that there is no millennium, no rest no perpetual peace till that fury has burnt itself out.' [17] Smith's final dream of happiness is to possess 'the secret of that passionless, everlasting calm of beings who had forever outlived and left as immeasurably far behind as the instincts of the wolf and the ape the strongest emotion of which my heart was capable' (p. 302).

Sexual love is a nightmare from which he has to try to escape. He only does this through dying, though ironically it is at the moment at which his devotion is to be rewarded by selection for siring the new mother. Schopenhauer joins company with Arnold, and the strange rainbow lily which is the treasured flower of the new age 'comes when most flowers are dead, or have their bright colours tarnished' (p. 163). Nature is only present at an aesthetic distance. It is not surprising that Gissing was anxious to meet him.

Hudson's utopia works primarily because it is Malthusian (birth control is a major issue in the eighties). The mother of the house argues that if all women were equal and therefore had the right to motherhood, they would give birth to degenerates. The passionless calm not only frees the individual from his drives, it frees humanity from its self-destructive growth. When Smith tries to explain his individuating love for Yoletta by her beauty, she asks 'are not all people beautiful?' He thinks 'of certain London types, especially among the "criminal classes", and of the old women with withered simian faces and wearing shawls, slinking in or out of public-houses at the street corners; and also of some people of a better class I had known personally ... and I felt that I could not agree with her' (p. 95). Later it is clear that not only has the working class been eliminated, but so have the savages to whose condition the excesses of civilisation drive its members back. Impressed with the number of birds, Smith reflects that in the new world:

On this bright sunny morning I was amazed at the multitudes I saw during my walk: yet it was not strange that birds were so abundant considering that there were no longer any savages on the earth, with nothing to amuse their vacant minds except killing the feathered creatures with their bows and arrows, and no innumerable company of squaws clamorous for trophies – unchristian women with painted faces, insolence in their eyes, and for ornaments the feathered skins torn from slain birds on their heads. (p. 289)

Darkest London and the jungle are both cleaned away. The hysteria would be funny did it not echo the real life exterminism practised by the white races with such vigour throughout the world at the end of the nineteenth century. He has finally to renounce the passion of love itself which 'was so much in man's life ... but in that over-populated world, it divided the empire of his soul with a great ever-growing misery – the misery of the hungry ones whose minds were darkened, through long years of decadence, with a sullen rage against God and man' (p. 307). Hudson's perfected world is a specific neutralisation, but, of course, because it is in the future, the neutralisation is self-begotten.

The most immediate response to this reactionary teleology is to accept it and turn it into a positive, which is what Edward Carpenter does. Carpenter is undoubtedly underestimated as a writer[18] who from the start of the eighties was trying to construct an epic vision of triumphant democracy which is more often than sometimes allowed stunningly vivid (though there are portions too where it seems more stunned than stunning). 'Sunday Morning near a Manufacturing Town', in the second part of *Towards Democracy*, is a fine example of balance between observation and hope. But there is always uncertainty about the source of that hope. Is it something humanity strives for in history or is it already folded within the material limits of the present?

Civilisation: Its Cause and Cure and the third part of *Towards Democracy*, 'After Civilisation', appear in 1889 and 1892 respectively, immediately before and after the appearance of *News from Nowhere*. 'Civilisation' situates itself at the heart of the fitness discourse, as William Greenslade describes it,[19] by invoking with horror Kay Robinson's prediction that the future human will be without hair or teeth or toes, because it will not need such things. It specifically locates physical and mental disease as the product of civilisation. Disease is a loss of unity with self, with nature, with our fellow men, and it starts with civilisation which is the institution of property destroying the gens as a society of equals. Motheright is replaced by women as property of men; we become '*nations policies*'.[20]

Carpenter is explicitly drawing on Morgan and Engels, but he provides a psychic/cultural emphasis, citing Morgan's description of the arrival of writing as a sign that the fall of man is through self-consciousness. There is no possibility of recursion, however. Man has to face the frightful struggle of self-consciousness to know the true self from the fleeting. To realise health he must go through disease. Property must literally be corrupted, broken up. 'And how can we', he asks, deploying a vocabulary familiar from the degenerative discourse, 'gulfed as we are in this present *whirlpool* conceive rightly the glory which awaits us?' (p. 35, my emphasis). The lost Eden turns out only to be a model for the future. The process is inevitable: 'While for the first time in History, Civilisation is practically continuous over the globe, now also for the first time can we descry forming in continuous line within its very structure, the forces which are destined to destroy it and to bring about the new order.'

On the one hand all we have to do is take off our clothes (clothing of the soul, clothing of the body, housing of the self) because to rise we need to be naked, on the other hand 'the forces destined to destroy' civilisation are capable of leading Carpenter into the witness-box on behalf of the Walsall anarchists in 1892 who were victims of *agents provocateurs*.[21] This slippage from natural process to anarchic gesture is effected by the concept of exfoliation, invoked in the 1887 text *England's Ideal*: 'Think what a commotion there must be within the bud when the petals of a rose are forming! Think what arguments, what divisions, what recriminations, even among the atoms!' It is not difficult to see why Morris should want to distance himself from this sugary Jekyll and manipulable Hyde position, or why Carpenter should have exercised a surely ideologically disastrous influence on D. H. Lawrence. The question of agency is balked: 'How can such morality be spread? How does a plant grow? It *grows*.'[22]

Linked to this is the hazy relationship between collective and individual self-transformation. This is not a contradiction in Carpenter's theoretical position whose whole importance, as Sheila Rowbotham makes clear,[23] is that he tried to hold together personal and political wholeness, which he elaborates in 'A Note on *Towards Democracy*' in *The Labour Prophet* in 1894. It is in the transformation of the theory into action that the slippage appears and is manifest therefore in his written practice.[24] 'After Civilisation' begins with a revolutionary messenger, Lord Demos, but as it progresses becomes more and more concerned with personal deliverance, its vigorous politics subsumed in transcendental salvationism, a classic instance of the substitution of the body for the economy. At the beginning of the poem, the message is social, but by the end we are not so sure. The poem closes with meditations about suffering and death and finally offers itself as an empty house which the reader is encouraged to enter but only to go back and set his own house in order, and abandon it: 'then come thou forth to where I wait for thee'.[25]

Reading *Towards Democracy* is exhilarating and that is certainly its intended effect, but you end up feeling unsure about what you are to do with this exhilaration. Carpenter did not know, that is sure, and lived in an increasingly marginalised position. His vision is not merely recuperative as Jefferies' vague ending is, and it does not collapse back into despair like Hudson's. But if even the arguments lie folded in the atomic structure, there seems to be no need to take responsibility for action. For all the power of his writing, Carpenter has to be classed with a future writing that does not insist on making a difference, that offers a future that already lies buried in the present. We will see this if we can see that the apparently opposite evolutionary writing of Bellamy shares with catastrophism and exfoliation, a single ideological embarkation point.

Looking Backward and Waking Up

In his dismissive review of Morris 's last work Wells, referring to the mid-eighties, writes of the huge mass of feeling that Henry George and Bellamy helped to shape.[26] *Looking Backward* is the immediate provocation for *News from Nowhere* although its influence is hard to determine because of its resemblance to but distinction from the Fabians (the American edition of whose essays Bellamy was asked to introduce). But its sales were huge in Britain, and it had some notable converts, including A. R. Wallace, Darwin's co-evolutionist, and Ebenezer Howard, father of the garden city.[27]

It promises the settlement of the industrial question without the abandonment of industrial methods (on the contrary, social equality is the result of higher industrial development) and without violence (the followers of the red flag are regarded as the hirelings of conservatism). The sphinx's riddle of the nineteenth century, its sleeping hero is told shortly after waking up in 2000, 'may be said to have solved itself. The solution came as the result of a process of industrial revolution which could not have terminated otherwise. All that society had to do was to recognise and co-operate with that evolution when its tendency had become unmistakable.'[28] This basically happens when the concentration of capital becomes tyrannical but results in a prodigious increase of efficiency. The epoch of trusts ends in The Great Trust. Not surprisingly, this is a world of mail-order shopping, piped music, the credit card and early retirement, to which *Equality* (its sequel, 1897) adds postmodernist fashion and the heritage industry, which preserves 'a rookery as hygienic warning'.[29]

It is both very like and unlike Utopian Socialism as Marx and Engels discussed it. On the one hand it is an imposed solution, an 'organisation of society' which replaces 'the gradual spontaneous class organisation of the proletariat'.[30] On the other hand it is not, like classical Utopianism, 'critical'. It keeps saying that however oppressive society is, it is only because it does not see itself correctly. On the contrary, it explicitly states that the greed of the rich played no real part in this oppression: 'The folly of men, not their hard heartedness, was the great cause of the world's poverty' (p. 238).

Central to this is the idea, explicitly absent in the texts I've just discussed, that no change is required in human nature to bring this about. Twice Julian West, the time traveller from the nineteenth century who narrates *Looking Backward* and *Equality*, says that human nature must have changed for nationalisation to have taken place without corruption, but this is strongly denied. It turns out here that the national organisation is simply based on 'the principal of military service' (p. 49). Later, on wage differentials and incentives, West is told that there are more honourable incentives (the admiration of women is one). Individuals are socialised by 'a codification of the law of nature – the edict of Eden ... the operation of human nature under rational conditions' (p. 86). Among them are 'a complex mutual dependence' as 'a universal rule' (p. 97) and 'untrammelled sexual selection' (p. 196).

What underwrites this rationality, however, is a 'moral contrast'. At the end of the book a broadcast sermon elaborates this and shows that the target on the novel is the worried cultured man who, in imagery reminiscent of Jefferies and Hudson and of the urban degeneration discourse, is compared to 'one up to the neck in a nauseous bog solacing himself with a smelling bottle' (p. 162). The sermon rehearses a number of images which plug into the dominant critical discourse. The story of the Black Hole of Calcutta is taken to be 'a striking type of the society of their age' (p. 204). Since the prevailing view of the nineteenth century is that the anti-social and not the social qualities of men furnished the cohesive force of society, intellectuals suffered from 'profound pessimism', decay of religious belief ('pale and watery gleams, from skies thickly veiled by doubt and dread', p. 206) and 'conservatism of despair' (p. 207). Only after the most bloodless of revolutions had made the nation the sole capitalist did 'the depraved tendencies, which had previously overgrown and obscured the better to so large an extent ... [wither] like cellar fungi in the open air' (p. 209). The preacher goes on to compare humanity to 'a rosebush planted in a swamp, watered with black bog water, breathing miasmatic fogs by day, and chilled with poison dews at night'. Regular gardeners claim that it is ineradicably tainted. Some try to claim that it was good for the bush to struggle and might even be improving. Finally (for no obvious reason) those who had been suggesting that it should be transplanted are listened to. Humanity, to change the metaphor, has burst the chrysalis. These metaphors are striking because they make no appeal to the rosebush itself, only to its gardeners and non-gardeners, and they deploy the discourse of that gardening.

After this, West wakes up in the nineteenth century. In the rookeries of Boston he finds leering girls with brows of brass, children like starving bands of mongrel curs, dwellers in Inferno. But because of his dream of reason, he sees, as Jefferies' hero had, a common humanity: 'like a wavering translucent spirit face *superimposed* upon each of these brutish masks I saw the ideal, the possible face that would have been the actual if mind and soul had lived (p. 235, my emphasis). The power of these images and the strenuousness with which they dispatched as the dreams of a return should alert us to the fact that Bellamy is not merely a crass Benthamite, but that the imagination of the future is an importunate ideological demand.

The 'possible face' reminds us of his transcendentalist origins and invites comparison with the Whitmanic Carpenter. 'The Religion of Solidarity', an essay drafted in 1874 but annotated in 1887, presents a dualistic consciousness by which 'we dwell needlessly in the narrow grotto of individual life, counting as strange, angelic visitants the sunbeams that struggle hither'.[31] Reverie, ecstasy, desire of natural beauty amounting 'to a veritable orgasm' (p. 11) are signals of a consciousness outside individuality which beckons us to community and death. The rhetoric strikingly resembles the movement of 'After Civilisation'. The 'social machinery' which Williams rightly identifies as the means by which Bellamy confers on his 'willed social transformation' the character of merely 'technological transformation' has, nonetheless, its psychic progenitor.[32] This is most closely focused in the title which, of course, implies that the past is a bad memory.

A remarkable *nouvelle* of 1880, 'Dr Heidenhoff's Process', clarifies the negative potency of memory for Bellamy. A New England village prayer meeting is interrupted by a young man who has been guilty of embezzlement. He says that although he has repented his sins, he cannot forget them: the blood of Christ turns them from black to red but does not blot them out. That night he shoots himself. The story then seems to concern itself with the vagaries of a vacuous romance between Madeline, the village organist, a village lad called Henry and the slick Bostonian who arrives to replace the suicide as drug store clerk. Henry gives up and goes to the city resolving never to have news of his loved one. After eight or nine months, he can no longer resist going back and he discovers that Madeline has been ruined and has fled to Boston. He finds her but she is emotionally paralysed by the past just as the suicide had been: 'Her memory, like a ditch from a distant morass, emptied its vile stream of recollections into her heart, poisoning all the issues of life.'[33]

At this point the novel, having already changed from a Hawthorne-like paradigmatic fable to Howellsian genteel realism, seems to shift gear again into science fiction. Deciding in a state of deep depression to accept Henry's offer of marriage, Madeline suddenly finds an advertisement for the treatment of bad memory by galvanic batteries (Dr Heidenhoff's process). This is based on recent physiological accounts of the mind (G. H. Lewes, *The Physical Basis of Mind* appeared in 1877), and the eponymous German doctor enunciates the most frequently cited sentence of the novel: 'memory is the principle of moral degeneration' (p. 108). Believing that, because of this bondage to the past, current theories of moral responsibility are in 'utter confusion and contradiction', he adds, foreshadowing the narrative process and ideological project of *Looking Backward*, 'it is time the world was waked up on that subject' (p. 102). This is while Madeline is asleep after the battery has destroyed the morbid tissues of her grey matter. She wakes up herself, prelapsarian and ready to marry Henry, but strangely obsessed by what it is she has forgotten. Then Henry also wakes up. The process has been a dream, and he is left instead with her suicide note.

Thus Bellamy is fully aware that waking up and dreaming are not states with a clear boundary but are overlapped by possibility, which in turn has to do with the relationship between the individual and the whole. Before her fall Madeline has linked memory with personality – 'I wouldn't care to forget anything I've done ... I should be afraid if they were taken away that I shouldn't have any character left' (p. 18). Locked in the past she is unable to relate to anyone else. Waking up to the chivalric love of Henry she can only give him the free future of her death. The 'solidarity' in which the utopian future resides means society seeing the past and the present which it rules as a dream and the post-individual future as a present to be woken into. A story of 1886 has Martians who can see the future rejecting human literature because it is written 'in the past tense and relating exclusively to things that are ended' but this is also a view of the present since they look at the earth with melancholy because of 'the contrast ... between the radiance of the orb and the benighted condition of its inhabitants.'[34] Earth is known to them as 'the blindman's world'. Technological transformation and social machinery are metaphors for the discovery of a democratic oversoul freed from the *ancien regime* of the self.

Equality, the sequel to *Looking Backward*, moves firmly into the blueprint mode, but also clarifies both the extent and the manner of the transformation. It makes clear for example that the new world is without classes, and unlike the earlier text it does not fudge the gender issue, indeed fudges it a lot less than Morris. This clearer differentiation is supported by a much more diagnostic account of the nineteenth century and the historical transition which is to follow. Thus 'democratic government' is actually a 'plutocracy' (p. 10) and the market is 'an artificial thing' (p. 168). The vocabulary of critical social discourse is echoed so that the cities become 'great whirlpools' (p. 292) and prostitution is described as 'the maiden tribute levied upon the poorer classes for the gratification of the lusts of those who could pay' (pp. 85/86). More generally, it is not mere reason, but the period of economic distress beginning in 1873 that 'awoke Americans'. The historical change is repeatedly referred to as the Revolution.

Nevertheless it still avoids class conflict, dispossessing capitalists by stealth ('flanking' is the word used). They finally see that there is no future in wealth and give it up! The Revolution was 'more like a trial of a case in court than a revolution of the traditional blood and thunder sort' (p. 346). On the one hand it is mere economism, 'an evolution that must be fulfilled' (p. 260) by which 'the mechanical and industrial forces held in check by the profit system only required to be unleashed to transform the economic condition of the race *as if by magic*' (p. 188, my emphasis). On the other it is a 'triumph of moral forces' (p. 341). This is not a simple self-contradiction. The 'rational phase' of history is an about face by which man marches 'with the course of economic evolution not against it' (p. 333). Economic evolution leads from the division of labour to the centralisation of planning and therefore to co-operation. Self-interest is therefore both immoral and blind. On both moral and economic levels this transformation is immanent, already present, merely locked up by unawareness. The strikers of the eighties get their monument but not because they knew what they were doing, rather because they were 'foolish' (p. 209) vessels of God's, that is nature's, that is productive forces', will. Naturally enough, in 2000 workers have no direct control over the conditions of work, though they are said to effect those conditions by choosing and changing occupations. The 'vital idea' of industrial administration is its 'unitary character' (p. 56). The religion of solidarity, equality itself, is the oversoul made flesh.

Wells's *The Sleeper Awakes*, which first appeared in 1899, does not merely take Bellamy's dream and turn it into nightmare, though the sleeper explicitly invokes the latter as he enters the future – 'he thought of Bellamy, the hero of whose Socialistic Utopia had so oddly anticipated this actual experience'[35] – and though it is sometimes claimed to be the model for twentieth-century dystopias. It is true that the Great Trust, the Council, is a repressive oligarchy and that the Sleeper only overthrows it to find it replaced by manipulative demagogy. It is also true that the only solution is for the Sleeper to wrest control of the technology, though I think that is to overlook the note of absurd schoolboy romanticism which is being mocked. What is more interesting about this text is that he takes into this future a memory of the future intended. Confronting Ostrog, the populist dictator, the Sleeper says that he believes in the people but is told that this is because 'you are an anachronism ... you dream of human equality – you have all those worn out dreams of the nineteenth century fresh and vivid in your mind' (p. 162). Later, he turns this into a claim on the support of the masses – 'I come out of the past to you ... with the memory of an age that hoped' (p. 171). Whether we are supposed to think that this is realistic is not clear to me, but what is important is that Wells sees how memory, the consciousness of the hopes of history cannot be sloughed off like an incumbent skin. It is not the aeroplane that saves the masses, it is the survival of yearning, the explicit recall of the principle of hope which is the keyword of the novel.

It is ironic that in 1921, Wells dismissed this text as 'no more than a nightmare of Capitalism triumphant ... a fantastic possibility no longer possible' (p. 8). He now thought *Tono-Bungay* closer to reality. Fear and hope both shrank perhaps to more manageable proportions. But the pleasure cities and the labour department are certainly closer to our dualistic world than is comfortable, and much of Bellamy's blueprint has been realised in the manner feared by Wells so we surely have no excuse to overlook the dangers of amnesia. Looking backward now would mean recovering not the prediction but the impulse to predict as a force for ideological discontent.[36] It is because they make this explicit that the writings about the future of Wilde and Morris stand apart from those which abolish history with auguries of immanence.

If Only / Only If

It is the celebration of the utopian drive that constitutes the serious base of Wilde's 'Soul of Man Under Socialism' (1891). Even-handedly rejecting the 'industrial barracks' of Bellamy's 'Authoritarian Socialism' and taking up a critical position towards Morris's dignification of manual labour, Wilde asserts that 'civilisation requires slaves'.[37] As human slavery is wrong, the future must rely on the enslavement of the machine, which could only come about through the abolition of property. Rhetorically asking 'is this Utopian?', Wilde answers by affirming the importance of utopianism as such: 'A map of the world that does not include Utopia is not worth even glancing at, for it leaves out the one country at which Humanity is always landing. And when Humanity lands there, it looks out, and seeing a better country, sets sail. Progress is the realisation of Utopias' (p. 1028). Later he expands this by embracing the two characteristic objections to Utopias, that they are impractical and that they go against human nature. A practical scheme, he argues, would either already exist, or fit existing conditions which precisely need to be changed. And if conditions change, human nature will change for 'the only thing that one really knows about human nature is that it changes' (p. 1039).

Wilde thus puts himself completely outside the immanentist texts we have been concerned with. He does this specifically, though with characteristic indirection, when he seems to deviate from his theme to a defence of charges of morbidity and unhealthiness in modern art. Not surprisingly, since art is oppositional and 'seeks to disturb ... monotony of type, slavery of custom, tyranny of habit, and the reduction of man to the level of a machine' (p. 1030), the delivery of man from past and present is aesthetic, 'the future is what artists are' (p. 1039). What is more surprising (and not, of course, untinged with irony) is that the point of likeliest contact between the artist and the public is not in the domain of public opinion but of 'the physical force of the public'. The very violence of revolution confers grandeur: 'it was a fatal day when the public discovered that the pen is mightier than the paving-stone' (p. 1033). This is clearly more about theatre than history, but it shows the possible conjuncture of aesthetics and revolution which is the basis on which we have to read *News from Nowhere.*

Morris is commonly and correctly thought to have occupied a third position *vis-à-vis* on the one hand Bellamy's technocracy and on the other, as Suvin puts it,[38] the 'post catastrophe tale'. But in view of the continuity between these two ideological postures which I have demonstrated, this third position cannot be between them. On the contrary, it opposes both postures by calling into play the status of the text within the future-writing project.

Perry Anderson sees the polemical occasion of the text, the response to Bellamy, as an ideological constraint: 'the tourniquet of their opposition', he writes, 'is an old one.'[39] He goes on to separate two strands in the text and relate them to different values in Morris's work. On the one hand there is a romantic opposition to utilitarianism with its tendency towards simplicity.[40] On the other hand, embedded in 'How the Change Came', there is an original and instructive concern with strategy, evident in complex detail in the lectures and essays. But this ignores its sophisticated aesthetic posture by which the historical is embedded within a specific structure built out of pragmatic intent and mimetic constraint.

To try to understand why *News from Nowhere* remains perplexing and enriching means paying attention to mimetic constraints which cannot be relegated to technical efficiency, but which unlike the ideological constriction are enabling rather than marginalising. Morris shows in his lecture on the 'English Pre-Raphaelite School' (1891) that if he is prepared to deploy romantic ideology it is by no means innocently. The argument of this lecture is that it took a conventionality to demolish the conventional.[41] Explicitly designating the discourse into which he is entering 'utopian romance', Morris inserts his text into a specific convention with its own conditions. Moreover he insists, as Simon Dentith shows in a precise manner,[42] on its provisionality as 'news' with a specific function, to announce not The Future but an epoch of rest. Morris is enabled by these strategies to discuss the immediate issues of a socialist society without being accountable for a superimposed system. It is indeed, as Williams later says, light at the end of the tunnel,[43] but it is a carefully constructed light, not merely a sentimental or desperate outburst. Both its personal satisfactions to the persona of the actant and the limitations that flow from this are constantly reiterated. The epoch of rest is dominated by the sense of change, its light shrouded in double vision, reminders by contrast of the present from which he has escaped, most notably the past and present (i.e. present and future) fieldwoman and Ellen's own sense of herself as reconstituted *femme fatale*. This is not, of course, to create some ironic let out. It is rather to escape the acknowledged authoritarianism of the utopian process and retain nevertheless the utopianising drive. The gap between dream and vision remains to be filled up by the reader.

We also have a utopian text interrogating the aporia of nineteenth-century realism – the boundary of public and private life, and the narrative necessity of illusions to be lost, but it deploys the problematic point of view that arises from this interrogation to raise questions about utopias. We no more ask ourselves whether we would like the world that is given to Guest than we would imagine that we lived in Rastignac's Paris. But we do take the experience of the realist text into our own lives and we take the experience of the dream into our own dreaming. It is the fact that the text can provoke Anderson, for example, into opposing his own utopia that is a tribute to its effectivity.

Morris himself placed utopias firmly by suggesting that they were just an expression of a man's temperament.[44] Moreover, if we deconstruct the title a little more than Dentith, we have to pay attention not only to 'News' but to 'Nowhere' and 'from'. Nowhere translates Utopia: it can no more be a utopia than Wells's *A Modern Utopia* is. It is calling attention to the utopian process. Which is what Engels does in *Socialism, Utopian and Scientific*, which was available in French from 1880 and of which there are a number of traces in *News from Nowhere*. Engels is far from dismissive of the Utopians. On the contrary, in several detailed ways he shows that they anticipate the demands of scientific socialism. Above all they are seen to be radically critical of the productive process which emerged in the early 1800s and the consequent bourgeois institutions.[45] Of Fourier, the writer whom Morris most admires (though, as Paul Meier has shown, he specifically rejects the French utopian's proposals),[46] Engels writes, 'he lays bare remorselessly the material and moral misery of the bourgeois world'.[47]

Morris, in my view, is aware of the distinction between the utopia (literary genre) and utopianism (ideological position). Bellamy specifically is not meant to be utopian in this sense, but logical and realistic as the postscript to *Looking Backward* makes clear. The dream is no dream. Morris offers the story (realistic) of having a dream (convention of utopia used by Bellamy) to recuperate the utopian from the schemes of planners, primarily to lay bare the critical opposition of socialist values to the present. Its psychological project, 'if only', becomes 'only if'. If at the end of the decade *The Sleeper Awakes* demonstrates the impossibility of possibilism, Morris has already demonstrated its irrelevance. Socialism is not about transplanting rosebushes, it is about ending the material and moral misery of the bourgeois world.

Morris is very specific about the conditions which underlie the new life. The first human activity that Guest notices in Nowhere is the children in the woods. Which raises the question of human formations (what we call education). This consciously instates an enlightenment/romantic project – schooling is displaced by growth. But it is not, of course, Wordsworthian for it leads not to the unfeeling armour of old time, but to absolute freedom – the abolition of prisons, the abolition of constraint, a relationship between men and women based on the unthinkable, pleasure. Reproduction is now defined as 'pleasure begets pleasure'.[48] These are overarched by the abolition of the division of labour, between capital and labour (through the abolition of money), town and country (England is now a garden where nothing is wasted) and between manual and intellectual labour. Each of these is very specifically hostile to Bellamy, but they do not amount to spontaneous self-transcendence in the manner of Carpenter or a return to the past.

Morris's critics object to the thinness with which this is realised in the text and to his failure to give it a convincing futurity. Wells, in the review of 1896 which was effectively an obituary of Morris, speaks of his own callow belief in Morris as 'absurd younger days when we seriously imagined we were to be led anywhere but backward by this fine old scholar ... His dreamland was no futurity but an illuminated past'.[49] It is a verdict repeated by Bloch, who strangely seems to prefer Bellamy. They fail to recognise the fictional constraint *News from Nowhere* imposes on itself. This gives a very specific structure whereby Guest is a spectator with illusions to be lost, awaking to what he thinks is the fourteenth century, and learning through dialogue that it is quite the opposite – a picture, appearance and reality, is then supplemented by a history which releases the protagonist into the scene, creates the possibility of a personal story, which had flickered on the edge of *Looking Backward* only as light relief from the expository monologue. But Guest has not lived this history. He can only know its present as recuperation, going back upstream to alienated romance. Ellen is not, like West's Edith, a reincarnation of a lost love, but a woman who in the nineteenth century would have been a prostitute. This is another dimension of the 'if only'/'only if'. For how else personally do we recover our humanity except by recursion? For it to be here, we would need a revolution. That is, we would need to know the future as the history of which it is constituted. To know it only as dream is to recover childhood, but childhood itself is a process of living towards the future. Ellen herself sees the dangers of forgetting.

In 1891, the first edition of Marx's *Critique of the Gotha Programme* was published:

In a higher phase of communist society, after the enslaving subordination of the individual to the division of labour, and thereby also the antithesis between mental and physical labour has vanished; after labour has become not merely a means of life but life's prime want;

after the productive forces have also increased with the all-round development of the individual, and all the springs of common wealth flow more abundantly, only then can the narrow horizon of bourgeois right be crossed in its entirety and society inscribe on its banners: 'From each according to his abilities, to each according to his needs'.[50]

Meier has shown how Morris's text specifically presents this higher, second stage.[51] But I want to stress its absoluteness, *only then*. Anything less leaves us in the narrow horizon of bourgeois right. Until the history narrated proleptically in Guest's dream has been lived through, he can only see that world as personal vision, as romance. Not that he will, in the manner of bourgeois realism, lose his illusions: his illusions will lose him.

The only sense in which Morris's text bears back into the past is that it pays full tribute not only to the difference of the future but the difference of the subject to perceive it. What absolutely defines the difference of Guest and Ellen is that he sees past and present as loss and gain, and she as rhythm of work and rest. Understanding becomes participation. The pragmatic effect of *News from Nowhere* is certainly a call to action, but this depends on its strenuous demand as well as its offered repose. And the strenuous demand is composed of its complex mimetic commitment and its concomitant intertextuality.

Conclusion

Wells's review of Morris in 1896 is full of the new generation's contempt for the nice old duffers. Forty years later Wells will be less generously mocked for *his* utopianism by Christopher Caudwell, mainly on the grounds that Caudwell thought he had seen the real future happen in ways absurdly distant from Wells's several schemes.[52] Of course *that* future is also under threat in our nineties and my list of non-catastrophes at the beginning was deliberately silent about the emancipation of the serfs. We would not now share Caudwell's high-spirited 'realism'. But then it is not Morris that he is looking to, but Lenin. I do not share the present readiness to nominate Lenin as a defunct idol, though I think that major questions need to be asked. But this only increases my respect for Morris's text. The 'settled sentimental socialist', 'the fine old scholar', 'the happiest of poets' has in my view in 1990 what is currently if not the last word, as no word will ever be last and the future has certainly not arrived with Mr Gorbachov's naturalisation of the market, but a very late word: 'What is the object of Revolution?' Hammond asks. 'Surely to make people happy … How can you prevent the Counter Revolution from setting in except by making people happy?' How unrealistic reality is!

Notes

1. Ernst Bloch, *The Principle of Hope*, translated by Neville Plaice, Stephen Plaice and Paul Knight (Oxford: Basil Blackwell, 1986) p. 480.
2. A. L. Morton, *The English Utopia* (London: Lawrence and Wishart, 1952) p. 148.
3. Jameson, *The Ideologies of Theory, Essays 1971–1986* (London: Routledge, 1988) pp. 84–5.
4. The Right Hon. Lord Lytton, *The Coming Race* (London: George Routledge and Sons, n.d.) p. 225. Subsequent references are given in parenthesis.
5. Raymond Williams, *Problems in Materialism and Culture, Selected Essays* (London: Verso, 1980) p. 201.
6. George Levine, *Darwin and the Novelists, Patterns of Science in Victorian Fiction* (Cambridge, Massachusetts: Harvard University Press 1988) p. 157–62.
7. Jameson, op. cit., pp. 78–9.
8. F. Engels, *Socialism Utopian and Scientific*, K. Marx and F. Engels, *Collected Works*, Vol. 24, 1986, p. 290.
9. Norman Kelvin (ed.), *The Collected Letters of William Morris*, Vol. II, 1885–1888 (Princeton, New Jersey: Princeton University Press, 1987) p. 426.
10. Richard Jefferies, *After London* (Oxford: Oxford University Press, 1980) p. 157. Subsequent references are given in parenthesis.
11. J. R. Ebbatson, 'Visions of Wild England: William Morris and Richard Jefferies', *The Journal of the William Morris Society*, III, 3 (Spring, 1977), p. 20.
12. Jameson, op. cit., p. 82; Darko Suvin, *Metamorphoses of Science Fiction* (New Haven: Yale University Press) 1979, p. 188.
13. W. H. Hudson, *A Crystal Age* (London, Duckworth and Co., 1919) pp. v–vi. All subsequent references in the text are given in parenthesis.
14. John Lucas, 'Conservatism and Revolution in the 1880s', *Literature and Politics in the Nineteenth Century*, ed. John Lucas (London: Methuen and Co. 1971) pp. 173–219.
15. George Gissing, *London and the Life of Literature in Late Victorian England, The Diary of George Gissing, Novelist*, ed. Pierre Coustillas (Hassocks: The Harvester Press, 1978) p. 144.
16. Lewis Mumford, *The Story of Utopias* (New York: Boni and Liveright, 1922).
17. Quoted, J. T. Frederick, *William Henry Hudson* (New York: Twayne, 1972) p. 44.
18. Simon Dentith's, *A Rhetoric of the Real* (Hemel Hempstead: Harvester Press, 1990) does much to rectify this. Also see Tony Brown (ed.), *Edward Carpenter and Late Victorian Radicalism* (London: Frank Cass, 1990) which appeared too late for consideration but which is primarily concerned with Carpenter's ideological importance already strongly argued by Sheila Rowbotham (see below note 23).
19. See W. Greenslade, 'Fitness and the Fin de Siècle', in *Fin de Siècle/Fin du Globe*, edited by John Stokes (London: Macmillan, 1992), pp.37–51.

20. Edward Carpenter, *Civilisation: Its Cause and Its Cure* (London: Swan Sonnenschein & Co, 1889) p. 4. Subsequent references are given in parenthesis.

21. Chushiki Tsuzuki, *Edward Carpenter, 1844–1929, Prophet of Human Friendship* (Cambridge: Cambridge University Press, 1980) pp. 99–107.

22. Edward Carpenter, *England's Ideal, and Other Papers* (London: Swan Sonnenschein & Co., 1889) p. 49; p. 59.

23. Sheila Rowbotham, 'Edward Carpenter, Prophet of the New Life', in Sheila Rowbotham and Jeffrey Weeks, *Socialism and the New Life, The Personal and Sexual Politics of Edward Carpenter and Havelock Ellis* (London: Pluto Press, 1977) p. 114.

24. Dentith, op. cit., pp. 139–41.

25. Edward Carpenter, *Towards Democracy* (London: George Allen and Unwin Ltd., 1918) p. 366. Subsequent references are given in parenthesis.

26. Patrick Parrinder and Robert M. Philmus (eds), *H. G. Wells's Literary Criticism* (Brighton: Harvester Press, 1980) p. 111.

27. Peter Marshall, 'A British Sensation', in Sylvia Bowman (ed), *Edward Bellamy Abroad, An American Prophet's Influence* (New York: Twayne, 1962) pp. 111–13.

28. Edward Bellamy, *Looking Backward* (London: George Routledge & Sons, n.d.) p. 39. Subsequent references are given in parenthesis.

29. Edward Bellamy, *Equality* (New York: D. Appleton-Century Corp. Inc., 1934) p. 64. Subsequent references are given in parenthesis.

30. K. Marx, F. Engels, *Manifesto of the Communist Party, Collected Works* (London: Lawrence and Wishart 1976) Vol. 6, p. 515.

31. Edward Bellamy, *The Religion of Solidarity* (Yellow Springs, Ohio: Antioch Bookplate Company, 1940) p. 21.

32. Williams, op. cit., p. 203.

33. Edward Bellamy, *Dr Heidenhoff's Process* (London: Frederick Warne, n.d.) p. 78.

34. Edward Bellamy, 'The Blindman's World', H. Bruce Franklin, *Future Perfect: American Science Fiction of the Nineteenth Century* (London: Oxford University Press, 1978) pp. 308–10.

35. H. G. Wells, *The Sleeper Awakes and Men Like Gods* (London: Odhams, n.d.) p. 50.

36. Ruth Levitas, *The Concept of Utopia* (New York: Philip Allen, 1990) p. 8, also pp. 179–200. This important book appeared too late to receive the consideration it deserves. Levitas stresses the relevance of utopian thinking to the problem of agency.

37. Oscar Wilde, *The Soul of Man under Socialism, Complete Works of Oscar Wilde* (London and Glasgow: Collins, 1971) p. 1028.

38. Suvin, op. cit., p. 187.

39. Perry Anderson, *Arguments within English Marxism* (London: Verso, 1980) p. 169.

40. Raymond Williams, *Politics and Letters* (London: Verso, 1979) p. 128.

41. May Morris (ed.), *William Morris, Artist Writer and Socialist* (New York: Russell and Russell, 1966) Vol. 1, p. 301.

42. Dentith, op. cit., p. 150.

43.   Williams, *Problems of Materialism*, op. cit., p. 204.

44.   Morris, *Artist, Writer and Socialist*, Vol. II, p. 502.

45.   F. Engels, *Socialism, Utopian and Scientific*, op. cit., pp. 288–90.

46.   Paul Meier, *William Morris, The Marxist Dreamer* (Hassocks: Harvester Press, 1978) Vol. 1, pp. 172–85.

47.   Engels, op. cit., p. 292.

48.   William Morris, *News from Nowhere, Collected Works*. Subsequent references are given in parenthesis.

49.   *H. G. Wells's Literary Criticism*, op. cit., loc. cit.

50.   Karl Marx, *Critique of the Gotha Programme*, Marx, Engels, *Collected Works*, Vol. 24, op. cit., p. 87.

51.   Meier, op. cit., Vol. II, pp. 306–327.

52.   Christopher Caudwell, *Studies in A Dying Culture* (London: John Lane, The Bodley Head, 1938) pp. 73–95.

CHAPTER 16

Margaret Harkness and the Socialist Novel

I Socialism and Literature in the 1880s

The 1880s is the decade in which the modern Labour movement begins to take shape. On the political level it begins with the founding of the Democratic Federation, the first political organisation to adopt the principles of revolutionary socialism, and ends with the first conference of the Scottish Labour Party in 1888 with its foreshadowing of the movement resulting in the foundation of the ILP in 1893. On the industrial level, the 'new unionism' sees the mass organisation of urban unskilled workers and reaches a climax in the Dock Strike of 1889. And on a sociological level, it is the decade of 'outcast London' and the visions of urban poverty which finally result in Booth's 'scientific' enquiry *Life and Labour of the People in London* which began to appear in 1889. The triad of concepts which motivate the present Labour movement – the concept of a working-class politics, the concept of trades union power and the concept of welfare – gets its first firm start.[1]

The most striking feature of this complex history is that in the interaction of these levels and in their separate developments, all the unsolved problems of the Labour movement are rehearsed in microscopic form. The political organisation was minute (Pelling describes it as a 'stage army'[2]), nevertheless there is an immediate tendency to schism. The Democratic Federation became explicitly socialist in 1883, and the breakaway Socialist league with its own tensions between Marxists and anarchists, and its own later fissures, was formed in 1884. The right wing of the remaining SDF formed the Socialist Union in 1885, and Hyndman's right-hand man, H. H. Champion, broke away finally in 1888 to work towards the ILP, only to find himself deserted by Burns and Mann and their supporters in 1890. This fissuring tendency was related to the essentially middle-class base of the political organisation, and the fact that it drew support from disaffected Conservatives, such as Hyndman, as well as disaffected Liberals, such as Morris. Given its funding from private wealth, such as that of Hyndman, Champion, Morris and Carpenter, and its relative insignificance for the working class it served, political issues tended to be highly abstract on the one hand and highly personal on the other. The questions of palliatives, parliamentarianism, grass roots organisation were not anchored in a concrete situation and thus play a freewheeling part in the rhetoric of contending factions. Most obviously fraught was the relationship with what was the most solid achievement of the decade – the new unionism, and this too is fraught with its own problems. The Dock Strike of 1889, for example, was certainly a triumph for independent working-class action and a blow for the power of labour against capitalism, but its resolution was the result of 'non-political' intervention from the outside (i.e., Cardinal Manning). The vexed history of the 'nonpolitical' strike is evident here – the new unionism was faced with an extremely complex mode of incorporation, which can be most graphically illustrated by the fact that the energies of Tom Mann in the promotion of the Eight Hour Day are diverted by the need to establish better wages. And the embroilment of the Fabians with the positivist sociology of Booth is another barrier, although no one would want to deny the importance of its implications for welfare. Every achievement is equally a defeat, which does not mean that we can simply write it off.

Given this complexity, it is not surprising that the literary response to the new social reality came more readily from conservative sources. A well-documented theoretical challenge to the ideology,[3] the sudden realisation of the depth and extent of urban poverty and the vague rumblings of working-class organisation, but without a certain relationship between all three, was a reality most easily construed as threat of 'anarchy' (Gissing, James) or appeal to complacent benevolence (Besant) depending on whether the political potential of the situation or the abject misery of the people who were caught in it struck the writer as predominant.[4] It is interesting that the two writers of substance who did identify themselves with socialism, Morris and Shaw, both felt compelled to work in a different aesthetic frame from that of the realist novel. On a general level, of course, this merely responds to the fact that realism is not available to socialist writers in its classic form because it assumes that reality is merely to be perceived and not made. But this does not answer the specific question of why these writers did not make more use of the transformations of realism already achieved by other writers, most notably Zola, but also in England in different ways by Meredith, Rutherford, Pater and indeed Gissing and James themselves. Morris and Shaw cannot, of course, be bracketed together by the decisions they made, but *A Dream of John Ball* and *An Unsocial Socialist* can be seen as responses to a common problem. The non-socialist writers I have mentioned respond to the new reality by a relativist displacement. They escape the realist assumption of personal complexity by deepening the personalisation of experience, and hence, in different ways, escalating the determinism of the given: this is true even of Meredith and Rutherford in spite of their consequent insistence on the active role of fiction in exposing the fictionality of that personalisation.[5] When Morris writes of nineteenth-century novels in *News from Nowhere* it is precisely to draw attention to the limits of the individuation of experience,[6] and Sidney Trefusis in his appendix to Shaw's novel points to the same inevitable limitations of the form itself:

> I cannot help feeling that, in presenting the facts in the guise of fiction, you have, in spite of yourself, shown them in a false light. Actions described in novels are judged by a romantic system of morals as fictitious as the actions themselves. The traditional parts of this system are, as Cervantes tried to show, for the chief part barbarous and obsolete: the modern additions are largely due to the novel readers and writers of our own century – most of them half-educated women, rebelliously slavish, superstitious, sentimental, full of the intense egotism fostered by their struggle for personal liberty, and. outside their families, with absolutely no social sentiment except love. Meanwhile, man, having fought and won his fight for this personal liberty, only to find himself a more abject slave than before, is turning with loathing from his egotist's dream of a independence to the collective interests of society, with he which he now perceives his own happiness to be inextricably bound up. But man in this phase (would that all had reached it!) has not yet leisure to write or read novels.[7]

The apparent sexism of this is only part of Shaw's 'irony' – the attack on the 'feminine' values of romantic fiction must be taken in the context of a sequence of novels which very clearly indicate the cultural conditioning of women to confine them within the ambience of the personal life. This means that although Trefusis seems to be attacking only sentimental fiction, in doing so he challenges the frontier of fiction itself, for as long as it confines itself to the 'fight for personal liberty' the novel cannot acknowledge the 'collective interests of society' except, as in the cases of Meredith and Rutherford, as a function of that liberty. Radical and important as their novels of the 1880s are, these writers (and I would want to add the author of *Marius the Epicurean*) do not write socialist novels. The implication in this passage and in the practice as well of Morris, is that there can be no such thing.

I am fully aware of the many questions this analysis fails to meet, but I am simply trying to clear a space for the specific tasks of a socialist fiction. Transcending the limits of the personal vision is a condition of socialist writing but it does not constitute socialist writing. It merely brings the writer to the point of retreating into a culturalist sublimation of the opposing self, or of projecting into a corporatist ideology – social Darwinism, pessimism, vitalism and so on.

The most obviously socialist text of the 1880s is *Germinal*, which brings relativism to the service of a revolutionary concept (the title, of course, is naturalistic but it alludes to the revolutionary calendar). Zola's novels were not understood in England as experimental novels which produce reality but as extensions of realism and at best encouraged a 'combative realism'[8] which needs to be socialised by socialist literary history. Nevertheless, there is one writer who was inspired by Zola and who did, I want to argue, produce at least one socialist novel. In a late autobiographical novel, *George Eastmont, Wanderer*, Margaret Harkness writes of her hero in the 1880s: 'A course of Zola would probably have taught him more than Maurice or Kingsley. He had just returned from a visit to the mines in Scotland, and there he found *Germinal* better than any guide book.'[9]

Her first novel, *A City Girl* appeared in 1887, a year or so after *Germinal* and was published by Zola's English publisher, Henry Vizetelly. We know of it because the author sent it to Engels, and although it is not obviously a Zola-esque novel, it provoked Engels' famous elaboration of his preference for Balzac over Zola. She went on to write three more novels in the 1880s and it is the object of this essay to introduce some of them as real attempts to achieve a specifically Socialist fiction building on rather than rejecting the forms of critical realism, by trying to negotiate the three levels of 'socialist' discourse I have mentioned, not as an ideological entity but as the problematic which confronted socialists at the beginning of their history.

II Who was Margaret Harkness?

There is no clear answer to this question because the evidence about her is muddled and confusing. [10] We know that she was a cousin and very close friend of Beatrice Potter who went with her on a trip to Austria in 1884 after the latter's emotional crisis over her relationship with Joseph Chamberlain and who introduced her to Sidney Webb in 1890. Beatrice Webb's diaries give very graphic accounts of her but they are contradictory and clearly subjective, and we know that although she bequeathed her books and pictures to Harkness in 1886, she quarrelled with her definitely in 1891, after a long time of suspecting the novelist of unreliability. We know that she became a close friend of Eleanor Marx who relied on her for information about the London poor, but she attacked Aveling and so lost that friendship. We know that just before and for a short time after the Dock Strike, she worked closely with Tom Mann and John Burns but quarrelled with them as well. We know that she was active in the SDF and later in the moves to create an Independent Labour Party but that by 1891, she was describing socialism as 'foolish' and 'wrong'. We also know that she befriended Olive Schreiner and Annie Besant, but that she also worked with religious institutions and edited an important series of articles, 'Toilers of London' for the *British Weekly*; a dissenting journal. What we don't know is whether she was a woman of consistent ideas who worked opportunistically in a series of alliances (her own image of herself), a radical feminist converted to socialism in the mid-1880s and disillusioned by it in the early 1890s, or simply a neurotic of wide but volatile sympathies vacillating between seeing herself as a journalist in pursuit of 'cold-blooded copy' and a rejected saviour of the working class. All these images are made possible by the patchy chronicle I have been able to construct.

According to Beatrice Webb, Margaret Harkness was the child of 'clerical and conventional parents' who 'tried to repress her extraordinary activity of mind'.[11] She emancipated herself from them by doing 'literary piecework' and living with the Poole family near the British Museum. Her life in the early 1880s seems to have been very much part of the world evoked in Gissing's *New Grub Street* (which, of course, is set in 1884): 'there you get', says Beatrice Webb, 'real intellectual drudgery'.[12] She wrote several articles on social questions, 'Women as Civil Servants' (1881) and 'Railway Labour' (1882) for the *Nineteenth Century* and two articles on 'The Municipality of London' for the Conservative *National Review* in 1883. At the same time she produced two books on British Museum antiquities for the Religious Tract Society's *Bypaths* of *Bible Knowledge* series on Assyrian and Egyptian life (the former has no date but precedes the latter which is 1884). None of these forecast the socialist novel except in so far that a concern for social issues is revealed. The first merely commends the Post Office decision to employ a small number of safely middle-class lady clerks, mildly criticising the social exclusiveness and low rate of pay and tentatively aligning itself with a liberal feminism close to that which emerged from the 1850s: 'Patience is all that is needed and a bond of mutual helpfulness, binding together all women irrespective of class to meet the obstacles incident to a changing world'.[13] The phrase 'irrespective of class' is the nearest we come to any radical perspective in these articles; those which follow move to a more overtly conservative position. She recommends the amelioration of the conditions of the railway workers and even describes the safely past period of 1866–71 as one of 'white slavery', but she explicitly denies the prospect of independent working-class initiative:

> I entirely agree with the men themselves in their conviction that they may trust implicitly to the railway companies for the ultimate solution of their difficulties, and for the redress of the grievances and hardships of which they very justly complain.[14]

and concludes with a classic formulation of the division of labour 'Those who think must govern those who toil'.[15] The articles on the government

of London in the *National Review* are largely a detailed history but attack
current proposals for reform along orthodox conservative lines, objecting
to centralisation (because it is unEnglish), paid government officials and
anything which enhances democratisation:

> Politics would be introduced into municipal elections, for the political
> value of municipal power would lead to the exclusion of unobtrusive
> men willing to work conscientiously for the welfare of the community
> in favour of political demagogues, who might, as in Paris, prove a
> danger to the State, or as, for many years, in another capital, misap-
> propriate public funds.[16]

The problem is how to read this work in connection with her later
commitment. On the one hand, they all have the note of hack work
(especially the history of London which resembles some of Walter Besant's
romanticisation of the past). The two books written for the Religious Tract
Society are overt vulgarisations of the work of more serious scholars, and
in so far as attitudes appear at all, they seem to have vestiges of a radical
position, such as the insistence on sexual equality among the Assyrians or
the praise of the humanity of the Egyptian legal code which 'is shown by
a clause which protects the labouring man against the exaction of more
than his day's labour'.[17] And at times she seems to admire the secular
tendencies of their religious attitudes. But at the same time she does praise
the superiority of the Hebrew religion because of its sense of sin and its
conception of a Divinity which is remote but in control of the 'smallest
events'.[18] In her diary, Beatrice Webb says that although, in 1883,
Harkness is logically a rationalist, she believed in a 'personal adoration of
Christ',[19] and though her novels sustain a radical critique of religious
institutions (the Catholic Church in *City Girl*, the Methodists in *Out
of Work*, the Anglicans in *Captain Lobe*) she shows a great respect for
religious people – notably the soldiers of the Salvation Army. She is even
said, by one historian, to have gone to Cardinal Manning to persuade
him to intervene in the Dock Strike,[20] and it may be indicative that her
late novel *George Eastmont, Wanderer* (1905) was published by Burns and
Oates. Was she a Christian radical or a humanist following in George
Eliot's footsteps? The same question is raised by the development of her
political attitudes. For although the early articles just discussed bear
no relation to the socialist commitment in evidence later, her critique
of socialism in the 1890s, especially in two articles written for the *New
Review* in 1891 and 1893, 'A Year of My Life' and 'Children of the
Unemployed' stress patience, evolution, hope against the threat of violent
change. Conservatism was one known starting point of middle-class
members of the SDF. On the other hand, when Beatrice Webb does

identify her cousin as 'a strong socialist' she adds that she is 'apparently uninterested' in economic facts. 'She says that when I argue I am unattractively combative'.[21] It suggests that her involvement with socialism may have been emotive rather than thought out, and with the usual corollary that sentimental commitment tends towards opportunistic alliance. 'A Year of My Life' seems to confirm this to some extent. Writing that she had wanted to work as a member of the English Labour Party she goes on to explain the 'brief success of the Socialist Party in England' as 'due to its advocacy of the cause of the unskilled worker just before he broke his shell and became a "divine animal"'.[22]

On the other hand, it is difficult to believe that a writer as deeply paternalistic as these early and late essays could have so fully entered into the consciousness of her working class protagonists, and there is a possible political explanation for these shifts of position. It is clear that the man with whom she most closely worked in the SDF was H. H. Champion. He, of course, was himself a highly enigmatic figure. Upper class and military in background, he financed the publication of much socialist material and was until the late 1880s secretary of the SDF. He was also involved in the Tory gold scandal of 1885 and left the SDF after Hyndman had accused him in *Justice* in 1888 of being a tool of the Tory agent Maltman Barry. There is also some evidence that he used Tory funds to finance Keir Hardie's mid-Lanark election expenses in 1889. But one way of seeing Champion's position is that he foresaw the need of an independent Labour party. He certainly published Tom Mann's pamphlet advocating an eight-hour day. Like Mann, Burns and others, he saw the need to establish a political expression of the new unionism. Certainly, as late as 1889, he was very much in Engels' favour, as seems to have been Harkness herself until she attacked Aveling in November. Both of them worked very closely with Mann and Burns both during the Dock Strike and during the early years of the independent Labour movement. This is not to exonerate Harkness' apparent unreliability but rather to suggest that it puts her at the point of the many tensions of the Labour movement at that time. There was a great deal of poverty and hardship, and the beginnings of an organisation to combat it. But the politics of that organisation was a matter of deep controversy. If Champion was devious, wasn't Hyndman too dogmatic and Morris too pure? Beatrice Webb complains of Margaret Harkness' treachery and later says that Tom Mann distrusted her because of her cousin's calumny. But this might reflect not just on her own instability but the instability of the Labour movement at this point.

A complete profile of Margaret Harkness would, I believe, be a fascinating case study of the fraught conjuncture of radical feminism and socialism, and of the role of the intellectual in the Labour movement. I cannot complete that profile without much more evidence. Beatrice Webb wrote in 1899:

She is typical of the emancipated woman who has broken ties and struggled against the prejudice and oppression of bigoted and conventional relations to gain her freedom but who has never been disciplined by a Public Opinion which expects a woman to work with the masculine standard of honour and integrity.[23]

But she has just admitted that she has 'splendid opportunities' for observation. Perhaps it is precisely because she was required to live by cold-blooded copy, that she had a complex sympathy for those who struggle and that like the working class themselves she was not yet disciplined by public opinion that Harkness produced a sequence of remarkable novels. For puzzling as she is, she is alive to the puzzle of a new reality and she makes, in my view, a new mode of fiction out of the instability.

As these novels will be unknown to most readers, I propose to write about each of them separately trying to show how she progressively abandons fictional forms as she progressively politicises the 'reality' she evokes.

III *A City Girl* (1887)

Engels praises this first novel because of the 'truthfulness of presentation'[24] by which 'the old, old story of the proletarian girl seduced by a man from the middle class', is made new. This is a very accurate analysis of the first half of the novel. The constituents of the newness form a 'new' reality which is the cause, not merely the site of this story. The 'city' is established with great visual accuracy but it is defined in terms of relationships. The opening, for example, is a description of Charlotte's Buildings which is the physical embodiment of a rent relationship and the picture is framed by that sense. The heroine's 'real' is defined by these buildings, the sweatshop in which she works and the family for whom her sole value is as a wage earner. The seduction is made inevitable by this 'real', because it responds to a subjectivity that is repressed by it (it is thus at a second level of potential subjection).

This is stressed by the fact that the material base is offered primarily as the provocation of ideological formations. The opening chapter rapidly moves from naturalistic description to the voices which emerge from the picture:

Charlotte's Buildings were, at that time, about two years old. They had been built by a company of gentlemen to hold casuals. The greater number of people who lived in them thought that they belonged to a company of ladies.

Why?

'Because they are built cheap and nasty', said the men. 'Women don't understand business. Depend upon it, some West End ladies fluked money in them.'

'Because ladies collect the rents', said the women.[25]

This is followed by the activities of the rent collectors and the comments that follow them, by the Irishwoman's speculations on what the rich think of them, and by the children's myths about the nearby reservoir. This gives way to an indication of the dominant catholicism and the dominant violence of the tenants' lives. It is a total scene into which Nelly is introduced, but one which is less pictorial than choric. Separate conscious articulations of the environment play through the novel, such as George, the good lover's single norm of military stability, or Father O'Hara's wrapping his intellect in a napkin. The East End is not made exotic, as it is in the later cockney school.[26] It is negotiable and determining. It is the source of Nelly's formation.

She is offered as innocent victim, but again Harkness does not, as with other 'realists', offer her as a consciousness which somehow transcends this environment. On the contrary, the seduction is fully portrayed as the effect of her trying to live within the given. She is special only because she is 'the masher', capable of a vitality contradicting her world's oppression in ways which are permitted and shared by her class. Her first concern is with buying a feather for her Sunday hat. The bedroom which centres on the mirror, the market and Petticoat Lane are the site of her own identity. The seduction begins effectively during a day out in Battersea Park. She sees it as 'a picture in a book' as he tries to recall which painting she reminds him of. The park and the palace are artefacts containing the natural and the romantic:

> As Nelly sat there eating cake, and listening to the music, she felt in Paradise; work and trouble were forgotten in the joys of the present, sweaters and trousers became things of the past; mother and brother were changed into fond relations; her companions were no longer George, Jack and Mr. Grant, but the handsomest, the best, the kindest men on the face of the earth.[27]

There is nothing patronising about this illusion: it is won out of the relief from oppression meticulously recorded earlier. It needs to be contrasted with the Crystal Palace episode in *The Nether World* which simply sees the 'holiday' as a momentary unleashing of degenerate instincts. Nelly's day out is a day of dreams but the dreams are of the ideology of civilisation – art, the family, chivalry. Parks are constructed to sustain such illusions; they fence in 'nature'. Later, Arthur Grant takes her to a theatre which further compounds the alienated illusion. The play is about a wronged

wife and her sorrowing husband. Nelly feels treated 'like a lady'. She
dreams what she is supposed to dream and because Grant enables her to
do it: 'she saw herself far away from the buildings'.[28] Further meetings are
at Kew and Greenwich, the excursion spaces within the city that allow for
and enclose what the 'buildings' exclude.

This evolution of a city consciousness – at once one of many voices and
articulated in terms of the specially individuated dream – is responded to
by the urban consciousness of Arthur Grant. Engels is right to say 'your
Mr. Grant is a masterpiece'. In four pages in the centre of the Battersea
Park episode, this middle-class radical is shown to be not wicked but
highly conditioned, comfortably married and 'playing truant'. Nelly thus
appears to him as an object of truancy and it is not accidental that it is in
the theatre that she overwhelms him with her beauty:

> Her complexion was dazzling by gas-light, and excitement made her
> eyes sparkle between their long dark lashes. Absolutely unselfcon-
> scious, trembling with pleasure, she was a picture worth looking at.[29]

Later she hides her face in red velvet cushions. It is not merely that she is
'a picture', an object, but that, linked with gaslight and red cushions,
she is the licensed object of his truancy. Later, we are told that he writes
novels which base themselves on psychological studies, but this does not
extend to Nelly because it does not extend to her class: 'She was no psychological study, this little Whitechapel girl, only something pretty to
look at'.[30] Again, she poses for him: 'she put on her wreath and looked like
a woodnymph.' If the park is for her a licensed day which she takes too far,
she is for him a licensed consumable.

This process of voices and image making within the material base of
wages and rents governs the novel at least for the first six chapters. The
problems arise with the second half. Engels claims that it is not realistic
enough because it shows the working class as a mere passive mass. To
some extent, and, in fact, in the final instance, this is true, but it is more
complex than that. Chapter VI, entitled 'East and West', contains all the
radical ironies of the first part. We move into winter, allusions to philanthropic concerts and invitations to wedding breakfasts are juxtaposed
against the pregnant Nelly's drudgery while she tries to seek some contact
through confession and instead goes to seek Grant in West Kensington,
where through the window she sees him shut in by 'the golden gates of
domestic peace and happiness'[31] (it is another highly wrought image). This
brings her to realise the immense gulf between East and West, and she
also is without money to return. She is forced to beg and predictably a
policeman suspects her of soliciting. On the edge of this abyss, the man
she begs from happens to be a well-known philanthropic lawyer. Then she
is beaten up by her brother because she has been sacked and is taken by

her good unrequited lover to a Salvation Army captain. All this bears out what Engels is saying. Harkness can neither push her into the abyss of the fallen woman, nor see how, in any way, energies of survival and improvement can come from within Nelly's own class. Except for her lover, George, who is in any case trained outside as a soldier, Nelly is taken out of that abyss by outside help.

But these interventions are strictly limited. The philanthropic lawyer only provides her bus fare back. Captain Lobe only takes her to decent lodgings and gets her more sweated work. More importantly, the rescue enables Nelly to move to a new phase of consciousness which the author of the *Origins of the Family* should have seen. When Father O'Hara asks Nelly whose child she has had, she replies 'mine'. Like Tess later, she is prepared to christen it herself. She maintains this stand in the face of her rejection by the 'supportive' institutions, the sweatshop and her family. But it goes further than this: it actually raises the question of monogamy and sexual equality as a question. George too wants to know the father's name, but Captain Lobe resists the implication of this: '"Well, I don't see myself why women should have only one sweetheart and men half-a-dozen", remarked the Captain. "In the Army we have the same set of rules for both men and women. The general favours neither sex"'.[32] What seems to privatise Nelly's story (the rescue) serves in fact to become the instrument of a sexual political affirmation. The episodes which follow, when the baby becomes ill and she has to face the institutional indifference of hospitals, show her locked in a solitary struggle with the powers that be.

Nevertheless, if she is taken out of passivity by what happens, she is not, of course, taken out of individual isolation. Engels admitted that East End society was the most passive working class he had known. Only in the very last years of the decade with the Match Girls' strike and the Dock Strike is there much sense of organised resistance. And, as has often been pointed out, it is significant that it is a women's union that starts the whole process. But *A City Girl*, if it foreshadows that in an indirect way, has a largely rhetorical feminism of protest. Oddly it is precisely the taking of Nelly out of passivity into the loneliness of single parenthood which contains both the novel's political thrust and writes it back into a recognisable fictional shape. For if the story of the fallen woman is thwarted in order to make a feminist affirmation, the illness and death of the child are the fictional means by which, for the reader, a compensating pathos is generated, and, for George, the way is made clear to 'forgive' and redeem Nelly. This trite ending, however, does nothing to make up for the radical documentary of the hospital and its alienating attitude. The ending is so muted that the sense of anger generated by the picture of social injustice is unrelieved by moral purgation. The political consciousness is uncontained by the narrative sequence.

IV *Out of Work* (1888)

Harkness' second novel shows many signs of a sophisticated response to Engels's critique. It does not become more Balzacian but rather is beyond Zola's experiment, breaking open the fictional frame to embrace an unfictionalised actuality. It opens, for example, with the Queen's Jubilee visit to Whitechapel and reaches a climax with the Trafalgar Square riots of November 1887, and between these events offers a picture, not, like *A City Girl* of a social *section*, but of a social *situation*, the consequences of unemployment. Its protagonist becomes the register of vividly rendered experiences of the doss house, the dock gates and the casual ward. Its incorporation of documentary in this sense looks forward to the Orwell of the 1930s and to the non-fiction novel of recent years. But the function of the documentary is strictly to gain access to kinds of experience denied by the parameters of hermetic fiction. Harkness makes it obvious from the start that she is concerned not with actuality but versions of it and their ideological role. Thus the opening centres precisely on the crowd around the People's Palace which in itself stands for one version of the critical alienation of the working class. In *All Sorts and Conditions of Men*, Walter Besant had depicted an East End likely to become dangerously political if the diversions of civilisation were not made available. Strangely enough, the novel's recommendations inspired enough fear and complacency to become one of the many programmes of the ruling class to prevent the politicisation of the poor; Harkness is immediately on to the ironies of this – the way in which it supplies reassuring versions of the situation:

> Reporters were busy at work concocting stories of the royal progress through the East End for the Monday papers; artists were preparing for the illustrated weekly papers pictures of Whitechapel as it may possibly appear in the Millennium. No one would speak about the hisses which the denizens of the slums had mingled with faint applause as Her Majesty neared her destination; no one would hint that the crowd about the Palace of Delight had had a sullen, ugly look which may a year or so hence prove dangerous. The ladies on their way to the Queen's Hall, who had leant back in their carriages, heedless of ragged men, hungry women and dirty little children, the *blasé* frequenters of Hyde Park and the clubs, who had glanced carelessly at the people as they accompanied their wives and daughters to the People's Palace, would be quoted by philanthropic persons intent on ministering to the poor by the unction of their presence, and represented by the artists as so many unselfish ladies and gentlemen who had given up an afternoon's pleasure-hunting in order to gratify the eyes of under-paid men and over-worked women by their shining hats and charming bonnets.[33]

On one level reporters, artists and philanthropic persons are making the episode into an *event* with its built-in reading. On the level of the situation itself, the ruling classes are looking at the working class who have come to look and comment on them. Later, this image of the crowd is complemented by working-class comments in the Queen. What immediately clinches the irony, however, is that 'Millennium' and 'unction' lead to the comment which follows this, that, as it is Sunday, the bells are calling upon the people to forget earth and think of heaven'. This novel will not forget earth, nor will it allow report, picture and comment to hold the sullen crowd at bay. We move immediately to a Methodist service, disrupted by a down-and-out who asks the minister if he has ever been hungry.

Of course, there is nothing specifically radical about this kind of irony: it simply calls attention to ruling class complacency and that can be and was a rhetoric used both by philanthropists and conservatives. But this is only the prelude to the much more radical fictional strategies: the secularisation of values by the inversion of fictional possibilities and the socialisation of experience by the contextualisation of consciousness as a voice among many anonymous voices. In *A City Girl*, a very conventional story is completed – it has a 'happy' (individual) ending. I have argued that this story is marginalised by the experience Nelly has to go through and the specific form of resistance which she has to develop to withstand it. *Out of Work* goes much further. Again the story is of a young girl caught between two men, but there is no question here of a steady lover able to rescue the trapped female victim. On the contrary, the 'steady' lover is a lugubrious Methodist teacher who uses his influence to gain his own ends, who works in the Mint because his father did before him, who is sexually nauseating to the heroine and whom she chooses in the end simply because: 'I'm going to marry a godly young man with a settled income'.[34] The unemployed hero is thus faced with his own social condition as an ultimate measure of love, and his own comment 'you little hypocrite' and the author's chapter title 'She Jilts Him' starkly challenge the reader's romantic speculations which have been encouraged by the rendering of the heroine's awareness of her feelings for him and revulsion from the man she will marry. As though to emphasise this by reference to *A City Girl* the steady lover of the earlier novel is an ex-soldier who retains a military integrity, and in this novel, there is an ex-soldier who is merely one of the anonymous victims of the recession, a man with a character reference who, because of that, is rejected by the envious dock gangers and whose presence is ultimately registered by a protesting inscription on the cell wall of the casual ward. Furthermore, the heroine has a wise sceptical Jewish 'uncle' from whom she seeks advice and who has no effect on events whatever. Early in the novel, Harkness offers a social Darwinian perspective which is presented ironically as though the novel will ultimately disprove it: 'it is a law of existence that the weakest must go to the wall, and a dogma, established by experience, that mind rules matter, no matter how strong matter may be'.[35] But the novel enacts this bitter conjunction of Darwinism and idealism. The ex-soldier and the hero, both strong capable men, cannot cope as weaker types can with the work of the casual ward. The deep commitment of the novel as a form to the survival of 'nature' is overturned by a more potent social reality.

This is matched in the life of Jos, the country boy driven by economic necessity into the army of casual labour in the city, by an inverted pastoral. From the beginning, what defines him is his sense that beyond the misery of urban experience lies a solider world of belonging and peace in the village where he has grown up. At the point of greatest misery, he decides to return to his home, but it is only to die, and the death is no release. It is stressed that there is no work in the village, and that Jos's mother and the rector who had shown some concern are both dead. The return is therefore a desperate illusion: 'Now that Polly had jilted him, the "lone" woman's memory was something to fall back upon, and he recalled numberless traits of tenderness, little things he had almost forgotten until that evening.'[36] But the comment on this is:

> Human nature *must* have a fetish.
> If a man does not worship his own shadow, he falls down before the shadow of someone else. When these things fail to satisfy, he calls out for God Almighty, be it Humanity, Zeus or Justice.[37]

His own death is specific, not reconciling – he dies of starvation. The 'peace', the 'home' he reaches is ironic – a meeting with 'the Absolute', but a burial by a stranger. As though to deepen the sense of anger, Jos does have a strange relationship with a petty thief known only as the Squirrel. Her final act of devotion is suicide. The end of the novel, final as it is, drawing on the rhetoric of catharsis as it does, only stresses the specific injustice which has brought it about. There is no 'so be it'.

This kind of analysis only takes us to a certain point. I have shown elsewhere how Gissing, especially in *The Nether World*, also sets up fictional expectations which are defeated by the specific recalcitrance of the social actuality. This merely brings Harkness into the category of a combative realism. But *Out of Work* is combative in a sense which seems to me to be specifically Socialist. Partly I mean by this that the realism generates as its most coherent gloss a socialist discourse embodied by Jos's docker friend and by a speaker on Mile End Waste at the end of Chapter Four when the ironies of the Jubilee, the chapel and Victoria Park (versions of Sunday release) give way to the unsolved problems of unemployment. The speaker stresses that the misery is caused by the Age of Competition which is really at an end. This theme is picked up again and again, on the level of romance, as I have indicated, by the distortion of social Darwinism and

its allegiance with Christian self-righteousness, on the level of industry
by the focus on dock labour: 'He began to realise that a job could only be
obtained by physical strength, that he had no chance until his leg was well
again',[38] and on a general social level by the description of Jos's social place
as among 'the great army that goes marching on, heedless of stragglers,
whose commander-in-chief is laissez faire.' Jos's way out of this becomes
gin, but that is firmly contextualised. He takes to gin when the hunger is
so bad he faints at the home of his docker friend who gives him spirits to
revive him. Likewise, he is supported through his misery by a petty thief.
Crime and drink are not merely seen as the bad consequences of poverty,
they are linked with the repressed corporateness which the Socialist on
Mile End Waste says will replace competition. Before the fight for work
at the dock gates, travelling to the battle, men are able momentarily to
show a camaraderie: 'the only good thing that comes of being unemployed is "I help you, and you help me, because we've no place in
society"'.[39] Socialism is not an imported utopian answer, it emerges as a
necessity and a possibility. The novel's finest passage is the build-up to the
Trafalgar Square demonstration. The unemployed resort to the Square as
a place to sleep. They are watched by the ruling class night after night.
It is impossible to convey by quotation how concretely Harkness renders
this breaking out of misery and its encampment in the arena of the
oppressor. It is as though a truth has broken its bounds, geographically
and socially. And given that the alternative to the Square for Jos is the
casual ward (again rendered with horrifying concreteness as a personal
experience) the reader is projected towards sharing the release of the riot.

The novel goes further than this. It overcomes one of the most obvious
problems for the socialist writer. Fiction has as one of its primary values
the personalisation of social experience but this is why it remains such
a bourgeois form, because Socialism clearly demands the extra-mural
sharing of consciousness. Jos's story is highly individualised, but it is not
declassed. On the contrary, Harkness carefully inserts what he learns into
a context of anonymous voices. The man at the Methodist service is merely
a voice challenging one level of coherence. The dock labourer radical is
never named. The ex-soldier is represented only by his graffiti. No little
community is set up to mark the specialness of the individual case. Jos's
story is specific but it is the story of the unemployed – not because that
story can be concentrated in that one life, but because it belongs with all
other separate lives which intersect his path. This is the very opposite of
the complexity which is the primary aesthetic end of the bourgeois
realism. Depressing as this novel is, and lonely as the social rejection
leaves the hero, all the other versions of defeat and loneliness are brought
together as a common pool of experiences and defeats. The novel itself by
its form organises this sense of oppression and in doing so secularises it.
Jos dreams of 'home', but he does not take his comrade with him. She only

knows that he has gone away. Jos perceives the stars as a mocking universe but that indifference is also glossed as the social system. And very briefly the common pool is articulated in Trafalgar Square. This brings us back to the first point – that the documentary in the novel is not of place but of event. Inarticulate as the voice of the unemployed is in the face of the institutions which silence it, royalty, Methodism, casual labour, poor relief, we see it in the process of becoming history. That is why, I think, Harkness thought about and assimilated Engels' criticism. Zola showed that working-class history could not be embodied in the protagonist, but he has to make it as did in his very different way, Morris, a matter of vision. Harkness goes a long way towards making it the voice of many voices.

V *Captain Lobe* (1889)

After *Out of Work*, *Captain Lobe* is inevitably disappointing but the reasons why it is so are not simple. The decision to use the Salvation Army as a focus for a novel about 'darkest London' does not seem strange if we bear in mind Engels's comment on its appearance in *A City Girl* when he praises 'your sharp repudiation of the conception of the self-satisfied philistines, who will learn from your story, perhaps for the first time, why the Salvation Army finds such support among the masses of the people.' General Booth wrote an appreciative preface to the novel, but he clearly recognises that it is not written by an author who shares his values. The motive is rather surely that the Army, more than any socialist organisation, had a structure sited within working-class London and thus has access to a reality which can otherwise be seen only hazily. What is more disturbing is the positive use of a melodramatic plot, a heroine who by virtue of her inheritance is only an observer and later benefactor of the working-class girls employed in the factory she owns, and the overall marginalisation of political readings to two outside voices who present their case episodically as a single contained discourse. At the same time, it is a novel whose documentary aim seems to take over – as for example when space is given to the tattooed man to relate his 'history' at length as though we were simply taken to the entertainment and left to look on.

But this is not to deny the strengths which are quite different from those of *Out of Work*. The Army, for example, is used in a brilliantly complex way both to act as a critical organisation and to be seen as being unable to meet the material case of poverty. The most striking episode of the book is Ruth's guided tour by two Army lassies through Seven Dials in the Fifth and Sixth Chapters. It is preluded by a rare account of the conversion of a stockbroker who is brought to salvation by a dream of social guilt. Captain Lobe himself is presented as an ascetic whose concern for the souls of the poor is underwritten by his awareness of what he terms 'lust of the spirit' in the rich, and his closest friends are an agnostic lady who, despite her scepticism about existing socialist organisations, urges that socialism is in the air, and a doctor who, contemptuous of his West End colleagues, quotes Engels and reveals an ambition to be a constitutional socialist. Lobe himself has to keep thanking God that he has no intellect:

> Salvationists do not attempt to reason; they appeal to a man's heart, and think the intellect a little thing that requires wheedling. Consequently, few educated men and women join their ranks, and they cannot point to one scholar in their camp of any importance. But in slums and allies their work is a real force, for the inhabitants of these places recognise their sincerity of purpose, and do not approach them in a critical spirit.[40]

The Army then is not sentimentalised – it is rather a mode of insight, which has to be theorised.

Equally it is a mode which meets continual resistance. The slum sisters meet not merely an unregenerated lumpenproletariat but also an articulate 'materialism' to which they have no answer.

> 'Are you saved, brother?' they asked a man with a white face and bloodless lips, whose clothes hung loosely on his emaciated body.
>
> 'If starving will save me, I ought to have been saved long before this', the man answered.
>
> 'You must give up your sins; then God will send you food', was the reply.
>
> The man shook his head, and said 'The Bible calls God a father and no father would starve his son for sinning. He would give him food first, and speak about his sin afterwards.'[41]

The dialogue continues but the man has the last word – 'I'm hungry.' Later Captain Lobe regrets having to consign his people to damnation, and we are told that: 'He had no great affection for the Salvation Army. But he did not know any other organisation that worked so hard'.[42] From the novelist's point of view, because it works so hard in darkest London, its very failure to make headway (which is what is stressed) exposes the nature of the problem, and both of Lobe's confidants express an alternative to salvation – socialism makes more sense in terms of what we have seen.

The real limitations of this privilege are precisely that at the novel tends to become a series of tableaux, brilliant and angry but the static and without much development. This is true as well of the later stages when Ruth is taken to the homes and the places of entertainment of her workplace by the confused socialist/feminist forewoman, Jane Hardy. Equally, as this suggests, characters tend to become very static. In fact the novel gravitates towards the spectacle of the penny gaff and although the hop-picking episode has more movement it is still within the terms of a contained sequence.

The reasons for these limitations are not difficult to define. What has given the earlier novels their specific effectivity, the cutting into the picture of voices which promise the voice of the working class has now been abandoned. On the one hand there are radical *versions*, *articulate* but from an *outside* middle class. On the other, the proletarian world itself is only allowed to speak in contained theatres – the doss house or the police court. Clearly Harkness wanted to articulate a more specific political pro-gramme and equally clearly she couldn't. Only the ideology of the Army set against the resistance of the working class (that is the most depressed among them). The melodrama of Captain Lobe rushing back to marry Ruth displaces any political action, but it is almost necessary to sidetrack the stalemate between what is effectively constituted as the ideological organisation of the poor and the hunger of the poor.

There are many ways in which this might reflect Harkness' own polit-ical confusion as the arguments of the late 1880s come to a head. But it also reflects on the difficulty of following *Out of Work* with a novel which could build on its positivity without being utopian. By seeing the truth through the alien utopia of the Salvation Army, Margaret Harkness seems to wish to correct the possible vagueness of her own political perspective She succeeds almost too well, and produces an endless documentary within the confines of a terminated story. But what I insist on is that like *A City Girl* and *Out of Work*, *Captain Lobe* ought to be read by anyone concerned with the implications for the literary production of the socialist movement.

Notes

1.   The historical details in this paper derive largely from Henry Pelling, *The Origins of the Labour Party* 1880–1900 (London, 1954), but I have also found E. P. Thompson, *William Morris, Romantic to Revolutionary* (London, 1955), Chushichi Tsuzuki, *H. M. Hyndman and British Socialism* (Oxford, 1961), Dona Torr, *Tom Mann and His Times* (London, 1956) useful in forming a general perspective. The synthesis offered here makes no claims to originality, but it is my own and I am only too aware of its eclecticism and simplification.

2.   Pelling, *op. cit.*, p. 48.

3.   Pelling, *op. cit.*: 'The fact was that, although it was to the interest of the working class that the Socialists appealed, there was a very high propor-tion of middle-class people among the converts of this period, and what

the societies lacked in numbers they made up in the comparative energy, ability and financial generosity of their members. This alone can account for the flood of Socialist periodicals and pamphlets which already poured from the presses.'

4. See my 'Gissing, Morris and English Socialism', *Victorian Studies*, XII, 1968, pp. 432–40, and John Lucas, 'Conservatism and Revolution in the 1880's', in John Lucas (ed.), *Literature and Politics in the Nineteenth Century* (London, 1971), pp. 173–219. [And now published here.]

5. I don't wish to underestimate the quite remarkable achievements of Meredith and Rutherford, nor indeed to suggest that in more than this strictly limited local context they can be bracketed together. See John Lucas, *The Literature of Change* (Hassocks, 1977), Chapter II for Rutherford.

6. In Chapter XVI. See my essay on Morris in Lucas, *Literature and Politics*, p. 232. [And now published here.]

7. Bernard Shaw, *An Unsocial Socialist* (London, 1914), pp. 324–5.

8. The term is Gissing's. See my *George Gissing: Fiction and Ideology* (London, 1978). Chapter 1.

9. John Law (i.e. Margaret Harkness), *George Eastmont, Wanderer* (London, 1905), p. 125. All of Margaret Harkness' novels were published under the pseudonym of John Law.

10. The main source of this section is the unpublished diary of Beatrice Webb. I have also found Norman Mackenzie (ed.). *The Letters of Sidney and Beatrice Webb* (London, 1978), Vol. I useful. For her relationship with Eleanor Marx see Yvonne Kapp. *The Crowded Years* (London, 1976).

11. Unpublished diary, entry of 24 March 1883.

12. *Ibid.*, 13 February 1882.

13. 'Women as 'Civil Servants', *Nineteenth Century*, X (1880), p. 381.

14. 'Railway Labour', *Nineteenth Century*, XII (1882), p. 72.

15. *Ibid.*, p. 732.

16. 'The Municipality of London', *National Review*, n.s., 2 (1883), p. 105.

17. *Egyptian Life and History* (London, 1884), p. 54.

18. *Ibid.*, p. 68.

19. Unpublished diary, entry of 24 March 1883.

20. Ann Stafford, *A Match to Fire the Thames* (London, 1961), p. 155.

21. Unpublished diary, entry of 18 October 1887.

22. 'A Year of My Life', *New Review*, 5 (1893), p. 376.

23. Unpublished diary entry, of 13 November 1889.

24. Karl Marx and Frederick Engels, *Literature and Art* (Bombay, 1956), pp. 35–8.

25. John Law, *A City Girl* (London, 1887), p. 9.

26. See Adrian Poole, *Gissing in Context* (London, 1975), for a discussion of this group of writers.

27. *A City Girl, op. cit.*, p. 47.

28. *Ibid.*, p. 70.

29. *Ibid.*, pp. 66–7.

30. *Ibid.*, p. 76.

31. *Ibid.*, p. 100.

32. *Ibid.*, p. 126.
33. John Law, *Out of Work* (London, 1888), p. 2.
34. *Ibid.*, p. 221.
35. *Ibid.*, pp. 18–19.
36. *Ibid.*, p. 240.
37. *Ibid.*, p. 241.
38. *Ibid.*, p. 163.
39. *Ibid.*, p. 129.
40. John Law, *Captain Lobe* (London, 1889), pp. 33–4.
41. *Ibid.*, p. 50.
42. *Ibid.*, p. 226.

CHAPTER 17

Mark Rutherford
and Spinoza

This essay is concerned with the presence of Spinoza in a sequence of fictions written by a fictional author "Mark Rutherford," rather than with the larger, more diffuse question of Spinoza's influence on William Hale White. Fictions are not reproductions of philosophic positions, and John Lucas is right to point out the danger of reducing these texts to the schematic horizons from which their representation of "reality" sometimes explicitly takes its bearings.[1] In any case Spinoza is not an easy philosopher and even had White claimed to be a Spinozan, and even if Rutherford was transparently White, we would not be able to designate their content "Spinozan" without much ramification.

Nevertheless, White's relationship to Rutherford is important and problematic and his involvement with Spinoza is deeply bound up with the production of the fictions. Although he claims to have translated *Ethic* in the 1860s, the first edition was published in 1883, between *The Autobiography* and *Deliverance*. The second, revised edition, with its much expanded preface, was published in 1894 between the last two novels, *Catharine Furze* and *Clara Hopgood*. *Pages from a Journal* and *More Pages* are also strictly part of the fictional sequence, and the last essay explicitly on Spinoza appears in the former.

Moreover, there are very marked traces of Spinoza in the texts, besides the obvious fictional re-incarnation of the philosopher himself in Baruch Cohen. The most acclaimed late nineteenth-century explicator of Spinoza, Frederick Pollock, called his account of the fifth book of *Ethic*, "The Deliverance of Man"[2] (White himself called it "Human Liberty").[3] "Revolution" is a word associated with Spinoza in both the 1883 preface and more explicitly in the late essay of the title.[4] And, of course, there are many direct echoes of Spinoza in the texts. Miriam's schooling among the stars, for example, is clearly a case of moving from inadequate thought (imagination) to reason (understanding). But these traces are less interesting than the influence of Spinoza on the fictional project itself. This is not straightforward. As Rutherford opposes *and* reflects White, Spinoza is a negative as well as positive presence. In either case, it certainly enriches our reading of the fictions to read Spinoza in conjunction with them.

No other writer in English fiction has so strong a relationship to a specific philosophic enterprise.

This however, would only be a matter of footnotes, did it not throw light on a larger issue, the question of the legibility of the Rutherford fictions. His texts are still so little read, and so often merely as thinly disguised documents in the history of ideas.[5] Spinozan explorations threaten to confirm this and, even worse, to depoliticize and dehistoricise the ideas, so that Rutherford/White ends up looking like a vulgariser of immutable truths. This essay assumes that Rutherford's novels are major texts in the history of fiction, challenging the organicist aesthetic of conservative modernism as well as demanding a re-reading of nineteenth-century history. (Was it possible to understand *The Revolution in Tanner's Lane* before *The Making of the English Working Class*?) But we need to understand fully the conditions on which the fictional project is based and the problematic way it relates to the realistic novel.

Spinoza can help us clarify this. He helps White through the ideological crisis which becomes increasingly manifest once the Second Reform Act has made it clear that self-help is not compatible with social stability, and enables him to test and reconstruct the resources of the realist novel which had centred on a social world composed of free but consenting adults, of which *Middlemarch* was the last, most vexed example. This does not mean that Spinoza provides an ideology, but that he defers specific closures which in other writers disintegrate the parameters of experience in irony and symbol.

The scientific revolution of the seventeenth century split philosophy into two major tendencies, rationalism and empiricism. Antithetical as they appear to be, however, they are politically both epistemologies of dominance. The mind is granted mastery or possession on condition that it can afford to withdraw from matter. For the dispossessed there needed to be accounts of the self which could be negotiated within an overarching system, and ready to hand are Positivism by which the self is absorbed into social morphology and Hegelianism by which, in its English version, the self is spirited away into the Absolute from whence it comes. Eliot and to some extent Hardy and Gissing are attracted to Positivism, and it is its manifest failure that sends the younger novelists into the arms of cosmic pessimism. White never seems to engage with Positivism although, of course, in *The Autobiography* Mark meets a woman vaguely like Marian Evans.

Hegelianism is a different matter. White revealed the true authorship of *The Autobiography*, it is said, to George Jacob Holyoake and to J. H. Stirling.[6] The former is not surprising, for the political and social concerns of the 80s mark all these historical texts. Stirling is more problematic. On the one hand he was certainly a major influence on White, and the latter's surprising lack of interest in Positivism when it had such a direct bearing on his political tendencies may be explained by the fact that Stirling in his supplementary notes to his translation of Schwegler's *History of Philosophy* which White claimed in 1883 contained the best introduction to Spinoza; it opens with a section entitled "Why Philosophy stops with Hegel and not with Comte."[7] On the other hand, his own *Secret of Hegel* runs counter to everything in Rutherford. "In one word," he states, "the principle must not be subjective will, but one will," and he recommends Hegel as compensation for the failure of the revolutions of 1848.[8] Stirling's note on Spinoza in Schwegler is dismissive – Spinoza only managed to construct a massive metaphor.[9] White cannot have been encouraged to devote so much energy to Spinoza by Stirling even though the latter's daughter helped him with the translation. Perhaps sending *The Autobiography* to him was as much a way of disagreeing as a tribute to his friendship. This would suggest that Spinoza was a way of resisting Hegelian absorption because he postulates a radically different scientificity from Positivism.

There are three problems to which Spinoza provides answers which open up the conditions on which the Rutherford texts are produced. The first is the relationship of narrative, history and experience to knowledge. Both the *Tractatus* and the *Ethic* enable Rutherford to construct a history which is neither gradualist nor teleological. Secondly, Spinoza problematises the formation of self/character without dissolving or absolving the subject. Finally, Rutherford keeps open the ideological problem of structure and agency by providing a fictional representation motivated by Spinoza's arguments about the relations of body and mind. Far from exhausting the novels this analysis aims merely to open them up and demonstrate that Rutherford both demolishes and reconstructs the parameters of realist fiction.

Picture and Thought

There is a basic tension between the programme of Rutherford's novels and White's involvement in Spinoza. In the preface to his translation of the *Tractatus de Intellectus Emendatione*, 1895, White writes: "The distinction between picture and thought is one on which Spinoza earnestly insists, ... and it may be said that it is impossible to proceed a single step with him unless this distinction be recognised."[10] Error is the product of the "imagined idea or image" or even merely of "the power of words." We must therefore see Rutherford's choice of narrative, which of course becomes more overtly fictional as it moves from the apparent "truth" of autobiography to the third person, cross gendered, historical stories of Catharine Furze and Clara Hopgood, as a counterpoint, even an act of defiance when set against the work done on Spinoza which coincides with it.[11] This tension, so far from damaging the novels, however, is a precondition of their strange effectiveness.

The most overtly anti-Spinozan text is *Catharine Furze* published in the year before the second edition of *Ethic* which, we are told, had entailed a thorough re-reading of Spinoza. It is true that two of the most endorsed characters in the novel are based on Spinozan insights. Mrs. Bellamy says that she comes to terms with her own distress by recognising that the apparent object of her misery is not the real cause.[12] This echoes the way out of human bondage. It is not by suppressing our passions any more than by indulging them that we are released from the bondage; it is by recognising that to be affected by an external cause is to suffer and that to recognise desire is internally motivated is to recognise passion as passion. Similarly, Dr. Turnbull says that any thought is evil if it "maims" us.[13] Bellamy and Turnbull both thus stand outside the attempts, by Mrs. Furze and later by Cardew, to manipulate Catharine's emotions and are thus instrumental in saving her. Or at least they seem to echo values that should save her. But neither of them are products of philosophy. Mrs. Bellamy reaches this insight by instinct and is never understood, though it may be a further irony that she explains her mental processes in a phrase that parodies White's praise of Spinoza's intellectual rigour: "for one thing always seems to draw me on to another."[14] Perhaps Spinozan intelligence is pushed to the margins by the conventional wisdom. Dr. Turnbull, although not uneducated, is not a metaphysician either, being explicitly designated a materialist.

Nor do Bellamy and Turnbull save Catharine. In fact Mrs. Bellamy's emancipation strikes Catharine as completely irrelevant to her own case, and Dr. Turnbull's practical advice leads to self-destructive altruism. They are marginal catalysts in the plot at most, just as they are marginal to society.

On the other hand, Cardew is clearly limited by his abstraction and focus on universals. The wife whose "pagan common sense"[15] irritates him so much is in need of empirical criticism, not Spinozan rationality. He is not himself Spinozan since the philosopher thought of universals as compound inadequate ideas, and refused to divorce body and mind, but he is redeemed by the "picture" of Catharine that remains with him:

> Some men are determined by principles, and others are drawn and directed by a vision or a face. Before Mr. Cardew was set for evermore the face which he saw white and saintly at Chapel Farm that May Sunday morning when death had entered, and it controlled and moulded him with an all-pervading power more subtle and penetrating than that which could have been exercised by theology or ethics.[16]

This, the last word of the novel, is surely significant. Mr. Cardew is redeemed by what in Spinoza's terms is a classic instance of an inadequate idea.

More than this, the possibility of redemption comes from his vulnerability to passion: "it is a fact," we are told, "that vitality means passion," and Mr. Cardew is compared in this with David. For Spinoza passion is the very reverse of vitality since it is other directed (sexual passion particularly so).

Cardew's own tale of Charmides is also an inversion of Spinozan enlightenment. He resists the "Jews" because they "actually believed in miracles." The Pauline epistle he reads is confused by metaphor and "illogical muddles," and he recognises that to become involved with Christianity is to reject the enlightenment of Apollo and the "order and sequence of Lucretius." The gospel tale is superstitious, but he is haunted by the fact of Demariste. His love for her is what motivates his ambiguous martyrdom – again it is an image. Faith, which he cannot connect with his own philosophy, is the only new spring of action.[17]

We should not explain this divergence with naïve biographical surmise, as Stone tends to.[18] Cardew is not Rutherford and Rutherford is not White. These affirmations of the power of imagination are refracted through speculative authority. But it shows that Spinoza is not there in the texts only as a set of influences, but also as a possibility against which the text is sometimes constructed.

One of the major differences between the first and second edition prefaces is that in the latter White discusses the *Tractatus Theologico Politicus*. This text subjects the Bible to analytic scrutiny and has two major points for us. First it makes a rigorous distinction between philosophy whose object is knowledge, and faith whose object is obedience. Faith is revealed through prophecy and miracle. Spinoza rejects miracle altogether, saying that historical factors must account for the perception of strange happenings. Prophecy, however, is taken as having a precise function in the establishment and preservation of obedience. Insofar as it promotes obedience to the laws of justice and love, prophecy has an important function which reason, unable to demonstrate that obedience is the means of salvation, cannot fulfill.

Prophecy is based on imagination: "that is, by words and figures either real or imaginary."[19] Words and figures enable prophets to go beyond the boundary of the intellect. White is surprised at the concessive attitude of Spinoza to the Bible, and is puzzled to know where Spinoza actually stands in regard to the truth of prophecy as opposed to its validity. It seems clear enough, however, that faith is available because reason is defective. More importantly, divine law, as opposed to human law which is a form of expedience, needs no validation from the past: "The truth of a historical narrative, however assured, cannot give us the knowledge, nor consequently the love of God, for the love of God springs from knowledge of Him, and knowledge of Him should be derived from general ideas …"[20] He goes on to concede that reading histories is useful "with a view to life in the world," by which he means to enable reason to help us adapt our actions to living in the world. Witness, prophecy, narrative are modes of integration and negotiation. They tell us about the human law, not the divine law. The thrust of *Catharine Furze* seems different. But this does not mean that the novelist Mark Rutherford who is not White and certainly not a Spinozan is independent of White or of the Spinozan questionings that he is capable of putting to the "truth" of historical witness, and human experience.

Although the remarks on *Tractatus* did not appear until 1894, it seems very unlikely that the translator of *Ethic* would not have read this most famous text before he embarked on the Rutherford novels. Indeed there are signs from the beginning of at least some reference. Thus Mark's meditation on Balaam [21] resembles the importance Spinoza gives him as one of the gentile prophets. And to follow *Deliverance* with "Job" as to preface *Miriam's Schooling* with "Gideon," "Samuel," and "Saul," who all feature very significantly in *Tractatus*, cannot be coincidence. It is precisely in these biblical re-narratives that the tension between philosophy and revelation is rehearsed and resolved.

The key texts here are the biblical narratives which precede *Miriam's Schooling* but they should be seen as part of the continuous sequence of Rutherford fictions arising from the need to elucidate and transcend the aporia of the preceding texts. And this takes us back to *Deliverance*. It is positive on balance, as the next section will show: starting from "I" of the autobiography it takes Rutherford beyond it. But *Deliverance* ends in ambiguity. Rutherford's deliverance is finally not merely from himself but from life. The "actual joy" with which the narrative ends is severely qualified by Shapcott's editorial closure. The actual joy only results in some papers, the first of which is "Notes on the Book of Job." Job resembles Spinoza or at least White's account of him as "the type of those great thinkers who cannot compromise ... who faithfully follow their intellect to its very last results" and in whose refusal to be comforted "lies the whole contention of the philosophers against the preachers." [22] The personal parallel Rutherford invokes is of the German woman who gives birth to a child who dies at one year old and who then dies herself at twenty-six, bears on Rutherford's own case. How can you define the meaning of the struggle towards life if it is met with death? Job gets no answer except that God will not be accountable to him, and he thus echoes Goethe's comment on the value of Spinoza. [23] Job nevertheless has a vision of God, sees rather than only hears him.

The *Tractatus* makes a great deal of play about the voices of the prophets (surprisingly it does not give much attention to Job and even doubts the validity of his witness). Job then leads to "Principles" and "Mysterious Portrait" both of which keep the need for personal example at play with the commitment to abstract truth. "Principles" vexes itself about rigour, compromise and change but ends with a role model. "Mysterious Portrait" retreats entirely into the saving grace of memory. Nonetheless, Job, who is not only the type of the philosopher but who expresses "the soul of the Revolution",[24] poses another possibility, the transmission of a tradition not confined to the inadequate idea of the personal memory, but capable of revealing what Spinoza means by the divine law.

This entails two interpretations of Spinoza which White seemed to hold, though they may not be incompatible. The first is that when Spinoza argues that we should scrutinise the Scriptures for their meaning and not their truth, he is effectively admitting that the Divine Law is transmitted in however obscure a form by prophecy insofar as it is critically read (thus Rutherford does not quote "Job" but interprets it). Second, that this truth survives the limited version of the individual vision. Certainly in Rutherford's fictive world death is a precondition of insight. Experience teaches us very little about our own lives but the transmitted experiences of those who have struggled form a meaningful historical record. This is how White reads the fifth book of the *Ethic* – there is an eternity of mind which means that revelation, though not philosophy, is meaningful for philosophy.

Assuming that the Rutherford texts are a meaningful sequence, this would give an important articulation to the development of the narrative. *The Revolution in Tanner's Lane* is composed of radical discontinuities of time and space (which can, it is true, be justified historically) bridged and emphasised at once by the inspirational succession of Paulines which offer an image of energising as opposed to closing womanhood. Rutherford is not saying that if only personal relations were more open and equal, revolution would be less liable to failure. On the contrary, it is an index of both Zachariah's and George's limitations that they do not understand Jane and Priscilla who both have sensibilities which play no part in their marriages. What is positive is that the revolutionary need recurs and is transmitted across the gaps of history.

The crucial development is from *Revolution in Tanner's Lane* to *Miriam's Schooling* because it takes Rutherford from a masculine narrative position to a feminine one. In *The Autobiography*, *Deliverance* and *Revolution*, woman is the agent of male liberation or suffering. She is always in the predicate of the subject's articulation. *Miriam*, *Catharine Furze* and *Clara Hopgood* invert that position. Again we might see this as a challenge to Spinoza who has a very poor estimate of women. But it also grows out of a Spinozan articulation. We must return to "Gideon."

Gideon in Spinoza's *Tractatus* is a clear demonstration that "Imagination does not, in its own nature, involve any certainty of truth, such as is implied in every clear and distinct idea, but requires some extrinsic reason to assure us of its objective reality."[25] Gideon asks God for a sign so that he can know that it is God and not another who tells him to shed most of his army and mount a guerilla attack.[26] Because he refuses to rule (thus qualifying for a certain Spinozan integrity because much of the polemic of the *Tractatus* is directed against theocracy), he is neglected by the Israelites and his family is destroyed. What is important is that in Rutherford's version this story is told not by Gideon himself who disappears with his sign and the emblems of his victory into the mists of time, but by a son who has no faith and who sees the father as having no faith. It is a story of failure and despair, redeemed only when it is given meaning 1400 years later in the Epistle to the Hebrews and later still in Scott's *Old Mortality*. Gideon, that is, speaks to man through time not because he has answers but because he is involved in struggle. That this is a political and not merely personal moral is confirmed by the allusion to Scott who himself presses the analogy between the Covenanters and the Revolution.[27] Gideon is an image of revolutionary integrity, doomed by his own political honesty, but transmitted in the sceptical recall through history.

The *Miriam's Schooling* volume then effects a startling transition. Samuel, who is singled out by Spinoza as a prophet particularly subject to imagination, is offered by Rutherford as a prophet coming from humble origins, not requiring a sign and being committed to republican integrity. The coming of Saul forces him into a specialised role as guardian of the Law (as opposed to the law), insisting on it being followed in every detail. Thus an opposition is set up between prophecy and priesthood. But Rutherford is not content with the Samuel perspective. He opposes it not with Saul but Saul's wife Rizpah's monologue which follows Samuel. She laments Saul's Terror, his lack of joy, but finally defends him against the antisocial Samuel and the wayward David.

There is nothing in Rizpah's narrative to suggest that she is being ironised. She does not fully vindicate Saul the secular tyrant against Samuel the uncompromising theocrat. But she adds a further dimension to the tension between revelation and political practice. It is a crucial transition in Rutherford's work, in a sense making it more pessimistically tied to the insoluble conflict between reason and experience and between love and science. From this point on it is woman who is put at the centre of this conflict both because there is an expected solution within the dedication available to the renouncing woman and, equally, because of the self obliteration that dedication threatens.

Miriam's Schooling itself works through this problematic. It is, as Lucas says,[28] the nearest Rutherford comes to offering a protagonist up to the egoism/altruism trajectory. It is, however, a long way from it as well. Miriam has to learn to go beyond the bounds of the self but it is not into self-sacrifice that she finally falls. Her banal marriage is in the end a genuine schooling. Finding in astronomy a sense of the infinite and recovering through this some of the energy that has hitherto misled her, she is not allowed to sublimate it into quietist awe. On the contrary, she is required to learn about and understand the heavens. Her journeyman husband is instrumental in this because he can make the necessary tools. It is an episode reminiscent of one of the most striking passages of Spinoza's essay on *The Emendation of the Intellect*, which White published in 1895. Spinoza rejects the Cartesian idea that we need to question our method back to infinity:

> After we have discovered what kind of knowledge is necessary for us, the way and method are to be exhibited by which the things which are to be known may be known by this kind of knowledge. To this end, we must first consider that there is no search *ad infinitum*; that is to say, in order that the best method of discovering the truth may be found, there is no need of another method for investigating the method of investigating the truth, and in order that the second method may be investigated there is no need of a third and so on *ad infinitum*; for in this way we shall never arrive at a knowledge of the truth, nor indeed at any knowledge. It is the same with tools; and the argument proceeds in the same way. For example, in order that iron may be forged, we need a hammer; and if we are to have a hammer we must make one. To this end we need another hammer and other instruments; and to obtain these we shall need other instruments and so on *ad infinitum*. Thus anybody might fruitlessly endeavour to prove that men are unable to forge iron. But inasmuch as men at the beginning, with instruments furnished by nature, were able to make certain very easy things, although with great labour and imperfectly, and with these, when they were finished, made other and more difficult things with less labour, and more perfectly, and thus by degrees, advancing from the most simple productions to tools, and from tools to other productions and tools, were able to accomplish with small labour so many and such difficult things, so also the intellect, by its own native force, forms for itself intellectual instruments by which it acquires additional strength for other intellectual works, and from these works, other instruments or power of further discovery, and thus by degrees advances until it reaches the pinnacle of wisdom.[29]

Miriam is "schooled" by the realisation that her boring husband has skills without which she cannot pursue the understanding she seeks. It places the whole fictive enterprise in a proper light.

Rutherford does not write Spinozan novels. Such a thing would be a contradiction in terms: "the truth of historical narrative … cannot give us the knowledge nor consequently the love of God, for the love of God springs from knowledge of Him, and knowledge of Him should be derived from general ideas, in themselves certain and known."[30] To write narratives at all is to acknowledge that "sure knowledge" can only be revealed by a sign and accepted in the end by simple faith. Nevertheless what narrative shows is the struggle to find the divine law and the correct interpretation of the meaning of that struggle as it is revealed in partial flawed histories and experiences is an index of the eternity of mind. It is in fact a glimpse of reason. Mark Rutherford is certainly not a flawless narrator.[31] We must read his texts in terms of the gaps imposed by imperfect record and the mark of death. History is not reason. Its only access to reason is interpretation. If we ignore the framework that Spinoza provides we may miss both the rationale of form and the challenge to prevailing ideology that the novels offer, beginning with a radical revision of the concept of identity.

The Empty "I"

In two of the articles he wrote for the *Secular Review* in 1880, White makes it clear that for him as for other major moralists of the seventies, Bradley, Spencer, Sidgwick, Eliot, the function of ethics was self-transcendence, "that self annihilation," as he puts it in "Ixion," "which is the goal of all ethics."[32] However, this is not altruism or self-immersion in a higher good. An earlier essay cites Whitman as reaching "the highest point of self negation" at the end of "Prayer of Columbus" which he glosses as "I am perfectly content if only the evolution goes on which my existence has helped," and this is "the goal of all ethics."[33] When we read the introduction to the 1883 *Ethic* we find an explicit distancing from renunciatory ethics: "the desires which we accuse so bitterly are really indispensable to our purification." A little before this he has argued that the desire to appropriate is good but "man has other desires, and the desire to appropriate brought under their influence is altered and becomes moral."[34] This is a vague paraphrase of Spinoza's argument in *Ethic IV*, but it is precise enough to preempt both a positivist evolution into social being and Hegelian self-transcendence. *The Autobiography* represents the emergence of the self from ideological obliteration. In Spinozan terms it is the uncovering of the "*conatus*" or "endeavour" by which "each thing, in so far as it is in itself, endeavours to persevere in its being."[35]

There are two ways of reading *The Autobiography*. "Shapcott," in his preface to the second edition, interprets it negatively as a warning against over intellectualisation for the mediocre mind. The ambiguous implication of the quotation from *Ecclesiastes* with which he closes surely means that if this is not a false gloss it is at least a premature foreclosure on Rutherford's story. Rutherford himself, on the contrary, stresses that the very ordinariness of the story told, "a tale of a commonplace life, perplexed by many problems I have never solved," may free others from "that sense of solitude" with which he has had to "face that perplexity."[36] There is no release from the solitude of the perplexity within the text and the ending confirms this, given over, as it is to the secular preacher at Mardon's funeral who neither speaks *for* Rutherford nor offers any illumination on his individual death, saying only that eternal life for the individual would be unendurable. In between, however, what has emerged and survived is a self not triumphant over human bondage, very much not delivered, but persistent and at the threshold of sustaining knowledge.

In *The Treatise Concerning the Emendation of the Intellect*, Spinoza identifies four kinds of knowledge, the first two of which are merged in *Ethic* to constitute imagination. In the preface to his translation of *The Emendation*, White enumerates these as follows: (1) by hearsay, tradition, or on authority, (2) by loose experience, (3) by inference of a cause from an effect, (4) by perception through essence, or knowledge of a proximate cause.[37] This last is what Pollock defines as man's "deliverance" and is clearly relevant to the second part of the autobiographical narrative. *The Autobiography* is concerned with the transition from the first to the second and the difficult and tentative groping towards the third, towards "reason."

The fundamental irony of this text is that the integrity of dissenting experience is offered Mark only as a self-denying institution which the dissent originated to overthrow. The context of autobiography entails the possibility of conversion, but here the conversion motif is institutionalised. The hypocrisy he identifies this as is internalised, "in the sense that I professed it to myself."[38] What he professes are convictions he is supposed to have of sin, the efficacy of atonement, forgiveness "and ... a great many other things which were the merest phrases." This is clearly knowledge by hearsay. The possibility of its truth is not denied, such things might once have happened, "under the preaching of Paul" and might still happen "by attachment to some woman," but this is not truth in Spinoza's or Rutherford's sense of the word because it is not gained by knowledge. Indeed Mark is excused from "experience" on the grounds of his parents' piety. Moreover, conversion is supposedly a miracle, so that its Spinozan invalidity is doubled. Later at college, Mark finds it impossible to talk about subjects which have no genuine connection with himself, and the prime example of this is "the artificial, the merely miraculous, the event which had no inner meaning."[39]

Mark's real conversion is caused by the *Lyrical Ballads* but his gloss on this is not strikingly Wordsworthian: "Wordsworth would have been the last man to say that he had lost his faith in the God of his fathers. But his real God is not the God of the Church, but the God of the hills, the *abstraction* Nature, and to this my reverence was transferred."[40] This Spinozan secularisation recurs when Rutherford ascribes "nearly every doctrine in the college creed" to "a natural origin in the necessities of human nature" and that he wishes to reach through to that original necessity, rather than "accept dogmas as communications from without."[41] This echoes *Tractatus* and *Ethic*. Spinoza argues for the transparency of the divine law in the scripture and the opacity of its presentation to particular human needs. The depersonalization and disinstitutionalization of God is strongly reminiscent of the whole thrust of *Ethic* but so, more specifically, is his comment on the atonement which on the face of it looks like a contradiction of "*conatus*." Rutherford's justification of atonement is in terms of its necessity not its moral desirability. He is not endorsing martyrdom. It is an aspect of the unity of things: "This was part of the scheme of the world, and we might dislike it or not, we could not get ride of it." He goes on to add that it is "a sublime summing up ... of what sublime men have done for their race," but this is glossed as an exemplification, not a contradiction of Nature.[42]

This point is crucial to the *The Autobiography* which, committed as it declares itself to be to the portrayal of failure is, at another level, the story of secular atonement. Mark is thrust from the hearsay of the religious institution not into the secure world of rationality but into worse isolation and despair. Deliverance is deferred on two levels. First, there is the ambiguous disappointment of unrequited love, emphasised by its double occurrence. Over and against the intellectual emancipation is an unfulfilled desire for "a perfect friendship," based on mutual readiness for utter sacrifice.[43] At first he explains this as a callow dream: "Only when I got much older did I discern the duty of accepting life as God made it, and thankfully receiving any scrap of love offered to me." Towards the end of the novel, however, it recurs when, among the Unitarians, he reflects that his "existence was of no earthly importance to anybody."[44] It is classed as weakness, but not as one from which he will ever be free: "The desire has not died ... it has been forcibly suppressed and that is all." In one of those resonant phrases by which Rutherford walks out of the frame of moral discourse, and into a startling socio-psychic analysis, he writes: "I have been repulsed into self-reliance, and reserve, having learned wisdom by experience." "Repulsed" surely undermines the force of the implicitly stoic "wisdom," and it is not accepting life as God made it because unlike, for example, the abstinence from wine, it does not derive from "a susceptibility to nobler joys."[45] Self-reliance, here, is a Spinozan pain.

Secondly, the abstraction which liberates him from the God of the Church is clearly limited in its power to help him to the right decision. Thus his rejection of Ellen is rational but abstracting: "I said to myself that instinct is all very well, but for what purpose is reason given us if not to reason with it; and reasoning in the main is a correction of what is called instinct, and of hasty first impressions."[46] Of course, it is not at all clear that breaking off the engagement with Ellen is wrong since their reconciliation is the result of their separate intervening experiences. But it conflicts with Spinoza's view of knowledge in two ways. First, he is not completely dismissive of imagination which is helpful for everyday matters. Secondly, and ultimately more importantly, reason has limited power in the liberation of man from his bondage. At the end of the process it is scientific intuition that releases him.

This is not articulately available to Mark in *The Autobiography*. Indeed Theresa's ardour, Mardon's secularism and the butterfly catcher's scientific endeavour are seen to be only makeshift solutions, though they close off facile escape routes. Thus the butterfly catcher satirises those who try to think their way through death with a Spinozan scorn of sloppy thinking: "there is a strange fascination about these topics to many people because they are topics which permit a great deal of dreaming but very little thinking; in fact true thinking, in the proper sense of the word, is impossible in dealing with them. There is no rigorous advance from one position to another, which is really all that makes thinking worth the novel."[47] Systematic procedure is what White in the preface to his first edition of *Ethic* first admires about Spinoza. The butterfly catcher nevertheless has no general view to offer in its stead. Listening to him, Mark finds him "incomprehensible,"[48] and it is only when he learns the man's story that he comes to understand. The butterfly catcher bears witness, he does not enunciate the truth, except by negating the false.

At the end of the narrative, Mark is in no better situation than he has been from the beginning. By the end of chapter eight his successive resistance to compromising the truth has left him an utterly isolated schoolteacher in Stoke Newington. It is a crisis of human bondage, the memory inadequate to the task of recall, the dominant note a fear of external interruption ("lest anything should arrest me"). And finally, as he passes from one state to a better, from the job to unemployment, he cries tears of joy. But both oppression and liberation are judged to be internal: "I am constrained now to admit that my trouble was but a bubble blown of air, and I doubt whether I have done any good by dwelling on it."[49] All that happens in the subsequent chapter is in fragmentary and temporary mitigation of that isolation. Crucially, however, Mark atones for the compromises he cannot make, and thus makes himself part of a rational whole.

Two propositions from the *Ethic* clarify this, and fill up the narrative gap. The first connects "*conatus*" with absolute integrity, with which at a certain point it may seem to clash (and indeed in an unaltered state of nature would clash). *Ethic IV* proposition LXXII, "a free man never acts deceitfully, but always honourably," has the following Scholium:

> If it be asked whether, if a man by breach of faith could escape from the danger of instant death, reason does not counsel him, for the preservation of his being, to break faith; I reply in the same way, that if reason gives such counsel, she gives it to all men, and reason therefore generally counsels men to make no agreements for uniting their strength and possessing laws in common except deceitfully, that is to say, to have in reality, no common laws, which is absurd.[50]

For Spinoza, man's social being resides in his absolute personal integrity, not as is sometimes assumed in his ability to compromise. Although in becoming sociable, man divests himself of rights which he accords to the State and therefore gives the State powers of coercion, this is in order to enhance his own existence, not to impede it. It is forgoing a lower for a higher desire (not as it happens only security, but also because it gives man pleasure not to have that pleasure at the expense of others). The only unqualified virtue Mark learns from his Calvinist upbringing is "a rigid regard for truthfulness."[51] This is both the source of his survival through the self-annihilation Calvinism demands, and the cause of his progressive isolation. But it is finally, too, a sign of his social being. The abrupt untidy end of *The Autobiography* and the quantum leap into a whole different way of relating to the world in *Deliverance* is not merely the fictional guarantee of "authenticity" but also a different aspect of something that is positively emerging in the earlier text. The atonement Mark makes is not for the individual against social man but for man's social capability against the inadequate knowledge that makes him shiver inside his bad faith.

As with *The Autobiography*, the title *Deliverance* is a manifest tease. What is Mark's deliverance? Is it the release from the isolation of the countryside and the purposeful life in the city? Is it release from the grinding horror of work through the reconstituted family and the holiday? Is it death itself? Nowhere in this text are we told that Mark is definitely delivered nor from what he is delivered. The *Ethic* will not heal this clearly interrogative silence, but I think it will help us identify its questions. In the context of late nineteenth-century thought, the *Ethic* is striking because it postulates the absolute unity of existence, but insists by its methods of argument on the absolute rational consent of the individual mind to perceive this. The reason has no peace either from its splendid isolation as "mind" or from its self-obliteration in a higher mind.

If the title alludes to Pollock's description of the fifth part of *Ethic*, it is clear that in terms of actual correspondence, Spinoza is only one preference among many that operate in the text, and that when he is present it is not always coherently or extendedly. Thus Mark, for example, seems to find a way out of his own misery by working with McKay, and McKay in his private capacity seems to start from a Spinozan demand that language should correspond unpersuasively with its meaning. McKay, however, is not only forced by circumstance to adopt a completely different posture in his professional writing, his linguistic puritanism is itself an inhibition from the clear idea he might have of the wife he constantly silences, so in that respect he merely operates intellectual rigour as self-indulgent passion. This is indeed borne out by his practice in Drury Lane which with its complaints about distraction and anarchy bears more resemblance to Arnold than Spinoza (though, of course, Arnold had made his own assimilation).[52] Rutherford places his activity as an overall repetition of the past rather than the new scientific approach currently needed. Nevertheless, having shown that McKay is unable to pursue a Spinozan clarity, the chapter "Drury Lane Theology" seems to vindicate on pragmatic grounds the philosophically dubious remedies proposed here.

The comment which follows this vindication seems to engage explicitly with the *Ethic*:

> We endeavoured to follow Christianity in the depth of its distinction between right and wrong. Here this religion is of priceless value. Philosophy proclaims the unity of our nature. To philosophy every passion is as natural as every act of saint-like negation, and one of the usual effects or thinking or philosophizing is to bring together all that is apparently contrary in man, and to show how it really proceeds from one centre. But Christianity had not to propound a theory of man; it had to redeem the world.[53]

This does not read like a repetition of the allotment of specific roles to theology and philosophy in the *Tractatus*. White's preface of 1883 asks of Spinoza's *Ethic*, "wherein can you help me?" If Drury Lane theology is helpful and "philosophy" merely theoretical, then we must see *Deliverance* as a rejection of the kind of knowledge Spinoza makes available. Certainly it is posing questions against it, and the way in which characters survive in the novel is not formulaic. Nevertheless, if we are aware that White has translated Spinoza by the time he publishes *Deliverance* we can see that the inadequacy of Drury Lane theology to account for "what it all came to" is a deliberate effect of the novel's structure.

This is related to two features, one structural and one representational. Structurally the text develops straightforwardly from Mark's arrival in Camden Town to his friendship with McKay, the setting up of Drury Lane and the first sermon. It then reaches a strange silence, the suppression of Mrs. McKay's comment on the ineffectiveness of McKay's Arnoldian message. We then abruptly turn to the story of Miss Leroy which reverts to Mark's home, the past and the portrayal of two marriages in two generations. This is in turn dropped and two further chapters deal with the outcome and the theology of Drury Lane. These three parts are of equal length and occupy two thirds of the text. The remaining third is, narratively, a sequel to the Miss Leroy story, culminating in the meeting and marriage of Mark and Ellen, the story of "a Helot's love"[54] constantly needing to be kept alive,[55] deliberately restricted (so as to make no mention of work, for example) and reaching "actual joy" only in a brief holiday, a reprise of the earlier break which had resulted in Ellen getting typhoid fever. This structure, or apparent lack of it, is clearly an authenticating device. This is supposed to be a manuscript discovered by Shapcott unexpectedly (since *The Autobiography* has ended with the claim that no more has been found). Like the papers which follow, it is fragmentary and Rutherford himself is at pains to point out that if he were writing a novel he would have more chance of coherence.[56] These disclaimers would in an eighteenth-century or modern author be seen to be devices calling attention to the fictionality of the text, though perversely enough, it seems to encourage Rutherford's readers to treat it as thinly disguised polemic.

Surely it rather calls into question the concrete validity of the polemic. What ought to challenge the theology, and what does at the end of the second chapter, is the social degradation of the people at which it is aimed, in whose lives as Mark, who is more like Morris than Arnold, points out there is no place even for the margin of imagination granted to undertakers in the decoration of their coffins. This is intensified by the gendered power structure which does not allow McKay's wife to express her recognition of this irrelevance. The gendering is confirmed by the two subsequent stories of Miss Leroy who protects her own feminine independence by marrying a dullard and Ellen whose life is reduced to minimal self-justification by the oppression of Miss Leroy's son. It then enters the first story by the production of Mrs. Cardinal and later Mrs. Taylor and is of course made dominant by the story of Ellen.

But so is the mood of social misery and despair. Before the theology, Drury Lane is defined by the terrible stories of its members, epitomised by the generically named Clark who foreshadows what Mark has to turn into in order to protect his marriage in material terms. And that in itself reminds us that the theology, far from being a point of rest, is transcended by the more complex positions that have to be taken up in the anomalous situation Mark finds himself in the end where he reaches the "novel's" traditional happy ending only to step on to the treadmill of destructive labour. It has become a novel about much wider issues than those realised in *The Autobiography* and the theological making the best of it must be seen, therefore, not as the answer to doubt but an answer which has to serve doubt in default of more coherence. Outside the text, as Shapcott's note attests, there is the hope of a political solution.

Both the narrative structure and the representational range of *Deliverance* are clarified by Spinoza's analysis of the relationship of the individual to the whole and by this to his own nature.

First, it is important to stress that Spinoza did not see his own version of human liberty either as easy in itself or as making any appeal to most people. In the Scholium to V.x, which White refers to early in his 1883 preface, Spinoza seems to foreshadow the provisional nature not only of Drury Lane "theology" but of all the religious props on which the characters of the text find themselves forced to lean: "The best thing, therefore, we can do, *so long as we lack a perfect knowledge* of our affects, is to conceive a right rule of life, or sure maxims (*dogmata*) of life, – to commit these to memory, and constantly to apply them to the particular cases which frequently meet us in life, so that *our imagination may be widely affected* by them, and they may always be ready to hand."[57] Individual survival is by whoever is to hand – McKay, Ellen, Mark for others – but no one is adequate on his own. Although the 1883 preface asserts that "the power to go from one ascertained point to another point and so on is what makes the strength of the human mind,"[58] in *Deliverance* personal coherence is seen to be unreliable especially as it defines itself in time, as experience. Thus memory and hope are both deplored. The "dogma of a personal calling" which Rutherford praises in Ellen is "a great truth" not because individuals can work out the universe for themselves. On the contrary it is paradoxically our propensity to doubt that calling because we cannot outstrip the limits of our mind: "But the truth of truths is that the mind of the universe is not our mind."[59] Later, by way of preface to the Drury Lane theology he describes infinity as a liberation from the tyranny both of the senses and the conclusions of logic. If he is echoing Whitman here, he is just as surely so calling on Spinoza: "one thing we cannot help believing as irresistibly as if by geometrical deduction – that the sphere of that understanding of ours, whose function it seems to be to imprison us, is limited."[60] This, rather than the sense of a higher order, is the basis on which the self is delivered from its isolation in the sequel. Mark's life is not worked through – rather is he absorbed into the life of others. That is the obvious "quantum leap" from one text to the other. It is less and less about himself. The self is not thereby transcended because it is into the individual lives of others that it is projected either as observer or as friend or as lover. As its most extreme this even modifies isolation. When Mark works as a clerk he is totally isolated from the obscene conversation of his colleagues. Once they have acknowledged that isolation (they decide he must be religious) he understands that their obscenity springs as much from necessity as his own playreadings to Ellen; they all need a stimulus apart from the monotony of labour (this has been foreshadowed by Clark whom Mark recalls). It is an entirely different social cohesion from those which like Hegelian statism and Positivist evolution consign the miseries of the individual to a teleology.

The recognitions that the city throws up are proleptic flickerings of solidarity. But that solidarity is underwritten philosophically in the *Ethic*. Spinoza's analysis of the relationships of individuals to wholes is in the Second Part, Proposition XIII, especially the Scholium to Lemma VII which sees individuals as themselves wholes composed of less complex individuals *ad infinitum*. Thus the possibility exists of individuals being affected by the change of its parts without undergoing the change of form. This is primarily about bodies and it is in Fourth Part, Scholium to Proposition XVIII, that Spinoza spells out the moral consequences of this interrelationship: "Again from Post. 4 pt. 2, it follows that we can never free ourselves from the need of something outside us for the preservation of our being …. There are many things outside us which are useful to us, and which, therefore are to be sought. Of all these, none more excellent can be discovered than those which exactly agree with our nature … Nothing, therefore is more useful to man than man." [61] This interdependence is further expanded on in XXXVI and XXXVII. It is not only God (nature) that individuals are part of, but in nature closest to one another: "It is very seldom indeed that men live according to the guidance of reason: on the contrary they are generally envious and injurious to one another. But, nevertheless, they are scarcely ever able to lead a solitary life …" [62]

Deliverance is thus not the salvation of an individual but the recognition that the self is part of a larger whole composed of, and not transcendent of, other selves. For what Mark learns from those he meets is not an answer to his own problems but their problems and their answers. In this respect it is impossible to adjudicate between characters, especially in the light of Spinoza's basic ethical notion of "*conatus*" which this text seems to explore. "*Conatus*," usually translated "endeavour," is the state by which everything strives to persist in its own being. Virtue is not a denial, a repression but a transmission of appetite into desire (which is an appetite made conscious) and the command of that desire as an internal motivation rather than as something externally affected (passion). All the characters attempt to persist in their own being. Miss Leroy, for example, marries George so that she can be untrammelled by the narrow society which disapproves of her sleeping with her bedroom window open. Ellen's "Calvinism" is a mode of surviving through the pain inflicted by Clem's infidelity, and even Clem, before he becomes an obstacle to Ellen's happiness, himself misled by idle passion, evolves his inadequate worldview as a means of self-preservation and Rutherford is very ambiguous about condemning him until he betrays Ellen. The same is true of McKay. This is made explicit by the Drury Lane colleagues all of whom have to make some resistant shell against what threatens to crush them (in a sense this is even true of Taylor: he does not withhold his anger out of fear but out of the knowledge that he must remain silent to go on living).

None of this, however, is made any less provisional than the theology itself. There is a limit to the ability of the self to resist oppression. Rutherford says of Taylor that he "would have been patient under any ordinance of nature but he could not lie still under contempt." [63] What is resilient about it is the knowledge that comes of the limited "*conatus*" of others. Mark himself dies a victim to emotion. After the "actual joy" of the day out in Surrey, he succumbs to the internalised anger at his work. But this does not destroy the eternity of that struggle because eternity, in this sense, has nothing to do with everlastingness. However momentary the "actual joy" was, it always will have been actual joy and that has come from the recognition in the child of Ellen of a love even greater than a love for woman, and the sense of the universe having its own kind of laws as replication. *Deliverance*, however, makes it clear that for Rutherford, as for Spinoza, such affirmation is critical of and not quiescent before the social oppression which makes such joy so hard won and so incidental. White's final essay mentioning Spinoza was called "Revolution," and, though one must not assume that his views never changed, it is no accident, I think, that beyond the deliverance lies the political and moral revolution in London and Tanner's Lane.

Body and Mind

The Revolution in Tanner's Lane encapsulates both the structural tension between narrative and knowledge and this radical restructuring of self and other. For the two dimensions of its articulation are, first, the persistence of revolutionary energy in time, not *through* history but *across* it as the recurrence of the same values even when that history is driven underground, and, second, the linked and problematic articulation of individual emancipation with the social movement.

But there is a third issue, the re-ordering of the relation of body and mind. Not only does this mean that both Paulines are as much agencies as the Major and his theories, or George and his politics, but also that, for example, Zachariah's wife, Jane, potentially freed as she is by her desire for the Major, and Priscilla, the wife of George who reveals her real love too late, are signs of the revolution's phallocentric limitations. The texts which follow this novel are partly concerned to bring woman off the margin.

No more fully does Rutherford do this than in *Clara Hopgood*, paradoxically his most feminist and, as Linda Hughes noted,[64] his most Spinozan novel. This is not merely because one of its protagonists is a Jewish monist craftsman called Baruch, but because echoes of Spinoza come up again and again with the thoughts that characters have and even more within the concrete dilemmas they face. Hughes deserves credit for making this clear, but we must not, as she does, turn a complex historical novel into a Spinozan moral fable. Geometric as Spinoza's method of argument is, he does not deliver answers to specific moral situations but reconstitutes the basis on which moral situations are to be understood. Rutherford's novel poses large philosophical questions, most notably about choice of action, but although they are enunciated in thought or dialogue at certain points, they occur also in concrete day to day decisions about "practical problems"[65] from the most private, such as whether to marry your child's father, to the most public such as whether to join the Chartists or Mazzini. Reading Spinoza does not unearth a buried ethical pattern which dissolves the actual lives of the protagonists into abstractions, but clarifies the remarkable originality by which Rutherford articulates these choices, throwing away the realist key which unlocks the personal cottage door, but refusing to sit down on the side of the road and close his eyes and dream. Specifically Spinoza clarifies the moral choice as a reconstruction of the relation of body and mind.

Again we are faced with an obvious formal problem in this novel, declared in its title which identifies one character as central but contradicts this by focusing the reading experience first on Madge, then on Baruch Cohen and only at the very end on Clara. It is tempting therefore to see Clara as emerging from behind the unresolved dilemmas of her sister and lover to produce an answer which has really been there all the time. This is how Hughes construes the novel. Madge is assigned to Spinoza's inadequate ideas, Clara to "reason" which triumphs in the end. (Hughes does not consider Baruch's dilemma.) This is not an accurate reflection either of Spinoza or the novel. First, Spinoza has three kinds of knowledge, not two, and the third and highest is described as "*scienza intuiva.*" To ascribe Madge's defence of intuitiveness to inadequate ideas overlooks both the fact that she is clearly as intelligent as Clara (who loses the game of chess over which this argument is played out) and that Clara's "reason" leads her only to recommend the wrong choice for Madge, while her own life choice (not to marry Baruch) is made without rational procedures: "Something fell and flashed before her like lightening from a cloud overhead, divinely beautiful, but divinely terrible."[66] It cannot fail to remind us of the "flash of forked lightning"[67] which drives Frank and Madge into the barn.

The "error" of Madge's pregnancy is not an error of intuition or impulse. Her intuition about Frank is right. Her impulse towards him is a fact, not right or wrong. It is her imagination that betrays her because she thinks that she feels sorry for him when he reveals that he has learnt the wrong Wordsworth poem for her. His own experience of love (see the end of Chapter V) is sentimental and morose but it is legitimated by the social world's equally sentimental construction, for its "entertainment," of a fictional romance out of a striking picture, *The Tempest* tableau. In fact, Madge reasons herself into love. What she clearly feels is sexual desire. It is an impulse of her own body which the imagination tries to construe into a response to reality.

Once she has experienced Frank's body and become pregnant Madge returns to her intuitive sanity. This is not, of course, without pain, first because she does recognise that the world imagines that pregnant women should marry the putative father and that it can penalise those who refuse. One critic has even argued that Madge is responsible for her mother's death, but this is nonsense. It is the world's opinion of her correct recognition of the fact that it would be a crime to marry Frank that prompts the landlady to evict them, and Mrs. Hopgood to make a journey she cannot afford, without adequate protection. This opinion is buttressed cruelly by Clara's reasoning which prompts her to make a doubly false remark,

"Frank loves Madge." It is false because Clara cannot know how Frank felt and also because even if it were true it is not a reason for Madge to marry him. This threatens to crucify Madge ("you know not what you do") because it confronts her both with her actual sexual desire ("she felt once more Frank's burning caresses") and her sense that she gave herself to him ("the movement of that which belonged to him").[68] When Mrs. Caffyn adds her reasoning, Madge recalls Clara's supposed good sense. But they are "her foes ... ranged ... against her" and within a few minutes she is "once more victorious," one of "those divine souls, to whom that which is aerial is substantial, the only true substance; those for whom a pale vision possesses an authority they are forced unconditionally to obey."[69] This vision is *scienza intuiva*, as the vocabulary, "divine," "substance," and the precarious but absolute awareness, should tell us.

This is not to replace Hughes's schematic reading with another, merely to indicate that the issue is much more complex than a simple division into right and wrong suggests. Madge's "pale vision" is only more "right" because it is her own knowledge and not hearsay or the reading of signs. More importantly it shows us that the deferred eponymity of Clara is not a moral rabbit out of the hat but the result of Rutherford trying to show that an uncommon decision, the commitment to Mazzini, is part of a process in which all major decisions, however common they are statistically, are complex and difficult processes requiring a great deal of clarity. Both Baruch and Clara go through ordeals which are parallel to that of Madge, and which we could not understand if it were not for that precedent.

However much he is an echo of Spinoza's personality, and however many of Spinoza's views Baruch has assimilated, he is far from being a normative character. Groping towards some philosophical view of the universe through monism, a commitment to the order of nature and by the separation of the concatenation of earth and sky, Baruch cannot, nevertheless, solve his personal problems of solitude and commitment by rationality. He is overwhelmed by his son's apparent indifference, and depressed by his own lack of enthusiasm for the Chartists. His exit from his dilemma is emotive, the vision of Clara and the prospect of love. But he has no real grasp on this desire, unable as he is to distinguish between his attraction to Clara and mere passion: "he was once more like one of the possessed. It was not Clara Hopgood who was before-him, it was hair, lips, eyes, just as it was twenty years ago, just as it was with the commonest shop boy he met ..."[70] As Clara's lightening establishes a community with Madge, so this surely links Baruch with Frank. It demolishes any easy hierarchy of moral position. We all endeavour to persist in our own being, and it is the nature of man to eschew solitude. Right conduct is the proper understanding of desire.

If we can understand that the novel has a corporate rather than hierarchical moral structure, we will also begin to understand Clara's decision, and to see how it relates to a fuller understanding of body and mind and hence structure and agency. I have already stressed that Clara's resistance to Baruch's clear opening echoes Madge's "fall" in its imagery. This should warn us against seeing it as a renunciation which is, of course, how the romantic reader seeking personal solutions even to fictional problems, is disposed to see it. There are at least two good reasons why Clara should *selfishly* turn him down. First of all his proposal comes in the form of an untruth: "Do you know Miss Hopgood, I can never talk to anybody as I can to you."[71] Clara has just witnessed Baruch talking very animatedly to her sister, so that she may see here that Baruch has other possible needs than herself. But more certainly this provokes in her an *image*, "A little house rose before her eyes as if by Arabian enchantment." Just as Clara is "Hair, lips, eyes" to Baruch, so he is domestic bliss for her. It is not him that provokes this image. The image comes from within herself in association with the kind of demand he is making on her. Worse, it is not even a positive image of domestic bliss but a screen whose denial would be another image, "solitude, silence, and childless old age." Her response, in other words, would be one of fear.

Her return to Mazzini is arguably positive. Only arguably because we learn nothing about it. She is not going to be a martyr but a spy, and although Mazzini accepts that even were her motives negative (disappointment in earthly love) this by analogy with Catholic martyrdom would be acceptable, she responds that her motives are "pure." This can only mean free from escapism and self-pity. But the novel is a narrative. It cannot answer for the objective value of Clara's act. But the function of narrative in these fictions is to recall human actions in order to give them eternal meaning. Hence, though we learn nothing of Clara's experience, we know about the meaning of her decision through Baruch's telling it to little Clara. And this is perfect because it links Clara's decision with Madge's most positive act in the novel, to bring up the baby outside marriage.

These strange and sudden leaps into a different kind of self-understanding are not leaps into a clear philosophic light which Spinoza himself does not seem to think is available except in fitful ways, but into an insight into the relationship between the physical world and our consciousness of it.[72] One of the specific questions raised in the novel is about the nature of individual choice in a wider social and natural world. Baruch and Clara discuss this on the streets of London, and Baruch also answers questions put by Madge about her atomic identity. I do not think he answers these very well and in the case of Madge he seems to recognise this. What gives a clearer answer is the novel itself.

It is concerned with the false and true apprehension of experience, but this is not for its own sake but as a decision-making process. Error in the novel is not derived from lack of principle or failure to apply the right principles (this is a novel without any but the most marginal blame).

It derives from mental elaborations which fail to recognise the relations of mind to the physical, external world. This is explicitly raised in Baruch's two parallel dialogues with Clara and Madge. In the first Clara says she is depressed by the apparent atomism of London (XXIV) which he counters not very effectively by arguing that number is applicable only to sensuous objects. Later when Madge asks him to teach her how "to submit to be useless",[73] he again argues for the radical difference of mental and bodily values. This is more successful though how he squares this with his commitment to a monistic world is not so clear.

The novel, however, offers the clarifications that Baruch and his mentor Robinson only glimpse at imperfectly. For Spinoza, mind and body were not, as for Descartes, separate substances, but the only two attributes of substance knowable to humanity. This means that they relate to one another as two aspects of one truth. They are not independent, as Baruch thinks, but neither can there be cause/effect transactions between them (otherwise one would be a mode of the other and therefore finite). Imagination is an unreliable faculty because it implies such a transaction – images are products of the assumption that the external world causes effects in thought. Of course the effects in thought are closely related to the effects in the body but are not caused by it. Equally imagination grafts volitions onto the physical world which is again specious. Error in this novel is not from privileging the body over the mind but of constructing an imaginary view, such as being in love, to account for changes in the body (sexual desire, pregnancy, etc.).

Madge experiences the most dramatic and immediate bodily change. She feels and yields to sexual desire and becomes pregnant and has a baby. She thinks that she falls in love or responds to love and gives herself to Frank. As long as she is in this pea soup of inadequate ideas she is muddled, though only in the way that the everyday world around her is muddled. But once she has made the break with it she is able to distinguish between real fear, the recognition that the pregnancy will bring problems to her mother and sister, and the special egoism of repentance. When she goes into the country in such despair therefore she is able to look into the mill pond and not think of suicide but to understand its vigorous motion and herself move on. In the church she is "overshadowed" by a larger pity than the one by which she feels her own misery.[74] At this point she meets Mrs. Caffyn and the novel turns into a kind of deliverance – the intense isolated situation of the Hopgood family becoming absorbed into the little community of the Caffyn-Marshall household and through them into the wider world of social struggle .

Madge's ordeal has to precede Clara's because otherwise we will misread it. Rutherford stresses the parallelism on a number of occasions, the lightning being the most important. But if Madge has to see through romance, so Clara can only see the stars when a volume of Calvin is removed. Both sisters are on the visit to Mazzini and Madge specifically poses the question of a woman's freedom to choose to Baruch. So that in choosing Mazzini, Clara is choosing to become a woman in freedom not in captivity. It is her own "*conatus*." But this is not an isolated decision. Above all it is evolved in the context of the idea as opposed to the image of the universe she confronts, once she has begun to make her decision. Chapter XXIX begins with her watching the dawn break over the rural holiday scene she has initiated. Hughes calls it an epiphany but it is not a static image and she is moved "by something more than beauty."[75] It is compared to Revelations IV (though more accurately to an interpretation of it which implies that the "One" transcends the visual effect). Like Madge she is "overshadowed" though by peace rather than pity. Later she sees Madge and Baruch and knows that they are right to be together. Once this is made explicit, Clara has her larger, fuller, but parallel mill pond experience.

> The river, for some reason of its own, had bitten into the western bank, and had scooped out a great piece of it into an island. The main current went round the island like a shallow, swift ripple, instead of going through the pool, as it might have done, for there was a clear channel for it... On the island were aspens and alders... Every one was as dense with foliage as if there had been no struggle for life, and the leaves sang their sweet song, just perceptible for a moment every now and then variations of the louder music below them. It is curious that the sound of a weir is never uniform, but is perpetually changing in the ear even of a person who stands close by it ... Clara ... watched that wonderful sight – the plunge of a smooth, pure stream into the great cup which it has hollowed out for itself.[76]

We are kept away from the details of Clara's mental crises as she decides not for Baruch, philosophy and domestic peace, but for Mazzini and the poor people of Italy. This passage is not metaphoric in any normal sense. It is not coherent enough to objectify Clara's own thoughts and she does not understand it ("for some reason of its own"). Yet it explains everything that has happened and that will. The stream driving its way irrationally through the earth and vegetation is complex and profuse but also unified and continuous. Clara is watching that complexity, not trying to take possession of it through ascribing meaning or evaluation. It is the very opposite of Daedalus's epiphanies which triumph over process with sudden stasis. It is the intuition of science.

But it is also opposite, I think, from the metaphoric organicism by which prose and passion is made to connect at the close of *Howard's End*, the children playing in the hay.[77] Clara's political decision will take her away from the immediate community, and yet it is a condition of its existence, just as the physical life of the community is a condition of her political effectivity, as Baruch first got Madge to agree, earlier in the chapter.

In his essay "Spinoza's Doctrine of the Relationship Between Mind to Body," 1896, White writes "The body and mind *are the same thing* so considered under two different aspects ... There is no such thing as an abstract mind issuing its orders to the body, and no such thing as an abstract body controlling the mind. Abstract mind and abstract body are impossible unrealities."[78] This constitutes a radical critique of romantic realism in which the protagonist has constantly to search for an accommodation between his perceptions and the external world. Clara here allows the river its own reasons, and can therefore think her own life through also. But she can only do it because Madge, and in a sense, Baruch, have done the same.

This only scratches the surface of this remarkable novel, and it is difficult to communicate the clarity with which it handles complex issues. But it would begin to come into the light if the fact that Spinoza could advance on Cartesian thought without trying to recuperate the world of signs that Descartes called in doubt, were seen to be enabling the Rutherford text to advance the realist mode it constantly calls in question.

Notes

1. John Lucas, *The Literature of Change: Studies in the Nineteenth Century Provincial Novel* (Hassocks, Harvester Press, 1977), 110.

2. Frederick Pollock, *Spinoza: His Life and Philosophy* (1880; London, Duckworth, 1899), 260–88.

3. Benedict de Spinoza: *Ethic*, William Hale White, trans., trans. rev. by Amelia Hutchison Stirling (London: Oxford University Press, 1937, 4th ed.), 250. All references are to this edition first published in 1910, unless otherwise stated.

4. Mark Rutherford, *Pages from a Journal: with Other Papers* (London: Oxford University Press, 1910), 32–58.

5. However, John Lucas and Charles Swann have begun to change this state of affairs. Catharine R. Harland's *Mark Rutherford: The Art and Mind of William Hale White* (Columbus: Ohio State University Press, 1988) is a welcome new monograph, but it does little to advance the recognition of White's political intelligence or his literary sophistication.

6. Catharine Macdonald Maclean, *Mark Rutherford* (London: Macdonald, 1955), 222.

7. Albert Schwegler, *Handbook of the History of Philosophy*, James Hutchison Stirling, trans. and annotated (Edinburgh: Oliver and Boyd, 1868), 446–67.

8. J. H. Stirling, *The Secret of Hegel: Being the Hegelian System in Origin, Principle, Form and Matter* (London: Longmans Green, 1902), Lxviii, Lxi.

9. Schwegler, 410.

10. Benedict de Spinoza, *Tractatus de Intellectus Emendatione*, W. Hale White, trans., trans. rev. by Amelia Hutchison Stirling (London: T. Fisher Unwin, 1895), xxiii.

11. The clearest definition of the sustained tension between "that *asquiescentia mentis*" Rutherford feels toward Spinoza, and the applicability of his truth to experience is in the remarkable "Supplementary Note on the Devil" which follows the essay on Spinoza in *Pages from a Journal*, pp. 58–63.

12. Mark Rutherford, *Catharine Furze, Reuben Shapcott, ed.* (London: T. Fisher Unwin, n.d.), 87. It is true that in reply to Catharine, Mrs. Bellamy admits her irrelevance and explains it with a parody of White's praise of Spinoza's rigour: "For one thing seems always to draw me on to another". Perhaps Spinozan wisdom is hidden in marginal and unrecognised intelligence.

13. Ibid., 311.

14. Ibid., 88.

15. Ibid., 124.

16. Ibid., 366.

17. Ibid., 148–70.

18. Wilfred H. Stone, *Religion and Art of William Hale White* (Stanford University Press, 1954), 132. Stone remains the best general introduction to White.

19. Benedict de Spinoza, *A Theologico-Political Treatise and a Political Treatise*, R. H. M. Elwes, trans. (New York: Dover, 1951), 25. I follow the convention of referring to this text by its Latin short title, *Tractatus*.

20. Ibid., 61.

21. *The Autobiography of Mark Rutherford, Reuben Shapcott, ed.* (London: T. Fisher Unwin, n.d., 12th ed.), 42. All references are to this edition.

22. *Mark Rutherford's Deliverance, Reuben Shapcott, ed.* (London: T. Fisher Unwin, n.d.), 140. All references are to this edition.

23. J. W. von Goethe, *Poetry and Truth from my Life*, R. O. Moon, trans. (London: Alston Rivers, 1932), 554.

24. *Deliverance*, 151.

25. *Tractatus*, 28.

26. Judges, 6–8.

27. Sir Walter Scott, *Old Mortality* (Harmondsworth: Penguin Books, 1975), Chapter 16.

28. Lucas, *Literature of Change*, 100.

29. *Tractatus*, 14–16.

30. Ibid., 61.

31. See Charles Swann, "Re-Forming the Novel: Politics, History and Narrative Structure in *The Revolution in Tanner's Lane*," *ELT*, 34: 1 (1991), 45–69.

32. "Ixion," *Secular Review*, 11 September 1880, 164.

33. "The Genius of Walt Whitman," *Secular Review*, 20 March 1880, 182.

34. Preface to *Ethic* (London: Trubner and Co., 1883, 1st ed.), xii.

35. *Ethic*, 4th ed., 114.

36. *The Autobiography*, 2.

37. *Tractatus*, xii–xiii.

38. *The Autobiography*, 10.

39.   Ibid., 21.
40.   My emphasis. Ibid., 19.
41.   Ibid., 21.
42.   Ibid., 22.
43.   Ibid., 25.
44.   Ibid., 110.
45.   Ibid., 39. A direct echo of the *Ethic*.
46.   Ibid., 70–71.
47.   Ibid., 106.
48.   Ibid., 108.
49.   Ibid., 115.
50.   Ethic, 239.
51.   *The Autobiography*, 8.
52.   Matthew Arnold, "Spinoza and the Bible," *Complete Prose Works*, R. H. Super, ed. (Ann Arbor: University of Michigan Press, 1962), 158–82.
53.   *Deliverance*, 90.
54.   Ibid., 108.
55.   Ibid., 113.
56.   Ibid., 102.
57.   My emphasis. *Ethic*, 1st ed., xxiii.
58.   Ibid., ix.
59.   *Deliverance*, 63.
60.   Ibid., 87.
61.   *Ethic*, 194.
62.   Ibid., 206.
63.   *Deliverance*, 69.
64.   Linda K. Hughes, "Madge and Clara Hopgood: William Hale White's Spinozan Sisters." *Victorian Studies*, 18 (1974), 57–75.
65.   "But if a philosophical doctrine be true, it does not follow that as it stands it is applicable to practical problems." "Supplementary Note on the Devil." *Pages from a Journal*, p. 58. See above n.11.
66.   Mark Rutherford, *Clara Hopgood, Reuben Shapcott, ed.* (London: T. Fisher Unwin, n.d.), 265.
67.   *Clara Hopgood*, 95.
68.   Ibid., 172–73.
69.   Ibid., 197.
70.   Ibid., 232.
71.   Ibid., 265.
72.   G. H. R. Parkinson, *Spinoza, Reason and Experience* (Milton Keynes: The Open University Press, 1983), 32–44, gives the clearest account I know of this problem.
73.   *Clara Hopgood*, 276.
74.   Ibid., 111.
75.   Ibid., 284.
76.   Ibid., 294–95.
77.   The comparison is made by Hughes and Lucas.
78.   "Spinoza's Doctrine of the relationship between Mind and Body," *International Journal of Ethics*, 6 (4 July 1896), 516–17.

CHAPTER 18

D. H. Lawrence

It seems blindingly obvious now that Lawrence is a very great novelist and that critics who try to claim otherwise are either exhibitionist or oblivious, yet the first coherent claim for his major status was not made until twenty-five years after his death, by F. R. Leavis. It is not difficult to see why: in two ways, Lawrence is isolated from the mainstream of critical theory which derives from the modern movement. In his last novel, *Lady Chatterley's Lover*, he gives a definition of the value of fiction which exactly places him in relation to his contemporaries:

> It is the way our sympathy flows and recoils that really determines our lives. And here lies the vast importance of the novel, properly handled. It can inform and lead into new places the flow of our sympathetic consciousness, and it can lead our sympathy away in recoil from things gone dead. (IX)[1]

'Sympathy' takes us straight back to George Eliot (see, for example, her essay 'The Natural History of German Life' where she advocates realism on the grounds that it enables an extension of our sympathies). It implies an essentially *secular* view of art, in which creative achievement has no absolute intrinsic value. 'I do write,' Lawrence said in a letter of 1913, 'because I want folk – English folk – to alter, and have more sense'. At the same time, much of his criticism, particularly in the twenties, is directed against didacticism. In 1914, he wrote to Sir Thomas Dunlop: 'You asked me once what my message was. I haven't got any general message, because I believe a general message is a general means of sidetracking one's own personal difficulties.' There is no contradiction: the kind of didacticism Lawrence deplores is that which tries to impose a moral order on experience, not that which, like his own, tries above all to *depose* order and discover instead the meaning for the individual of the flux of life itself. And this makes for the second factor in his dis-orientation from the major impetus of modern art – there is no rage for order, no seeking after values which transcend historical change. In a way which makes Lawrence alien to his major contemporaries, he is a relativist: 'Einstein,' he wrote in 1921, 'isn't so metaphysically marvellous, but I like him for taking out the pin which fixed down our fluttering little physical universe.' To measure the deterioration of modern life or to impose order on its flux by values derived from the past, the cultural tradition, is, for Lawrence, to get the dead to bury the dead.

Leavis's definitive evaluation grows precisely out of his recognition of the centrality of the major pre-modern novelists, Jane Austen and George Eliot, for example. This is, without doubt, the right perspective in which to place the achievement of Lawrence against that of T. S. Eliot or James Joyce. It is, however, a very problematic perspective. Significantly, the quotation with which we began is from a novel which is overtly immoral by any standards which are to be derived from 'the great tradition' (we ought not to be surprised that Leavis finds the book intolerable). It explicitly attacks the whole range of moral positives (from duty, to tolerance of other people's weakness) which affirm in any way the relevance of social institutions (from marriage to intelligent conversation). We need to note how positive, in that quotation, is the concept of 'recoil'. Of course, revulsion from what has gone dead is an important effect of George Eliot's fiction too (we recoil from Casaubon as much as from Sir Clifford Chatterley), but it is not a positive function of the novel, equal to its affirmations. Once the discriminations have been made, the effect of *Middlemarch* is to establish large areas of tolerance (for example, for such figures as Cecilia and Sir James).

And the recoil is, throughout Lawrence's work, precisely from those values, values which make for integrity and accommodation, that we find in Jane Austen and George Eliot. In *À Propos Lady Chatterley's Lover*, Lawrence writes:

This, again, is the tragedy of social life today. In the old England, the curious blood-connection held the classes together ... We feel it in Defoe or Fielding. And then, in the mean Jane Austen, it is gone. Already this old maid typifies 'personality' instead of character, the sharp knowing in apartness instead of knowing in togetherness ...

(*Phoenix* II p. 513)

This was in 1930, and it has its particular context. But it is congruent with much earlier criticism, in that it sees the nineteenth century as an epoch of egoism accommodated, through 'personality', in society, followed by an epoch in which the social institutions of personality have to be destroyed. An important review of 1913, '*Georgian Poetry 1912–1913*', sees that anthology (to which he contributed himself) as an affirmation of life against the nihilism of Flaubert, Nietzsche and Hardy, but sees too that it could only come about because of that nihilism:

The last years have been years of demolition. Because faith and belief were getting pot-bound, and the Temple was made a place to barter sacrifices, therefore faith and belief and the Temple must be broken. This time art fought the battle, rather than science or any new religious faction. And art has been demolishing for us: Nietzsche, the Christian religion as it stood; Hardy, our faith in our own endeavour; Flaubert, our belief in love. Now, for us, it is all smashed, we can see the whole again. We were in prison, peeping at the sky through loop-holes. The great prisoners smashed at the loop-holes, for lying to us. And behold, out of the ruins leaps the whole sky.

The evaluation is carefully historical. If Flaubert and Dostoevsky have to be attacked more vigorously than Jane Austen or George Eliot, it is not because the latter pair are more moral or life enhancing, it is because they are more irrelevant historically – they have been demolished already. Flowers of evil are more valuable than the innerly corrupt cabbages of the self-contained personality.

The only relevance finally of the great tradition is that it is an opposite. In some ways, *Mansfield Park* is a perfect bourgeois novel because the house whose values are affirmed can accommodate personality – Fanny Price is granted integration through the discovery of a role (duty) and the sanctity of a retreat (her private room) in which the inner being can remain unviolated. Such a compact is not possible in Lawrence, and it is to the affirmation of modes of being alien to those which Jane Austen affirmed that we must pay most attention.

I. 1885–1912

Lawrence was born in 1885 in Eastwood, a small mining village outside Nottingham, the fourth child of a collier. Though his world was industrial, it was not really urban since a little beyond Eastwood there was an unmolested rural world which was as much a part of Lawrence's childhood landscape as the colliery: 'so that the life,' he wrote in later years, 'was a curious cross between industrialism and the old agricultural England of Shakespeare and Milton and Fielding and George Eliot' (*Phoenix* p. 135). To the tension which resulted from this dual environment was added the violent social tension evident in his parents' marriage. Mrs. Lawrence was a Nonconformist with middle-class antecedents whose response to the spontaneous but irresponsible world of her husband was a conventional social aspiration realized vicariously through her children. 'I am sure,' Lawrence wrote, 'my mother never dreamed a dream that wasn't well off' (*Phoenix* p. 822). She it was who strove to ensure that he had an education that would displace him from the working class milieu in which he was brought up. But there is a third tension in Lawrence's early life which both derives from that education and through the relationship that he formed in 1901 with Jessie Chambers, and that was the equally bourgeois but 'unconventional' aspiration to a higher plane than social reality; 'a world apart,' Jessie wrote in her memoir, 'where feeling and thought were intense, and we seemed to touch a reality that was beyond the ordinary workaday world'. Lawrence's identity then grows in relation to a threefold antithesis, industrial and rural, community and social aspiration, convention and idealism. It makes for a pervasive and complex rhythm in his work between a powerful need for human relationship and an intense dynamic of self-realization.

It is a rhythm made more complex by his specific historical situation. Lawrence's career is at once a tribute to and indictment of the Forster Education Act (1870) which definitively established a national system of elementary education. From the Board School which was that Act's creation, Lawrence won a scholarship to Nottingham High School in 1898, but the scholarship was not enough to cover his expenses so that much of the Lawrence family income had to be directed towards providing an education which would separate their child from them. He worked as a clerk for a few months in 1901, but ill health forced him to give up the post. In Autumn, 1902, on the advice of his mother's Congregationalist minister, Lawrence re-entered the educational system as a pupil teacher. Under a scheme set up by the Balfour Education Act of that year, he was, in 1903, drafted to the Pupil Teacher Centre in Ilkeston where he was able to matriculate. For financial reasons, however, he had to defer taking up a place at Nottingham University College for a further year. He got to Nottingham in 1906 and gained his teacher's certificate there two years later. These years are crucial in Lawrence's development. The national education system gave him an opportunity unavailable to previous generations to achieve middle-class status. But it meant much hard work and self denial for an education which an intelligent boy could see was inadequate. In 'Education of the People', an essay Lawrence wrote at the end of the First World War, Lawrence offers a very sharp diagnosis of the contradictions inherent in the system: theoretically, education is about disinterested ideals, but in fact the whole system is geared to the material needs of society so that it is caught hopelessly between sentimentalism and vulgar utilitarianism. Negatively, Lawrence's education taught him the intellectual poverty of the academic mind; positively, it put him in touch with the major intellectual currents of his time, Darwin, Schopenhauer, William James, which displaced him both from the working-class world of his father and the middle-class values, sustained by Christianity, which his mother cherished. It demanded too a kind of integrity which neither these values nor the romantic withdrawal of Jessie Chambers could accommodate. But at the same time, because of her, he was turning towards a profession which the national education system was hardly designed to encourage: he seems to have begun *The White Peacock* in 1906, and, in 1907, he submitted three stories to the *Nottingham Guardian*, one of which, under Jessie's name, was published ('A Prelude'). By the time Lawrence left Eastwood, in 1908, to take up a teaching post at Davidson Road School, Croydon, he was already caught up in the painful process of deracination which is inevitable for the working-class or lower-middle-class intellectual.

Describing his mother's concept of success in an essay of 1929, Lawrence wrote: 'Flights of genius were nonsense – you had to be clever & rise in the world, step by step.' (*Phoenix* II p. 301). Lawrence's London years mocked her wisdom. The step-by-step career at Davidson Road was morally crippling because Lawrence found that the system did not allow him to develop a non-institutional relationship with the boys (the sequence of poems called 'The Schoolmaster' registers his predicament at this time). On the other hand, the flights of genius had some success. Jessie Chambers sent some of his work to Ford Madox Hueffer (later Ford), editor of *The English Review* in 1909. Hueffer did not only publish Lawrence (at first in the November issue) but also introduced him into the literary world. During 1910, Lawrence finished his first two novels, *The White Peacock* and *The Trespasser* and seems to have had little difficulty in getting them published (in 1911 and 1912 respectively). In June 1911 Martin Secker was asking him for a volume of short stories: as a writer he had arrived. It is not surprising that Lawrence found himself alien to the bourgeois morality of his mother, and, perhaps, the last link with that morality was severed when, in December 1910, she died. In November of the following year, pneumonia forced Lawrence to give up his post at Davidson Road and from then on he never returned to a 'regular' profession. And, as though it were a final dramatic gesture against the world his mother had dreamed of for him, Lawrence met and eloped with the wife of the Professor of Modern Languages at Nottingham, Frieda Von Richthofen, early in 1912. They went to Germany, her homeland, and spent most of the next two years travelling in Europe. Exile was to become the dominant note of Lawrence's life from this point, and by the end of 1912, he had completed the novel that was to present the inevitability and representativeness of that exile and was also his first great work, *Sons and Lovers*.

During these years, as we have seen, Lawrence saw his own role as that of the new affirmer after the total negation of bourgeois morality by Flaubert and Hardy. There was no return to the dualistic 'personality' of Jane Austen and George Eliot. The apart, inner self that their *modus vivendi* relies on ultimately takes refuge in mental consciousness, and this, Lawrence realized, was only destructive since it could only make of the 'inner self' a mirror image of the social being from which it is withdrawn.

The inner self might be the antithesis of social being, but this too is just another kind of reflection. The early short stories (all collected in *The Prussian Officer*) affirm a different order of being which can make no compact with the social world but which must either subvert that world or atrophy within it.

This process is most schematically evident in 'The Daughters of the Vicar'. The vicar's family live in a situation which is for them socially degrading: one of the daughters who has 'a proud pure look of submission to a high fate', marries a clever and wealthy but physically monstrous clergyman in order to create for herself a place in the world within which she can exist unviolated. The second finds herself nursing a lower-class woman through her last illness and through this being forced into physical intimacy with the woman's son, a collier. It is partly a story which affirms the priority of sexual love over class convention, but more it is the dramatic realization of an order of being which class convention will not accommodate. When she finds herself washing the back of the collier she feels 'the almost repulsive intimacy being forced upon her. It was all so common, so like herding. She lost her own distinctness'. Through her relationship with the son she is to find another kind of distinctness, but it is only after the individualism of bourgeois convention has been totally subverted. The new distinctness is one which acknowledges a relationship which the conventional world tries to make merely a function of itself.

But 'class' is only one of the social mediations which Lawrence sees as a destructive force which has to be overcome by a new vitality. A less schematic and more powerful story than 'The Daughters of the Vicar', 'The Christening', presents a world in which the compact between inner and outer worlds is seen in a context of the very idea of family itself. It is hardly a story at all: a collier smitten with locomotor ataxy has three daughters drifting into spinsterhood. One of them has an illegitimate baby, and the clergyman is called to christen it; during the ceremony, the collier speaks a strange prayer rejoicing that the child has no father: 'Aye an' I wish it had been so with my children, that they'd had no father but Thee. For I've been like a stone upon them, and they rise up and curse me in their wickedness'. The family, enacting the will of the father, is well to do and different from 'the common collier folk', but the rise in the world, the transformation of the father's 'pride' into the group identity of social being, has crushed the individuality of the children: 'They had never lived; his life, his will had always been upon them and contained them. They were only half-individuals.' The bastard is only a pathetic gesture at individual assertion (for its mother hates the man who is its father), and it is, paradoxically, at the end, the broken-down father, still exercising his will through his debility, who affirms 'joy in life' – a pride of being not thwarted by the sense of group responsibility. The paradox enables us to see how much more Lawrence is concerned with than simply the realization of the price of conformity. The father's will is not morally condemned: it is simply the unnatural distortion of his pride, his vitality, through the very fact of fatherhood. We are witnessing not the struggle of the emergent individual against the static group, but the inextricable involvement of the emergent individual with the *emergent* group – itself the medium of individual vitality.

Both of these stories illustrate how much the Lawrencean affirmation of vitality demolishes the equilibrium between 'inner' and 'outer' being which is the basis of characterization in the nineteenth century novel, and we ought to cite other stories, 'The White Stocking', 'Odour of Chrysanthemums', 'The Prussian Officer' and 'The Thorn in the Flesh', which, though they have very different immediate concerns, demonstrate the same dramatic realization of the collision between incompatible orders of being. In three of these stories a new kind of 'self' emerges unmediated by its given role (husband or subordinate, for example) to disrupt a precariously controlled social situation. In the fourth, 'Odour of Chrysanthemums', this naked self, the undamaged body of a collier asphyxiated in the mine, brings to his wife, as she prepares him for burial, the recognition of the gap between her socially conditioned vision of his failure and his 'real' being. This is the moment of her true marriage in which she acknowledges his separateness, but it belongs to death and she has still to go on living. The continuity of the past which was between them is a death-in-life: 'The child was like ice in her womb'. And, although she turns back to life, it is in the knowledge that the reality of her life, 'her ultimate master', is utterly separate from her existence, is death. The recognition has been foreshadowed by her half-conscious gesture of wearing the chrysanthemums her child has torn up: later in the story, she links the flower with the failure of her marriage, but her spontaneous gesture is all that gives life to her drab, defeated appearance. and it binds her to the man's reality.

The awareness registered in these stories is undoubtedly more articulate because both Meredith and Hardy had realized it in their novels. But already, Lawrence has gone much further than they. Because he has a much deeper sense of human *groups* than Meredith, there is never any reduction to a theatrical antithesis between personal vitality and social rigidity. And, unlike Hardy, Lawrence does not find it necessary to dramatize this sense in terms of an already dying society. The great achievement of these stories is that they realize an interaction between the individual and his social context which is both eruptive and diurnal, a salient feature of the modern provincial world. But, of course, the stories necessarily simplify, because although the social order is not rigid, we cannot fully recognize that it is the product not only of changing individuals but also of changing groups. It is only when we turn to the novels that we become aware of a threefold dynamic growing from the relationship between the social order, the human group and the emergent individual.

The White Peacock already shows a remarkable grasp of these complexities. Critics from Lawrence himself onwards have habitually regarded it with contempt, and it is undeniable that it is very uneven and, finally, incoherent. But this is because of what Lawrence is trying to do – to use a medium which is essentially that of personal relationships (the declared model was George Eliot) to register forces which are beyond 'personality' and which determine the development not merely of single individuals but also of the human group in which they have their being. So that Lawrence finds it necessary to intersperse the fragmented drama with choric prose-poems, structurally irrelevant set scenes and a vast network of literary allusions. But if the technique is painfully improvised, it looks forward to the later novels in its effort to articulate rhythms which will not be contained in the conscious life of the individual, and it initiates themes which are going to remain crucial throughout Lawrence's work.

The opening chapter impressively announces the overt moral scheme of the novel through the invocation of the drama's setting. Nethermere is a world of somnolence: 'the whole place was gathered in the musing of old age' (Part One, I), and this is emphasized by verbal echoes – 'the water slid *sleepily* among them', 'the low red house … *dozed* in sunlight.' But if it is a world of the past, the figures in the landscape are young, on the edge of life, and though the central figure, George Saxton, participates in the somnolence of Nethermere, this is seen not as a retreat into the static but a precarious unconsciousness of what life is to be about: 'Your life is nothing else but a doss. I shall laugh when somebody jerks you awake'. The dominating tension of the novel is already before us: the characters, held in the pastoral fixity of Nethermere, belong not to the past but to the future – awakening will mean separation from the landscape and growth will mean uprooting. So we have, in these opening pages, beneath the quiet surface, the irritated buzzing of young bees, some of whom, with the lazy curiosity which is to be his own destruction, George kills. And later in the chapter the other main figure, Letty, whose life is also to be a kind of ruin, expends her vibrant but trivial energy on a battered piano. Both George and Letty come into being within the world of the past, but for both of them it means not nourishment but distortion. Letty summarizes the whole theme of the novel when she says to George:

> You never grow up, like bulbs which spend all summer getting fat and fleshy, but never wakening the germ of a flower. As for me, the flower is born in me, but it wants bringing forth.
>
> (Part One, III)

The flower is a pervasive metaphor of being in Lawrence because it implies both rootedness in a common soil and highly individual blossoming. But it is an ideal relating only two of the terms which we have noted in the

Lawrencean vision – the group and the individual. In actuality what relates them is the social structure which they create between them, and in *The White Peacock*, the flower of being is distorted because of the social structure. George is to sink his roots deeper and deeper in the declining provincial world and to rot inwardly; Letty, whom George fails to 'bring forth', is to turn outwards to the world of the industrialist and to become a forced growth taking refuge in the being of others. Both recoil from the torture which it is 'to each of them to look thus *nakedly* at the other.'

Growth becomes, therefore, deeply implicated with the destruction of the group. George is, in some respects, the representative of the pastoral world of Nethermere. There is, for example, a straightforward antithesis between his home and the strident sophistication of the home of Letty's industrialist in 'The Riot of Christmas': after the cake-making, the reading aloud and the dance in stockinged feet, we have the high-flown talk with its allusions to Maeterlinck and the correct and coy kissing under the mistletoe. And, of course, in terms of the social structure of the novel, it is the second party which embodies supremacy. In personal terms, it is so because the will of Letty searches for a personal role. On the way to the party, the protagonists meet two boy mineworkers who are reminders that the gaiety which is to come is paid for by impersonal exploitation; Letty's response personalizes the impersonal: 'Fancy ... those boys are working for me!' (Part One, VIII). A little later, at the party, we explicitly see Letty coming to love Leslie, the industrialist, because the social order he commands gives her an opportunity of playing a role, of masking the naked self in the personalized impersonality of social being: 'Letty was enjoying her public demonstration immensely: it exhilarated her into quite a vivid love for him'. The determinative need to play a social role is not fully explored in terms of Letty's character, and this is one of the faults of the novel, but it is also part of its striking originality. It is clear that it is partly because her vitality demands a more powerful relationship than George can offer her – for if he is a noble peasant, Letty's 'taureau', he is one who is rotting internally because the pastoral world is not the world of youth. Letty's response to his inertia is to escape into social determinism; having confessed to George that dancing with him is 'real', she goes on to justify her engagement to Leslie in these terms: 'I have been brought up to expect it – everybody expected it – and you're bound to do what people expect you to do – you can't help it. We can't help ourselves, we're all chess-men' (Part One, IX). The reality can only be momentary: in the world of the actual, George is impotent. It is not insignificant that Letty is finally thrown on to Leslie by a combination of mechanization and chance – his motor car accident from which, with the false maternal relationship Lawrence saw as characteristic of bourgeois marriage, she has to nurse him. But we cannot separate the mechanization of Letty from the general breaking up of Nethermere. Letty's own family, for example, has a stability, made precarious by the death of the father whose corpse lies in a squalid urban backstreet evoked with elaborate realism. After this discovery, the pastoral of the novel is always flawed. The Saxton farm is being ruined by the rabbits with which the Squire infests his estate, and George only stirs himself to contemplate emigrating. This is not simply elegiac, however. Within the pastoral world, there is always a sense of violence underneath; the surface: the drowned cat, the hunted rabbits, the mad dog. 'If we move,' says Letty, 'the blood rises in our heel-prints' (Part One, II). The violence is part of the reality, but it remains unassimilated by the characters so that their awakening must also become a turning away. The unassimilated violence is present in Annable, the gamekeeper who stands as a reminder to the main characters of the reality which, in their awakening, they reject. But he can be no more than a reminder because he is only a very literary symbol. In actuality, he is an agent of Nethermere's destruction, since it is his job to protect the rabbits. His commitment to animal vitality is highly self-conscious and, after his death, his family is reduced to an urban slum. Annable is a bitter joke: what he stands for is not even available to himself. After his death, the novel becomes an exercise in realism, acting out the inevitable distortions of being implicit in the first half. George drifts into a highly sensual marriage, compensates with a momentary socialism and finally collapses into alcoholism, 'like a tree that is going soft'. Letty becomes just a social being. The children of Nethermere, necessarily growing out of the hollow which cannot contain them, have to cast themselves 'each one into separate exile'. It is in this atrophied way that the violence of vitality finds its way into their lives, not through the organic wholeness that Annable stands for. In this novel, becoming is an uprooting: it grows out of the group, but it flowers only in the city, and the flower is rotten, wasteful: 'What did it matter to them what they broke or crushed ... What did it matter, when all the great red apples were being shaken from the Tree to be left to rot.' (Part Two, VII).

The White Peacock is finally incoherent, however, because none of the individual characters in the novel are capable of experiencing *subjectively* the full implications of the changes which the novel registers (the first person narrator hardly exists as a character within the novel at all), and it comes to seem over-deterministic. It is not until we reach *Sons and Lovers* that the complexities we have already noted can be made coherent through the extension of consciousness within the protagonists so that they become subjects of these complexities and not merely objects. It is, of course, an autobiographical novel based on Lawrence's own early life, but he was right, I think, to describe it as 'impersonal'. It is impersonal in the sense that the subjectivity portrayed in the novel belongs to the characters and not to the narrator. Paul Morel's experience is fully coherent with the world realized in the novel so that its coincidence with Lawrence's own is only a matter of curiosity. The more so since the subjectivity of Paul is a highly representative one in that it is responsive to the most salient features of the historical world which the novel imitates. Of course, Paul is, like Lawrence himself, very exceptional, but it is only possible to realize the whole truth of a social world in fictional terms through the exceptional man; the character who is realized as 'average' in a novel can only, obviously, embody part of the truth. *Sons and Lovers* is a portrait of the artist as a young man, but the portrait can stand for the landscape of a whole epoch. In the particular case, it is the only way in which the epoch can be recorded since it is an epoch in which the working class emerges not as a *class* but as separate individuals nurtured and uprooted by the new aspirations and opportunities offered by the post-Forsterian 'democracy'.

This is not merely a matter of content but of the very form of the novel. We are to witness the working class boy emerge as the bourgeois hero, and whereas *The White Peacock* fails because Lawrence tries to engraft an impersonal range of experience onto a personal form, *Sons and Lovers* is a great novel because it *transforms* a bourgeois fictional structure. It is a structure in which the education of the hero is achieved by exile from the sanctity of childhood and a search for values 'in the world' which will accommodate his integrity and aspirations. The major instances in English are *Tom Jones* and *Great Expectations*, but in them the hero's exile is external: neither Tom nor Pip have a family. *Sons and Lovers* is a radical transformation because the exile cannot be referred to that particularity; on the contrary, Paul's exile takes place from within the family because the family itself is changing. We are aware, above all, not of personal and moral alienation from a static ideal, but of a series of cultural dislocations which create and demand a particular kind of personal integrity.

The first of the major cultural dislocations is within the marriage of Paul's parents. Mrs. Morel has been drawn into her marriage by the need for an experience which is outside the narrow confines of her puritan upbringing. But it is not simply an atavistic reaction against her father's middle class values: the 'dusky, golden softness' of Morel's 'sensuous flame of life' belongs to his working class vitality but she sees it in terms of expansion, 'something wonderful, beyond her' (I), so that as soon as it is seen, socially, as a contraction of possibilities, she becomes alien to their relationship. She can only relate to Morel subjectively, trying to change him into her own image: 'His nature was purely sensuous, and she strove to make him moral, religious. She tried to force him to face things. He could not endure it – it drove him out of his mind'. The verbs, 'strove' 'tried to force' are verbs of an imposed will bent on assimilating their relationship to the social reality, and later in the chapter, we have 'She was almost a *fanatic* with him … she tortured him … she destroyed him'. Lawrence later felt that he had been unfair to Morel, but the reservations are clearly there. It is not that the novel is unbiased – it cannot be because it is to be about Paul's experience, and Paul is given his identity by his mother – it is that the bias is registered as a socially specific mode of consciousness. For Mrs. Morel's vision of the family is culturally special-ized: she sees it as an agent of social mobility. In a significant glimpse into her past, Lawrence relates how she rebuked her middle-class lover, John Field, for not going into the ministry because of his father's pressure to go into business with 'But if you're a *man*?' But she now recognizes that being a man is not enough, and it is significant that she calls Barker, Morel's colleague, more of a man than her husband although he is physi-cally inferior – she can admire Barker for his ability to do his wife's chores when she is in childbirth. She sublimates a primarily physical relationship into a socially efficient one. Of course, Morel *is* a failure and it is to sentimentalize the novel to see him as the embodiment of 'organic' values. Nevertheless through him we are alerted to other possibilities of family life. Paradoxically, the most fully realized moment is immediately after he has been definitively placed in relation to his own family: 'He was an outsider. He had denied the God in him' (IV). The phrase adumbrates a kind of social Calvinism – through his irresponsibility he has cut himself off from grace, from the elect in a world of social mobility (it comes after he has found out that Paul has won a prize). But immediately after this we see him inaugurating a Ruskinian idyll in which he unites the whole family through their participation in craftsmanship. This is followed by Paul's most transparently unfair rejection of Morel during his illness. Lawrence is not being inconsistent here. Morel *can* achieve an organic relationship with his family, but it is only vestigial: through his lack of moral rigour in a world of social hardship, he is beyond redemption. But so too is the kind of familiar order his craftsmanship memorializes, for it is marginal to his real social life as a miner. We are in a world in which the only meaningful social unit is Mrs. Morel's vision of the family.

It is this vision which gives Paul his identity. The process of individ-uation for Mrs. Morel is through her family She has her own ways out – significantly through the moral vitality of the chapel and the feminist emancipation of the Women's Guild, but these are only consolatory. The very naming of Paul is an act of self-realization. She takes the baby to the cricket field, a pastoral island in the urban prison of her marriage, and thinks of her child as a future Joseph, an exile who was to save a nation and his own family. Momentarily, she offers him up to the sun, to the impersonal world from whence he came, but immediately she clutches him to her bosom, to the particular individuality of his origin. And she names him Paul, after the only theologian her father had felt sympathy with, so that it means a recommitment to his narrow individualistic values – St. Paul, of course, is not, like Joseph, the hero of social salvation, but of personal salvation. Paul's exile is not to be that of the leader, but of the isolate self. After she has settled Paul in his first job, Mrs. Morel thinks proudly of her two sons: 'Now she had two sons in the world. She could think of two places, great centres of industry, and feel that she had put a man into each of them' (V). 'In the world', in this context, is a cliché of the self-made man, and when Paul tells her about his work, it is like a tale from the *Arabian Nights* to her: she discovers her 'beyond' in the modern social structure, the centre of industry.

Of course, the realization of Paul's relationship with his mother is much more profound than such an analysis suggests. It is not just the product of the social order, it is the creation of a cultural world, a new human group. Soon after Morel has asserted his relatedness through craftsmanship, we have a glimpse of a pastoral communion between Mrs. Morel and Paul when she brings home a small cornflower dish from the market – it is a reminder that Mrs. Morel is not just putting sons into the world, but creating a home for them to return to. But there is a very significant difference between this moment and the vestigial, communal sense created by Morel: the latter has to do with work, the former with a possession. It is as though the tenor of the relationship between Paul and his mother were communal, but its inevitable vehicle of expression acquisitive. What most immediately identifies Paul as separate from the environment he confronts, is the class-based social mediation which has been granted to him by his mother's aspiration (Mr. Braithwaite drops his 'h's, Mr. Jordan is 'common'). It is this context which we should bear in mind when we consider the quality of their relationship. Inevitably it has been seen as Oedipal, and certainly it is very close: they sleep together, Mrs. Morel fights bitterly to prevent Paul from being taken from her by Miriam, and Paul finally has to kill her to release himself from her posses-sive will. But the most overtly Oedipal moments in the novel, when they both go to Paul's interview, and when they go for the first time to Leivers' farm are surely too conscious to suggest repression: 'She was gay, like a sweetheart' (V); 'You *are* a fine little woman to go jaunting out with' (VI). Moreover, the language, 'sweetheart', 'jaunting', suggests less sexual love than the social *appearance* of sexual love. And the episodes in which it occurs confirm this: both are scenes in which Paul, through his mother, establishes emancipation from the world of Morel. In the first he is going to get a job which takes him out of the mining community, and, in the second, mother and son are going to re-establish a friendship made through the chapel in the rural world beyond the industrial reality of Bestwood (we note that Mr. Leivers is another of the men Mrs. Morel feels she could have been a good wife to). The texture of Paul's relationship with his mother is one of an intimacy so close that the only adequate means of expression are sexual, but its structure is throughout one of social aspiration. The texture is determined by the distortion of family relation-ships caused by the cultural dislocation between the working man and his aspiring wife. When Morel is ill because of an accident caused by his own irresponsibility, Paul talks of himself as the man in the house. Later, when Mrs. Morel complains that her husband is giving her less money because Paul is working, Paul grows angry because she still cares about Morel's responsibility when he feels that it is a role that he himself can fill. Whatever quasi-sexual relationship there is between Paul and his mother, is thus determined by the changing structure of the family. The Morel family is neither an organic cultural unit because of the father's inability to establish its unity, nor is it straightforwardly an agent of social mobility because Mrs. Morel cannot establish her own kind of relationship with Morel, and has to replace it first by her relationship with William and then with Paul. And Paul becomes so meaningful because he is able, like Barker and like John Field, to be, for his mother, more than a man – a domestic help-meet (the bread-baking emphasizes this, and when Paul burns the bread it is the first crisis in the break-up of the relationship) and a social success. We shall only make the mistake of devaluating Mrs. Morel if we trivialize her social aspiration with a word like snobbery. Lawrence knows better, and he is able to dramatize the deep inner pressure towards individuation in terms of the social structure with such force that it is right to say, as Keith Sagar puts it, that Paul is 'kindled into life by his mother'. But we shall not make sense of the rest of the novel unless we are aware as well that this does not mean that Mrs. Morel's values are a moral norm. For it is a particular mode of life that she kindles Paul into – one determined by the Congregational Chapel and the bour-geois vitality of her father. And it is a mode that Paul has to grow beyond to rediscover his manhood.

This is a simplifying formula and the process which the novel records involves a more complex evolution than it suggests. In the first place, we have a second cultural dislocation, between Paul and his mother, which is dramatized through his relationship with Miriam, the girl he meets at the farm to which his mother takes him. It is predicted already on their walk to the farm. Paul rhapsodizes over the pit in the distant landscape while his mother remains utilitarian about it. Paul's response is aesthetic and humanist – 'There's a feel of men about trucks' (VI) and it is the kind of romanticism which only those who are already emancipated from the social world of the colliery can afford. The individuality conferred on Paul by his mother and his job takes him beyond both, into the realm of the ideal. The exact process is made clear by a comment on his art: 'From his mother he drew the life-warmth, the strength to produce; Miriam urged this warmth into intensity like a white light (VII). The distinction here is not very different from the distinction Arnold makes between Hebraic and Hellenic qualities which differentiate middle-class and cultured virtues – the distinction between energy and light. At the climax of the quarrel with his mother about Miriam, Paul overtly defines his estrange-ment in cultural terms: 'You don't care about Herbert Spencer' (VIII).

Unlike the dislocation between Paul's parents, however, this is not one of class but of generation: 'You're old, mother, and we're young.' The movement from Mrs. Morel to Miriam, and the shift of interest from the work at Jordan's to the pastoral world of the farm, is a development from one phase – of middle-class aspiration to another – from a desire for self-realization by 'facing' the world (society) to a desire for self-realization in a world that the self shapes, a movement, in the vocabulary Lawrence knew from Schopenhauer, from will to idea.

It is a move to an inevitable but expendable phase in Paul's individuation. The relationship with Miriam is doomed because it does not release Paul from his mother's subjectivity but merely offers a rival imposed image, more narrowly subjective because it is more atrophied from reality. Miriam remains coiled up against reality and she uses Paul to mediate with the world without coming to terms with it. In scene after scene we see that Miriam relates only to a specialized image of Paul, always having to make allowance for a 'lower' (physical and societal) self which has nothing to do with her. Finally she has to hand over this lower self to Clara Dawes, and it is after Paul has showered Clara with flowers in a dionysiac ritual which transcends Miriam's dualistic being that Paul begins to grow free of his mother in more than intellectual terms. He takes her to Lincoln Cathedral and there realizes that his 'woman' is old and cannot share his life anymore. At the end of the same chapter (IX), the Morel family disintegrates – Paul's sister gets married, his younger brother finds a sweetheart and Paul begins to feel that he must leave. After this, the novel becomes a painful record of Paul's search for a total self which is neither his mother's nor Miriam's.

Nor Clara's. Through her he finds 'a baptism of fire in passion', but this is a single rite which is unrepeatable and transitional. Their relationship is simply, for Paul, a release from other subjectivities. It involves, above all, a descent from the other-created self into oblivion: 'She wanted to soothe him into forgetfulness' (XIII). During their first walk together, they watch the landscape merge into a one-ness which obliterates all the individual life of Paul into indistinctness. Only an impersonal relationship can release him from personality. But, of course, Clara is a person – 'About *me* you know nothing' (XIII) and as soon as she demands a personal relationship, he has to retreat into the dualism of a day-time world of work, and a night-time of love. The womanliness of Clara gives Paul his manhood, makes possible for him the kind of vitality that had once existed between his parents and that had momentarily flickered up again in the scene immediately before Paul's quarrel with his mother about Miriam as a reminder both of what the parents might have achieved and of what Paul's relationship with Miriam necessarily leaves out of account. But Clara has to return to her husband for a permanent relationship, and, indeed, it is only through her husband that Paul can discover his manhood as an isolate being, Fighting him, he becomes aware of himself as a machine, and after the fight, Lawrence habitually calls him not Paul, but Morel. In a more meaningful sense than before he has become the man in the house, for he has learnt the physical intimacy and separateness which is part of the vitality of manhood but which for the collier is confined to the mine. Clara and Baxter give Paul not a new self, but a knowledge of the impersonality and separateness that a truly self-created being must take account of. Both his mother and Miriam remain to be fully rejected in the closing pages of the novel. And, paradoxically, in releasing himself from their subjectivities through a brutal self assertion, he becomes more nakedly bourgeois than either – a kind of Robinson Crusoe figure, stripped of everything but the shut fist and the clenched mouth, turning his back on the proffered oblivion in his mother's death 'towards the faintly humming, glowing town'. For all that it is a journey towards self discovery there is no discovery at the end of *Sons and Lovers*, for Paul asserts his selfhood, not like Robinson Crusoe in an unknown land, but in the old world of men and the city: it is merely a renewed determination to go on 'quickly' without the mediating relationships offered by the subjectivities around him. And this takes us to the heart of the Lawrencean moral agony: for in the escape from the dualistic 'personality' which transforms its vitality into an energy within the social machine or tries to hold it apart in mystic evasion, the hero has to recognize more radically his own apartness. The intensity and completeness with which this agony is realized seem to me to make *Sons and Lovers* a very great novel indeed, and although we must see *The Rainbow* and *Women in Love* as necessary progressions following it, it is surely a futile and academic exercise to try to arrange a hierarchy of value between the three.

II. 1913–1919

The first four years after the elopement with Frieda (whom he married in 1914) are, for Lawrence, years of an amazing creative energy which was richly productive. In January, 1913, he began work on what was to become *The Lost Girl*, but set this aside for 'The Sisters' which was to become both *The Rainbow* (finished in March, 1915) and *Women in Love* (finished in June, 1916, though probably revised thereafter). In addition he wrote some of his greatest stories – 'The Prussian Officer', 'Thorn in the Flesh' and 'England My England' – and three of the major prose essays which form the ideological framework of his greatest novels – 'A Study of Thomas Hardy' (written 1914), *Twilight in Italy* (written between 1913 and 1915, published 1916), and 'The Crown' (written and published in 1915). These, together with the later essay, *Psychoanalysis and the Unconscious* (1921) repay the careful reading that their rhetoric demands and illuminate sharply the concepts which underly Lawrence's fictional characterization. The sources of the massive impetus of these years are obvious – the effective release from the inhibitions of the past through the relationship with Frieda, the positive strength which seems to have come from that relationship (see the volume of poems entitled *Look! We have Come Through!*), and, more problematically, a sense of the possibility of finding a sympathetic community among the intelligentsia.

By 1914, Lawrence had a wide ranging circle of friends both literary and aristocratic – the Garnetts, Edward Marsh (editor of *Georgian Poetry*), the imagist poets, H. D. and Amy Lowell, John Middleton Murry and Lady Cynthia Asquith. In the following year, he met Lady Ottoline Morrell who introduced him to E. M. Forster and Bertrand Russell. The importance of this is more than casual. Lawrence spent the early months of 1915 trying to set up a dialogue with Russell which would provide a political solution to the situation precipitated by the war, and later in the year he tried to get going, with Middleton Murry and Katherine Mansfield, a little magazine, *The Signature*. Both efforts were attempts to create a social role within the context of a minority culture. Both failed. By August, 1915, he had quarrelled with Russell and Lady Ottoline: 'they are static, static, static ... they filch my life for a sensation unto themselves'. On the surface the quarrel was with Russell's liberalism, but not far beneath there is a personal incompatibility which reflects an inescapable class antagonism (made dramatically clear by a disastrous weekend Lawrence spent at Cambridge, with Russell and J. M. Keynes). *The Signature* ran only for three issues. The events of 1915 show how little, really, Lawrence could be assimilated into the minority culture to which his becoming a writer inevitably drew him. The story of his later career is partly the story of his cultural marginalization – from the wide circle of 1914–15 to the narrow one of Middleton Murry and Katherine Mansfield, and finally to the bizarre cult-world of Mabel Dodge Luhan and the Honourable Dorothy Brett. And however much this is explained away by Lawrence's 'temperament', it is bound up with his objective insight into the inextricable relationship between the minority culture and the 'mass-civilization' it tries to reject.

1915 was also the year which brought the definitive declaration of war between Lawrence and the bourgeois reading public. In November, *The Rainbow* was suppressed for indecency. And the years which follow are years of a more insidiously personal persecution. At the end of 1915, Lawrence was lent a house in Cornwall (one of his congenital problems was finding somewhere agreeable to live) and it seems to have been a place he could like. But since, though he was not a conscientious objector, he was openly opposed to the war, and since also he was married to a German, he was suspected of spying and finally, in October 1917, forbidden to live in Cornwall which, obviously, was strategically important for any potential invasion (the whole traumatic episode is recorded, rather hysterically, in chapter IX of *Kangaroo*). Not surprisingly, as soon as the war was over, Lawrence's first concern was to get out of England. It took him until October, 1919 when he went to Germany.

Because *Sons and Lovers* is about self-discovery, it can have no end, for the only self that can be 'discovered' with finality is the static self of egoism. 'When I assert an identity in the temporal flux, I become like a cabbage which folds over itself in its effort to contain the flux in static individuation.' This image is from 'The Crown', Lawrence's most explicit discourse on the nature of being: 'Whilst I am temporal and mortal,' he writes, 'I am framed in the struggle and embrace of the two opposite waves of darkness and of light' (*Phoenix* II. p. 377). There is an Absolute of being but it is in the consummation of this struggle:

> It is that which comes when night clashes on day, the rainbow, the yellow and rose and blue and purple of dawn and sunset, which leaps out of the breaking of light upon darkness, of darkness upon light, absolute beyond day or night.
>
> (ibid. p. 373)

In time, the Absolute is attainable only as a moment of consummation in relationship. We must, as individuals, recede from the consummation towards the relative eternities of light (love) or darkness (power). And therefore the consummation must be imperfect and what remains of it is the residue, the child – who will also strive towards the meeting of the two waves of the tide. This is an ontology which is discovered after *Sons and Lovers*, but the novel clearly moves towards it: Paul cannot go into the tide of his mother's own recession into darkness; having once reached perfection in love and once in battle, he must turn towards the light-and-darkness of the town. But equally, Lawrence needs to create a new structure to realize fictionally the full implications of this vision of being. *The Rainbow* is both an extension and a re-focusing. From a single family in a particular historical phase, we move to a whole cycle of over-lapping generations who live through more than half the nineteenth century. And from biography we move, logically, to the history of *relationships* within that generational cycle.

The rainbow as an image is the symbol of consummated relationship, the perfect arch, different from either of the beings whose relationship creates it, but perceptible in the temporal world only as a transient vision. And it is also out of Genesis, God's covenant to Noah that generation will not cease. There is sensible discussion of its significance both by Arnold Kettle and Keith Sagar. But though it is helpful to keep it in mind, it is necessary to forgo discussion here when there is so much to be said about the basic pattern of the novel. For, I think, it is less than central to the totality of the novel. It does not occur *explicitly* until the visionary rhetoric of the final pages: insofar as it occurs positively, it is in the implicit, inarticulate feeling Tom Brangwen has about his relationship with Lydia Lensky; insofar as it becomes conscious, it is in the *false* arches of Will's Cathedral or Anna's commitment to the arch of daylight, dawn and sunset. Since it is a non-temporal absolute, and since the primary affirmation of the novel is that humans live in time, it can obviously be no more than a point of reference – it cannot be a controlling structural device. And it is to the 'structure' of the novel that we must first be attentive. The diffi-culty here is that 'structure' as an aesthetic term suggesting architectural unity has little relevance to a novel so much enacting the rhythms of time: we are confronted rather with a process in which the controlling motive is the movement from one generation to another. It is a twofold movement – we can talk, helpfully, of a pattern of change and continuity, but this does not suggest that we are confronted in this novel with two kinds of change. It is better to think of historical change (which enacts the changing environment of man) and evolutionary change (which enacts the chang-ing nature of man). Both establish a dialectic between continuity and change – between, on the one hand, the Brangwen vitality and the coming of urban society, and, on the other, between the constant Brangwen aspi-ration towards new modes of being and the evolving individuation of the Brangwen vitality. But finally what the novel is about is the relationship between these two changing spheres – a changing world is in collision with changing man.

The first perspective of change is the record of man's vitality being distorted by his entry into the social world. The Brangwens stand not for a social myth, like 'community', but presocial man, for whom life is fully integrated with the rhythms of nature: 'working hard because of the life that was in them, not for want of the money' (I). The women who face 'outwards to where men moved dominant and creative', express a social aspiration which, though, as Leavis says, it is not ironized since it is a process of becoming more human, is destructive of this integration, for it is less to the *outer* world that they look than the world *beyond*, the world of social consciousness attainable by 'education and experience'. It is experi-enced as fantasy ('the magic land') by the mind apart from its world and it is a fantasy of self distortion – she *strained* her eyes to see', 'she *craved* to know'. Knowledge is to be the ultimate destructive agent of Ursula's relationship with Skrebensky: 'she knew him all round, not on any side did he lead into the unknown' (XV). Moreover, like Mrs. Morel, they enact their aspiration vicariously through their children. But this is not to be the portrayal of aspiration within the social system; it is a brief statement of the Brangwens' entry into the social system. The narrative of the novel begins with historical specificity, the coming of the canal in 1840, and already we have a changed image of the Brangwens – they make money from the trespass across their land; they grow richer by supplying the new town beyond – 'they were almost tradesmen'. The land becomes 'property' and the new generation of Brangwens move into society – Alfred becomes a draftsman, crushing the life within him, becoming successful and cultivating a mistress: his brother becomes a butcher and a drunkard and his sister marries a collier. Tom Brangwen is sent by his mother to Grammar School and made to feel 'guilty of his own nature'. As soon as they enter the world, fulfilling the dream of the women,. the Brangwens are split beings.

In Tom, the duality can be resolved. It takes the form, merely, of an inherited female need for the 'beyond', and this can be supplied by the 'Polish Lady', Lydia Lensky, who is foreign but alienated from her own world and finds in Tom a stability which enables her to relate again to what is outside her. Thus she can be assimilated into the Marsh Farm, and they finally achieve a rootedness in separation which is the basis of human relationship. Nevertheless it is a limited integration, private and inarticulate. Tom becomes atrophied from the farm world, a gentleman farmer whose only real activity is getting drunk and whose individuality is only finally asserted in death. Lydia never belongs fully to the farm at all, and after Tom's death, she retreats into the world of her past. What is the 'making' of Tom, the confrontation of the unknown, is also the defeat of the Brangwen integration with the land. The duality between inner and outer worlds becomes increasingly insoluble. Anna and Will are only related in their withdrawal from the world, and once they redescend to it, their relationship disintegrates until unity means only predatory victory of one over the other. Both are more specifically social beings than Tom. Will, the son of Alfred, is already urban and his creative vitality is thwarted both by a dualism within himself and by his polarization from Anna. Anna too is unable to create a relationship with the outer world. She finds the Brangwen household constricting because it 'belittles' her, but its very qualities alienate her from the outer social world. She can only relate to society through fantasy: she holds herself aloof from the world around her not, like her mother, because she is prepared to accept the limited horizons of the Marsh Farm in exchange for stability, but because she identifies with high society – the Princess Alexandra. She is drawn to Will because 'he was the hole in the wall, *beyond* which the sunshine blazed on an outside world' (IV) and when he fails to offer the relationship which will take her beyond the immediate world, she has to cast him off and withdraw into her own pregnancy. The stability she finds in the end is much less inclusive and more private than Lydia and Tom find: it is a retreat into the 'trance of motherhood', to a daylight world. The darkness she leaves to Will who holds it coiled inside him so that it appears only in outbursts of violence against his daughter.

Out of this spirit, Ursula's own relationship to the world grows, and the process of alienation becomes more inexorable and more complex. She recoils from her mother's fecundity, and she recognizes her own apartness because of the treacherous violence of her father. Being alone in her selfhood, Ursula is compelled to seek her being in the outer world from which Anna retracts, and it is a search which discovers no mode of relationship because it has to take place in a world which has institution-alized relationships. The key chapter here is the one describing her life as a schoolteacher, significantly and justifiably entitled 'The Man's World' since it offers a paradigm of the new urban world Ursula has to confront. It is a great chapter because Lawrence does not simplify the issue, as Dickens does in *Hard Times*, by confusing the system with its agents. Even Harby, the odious headmaster who is most fully committed to making the system work, is not allowed to become mechanical: 'He seemed to have some cruel, stubborn, evil spirit, he was imprisoned in a task too small and petty for him, which yet, in a servile acquiescence, he would fulfil, because he had to earn his living' (XIII). There is no sentimentalization – Harby the man is not simply separated from Harby the headmaster – but the word 'imprisoned' discriminates the two: his very 'evil spirit', harnessed as it is to the system, is too big for the system, and we have throughout the chapter a sense that there is an ominous gap between the system and the vitality it demands. It is precisely this local greatness which gives the chapter its function in the novel as a whole. For Lawrence is thus able to give us Ursula caught up in the system without destroying her as an established and developing character: Harby is not only her enemy but also her mentor. It is not people that the system mechanizes, but the relationships between people, as the episode with Williams shows. And that is precisely the point towards which the novel has been moving – the increasing separation of the inner being from the relationships by which it forms itself, so that being becomes, in the end, a distorted recoil from relationship. As the Brangwens move into society, and as society moves towards the Boer War, what has, from the beginning, been postulated as the only mode of being which does not falsify relationships, the rhythmic flow of 'blood-intimacy' which realizes the rainbow, has been destroyed. But Ursula's alienation is not merely the distortion of her vitality through the changing nature of social relationships. If we are content with this perspective, the end of the novel becomes, as S. L. Goldberg argues, less of a diagnosis of the modern world in terms of the vitality which Ursula inherits than a protest against it: the modern world crumbles too quickly before the 'chosen vessel of vitality'. We need to be aware as well of the changing nature of the vitality, of the modes of being in which the protag-onists discover themselves, which evolve progressively from generation to generation. And Ursula inherits three developing needs. First, as the third Lensky woman, she seeks in man a mediator with the outer world.

For Lydia this means seeking a separate existence which can give her rootedness, and she has to bring Tom to *submit* not to herself, but to the recognition of her own separateness. For Anna, Will is an agent of her relationship with the outer world: it is only *part* of him that she needs and as soon as his agency ceases to be effective she casts him off – we move from submission to defeat, 'Anna Victrix'. Ursula, as we have seen, is compelled to discover herself as an isolate being, and she seeks in Skrebensky an image of what she wishes to become: 'He seemed simply acquiescent in the fact of his own being, as if he were beyond any change or question. He was himself' (XI). And once she has asserted herself against him, she can only destroy him. Submission, defeat, destruction – this is the most obvious evolutionary pattern. But Ursula is also the heir of Tom and Will, and this means that in seeking herself, she must also seek physical identity, the blood intimacy of the male Brangwens. In Tom's case, this means submission to the darkness which he does not understand; in Will's case this means containing the darkness within himself and relieving it through sensuality or violence. For Ursula no such dualism is possible: she is compelled to seek ecstasy, the fulfilment of the physical being within the isolation of her individuation. And this is involved with the third inherited force, that of the female Brangwens. When she is, early on, seeking her 'real self' (the reiterated concept in Ursula's story) she comes across Genesis VI which suddenly refers to the 'Sons of God', and she construes this to mean that there was a race of men other than the sons of Adam: she conceives of herself as one of the beautiful women who was taken by these antediluvian giants. Later, she mocks the Genesis story of the flood on the same grounds as T. H. Huxley, who argued that the flood was merely a local event. This links with the drowning of Tom to whom the flood at the farm has seemed all-engulfing: Tom is not Noah, since he drowns, but he *is* one of the sons of Adam. Her mockery comes after she has met Skrebensky whom she sees as one of the sons of God. The Skrebenskys have come to stand, after Anna's visit, for a reality beyond the suffocating intimacy of the Brangwen farm. Enacting the female Brangwen aspiration to the beyond, Ursula seeks her real being in a mode beyond the Brangwens and ultimately beyond the human.

This is surely why the world in which she is compelled to seeks her identity crumbles before her so quickly. The whole of her relationship with Skrebensky is summed up in their dance at Fred Brangwen's wedding. Like the corn harvest in which Will and Anna come together, this is a moonlight ritual of sexual ecstacy. But whereas the first scene is a rhythmic enactment of sexual vitality in which unity is never quite realized, the second is a scene in which Ursula meets Skrebensky to go beyond him to seek out 'pure being' through her relationship with the moon: 'She wanted the moon to fill her, she wanted more, more communion with the moon, consummation' (XI). And she returns to Skrebensky only to destroy him, like a corrosive salt. Ursula takes her being from the moon (a theme which is importantly continued in *Women in Love*), and this is not Lawrencean mystagogy – it is a validated metaphor for the destructive vitality of 'pure being' which emancipates itself from the world of man. Thus the Brangwen vitality becomes not simply the value against which 'modern' life is measured, it is also an agent of that life. Skrebensky is not merely a 'nullity' – he is made a nullity by Ursula's vitality. The continuity between the generations is an evolution towards death and extinction.

It is the relationship between the two processes we have noted that gives *The Rainbow* its coherence. For it means that we have, not a historical novel opposing 'traditional' values to social change, but a complex portrayal of man's descent into history and his evolution towards and beyond the forms of being which that descent encounters. Of course, it is modern history that Lawrence is concerned with, but the novel's enquiry is into the nature of historical man, and through this into the relationship between 'objective' reality and 'subjective' being. Man is agent and patient of his own destiny. And the end of the novel seems to me to be perfectly coherent with the realization of this relationship. Ursula, pregnant by Skrebensky who has deserted her for social integration, is surrounded by unseen horses as she walks in the rain. She climbs a tree to escape them and has a miscarriage. After a long and obscure illness, she awakes to a new sense of being, denuded of social reality, like a kernel which has burst its shell. Looking out from her parents' new house over the industrial waste land of Beldover, she sees the corruption of a people bowed down by industrialism. But she sees too a rainbow arched over the town and feels that it is arched in the blood of the working people. The horses are clearly the unacknowledged forces of her inner being – the darkness which had sought and failed to discover the unknown in Skrebensky. But they appear as nightmare, and though, like Tom's drowning, it is a consummation of her being, it is utterly private. We have moved into an era in which the 'blood intimacy' of the Brangwens is buried in the inner being of the isolate self. But also, by causing the miscarriage, the horses acknowledge the end of 'generation' and hence the end of the old bases of personal relationship. Finally, they seem to be 'running against the walls of time', affirming that is the vitality of change against the 'Absolute' of 'pure being'. So that they are at once a challenge and an affirmation: a challenge to the absorption of being in the outer world and to the family as an agent of aspiration and continuity – an affirmation of new potentials of being in time. So that the naked kernel of being is able to discover a new sense of the human group, of relationship beyond the social order, in the rainbow – 'the very iris of my being'. This is not utopian because it is not a glimpse of a new social order, but an inward vision of something beyond pure individuality: it is an image of what the new self needs to create, but the rainbow is a momentary image, and it presupposes that the deluge will precede it. From this point, Lawrence has to move on from the portrayal of the creation of social man to the portrayal of the society he creates moving towards its destiny in destruction. And this means moving from saga to panorama, and from the symbol which is a referential covenant to a structural system of symbols which are the signals of social destiny. The end of *The Rainbow* takes us straight to *Women in Love*.

It is, in fact, a massive and necessary prelude to *Women in Love* in that, as a recreation of man's entry into the historical world, it gives a large temporal perspective to what is to be the final judgement on that world affected by the Brangwen sisters who wait, at the opening, with slightly pretentious boredom to discover a role in the present. *Women in Love* is, in a way that *The Rainbow* cannot be, a historical novel specifically narrating the death of a society. And this means that it is concerned not simply with the coming of social change and the consequent erosion of ethical values (as, for example, a novel by Scott or Balzac might be) but with the death of ways of being, a death precisely caused by the very evolution of vitality that is registered in *The Rainbow*. The best preparation for the study of *Women in Love* is George Dangerfield's history of the years 1910–1914, *The Strange Death of Liberal England*. Dangerfield finds it necessary to talk of the 'neurosis' of a whole society, and his picture is essentially one of institutions dying in the face of an unaccommodated vitality; this is what is happening in *Women in Love*. Gerald, both through the determinant role of his own vitality and through its need to relate to the destructive critical vigour of Gudrun, goes to his death in the navel of the world, and his death, we are made to feel, is an apocalyptic image of the end of the social world which he dominates and by which he is created. But the link with Dangerfield's book is more than one of content: for a historical narrative, its organization is surprisingly spatial – Dangerfield moves rather from one social area to another than through successive points in time. And *Women in Love* has, in its central portions, this sense too – we move from Shortlands to the Café de Pompadour to Breadalby to Beldover and back to Shortlands. Each location contains a part of the society Lawrence is portraying. Again, we are confronted with a transformed nineteenth century form – the panoramic novel – and as a social picture it is bound to be rather static. This is one reason why we cannot separate it from *The Rainbow* – without the temporal prelude of the earlier novel we are likely to look on *Women in Love* as an organism of related moral values, as a 'fable' with social significance. Whereas it is a chronicle of a moment in history.

This means that primarily we should be concerned with the novel's presentation of a world moving to its death, rather than with the moral values with which Lawrence is measuring that world. Although it was written during the war, and although its conception was involved with the sense Lawrence gained from the war of the drift of societal ideologies towards social destruction, it importantly is not a novel *about* the war; it is about the social world which was obliterated by it. It is, that is to say, a novel about a world which has already gone. Its going is recognized to be inevitable, not because of the coming of an external historical event, but because of its inherent characteristics. It is central to Lawrence's pur--pose to realize this inherentness because his history is not of 'events' but of the evolution of consciousness within a static order. This is why Birkin and Ursula seem so unsatisfactory as representatives of 'normative' values: what they stand for is no real alternative to what is taking place, for the death is inevitable and even desirable. We can see clearly how much Lawrence is concerned to preserve a sense of historical inevitability if we consider *Twilight in Italy* which in many detailed ways is a trial run for the novel. It is a remarkably concrete and vivid record of the erosion of the spontaneous vitality of the Italian soul by the encroachment of Northern efficiency and Northern consciousness. The village players who act Ibsen and Hamlet ('tragedy of the convulsed reaction of the mind from the flesh, of the spirit from the self'), the *padrone* of the Lemon Gardens who frets about his new spring lock, the peasants who go to America and return up-rooted and vacant and the Italian exiles in Switzerland who drift into a mechanical anarchism – all these are signs of the coming of a new era of self-consciousness and mechanical dualism to a way of life which has always been of the 'shadow', vital and physical. And there are constant digressions on the corruption of England by the Industrial Revolution. Lawrence's moral attitude is clear, but it exists within a bitter and tenacious recognition that this has to be, not simply because it has happened and is undeniable, but also because it is part of human evolution. The Italian 'soul' is a regression, and, as he says, 'It is better to go forward into error than to stay fixed inextricably in the past'. *Women in Love* maintains the same balance of attitudes: the world of the Criches must go forward to meet its destiny in violent death because of its very vitality.

We can say 'the Crich world' because although the novel is panoramic, the social centres which are established exist as functions of the hegemonic world of Shortlands. Shortlands, the seat of industrial power, determines the dominant modes of consciousness of the novel. It depends on a rigorously imposed order maintained by the kind of vitality exemplified in Gerald's determination to make the Arab mare face the train which frightens her; on, that is, the violent subjugation of physical energy to the machine. But it is also, clearly, a dualistic world. The first generation of Criches simply assimilate their energy into the creation of industrial prosperity, but Gerald's father attempts to mitigate this energy with a hopelessly paralytic philanthropism. As the leader of the third generation, Gerald becomes the agent of power, shaping the family affairs into a highly mechanized efficiency. But not all of Gerald can be absorbed into this creation of his outer being: his is a power which cannot be contained by the outer world, and through him the order of Shortlands comes to be dependent on an underworld of degenerate centres – the darkness of Beldover, the mindlessness of the Pompadour and the dissolution of being into 'talk' which is Breadalby. Thus, in this perspective, *Women in Love* establishes a 'social statics' in which the hegemonic consciousness of industrial power has escape routes into decadence.

But there is too a 'social dynamics' and this is realized by what transforms the novel from panorama to apocalypse – the complex patterns of symbols and symbolic scenes which have been discussed most fully by Leavis. It is impossible, in an essay of this scope, to go beyond what he offers as analysis, but it is necessary to say something about the function of symbolism in *Women in Love*, for Lawrence's kind of symbolism is very different from 'literary' symbolism. He had experimented with a symbolic structure in *The Trespasser* (1912) which moves from a depressing social environment to the Isle of Wight, a landscape in which the main characters act out the implications of their situations in mythic terms. It is clear that Lawrence moves towards symbolism in an attempt to cater for the aspects of self which are not available to a socially defined consciousness (personality). It is not so much a rhetorical device as part of the vision which is being realized. In *Women in Love* we do not have two co-existing levels of reality, the actual and the symbolic, but we have a process in which the actual modulates into the symbolic as it plays out its implications without the defence of social mediation. Again and again there are scenes which begin as panoramic realism and come to focus on symbolic gesture or theme. Thus at the wedding which opens the novel, we have Gerald, at this stage insisting on social conformity, and suddenly summoning the guests to the breakfast with a conch shell, which embodies the nature of his vitality – the primitive assertion of tribal domination. Again, at Breadalby, we have a country house party sharply realized in terms of social types and the 'stream of conversation' by which they declare their own abstraction and stagnation. When Hermione, mechanically asserting her will after her defeated attempt to crush the vitality in Birkin, suggests that her guests go swimming, the party resolves itself into a tableau of stagnant pastoralism: 'one wanted to swoon into the bygone perfection of it all' (VIII). But the image recedes in time beyond its human context: 'Don't they look saurian? They are just like great lizards'. It is an image of a primeval world obliterated by evolution. Significantly, it is Gudrun who makes this remark for it is she who is to demolish this escape route for Gerald, as she draws him into the destructive impetus of his own dualism (Gerald has joined the swimmers, but he is fascinated by her destructive criticism of it). Similarly, the Café de Pompadour moves towards its definitive symbol of the African fetish, the disintegration into mindlessness (this is another world which Gudrun finally places and overtakes). This modulation operates too on a personal level – Birkin discovers his image of the relationship he wants with Ursula in his cat's attitude towards the wild female Gerald and Gudrun recognize their desire for mutual destruction in the violence of the rabbit.

Too much of the symbolism is bound up with the freedom of the characters in the novel for us to think of it as the author's way of giving order to the reality he is imitating. They *choose* their symbolic acts and images as ways of declaring their relationship with the outer world and of indicating the direction of their vitality. The best analogy is perhaps from anthropology. One of the major debates in this field at the turn of the century was the nature of totemism (Sir James Frazer had published two books on the subject in 1887 and 1910; Freud had related the problem of totemism to psychoanalysis in *Totem* and *Taboo*, 1913). Malinowski in an essay on Frazer writes:

> totemism expresses ritually and mythologically man's selective interest in a number of animal or plant species: it discloses the primitive's profound conviction that he is in body and mind akin to the relevant factors of his environment.
>
> (*Sex, Culture and Myth*, 1963, p. 281)

Women in Love is the portrait of a society seeking out the relevant factors of its environment: the characters, especially Gerald, are compelled by the dynamics of their own vitality to break through the static world of contained social consciousness and act out the violence and destruction implicit in the mode of being which gives them their hegemony. The massive coda of the novel discovers the landscape, the new world of frozen mountains, where the society is dominated by Loerke the artist whose work is at once the most extreme product of industrialism and the most conscious satire of it. Gerald has used Gudrun as an escape from the pressure of the external world of Shortlands on the inner vacuum of his being (his first intercourse with her is both a release from consciousness, a kind of masturbation, and a return to the womb), and then, once he has realized that she is no Minette, he tries to assimilate her into his dualism, thinking of her as the wife to whom he will be unfaithful. But through the mountains and through the extreme, corrupt and satiric consciousness of Loerke, Gudrun selects her own, reductive and anti-static kinship with her environment. Loerke is *her* 'totem', and in his defence, she delivers Gerald the blow which sends him to his death. His frozen body is the image of what the consciousness of the world of Shortlands implies.

I have offered an account of the way in which we need to approach the form of *Women in Love*, but it would be simply dishonest of me to pretend to give even the same perfunctory account of its themes as I have tried to do in the discussion of other novels. The overall theme of *Women in Love* is easier to describe than that of *The Rainbow* or even *Sons and Lovers*: it is the study of the dynamic implications of the modes of consciousness created by a static but dying society realized in the sexual relationships which exist within that society. But, of course, what is important is the detailed realization of this theme and that requires a prohibitively extensive analysis. There is an important problem, however, which must be discussed, and this has to do generally with the kind of 'historical' novel *Women in Love* is, and in particular with the structural importance of the relationship between Ursula and Birkin.

A novel which claims to have historical significance, as I think *Women in Love* does, ought to realize an awareness of potential change. Yet we have noted that the sense of development that there is in the novel has to do not with historical change but only with the symbolic realization of the *terminus ad quem* of a particular epoch: the future seems to be only an ending. Ursula and Birkin do seem, on the face of it, to be intended to offer an alternative mode of relationship, one which is not only beyond corrupt possessiveness, but also beyond 'love' – that is mutual absorption. Yet nobody has satisfactorily answered Leavis's objections to Lawrence's portrayal of this relationship – that it is a rhetoric of assertion rather than realization, and that it is limited by an overbearing jargon (the chapter called 'Excurse' gives sufficient examples of this). We surely have to admit that this is a very problematic aspect of the novel.

But also, we must recognize how much Lawrence recognizes the limits of what Ursula and Birkin achieve. Although he is very explicit about their struggle towards a viable relationship, says very little of their marriage, except to define its limitations. In the first place, Birkin is looking for a more than private relationship: he aspires to be free 'with a few other people', that is to make his relationship with Ursula the basis for a new society. This is linked with his failed desire to achieve a deep relationship with Gerald. It is an unresolved aspiration – Birkin has to give in, at least temporarily, to Ursula's contentment with privacy. Secondly, their first act under the new dispensation is to disrobe themselves of their social being altogether by resigning their educational posts. They opt, that is for exile, not for the kind of regeneration through education which had been glimpsed early in the novel in Ursula's classroom. Finally, Birkin's major consolation for his despair about Gerald is a Darwinian faith that the human race will be totally destroyed and replaced.

These qualifications do not contest the obvious fact that Birkin is close to Lawrence's own view. But they do *place* Birkin in the world which is being destroyed. Nobody can fail to have been struck by Birkin's irresoluteness for much of the novel – the difficulty he has in ending his relationship with Hermione, and the way in which, for all his ideas, he participates in the talk and the social pretence of Breadalby and the Pompadour (Minette revealingly thinks of him in the same group as Halliday).

It is significant that Birkin is finally driven out of these groups, by
Hermione's violence and Halliday's mockery, rather than by his own
decision. Birkin is very much (dramatically if not ideologically) part of the
world whose destruction is being enacted. Indeed we must go further
and say that the social world which is portrayed is for the purposes of the
novel, the *human* world. To escape from it is to escape from humanity.

This enables us to define the quality of the novel which is both its
strength and its limit. When we say that *Women in Love* is about the death
of a whole society, we must note too that Lawrence's social vision is almost
entirely hegemonic. That is to say, the nature of a society defines itself
for him by the structures of consciousness created by the classes which
dominate it. This has been increasingly true since *Sons and Lovers* –
Lawrence's interest has been primarily in those impulses towards self-
realization which are the *making* of a social structure. This is recognized,
I think, in a small scene in *Women in Love*. Shortly before they leave
England, Birkin and Ursula discover a chair in a market which they see as
the survival of pre-industrial England, a more productive age. They buy
it, but then decide that the continuity with the past it represents is not for
them – they must opt out of the world of possessions altogether. So they
give it to a poor man and the pregnant girl he is about to marry. They are
urban England, subdued and miserable, yet they have also a certain
singular vitality which is appealing. It is as though Birkin and Ursula were
giving up society but laying a stake in the future by bequeathing their
most valuable possession to a class which is not present in the novel except
as part of the dualistic world of Shortlands. It is a very slight reminder that
there is a humanity beyond the Crich world, although it is one which
the Criches hold in their power. And surely this is the right perspective.
It would have been quite sentimental for Lawrence to have shown a 'new'
humanity *replacing* that of Shortlands. As Birkin says to Ursula, it is not
possible to be of the end and of the beginning. Equally, however, we
know that it is the end of a *particular* world. And the end must seem to
be complete, for it is only possible to conceive of being in terms which are
consciously available within human society, and human society is determined by its possessors. The new heaven and the new earth cannot be of
this vocabulary. It suggests a vision which is limited, but the vision would
be weakened if it were dissipated by Utopian projections.

III. 1919–1930

From 1919 to 1922, Lawrence stayed on the Continent, largely in Sicily.
It is another fruitful phase which includes the completion of *The Lost Girl*
(May, 1920) and *Aaron's Rod* (May, 1921) and the writing of two important
tales, 'The Fox' and 'The Captain's Doll' (both finished in 1921). He also

wrote two important essays on the theory of personality, *Psychoanalysis and the Unconscious* (1920) and *Fantasia of the Unconscious* (1921) the second of his remarkable travelogues, *Sea and Sardinia* (1921) and most of the poems of his best volume, *Birds, Beasts and Flowers*. The pattern of his career is clear at this point: there is a new initiative and a new determination to discover an audience. In January, 1920, we find him refusing to accept an offer of £200 for the rights of *The Rainbow*, partly because 'I believe in my books and their future'. In February, he is impressing on his American agent the urgency of securing a public in America, and, in May, he is looking for an opportunity to serialize *The Lost Girl*. At the same time there is a co-existent despair. In February of the same year, he writes to Amy Lowell, 'Why can't I earn enough, I've done the work'. By May, 1921, the short-lived concern for and faith in a public has evaporated: 'I have *nearly* finished my novel *Aaron's Rod* ...', he writes to S. L. Koteliansky, 'But it won't be popular.' *The Lost Girl* had sold only 2,300 copies, and *Women in Love* (published in England in 1921) was branded as indecent by the popular press. Lawrence was never a willing cultural martyr, and such alienation was damaging. The preface to *Fantasia of the Unconscious* is an embarrassing attempt to be indifferent to 'the general reader', and the violent, assertive rhetoric of the book contrasts dismally with the lucidity of the earlier essay on psychoanalysis.

This is certainly one factor in the decision to accept a more disastrous exile than that of Europe. In 1922, after a good deal of vacillation between rival invitations to Ceylon and New Mexico, Lawrence sailed east. As soon as he arrived, he disliked Ceylon and moved to Australia. After three months there, he finally arrived in Taos, New Mexico in September to take up an offer of a house by a wealthy American admirer, Mabel Dodge Sterne (later Luhan). There he was based until he finally returned to Europe in September, 1925, but Harry T. Moore has computed that he only stayed there for a total of eighty weeks in those three years. In this tragically unsettled phase, the only major fiction of real merit is 'St. Mawr' which seems to ironize bitterly every character in the story (including, I think, the horse). The novels of these years are simply bad: *Kangaroo* (1923), despite sharp insights into Australian society, is uncontrolled autobiography: *The Boy in the Bush* and *The Plumed Serpent* are barely readable because of a self-indulgent didacticism. The danger signs in Lawrence's alienation had long been evident. In the lonely years at the end of the First World War, in essays such as 'Education of the People' and 'Democracy', we see a tired mind which has a very sharp sense of the problems of modern society reaching desperately for a simple solution. He had found it mainly in a mystic (and mystifying) concept of social leadership. This takes, however, a long time to get into the novels. In *Aaron's Rod* it is a marginal and unrelated theme, in *Kangaroo* it is dominant, but the novel is largely concerned with its rejection. Only in *The Plumed*

Serpent does it become programmatic, and that is a novel that Lawrence himself was later to reject. His fictional imagination resisted as long as possible the subjective ideology that his isolation led him to, and it is significant that only when he has cut himself off from the ineluctable reality of Europe can Lawrence fully indulge himself. Lawrence, it needs to be insisted, found himself in a dilemma that was barely soluble. He recognized, as soon as he left Europe, that exile was dangerous. From Ceylon, he wrote:

> But I do think, still more now I am out here, that we make a mistake forsaking England and moving out into the periphery of life. After all, Taormina, Ceylon, Africa, America – as far as *we* go, they are only the negation of what we ourselves stand for.

He felt also that Australia and America failed to provide the self with any kind of societal reality (of course, he was kept very much on the fringe of American society in the bogus primitivism and opulent bohemianism of Mabel Dodge Luhan's cultural menagerie). At the same time, he couldn't bring himself to encounter the old chagrin of living in England ('But I feel England has insulted me, and I stomach that badly'). So, throughout 1923, we find him making plans to return to Europe, but finally letting Frieda go alone only joining her at the end of November. And as soon as he is in London, he wants to return to America. He sailed back in March 1924. One reason that he must have been drawn back was simply that in America he had an audience. He wrote to Secker in 1922 that whereas from the sale of the whole of his work in England he was getting about £120 a year, he had been offered in America $1,000 for the magazine rights of 'The Captain's Doll' alone, and, in the same year, he learnt that *Women in Love* had sold 15,000 copies in America. There is no reason to assume that these sales would have diminished if Lawrence had not lived there, but Lawrence was a writer who was socially responsive enough to be drawn to where he was wanted.

Illness, however, was soon to become the major fact of his life. In Mexico, in February 1925, tuberculosis was definitively diagnosed, and in September he crossed the Atlantic again this time for good. The next four years, frighteningly restless though they were, see a final creative phase. 'Sun' was written in 1925; *The Virgin and the Gypsy* and 'The Man Who Loved Islands' in 1926; and 'The Escaped Cock' ('The Man Who Died') in 1927–8: *Lady Chatterley's Lover* was begun in October, 1926 and finished in December 1927. It is also a period of great essays. The attack on Galsworthy, 'Pornography and Obscenity' and a moving series of pieces about his home country, 'Autobiographical Fragment', 'Nottingham and the Mining Country' and 'Autobiographical Sketch'. Both the creativity and its particular direction suggest a renewed determination to resume battle with the particular world in which he was so deeply rooted, and whose institutions and culture drove him into exile. And he achieved a kind of victory. *Lady Chatterley's Lover*, though it was privately published, was seized by the police in October, 1928 (and it remained a classic underground book until 1960). In January, 1929, the manuscript of his satiric poems, *Pansies*, was seized by the Post Office (with very doubtful legal justification), and in July, the police carried off thirteen of his paintings from an exhibition in London. Lawrence became the only modern writer to become, like Dickens, a household name.

It is almost inevitable that, after *Women in Love*, Lawrence's work should seem disappointing (though this is a highly relative statement). It is not simply that it would be very difficult for any writer to transcend the achievement of the three novels we have most fully discussed, it is also that the very nature of *Women in Love* demands a progression which inevitably places Lawrence historically. Although, as he himself said, it is a destructive novel, it is not pessimistic because it is so much a novel about the past. You cannot really be pessimistic about the past, only about the future: if, somehow, life goes on, you are compelled to discover a basis for the affirmation of its continuity. This is complicated by the war, which, for Lawrence asserted the pastness of the world he knew, and, despite its horror, granted new hope for a totally new future. And fiction must move from the 'destructive' to the programmatic. Because of the limitations of Lawrence's vision, the programme is full of difficulties.

This is an oversimplifying formula because it suggests that 'the programme' is an imposition of absolute moral values on the world of the novel. Whereas, at least in *The Lost Girl*, it is much more an affirmation of a new centre of vitality which is discovered within the portrayed historical situation. Alvina Houghton is a powerfully realized study in alienation. Externally, she is entirely the product of her father's megalomaniac but trivial business world, and she has to learn first to become an outsider by marrying a theatrical Italian, and second to confront the landscape which has made him, a landscape which is an eternal negation of human effort, before she can realize her own being, not in a futile antithetical struggle with society, but in relation to the 'pre-world' against which man has to assert his significance. She has to be lost to society, to her former being in order to discover the reality of human relationships which social institutions disguise. But it is not this thematic coherence which gives the novel its impressiveness: it is simply the density with which Alvina's social world is realized. The petty bourgeois world with its pretentiousness and its commodity-fetishism is so much on top of us, that we recognize Alvina's escape to Italy with Cicio not as a romantic gesture of defiance but as a real necessity – the only way to avoid becoming one of Woodhouse's old maids. If Cicio were not there, he would have to be invented.

And yet here, in its very convincingness, is the problem which confronts us in the later Lawrence. Symbolically, Cicio stands for the masculine force of darkness, the reaffirmed rootedness of being in 'unconscious' sexual relationship. But Cicio is *realized* as something less than what he has to stand for. In the first place, he comes to Woodhouse with the tawdry and absurd 'Red-indian' troop, the Natcha-kee-Tawaras (we do not have to read the novel very closely to see that they are meant to be tawdry and absurd): this means that he is not only the primitive principle of blood consciousness but that he is playing at being such a symbol – his presocial subversiveness is part of his social being. And thus he is almost comically dualistic – if he is capable of taking Alvina out of Woodhouse, he is also capable of being impressed by its affluence, and Alvina is both a social and a sexual 'catch'. This is partly explained by the 'modern education' which makes 'money and independence an *idée fixe*' (X), but we should note that Lawrence recognizes that this is 'more efficacious' than the 'old instinct' which it overlays, and, more importantly, that the old instinct is 'an instinct of the world's meaninglessness' – it is not realized as more than a negation. When we arrive in *his* world, Califano, he becomes a radically diminished symbol: it is not he, but the landscape which creates a new sense of being outside social convention. And the predominant sense that Alvina has is that of a '*lapse* of life' (XV). At the end, Cicio goes off to the war and we are not certain that he will come back. We cannot be sure whether Alvina is lost to society or lost completely. The necessary affirmation of a life apart from social institutions is 'perilously' near to death. Lawrence must inevitably proceed from the negation of *Women in Love* to the discovery of new orders of vitality, but although vitality is *conceptually* clearly defined in 'The Crown' and *Psychoanalysis and the Unconscious*, its realization in *fictional* terms is difficult.

We find it best realized in the stories – in 'The Horse Dealer's Daughter', 'You Touched Me', and 'The Captain's Doll', for example. But this is significant – the short story does not have to confront the problem of the *duration* of what it affirms. Indeed the first two stories just mentioned depend for their whole strength on a tension, at the end, between an unambiguous momentary affirmation of the reality of physical communion and utter doubt about that moment's duration in time. The novel cannot be so ambiguous about duration, and by the nature of Lawrence's concern for human life which is not atrophied by the individualism of bourgeois morality, the durational realization of the new order of vitality must mean that we move from a moral issue to a social one.

The key text here is *Aaron's Rod*, which is a much better novel than is usually thought. Aaron, caught in the dualism of work and family on the one hand, and self indulgent escape on the other, has to break out or rot inwardly. His problem may be, as Moynahan dismissively says, boredom, but boredom can be very complex, and in Aaron's case it involves an integrity which refuses to be absorbed in the conventionally ordered world, a separate self which cannot be held in apartness but which must be responded to in action. The vivid portrayal of his home life in the opening chapters makes us feel that self-exile is the only integrity. The difficulty begins with the exile itself. Unlike Wells' Mr. Polly, Aaron finds no retreat. The only other world is that of his sophisticated patrons, and that is a world as oppressive and as alienating as that of his home. We see this most clearly in the scene in which Sir William Franks ceremoniously displays his medals: we are still in a world of social labels and Aaron, having no label himself, has to look on. He has not escaped, he has only become invisible. The ambiguities of *The Lost Girl* become central, and the very structure of the novel becomes an aimless wandering from set to set. It is as though Aaron's self-discovery and flight to freedom can have no meaning beyond the single act of going away. And this is clearly because there is no social order which can contain the basis of the regenerated human group. The isolate self becomes absolute but not more 'free' in its cutting loose.

The novel works best, I think, if we see it as totally directionless. It then becomes a vivid portrayal of the man of personal integrity picking his way among the ruins of the post-war world. But there is a direction – marginal and unrelated – in that Aaron is vaguely searching for Rawdon Lilly. Lilly, who is an idealization of Lawrence, offers him a relationship which is meaningful outside the social consciousness. But, it is also clear that it is a relationship which is contradictory. At the end of the novel, Lilly is trying to explain that he believes in both the idea of natural superiority and its concomitant idea of submission, *and* that every man is 'a sacred and a holy individual, *never* to be violated' (XX). The ideological difficulty is resolved by a loud explosion from a political bomb which obliterates the conversation. Aaron's flute is broken, his individuality violated. Freedom from social reality is impossible. More than this, Lilly's own mode of relationship is essentially one of violation. Personal sufficiency, he tells Aaron at the end, is not enough: Aaron must submit to some higher being. The message is clear: the emancipated self needs to discover real contact and real community. But dramatically, Lilly cannot offer this new sense of relationship because he is too much a part of the intellectual set in which Aaron discovers his inexorable isolation. The only way in which Lawrence can bring out the possibilities that Lilly is meant to offer is by making him give a sermon at the end: it is crude, but significantly crude – Lilly can only oppose the corrupt intellectual world against which he is meant to offer alternative values with talk, and talk is the safety valve by which the sophisticated world which Aaron has encountered, survives. Lilly is *dramatically* no more meaningful to Aaron's predicament than Sir William Franks, except, that is, in the finite interval of consummated intimacy in Covent Garden when Lilly nurses the sick Aaron back to life. Lilly may be as a character an idealization of Lawrence, but his social importance is assessed with a realism which is inescapable. It leaves Lilly chattering away while the bombs go off.

We are confronted then finally with the incoherence of Lawrence's social vision. Throughout the tales of the period which follows *Aaron's Rod*, we find a more and more lucidly realized sense of the moral relationship between the kind of integrity discovered by Alvina and Aaron and the meaningful human contact within which it can survive. But in the novels, *Kangaroo* and *The Plumed Serpent* especially, we find a desperate but inevitable attempt to envisage fictionally the new society which such a morality demands. In the process, the morality is distorted into propaganda: vitality becomes order. It is not until we reach *Lady Chatterley's Lover* and Lawrence returns again to the historical problem which is his most central concern, the changing consciousness of those who inhabit an industrial society, that we get a real sense of what he was trying to make articulate.

It is a failure, but it remains one of the few really challenging texts about the values inherent in modern society, and the source of its failure is also a source of its strength. Sir Clifford Chatterley is a Gerald who has survived the war, and is thus unmanned, an anachronism whose only motive for survival is an atrophied social will. His own concept of integrity is precisely that of 'personality', the living in apartness which Lawrence finds so nauseating in Jane Austen: 'Isn't the whole problem of life,' he says, 'the slow building up of an integral personality, through the years? living an integrated life?' (V). Such an integrity is entirely mental and, as Connie realizes, 'out of touch' (in all possible ways) with any sense of human community. It is a sterility reflected at one level by the mechanical orderliness of Wragby and the dreary standardization of Tevershall, and at another by the futile talk of Sir Clifford's friends. It is an undeniably powerful realization of a bourgeois mode of being. Lawrence has been criticized for making Sir Clifford a cripple, and thus simplifying the moral situation by a symbolic accident. But, though the physical debility is symbolic, it seems to me to be justifiable in historical terms: his wound is a war wound, and the war was fought in the interests of Sir Clifford's class. He is not sterile because he is a cripple, but a cripple because he is sterile – because, that is, he accepted the role offered him by his class. It does not need demonstrating that in scene after scene, Sir Clifford defines himself as a totally class-conscious being, and as something less than human, so that in this novel about tenderness, we do not find it shocking that Connie feels 'as if he ought to be obliterated from the face of the earth' (XIII). Sir Clifford is of a different species from the humanity that Lawrence is trying to realize in the relationship between Connie and Mellors: he has no more place in their world than a dinosaur, and to feel sorry for Sir Clifford is to be sentimental and not see that he is totally, through his own effort of will, a class product.

What one wonders, on the contrary, is why, if he is such an anachronism, Sir Clifford takes quite so much exterminating. He is so weak and pathetic that though we can believe in his odiousness, it is difficult to believe in his capacity for survival. Many of the scenes in which he appears are brilliantly realized, but they hardly add to one another – Sir Clifford is definitively placed as soon as he appears. Of course, industrialism was not about to disappear in 1928, but we get very little sense of its power within the novel.

The difficulty arises from the ambiguity of Mellors. In a brilliant review of the novel, in 1929, Edmund Wilson hailed the sexual language Mellors uses as a breakthrough both for Lawrence and for the novelist in general. 'It gets rid,' he wrote, 'of a good deal of the verbosity, the apocalyptic grandiloquence, into which [Lawrence's] subject has so often led him, and it keeps the love scenes human'. This seems to me to be undeniable, as long as we are thinking of the novel as a moral act. The trouble is that the language is part of the social vision because it is not merely the authentic language of sexuality, but also a consciously adopted working-class dialect which is to make the relationship with Connie subversive of Sir Clifford's class hegemony. And in *this* perspective, the language is not a breakthrough but a regression. Mellors adopts dialect not spontaneously but as a conscious atavistic gesture of defiance. And we have to come back again to a point that we have made earlier. For Lawrence, we have seen, the idea of a cultural absolute to measure the impoverishment of the modern world is contradictory: it is using the dead to bury the dead. But in the end, the four-letter words come to have a role remarkably similar to that of the literary tradition in *The Waste Land*. And this applies too to the sexuality itself: it is a retreat to the woods, to a pastoral world, and thus it comes to seem not a social force but a *standard*, absolute but without visible presence in actuality. Mellors himself is an anachronism: 'He was a man in dark green velveteens and gaiters … the old style, with a red face and red moustache and distant eyes' (V). And though he is from the working class, as much of his rhetoric is directed against it as it is against the world of Sir Clifford. So that the opposition between himself and Sir Clifford remains a very personal one. Socially it is not very effective. By the end of the novel, the moral values are clearly and explicitly defined in Mellors' letters to Connie, but it is significant that it is letters we have, for the whole situation remains unresolved – they are still apart, and Sir Clifford survives. Connie and Mellors are as impotent socially as Sir Clifford is morally.

It is indeed Sir Clifford who makes the sharpest social affirmation in the novel: 'An individual may emerge from the masses. But the emergence doesn't alter the mass. The masses are unalterable' (XIII). Mellors is effective only as long as he is an individual who has emerged – he cannot challenge the hegemony of the impotent except by getting away. He is, after all, a gamekeeper, a man whose job it is to preserve life for 'fat men' to take again at their leisure. Connie feels that Clifford's remark is 'a truth that killed', and this is devastating – for it places Mellors exactly: he is the lie that heals, the myth of the organic past. We cannot rationalize these limitations by seeing Mellors as another Birkin: Birkin is a social saviour, but this is part of him that is mocked by the novel. His business is not salvation but survival. Mellors, however, has to be more: he stands outside society to offer a direct challenge to its conventions. It is radically limiting that his programme is carried not to society but apart from it.

We are now openly facing the central limitation of Lawrence's hegemonic vision. In *Women in Love*, there is an oddly assertive passage which describes the workers' response to Gerald's cult of efficiency, we are told simply that they accept it because they too worship the machine. It is isolated and structurally unimportant, but this kind of assertive blurring is much more evident in *Lady Chatterley's Lover*. Mellors, for example, laments the industrialization of the working class: 'It's all a steady sort of bolshevism just killing off the human thing, and worshipping the mechanical thing' (XV). In Lawrence, essentially, there can be no conflict of social forces, because all social forces are determined unilaterally by the dominant class – bolshevists are only capitalists. In the case of *Women in Love*, this hardly matters since we are concerned only with the death of society. But in *Lady Chatterley's Lover*, we are confronted with the struggle between the forces which make for death and those which make for life. At the very least, in such a struggle, it seems anachronistic, after the General Strike, to write a novel in which working-class consciousness is merely an extension of bourgeois consciousness, and which might therefore simply be ignored. It makes Mellors' job a simpler one: his values might not stand up so easily to those of a collier's wife. But it makes it also a curiously irrelevant one.

This is, however, to ignore the most interesting character in the novel, Mrs. Bolton. As Sir Clifford's housekeeper, she takes over the role of wife, because she is able to be both slave and *magna mater* to her employer. Her success is primarily a sign of his corrupt infantilism. But Connie too is drawn to her, and when Mrs. Bolton tells her the story of her husband's death in the mine and the loss of physical relationship she endured because of it, Connie feels that she is, like Mellors, 'another passionate one out of Tevershall' (XI). Moreover, it is 'them as runs the pit' that Mrs. Bolton explicitly blames for this loss to her of human contact. When she discovers that Mellors is Connie's lover, she is gratified by the implied social revenge: 'A Tevershall lad … My word, that was a slap back at the high-and-mighty Chatterleys!' (X). And her relationship with Sir Clifford is detached and shrewd: 'in some corner of her weird female soul, how she despised him and hated him! … The merest tramp was better than he' (XIX). These moments make Mrs. Bolton neither more sympathetic nor more contradictory, but they mean that she is, as much as Connie and Mellors, a challenge to the power of Sir Clifford. And in one way a more effective challenge – they escape him, she takes him over. It is not insignificant that she, rather than Mellors, becomes Connie's source of information about the working people, for, upstart as she is, she is not so much of a class renegade as Mellors. So that if, through Mellors, Lawrence has bypassed the main social issue in the themes with which he is dealing, he creates, through Mrs. Bolton, a fragmentary image of the class conflict to which he tried to become indifferent. The real challenge that Lawrence needed to face in the late twenties, was not that of the class whose inner death he had registered in *Women in Love*, but that of the class from which he came.

There are signs, in the later essays, of a new appraisal of his own society. And we even find him stepping out of the tradition of social thought which dominates English literature from Carlyle to Leavis and takes refuge in a golden age of a preindustrial 'organic community': in 'Nottingham and the Mining Countryside' he blames the squalor of England not on urbanism but on the attempt to impose the village on industrial society and the failure to build radial cities. It is one crucial index of Lawrence's new engagement with the world in which he had his being. But the real confrontation never came. Lawrence's health had deteriorated steadily since 1925. In 1928, he was forced to go to Switzerland because of his lungs, and in the following year moved to the South of France. He died on March 2nd, 1930, aged 44.

Bibliography

A. Works by Lawrence

(i) *Fiction*. There is no authoritative edition. [True when written. Now Cambridge University Press is filling the gap.] All the novels have been available in Penguin, and all but nine of the stories. *The Phoenix* Edition (London, 1954 onwards) has all the novels except *The Boy in The Bush*, and all but one of the stories. The texts of *The Rainbow* and *The Lost Girl* are incomplete in this edition.

The White Peacock	London, 1911
The Trespasser	London, 1912
Sons and Lovers	London, 1913
The Prussian Officer and Other Stories	London, 1914
The Rainbow	London, 1915
Women in Love	New York, 1920
The Lost Girl	London, 1920

Aaron's Rod	London, 1922
England My England (stories)	London, 1922
The Ladybird (stories)	London, 1923
Kangaroo	London, 1923
The Boy in the Bush (with M. L. Skinner)	London, 1924
St. Mawr, together with The Princess	London, 1925
The Plumed Serpent	London, 1926
The Woman Who Rode Away (stories)	London, 1928
Lady Chatterley's Lover	Florence, 1928
Sun (1st unexpurgated edn.)	Paris, 1928
The Escaped Cock	Paris, 1929
The Virgin and The Gypsy	London, 1930
Love Among the Haystacks (stories)	London, 1930

(ii) Other Works

The Complete Poems ed. Pinto and Roberts. 2 Vols. (London and New York, 1964).

The Complete Plays (London, 1965; New York, 1966).

Three Plays (introduction by Raymond Williams; Harmondsworth, 1969).

Twilight in Italy (London, 1916; New York, 1916).

Sea and Sardinia (London, 1923; New York, 1921).

Mornings in Mexico (London, 1927; New York, 1927).

Etruscan Places (London, 1932; New York, 1957).

(Note, these four travel books are available in both the Penguin and Phoenix editions.)

Fantasia of The Unconscious and Psychoanalysis and the Unconscious, in one volume (London, 1961; New York, 1960).

Phoenix (essays) (London and New York, 1936).

Phoenix II (London, 1968; New York, 1967).

Studies in Classic American Literature, Mercury Books, London, 1965. (Originally published in 1923).

(iii) *Bibliography*. Warren Roberts: *A Bibliography of D. H. Lawrence* (London, 1963).

B. Biographical Material

(i) *Letters*

The Collected Letters of D. H. Lawrence, edited by Harry T. Moore, 2 Vols. (London, 1962). (This is by no means complete. Not only are there uncollected letters scattered through various memoirs and periodicals, but the Huxley volume, mentioned below, has many, and important letters not reprinted here.)

The Letters of D. H. Lawrence, edited by Aldous Huxley (London and New York, 1932). (Huxley's Introduction is one of the best early essays on Lawrence).

(ii) *Secondary Material*

The Intelligent Heart by Harry T. Moore (Revised Edition, London, 1960; New York, 1962). (The most reliable of the many biographies.)

D. H. Lawrence: A Composite Biography, edited by Edward Nehls, 3 Vols. (Madison, Wisconsin, 1957–1959). (A collection of documents, some previously unpublished, from memoirs of Lawrence. Some of it is illuminating, much of it is trivial. It is worth consulting for reference, and a sustained reading of almost any section gives a good idea of the inadequacy and egoism of most of Lawrence's friends and enemies.)

D. H. Lawrence, A Personal Record by 'E. T.' (London, 1932; New York, 1936). (This is Jessie Chambers' memoir. It gives a lucid, though of course, subjective account of her relationship with Lawrence. More importantly, it gives us some sense of the kind of cultural milieu in which the adolescent Lawrence found himself.)

C. Critical Material

(a) *Books*

F. R. Leavis: *D. H. Lawrence, Novelist* (London, 1955; New York, 1956). (The first extended critical assessment of Lawrence by a major critic. It is still the most important book on Lawrence, and it is also Leavis's best work.)

Mark Spilka: *The Love Ethic of D. H. Lawrence* (Bloomington, Indiana, 1955).

H. M. Daleski: *The Forked Flame: A Study of D. H. Lawrence* (London and Evanston, Illinois, 1965). (Although this is rather pedestrian, it makes useful connections between the discursive prose and the fiction, so that it is always worth consulting on particular issues.)

Julian Moynahan: *The Deed of Life: The Novels and Tales of D. H. Lawrence* (Princeton 1966). (The best critical book on Lawrence since Leavis. Particularly it is good on the novels Leavis underestimates – *Sons and Lovers*, *The Lost Girl* and *Lady Chatterley's Lover*.)

Keith Sagar: *The Art of D. H. Lawrence* (Cambridge, 1966). (This has a good, detailed chronology and a full bibliography. The criticism is sensible and informative.)

Gamini Salgado: *D. H. Lawrence's Sons and Lovers* (London, 1966).
Colin Clarke: *River of Dissolution: D. H. Lawrence and English Romanticism* (London, 1969).

(b) *Collections*

Harry T. Moore and Frederick Hoffman (eds.): *The Achievement of D. H. Lawrence* (Norman, Oklahoma, 1953). (Contains a useful sample of early essays on Lawrence, and above all, Edmund Wilson's review of *Lady Chatterley's Lover*.)

Mark Spilka (ed.): *D. H. Lawrence: A Collection of Critical Essays* (Englewood Cliffs, New Jersey, 1963). (Notably reprints Marvin Mudrick's essay on *The Rainbow*, and Raymond Williams' account of Lawrence's social thinking.)

'*Sons and Lovers*': a Casebook, ed. Gamini Salgado (London, 1969).

'*The Rainbow*' and '*Women in Love*': a Casebook, ed. Colin Clarke (London, 1969).

(c) *Single essays*

Arnold Kettle: *An Introduction to the English Novel*, Volume Two (London, 1953) (on *The Rainbow*).

S. L. Goldberg: '*The Rainbow*: Fiddle Bow and Sand' in *Essays in Criticism*, xi (October, 1961).

Frank Kermode: 'D. H. Lawrence and the Apocalyptic Types' in *Continuities* (London, 1968).

Mark Kinkead-Weekes: 'The Marble and the Statue: The Exploratory Imagination of D. H. Lawrence' in *Imagined Worlds*, ed. Maynard Mack and Ian Gregor (London, 1968).

Note

1. Since there was no authoritative edition of Lawrence's novels, references are to the chapter in which the quotation occurs. This is indicated by a Roman numeral in parenthesis after the quotation. Where there is an unbroken series of quotations from one chapter, the reference is given only after the first quotation in the series.

CHAPTER 19

'The Uninteresting Actual Frog', or Is There Life After Postmodernism?

One result of the seemingly endless deferral of this lecture is that I have had the title in my head since soon after I arrived here in 1989, expecting at any moment that the Vice-Chancellor would spring out of his office and tell me to do an inaugural next week. By the time I learnt that it was no good exercising the skill, naturally acquired researching Victorian literature, in being a wallflower, I began to think my subtitle would be so old fashioned that nobody would be able to keep awake long enough to listen to it or read it, besides the uncomfortable fact that David Lodge then brought out a book subtitled *Is There Life After Deconstruction?* and as though supernaturally pointing at me was writing on plagiarism in *The Independent* last week. But an even worse crime than being thought a plagiarist is to be thought out of date and, in the interim, Terry Eagleton demolished postmodernism in the last chapter of *The Ideology of the Aesthetic*. Christopher Norris published at least two books showing what's wrong with postmodernism, and Laurie Taylor wrote a spoof list of conferences on postpostmodernism. Worse still, in some ways, Fredric Jameson brought out a volume so exhaustive that even the Vice-Chancellor took pity on me for having to carry it around (or did he just allow himself the faint hope that I might have written it myself?). Those of you who haven't yet caught up with what postmodernism is may be forgiven for thinking, as some men thought in the early seventies when flared trousers appeared, you had only to hesitate long enough for them to go the way of all daft ideas and you could leap back into your drainpipes.

I make no apology for my title, and my frog will indeed leap into the lecture. But I'm sorry to go on like everybody else about postmodernism: I felt that I had to.

I thought that as this is a Chair of English refilled after a lapse of time I ought to respond to that signal of Keele's recognition of the subject's importance in the future of Higher Education by addressing the question of its place in the world today. Of course by 'English' I mean the study of literature and I have to add that I regard English as a language community and not as the property of a nation state.

Addressing its place in the present means looking at two problems which are, I think, related. First is the question of its own self definition as a discipline. Second is the kind of intervention it should make in the changing cultural environment which I will identify as that of 'postmodernity'.

English as a subject has experienced a double crisis in the last two decades, a crisis neatly summarised in the title of my colleague Bernard Bergonzi's book, *Exploding English*. This title indicates both the rapid expansion of the subject but also that this expansion is coupled with a tendency to self-destruct. The more widespread the subject has become the more its very activity and especially the object of its proper knowledge, 'literature', has been brought into question. As more and more people do it, more and more doubt is thrown on its validity as a form of knowledge.

We should keep this in perspective. The central activity of literary studies is criticism, and criticism is about bringing things to a state of crisis. *Angst* is not an occupational hazard of the literary scholar, it is his/her *raison d'être*. Moreover, literary studies has always been deeply bound up with education, but education in this country has always had a double identity – imparting knowledge has to share the timetable with forming character. Carlyle recommended education as a solution to the class war because it would impart wisdom by which he meant reverence. J. G. Farrell's arch liberal utilitarian, the Collector Hopkins in *The Siege of Krishnapur*, not only regards the Great Exhibition as the height of civilisation but believes in the ennobling effect of literature. This idea that the chief role of literature is to provide a wholesome and fortifying counter to all the hard nosed truths you get from other disciplines has always made it liable to disintegration and its place in the higher reaches of education was secured in the twenties and thirties by ensuring that it was a dissenting activity. Its very success therefore is a kind of defeat. How can dissenters become the normative group without ceasing to be dissenters?

But the real disaster for English Literature is not the simple attraction of its discipline, but the arrival of postmodernism – by which for the moment I simply mean that intellectual posture which sees the world, or at least our understanding of it as postmodern. The most obvious move of this posture is to make the world a text. Thus in the first instance, the modes of understanding, history, philosophy, psychology and so on, become discourses, like a sonnet is a discourse. You don't ask whether Shakespeare really had a mistress whose eyes were nothing like the sun or even whether he thought he had. You analyse the way he orchestrates a theme, of which this statement is a part in relation to the sonnet form and the conventions it displays.

You can clearly do this with historical accounts or philosophical positions. And this is not only, of course, something that is happening in intellectual discourses. It is happening also in discourses of social interaction such as law. And finally it extends to the external environment itself. Charles Jencks, one of the earliest writers on postmodernism, argued that buildings should be read like texts, and in particular that stylistic features of architecture were to be taken as metaphors. It does not take very much imagination then to see the built environment as a whole as a system of signs, not standing for some external reality, but constituting themselves as a kind of reality to be understood rather than translated into something else. I suppose the clearest if rather trivial index of that is (was?) designer clothing, where the label is more important than the utility of the garment. I am still pre-postmodernist enough myself to find the idea of carrying a free advertisement for Benetton on my chest faintly immoral, but this is clearly deluded.

Now if everything is to be read like a text, including the 'reality' texts used to be separate from, this is good news for literary students' imperialist dreams, but not so good for their waking up. For in the end this means that everyone in any discipline has to acquire skills of literary analysis, in which case is there any need for specialists not condemned to repeating training programmes? That is, do we actually need literary research, do we need Professors of English? This is a high risk question, but we should be adventurous.

I shall be very selective about what I treat as the significant features of postmodernism. Partly this is time, partly as well, however, it is because I think some of them such as self-reflexivity especially about language, and intertextuality, the idea that texts are begotten of other texts and have no direct access to an original 'reality', are familiar to any reader of Shakespeare, as Ann Righter and Philip Edwards long ago showed. These concepts are central to the literary project itself. What is new is that they have become the focus of attention, the whole substance of some literary texts, and that they have transgressed the specific literary boundary, so that, for example, buildings may be seen not to fill space or serve functions but to allude to other buildings.

Lyotard's argument that the chief feature of the postmodern condition is the break up of totalising, explanatory, 'grand' narratives, such as the idea of progress, is certainly more interesting. It is worth comparing *The Postmodern Condition*, a report on knowledge for the Canadian Government, with the recent White Paper on Higher Education. His argument that consensus puts paid to knowledge as opposed to performativity is highly relevant to the unthinking rhetoric about quality control which seems to me to be a way to guarantee mediocrity. Nevertheless there is nothing very challenging to the reader of novels in the idea of the break up of the grand narratives. Think only of the irony of the title of *Great Expectations* placed against the text that was nearly its contemporary, Samuel Smiles' *Self Help*, now available incidentally as a management text book (abbreviated) with an introduction by Keith Joseph. Or think of the foundation text of the European novel itself: *Don Quixote* plays two grand narratives, chivalric romance and the realism of comic banality against one another (without letting either triumph – realism is no more true than chivalry in the end).

What really convinced me that I ought to give some attention to the question of the postmodern was a book by a geographer I have admired since the appearance of *Social Justice and the City* in 1973: David Harvey's *The Condition of Post Modernity*. This forces us to see postmodernism not as a moment in the history of styles, a reaction against previous practice, as, say, Hassan or Jencks or even Lyotard do, but as the response to a new situation, the postmodern condition. These other writers seemed to be saying that non literary phenomena should be treated (with the same knowing scepticism) as literary phenomena, which is obvious enough since all disciplines operate through language and even physical objects like buildings (especially if you accept Volosinov's views that there is no consciousness that is prior to language) are the objects of reading. Post-modernist literature then seemed no more than a kind of masochistic narcissism (we are writing novels only to show how clever and naughty we are for writing novels because, *hypocrite lecteur*, surprise surprise, they lie).

Harvey convinced me (more than Jameson's original 1984 essay, exciting as it was) that what underlay this ubiquitous textualisation of intellectual production was an important shift in the perception of the world.

I should be more explicit now about what I think postmodernism is, and I shall be drawing very largely on Harvey. Postmodernism is defined by its relation to three other words – 'modernity', 'modernism' and 'post-modernity'. What you have to accept here is that there is something meaningfully designated 'modernity'. Modernity is a mode of conscious-ness. It means the awareness that what is specific to our age is different enough from what has preceded us to offer itself as *the* characteristic of it. All ages have something specific to them but we do not feel that the fact of specificity itself is the most important thing about them. Modernity is a double consciousness, consciousness first of vertiginous liberation – economic through the coming of industry, intellectual through the triumph of the enlightenment, political through the enfranchisement of the individual subject. 'All that is solid,' in the phrase Marshall Berman quotes from Marx, 'melts into air'. But with this dizzying unpinning of the universe, there is an opposite feeling of overwhelmingly powerful determining forces, a nature much older than man had ever dreamt and with laws inimical to human reason and affection, an economy dependent on dehumanising machines, a self driven by psychological forces it barely knows. This consciousness is frequently associated with a technological and economic process, modernization, which also combines tremendous liberation from physical constraints with equally tremendous constraints – mechanical efficiency and the drive for profit.

Modernity provokes an aesthetic response, modernism. This is a set of artistic strategies in every field combining recognition of the modern with resistance to it. Thus Eliot's *The Waste Land* is at once, in form and theme, a recognition of the alienation of modernity and by its unity of structure and its command of allusion, a co-ordination of residual traditions. And, in a more practical way, Le Corbusier's architecture is a recognition that you can't pretend that men can live in houses and cottages any more but you can constitute integrated communities within the great impersonal whole.

Postmodernity would then be a development of modernity. First on the level of consciousness: if modernity is an acute sense of historicity (the feeling that the now is radically different from the then), postmodernity first of all throws doubt on this sense of order not because it denies the radical break with the past but because it denies that the break can be described within a single narrative sequence – there is no then and no now, no origin and no totality of this specific 'now'. All total explanation is totalitarian, as Lyotard argues. But it registers also shifts in the reality, in the degree of modernisation. The balance of man and nature is no longer the evenly matched struggle it was in the height of the industrial period but there is a degree of human control which is felt to be out of control, urbanisation, finance capital, globalisation of markets and com-munications. Psychology demolishes rather than explains the individual subject. Above all, the signs by which consciousness thinks it knows the world are wrenched apart from the 'referent', what we think of as the world itself. So that consciousness becomes not a decoding of signs, but an adventure or ordeal among signs. Television is a clear index of this. Promising us infinite access to the events of the world as they happen, it manipulates those events to form a meaningful sequence of pictures, 'Reality' itseif is a text.

It is important to keep modernity distinct from modernism, and post-modernity distinct from postmodernism. You can be aware of modernity without being a modernist (as Matthew Arnold or Hardy were), and pre-sumably it is theoretically possible to be aware of postmodernity without being a postmodernist (though unlikely, because whereas what is stressed in modernism is the strategic rejection of modernity, what is stressed by post-modernism is the need for recognition). But I need to stress that I don't agree with Lynda Hutcheon that the two sets of terms relate as ground and response. Modernity and postmodernity are not grounds, they are ideas, responding, interpreting, mistaking, overlooking, as do any other patterns of ideas, as does consciousness in general. The 'isms' are thus practices related to those ideas, practices also governed by material and economic constraints which have nothing to do with the perceived condi-tion. Even if you say, as Harvey and Jameson do, that both modernity and postmodernity are phases of a social process, modernisation, this gets us no nearer the ground because modernisation too is reflective. Fordism, for example, which is a major component of the first phase of modernisation, is not a real relationship, it is a system, even a theory designed to respond to a felt need.

Because this is purely on the level of the superstructure, it is obvious that the moment of change will be very variable. Indeed, Harvey would argue that both modernist and postmodernist responses are visible in the original response to the modern. And I would certainly agree with that. In fact, somewhat naively, in 1978, I wrote an article which attributed some of the characteristics of the postmodern, particularly its despair of totalities, to the premodernist 'decadence' of the late nineteenth century, and argued that modernism was a betrayal of that advance. It was presumably a kind of postmodernist essay, that is, I was able to see the value of what through no fault of mine was called 'the decadent producer' because I felt critical of the modernist preoccupation with organic form, with totality.

Postmodernism would then be, in parallel with modernism, not merely the consciousness of this change, but a strategy in relation to it. And so it is, but it is complicated by the fact that it has as its pre-history the epic and many would say futile struggle to overcome modernity in modernism. Modernism is indeed frequently seen as a totalitarian grand narrative. In this respect, *Waiting for Godot* in 1956, and the collapse of Ronan Point, the high rise flats, in 1968, mark the beginning and end of a decisive attack on the modernist project, the blessed rage for order. For Beckett presents the superb richness of language in a timeless (almost) trap by which it marks nothing but its own delusions of philosophical grandeur. And Ronan Point seemed to mark literally the collapse of modernist structuring of the community (Le Corbusier's commitment to high rise was based on the urge to maximise communal and green space).

Language and architecture now become free from the formless referent they seek to structure, but free only to explore themselves. They no longer claim to be interventionist. Postmodernism's strategy seems to move between helplessness and celebration. It is this difference which is for me crucial, for you can throw up many variations of style which get earmarked as modernist or postmodernist, and they will contradict one another. This follows from my earlier point that by the time we are talking about postmodernism we are talking about an extremely mediated discourse, a strategic response to a condition which in turn is a response to a process which is a response. That is why, for example, Kuspitt who sees postmodern architecture as a project of humanisation after the commissar stance of modernism, and Davies who sees it as the product of the excessive accumulation of capital could both be right.

The important difference is in the strategic function of the artefact, not its distinctive features. The difference between the modernist and the postmodernist is most crucial, for me, as a difference in the relation of their situation as producers.

One of the strongest criticisms of postmodernist methodology is that in questioning the grand narratives by which knowledge has been imprisoned, it sacrifices historicity altogether, presenting the past as a more or less meaningless simulacrum (as Jameson puts it) of interchangeable images, rather as the video offers endless possibilities of the manipulation of time. This is clearly a reduction of time to a commodity and although it offers possibilities of retrieval and selectivity which looks like a gain to the historian, it also empties history of its potency. If we can always rewrite it in whatever way is convenient, or rather replay it whenever we need it and at whatever pace, it is going to be inoculated from our actual lives.

Meanwhile our own actual history can be concealed from us, or rather developed in a manipulated way. The inoculation of the past is signalled in the heritage industry which can enable us at will to experience what it smelt like to be a Viking or offer us actresses with dirty faces pretending to be pauper children at Quarry Bank Mill, while the manipulation of the present was clear in the extraordinary fabrication of the Gulf War in which a phoney epic was staged on the pretext of destroying a genocidal dictator (still very much in power, despite the apparent victory) whose real purpose was to re-instal a valuable family of investors to their fake feudal dignity. It is not surprising that the main allied casualties were from friendly fire or that long term victims are the Kurds and Shi-ites whose oppression the whole rhetoric exploited.

If history has had a bad time at the hands of postmodernism (of course, I mean a certain kind of history, the kind which tells stories or rather the story, which much contemporary history no longer does), geography has come into its own. Aside from Harvey, Soja's *Postmodern Geographies* is one of the strongest radical arguments for postmodernist methodology. Soja presents the postmodern as the revenge of space on the modernist privileging of time.

This new geography has clarified a long standing aporia in my own research between its privileged object and the available methodology. My first research interest was in the late Victorian novelist, George Gissing whose importance is that his novels seemed to register a new experience, wholly urban in its nature, that is to say not the experience of the city which has a long history, but the urban experience of city life, one whose differentials are entirely urban – slum is opposed to suburb, labour to leisure, rather than to a less alien form of labour. When he does take his characters outside the city, it is to urban extensions such as the seaside. Before him, even Dickens had grounded his values in a rural primal scene. Now the difficulty for me was that the most congenial available methodology came from Lukács who analyses the novel in terms of its capacity to register the coming of history into modern life with the French revolution. Gissing's novels lack any real historical sense, except incidentally. The urban landscape is a structure which seems endlessly present – change is spatial. This is true of many other writers of the period 1880–1930 too. The only way to explain this in Lukácsian terms would be to argue, as he does of modernism in general, that it is helplessly trapped in the alien world to which they were responding. This is his account of all forms of modernism from Zola to Joyce. But this made no real sense to me since a writer such as Gissing, and even more Zola and Joyce, would not be able to give us this clear register of experience if they were helplessly installed in it – you can only see what is outside you. Modernist writers resist the modern, as I have suggested, but not by endowing it with the history it conceals. On the contrary, as several critics have suggested, they spatialise time, which we can easily see if we recall that *Ulysses*, the modern epic, takes place within a single day, as does *Mrs Dalloway* and even Proust's massive reclamation of the past is conjured into being by a geographical specificity, *Du Côté de Chez Swann*.

The resistance, to be sure, is in the name of history, the totality of European culture from Homer to Paul de Kock in Joyce, and the unity of personal growth in Woolf, but history is posed against the disintegrating present as a metaphor, an ever present alternative space, like Eliot's idea of tradition, the 'existing monuments' as he puts it. Monuments are what civic rulers build to incorporate the past into the present structure. Both Joyce and Woolf at least know the ironies in this. *The Odyssey* is as much invoked for its absence as its presence – it is a shadow on the text, and time is registered in *Mrs Dalloway* by the spatial landmark of Big Ben.

Failing to take account of the dialectical relation of modernist aesthetic production to the ideological trends of the turn of the century, Soja sees modernism to be guilty of 'occlusive historicism', one of the major culprits being Lukács. 'Historicism', his grand narrative, occludes space as an agent of social differentiation and structuration. Concepts such as uneven development, centralisation and peripheralisation complicate and contest the simplifying grand narratives of historical destiny. You cannot understand Los Angeles by describing its development as well as you can by flying over it. Its meaning is semiotic – it has to be read.

One of the major theories he invokes in support of this thesis is Henri Lefebvre's theory of the urban revolution. As I think that it will help us both understand postmodernism and help us get beyond it, I must offer a very simplified version of this. There are four phases of urban development. First the city comes into being as a defensive and administrative centre, it is where you can withdraw to when under attack and it is also a place in which the laws and political decisions can be made. Then it becomes also a place of commerce. At this stage, the city is still at the service of a rural economy.

Of course, it does not take much for the productive hierarchy to be reversed and for the rural producers to appear subservient to the military, administrative and mercantile classes, but these latter are still justified

because they support the country in its productive capacity. With industrialisation this changes. Production now goes on within the city as well as
within the country. By the time industrial production comes to dominate
the economy, the rural production is to service the town. The first division
of labour, between town and country, is replicated in both spaces. The
graphic image of this is Zola's novel, *La Ventre de Paris*, with its centrifugal
image of Les Halles.

But then, according to Lefebvre, there is a third stage in which industrialisation is transformed into urbanisation. The city no longer functions
merely as a support nor as an increasingly dominant annex to production
– it becomes the social condition itself. The distinction between city and
country disappears – the 'rural' world is urbanised, farming becomes
another branch of industry, subject to rationalisation and planning, space
itself is no longer deployed according to its effectiveness, it is actually
created. You can get some sense of this if you think of the park. The city
park is a deliberately enclosed 'memory' of rural life, part of the incorporated rhythm of zoning and mobility by which the citizen is constructed
as worker and consumer. But then this extends to the countryside, the
national park is a deliberately engineered space of small scale rural
production to preserve for tourists an illusion that there is a more natural
life to be had beyond their immediate horizon. A construction engineer
I know spent four years in the late seventies returning the site of the steel
works at Consett to a state of nature, wiping out for ever its industrial
history. If Lady Chatterley wanted to revitalise her love life today she
would be less likely to find a gamekeeper than an environment manager.

As Harvey said in 1973, this thesis has yet to be proved. It might be
difficult to experience the urban revolution in Bolivia, and the strip
farming and horsedrawn ploughs which seemed so quaint to me on my
journey from Wrocklaw to Warsaw in the mid eighties were for real. But
the spread of this revolution over large enough regions for it to have at
least the illusion of a global phenomenon, not to speak of the fact that
satellite television communication has the potential for the urban penetration of the most remote regions, makes it a valuable explanation of a
certain 'structure of feeling'.

Now urbanisation is in complex relation with history, since the flow of
populations to the city is in flight from their manifest historical destiny
(Upton Sinclair's novel, *The Jungle*, gives a very good sense of this with its
successive migratory waves which disappear into the exploitative system
of Chicago). The city itself has a history but this is at loggerheads with the
people hidden in its streets who flow around one another without needing
to know where they come from. The city covers the ground of its past
which it can simply demolish, as my own city of Birmingham has done
once and is now in process of doing again. The text which most sharply
reflects this is Walter Abish's novel *How German Is It?* which has a new

city built on the site of a concentration camp with all the ironies that that implies.

Furthermore the city can reconstruct the past not only with its museums and imitation pre-industrial enclaves like Tontines in Hanley, but also through its manifest restorations. Frankfurt has a street of postmodernist houses, but the most postmodernist thing about Frankfurt is its old quarter, rebuilt, scrubbed clean and made into an attractive centre of food consumption. Cologne too has a whole system of reconstructed Romanesque churches which at least arose out of the ruins. Warsaw built its old quarter from scratch. I don't especially lament these things. It is good that communities can control their own environment. The question about them is, to adapt Abish's title, how realist is it? Lukács, following Hegel, argued that the importance of the French Revolution is that it involved the masses as agents of their own history. The post war boom has incorporated into the cities of the people simulacra of their own past and this might make history hard to find precisely because it is so easy to see. And what is true of the past is surely even more true of the present in which history is being made. We have such sophisticated communications that everything that happens can be instantly available and yet, as we know that only gives us the sense that the history of the present is being managed for us. But the Gulf War could have been played out in our living rooms, which was why the news management had to be so carefully organised. Of course, there are plenty of ways we can uncover history if we have a mind to. The importance of the postmodern situation is not that history is concealed or distorted. That has happened in every culture of which we are aware.

What is new is that the primary experience is that, wherever we turn, we know we are lost. This is a feature of the built environment as Jameson points out about the Bonaventura building in Los Angeles (and indeed the Potteries centre itself – do you ever know where you really are in there? It is full of signs but they all indicate where you have arrived at rather than where you have come from or wish to go. And of course, you are certainly not meant to know where you are in relation to the outside). But this knowing that we don't know is not confined to the built environment. It extends also to the social discourses which wilfully abdicate their truth claims in the interests of pragmatism.

As I say, I am far from merely critical of this, and in this sense, I think, differ from both Eagleton and Norris (though I endorse many of the very acute things they say about postmodernism). Most truth claims are more or less disguised bids for power. The question is whether knowing that we don't know is a liberation from ideological slavery or another form of it. This is not a rhetorical question. My answer will be that it depends. But the argument that postmodernism is a response enables me to pull the test out of its background even if I agree that the dominant feature of this background is its textuality. It enables me to restore what I think is the primary condition of literary analysis, what Stephen Daedalus would call the *integritas* of the text, the line drawn around it which makes it different from its environment. This is a modernist concept, of course, but it moves beyond modernism, unlike the second and third qualities, *consonantia* and *claritas* which belong more strongly to the blessed rage for order. *Integritas* relates to the work of art as a project, a specific productive act, and it relates backwards to Pater's critique of Coleridge's naturalisation of aesthetic production and forward to Benjamin. It enables me to read these texts with more understanding as interventions and it also demands that I make discriminations.

One of the most ambitious fictional responses to the postmodern environment in this country in recent years is Martin Amis's *London Fields*, a title which clearly refers the contemporary metropolis to the past it has deleted as in Coldbath Fields, and, given the world news alluded to in the text, the repressed third world Other, the killing fields of Cambodia. Picking up the self-referentiality and self-questioning nature of postmodernist discourse, this 'true' story is told by an American novelist living in the vacated flat of a successful novelist. It is a 'true' murder story, but although the novelist, Sam, finds a 'murderee' and at least two suspects, he finally has to commit the murder himself, thus leaving us to wonder whether this true story told by a fictional author is anything but a simulacrum with no external reference. Thus anything you say about the values rehearsed in the book cannot be taken and used in evidence. Amis, the actual author, is covered. Nevertheless, you have the sense of an extremely moral tale, and when, near the end the absent M.A. (after pages of unrepresented pornography) states that nobody wants truth any more, you feel that is what you have read the book to agree with. And in fact, the rather thin plot becomes a peg for someone, narrator or author – does it matter? – to hang all his hangups on from cosmic decay to double-parking. Moreover the characters are nothing if not representative (clearly intended by their names) and except for the nice inept romantic rich Guy (his name and nature) are the receptacles of someone's hatred – in order of obnoxiousness – the working class, single women, wives, blacks and babies (or at least hyperactive ones).

It wears the trappings of postmodernist cleverness like I wear a suit. It really is the victim of the postmodern condition, and has had to give up on history (thus linking the present to the past and the presence to the Other only by metaphor, fields). 'Perhaps', says the narrator, 'because of their addiction to form, writers always lag behind the contemporary formlessness, they write about an old reality in a language that's even older ... In this sense all novels are historical novels'. The past is merely form, the present formless. History is merely aestheticised, and indeed time brings not change but only dissolution and decay: 'Everything is winding down ... Who stitched us up with all these design flaws? Entropy, time's arrow

– ravenous disorder.... Time takes from you ... things just disappear into it'. A modish echo of contemporary physics is the only perspective in which the succession of phantasmagoric images occur; a worker who is out of work, a harlot who never has sex, a mother who always absconds leaving the man holding the baby, an overcrowded, overheated city which has successfully convinced its portrayer that its formlessness is real, and without explanatory precedent, and with only a future of erasure.

It is worth contrasting this novel with George Perec's even more thoroughly metropolitan and postmodern novel, *La Vie, Mode d'Emploi*, translated into English as *Life, A User's Manual*. This presents us with a Parisian apartment block at a single moment in time. It is through the meticulous exploration of its individual spaces that the stories associated with its inmates are recovered, (a familiar device, seen in films such as *Sous Les Toits de Paris*, and Simenon novels, so this too is less a response to reality that a reworking of other discourses).

The recovery is questioned and mocked by every formal device of the text. The most wealthy inhabitant, Bartlebooth, having decided to plan his life on a rational basis, spends ten years learning how to paint water colours from another tenant, ten years travelling around the world painting scenes which he sends back to another fellow tenant to make into jigsaw puzzles and returns to spend twenty years doing the puzzles, after which the pictures are erased. The enterprise mocks the realist reliance on experience, its representation and its reconstruction in memory. Then the stories having been told, the elements of the narrative are spatially recomposed as diagram (of the *immeuble*), chronological table, general index, and alphabetical checklist of tales within the narrative. The individual stories are interwoven with one another so that in both senses of the word, they are yarns. Personal histories are broken up – the collective history is repatterned in space. The only change, the history of the building itself, is moving towards erasure as the city develops. There is no feeling of moral outrage at this fragmentation – on the contrary the whole form of the book is a huge joke. But neither is history erased.

This is partly confirmed by the end. Bartlebooth dies holding the last piece which would not have fitted anyway since the last hole was shaped like an X and the piece is shaped like a W. These two letters dominate an earlier and very strange text, *W, ou le Souvenir d'Enfance*. This intercalates the lost history of the author's childhood which is bound up with the Nazi extermination of the Jews, and the childhood fantasies with which he consoles himself and which in grotesque form reflect the racism of which he is unknowingly the victim. It is a text almost illustrating Santayana's dictum that a people that forgets its history is condemned to relive it. For the interwoven yarns, spatialised though they are nevertheless incorporate the individual histories which form the collective history embodied in but unrecorded by the *immeuble*.

In other words, if we are conscious that the grand narrative of the collective past has been recomposed in space, we are conscious that it has been recomposed, and I am sure that I am not the only reader who reads this text in the same way that I read the interlocking stories of Dickens and Balzac, to give me the sense of an epoch and an environment. And this is not to read against the grain of the text: the very spatialisation effect calls attention to the item it is deleting. I get the same sense when the heroine of Caryl Churchill's great play, *Top Girls*, invites the women of the past to dinner. It has the air of ultimate metropolitanisation, especially as she has won the right to participate in this simulated feminist history by erasing her own roots in the rural world, even abandoning her daughter to her less ambitious sister. But it is the sense that history has been acclimatised that is important. What the spatialisation enforced by the presence of these simulacra enforces is that they are not the history they literally embody.

Other texts register this spatialisation with the same sense of loss. In Graham Swift's *Waterland*, which has a present dominated by a retiring history teacher who feels that his discipline is being made redundant and whose wife has committed that most urban of sins, baby-snatching, registers the presence of the historical not merely or even ultimately by tracing the social history of the individuals trapped in the modern world, but by the presence of a landscape and its provisions and deprivations. The spatialisation means loss of agency because it naturalises change, but the sense of this loss is always present.

The text which develops this shadow of absence most fully is, I think Pynchon's *Vineland*. This is a novel in which the world is urbanised, a kind of paranoid global thriller dominated by electronic communications and history, as a result, reduced to image. Thus four generations of a radical family move from lumber camp organisers to Hollywood unions, to student protest and finally to the feckless incorporation of the eighties. The novel opens in the present with an ageing hippie preparing to make his annual act of protest, and so ensure the continuation of his social welfare payments, by performing a transfenestration in drag. This parodic gesture of radical containment is matched more depressingly by the transformation of his ex-wife from investigative journalist, fighting the revolution two generations of her family have already fought, to agent of surveillance. This assimilation is represented in other ways by addictive television watching, a community of compulsive nostalgics called Thanatoids, and the relegation of radical politics to a secret organisation based on ninja). What is worse is that this works retroactively. The heroic radical politics of labour in the great-grandparent generation is reduced to an annual picnic of the original clans, whose ideology is stated in a reading from Emerson which the leader had found quoted in William James' *Varieties of Religious Experience*, a copy of which he found in jail, a surely symbolic

Foucauldian representation of the idea of freedom, imprisoned in a pseudo-scientific text, imprisoned in a physical jail. On the face of it, it seems a thoroughly depressing book.

The difference is that the pessimism is not sardonic because it constantly invokes the absent history it sees trapped in the electronic system of control. There is a powerful metaphoric representation of this in one of the ironic highlights of the old left's convention, a put down but with a final twist:

> And other grandfolks could be heard arguing the perennial question of whether the United States still lingered in a prefascist twilight, or whether that darkness had fallen long stupefied years ago, and the light they thought they saw was coming only from millions of Tubes [i.e. TVs] all showing the same bright colored shadows. One by one, as other voices joined in, the names began – some shouted, some accompanied by spit, the old reliable names good for hours of contention, stomach distress, and insomnia – Hitler, Roosevelt, Kennedy, Nixon, Hoover, Mafia, CIA, Reagan, Kissinger, that collection of names and their tragic interweaving that stood not constellated above in any nightwide remoteness of light, but below, diminished to the last unfaceable American secret, to be pressed, each time deeper, again and again beneath the meanest of random soles, one blackly fermenting leaf on the forest floor that nobody wanted to turn over, because of all that lived, virulent, waiting, just beneath.

This is doubly pessimistic, first because the elegiac note is surely being sent up. The political culture here is self-indulgent (the old reliable names good for hours of contention). More importantly, the only way that the energy is described is metaphoric. Nevertheless I find that though any sentimentalisation is undercut, the rejection of the constellation pays some kind of tribute to what endures in this novel in spite of the electronic imprisonment which pervades it. The fermenting leaf is surely a reminder that death is more important than eternity in generating history. For however deep you bury the corpse of human aspiration it does not cease to ferment.

Just as in modernism, time is privileged only as the metaphor of spatial relations, so in the postmodernist fictions, the dominance of space is only acknowledged through a deconstruction of time. And this leads me to question the spatialisation of discourse which Soja sees as the necessary transformation of postmodernist analysis. As he argues, when he speaks of space he means social space, not space in the abstract. In Lefebvre's terms it is created space, as opposed to effective space, that leads someone trained in the analysis of literature to see it rather as the negation of space.

Literary language is not merely or primarily about the meaning it functions to convey, it is about the exclusion of all the other ways of conveying the same message: why this diction, this metaphor, rather than any other? Social space by the same token is the specific using up of space, which is always at the expense of somebody else. Created space is not really created; it is space used up. Soja would have no difficulty in assenting to this. His flight around Los Angeles with its observation of the boundary punctuated with defence establishments is just such a picture of space commandeered by the military.

But in the same way, history is not time, but the negation of time, time used up, the time of the managed, used up, as Hardy might put it, by the managers. Some modern historians, Caroline Steedman and David Vincent eminently among them, precisely try to restore that lost time to the unrecorded lives from which history, as the narrative of power, has been stolen. So when I said 'it depends' I was talking about two kinds of space and two kinds of history. And just as history needs its unrecorded spear carriers, so the built urban environment needs its open squares and back alleys. Which brings me to my frog.

I've said before that many of the features of the postmodern are clearly evident in pre-modern texts – self-referentiality, awareness of discourse and its limits. The frog is not mine but belongs to one of the great poets of the late nineteenth century and one who significantly haunts at least two postmodernist novels, *The French Lieutenant's Woman*, and A. S. Byatt's *Possession*. My title is from a poem by Christina Rossetti called *A Frog's Fate*.

> CONTEMPTUOUS of his home beyond
> The village and the village-pond,
> A large-souled Frog who spurned each byeway
> Hopped along the imperial highway.
>
> Nor grunting pig nor barking dog
> Could disconcert so great a Frog.
> The morning dew was lingering yet,
> His sides to cool, his tongue to wet:
> The night-dew, when the night should come,
> A travelled Frog would send him home.
>
> Not so, alas! The wayside grass
> Sees him no more: not so, alas!
> A broad-wheeled waggon unawares
> Ran him down, his joys, his cares.
> From dying choke one feeble croak
> The Frog's perpetual silence broke:—
> 'Ye buoyant Frogs, ye great and small,

Even I am mortal after all!
My road to fame turns out a wry way;
I perish on the hideous highway;
Oh for my old familiar byeway!'

The choking Frog sobbed and was gone;
The Waggoner strode whistling on.
Unconscious of the carnage done,
Whistling that Waggoner strode on—
Whistling (it may have happened so)
'A froggy would a-wooing go.'
A hypothetic frog trolled he,
Obtuse to a reality.

O rich and poor, O great and small,
Such oversights beset us all.
The mangled Frog abides incog,
The uninteresting actual frog:
The hypothetic frog alone
Is the one frog we dwell upon.

                (1885)

Now the frog hopping onto the imperial highway may only be making for the village, but pro-rata he is urbanising himself, searching to become a travelled frog. Failing to return, he is given the unlikely chance to moralise his fate, but his one feeble croak certainly does not persist in the perpetual silence which follows. Both his aspiration and his education are lost in the actual disposition of power. In its way, it is as depressing and funny as *Vineland*. But it is the form of the poem to which I want to draw attention. It is certainly locked in its own discourse. Nothing assures us that this Frog, the subject of Rossetti's narrative, is any less hypothetic than the Waggoner's, as the last two lines, 'the one frog we dwell upon' tells us. Nor is the uninteresting actual frog any nearer, presented to us as it is in an oxymoron by which the first adjective, 'uninteresting' is belied by the second, 'actual' (since we cannot really profess uninterest in the actual). So in no way does the poem pretend to deliver us the real frog. What it does is draw our attention to the importunate presence, which the history has deleted, of 'a reality', 'the actual'. The uninteresting actual frog is as hypothetical as the large-souled Frog and the frog of the Waggoner's song. And yet we end up with a very clear commitment to the actual frog.

We all know that truth, like beauty, is not merely in the eye of the beholder but in the grip of those to whom we are beholden. But the actual eludes that grasp, filling the spaces of the city and the gaps in the history with the echoes of its erasure. At its most complacent, the discourse of the postmodern tells us that history is over, and it is true that frogs can be reconstructed in the image of our culture. But we know that it is hypothetical. A reality, *the* actual remains.

Ernst Bloch argued that the urge towards the future, the motive of utopia started in hunger. Hunger is not only human, of course, but there is a specifically human way of dealing with hunger which has to do with planning and imagining and abstraction. Which is why hungering and thirsting after righteousness is a metaphor which can travel back to its literal origins. That double hunger is what keeps history going in spite of attempts on every level to write history up according to the wishes of the less hungry, a writing up which finally means erasure, preservation in monuments. But the hunger keeps on coming, migration, shanty towns, the so called 'underclass' (a repetition of the *fin de siècle* too. Charles Booth in his *Life and Labour of the People of London* liked to speak of the submerged tenth, the underclass is the same kind of disguise).

Of course, the actual does not always seem as likeable as it is in the form of the frog. I think the case of Salman Rushdie's *The Satanic Verses* is a reminder that the actual remains outside our attempts to incorporate it in discourse. For it does not take much imagination to understand how a hard working and harassed corner shop-keeper might feel if he were to learn that £400,000 advance royalties had been paid for a novel attacking his religion. It was odd last week to listen to writers in defence of Rushdie's cause speaking as though the issue were simply one of the relationship between the West and Iran. The *fatwa* was only an opportunist use of a more local upsurge. It is not, as Stoppard would imply, merely a conflict of mind-sets. Of course, I totally agree with Rushdie's friends that Britain should not have any relations with Iran before the *fatwa* is rescinded. Rushdie is victimised. But it is too complacently within the enlightenment project to suppose he is the victim of religious fanaticism. He is the victim of the economic and racial oppression that has given that fanaticism its lease of life.

However problematised the truth becomes, as the grand narratives reveal themselves to be the constructs of power, however bewildering the mirrors which reflect back on us and relocate our visions so that it can never find its place or rather who put the place there, the actual exists shadowed forth only it may be by its absence. I would like to illustrate this by considering briefly Don De Lillo's novel, *Libra*, a novel, like Stone's movie *JFK*, going over the traumatic assassination of Kennedy. Aside from the theme, however, it could not be more different. The movie exploits certain postmodernist paraphernalia, particularly the use of bogus old film (black and white, out of focus, but clearly featuring the modern actors). But it is firmly within a realist tradition. It offers the truth, a solution to the mystery of the assassination which makes it absolutely coherent. The truth is not however, 'who shot JFK?' This is pure fiction in its totality. The inclusion of some facts can only be designed to confuse and alert us, as Balzac's assertion of the truth of *Père Goriot*. The truth of this movie is rather announced in the Eisenhower speech at its opening which is about the dangerous prevalence of the industrial military complex in the U.S.A. The uncovering of the plot to assassinate Kennedy (part of which is to show how, beyond a certain point in the hierarchy, connection could not be established because no active involvement was taken) is to show the true nature of American society in the post-Kennedy era. It would no more matter if the speculation were wholly false, than it mattered to *Little Dorrit* that Humphrey House discovered that much of its social criticism was a generation behind the times. That is, it matters because it shows something about the making of the book, but it does not matter to the project or indeed the effect of the book. In other words, the 'reality' of the film is its parallel with the actual, not its contiguity with it. You will find the movie convincing if you find its politics convincing, not if you think Jim Garrison, the investigator (who is, I think, placed as a southern gentleman) is right.

De Lillo's novel is much more sophisticated and lays no claim that historical reconstruction is a way to truth. To begin with, the story of the assassination itself is nested within the project of the historian Nicholas Branch, who is employed by the CIA, and who therefore has more than enough evidence. The very extent and complexity of the evidence is overwhelming. Sitting in his room is sitting in the 'room of theories'. But our first glimpse of him is juxtaposed with the first glimpse of Win Everett, another retired CIA man who designs the whole conspiracy like a novel, inventing characters, laying false clues: 'we are characters in plots ... Our lives examined carefully in all their affinities and links, abound with suggestive meaning, with themes and involute turnings we have not allowed ourselves to see completely. He would show the secret symmetries in a nondescript life'. So Branch for fifteen years has been trying to decipher the fiction Everett plans for the future in 1963. This is a novel in which history is caught up in the process of urbanisation, where it is either invisible or manipulable. Time and space are problematised by the very structure of the book which is divided into chapters that alternate place names and dates. Thus the first five sections read, 'In the Bronx', '17 April', 'In New Orleans', '26 April', 'In Atsugi' and so on. The dates are all days in 1963 so concern themselves with the immediate. The past has to be recapitulated by its location, so the 'In the Bronx' is about Lee Harvey Oswald's childhood, 'In Atsugi' about his time in the marines. The assassination itself is as much a function of territory as it is of historical conjecture. It is Oswald's trajectory from the Bronx to Dallas via Japan and Moscow, and his social migrations that determine his presence as an employee in the book warehouse, and it is the President's strange route that brings him to Dallas at all. Branch concludes that the conspiracy was 'a rambling affair that succeeded in the short term due mainly to chance'.

The idea of history itself is enunciated in the text mainly as a fascist concept. One of the conspirators, Guy Banister, says to another, 'I believe deeply that there are forces in the air that compel men to act. Call it history or necessity or anything you like'. Later, another conspirator, Donald Ferrie, tries to persuade Oswald that his act is inevitable, 'Think of two parallel lines'. Both of these remind me of the vision of history in Yeats' 'Leda and the Swan'. 'Did she put on his knowledge with his power ...?' And yet there is another more radical way that history becomes actual, and that is through the portrayal of Oswald himself. Nested within Branch's retrospective reconstruction of Everett's proleptic conspiracy is the 'actual' story of Oswald, realised with all the traditional resources of realist fiction, focalisation, free direct discourse, conjuncture of several points of view. And the life is detailed from the cradle to the grave. Oswald seeks to enter history to escape the small rooms within which he is trapped by poverty and his mother's isolation. So it is a double aspiration, to make himself different, or to make a difference, on the one hand and to merge on the other. 'Happiness,' he is quoted as writing to his brother in the epigraph, 'is taking part in the struggle, where there is no borderline between one's own personal world and the world in general'. 'History,' he thinks later 'means to merge' and yet 'we live forever in history'. Finding no role in time, Oswald finds it spatially. Thus for example in Japan, where he has learnt some Marxism from a Japanese socialist, he recalls that Trotsky had spent some time in the Bronx not far from where he had lived as a child. Later, Donald Ferrie starts to call him Leon. Because there is no career open to him, Oswald is free to move anywhere – even back and forth from the Soviet Union – and free too to choose his own identity, adopting several different names. But at the same time he is available and reproducible. The conspirators invent several duplicate Oswalds. He is, in the end, one of the crowd: 'Hundreds of thousands come from so many histories and systems of being' here in Dallas momentarily united to be an event. Equally, of course, he is *one* in the crowd, separated by his own role, chosen to make the event what it became. We know this is merely contingent. De Lillo doesn't suggest, for example, as Stone does, that Oswald's job in the Dallas warehouse is part of the conspiracy. He just turns up and, if he hadn't, he could have been invented. Except that the dense realisation of the larger casualty of poverty and alienation (literal since his mother doesn't speak very good English) makes this contingency merely a matter of appearances, or rather a product of the erasure of so many histories. At one point, the narrator says the Agency is god – he means the CIA is constantly seeking to produce the intelligence it is supposed to find. But in a larger sense this is a novel about agency, about the way men make their own history in spite of all attempts to ensure that history is locked up in monuments. Oswald is a frog. Seeking a place on the highway, he is too uninteresting to be remarked, but, like the frog, he is actual, acting, out of hunger and dream. It is, of course, a fiction. It is not the real Oswald, nor does the book resolve the mystery of the assassination. But it throws up the shadow of its absences.

One of the striking moments in Lyotard's text is when he talks about justice. 'Consensus', he says, 'has become an outmoded and suspect value. But justice as a value is neither outmoded or suspect.' It wouldn't be difficult to argue that this was another grand narrative: it is the central idea after all of that early argument for repression, Plato's *Republic*, and the sardonic ending of Hardy's *Tess of the D'Urbervilles*, 'Justice was done and the President of the Immortals (in Aeschylean phrase) had ended his sport with Tess' seems to give strength to that. Like truth and beauty, it is easily highjacked by the ruling powers. But I think that it is justice that these shadows of the actual seek.

Underclass, assassin, terrorist, even yuppie are labels which easily cover both the particularity of those who move across our cities, our global city, and the general universal determination that all embody to seek for themselves the access to resources they are denied. As long as there is injustice, there will be history. The thing about literary texts is that, although they articulate signs which have a problematic relationship to what they represent, they know it, or at least there is no excuse for the reader not knowing it. They constitute a hyperreality in relation to whatever they stand out from, and this means that however hyperreal the real may seem to be, they always signal that there is something else. Lyotard also praises the postmodern because it bears witness to the unpresentable, and that is what I have been finding to admire in the texts I have looked at. But he goes on to say, let us activate the differences, and I would want to turn that into *the difference*. Fictive texts as a whole call attention to what it means to be fully human, and to how far we all are from that, but how much further some are than others. The hypothetic that literature is exists only to call attention to the uninteresting it isn't – and to remind us that it is actual.

Index

Abensour, W., 333
Abish, Walter, 471–2
Adam, Villiers de Lisle, 350
Alexander, Sally, 224
Allen, Grant, 166, 178, 201–5, 254
Althusser, Louis, 185, 229, 347, 351
Amis, Kingsley, 88
Amis, Martin, 473–4
Anderson, Perry, 224, 334, 368
Anstey, F., 251
Aquinas, Thomas, 351
Armstrong, Nancy, 227
Arnold, Matthew, 7, 8–10, 14–15, 20 ff., 27, 33, 39, 44, 155, 158, 160, 231, 260, 343, 358, 408, 410, 435
Arnold, Thomas, 7, 11–16, 20
Asquith, Cynthia, 421
Auden, W.H., 196, 197–203
Auerbach, Eric, 111, 112–13
Auerbach, Nina, 223
Austen, Jane, 228, 327, 423, 424, 456
Austen, Zelda, 232
Aveling, Edward, 381

Bagehot, Walter, 3–4, 6, 9
Balzac, Honoré de, 102, 111, 131, 228, 233 f., 369, 375, 378, 381, 445, 480
Barret, Walter, 116
Barthes, Roland, 232

Baudelaire, Charles, 337, 350, 352
Bax, Belfort, 162, 282, 322
Bayley, John, 81, 83, 94
Beaumarchais, P.A.C., 219–20
Beckett, Samuel, 468
Beer, Gillian, 232
Beesley, Edward, 162
Bellamy, Edward, 268, 312–13, 315–16, 324, 326, 329, 331, 333, 355, 362–70
Belsey, K., 227, 233
Benjamin, Walter, 337, 351, 473
Bennett, Arnold, 241, 350
Berger, John, 243
Bergonzi, Bernard, 464
Bergson, H., 243
Berman, M., 466
Besant, Annie, 162, 241, 378
Besant, Walter, 163, 254, 342, 344–5, 380, 386
Bewley, Marius, 93–4, 123
Blake, William, 323
Bloch, Ernst, 331, 370, 479
Bodichon, Barbara, 64, 68, 74
Boos, F.S., 321
Booth, Charles, 254, 375, 376, 479
Boumelha, Penny, 155, 227, 229, 230, 232, 239
Bradley, A.C., 81
Bradley, F.H., 89, 94, 351, 404
Brantlinger, P., 327
Bray, Charles, 64
Brecht, B., 327, 351

Brett, Dorothy, 438
Briggs, Asa, 158
Bright, John, 2, 283
Brontë, Charlotte, 3, 65, 67, 68,
    227 ff., 231, 252
Brontë, Emily, 231, 241, 242
Brougham, Henry, 5
Browning, Robert, 20–1, 155, 358
Buick, Adam, 322
Buonaparte, Felicia, 72
Burgess, Joseph, 255
Burke, Edmund, 4, 293
Burns, John, 254–5, 263, 375,
    378, 381
Butler, A. J., 347
Byatt, A. S., 477
Byron, George Gordon, 345, 352

Caird, Mona, 200
Carlyle, Thomas, 2, 13, 22, 36, 47,
    58, 231, 264, 272, 325, 350
Carpenter, Edward, 162, 357,
    360–2, 364, 370, 375
Caudwell, Christopher, 154, 155,
    164, 371
Cavour, C. B., 73, 78
Cervantes, M., 233, 465–6
Chamberlain, Joseph, 378
Chambers, Jessie, 425–6
Champion, H. H., 375, 381
Chorley, H. F., 27
Clough, A. H., 6–26
    Amours de Voyage, 6, 22, 27–44
    Blank Misgivings of a Creature
        Moving about in Worlds Not
        Realized, 11, 29
    Bothie of Tober Na Vuolich, The,
        8, 11, 16–21, 23
    Dipsychus, 6, 22–3
    Jacob's Wives, 21–2
    Natura Naturans, 11
Cobban, Alfred, 1
Cole, G. D. H., 300
Coleman, Stephen, 321–2

Coleridge, S. T., 49, 339–41, 345,
    473
Collins, Wilkie, 251, 342, 343
Comte, Auguste, 60, 264
Conrad, Joseph, 355
Crackanthorpe, Hubert, 338–9,
    346
Creeger, C., 52
Cunningham, A. R., 178

Da Ponte, Abbé Lorenzo, 219–21
Dangerfield, G., 445
Darwin, Charles, 230, 233, 425
David, Deirdre, 231
Davidoff, Leonore, 226, 236, 237,
    238
Davidson, John, 349
Davies, Mike, 468
De Lillo, Don, 479–82
Demetz, Peter, 274–5
Dentith, Simon, 332, 333, 368–9
Descartes, R., 417
Dickens, Charles, 2, 148, 195,
    327, 345, 432, 442, 453, 465,
    469, 480
Dinesen, I., 243
Disraeli, Benjamin, 12, 264
Dostoevsky, F., 424
Droz, Jacques, 1
Duhring, C. K., 249
Du Maurier, George, 346–7

Eagleton, Terry, 73, 154–5, 161,
    176, 227, 337, 463, 472
Ebbatson, Roger, 357
Edwards, Philip, 465
Egerton, George, 178, 181–2,
    239, 242
Einstein, Albert, 422
Eliot, George, 28, 101–2, 105,
    327, 329–30, 396, 404, 422–4
    Adam Bede, 45–63, 235
    Daniel Deronda, 60, 65–8,
        77–80, 160, 230, 234, 238

Felix Holt, 72, 235
Impressions of Theophrastus Such, The, 78, 79
Middlemarch, 60, 231–8
Mill on the Floss, The, 67–71, 74, 77, 235
Romola, 68, 72–7, 79–80, 235
Eliot, T.S., 27–8, 43, 102, 105, 350, 351, 423, 457, 467, 470
Ellis, Havelock, 155, 162, 165, 172, 339
Emerson, R.W., 30, 32, 115, 119, 120, 132, 136, 180–1, 478
Empson, William, 196
Engels, F., 153, 195, 225, 268 f., 274–5, 292, 296, 305, 307, 312, 323, 328, 356 f., 360, 362, 369, 381 f., 384–5, 386

Farrell, J.G., 464
Feuerbach, C.A., 56, 60–1, 64
Fielding, Henry, 49, 233, 243, 424, 432
Flaubert, Gustave, 102, 241, 344–5, 352, 423, 424, 426
Ford, Ford Madox, 426
Forster, E.M. 102, 418, 438
Foucault, M., 340
Fourier, F.M.C., 356, 369
Fowles, John, 166, 477
Franklin, Benjamin, 59
Fraser, James, 448
Freeman, E.A., 305
Freud, Sigmund, 184, 224, 229, 230

Galbraith, J.K., 315
Galsworthy, John, 241, 452
Garibaldi, G., 74
Garnett, E., 438
Gaskell, Elizabeth, 53–4, 57, 60, 73, 252, 260, 261
Geismar, Maxwell, 93
George, Henry, 259, 362

Gibbon, Edward, 134–5, 325
Gilbert, S., 223, 243
Gilman, Charlotte Perkins, 356
Gissing, George, 202, 282, 313, 358, 376, 396, 469–70
Born in Exile, 279
Demos, 162, 247–71, 275–6
Denziel Quarrier, 279
Mrs. Grundy's Enemies, 248
Nether World, The, 249, 267, 269, 283, 383, 388
New Grub Street, 248, 276–9, 379
Odd Women, The, 208–11
Private Papers of Henry Ryecroft, The, 279
Unclassed, The, 163
Workers in the Dawn, 249
Godwin, W., 321
Goethe, W., 35–6, 39–40
Gogol, N.V., 233
Goldberg, S.L., 442
Gombrich, E.H., 47
Grand, Sarah, 178
Gramsci, A., 161, 304, 337, 351
Gray, John, 341, 349
Green, J.R., 293–5
Greenslade, Walter, 163, 360
Gregor, Ian, 45, 57–8
Gubar, S., 243
Gueunier, Nicole, 353

Haeckel, E.H., 351
Haggard, Rider, 198–200
Hall, Catherine, 226, 236, 237, 238
Hall, Peter, 221
Hampton, Christopher, 321
Hardie, Keir, 381
Hardy, Barbara, 62, 82
Hardy, Thomas, 5, 52, 152–70, 202, 280–1, 282, 313, 318, 328, 345, 396, 423, 426, 428, 467, 482

Desperate Remedies, 157–8, 159
Dynasts, The, 153–4, 167–9
Far from the Madding Crowd,
    155, 159–60, 171, 174, 195,
    280
Hand of Ethelberta, The, 157,
    159–60
Human Shows, Far Phantasies,
    153
'Indiscretion in the Life of an
    Heiress, An', 156
Jude the Obscure, 155, 160, 165,
    167, 171–9, 205, 280–1, 283,
    346–9
Life, The, 155–6, 158
Life's Little Ironies, 166
Mayor of Casterbridge, The, 155,
    161, 162–3
Pair of Blue Eyes, A, 156–7
Poor Man and the Lady, The, 155,
    158
Return of the Native, 160, 161
Tess of the d'Urbervilles, 155, 161,
    164–6, 167, 208, 211–14
Two on a Tower, 161
Well-Beloved, The, 155, 166–7
Woodlanders, The, 162–4
Harkness, Margaret (John Law),
    162, 241–2, 268, 274–5, 375
    Captain Lobe, 380, 390–2
    'Children of the Unemployed',
    380
    City Girl, A, 378, 380, 382–5
    George Eastmount, Wanderer,
    378, 380
    'Municipality of London, The',
    379
    Out of Work, 380, 386–90
    'Railway Labour', 379
    'Women as Civil Servants', 379
    'Year of My Life, A', 38
Harrison, F., 254, 264
Harrison, Royden, 1, 161–2, 249
Harvey, David, 466, 467–71

Harvey, W.J., 81–2, 84, 85, 101,
    232
Hassan, I., 466
Hawthorne, Nathaniel, 123
H.D., 438
Hegel, G.W.F., 13
Heilman, Robert, 95
Heine, H., 24
Hello, Ernst, 348
Henley, W.H., 338, 349
Hennell, Sara, 72
Herzen, A., 337
Holland, L.,133
Hollingshead, J., 343
Holtby, Winifred, 243, 244
Holyoake, George Jacob, 396
Homer, 470
Hopkins, G.M., 27
Horace, 31, 34, 35, 41
Houghton, Walter, 27, 31, 38, 39
Howard, Ebenezer, 362
Howells, W.D., 117–19, 121–3
Hudson, W.H., 322, 331, 362, 363
    Crystal Age, A, 355, 358–60
Hughes, Linda, 413, 414, 415
Hutcheon, L., 467, 470
Hutton, R.H., 10
Hume, David, 39
Huxley, T.H. , 443
Huysmans, J.K., 341
Hyndman, H.M., 162, 254, 255,
    259, 261, 263, 294

Ibsen, H., 178, 182, 241, 446

Jacobus, Mary, 223
Jakobson, Roman, 214
James, Henry, 44, 153, 163, 280,
    358, 376
    Ambassadors, The, 85–92,
    99–100, 107
    American, The, 84
    'Author of "Beltraffio", The', 84
    Bostonians, The, 84

Golden Bowl, The, 83, 92–9, 107
Notes of a Son and Brother, 120
Portrait of a Lady, The, 81–103
    passim, 106, 192–4
Princess Casamassima, The, 93,
    162, 254, 260
Roderick Hudson, 83, 84
Spoils of Poynton, The, 94–5
Turn of the Screw, The, 92–9
Washington Square, 83
Wings of the Dove, The, 105–52
James, William, 89, 106, 143, 425,
    475
Jameson, F., 356, 358, 367, 463,
    466–7, 469, 472
Jardine, Alice, 223
Jefferies, Richard, 322, 362, 363
    After London, 355, 357–8
Jencks, Charles, 465, 466
Johnson, Lionel, 338–9, 348
Joseph, Keith, 465
Jowett, Benjamin, 4–5
Joyce, James, 239, 350, 470, 473
Jump, John, 27

Kaplan, Cora, 229
Kautsky, Minna, 274–5
Kempis, Thomas à, 70, 71
Kettle, Arnold, 155, 157, 439
Keynes, J.M., 438
Kingsley, Charles, 252
Knight, G. Wilson, 81
Kuspitt, D., 468

Laforgue, Jules, 350
Lassalle, F., 257
Laveleye, E.L.V., 162, 257, 262
Lawrence, D.H., 102, 172, 173,
    195, 239–40, 351, 361, 422–62
    Aaron's Rod, 450, 451, 454–6
    A Propos Lady Chatterley's Lover,
    423
    'Autobiographical Fragment',
    452

'Autobiographical Sketch', 452
Birds, Beasts and Flowers, 451
Boy in the Bush, The, 451
'Captain's Doll, The', 450, 452,
    454
'Christening, The', 427–8
'Crown, The', 439
'Daughters of the Vicar, The',
    427
'Democracy', 451
'Education of the People', 425,
    451
'England, My England', 437
Fantasia of the Unconscious, 451
'Fox, The', 450
Georgian Poetry 1912–1913, 423
'Horse Dealer's Daughter, The',
    454
Kangaroo, 439, 456
Lady Chatterley's Lover, 452, 453,
    456–9
Look! We Have Come Through!,
    438
Lost Girl, The, 437, 450, 451,
    455
'Man Who Died, The' ('The
    Escaped Cock'), 452
'Man Who Loved Islands, The',
    452
'Nottingham and the Mining
    Country', 452
'Odour of Chrysanthemums',
    428
Pansies, 453
Phoenix II, 439
Plumed Serpent, The, 451–2, 456
'Pornography and Obscenity',
    452
Prussian Officer, The, 427
'Prussian Officer, The', 428, 437
Psychoanalysis and the Unconscious,
    437, 451, 454
Rainbow, The, 308, 437, 438,
    439–45, 449, 451

'St. Mawr', 451
'Schoolmaster, The', 426
Sea and Sardinia, 451
Sons and Lovers, 426, 431–7, 439, 449, 450
'Study of Thomas Hardy, A', 437
'Sun', 452
'Thorn in the Flesh, The', 428, 437
Trespasser, The, 426, 447
Twilight in Italy, 437, 445
Virgin and the Gypsy, The, 452
White Peacock, The, 426, 429–31
'White Stocking, The', 428
Women in Love, 287, 445–50, 451 ff., 458 f.
'You Touched Me', 454
Leavis, F.R., 81, 82–3, 228, 232, 422–3, 440
Leavis, Q.D., 248, 342
Lebowitz, N., 125
Le Corbusier, 467–8
Lee, Brian, 106
Lefebvre, H., 470–1, 476
Le Gallienne, R., 338
Lenin, V.I., 153, 371
Lessing, Doris, 243, 244
Levine, George, 73, 356
Lévi-Strauss, C., 229
Levitas, Ruth, 333–4
Lewes, G.H., 63, 364
Lewis, C.S., 103, 196, 232
Linton, E. Lynn, 186–8, 195
Lloyd, Henry Demarest, 121
Locke, John, 5
Lodge, David, 232, 463
Louis Napoleon, 3–4, 6
Lovell, Terry, 223, 224, 225, 227, 228, 240
Lowell, Amy, 438
Loyola, Ignatius, 32
Lucas, John, 173, 176, 395
Luhan, Mabel Dodge, 438, 452

Lukács, G., 21, 223, 240, 328, 469–70
Luther, Martin, 32
Lyell, C., 36
Lyotard, J.-F., 465–7, 482
Lytton, Bulwer, 356

McCabe, 232, 234
Macdonald, George, 195–8
Macherey, P., 214, 351
Maeterlinck, M. 131–2, 143, 350
Machiavelli, N., 74
Mahaffy, J.P., 168
Maine, J.S., 305
Malinowski, B., 448
Mallarmé, S., 350
Mallock, W.H., 248, 253–4, 260, 263
Mann, Tom, 254, 259, 263, 376, 378, 381
Manning, H.E., 376, 380
Mansfield, Katherine, 239, 438
Marcuse, H., 225
Mario, Jesse White, 74, 78
Marsh, E., 438
Marsh, Jan, 321
Marx, Eleanor, 162, 241, 378
Marx, Karl, 3, 7, 61, 152–70, 230, 249, 252, 273, 283, 295, 297, 299, 305, 335, 341, 344, 352, 356, 362, 370–1, 466
Maurice, C. Edmund, 294
Mazzini, G., 28, 32, 34, 73, 78, 413, 416, 418
Meier, P., 331, 332, 369, 371
Meredith, George, 28, 73, 148–9, 155, 202, 248, 338, 342, 362, 376, 428
Beauchamp's Career, 160
Diana of the Crossways, 203–7
Egoist, The, 203
Emilia in England, 73
One of Our Conquerors, 148–9
Rhoda Fleming, 203

Vittoria, 73, 203
Michelangelo, 32
Michelet, 221
Mill, J.S., 5–6, 70, 74, 176, 182, 200, 203, 241, 321
Miller, J. Hillis, 166, 232
Millett, Kate, 173, 185, 228
Milton, John, 168, 293, 323, 352, 424
Mitchell, Juliet, 223, 224–5
More, Thomas, 333
Morgan, L.H., 305, 307, 360
Morley, John, 254
Morrell, Ottoline, 438
Morrell, Roy, 155
Morris, William, 165, 247, 250–70, 321–35, 375, 376–7, 381, 410
   'Address on the Collection of Paintings of the English Pre-Raphaelite School', 324
   'Art and the Beauty of the Earth', 262
   'Art and Socialism', 325
   'Art under Plutocracy', 325
   'Communism', 331
   Defence of Guinevere, The, 324
   Dream of John Ball, A, 162, 293–305, 307, 309, 311, 314–15, 325, 326, 358
   Earthly Paradise, The, 262
   Hopes and Fears for Art, 250, 261, 262
   'Hope of Civilization, The', 256
   'Hopes of Civilization, The', 326
   'How I Became a Socialist', 285–6
   'How Shall We Live Then?', 333
   'How We Live and How We Might Live', 163, 283–4
   House of Wulfings, The, 306–11, 313, 326
   'Lesser Arts, The', 262
   'Misery and the Way Out', 268, 282–3
   News from Nowhere, 249, 269, 281, 293, 314–18, 323, 327–35, 355, 356–8, 362, 368–70
   Novel on Blue Paper, 325
   Pilgrims of Hope, 162, 325, 326
   Roots of the Mountains, The, 313–14, 326
   Signs of Change, 162, 249, 293
   Sigurd the Volsung, 163, 287–92, 309, 324–5, 326
   'Society of the Future, The', 333
   Story of the Glittering Plain, The, 318
   'Useful Work versus Useless Toil', 162, 262
Morton, A.L., 314, 355
Mozart, W.A., 219–21
Murdoch, Iris, 81, 82, 101, 232
Murry, J.M., 438
Myers, Gustavus, 116

Nietzche, F., 423
Nerval, G., 350
Norris, C., 463, 472
Norton, Grace, 89

Oliphant, M., 172, 189–92, 194
Orwell, George, 258, 386
O'Sullivan, Paddy, 321–2
Orpen, Goddard H., 262
Ouida, 251
Owen, Robert, 256, 322, 356

Paine, T., 321
Pater, Walter, 86, 114, 132–4, 135, 155, 160, 193, 338, 339–41, 348, 351, 352, 376, 377, 473
Pearson, Mark, 322
Pelling, Henry, 375

Perec, G., 474
Plato, 482
Poggioli, R., 337, 341
Poirier, Richard, 104, 106
Pollock, Frederick, 395, 408
Poovey, Mary, 226
Pope, Alexander, 40, 41, 49
Proudhon, P.J., 252
Proust, Marcel, 102, 167, 470
Pynchon, T., 475–6, 478

Quilter, Harry, 188

Rahv, Philip, 119
Rattle, Simon, 219, 221
Reade, Charles, 342
Richardson, Samuel, 228
Riehl, W.H., 44–5
Righter, A., 465
Rimbaud, A., 350
Rogers, Thorold, 293–4, 301
Rossetti, Christina, 477–9
Rossetti, D.G., 196
Rowbotham, Sheila, 361
Rushdie, Salman, 479
Ruskin, John, 134, 160, 251, 272,
    321, 322, 325
Rutherford, Mark (W. Hale
    White), 155, 282, 376, 377,
    395–421
    Autobiography, The, 395, 396,
       401, 404–8
    Catharine Furze, 395, 397,
       400–1
    Clara Hopgood, 395, 397, 401,
       413–19
    Deliverance, 385, 400–3, 408–13
    'Genius of Walt Whitman,
       The', 404
    'Ixion', 404
    *Miriam's Schooling and Other
       Papers*, 402–4
    More Pages from a Journal, 395
    'Notes on the Book of Job', 400

Pages from a Journal, 395
Revolution in Tanner's Lane, The,
    396, 401, 413

Sagar, K., 435, 439
St Beuve, C.-A., 138
St Simon, C.H., 252, 356
Sandeen, E.,124
Sartre, Jean-Paul, 101–2, 336–7
Schaeffle, Albert, 249, 257
Schopenhauer, A., 153, 249, 266,
    358, 425, 435
Schreiner, Olive, 155, 162,
    179–81, 242–4, 378
Schwegler, Albert, 397
Scott, Walter, 327, 328, 345, 402,
    445
Shakespeare, William, 37, 424,
    446
Sharratt, Bernard, 327
Shaw, G.B., 158, 162, 323, 328,
    376–7
Shelley, Mary, 202, 231, 241
Shelley, P.B., 155, 162, 177, 241,
    323
Sherman, G.W., 155
Showalter, Elaine, 64, 65, 68, 71,
    178, 179, 223, 232, 243
Shuttleworth, Sally, 70
Sidgwick, H., 404
Sillitoe, A., 222
Sinclair, Upton, 471
Smiles, Samuel, 63, 465
Smith, F.B., 2
Smith, George, 344
Smith, Paul, 223
Smith, Samuel, 259
Soja, E., 469–70, 476–7
Spencer, Herbert, 51, 53, 59, 209,
    265–6, 404, 435
Spenser, Edmund, 52
Spinoza, B., 63, 395–421 *passim*
Sprigge, S. Squire, 342–3
Stanley, A.P., 7

Steedman, C., 477
Stendhal, 229, 233
Stephen, Leslie, 4
Stevenson, R.L., 251, 361
Stirling, J.H., 396–7
Stokes, John, 212
Stone, Oliver, 479
Stoppard, T., 479
Stubbs, W., 293–5
Suvin, Darko, 358
Swann, Charles, 154–6
Swedenborg, E., 105, 351
Swift, Graham, 475
Swift, Jonathan, 40
Swinburne, A.C., 155, 339, 348
Symonds, J.A., 135, 155, 162
Symons, Arthur, 132, 336, 338–9,
    348, 349–51

Taine, H., 111
Tanner, Tony, 325
Taylor, Barbara, 226
Taylor, Harriet, 74
Tennyson, Alfred, 27, 39, 44, 117,
    342
Tillotson, Kathleen, 248
Todd, Janet, 223
Tolkien, J.R.R., 196
Tolstoy, Leo, 101, 233, 327–8,
    329–30
Thompson, E.P., 3, 223, 227, 255,
    262, 268, 273, 314, 321, 322,
    332, 333, 396
Trevelyan, G.M., 44
Trollope, Anthony, 148
Trotsky, L., 353
Tyrell, R.Y., 172

Uglow, Jennifer, 232

Veblen, Thorstein, 117–19, 121
Verlaine, P., 350
Veyriras, Paul, 27, 28
Vincent, David, 477

Virgil, 40
Vizetelly, H., 378

Wagner, Adolph, 249
Wain, John, 168
Wallace, A.R., 362
Walters, Margaret, 223
Ward, James, 86, 89
Watkinson, Ray, 322
Watt, Ian, 228
Waugh, Arthur, 339
Webb, Beatrice, 241, 378, 379,
    380–1
Webb, Sidney, 378
Wedgwood, Julia, 252
Wells, H.G., 241, 323, 356, 362,
    366–7, 369–70, 371, 455
Wesker, Arnold, 222
Westminster, Duke of, 259
White, William Hale, see Mark
    Rutherford
Whitman, Walt, 404
Wilde, Oscar, 367–8
Wilding, M., 326
Williams, Raymond, 154–5, 157,
    223, 235, 247, 272–3, 321,
    332, 334, 356, 365, 368
Wilson, Edmund, 82, 457
Wilson, Elizabeth, 225
Wolff, Janet, 228, 239
Wollheim, Richard, 89
Wollstonecroft, Mary, 229, 230,
    241
Woolf, Virginia, 239–40, 244, 470
Wotton, George, 155
Wordsworth, William, 39, 43, 49,
    405

Yeats, W.B., 153, 310, 336, 338,
    350, 351
Yonge, C., 342
Young, Arthur, 49

Zola, Emile, 241, 328, 378, 386,
    470–1

Hermetic Fictions
Alchemy and Irony
in the Modern Novel

DAVID MEAKIN

This fascinating study of hermetic symbolism brings together an extensive range of major European novelists – from Goethe to Umberto Eco, via such major figures as Zola, Verne, Proust, Thomas Mann, Joyce and Butor – and offers a detailed rereading of key novels of the last 150 years.

In the light of twentieth-century re-evaluations of the hermetic tradition by Jung, Eliade and Bachelard, David Meakin analyses the underlying myth structure of these novels, in which the hermetic and the initiatory is held in tension with the ironic. This tension, argues Meakin, comes increasingly to the fore in the ironic and playful self-consciousness of the modern period and it provides the main focus of his study.

By investigating the remarkable persistence and richness of initiatory – and specifically alchemical – structures in modern fiction, this work makes a significant contribution to the theory of the European novel as well as the field of comparative literature. It will be of value to both specialist and non-specialist readers interested in the European novel or the hermetic tradition itself, with its long and problematic fascination.

David Meakin is Senior Lecturer in French at Bristol University. He is a comparative literature specialist and author of *Man and Work: Literature and Culture in Industrial Society*, numerous articles, chiefly on the modern novel, and editor of Alain Robbe-Grillet, *Dans le labyrinthe*.

For a complete list of publications please write to:
Keele University Press, Keele University,
Staffordshire ST5 5BG, England

News from Nowhere: Theory and Politics of Romanticism
1995 volume – Romanticism : Theory : Gender
Edited by Tony Pinkney, Keith Hanley and Fred Botting

Harold Hobson: Witness and Judge
Dominic Shellard

Harold Hobson: The Complete Catalogue 1922–1988
Dominic Shellard

Sir Henry Irving: Theatre, Culture and Society
Edited by Jeffrey Richards

Thomas Lodge: Rosalynd
Edited by Brian Nellist

Private Voices:
The Diaries of Elizabeth Gaskell and Sophia Holland
Edited and annotated by J A V Chapple
with an introduction by Anita C Wilson

Thomas Hardy: Moments of Vision
Edited by Alan Shelston

Thomas Hardy: Wessex Poems
Edited by Trevor Johnson

John Ruskin: Praeterita
Edited by A O J Cockshut

Edmund Gosse: Father and Son
Edited by A O J Cockshut

The Autobiography of John Stuart Mill
Edited by A O J Cockshut

Elizabeth Gaskell: Mary Barton
Edited by Angus Easson

George Gissing: New Grub Street
Edited by John Halperin

Harriet Beecher Stowe: Dred
Edited by Judie Newman

Edward Gibbon: Memoirs of My Life and Writings
Ed. A O J Cockshut and Stephen Constantine